And they shall not teach every man his neighbour, and every man his brother, saying, Know the Lord: for all shall know me, from the least to the greatest.

Hebrews 8:11

Daily Bible Study 101: Q&A

BRIDAN
PUBLISHING

DAILY BIBLE STUDY 101: Q&A
By Reggie Casaus

BRIDAN PUBLISHING
Post Office Box 25
Kingston, TN 37763 U.S.A.
bridanpublishing.com

All rights reserved. No part of this book may be reproduced or transmitted in any form or by any means—graphic, electronic, mechanical, including photocopying, recording, taping, Web distribution, or by any information storage and retrieval system, or otherwise—without prior written permission from the author, except for the inclusion of brief quotations in a review.

Sales of this book without a front cover may be unauthorized. If this book is coverless, it may have been reported to the publisher as "unsold or destroyed" and neither the author nor the publisher may have received payment for it.

Copyright © 2016 by Bridan Publishing

All scripture quotations are taken from the Authorized King James Version of the Bible.

ISBN   978-0-9979638-3-0

Printed in the United States of America

Cover and interior art © Shutterstock | www.shutterstock.com

Cover design by Jeff Jansen

Dedicated to those whose names are written in the book of life.

The words of the LORD *are pure words: as silver tried in a furnace of earth, purified seven times. Thou shalt keep them, O* LORD, *thou shalt preserve them from this generation for ever.*

Psalm 12:6-7

Table of Contents

Preface   xix

Date	Lesson	Scriptures	Page
January 1	1	Genesis 1–3	21
January 2	2	Genesis 4–7	23
January 3	3	Genesis 8–11	25
January 4	4	Genesis 12–15	27
January 5	5	Genesis 16–18	29
January 6	6	Genesis 19–20	31
January 7	7	Genesis 21–23	33
January 8	8	Genesis 24–25	35
January 9	9	Genesis 26–28	37
January 10	10	Genesis 29–30	39
January 11	11	Genesis 31–32	41
January 12	12	Genesis 33–35	43
January 13	13	Genesis 36–38	45
January 14	14	Genesis 39–41	47
January 15	15	Genesis 42–44	49
January 16	16	Genesis 45–47	51
January 17	17	Genesis 48–50	53
January 18	18	Exodus 1–3	55
January 19	19	Exodus 4–6	57
January 20	20	Exodus 7–9	59
January 21	21	Exodus 10–12	61
January 22	22	Exodus 13–15	63
January 23	23	Exodus 16–18	65
January 24	24	Exodus 19–21	67
January 25	25	Exodus 22–24	69
January 26	26	Exodus 25–27	71
January 27	27	Exodus 28–29	73
January 28	28	Exodus 30–32	75
January 29	29	Exodus 33–35	77
January 30	30	Exodus 36–38	79
January 31	31	Exodus 39–40	81
February 1	32	Leviticus 1–4	83

Date	Lesson	Scriptures	Page
February 2	33	Leviticus 5–7	85
February 3	34	Leviticus 8–9	87
February 4	35	Leviticus 10–12	89
February 5	36	Leviticus 13	91
February 6	37	Leviticus 14–15	93
February 7	38	Leviticus 16–18	95
February 8	39	Leviticus 19–21	97
February 9	40	Leviticus 22–23	99
February 10	41	Leviticus 24–25	101
February 11	42	Leviticus 26–27	103
February 12	43	Numbers 1–2	105
February 13	44	Numbers 3–4	107
February 14	45	Numbers 5–6	109
February 15	46	Numbers 7	111
February 16	47	Numbers 8–10	113
February 17	48	Numbers 11–13	115
February 18	49	Numbers 14–15	117
February 19	50	Numbers 16–18	119
February 20	51	Numbers 19–21	121
February 21	52	Numbers 22–24	123
February 22	53	Numbers 25–26	125
February 23	54	Numbers 27–29	127
February 24	55	Numbers 30–31	129
February 25	56	Numbers 32–33	131
February 26	57	Numbers 34–36	133
February 27	58	Deuteronomy 1–2	135
February 28	59	Deuteronomy 3–4	137
March 1	60	Deuteronomy 5–7	139
March 2	61	Deuteronomy 8–10	141
March 3	62	Deuteronomy 11–13	143
March 4	63	Deuteronomy 14–17	145
March 5	64	Deuteronomy 18–20	147
March 6	65	Deuteronomy 21–23	149
March 7	66	Deuteronomy 24–26	151
March 8	67	Deuteronomy 27–28	153

Date	Lesson	Scriptures	Page
March 9	68	Deuteronomy 29–31	155
March 10	69	Deuteronomy 32–34	157
March 11	70	Joshua 1–4	159
March 12	71	Joshua 5–7	161
March 13	72	Joshua 8–9	163
March 14	73	Joshua 10–11	165
March 15	74	Joshua 12–14	167
March 16	75	Joshua 15–17	169
March 17	76	Joshua 18–20	171
March 18	77	Joshua 21–22	173
March 19	78	Joshua 23–24	175
March 20	79	Judges 1–3	177
March 21	80	Judges 4–6	179
March 22	81	Judges 7–8	181
March 23	82	Judges 9–10	183
March 24	83	Judges 11–13	185
March 25	84	Judges 14–16	187
March 26	85	Judges 17–19	189
March 27	86	Judges 20–21	191
March 28	87	Ruth 1–4	193
March 29	88	I Samuel 1–3	195
March 30	89	I Samuel 4–7	197
March 31	90	I Samuel 8–10	199
April 1	91	I Samuel 11–13	201
April 2	92	I Samuel 14–15	203
April 3	93	I Samuel 16–17	205
April 4	94	I Samuel 18–20	207
April 5	95	I Samuel 21–24	209
April 6	96	I Samuel 25–27	211
April 7	97	I Samuel 28–31	213
April 8	98	II Samuel 1–3	215
April 9	99	II Samuel 4–7	217
April 10	100	II Samuel 8–11	219
April 11	101	II Samuel 12–13	221
April 12	102	II Samuel 14–15	223

Date	Lesson	Scriptures	Page
April 13	103	II Samuel 16–17	225
April 14	104	II Samuel 18–19	227
April 15	105	II Samuel 20–22	229
April 16	106	II Samuel 23–24	231
April 17	107	I Kings 1	233
April 18	108	I Kings 2–3	235
April 19	109	I Kings 4–6	237
April 20	110	I Kings 7	239
April 21	111	I Kings 8	241
April 22	112	I Kings 9–10	243
April 23	113	I Kings 11–12	245
April 24	114	I Kings 13–14	247
April 25	115	I Kings 15–17	249
April 26	116	I Kings 18–19	251
April 27	117	I Kings 20–22	253
April 28	118	II Kings 1–2	255
April 29	119	II Kings 3–4	257
April 30	120	II Kings 5–7	259
May 1	121	II Kings 8–9	261
May 2	122	II Kings 10–12	263
May 3	123	II Kings 13–14	265
May 4	124	II Kings 15–16	267
May 5	125	II Kings 17–18	269
May 6	126	II Kings 19–21	271
May 7	127	II Kings 22–25	273
May 8	128	I Chronicles 1	275
May 9	129	I Chronicles 2–4	277
May 10	130	I Chronicles 5–6	279
May 11	131	I Chronicles 7–9	281
May 12	132	I Chronicles 10–12	283
May 13	133	I Chronicles 13–16	285
May 14	134	I Chronicles 17–19	287
May 15	135	I Chronicles 20–23	289
May 16	136	I Chronicles 24–26	291
May 17	137	I Chronicles 27–29	293

Date	Lesson	Scriptures	Page
May 18	138	II Chronicles 1–4	295
May 19	139	II Chronicles 5–7	297
May 20	140	II Chronicles 8–10	299
May 21	141	II Chronicles 11–14	301
May 22	142	II Chronicles 15–18	303
May 23	143	II Chronicles 19–22	305
May 24	144	II Chronicles 23–25	307
May 25	145	II Chronicles 26–28	309
May 26	146	II Chronicles 29–30	311
May 27	147	II Chronicles 31–33	313
May 28	148	II Chronicles 34–36	315
May 29	149	Ezra 1–2	317
May 30	150	Ezra 3–5	319
May 31	151	Ezra 6–8	321
June 1	152	Ezra 9–10	323
June 2	153	Nehemiah 1–3	325
June 3	154	Nehemiah 4–6	327
June 4	155	Nehemiah 7–8	329
June 5	156	Nehemiah 9–10	331
June 6	157	Nehemiah 11–13	333
June 7	158	Esther 1–3	335
June 8	159	Esther 4–7	337
June 9	160	Esther 8–10	339
June 10	161	Job 1–5	341
June 11	162	Job 6–10	343
June 12	163	Job 11–15	345
June 13	164	Job 16–21	347
June 14	165	Job 22–28	349
June 15	166	Job 29–33	351
June 16	167	Job 34–37	353
June 17	168	Job 38–42	355
June 18	169	Psalms 1–9	357
June 19	170	Psalms 10–17	359
June 20	171	Psalms 18–22	361
June 21	172	Psalms 23–31	363

Date	Lesson	Scriptures	Page
June 22	173	Psalms 32–37	365
June 23	174	Psalms 38–44	367
June 24	175	Psalms 45–51	369
June 25	176	Psalms 52–59	371
June 26	177	Psalms 60–67	373
June 27	178	Psalms 68–71	375
June 28	179	Psalms 72–77	377
June 29	180	Psalms 78–81	379
June 30	181	Psalms 82–89	381
July 1	182	Psalms 90–97	383
July 2	183	Psalms 98–104	385
July 3	184	Psalms 105–107	387
July 4	185	Psalms 108–112	389
July 5	186	Psalms 113–118	391
July 6	187	Psalms 119	393
July 7	188	Psalms 120–135	395
July 8	189	Psalms 136–142	397
July 9	190	Psalms 143–150	399
July 10	191	Proverbs 1–4	401
July 11	192	Proverbs 5–8	403
July 12	193	Proverbs 9–13	405
July 13	194	Proverbs 14–17	407
July 14	195	Proverbs 18–21	409
July 15	196	Proverbs 22–24	411
July 16	197	Proverbs 25–28	413
July 17	198	Proverbs 29–31	415
July 18	199	Ecclesiastes 1–6	417
July 19	200	Ecclesiastes 7–12	419
July 20	201	Song of Solomon 1–8	421
July 21	202	Isaiah 1–4	423
July 22	203	Isaiah 5–8	425
July 23	204	Isaiah 9–12	427
July 24	205	Isaiah 13–16	429
July 25	206	Isaiah 17–21	431
July 26	207	Isaiah 22–25	433

Date	Lesson	Scriptures	Page
July 27	208	Isaiah 26–28	435
July 28	209	Isaiah 29–31	437
July 29	210	Isaiah 32–35	439
July 30	211	Isaiah 36–38	441
July 31	212	Isaiah 39–42	443
August 1	213	Isaiah 43–47	445
August 2	214	Isaiah 48–51	447
August 3	215	Isaiah 52–56	449
August 4	216	Isaiah 57–59	451
August 5	217	Isaiah 60–63	453
August 6	218	Isaiah 64–66	455
August 7	219	Jeremiah 1–3	457
August 8	220	Jeremiah 4–6	459
August 9	221	Jeremiah 7–9	461
August 10	222	Jeremiah 10–12	463
August 11	223	Jeremiah 13–15	465
August 12	224	Jeremiah 16–18	467
August 13	225	Jeremiah 19–22	469
August 14	226	Jeremiah 23–24	471
August 15	227	Jeremiah 25–27	473
August 16	228	Jeremiah 28–30	475
August 17	229	Jeremiah 31–32	477
August 18	230	Jeremiah 33–35	479
August 19	231	Jeremiah 36–38	481
August 20	232	Jeremiah 39–41	483
August 21	233	Jeremiah 42–44	485
August 22	234	Jeremiah 45–48	487
August 23	235	Jeremiah 49–50	489
August 24	236	Jeremiah 51–52	491
August 25	237	Lamentations 1–2	493
August 26	238	Lamentations 3–5	495
August 27	239	Ezekial 1–4	497
August 28	240	Ezekial 5–8	499
August 29	241	Ezekial 9–12	501
August 30	242	Ezekial 13–15	503

Date	Lesson	Scriptures	Page
August 31	243	Ezekial 16	505
September 1	244	Ezekial 17–19	507
September 2	245	Ezekial 20–21	509
September 3	246	Ezekial 22–23	511
September 4	247	Ezekial 24–26	513
September 5	248	Ezekial 27–28	515
September 6	249	Ezekial 29–31	517
September 7	250	Ezekial 32–33	519
September 8	251	Ezekial 34–36	521
September 9	252	Ezekial 37–38	523
September 10	253	Ezekial 39–40	525
September 11	254	Ezekial 41–43	527
September 12	255	Ezekial 44–45	529
September 13	256	Ezekial 46–48	531
September 14	257	Daniel 1–2	533
September 15	258	Daniel 3–4	535
September 16	259	Daniel 5–6	537
September 17	260	Daniel 7–8	539
September 18	261	Daniel 9–10	541
September 19	262	Daniel 11–12	543
September 20	263	Hosea 1–6	545
September 21	264	Hosea 7–12	547
September 22	265	Hosea 13–14, Joel 1–3	549
September 23	266	Amos 1–5	551
September 24	267	Amos 6–9, Obadiah 1	553
September 25	268	Jonah 1–4, Micah 1–2	555
September 26	269	Micah 3–7	557
September 27	270	Nahum 1–3, Habakkuk 1–3	559
September 28	271	Zephaniah 1–3, Haggai 1–2	561
September 29	272	Zechariah 1–6	563
September 30	273	Zechariah 7–10	565
October 1	274	Zechariah 11–14	567
October 2	275	Malachi 1–4	569
October 3	276	Matthew 1–4	571
October 4	277	Matthew 5–6	573

Date	Lesson	Scriptures	Page
October 5	278	Matthew 7–9	575
October 6	279	Matthew 10–12	577
October 7	280	Matthew 13–14	579
October 8	281	Matthew 15–17	581
October 9	282	Matthew 18–20	583
October 10	283	Matthew 21–22	585
October 11	284	Matthew 23–24	587
October 12	285	Matthew 25–26	589
October 13	286	Matthew 27–28	591
October 14	287	Mark 1–3	593
October 15	288	Mark 4–5	595
October 16	289	Mark 6–7	597
October 17	290	Mark 8–9	599
October 18	291	Mark 10–11	601
October 19	292	Mark 12–13	603
October 20	293	Mark 14–16	605
October 21	294	Luke 1	607
October 22	295	Luke 2–3	609
October 23	296	Luke 4–5	611
October 24	297	Luke 6–7	613
October 25	298	Luke 8	615
October 26	299	Luke 9	617
October 27	300	Luke 10–11	619
October 28	301	Luke 12–13	621
October 29	302	Luke 14–16	623
October 30	303	Luke 17–18	625
October 31	304	Luke 19–20	627
November 1	305	Luke 21–22	629
November 2	306	Luke 23–24	631
November 3	307	John 1–3	633
November 4	308	John 4–5	635
November 5	309	John 6–7	637
November 6	310	John 8–9	639
November 7	311	John 10–11	641
November 8	312	John 12–13	643

Date	Lesson	Scriptures	Page
November 9	313	John 14–16	645
November 10	314	John 17–18	647
November 11	315	John 19–21	649
November 12	316	Acts 1–3	651
November 13	317	Acts 4–6	653
November 14	318	Acts 7–8	655
November 15	319	Acts 9–10	657
November 16	320	Acts 11–13	659
November 17	321	Acts 14–16	661
November 18	322	Acts 17–18	663
November 19	323	Acts 19–20	665
November 20	324	Acts 21–22	667
November 21	325	Acts 23–25	669
November 22	326	Acts 26–28	671
November 23	327	Romans 1–3	673
November 24	328	Romans 4–7	675
November 25	329	Romans 8–10	677
November 26	330	Romans 11–14	679
November 27	331	Romans 15–16	681
November 28	332	I Corinthians 1–4	683
November 29	333	I Corinthians 5–8	685
November 30	334	I Corinthians 9–11	687
December 1	335	I Corinthians 12–14	689
December 2	336	I Corinthians 15–16	691
December 3	337	II Corinthians 1–4	693
December 4	338	II Corinthians 5–8	695
December 5	339	II Corinthians 9–13	697
December 6	340	Galatians 1–6	699
December 7	341	Ephesians 1–3	701
December 8	342	Ephesians 4–6	703
December 9	343	Philippians 1–4	705
December 10	344	Colossians 1–4	707
December 11	345	I Thessalonians 1–5	709
December 12	346	II Thessalonians 1–3	711
December 13	347	I Timothy 1–4	713

Date	Lesson	Scriptures	Page
December 14	348	I Timothy 5–6	715
December 15	349	II Timothy 1–4	717
December 16	350	Titus 1–3, Philemon 1	719
December 17	351	Hebrews 1–5	721
December 18	352	Hebrews 6–9	723
December 19	353	Hebrews 10–11	725
December 20	354	Hebrews 12–13	727
December 21	355	James 1–5	729
December 22	356	I Peter 1–5	731
December 23	357	II Peter 1–3	733
December 24	358	I John 1–5	735
December 25	359	II John 1, III John 1, Jude 1	737
December 26	360	Revelation 1–3	739
December 27	361	Revelation 4–8	741
December 28	362	Revelation 9–12	743
December 29	363	Revelation 13–16	745
December 30	364	Revelation 17–19	747
December 31	365	Revelation 20–22	749
Answers			751
Notes			783
Works Cited			783
Permissions			783
Acknowledgments			784

"It is the duty of all nations to acknowledge the providence of Almighty God, to obey His will, to be grateful for His benefits, and humbly to implore His protection and favor."

George Washington

PREFACE

The purpose of this book is to help Bible scholars recall previously learned Bible scriptures. *Daily Bible Study 101: Q&A* uses a system of 20 multiple-choice questions and answers for each day of the year based upon the first of six cognitive domains of the Revised Bloom's Taxonomy. These six cognitive domains include Remembering, Understanding, Applying, Analyzing, Evaluating, and Creating. The first cognitive domain, *Remembering*, is used to exhibit memory of previously learned material by recalling facts, terms, basic concepts, and answers.[1] By building a solid foundation using the first domain, *Remembering*, the Bible student will develop a basic understanding of God's holy Word.

This book is designed to help ministers, Bible teachers, students enrolled in Sunday school classes, Bible study groups, students in college or high school Bible courses, and individuals discovering on their own the incredible Word of God. Ministers may use the book to help them recall key scripture points while preparing a sermon or a lesson plan for a Bible study class. Likewise, Bible teachers will find a treasure of questions and answers to help them prepare scholarly lesson plans. Since students tend to learn better when engaged during discussions, the questions in this book may be used during a lesson to elicit students' responses to promote a positive learning environment in the classroom.

Students enrolled in a high school or college course based upon the Bible may use this book as a supplement to other class texts and materials to gain further knowledge and a deeper understanding of the Bible. In addition, individuals will find the material helpful as they grow and discover God's holy words.

The book is not targeted toward any one particular Christian denomination; therefore, its purpose is not theology-based but instead concentrates on the literature in the Bible. Scripture verses in italics are included with each question to allow Bible learners a way to fact-check the answers to each question. The layout of the book is adapted to a structured daily Bible reading plan; however, a Bible study group could adapt the reading schedule to fit their time constraints. For example, a Bible study group may opt to study each lesson on a weekly basis to cover the various books of the Bible. A unique feature of *Daily Bible Study 101: Q&A* is an individual or group may begin their daily Bible studies at any time of the year, and still read the entire Bible in only twelve months.

World histories typically begin with prehistoric times and include vast theories on the age of the earth. Since no living mortal was alive during the days of Adam, expositors can only hypothesize the true age of the earth. The job of the archaeologist is to unearth the remnants of the villages of our ancestors; moreover, the anthropologist tries to reconstruct these lost worlds and rely upon an immeasurable amount of speculation on how our ancestors behaved, lived, and survived.[2] Historians also rely upon immeasurable amounts of speculation to explain who early man was, where he lived, what he did, and how and why he did it.[3] Furthermore, the lack of evidence prior to 2100 BC creates great difficulty for expositors to place exact dates and times on world events. Although, the period between 2100-1000 BC offers some evidence, most events still remain opaque, creating more questions than answers for expositors. After 1000 BC, dates become clearer due to the discovery of more ancient records and texts, but even much of these artifacts remain obscure due to missing pieces and various interpretations.[4] In short, theories as to the true age of the earth are tentative at best and based upon vast amounts of speculation.

Since the history of time cannot be repeated in a laboratory, the dates used in this book are primarily based upon the theories of Rev. Archbishop James Ussher,* to give the Bible learner a macroscopic view of when events during the course of time unfolded.[5] Young earth creationism is the theory that the earth is approximately 6000 years old and was created by God who is omnipotent.[6] It is logically the best choice since many events throughout prehistory and history remain a mystery, and most scientists rule out the miracles of the divine Creator since his ways do not always follow the laws of nature.[7] In addition, not all scientists agree the earth is millions or possibly even billions of years old.[8] Most scientists base their findings upon tangible evidence, which only allows explanations that are observable, palpable, testable, and based upon natural laws, thus ruling out the supernatural, which includes miracles such as God parting seas and the Virgin Mary giving birth to Jesus, who is the Christ.

At best, history is similar to a massive jigsaw puzzle with several pieces missing. As a result, the dates given in this book should serve as a guideline to the Bible learner until new evidence emerges.

An old cliché states that one usually gets out of something what one puts into it; the same can be said of *Daily Bible Study 101: Q&A*. For the Biblical scholar to get the most benefit from this book, the student should follow these guidelines:

1. Pray before studying.
2. Ask the Holy Ghost to instruct you.
3. Do not rush through the reading assignments.
4. Ask the Holy Ghost how the scriptures apply to you.
5. Study the Word faithfully every day.
6. Use a Bible dictionary.
7. Use a Bible atlas.
8. Use Bible commentaries written by reputable theologians.
9. Take notes.
10. End your study sessions with prayer.

In closing, the Biblical scholar is encouraged to follow the habits of the Bereans who received the word with readiness of mind and searched the scriptures *daily* to see whether the doctrines being taught were true[9]. In addition, the Israelites were told before entering the Promised Land to meditate upon the book of the law day and night and to be careful to do everything written in it, so that they would be prosperous and successful[10]. In addition, the Book of Mark states that Jesus taught *daily* in the Temple[11], a further sign that the Bible learner is to study the scriptures *daily*. Furthermore, when the early church met with one accord *daily* in the Temple, broke bread from house to house, baptized new believers, and followed the apostle's doctrine and fellowship, the Lord added to the church *daily* by saving those who were lost[12]. Finally, the true Biblical scholar should read and heed the Word of God *daily* in order to become prosperous and successful—not as defined by the world—but by the Almighty Father.

- Ussher, James. *The Annals of the World Deduced from the Origin of Time, and Continued to the Beginning of the Emperour Vespasians Reign, and the Totall Destruction and Abolition of the Temple and Common-wealth of the Jews: Containing the Historie of the Old and New Testament, with That of the Macchabees, Also the Most Memorable Affairs of Asia and Egypt, and the Rise of the Empire of the Roman Caesars under C. Julius, and Octavianus: Collected from All History, as Well Sacred, as Prophane, and Methodically Digested*. London: Printed by E. Tyler, for J. Crook ... and for G. Bedell ..., 1658. Print.

JANUARY 1

Lesson 1
Today's Reading: *Genesis 1–3*
Period of Time: Sunday evening, October 23, 4004 BC
Author: Moses

1. Who created the heaven and the earth?
   Genesis 1:1
   - **A.** Adam
   - **B.** Darwin
   - **C.** God
   - **D.** Satan

2. What moved upon the face of the waters?
   Genesis 1:2
   - **A.** Angel of God
   - **B.** Breath of God
   - **C.** Name of God
   - **D.** Spirit of God

3. What did God call the firmament?
   Genesis 1:8
   - **A.** Hades
   - **B.** Haven
   - **C.** Heaven
   - **D.** Hell

4. On which day did dry land appear?
   Genesis 1:9–13
   - **A.** 2nd day
   - **B.** 3rd day
   - **C.** 4th day
   - **D.** 5th day

5. On which day did the lights in the firmament appear?
   Genesis 1:14–19
   - **A.** 1st day
   - **B.** 4th day
   - **C.** 5th day
   - **D.** 6th day

6. What was made on the sixth day?
   Genesis 1:24–31
   - **A.** Fowl
   - **B.** Man
   - **C.** Seas
   - **D.** Whales

7. Which of the following foods was Adam permitted to eat?
   Genesis 1:29
   - **A.** Bread, locusts, and wild honey
   - **B.** Herbs, fruits, and nuts
   - **C.** Quail, manna, and grains
   - **D.** Vegetables, milk, and eggs

8. What watered the face of the ground in the beginning?
   Genesis 2:6
   - **A.** A mist
   - **B.** A river
   - **C.** A sea
   - **D.** An ocean

9. What did Adam become after he was created?
   Genesis 2:7
   - **A.** A cherubim
   - **B.** A god
   - **C.** A living soul
   - **D.** An angel

10. Where was the garden of God located?
    Genesis 2:8
    - **A.** Eden
    - **B.** Edom
    - **C.** Elon
    - **D.** Etam

11. What were the names of the four rivers that watered the garden?
    Genesis 2:10–14
    - **A.** Abana, Gihon, Kishon, and Arnon
    - **B.** Jordan, Ahava, Hiddekel, and Pharpar
    - **C.** Nile, Kanah, Jabbok, and Abana
    - **D.** Pishon, Gihon, Hiddekel, and Euphrates

12. Which knowledge tree was Adam forbidden to eat from?

    Genesis 2:17

    A. Good and evil
    B. Hot and cold
    C. Light and darkness
    D. Time and seasons

13. Who named every beast of the field?

    Genesis 2:19

    A. Adam
    B. God the Father
    C. God the Son
    D. Spirit of God

14. What was removed from Adam's body to make the first woman?

    Genesis 2:21–22

    A. A portion of his brain
    B. A portion of his heart
    C. One of his lungs
    D. One of his ribs

15. What was more subtle than any beast of the field?

    Genesis 3:1

    A. The fox
    B. The leopard
    C. The pig
    D. The serpent

16. What did Adam and his wife use to make aprons?

    Genesis 3:7

    A. Cotton
    B. Leaves
    C. Silk
    D. Wool

17. When did Adam and his wife hear the voice of the LORD God walking in the garden?

    Genesis 3:8

    A. As the shadow went back ten degrees
    B. During the ninth hour of the day
    C. In the cool of the day
    D. When the moon turned to blood

18. What name did Adam give to his wife?

    Genesis 3:20

    A. Eglah
    B. Elisabeth
    C. Esther
    D. Eve

19. What did God use to clothe Adam and his wife?

    Genesis 3:21

    A. Animal skins
    B. Camel's hair
    C. Coats of many colors
    D. Fine linen woven together

20. What did God place east of the garden to guard the special tree?

    Genesis 3:24

    A. A burning bush and thorny briers
    B. A chariot of fire and an angel
    C. A cherubim and a flaming sword
    D. A wall and a fire-breathing dragon

*Answers on page 751

Lesson 2
Today's Reading: *Genesis 4–7*
Period of Time: 3874 BC–Sunday, December 7, 2349 BC
Author: Moses

JANUARY 2

1. Who was Adam's firstborn son?
   Genesis 4:1
   A. Abel
   B. Cain
   C. Noah
   D. Seth

2. Who was Adam's secondborn son?
   Genesis 4:2
   A. Abel
   B. Cain
   C. Noah
   D. Seth

3. Who went to dwell in the land of Nod?
   Genesis 4:16
   A. Abel
   B. Cain
   C. Noah
   D. Seth

4. What were the names of Lamech's wives?
   Genesis 4:19
   A. Abigail and Zeruiah
   B. Adah and Zillah
   C. Anna and Zibiah
   D. Ariel and Zimri

5. Who was the father of the first musicians to play harps and organs?
   Genesis 4:21
   A. Jabal
   B. Jabez
   C. Jacob
   D. Jubal

6. After which child was born did men begin to call upon the name of the LORD?
   Genesis 4:26
   A. Enos
   B. Hazo
   C. Kore
   D. Maaz

7. How old was Adam when he died?
   Genesis 5:5
   A. 70 years old
   B. 450 years old
   C. 666 years old
   D. 930 years old

8. Who walked with God—and was not—for God took him?
   Genesis 5:24
   A. Enam
   B. Enan
   C. Enoch
   D. Enosh

9. How old was Methusaleh when he died?
   Genesis 5:27
   A. 969 years old
   B. 1,016 years old
   C. 1,357 years old
   D. 30,150 years old

10. What are the names of Noah's sons?
    Genesis 5:32
    A. Enoch, Enosh, and Enoth
    B. Jubal, Jabal, and Jobal
    C. Shem, Ham, and Japheth
    D. Benjamin, Jesse, and David

11. How many years did God say man would live—according to Genesis 6:3?
    Genesis 6:3
    A. 39
    B. 65
    C. 70
    D. 120

12. What type of wood was used to build the ark?
    Genesis 6:14
    A. Ash
    B. Balsam
    C. Elm
    D. Gopher

13. What were the dimensions of the ark measured in cubits?

    Genesis 6:15
    A. 150 x 75 x 25
    B. 300 x 50 x 30
    C. 450 x 150 x 64
    D. 800 x 300 x 108

14. How many windows did the ark have?

    Genesis 6:16
    A. 0
    B. 1
    C. 3
    D. 7

15. How many stories did the ark contain?

    Genesis 6:16
    A. 1
    B. 2
    C. 3
    D. 4

16. How many different *sorts* of every living thing of flesh was Noah told to bring onto the ark?

    Genesis 6:19
    A. 2
    B. 3
    C. 7
    D. 12

17. How old was Noah when the flood came?

    Genesis 7:6
    A. 200 years old
    B. 400 years old
    C. 600 years old
    D. 800 years old

18. How many people were inside the ark during the flood?

    Genesis 7:7, 7:13
    A. 8
    B. 10
    C. 12
    D. 14

19. How many days and nights did it rain upon the earth during the flood?

    Genesis 7:12, 7:17
    A. 10
    B. 20
    C. 30
    D. 40

20. How many days did the waters prevail upon the earth?

    Genesis 7:24
    A. 40
    B. 120
    C. 150
    D. 365

*Answers on page 751

Lesson 3
Today's Reading: *Genesis 8–11*
Period of Time: Wednesday, May 6, 2349–1922 BC
Author: Moses

JANUARY 3

1. Upon which mountains did the ark rest upon?
   Genesis 8:4
   A. Mountains of Ararat
   B. Mountains of Carmel
   C. Mountains of Olives
   D. Mountains of Pisgah

2. What bird did Noah send out first?
   Genesis 8:7
   A. Dove
   B. Eagle
   C. Pigeon
   D. Raven

3. How many birds did Noah send out?
   Genesis 8:7–8
   A. 1
   B. 2
   C. 3
   D. 4

4. Which bird brought Noah an olive leaf?
   Genesis 8:11
   A. Dove
   B. Eagle
   C. Pigeon
   D. Raven

5. What was to be the punishment for murder, whether by beast or by man?
   Genesis 9:6
   A. Blindness
   B. Castration
   C. Death
   D. Slavery

6. What token did God give when He promised he would never flood the earth again?
   Genesis 9:13
   A. A bow in the cloud
   B. An eclipse of the sun and moon
   C. Spring, summer, autumn, and winter
   D. The tides along the shorelines

7. Who is the father of Canaan?
   Genesis 9:18, 9:22
   A. Abel
   B. Cain
   C. Ham
   D. Kenan

8. Who drank too much wine and was found naked inside his tent?
   Genesis 9:20–21
   A. Japheth
   B. Noah
   C. Put
   D. Sidon

9. Whom did Noah curse?
   Genesis 9:22–25
   A. Balaam
   B. Canaan
   C. Japheth
   D. Shem

10. How many years did Noah live after the flood?
    Genesis 9:28
    A. 98
    B. 150
    C. 275
    D. 350

11. Who was a mighty hunter before the LORD?
    Genesis 10:9
    A. Anamim
    B. Diklah
    C. Nimrod
    D. Sabtah

12. Where was the city of Babel located?
    Genesis 10:10
    A. Land of Canaan
    B. Land of Gomorrah
    C. Land of Shinar
    D. Land of Sodom

13. Whom did the Philistim descend from?

    Genesis 10:14

    A. Casluhim
    B. Emim
    C. Lehabim
    D. Naphtuhim

14. During whose time was the earth divided?

    Genesis 10:25

    A. Accad
    B. Dedan
    C. Jerah
    D. Peleg

15. How many languages existed prior to the construction of the city of Babel and its tower?

    Genesis 11:1

    A. 1
    B. 7
    C. 32
    D. Unknown

16. What did the people use for mortar to build the city of Babel and its tower?

    Genesis 11:3

    A. Cement
    B. Clay
    C. Sap
    D. Slime

17. Who were Terah's three sons?

    Genesis 11:26

    A. Abraham, Martin, and John
    B. Abram, Nahor, and Haran
    C. Adam, Cain, and Seth
    D. Azariah, Adaiah, and Ahaziah

18. Who lived in Ur at the time of Terah?

    Genesis 11:28

    A. The Arabians
    B. The Bereans
    C. The Chaldeans
    D. The Egyptians

19. Who was Terah's grandson?

    Genesis 11:31

    A. Abe
    B. Dan
    C. Ely
    D. Lot

20. Where did Terah die?

    Genesis 11:32

    A. Babel
    B. Haran
    C. Nineveh
    D. Zeboiim

*Answers on page 751

JANUARY 4

Lesson 4
Today's Reading: *Genesis 12–15*
Period of Time: 1921–1912 BC
Author: Moses

1. Who did God say would be blessed through Abram?
   Genesis 12:3
   A. Families
   B. Gentiles
   C. Heathens
   D. Jews

2. How old was Abram when he departed Haran?
   Genesis 12:4
   A. 18
   B. 21
   C. 40
   D. 75

3. Who, besides his wife, left Haran with Abram?
   Genesis 12:5
   A. His brother
   B. His nephew
   C. His son
   D. His uncle

4. Which land did God promise to give to Abram?
   Genesis 12:5–7
   A. Canaan
   B. Egypt
   C. Greece
   D. Rome

5. What did Sarai tell the Egyptians her relationship was to Abram in order to spare his life?
   Genesis 12:11–13
   A. She was his aunt.
   B. She was his cousin.
   C. She was his sister.
   D. She was his wife.

6. What did Pharaoh do to Abram after God brought a plague upon Pharaoh and his house?
   Genesis 12:17–20
   A. Flogged him in public
   B. Made him a slave for 7 years
   C. Sent him away
   D. Threw him in jail for 6 months

7. After Abram left Egypt, between which two cities did he pitch his tent?
   Genesis 13:3
   A. Bethel and Hai
   B. Nineveh and Ur
   C. Sodom and Gomorrah
   D. Tyre and Sidon

8. Besides the Canaanites, what other group of people dwelled in the land of Canaan according to Genesis 13:7?
   Genesis 13:7
   A. The Elamites
   B. The Levites
   C. The Ninevites
   D. The Perizzites

9. When Abram separated from Lot, which direction did Lot go?
   Genesis 13:11
   A. East
   B. North
   C. South
   D. West

10. After he departed from Abram, near what city did Lot pitch his tent?
    Genesis 13:12
    A. Ai
    B. Jericho
    C. Sodom
    D. Tarsus

11. Where did Abram settle after he departed from Lot?

    Genesis 13:18
    A. Bethlehem
    B. Hebron
    C. Jerusalem
    D. Macedonia

12. Near what sea is the vale of Siddim located?

    Genesis 14:3
    A. Black sea
    B. Great sea
    C. Red sea
    D. Salt sea

13. What happened to the kings of Sodom and Gomorrah in the vale of Siddim?

    Genesis 14:10
    A. They died in an attack by a dragon.
    B. They died in lava from an active volcano.
    C. They fell into slimepits.
    D. They froze to death in a blizzard.

14. What name is Abram referred to in Genesis 14:13?

    Genesis 14:13
    A. The Gentile
    B. The Hebrew
    C. The Perrizzite
    D. The Sidonian

15. How many armed and trained servants did Abram use to rescue Lot?

    Genesis 14:14
    A. 40
    B. 70
    C. 232
    D. 318

16. Who was the priest of the most high God that came to meet Abram?

    Genesis 14:18–19
    A. Caiaphas
    B. Melchizedek
    C. Uzzi
    D. Zadok

17. What did Abram give the high priest of the most high God?

    Genesis 14:20
    A. Cattle
    B. Gold
    C. Silver
    D. Tithes

18. How did Abram feel when the LORD told him he would multiply his offspring?

    Genesis 15:6
    A. He did not believe the LORD; and he knew he was too old to father children.
    B. He did not believe the LORD; and he knew his wife was too old to bare children.
    C. He believed in the LORD; and he counted it to him for righteousness.
    D. He believed in the LORD; and he knew the offspring would come from Ishmael.

19. How many years did God say Abram's offspring would be slaves in a foreign land?

    Genesis 15:13
    A. 100
    B. 400
    C. 500
    D. 100

20. Whom was God referring to when he said their iniquity was **not** yet full?

    Genesis 15:16
    A. The Amorites
    B. The Hebrews
    C. The Philistines
    D. The Phoenicians

*Answers on page 751

JANUARY 5

Lesson 5
Today's Reading: *Genesis 16–18*
Period of Time: 1910–1897 BC
Author: Moses

1. Who was Sarai's handmaid?
   Genesis 16:1
   A. Delilah
   B. Hagar
   C. Leah
   D. Rachel

2. Who found Sarai's handmaid by a fountain of water in the wilderness?
   Genesis 16:7
   A. Abram
   B. An angel
   C. Lot
   D. Satan

3. What was the name of the handmaid's unborn child?
   Genesis 16:11, 16:15
   A. Aaron
   B. Esau
   C. Ishmael
   D. Jacob

4. How old was Abram when the handmaid's son was born?
   Genesis 16:16
   A. Twoscore and four years old
   B. Threescore and five years old
   C. Fourscore and six years old
   D. Fourscore and seven years old

5. How old was Abram when the LORD appeared unto him and told him, "I am the mighty God; walk before me and be thou perfect"?
   Genesis 17:1
   A. 66 years old
   B. 77 years old
   C. 88 years old
   D. 99 years old

6. What new name did God give to Abram?
   Genesis 17:5
   A. Abraham
   B. Isaac
   C. Jacob
   D. Joseph

7. What land did God promise to give to Abram?
   Genesis 17:8
   A. Asia Major
   B. Asia Minor
   C. Canaan
   D. Egypt

8. What was to be the sign of the covenant between God and Abram?
   Genesis 17:10
   A. A chariot of fire
   B. Circumcision
   C. Rainbows
   D. The Star of David

9. What new name did God give to Sarai?
   Genesis 17:15
   A. Sarah
   B. Tahpenes
   C. Tamar
   D. Zilpah

10. What was the name of the son that God promised to give to Abram and Sarai?
    Genesis 17:19
    A. Aaron
    B. David
    C. Gideon
    D. Isaac

11. What did Abram see as he sat in his tent doorway on the plains of Mamre?
    Genesis 18:1–2
    A. A dragon
    B. An angel of the LORD
    C. Robbers and thieves
    D. Three men

12. What did Abram serve his guests?
Genesis 18:4–8
   A. Bread, beef, butter, milk and water
   B. Cake, wine, chicken, raisins, and nuts
   C. Dates, bread, water, almonds, and fish
   D. Honey, raisin cakes, veal, milk, and beer

13. What did Sarai do when a guest prophesied she would give birth to a child in her old age?
Genesis 18:11–12
   A. Became angry
   B. Cried
   C. Jumped up and down
   D. Laughed

14. Which two cities' cries were great and their sin grievous?
Genesis 18:20
   A. Athens and Corinth
   B. Babylon and Nineveh
   C. Sodom and Gomorrah
   D. Tyre and Sidon

15. What did God promise Abram if 50 righteous people lived within the city? God would....
Genesis 18:23–26
   A. Spare the 50, but destroy the rest.
   B. Spare the 50, including their wives and children, but destroy the rest.
   C. Spare the entire city.
   D. Destroy the entire city.

16. What did God promise Abram if 45 righteous people lived within the city? God would....
Genesis 18:27–28
   A. Spare the entire city.
   B. Spare the 45, but destroy the rest.
   C. Spare the 45, including their wives and children, but destroy the rest.
   D. Destroy the entire city.

17. What did God promise Abram if 40 righteous people lived within the city? God would....
Genesis 18:29
   A. Spare the entire city.
   B. Spare the children, but destroy the rest.
   C. Spare the 40, including their wives and children, but destroy the rest.
   D. Destroy the entire city.

18. What did God promise Abram if 30 righteous people lived within the city? God would....
Genesis 18:30
   A. Spare the women and children, but destroy the rest.
   B. Spare the entire city.
   C. Spare the 30, but destroy the rest.
   D. Destroy the entire city.

19. What did God promise Abram if 20 righteous people lived within the city? God would....
Genesis 18:31
   A. Spare the 20, but destroy the rest.
   B. Spare the entire city.
   C. Spare the 20, including their wives and children, but destroy the rest.
   D. Destroy the entire city.

20. What did God promise Abram if 10 righteous people lived within the city? God would....
Genesis 18:32
   A. Spare the 10, but destroy the rest.
   B. Spare the 10 and newborn infants, but destroy the rest.
   C. Spare the 10, including their wives and children, but destroy the rest.
   D. Spare the entire city.

*Answers on page 751

JANUARY 6

Lesson 6
Today's Reading: *Genesis 19–20*
Period of Time: 1897 BC
Author: Moses

1. How many angels came to Sodom?
   Genesis 19:1
   A. 2
   B. 3
   C. 7
   D. 12

2. Where were the angels planning to spend the night?
   Genesis 19:2
   A. In a stable
   B. In an inn
   C. On the street
   D. On the threshing floor

3. What type of bread did Lot serve to the angels at the feast?
   Genesis 19:3
   A. Ezekiel
   B. Manna
   C. Unleavened
   D. Yeast

4. What did Lot offer to the men of Sodom in exchange for his guests?
   Genesis 19:8
   A. A talent of gold
   B. His two daughters
   C. Thirty pieces of silver
   D. Three baths of wine (18 gallons)

5. What did the angels do to the men of Sodom to protect themselves and Lot?
   Genesis 19:11
   A. Blinded them
   B. Gave them leprosy
   C. Got the men drunk on wine
   D. Served them poisonous mushrooms

6. Which of Lot's relatives did **not** believe the city was going to be destroyed?
   Genesis 19:14
   A. His daughters
   B. His daughters-in-law
   C. His sons
   D. His sons-in-law

7. How many people escaped from Sodom before it was destroyed?
   Genesis 19:15–16
   A. 3
   B. 4
   C. 8
   D. 70

8. What was the name of the city Lot fled to?
   Genesis 19:22
   A. Zaanannim
   B. Zebulon
   C. Ziklag
   D. Zoar

9. What did God use to destroy Sodom and Gomorrah?
   Genesis 19:24
   A. Avalanches and floods
   B. Brimstone and fire
   C. Pestilence and disease
   D. War and famine

10. What happened to Lot's wife?
    Genesis 19:26
    A. She was captured and given as a wife to Palti, son of Laish.
    B. She was thrown out of a window and her corpse was eaten by dogs.
    C. She was traded as a slave for barley and silver.
    D. She was turned into a pillar of salt after looking back.

11. Why did Lot live in the mountains?

    Genesis 19:30

    A. He feared living in the city.
    B. He knew there was gold in the hills.
    C. He wanted to build a mighty fortress.
    D. He was a lumberjack by trade.

12. What sin did Lot commit?

    Genesis 19:31–36

    A. Adultery
    B. Blasphemy
    C. Incest
    D. Murder

13. Who is the father of the Moabites?

    Genesis 19:37

    A. Ahab
    B. Joab
    C. Jonadab
    D. Moab

14. Who is the father of the children of Ammon?

    Genesis 19:38

    A. Amoammi
    B. Benammi
    C. Loammi
    D. Miammi

15. Who was the king of Gerar?

    Genesis 20:2

    A. King Abimelech
    B. King Chedorlaomer
    C. King Tidal
    D. King Zophar

16. What did Abraham tell the king of Gerar his relationship was to Sarah?

    Genesis 20:2

    A. She was his aunt.
    B. She was his cousin.
    C. She was his sister.
    D. She was his wife.

17. Who told the king of Gerar the truth about Abraham and Sarah?

    Genesis 20:3

    A. An angel of the LORD
    B. God
    C. One of the king's servants
    D. The king's astrologers

18. What did the king of Gerar give to Abraham?

    Genesis 20:14–16

    A. Camels, rubies, 10 talents of gold, and a title
    B. Donkeys, gold, silver, and wives
    C. Horses, chariots, soldiers, and weapons
    D. Sheep, oxen, servants, and 1,000 pieces of silver

19. What did Abraham do for the king of Gerar?

    Genesis 20:17

    A. Became his treasurer
    B. Led his army into battle
    C. Prayed for him
    D. Sent him 100 head of cattle

20. How had God punished the king of Gerar?

    Genesis 20:17–18

    A. He closed the wombs of the women.
    B. He forced him to eat grass like a cow.
    C. He made his hand leprous.
    D. He slew 153,000 of his soldiers.

Answers on page 751

JANUARY 7

Lesson 7
Today's Reading: *Genesis 21–23*
Period of Time: 1896–1859 BC
Author: Moses

1. How many days old was Isaac when he was circumcised?
   Genesis 21:4
   A. 3
   B. 7
   C. 8
   D. 12

2. How old was Abraham when Isaac was born?
   Genesis 21:5
   A. 18 years old
   B. 41 years old
   C. 65 years old
   D. 100 years old

3. Where did Hagar and her son go after she was forced to leave Abraham?
   Genesis 21:14
   A. Egypt
   B. Mount Carmel
   C. River of Jordan
   D. Wilderness of Beersheba

4. What did God give Hagar and her son after they left Abraham?
   Genesis 21:19
   A. A camel
   B. A knife
   C. A sack of cornmeal
   D. A well of water

5. What did Hagar's son become?
   Genesis 21:20
   A. An archer
   B. An engraver
   C. An innkeeper
   D. An oarsmen

6. Where did Hagar's son dwell?
   Genesis 21:20–21
   A. Along the great sea
   B. In army fortresses
   C. Mount Mariah
   D. Wilderness of Paran

7. Where did Hagar find her son's bride?
   Genesis 21:21
   A. Babylon
   B. Egypt
   C. Moab
   D. Ur

8. What did Abraham give to Abimelech as a witness to the well he dug in Beersheba?
   Genesis 21:28–30
   A. 5 crown jewels
   B. 7 ewe lambs
   C. 8 talents of gold
   D. 10 pieces of silver

9. Whose land did Abimelech and Phicol go to after making a covenant with Abraham?
   Genesis 21:32
   A. Land of the Philistines
   B. Land of the Sabeans
   C. Land of the Uzzielites
   D. Land of the Zamzummims

10. Where did God order Abraham to take Isaac and sacrifice him as a burnt offering?
    Genesis 22:2
    A. Mount Ararat
    B. Mount Carmel
    C. Mount Moriah
    D. Mount Nebo

11. Who stopped Abraham from sacrificing Isaac?
    Genesis 22:10–12
    A. An angel of the LORD
    B. Isaac
    C. Lot
    D. Sarah

12. What did Abraham use in place of Isaac for the burnt offering?

    Genesis 22:13

    A. A bull
    B. A dove
    C. A pigeon
    D. A ram

13. What did Abraham call the name of the place where he offered the burnt offering?

    Genesis 22:14

    A. Jehovah-jireh
    B. Jehovah-nissi
    C. Jehovah-rapha
    D. Jehovah-yahweh

14. What two symbols did God use when referring to multiplying the seed of Abraham?

    Genesis 22:15–18

    A. Cattle and sheep
    B. Stars and sand
    C. Trees and leaves
    D. Vines and Grapes

15. Who begot Rebekah?

    Genesis 22:23

    A. Balaam
    B. Belshazzar
    C. Bethuel
    D. Boaz

16. How old was Sarah when she died?

    Genesis 23:1–2

    A. 99 years old
    B. 127 years old
    C. 133 years old
    D. 149 years old

17. Where in the land of Canaan did Sarah die?

    Genesis 23:2

    A. Kabul
    B. Kedesh
    C. Kirjath-arba
    D. Kumukhu

18. Whom did Abraham buy the land from to bury Sarah's body?

    Genesis 23:3–16

    A. Elika the Harodite
    B. Ephron the Hittite
    C. Sanballat the Horonite
    D. Sibbechai the Hushathite

19. How much did Abraham pay for Sarah's gravesite?

    Genesis 23:16

    A. 2 wells of water
    B. 7 ewe lambs
    C. 400 shekels of silver
    D. 1,000 talents of gold

20. Where was Sarah's body laid to rest?

    Genesis 23:19

    A. In a cave in the field of Machpelah
    B. In a potter's field in the land of Canaan
    C. In a sepulcher along the river of Jordan
    D. In an unknown tomb

*Answers on page 751

Lesson 8
Today's Reading: *Genesis 24–25*
Period of Time: 1856–1804 BC
Author: Moses

JANUARY 8

1. Where did Abraham's servant place his hand when he made the oath?
   Genesis 24:2–9
   A. Over his heart
   B. Under Abraham's thigh
   C. Up in the air
   D. Upon the sacred scrolls

2. How many camels did Abraham's servant use for his journey?
   Genesis 24:10
   A. 10
   B. 40
   C. 70
   D. 90

3. Where did Abraham's servant travel to in his search to find Isaac a wife?
   Genesis 24:10
   A. Armenia
   B. Egypt
   C. India
   D. Mesopotamia

4. Near which city did Abraham's servant make the camels kneel by a well of water?
   Genesis 24:10–11
   A. Besor
   B. Endor
   C. Nahor
   D. Peor

5. What did Abraham's servant give Rebekah at the well of water?
   Genesis 24:22
   A. A golden earring and two golden bracelets
   B. A dozen camels and seven ewe lambs
   C. Silver necklaces and a white donkey
   D. Ten dresses and a coat of many colors

6. Who accompanied Rebekah to Canaan?
   Genesis 24:59
   A. Her bodyguard
   B. Her doctor
   C. Her nurse
   D. Her secretary

7. What did Isaac do when he met Rebekah?
   Genesis 24:67
   A. He led her into Sarah's tent and loved her.
   B. He scolded Abraham's servant and told him to take her back to her father.
   C. He treated her like a maidservant and not like a wife.
   D. He wept because she was so beautiful.

8. What was the name of Abraham's second wife?
   Genesis 25:1
   A. Azubah
   B. Delilah
   C. Hannah
   D. Keturah

9. How many children did Abraham and his second wife have?
   Genesis 25:2
   A. 0
   B. 6
   C. 8
   D. 12

10. How old was Abraham when he died?
    Genesis 25:7
    A. 120 years old
    B. 133 years old
    C. 149 years old
    D. 175 years old

11. Where was Abraham's body laid to rest?

    Genesis 25:9

    A. Cave of Machpelah
    B. City of Ur cemetery
    C. Near the river of Egypt
    D. Potter's field

12. Near which well did Isaac dwell?

    Genesis 25:11

    A. Jacob's well
    B. Lahairoi's well
    C. Rehoboth's well
    D. Sitnah's well

13. Who was the firstborn of Ishmael?

    Genesis 25:13

    A. Naaman
    B. Nathan
    C. Nebajoth
    D. Nebuchadnezzar

14. How many sons did Ishmael have?

    Genesis 25:16

    A. 7
    B. 12
    C. 27
    D. 113

15. How old was Ishmael when he died?

    Genesis 25:17

    A. 54 years old
    B. 99 years old
    C. 120 years old
    D. 137 years old

16. How old was Isaac when he took Rebekah as his wife?

    Genesis 25:20

    A. 20 years old
    B. 30 years old
    C. 40 years old
    D. 50 years old

17. What did Esau look like when he was born?

    Genesis 25:25

    A. Black like the night
    B. Red like a hairy garment
    C. White like the first snow
    D. Yellow like a daffodil

18. How old was Isaac when the twins were born?

    Genesis 25:26

    A. Threescore years old
    B. Fourscore years old
    C. Fivescore years old
    D. Sixscore years old

19. What other name was Esau called?

    Genesis 25:30

    A. Ebal
    B. Eder
    C. Edom
    D. Ehud

20. What did Jacob give Esau in exchange for his birthright?

    Genesis 25:29–34

    A. A bag full of diamonds and other precious stones
    B. A boar's head brush and tortoise shell comb
    C. A necklace and two bracelets made of gold
    D. A pottage of lentils served with bread

Answers on page 751

Lesson 9
Today's Reading: *Genesis 26–28*
Period of Time: 1804–1759 BC
Author: Moses

1. Where did Isaac dwell during the famine?
   Genesis 26:1
   A. Baaltamar
   B. Edar
   C. Gerar
   D. Tamar

2. What relationship did Isaac tell King Abimelech that Rebekah's relationship was to him?
   Genesis 26:6–11
   A. She was his cousin.
   B. She was his daughter.
   C. She was his niece.
   D. She was his sister.

3. How much did God bless Isaac in one year after he sowed a crop?
   Genesis 26:12
   A. A double fold
   B. A triple fold
   C. A hundred fold
   D. A thousand fold

4. Who envied Isaac?
   Genesis 26:14
   A. The Cyrenians
   B. The Egyptians
   C. The Libertines
   D. The Philistines

5. What did King Abimelech do to Isaac when Isaac became mightier than him?
   Genesis 26:16
   A. Commanded him to leave
   B. Lowered him into a pit
   C. Ordered his army to kill him
   D. Taxed him

6. Which well did Isaac and his herdsmen **not** dig?
   Genesis 26:17–22
   A. Esek
   B. Jacob
   C. Rehoboth
   D. Sitnah

7. Where was Isaac when the LORD appeared to him at night?
   Genesis 26:23–33
   A. Beer-sheba
   B. Kartan
   C. Pisgah
   D. Succoth

8. How old was Esau when he married two women?
   Genesis 26:34
   A. 33 years old
   B. 40 years old
   C. 45 years old
   D. 50 years old

9. What were the names of Esau's wives?
   Genesis 26:34
   A. Adah and Anna
   B. Judith and Bashemath
   C. Rachel and Leah
   D. Ruth and Orpah

10. What was Esau's wives' ethnicity?
    Genesis 26:34
    A. Buzite
    B. Eranite
    C. Hittite
    D. Oznite

11. What did Isaac tell Esau to bring him before he would give Esau his blessing?

    Genesis 27:1–4

    A. A drink of water from the well of Bethlehem
    B. A little balm, and a little honey, spices, and myrrh, nuts, and almonds
    C. A little bit of honey from the carcass of a dead lion
    D. A savory meal made with venison

12. Who helped Jacob steal Esau's birthright?

    Genesis 27:5–17

    A. Beeri
    B. Esau's wives
    C. King Abimelech
    D. Rebekah

13. How did Jacob fool blind Isaac?

    Genesis 27:15–27

    A. He covered his hands and neck with goatskins and wore Esau's clothes.
    B. He got Isaac drunk with wine and had him sign the official papers.
    C. He hired his cousin to act like Esau and trick Isaac into giving him the blessing.
    D. He made Isaac believe he heard the voice of God talking to him in his sleep.

14. Where did Jacob flee to when he found out Esau had plans to kill him after Isaac died?

    Genesis 27:41–28:5

    A. Padan-aram
    B. Pasdammim
    C. Perezuzzah
    D. Pihahiroth

15. Who was Rebekah's brother?

    Genesis 28:2

    A. Javan
    B. Laban
    C. Ornan
    D. Tartan

16. Who was Esau's third wife?

    Genesis 28:9

    A. Ephrath
    B. Mahalath
    C. Shimeath
    D. Taphath

17. What did Jacob use for pillows one night?

    Genesis 28:11

    A. Blankets
    B. Clothes
    C. Stones
    D. Wood

18. What did Jacob see in his dream?

    Genesis 28:12–15

    A. A ladder that reached up to heaven
    B. Seven fat kine coming out of a river
    C. Sheaves in a field bowing down to a sheaf
    D. The sun, moon, and eleven stars bowing down to him

19. What did Jacob name the place where he had his dream?

    Genesis 28:19

    A. Babel
    B. Betharbel
    C. Bethel
    D. Bethlehem

20. What vow did Jacob make when he woke from his sleep?

    Genesis 28:22

    A. He would change his name to Israel.
    B. He would eat pulse and drink water for ten days.
    C. He would fast for seven days, shave his hair, and avoid touching dead bodies.
    D. He would give God a tenth of everything God gave to him.

*Answers on page 751

JANUARY 10

Lesson 10
Today's Reading: *Genesis 29–30*
Period of Time: 1759–1739 BC
Author: Moses

1. Who was Laban's father?
   Genesis 29:5
   A. Hamor
   B. Nahor
   C. Nicanor
   D. Zippor

2. Whom did Jacob meet at the well?
   Genesis 29:6–9
   A. Bilhah
   B. Leah
   C. Rachel
   D. Zilpah

3. Who was Laban's eldest daughter?
   Genesis 29:16
   A. Bilhah
   B. Dinah
   C. Leah
   D. Zilpah

4. Who was considered beautiful and well favored?
   Genesis 29:17
   A. Dinah
   B. Leah
   C. Rachel
   D. Zilpah

5. How did Laban beguile Jacob?
   Genesis 29:18–26
   A. He deceived Jacob by having him marry his eldest daughter.
   B. He did not reveal his true identity and accused Jacob of being a spy.
   C. He falsely accused Jacob of trying to commit adultery with his wife.
   D. He lied to Jacob and told him his wife was his sister.

6. Who was Leah's handmaid?
   Genesis 29:24
   A. Bilhah
   B. Dinah
   C. Rachel
   D. Zilpah

7. How many years did Jacob work for Laban so that he could marry the woman he loved?
   Genesis 29:18–30
   A. 7
   B. 14
   C. 16
   D. 20

8. How many days did the honeymoon last after each wedding?
   Genesis 29:27–28
   A. 3
   B. 7
   C. 21
   D. 30

9. What was the name of Leah's firstborn son?
   Genesis 29:32
   A. Dan
   B. Gad
   C. Levi
   D. Reuben

10. What was the name of Leah's secondborn son?
    Genesis 29:33
    A. Asher
    B. Issachar
    C. Judah
    D. Simeon

11. What was the name of Leah's thirdborn son?
    Genesis 29:34
    A. Levi
    B. Naphtali
    C. Simeon
    D. Zebulun

12. What was the name of Leah's fourthborn son?
    Genesis 29:35
    A. Judah
    B. Levi
    C. Naphtali
    D. Reuben

13. What was the name of Bilhah's firstborn son?
    Genesis 30:1–6
    A. Asher
    B. Dan
    C. Gad
    D. Levi

14. What was the name of Bilhah's secondborn son?
    Genesis 30:7–8
    A. Issachar
    B. Reuben
    C. Simeon
    D. Naphtali

15. What was the name of Zilpah's firstborn son?
    Genesis 30:9–11
    A. Asher
    B. Dan
    C. Gad
    D. Judah

16. What was the name of Zilpah's secondborn son?
    Genesis 30:12–13
    A. Asher
    B. Naphtali
    C. Simeon
    D. Zebulun

17. Who brought mandrakes to his mother?
    Genesis 30:14–16
    A. Asher
    B. Levi
    C. Reuben
    D. Simeon

18. Who was Dinah's mother?
    Genesis 30:20–21
    A. Bilhah
    B. Leah
    C. Rachel
    D. Zilpah

19. What was the name of Rachel's firstborn son?
    Genesis 30:22–24
    A. Joseph
    B. Levi
    C. Naphtali
    D. Zebulun

20. How did Jacob cheat Laban out of livestock?
    Genesis 30:25–43
    A. He purchased Laban's meat at a lower price using false scales.
    B. He sacrificed Laban's scrawny animals to God and kept the best for himself.
    C. He turned Laban's cattle into steers by castrating them.
    D. He used the strongest animals to breed with his; and the weak ones with Laban's.

Answers on page 751

JANUARY 11

Lesson 11
Today's Reading: *Genesis 31–32*
Period of Time: 1739 BC
Author: Moses

1. Who told Jacob to return to Canaan?
   Genesis 31:3
   A. God
   B. Isaac
   C. Laban
   D. Reuben

2. How many times did Laban change Jacob's wages?
   Genesis 31:7
   A. 2
   B. 3
   C. 7
   D. 10

3. What did Jacob see in his dream prior to returning to Canaan?
   Genesis 31:10–13
   A. A man squeezing grapes into a cup
   B. Birds eating food out of a basket
   C. Rams leaping upon cattle
   D. Seven thin ears of corn eating seven fat ears of corn

4. Whom did God tell Jacob he was the God of?
   Genesis 31:13
   A. Amana
   B. Bethel
   C. Kirjath-arba
   D. Tyre

5. Who were Laban's two daughters?
   Genesis 31:14–16
   A. Bilhah and Dinah
   B. Leah and Rachel
   C. Martha and Mary
   D. Ruth and Naomi

6. Who stole Laban's images?
   Genesis 31:19
   A. Bilhah
   B. Jacob
   C. Rachel
   D. Zilpah

7. What was Laban's ethnicity?
   Genesis 31:20, 31:24
   A. Amorite
   B. Canaanite
   C. Perizzite
   D. Syrian

8. Which mountain did Jacob set his face toward?
   Genesis 31:23
   A. Mount Gilead
   B. Mount Naphtali
   C. Mount Paran
   D. Mount Perazim

9. Who told Laban **not** to harm Jacob?
   Genesis 31:24
   A. Abimelech–King of Gerar
   B. God
   C. Isaac
   D. Laban's wife

10. How many years did Jacob serve Laban?
    Genesis 31:38–41
    A. 10
    B. 14
    C. 19
    D. 20

11. What did Jacob call the place where he and Laban made a covenant with each other?
    Genesis 31:47–48
    A. Gadara
    B. Galatia
    C. Galeed
    D. Gallim

12. What did Jacob call the place where the angels met him?
    Genesis 32:1–2
    A. Mahanaim
    B. Makkedah
    C. Mamre
    D. Masada

13. Where in the land of Seir did Esau make his home?

    Genesis 32:3

    A. Ammon
    B. Edom
    C. Moab
    D. Midian

14. How many men did Esau send when he heard Jacob was in the land of Seir?

    Genesis 32:6

    A. 12
    B. 100
    C. 400
    D. 1000

15. Which peace offering did Jacob send to Esau?

    Genesis 32:13–21

    A. 10 bulls, 220 goats, 10 talents of gold, 40 rams, 60 camels, 10 kine, 20 swine, and 20 chickens
    B. 20 talents of gold, 20 pieces of silver, 8 ruby necklaces, 20 pearl bracelets, and 30 changes of clothes
    C. 100 talents of gold, 20 pieces of silver, 30 milk camels, 40 rams, 60 kine, and 200 goats
    D. 200 she goats, 20 he goats, 200 ewes, 20 rams, 30 milk camels, 40 kine, 10 bulls, and 10 foals

16. How many sons did Jacob have when he crossed the ford?

    Genesis 32:22

    A. 11
    B. 12
    C. 18
    D. 24

17. What was the name of the ford Jacob crossed?

    Genesis 32:22

    A. The Barada
    B. The Dan
    C. The Jabbok
    D. The Seven Streams

18. How did the man injure Jacob when he wrestled him?

    Genesis 32:25

    A. He dislocated Jacob's thigh joint.
    B. He knocked Jacob out with a blow to the head.
    C. He punched Jacob's ear causing him to go partially deaf.
    D. He stabbed Jacob in the stomach with a knife.

19. What new name did God give to Jacob?

    Genesis 32:28

    A. Dan
    B. Gad
    C. Heman
    D. Israel

20. What did Jacob call the place where he saw God face to face?

    Genesis 32:30

    A. Padan-aram
    B. Peniel
    C. Persia
    D. Phrygia

*Answers on page 751

Lesson 12
Today's Reading: *Genesis 33–35*
Period of Time: 1739–1716 BC
Author: Moses

JANUARY 12

1. When Jacob saw Esau and his 400 men approaching, how did he divide his people?
   Genesis 33:1–2
   A. Handmaids and their children first, Leah and her children second, and Rachel and Joseph last.
   B. Joseph first, handmaids second, Leah and Rachel third, and all of the children last.
   C. Leah and her children first, Rachel and Joseph second, and handmaids and their children last.
   D. Rachel and Joseph first, handmaids and their children second, and Leah and her children last.

2. How many times did Jacob bow to Esau?
   Genesis 33:3
   A. 3
   B. 7
   C. 10
   D. 12

3. Where did Jacob build a house for himself and booths for his cattle?
   Genesis 33:17
   A. Shalem
   B. Shechem
   C. Succoth
   D. Suphah

4. How many pieces of money did Jacob pay the sons of Hamor for the field?
   Genesis 33:18–19
   A. 10
   B. 20
   C. 50
   D. 100

5. What did Jacob call the place where he built an altar?
   Genesis 33:20
   A. El-elohe-Israel
   B. El Roi
   C. El Shaddai
   D. El Yonna Adonai

6. What was the name of Jacob's daughter that was defiled?
   Genesis 34:1–2
   A. Damaris
   B. Diana
   C. Dinah
   D. Dorcas

7. Who defiled Jacob's daughter?
   Genesis 34:2
   A. Amnon
   B. Joseph
   C. Lot
   D. Shechem

8. What did the Hivite men agree to do in order to marry into the family of Jacob?
   Genesis 34:6–24
   A. Become circumcised
   B. Make a vow to practice Judaism
   C. Pay a dowry to Jacob
   D. Serve Jacob for seven years

9. Which two of Jacob's sons slew all of the Hivite men in a city?
   Genesis 34:25
   A. Benjamin and Judah
   B. Levi and Simeon
   C. Naphtali and Joseph
   D. Reuben and Dan

10. What did the sons of Jacob do after the Hivite men in the city were slain?

    Genesis 34:27–29

    A. Begged God for forgiveness
    B. Built an altar unto God
    C. Paid a tithe to God
    D. Spoiled the city

11. Who did Jacob fear would kill him and his family for killing the Hivite men?

    Genesis 34:30

    A. Amorites and Kenizzites
    B. Bethelites and Shulamites
    C. Canaanites and Perrizzites
    D. Danites and Edomites

12. Where did God tell Jacob to go after the Hivite men were slain?

    Genesis 35:1

    A. Bethel
    B. Egypt
    C. Paddan-aram
    D. Shalem

13. What did Jacob tell his family prior to leaving their home near the Hivite city?

    Genesis 35:2

    A. "Go and wash in the river of Jordan seven times and you shall be clean."
    B. "Put away the strange gods that are among you, and be clean, and change your garments."
    C. "Sacrifice unto the LORD your God a sin offering for the evil you have done."
    D. "Take your families and go into the wilderness and ask the LORD for forgiveness and ye shall know the truth, and the truth shall make you free."

14. What did Jacob hide beneath an oak tree?

    Genesis 35:4

    A. The silver and gold amulets his sons took from the Hivite city.
    B. The silver idol he had bought from the Hivite men.
    C. The strange gods and earrings his children gave to him.
    D. The talents of gold he stole from Laban.

15. What is another name for Luz?

    Genesis 35:6

    A. Bethel
    B. Egypt
    C. Paddan-aram
    D. Shalem

16. Who was Rebekah's nurse?

    Genesis 35:8

    A. Abigail
    B. Bilhah
    C. Cozbi
    D. Deborah

17. What did Jacob name the son born to him and Rachel?

    Genesis 35:18

    A. Aaron
    B. Benjamin
    C. Caleb
    D. Dan

18. What is the other name for Bethlehem?

    Genesis 35:19

    A. Ephesus
    B. Ephrath
    C. Ephron
    D. Ethiopia

19. Which of Jacob's sons had a sexual relationship with one of Jacob's concubines?

    Genesis 35:22

    A. Judah
    B. Levi
    C. Reuben
    D. Simeon

20. How old was Isaac when he died?

    Genesis 35:28–29

    A. One hundred and twoscore plus seven years
    B. One hundred and twoscore plus eleven years
    C. One hundred and threescore plus three years
    D. One hundred and fourscore years

Answers on page 751

Lesson 13
Today's Reading: *Genesis 36–38*
Period of Time: 1728 BC
Author: Moses

1. Which nation is Esau the father of?
   Genesis 36:1, 36:8
   A. Edom
   B. Ekron
   C. Elam
   D. Eran

2. Who was Nebajoth's sister?
   Genesis 36:2–5
   A. Baara
   B. Bashemath
   C. Bathsheba
   D. Bazrah

3. Where did Esau move to after he and Jacob became so rich they could no longer dwell together on the same land?
   Genesis 36:7–8
   A. Mount Carmel
   B. Mount Horeb
   C. Mount Seir
   D. Mount Tabor

4. How many sons did Esau have?
   Genesis 36:4–14
   A. 5
   B. 8
   C. 12
   D. 17

5. What was Seir's ethnicity?
   Genesis 36:20
   A. Hebronite
   B. Hittite
   C. Horite
   D. Huphamite

6. What gift did Jacob make for Joseph that made Joseph's brothers jealous?
   Genesis 37:3–4
   A. A coat of many colours
   B. A house overlooking the sea
   C. A sword made of iron
   D. A vineyard

7. Whose sheaves made obeisance to Joseph's sheaves in his first dream?
   Genesis 37:6–7
   A. A baker's sheaves
   B. A king's sheaves
   C. An idol's sheaves
   D. His brothers' sheaves

8. Which of the following made obeisance to Joseph in his second dream?
   Genesis 37:9–10
   A. Earth, wind, and fire
   B. Insects, birds, and animals
   C. Kings, princes, and subjects
   D. Sun, moon, and eleven stars

9. Where did Joseph find his brothers tending sheep?
   Genesis 37:17
   A. Avith
   B. Dothan
   C. Masrekah
   D. Rehoboth

10. Which brother tried to rescue Joseph?
    Genesis 37:20–22
    A. Naphtali
    B. Reuben
    C. Simeon
    D. Zebulun

11. What were the men that purchased Joseph?
    Genesis 37:28
    A. Canaanites
    B. Edomites
    C. Hivites
    D. Ishmeelites

12. How much was Joseph sold for?
    Genesis 37:28
    A. 10 Arabian horses
    B. 12 talents of gold
    C. 20 pieces of silver
    D. 40 desert tents

13. How did Joseph die according to his brothers?
    Genesis 37:31–33
    A. An evil beast devoured him.
    B. An Ithrite thief stabbed him.
    C. An obelisk fell and crushed him.
    D. An old witch poisoned him.

14. Whom was Joseph sold to in Egypt?
    Genesis 37:36
    A. Pharaoh
    B. Potiphar
    C. Potipherah
    D. Publius

15. What was Hirah's ethnicity?
    Genesis 38:1
    A. Adullamite
    B. Amalekite
    C. Anakite
    D. Ashurite

16. What happened to Judah's firstborn son?
    Genesis 38:7
    A. He became a great leader in the land of Canaan and defeated the Philistines.
    B. He died at birth from a blood infection because of Judah's great sin.
    C. The LORD slew him for being so wicked.
    D. The Philistines adopted him.

17. What happened to Judah's secondborn son?
    Genesis 38:8–10
    A. A nurse dropped him at birth, crippling his foot.
    B. God killed him because he spilled his seed on the ground.
    C. He drowned in the river of Jordan trying to save his son.
    D. He led a revolt against Egypt and was killed in a battle.

18. Who was Judah's thirdborn son?
    Genesis 38:5, 38:11
    A. Chezib
    B. Er
    C. Onan
    D. Shelah

19. Whose Canaanite daughter did Judah marry?
    Genesis 38:2, 38:12
    A. Sheba's daughter
    B. Shelia's daughter
    C. Shomar's daughter
    D. Shua's daughter

20. Who was the father of the twins Perez and Zerah?
    Genesis 38:12–30
    A. Er
    B. Onan
    C. Judah
    D. Tamar

Answers on page 752

JANUARY 14

Lesson 14
Today's Reading: *Genesis 39–41*
Period of Time: 1728–1708 BC
Author: Moses

1. In which nation did the Ishmeelites sell Joseph?
   Genesis 39:1
   A. Canaan
   B. Egypt
   C. Syria
   D. Sumeria

2. Who purchased Joseph from the Ishmeelites?
   Genesis 39:1
   A. Asenath
   B. Manasseh
   C. Potiphar
   D. Zaphenathpanah

3. What was Joseph falsely accused of?
   Genesis 39:2–20
   A. Attempted kidnapping
   B. Attempted murder
   C. Attempted rape
   D. Attempted robbery

4. What did the chief butler dream?
   Genesis 40:1–11
   A. He anointed the next king of Egypt.
   B. He became the Pharaoh's top general.
   C. He delivered a flying scroll to the queen.
   D. He handed Pharaoh his cup.

5. What did the chief baker dream?
   Genesis 40:16–17
   A. He had three baskets upon his head.
   B. He married Pharaoh's daughter.
   C. He saved Pharaoh's life.
   D. He saw who murdered Pharaoh's son.

6. What happened to the chief butler?
   Genesis 40:20–21
   A. He attacked a guard and died in prison.
   B. He became chief butler once again.
   C. He fled to Midian.
   D. He was sold to the Ishmeelites.

7. What happened to the chief baker?
   Genesis 40:20–22
   A. He became the captain of the guard.
   B. He died in prison.
   C. He fled to Midian.
   D. He was hanged by Pharaoh.

8. What was Pharaoh's *first* dream?
   Genesis 41:1–4
   A. 7 lean kine ate 7 fat kine.
   B. 7 fat kine ate 7 lean kine.
   C. 7 full ear of corn ate 7 thin ear of corn.
   D. 7 thin ear of corn ate 7 fat ear of corn.

9. What was Pharaoh's *second* dream?
   Genesis 41:5–7
   A. 7 lean kine ate 7 fat kine.
   B. 7 fat kine ate 7 lean kine.
   C. 7 full ear of corn ate 7 thin ear of corn.
   D. 7 thin ear of corn ate 7 fat ear of corn.

10. What did Joseph tell Pharaoh regarding Pharaoh's dreams?
    Genesis 41:14–32
    A. Pharaoh would have 7 sons, but the 7 sons would die during a famine.
    B. 7 kings would rise against Pharaoh in 7 years, causing a severe famine.
    C. 7 wives would give Pharaoh 7 sons during the 7 years of famine.
    D. The land would have 7 years of abundance followed by 7 years of famine.

11. What did Joseph tell Pharaoh he should do to prepare for the famine?
    Genesis 41:33–36
    A. Appoint a person over Egypt to buy land and hoard food.
    B. Kill all the Hebrews, but keep the Hebrew girls as concubines.
    C. Make slaves of the Hebrews and force them to build silos to store the grain.
    D. Throw the newborn Hebrew males into the river of Egypt.

12. What did Pharaoh give to Joseph?

    Genesis 41:42

    A. Bondservants, his daughter to wed, and a new house
    B. Camels, slaves, and seven golden rings
    C. Clothes made of fine linen, a ring, and a gold necklace
    D. Made him captain of the guard, a wife, and a new house

13. What did Pharaoh call Joseph?

    Genesis 41:45

    A. Zadok
    B. Zaphnath-pa'aneah
    C. Zerubbabel
    D. Zurishaddai

14. Who was Potiphera's daughter?

    Genesis 41:45

    A. Asenath
    B. Orpah
    C. Vashti
    D. Zipporah

15. What was Potiphera's title?

    Genesis 41:45

    A. Captain of the guard
    B. Chief Butler
    C. General of Pharaoh's army
    D. Priest of On

16. How old was Joseph when he stood before Pharaoh?

    Genesis 41:46

    A. 18 years old
    B. 21 years old
    C. 30 years old
    D. 42 years old

17. What was the name of Joseph's firstborn son?

    Genesis 41:51

    A. Magog
    B. Manasseh
    C. Mark
    D. Matthias

18. Who was Joseph's secondborn son?

    Genesis 41:52

    A. Elisha
    B. Ephraim
    C. Ethan
    D. Ezra

19. What did Pharaoh tell the Egyptians when they asked him for bread?

    Genesis 41:55

    A. "Go unto Joseph; what he saith to you, do."
    B. "Go unto the Priests of Egypt; whatsoever they saith unto you, that you must do."
    C. "Sell me your cattle, goats, and pigs, and then I will give you a year's ration of corn."
    D. "Sell me your farms; then I will give you bread enough to eat."

20. How far did the famine spread?

    Genesis 41:56–57

    A. Egypt
    B. Egypt and Canaan
    C. All over the face of the earth
    D. All over the face of the earth, but not in North and South America

*Answers on page 752

JANUARY 15

Lesson 15
Today's Reading: *Genesis 42–44*
Period of Time: 1707–1706 BC
Author: Moses

1. How many of Joseph's brothers arrived in Egypt to buy corn?
   Genesis 42:3
   A. 3
   B. 7
   C. 10
   D. 12

2. Which one of Joseph's brothers did **not** go to Egypt to buy corn?
   Genesis 42:4
   A. Benjamin
   B. Dan
   C. Gad
   D. Levi

3. Where did Joseph's brothers tell the governor of Egypt they came from?
   Genesis 42:13
   A. Babylon
   B. Canaan
   C. Libya
   D. Sumeria

4. What did Joseph accuse his brothers of being?
   Genesis 42:14
   A. Adulterers
   B. Kidnappers
   C. Robbers
   D. Spies

5. How many days did Joseph's brothers stay in prison?
   Genesis 42:17
   A. 3
   B. 12
   C. 28
   D. 40

6. Why did Joseph use an interpreter when speaking to his brothers?
   Genesis 42:23
   A. He had been in Egypt so long he no longer understood Hebrew.
   B. Interpreters were required to be present when dealing with foreigners.
   C. It was forbidden for noblemen to speak directly to lower class subjects.
   D. It was part of his clever disguise.

7. Which one of Joseph's brothers remained in prison after the others were set free?
   Genesis 42:24
   A. Benjamin
   B. Judah
   C. Reuben
   D. Simeon

8. What did the brothers find in their grain sacks the first time they left Egypt?
   Genesis 42:25–28
   A. Diamonds
   B. Golden idols
   C. Money
   D. Silver cups

9. What did Reuben say he would give his father if harm were to come upon the youngest brother?
   Genesis 42:37
   A. All of the wells on the land he owned
   B. His two sons to slay
   C. The cattle on the 1000 hills he owned
   D. Spartacus, his slave and gladiator

10. Which brother said he would take the blame if any harm came upon the youngest brother?
    Genesis 43:3–9
    A. Judah
    B. Levi
    C. Reuben
    D. Simeon

11. Which of the following did Joseph's brothers take with them to Egypt on their second trip?
    Genesis 43:11–15
    A. Amulets, balm, cattle, clothe, gold, frankincense, and myrrh
    B. Balm, almonds, fruit, honey, money, myrrh, nuts, and spices
    C. Camels, diamonds, gold, horses, nuts, silver, swords, hooks, and tents
    D. Linens, beads, cinnamon, nutmeg, olive oil, pomegranates, knives, and rams

12. When were Joseph's brothers to meet Joseph at his house?
    Genesis 43:16, 43:25
    A. 9:00 a.m.
    B. 12:00 noon
    C. 6:00 p.m.
    D. 12:00 midnight

13. Why did Joseph weep?
    Genesis 43:29–30
    A. He found his youngest son floating in the river of Egypt.
    B. He saw his youngest brother.
    C. His brothers brought him gold, frankincense, and myrrh.
    D. His brothers had informed him of his mother's death.

14. What was an abomination to the Egyptians?
    Genesis 43:32
    A. Eating with Hebrews
    B. Fortunetelling
    C. Wearing clothing made from flax
    D. Worshipping idols

15. Which brother's mess was five times greater?
    Genesis 43:34
    A. Benjamin's mess
    B. Judah's mess
    C. Reuben's mess
    D. Zebulun's mess

16. Who filled the brother's sacks before they departed the second time from Egypt?
    Genesis 44:1
    A. The baker
    B. The banker
    C. The cook
    D. The steward

17. Where was Joseph's silver cup found?
    Genesis 44:12
    A. Inside the banker's house
    B. Inside the high priest's temple
    C. Inside the youngest brother's sack
    D. Inside the youngest silversmith's well

18. How did Joseph say he discovered who took his silver cup?
    Genesis 44:15
    A. He claimed a spy informed him.
    B. He found in his room the thief's sandal.
    C. He practiced divination.
    D. He witnessed the thief take it.

19. What punishment did Joseph say he would do to the person who stole his silver cup?
    Genesis 44:17
    A. Feed him to a den of starving lions
    B. Hang him
    C. Make him his servant
    D. Throw him in jail for life

20. Who offered to take the place of the accused thief?
    Genesis 44:18–34
    A. Benjamin
    B. Gad
    C. Levi
    D. Judah

*Answers on page 752

JANUARY 16

Lesson 16
Today's Reading: *Genesis 45–47*
Period of Time: 1706–1689 BC
Author: Moses

1. What did Joseph's brothers do to him?
   Genesis 45:4
   A. Lied to him about their mother's death
   B. Sold him into slavery
   C. Stole his birthright
   D. Stole his blessing from their father

2. What purpose did Joseph tell his brothers was the reason for him being in Egypt?
   Genesis 45:5
   A. To become a pharaoh
   B. To become wealthy
   C. To interpret dreams
   D. To preserve life

3. How many years had the famine been in the land when Joseph revealed himself to his brothers?
   Genesis 45:6
   A. 2
   B. 3
   C. 6
   D. 7

4. How many years did Joseph say there would be neither earing nor harvest?
   Genesis 45:6
   A. 2
   B. 3
   C. 5
   D. 10

5. What did Joseph tell his brothers God made him to Pharaoh?
   Genesis 45:8
   A. A brother
   B. A father
   C. A friend
   D. A god

6. Where did Joseph tell his family they could dwell?
   Genesis 45:10
   A. Cairo
   B. Goshen
   C. Memphis
   D. Thebes

7. What did Pharaoh tell Joseph he would give Joseph's family?
   Genesis 45:18
   A. A rod to rule over cobras and scorpions
   B. Straw and mud to make bricks
   C. The fat of the land to eat
   D. The feel of his whip on their backs

8. What two things did Pharaoh give Joseph's family for their move to Egypt?
   Genesis 45:19–21
   A. Camels and mules
   B. Hay and horses
   C. Soldiers and catapults
   D. Wagons and provisions

9. What did Pharaoh tell Joseph his family should do with their stuff?
   Genesis 45:20
   A. Bring it with them
   B. Leave it in Canaan
   C. Sell it to the Egyptians
   D. Use it for wood for a burnt offering

10. Which gifts did Joseph give to Benjamin?
    Genesis 45:22
    A. 300 pieces of silver and 5 changes of raiment
    B. 500 pieces of gold and 7 changes of raiment
    C. 750 pieces of ivory and 8 changes of raiment
    D. 1,000 pieces of gold and 10 changes of raiment

11. What convinced Jacob that Joseph was still alive?

    Genesis 45:25–28

    A. Feeling Pharaoh's inscriptions on the gold pieces
    B. Hearing the faithful word of Judah
    C. Joseph's scent on the coat of many colors
    D. Seeing wagons from Egypt

12. Where did Jacob offer sacrifices to God on his way to Egypt?

    Genesis 46:1

    A. Beersheba
    B. Kadesh-barnea
    C. Libya
    D. Macedonia

13. Who was **not** one of Jacob's sons?

    Genesis 46:8–25

    A. Asher
    B. Issachar
    C. Pelet
    D. Zebulun

14. What were the names of Joseph's two sons?

    Genesis 46:20

    A. Er and Onan
    B. Hanoch and Pallu
    C. Manasseh and Ephraim
    D. Merari and Kohath

15. How many souls of the house of Jacob came with him to Egypt?

    Genesis 46:27

    A. Twoscore and two
    B. Threescore and ten
    C. Fourscore and one
    D. Fourscore and six

16. Which occupation was an abomination to the Egyptians?

    Genesis 46:34

    A. Farmers
    B. Miners
    C. Ranchers
    D. Shepherds

17. How old was Jacob when he appeared before Pharaoh?

    Genesis 47:9

    A. 130 years old
    B. 143 years old
    C. 165 years old
    D. 187 years old

18. Where did Jacob and his family go to dwell in the land of Egypt?

    Genesis 47:11

    A. Land of Rameses
    B. Mount Sinai
    C. Thebes
    D. Valley of Charashim

19. What was the order in which the Egyptians paid Joseph for their bread?

    Genesis 47:13–26

    A. Crops, land, livestock, money
    B. Land, crops, livestock, money
    C. Livestock, crops, money, land
    D. Money, livestock, land, crops

20. Whom did Pharaoh **not** buy land from?

    Genesis 47:22, 47:26

    A. Doctors
    B. Masons
    C. Priests
    D. Soldiers

Answers on page 752

JANUARY 17

Lesson 17
Today's Reading: *Genesis 48–50*
Period of Time: 1689–1635 BC
Author: Moses

1. Where did God Almighty appear unto Jacob?
   Genesis 48:3
   A. Buz
   B. Gur
   C. Luz
   D. Uz

2. Who were Joseph's sons?
   Genesis 48:5
   A. Ephraim and Manasseh
   B. Levi and Judah
   C. Naphtali and Benjamin
   D. Rueben and Simeon

3. Where was Rachel's body laid to rest?
   Genesis 48:7
   A. Arpad
   B. Bethlehem
   C. Coos
   D. Damascus

4. What was the name of Joseph's firstborn son?
   Genesis 48:8–20
   A. Benjamin
   B. Judah
   C. Manasseh
   D. Reuben

5. Whom did Jacob say he took land from with his sword and bow?
   Genesis 48:22
   A. The Amalekites
   B. The Ammonites
   C. The Amorites
   D. The Amramites

6. Which two brothers did Jacob describe as having instruments of cruelty in their habitations?
   Genesis 49:5
   A. Asher and Benjamin
   B. Judah and Naphtali
   C. Reuben and Zebulun
   D. Simeon and Levi

7. Which son did Jacob say the scepter would **not** depart from?
   Genesis 49:10
   A. Issachar
   B. Judah
   C. Levi
   D. Simeon

8. Which son did Jacob say would be a haven for ships?
   Genesis 49:13
   A. Asher
   B. Gad
   C. Joseph
   D. Zebulun

9. Which son did Jacob say was a strong ass couching down between two burdens?
   Genesis 49:14
   A. Dan
   B. Issachar
   C. Naphtali
   D. Simeon

10. Which son did Jacob call a serpent that bites the horse's heels?
    Genesis 49:17
    A. Dan
    B. Gad
    C. Judah
    D. Levi

11. Which son did Jacob say a troop would overtake him, but he would overcome at the last?
    Genesis 49:19
    A. Dan
    B. Gad
    C. Issachar
    D. Judah

12. Which son did Jacob say would produce royal dainties?

    Genesis 49:20

    A. Asher
    B. Benjamin
    C. Dan
    D. Gad

13. Which son did Jacob say was a hind let loose and gives goodly words?

    Genesis 49:21

    A. Benjamin
    B. Issachar
    C. Naphtali
    D. Reuben

14. Which son did Jacob say was a fruitful bough?

    Genesis 49:22–26

    A. Asher
    B. Dan
    C. Issachar
    D. Joseph

15. How many tribes made up the tribes of Israel?

    Genesis 49:28

    A. 3
    B. 7
    C. 10
    D. 12

16. What did Jacob tell his sons he wanted done to his body when he died?

    Genesis 49:29–32

    A. Bury it in the cave that is in the field of Ephron the Hittite.
    B. Cremate it and scatter the ashes over Egypt.
    C. Drop it into the great sea for proper burial.
    D. Hide it in a pyramid located in the valley of the Kings.

17. How many days did the Egyptians mourn for Jacob after his death?

    Genesis 50:3

    A. Threescore and ten days
    B. Fourscore days
    C. Fourscore and ten days
    D. Fivescore days

18. Where in the land of Canaan did Joseph mourn for his father for seven days?

    Genesis 50:10–11

    A. Along the banks of the river of Jordan
    B. At the house of Rebekah
    C. At the threshing floor of Atad
    D. Under the great oak tree of Machpelah

19. How old was Joseph when he died?

    Genesis 50:26

    A. 45 years old
    B. 65 years old
    C. 90 years old
    D. 110 years old

20. What did they do with Joseph's body after he died?

    Genesis 50:26

    A. Put it in an urn after burning it
    B. Put it inside a coffin in Egypt
    C. Put it on a ship for proper burial at sea
    D. Put it under glass

*Answers on page 752

JANUARY 18

Lesson 18
Today's Reading: *Exodus 1–3*
Period of Time: 1635–1491 BC
Author: Moses

1. Which one of the following was **not** one of Jacob's sons?
   Exodus 1:2–4
   A. Andrew
   B. Levi
   C. Naphtali
   D. Reuben

2. How many souls did Jacob take with him to Egypt?
   Exodus 1:5
   A. 70
   B. 700
   C. 7000
   D. 7,000,000

3. Which two cities built for Pharaoh by slaves were treasure cities?
   Exodus 1:11
   A. Athens and Corinth
   B. Gibeon and Shiloh
   C. Pithom and Ramses
   D. Ur and Nazareth

4. Who were the Egyptian midwives that Pharaoh commanded to kill the male Hebrew newborns?
   Exodus 1:15–22
   A. Eglah and Zillah
   B. Damaris and Hazelelponi
   C. Jemima and Tahpenes
   D. Shiphra and Puah

5. What did Pharaoh tell the Egyptians to do with the Hebrew newborns that were males?
   Exodus 1:22
   A. Baptize them in water
   B. Circumcise them on the eighth day
   C. Sacrifice them to the Egyptian god Ra
   D. Toss them into the river

6. How many months did Moses' mother hide him before placing him in an ark?
   Exodus 2:1–2
   A. 2
   B. 3
   C. 4
   D. 5

7. What did Moses' mother use to build him an ark?
   Exodus 2:3
   A. Gum, resin, and twigs
   B. Mud, nails, and gopher wood
   C. Pitch, slime, and bulrushes
   D. Reeds, screws, and mud

8. Who asked Pharaoh's daughter if she wanted her to find a Hebrew woman to nurse the baby?
   Exodus 2:7
   A. Moses' mother
   B. Moses' sister
   C. The eldest brother to Pharaoh's daughter
   D. The physician to Pharaoh's daughter

9. Whom did Pharaoh's daughter pay to nurse the baby she named *Moses*?
   Exodus 2:8–9
   A. Moses' aunt
   B. Moses' cousin
   C. Moses' mother
   D. Moses' sister

10. Why did Pharaoh's daughter name the baby *Moses*?
    Exodus 2:10
    A. She considered him a gift from the gods
    B. She drew him out of the waters
    C. She knew he would be pharaoh one day
    D. She named him after her father

11. Why did Moses flee from Egypt?
    Exodus 2:11–15
    A. He assaulted Pharaoh's daughter.
    B. He raped a guard's wife.
    C. He robbed Pharaoh's tomb.
    D. He slew an Egyptian.

12. Where did Moses flee to?
    Exodus 2:15
    A. Midian
    B. Oboth
    C. Succoth
    D. Zair

13. What was the name of the father of the seven women Moses saved from the shepherds?
    Exodus 2:18
    A. Raamah
    B. Reba
    C. Reuel
    D. Rufus

14. Who was Moses' wife?
    Exodus 2:21
    A. Jedidah
    B. Mara
    C. Shua
    D. Zipporah

15. What was the name of Moses' firstborn son?
    Exodus 2:22
    A. Gershom
    B. Hoham
    C. Nahum
    D. Obededom

16. What was the name of Moses' father-in-law?
    Exodus 3:1
    A. Jesse
    B. Jethro
    C. Joel
    D. Joshua

17. Which title did Moses' father-in-law have?
    Exodus 3:1
    A. Apostle
    B. Priest
    C. Prophet
    D. Rabbi

18. Where did the angel of the Lord appear to Moses in a flaming bush that did **not** burn?
    Exodus 3:1–2
    A. Mount Carmel
    B. Mount Ebal
    C. Mount Horeb
    D. Mount Nebo

19. What name did God tell Moses to use when the people ask him who sent him to Egypt?
    Exodus 3:14
    A. I AM THAT I AM
    B. I AM THAT UNKNOWN GOD
    C. I AM THE ALMIGHTY
    D. I AM THE BREAD OF LIFE

20. What promise did God give to Moses that would be fulfilled when the Hebrews left Egypt?
    Exodus 3:21–22
    A. They would become the largest army in Africa and the Middle East.
    B. They would have God's holy ten commandments.
    C. They would leave with Pharaoh's chariots and horses.
    D. They would spoil the Egyptians of their riches.

*Answers on page 752

JANUARY 19

Lesson 19
Today's Reading: *Exodus 4–6*
Period of Time: 1491 BC
Author: Moses

1. What was the *first* sign God told Moses to use if the people did **not** believe God had sent him?
    Exodus 4:1–5
    A. Bring Lazarus back from the dead.
    B. Change Moses' rod into a serpent.
    C. Show them the burning bush.
    D. Turn water into wine.

2. What was the *second* sign God told Moses to use if the people did **not** believe God had sent him?
    Exodus 4:6–8
    A. Make his hand become leprous.
    B. Raise his son from the dead.
    C. Speak to his wife in tongues.
    D. Use mud to heal the blind.

3. What was the *third* sign God told Moses to use if the people did **not** believe God had sent him?
    Exodus 4:9
    A. At noon make the sun stand still and go back the span of one hour.
    B. Cause fire and hail to rain down from heaven.
    C. Fill their nostrils with a stench from dead frogs.
    D. Take water from the river and make it become blood upon the dry land.

4. What excuse did Moses give when God told him to free the Hebrew slaves?
    Exodus 4:10
    A. He was a murderer.
    B. He was an only child.
    C. He was slow of speech.
    D. He was too old.

5. Which tribe did Aaron belong to?
    Exodus 4:14
    A. Tribe of Issachar
    B. Tribe of Levi
    C. Tribe of Naphtali
    D. Tribe of Simeon

6. Who was Moses' father-in-law?
    Exodus 4:18
    A. Jethro
    B. Jeuel
    C. Jonah
    D. Jotham

7. Where did Moses begin his journey to Egypt?
    Exodus 4:19
    A. Bashan
    B. Dibon
    C. Hebron
    D. Midian

8. Why did God sought to kill Moses?
    Exodus 4:24–26
    A. Moses boarded a ship headed to Tarsus.
    B. Moses bowed down to a golden calf.
    C. Moses did not circumcise his son.
    D. Moses trimmed his beard.

9. Who was Moses' wife?
    Exodus 4:25
    A. Delilah
    B. Elizabeth
    C. Mary
    D. Zipporah

10. What punishment did Pharaoh give the Hebrews because of Moses?

    Exodus 5:1–19

    A. He forced them to collect their own straw to make bricks.
    B. He gave the Hebrew men 40 lashes across their backs.
    C. He ordered the taskmasters to take away their mules and wagons.
    D. He raised the rent on their homes and businesses.

11. Which name was God known as to Abraham, Isaac, and Jacob?

    Exodus 6:3

    A. Abba Father
    B. God Almighty
    C. JEHOVAH
    D. Omniscient God

12. What was part of the covenant God promised Abraham's descendants?

    Exodus 6:4–8

    A. The ancient world and the seven seas would belong to them.
    B. The Egyptians would become their slaves for 400 years.
    C. The land of Canaan would become theirs.
    D. They would own all of the rich oil fields in the Middle East.

13. Who was the firstborn son of Israel?

    Exodus 6:14

    A. Gad
    B. Levi
    C. Joseph
    D. Reuben

14. How old was Levi when he died?

    Exodus 6:16

    A. 129 years old
    B. 137 years old
    C. 141 years old
    D. 166 years old

15. How old was Kohath when he died?

    Exodus 6:18

    A. 118 years old
    B. 127 years old
    C. 133 years old
    D. 140 years old

16. Who were Amram's sons?

    Exodus 6:20

    A. Aaron and Moses
    B. Carmi and Hezron
    C. Ohad and Shaul
    D. Pallu and Zohar

17. How old was Amram when he died?

    Exodus 6:20

    A. 137 years old
    B. 142 years old
    C. 155 years old
    D. 161 years old

18. What were Assir, Elkanah, and Abiasaph?

    Exodus 6:24

    A. Ammonites
    B. Korahites
    C. Reubenites
    D. Simeonites

19. Who was Eleazar's father-in-law?

    Exodus 6:25

    A. Amram
    B. Gershon
    C. Izhar
    D. Putiel

20. Who was Eleazar's son?

    Exodus 6:25

    A. Aaron
    B. Jamin
    C. Phinehas
    D. Uzziel

*Answers on page 752

JANUARY 20

Lesson 20
Today's Reading: *Exodus 7–9*
Period of Time: 1491 BC
Author: Moses

1. Who did God say would be Moses' prophet?
   Exodus 7:1

   A. Aaron
   B. Jethro
   C. Pharaoh
   D. Zipporah

2. What did God promise to do in Egypt?
   Exodus 7:3–5

   A. Bless Pharaoh
   B. Give a foreign army victory over Egypt
   C. Lead the Israelites out of Egypt
   D. Soften Pharaoh's heart

3. How old was Moses when he returned to Egypt?
   Exodus 7:7

   A. Twoscore years
   B. Twoscore and ten plus six years
   C. Threescore and ten plus eight years
   D. Fourscore years

4. How old was Aaron when he returned to Egypt?
   Exodus 7:7

   A. Twoscore and three years
   B. Fourscore and three years
   C. Fourscore and ten plus three years
   D. Fivescore plus three years

5. What happened when the magicians threw down their rods?
   Exodus 7:10–12

   A. Aaron's rod swallowed them.
   B. Aaron's rod turned to salt.
   C. Their rods swallowed Aaron's rod.
   D. Their rods turned to salt.

6. When and where did God tell Moses to meet Pharaoh?
   Exodus 7:15

   A. At noon in Pharaoh's palace
   B. At midnight in the royal tombs
   C. In the evening in the royal gardens
   D. In the morning by the river's brink

7. What was the *first* plague upon Egypt?
   Exodus 7:14–25

   A. Death of all firstborn Egyptian males and their livestock
   B. Frogs covered the land
   C. Lice covered the land
   D. River turned into blood

8. How many days did the *first* plague last?
   Exodus 7:25

   A. 3
   B. 5
   C. 7
   D. 10

9. What was the *second* plague upon Egypt?
   Exodus 8:1–6

   A. Boils afflict Egyptians and their beasts
   B. Frogs covered the land
   C. Lightning and hail
   D. River turned into blood

10. What was the *third* plague upon Egypt?
    Exodus 8:16–19

    A. Lice covered the land
    B. Lightning and hail
    C. Locusts covered the land
    D. River turned into blood

11. What did the magicians say to Pharaoh when they could **not** duplicate the *third* plague?
    Exodus 8:19

    A. "Give us more time to figure it out."
    B. "Moses is a better magician."
    C. "This is the finger of God."
    D. "This Moses is no man."

12. What was the *fourth* plague upon Egypt?
    Exodus 8:20–24
    A. Boils afflict Egyptians and their beasts
    B. Flies invade the Egyptians
    C. River turned into blood
    D. Water turned into wine

13. What answer did Moses give to Pharaoh when Pharaoh told the Israelites to go and sacrifice to their God, but stay in the land of Egypt?
    Exodus 8:26
    A. Thank you.
    B. The Egyptians will stone us.
    C. There isn't enough wood in Egypt for the burnt offering.
    D. We cannot make an offering to our God on unholy soil.

14. What was the *fifth* plague upon Egypt?
    Exodus 9:1–7
    A. Flies invade the Egyptians
    B. Gnats covered the land
    C. Livestock died
    D. Locusts covered the land

15. What was the *sixth* plague upon Egypt?
    Exodus 9:8–12
    A. Boils afflict Egyptians and their beasts
    B. Lightning and hail
    C. Livestock died
    D. Locusts covered the land

16. What did Moses use to bring the *sixth* plague upon Egypt?
    Exodus 9:8–12
    A. A ram's horn
    B. A rod
    C. An elephant's tusk
    D. Ashes from a furnace

17. Which one of the following names of God did Moses use when he told Pharaoh that God said to let his people go so that they may serve God?
    Exodus 9:13
    A. God Almighty
    B. JEHOVAH
    C. The Great I AM
    D. The LORD God of the Hebrews

18. What was the *seventh* plague upon Egypt?
    Exodus 9:13–26
    A. Death of all firstborn Egyptian males and livestock
    B. Gnats covered the land
    C. Lightning and hail
    D. Livestock died

19. Which two Egyptian crops were **not** destroyed by the *seventh* plague?
    Exodus 9:32
    A. Barley and rice
    B. Rye and wheat
    C. Soybeans and corn
    D. Sugar beets and flax

20. How did Moses stop the *seventh* plague?
    Exodus 9:33
    A. He went out of the city and spread his arms apart unto the LORD.
    B. He went out of the palace and poured water from the Nile onto the ground.
    C. He went to the edge of a mountain and tossed his rod over the ledge.
    D. He went to the palace and prayed that God would drive away the locusts.

Answers on page 752

JANUARY 21

Lesson 21
Today's Reading: *Exodus 10–12*
Period of Time: 1491 BC
Author: Moses

1. What would sweep across the land bringing the next plague (eighth)?
   Exodus 10:1–6
   A. Bees
   B. Lice
   C. Locusts
   D. Wasps

2. What compromise did Pharaoh offer Moses to avoid the next plague (eighth)?
   Exodus 10:7–11
   A. Take your women and children with you, but be back in 3 days.
   B. Take only the Hebrew men and go serve the LORD.
   C. Take your families, go and worship your god and say a prayer for me.
   D. Take your families, but leave your livestock, and return to me in 7 days.

3. From which direction did the next plague (eighth) arrive?
   Exodus 10:12–13
   A. North
   B. South
   C. East
   D. West

4. From which direction did the next plague (eighth) leave?
   Exodus 10:19
   A. North
   B. South
   C. East
   D. West

5. How many days did darkness cover Egypt?
   Exodus 10:22
   A. 3
   B. 7
   C. 10
   D. 12

6. After the plague of darkness, what did Pharaoh want Moses to leave behind before going to serve the LORD?
   Exodus 10:24–26
   A. The elderly
   B. Their children
   C. Their flocks and herds
   D. Their wives

7. What did Pharaoh tell Moses following the plague of darkness?
   Exodus 10:28
   A. He claimed the magicians had brought the darkness upon Egypt.
   B. He invited Moses to dinner that evening to work out a deal.
   C. He offered Moses a job as governor of Egypt.
   D. The next time he saw Pharaoh's face he would die.

8. When would the firstborn Egyptian sons die?
   Exodus 11:4–6
   A. 12 midnight
   B. 9 a.m.
   C. 12 noon
   D. 3 p.m.

9. Why was the first passover so important?
   Exodus 12:1–2
   A. God had softened Pharaoh's heart.
   B. It became the first month of the year.
   C. The Hebrews became the Israelites.
   D. The Hebrews became the Jews.

10. What did the LORD command the Israelites to do on the 10th day of the first month?
    Exodus 12:3–5
    A. Fast the entire day
    B. Hold a feast day unto the LORD
    C. Offer the LORD a burnt offering
    D. Select a sacrificial lamb

11. What did the LORD command Israelites to do on the 14th day of the first month?

    Exodus 12:6

    A. Fast the entire day
    B. Kill the sacrificial lamb
    C. Offer the LORD a burnt offering
    D. Wash their bodies in the river of Egypt

12. What did the passover meal consist of?

    Exodus 12:7–11

    A. Baked ham, rye bread, and mixed vegetables and herbs
    B. Roasted lamb, bitter herbs, and unleavened bread
    C. Steamed vegetables, baked fish, and wheat bread
    D. Unleavened bread, broiled fish, and fried potatoes

13. How were the Israelites to eat the passover meal?

    Exodus 12:11

    A. At a table with seven white candles, and surrounded by chairs
    B. By the doors inside their homes, with swords at their hips, and feet shod
    C. Near the doors inside their homes, dressed in sackcloth and ashes
    D. With loins girded, shoes on their feet, and staffs in their hands

14. What type of blood was smeared on the door posts during the passover?

    Exodus 12:7–22

    A. Lamb's blood
    B. Ram's blood
    C. Sheep's blood
    D. Turkey's blood

15. Which sentence is true concerning the passover?

    Exodus 12:14

    A. Israelites are to keep it as a memorial.
    B. Israelites may eat leavened bread.
    C. Israelites must fast and confess their sins.
    D. Israelites remaining debts must be paid.

16. Which statement is true concerning the feast of unleavened bread?

    Exodus 12:17–20

    A. All bread must be fermented.
    B. Different breads are eaten each day.
    C. It begins on the 14th day of the month.
    D. Strangers are forbidden to eat bread.

17. Which sentence is true?

    Exodus 12:31–36

    A. A dove descended upon Moses.
    B. Half the Egyptians converted to Judaism.
    C. Pharaoh blessed the Hebrew children.
    D. The Israelites spoiled the Egyptians.

18. Where did the Israelites go after they departed the city of Rameses?

    Exodus 12:37

    A. Kitron
    B. Succoth
    C. Tolad
    D. Zobah

19. Approximately how many Israelite men left Egypt during the Exodus?

    Exodus 12:37

    A. 6,000
    B. 60,000
    C. 600,000
    D. 6,000,000

20. How many years had the Israelites sojourned in Egypt?

    Exodus 12:40–41

    A. 430
    B. 666
    C. 800
    D. 975

Answers on page 752

JANUARY 22

Lesson 22
Today's Reading: *Exodus 13–15*
Period of Time: 1491 BC
Author: Moses

1. What did the LORD command Moses to sanctify unto him?
   Exodus 13:2
   A. Firstborn of every man and beast
   B. Moses' family members
   C. Orphans and widows
   D. Slaves and servants

2. Which month were the Israelites set free?
   Exodus 13:4
   A. Ab
   B. Abib
   C. Adar
   D. Shebat

3. Which nations lived in the land that God was giving to the Israelites?
   Exodus 13:5
   A. Amorites, Parthians, Libyans, Samaritans, and Hittites
   B. Babylonians, Asians, Levites, Greeks, and Philistines
   C. Canaanites, Hittites, Amorites, Hivites, and Jebusites
   D. Romans, Jebusites, Medes, Barbarians, and Spaniards

4. How often were the Israelites to celebrate the feast of unleavened bread?
   Exodus 13:5–10
   A. Monthly
   B. Annually
   C. Biannually
   D. Every seven years

5. What was to be redeemed for every firstling of an ass?
   Exodus 13:13
   A. A dove
   B. A lamb
   C. A pigeon
   D. A ram

6. Why did God avoid leading the Israelites through the land of the Philistines?
   Exodus 13:17
   A. The Israelites would want to return to Egypt when they saw war.
   B. The King's Highway was the fastest and safest route to Canaan.
   C. The land contained dangerous tar pits.
   D. The land contained deadly quicksand.

7. Whose bones did the Israelites take with them when they left Egypt?
   Exodus 13:19
   A. Abraham's bones
   B. Adam's bones
   C. Isaac's bones
   D. Joseph's bones

8. Where did the Israelites go after they left Succoth?
   Exodus 13:20
   A. Aphekah
   B. Beth-haccherem
   C. Etham
   D. Gilead

9. What did the LORD use to lead the Israelites by day?
   Exodus 13:21
   A. A pillar of a cloud
   B. Homing pigeons
   C. Smoke from a meteor
   D. The North Star

10. What did the LORD use to lead the Israelites by night?
    Exodus 13:21
    A. A comet
    B. A pillar of fire
    C. Light from the moon
    D. The Stars

11. Why did God want the Israelites to camp at Pihahiroth?
    Exodus 14:2–4
    A. He wanted Pharaoh to believe the Israelites were trapped.
    B. The jungles and caves along the coast would allow the Israelites places to hide.
    C. The narrow passage allows a small army to defeat a large army.
    D. The mountains would provide protection for months against Pharaoh's army.

12. How many chosen chariots, besides the rest of the chariots in Egypt, did Pharaoh send to pursue the Israelites?
    Exodus 14:5–9
    A. 10
    B. 100
    C. 500
    D. 600

13. What happened to Pharaoh and his army?
    Exodus 14:15–31
    A. God sent snakes to torment them.
    B. Israelite archers killed them.
    C. Moses used boulders to crush them.
    D. They drowned in the sea.

14. What did the Israelites do after the Egyptian army was defeated?
    Exodus 15:1–19
    A. They begged Moses to return to Egypt.
    B. They built an altar with twelve stones.
    C. They made a molten calf of gold.
    D. They sang a song thanking the LORD.

15. Who was Aaron's sister?
    Exodus 15:20
    A. Bathsheba
    B. Jezebel
    C. Miriam
    D. Rachel

16. Which musical instrument did Aaron's sister play?
    Exodus 15:20
    A. Clarinet
    B. Harp
    C. Timbrel
    D. Trumpet

17. Where did the waters taste bitter?
    Exodus 15:22–23
    A. Artesia
    B. Gihon
    C. Marah
    D. Sweetwater

18. How were the waters made sweet?
    Exodus 15:25
    A. Aaron diluted the water with wine.
    B. Jethro added maple syrup to the water.
    C. Joshua mingled the waters with nectar.
    D. Moses cast a tree into the water.

19. What promise did God make to the Israelites if they did that which was right in his sight?
    Exodus 15:26
    A. The diseases that came upon the Egyptians would not come upon them.
    B. The firstborn males would receive plots of land to raise their families on.
    C. Their mothers would receive homes to raise their children.
    D. Their nation would become the most feared people in Canaan.

20. How many wells of water were in Elim?
    Exodus 15:27
    A. 10
    B. 12
    C. 25
    D. 50

*Answers on page 752

Lesson 23
Today's Reading: *Exodus 16–18*
Period of Time: 1491 BC
Author: Moses

JANUARY 23

1. Which wilderness did the Israelites travel to after they left Elim?
   Exodus 16:1
   A. Wilderness of Paran
   B. Wilderness of Shur
   C. Wilderness of Sin
   D. Wilderness of Zin

2. What did the Israelites accuse Moses of in the wilderness?
   Exodus 16:2–3
   A. Adultery with a foreign prostitute for 2 hins of water
   B. Blasphemy against God by offering a strange fire
   C. Giving aid and comfort to a captured Egyptian
   D. Leading them into the wilderness to starve them to death

3. What abundant food did the Israelites eat in the evenings?
   Exodus 16:13
   A. Chicken
   B. Duck
   C. Pheasant
   D. Quail

4. What did the Israelites name the bread from heaven they found every morning?
   Exodus 16:14–15
   A. Agape
   B. Manna
   C. Marah
   D. Shalom

5. What happened to the leftover bread from heaven?
   Exodus 16:20
   A. It bred worms and stank.
   B. It caramelized in the hot sun.
   C. It doubled in size and became elastic.
   D. It turned into a wafer.

6. Which day of the week were the Israelites to gather twice the amount of bread from heaven?
   Exodus 16:22
   A. 2nd day
   B. 3rd day
   C. 6th day
   D. 7th day

7. Which day of the week did the Israelites **not** find any bread from heaven?
   Exodus 16:23–26
   A. 1st day
   B. 3rd day
   C. 5th day
   D. 7th day

8. Which statement is true concerning the bread from heaven?
   Exodus 16:31
   A. It had a rough texture on the outside, but sweet and moist in the middle.
   B. It smelled like bread fresh from the oven; and its crust was tan in color.
   C. It tasted like milk and honey, and was in the shape of a loaf.
   D. It was like coriander seed, white; and tasted like wafers made with honey.

9. How much bread from heaven were the Israelites to store in a pot to show future generations?
   Exodus 16:32–34
   A. 1 kab
   B. 1 ephah
   C. 1 omer
   D. 1 seah

10. How many years did the Israelites eat the bread from heaven?

    Exodus 16:35

    A. 10
    B. 40
    C. 400
    D. 840

11. Where did the Israelites find water in Horeb?

    Exodus 17:6

    A. Inside a cactus
    B. Inside a cave
    C. Inside a rock
    D. Inside a well

12. Which two names did Moses give the place where the Israelites were given water in Horeb?

    Exodus 17:7

    A. Massah and Meribah
    B. Pisgah and Petra
    C. Ramoth-Gilead and Rhodes
    D. Siphmoth and Sychar

13. Who attacked the Israelites in Rephidim?

    Exodus 17:8

    A. Amalek
    B. Edom
    C. Moab
    D. Syria

14. Whom did Moses choose to lead the Israelite army against the enemy in Rephidim?

    Exodus 17:9–10

    A. Cornelius
    B. Joshua
    C. Naaman
    D. Uriah

15. Which two men accompanied Moses to the top of the hill in Rephidim?

    Exodus 17:10

    A. Aaron and Hur
    B. Iddo and Chilion
    C. Machir and Manasseh
    D. Omri and Joiarib

16. What did God order Moses to do after the Israelites defeated the enemy at Rephidim?

    Exodus 17:14

    A. Burn the dead bodies
    B. Sing a song
    C. Spoil the enemy
    D. Write a book

17. Who was Moses' father-in-law?

    Exodus 18:1

    A. Abimelech
    B. Jethro
    C. Rufus
    D. Shamgar

18. Where was Moses' father-in-law from?

    Exodus 18:1

    A. Arad
    B. Bethel
    C. Midian
    D. Philistia

19. What were the names of Moses' two sons?

    Exodus 18:3–4

    A. Gershom and Eliezer
    B. Jonas and Agabus
    C. Nathan and Hosea
    D. Zaavan and Tola

20. Who judged the most serious cases for the Israelites?

    Exodus 18:26

    A. Felix
    B. Moses
    C. Pilate
    D. Shamgar

Answers on page 752

JANUARY 24

Lesson 24
Today's Reading: *Exodus 19–21*
Period of Time: 1491 BC
Author: Moses

1. Which wilderness did the Israelites travel to three months after leaving Egypt?
   Exodus 19:1
   A. Wilderness of Shur
   B. Wilderness of Sin
   C. Wilderness of Sinai
   D. Wilderness of Zin

2. What did God say he would call the Israelites if they obeyed him and kept his covenant with them?
   Exodus 19:3–6
   A. A kingdom of priests
   B. A nation of judges
   C. A peculiar people
   D. Sons of thunder

3. What did the Israelites have to do before they could ascend the mountain to meet God?
   Exodus 19:10–15
   A. Bathe for three days, confess their sins, and trim their beards
   B. Be sanctified, wash their clothes, abstain from sexual intercourse with their wives
   C. Dress in sackcloth and ashes, offer a burnt offering, sing a song of praise
   D. Wash their clothes, bathe, and offer a drink offering

4. What was the name of the mountain where the Israelites were to meet God?
   Exodus 19:10–18
   A. Mount Carmel
   B. Mount Hebron
   C. Mount Nebo
   D. Mount Sinai

5. Which statement is true concerning the day the Israelites met God?
   Exodus 19:16
   A. The birds sang, dew fell upon the grass, and angels appeared in the sky.
   B. The ground shook, smoke appeared, and the mountain was divided.
   C. There was lots of sunshine, no clouds, and desert wild flowers bloomed.
   D. There was thunder and lightning, a thick cloud, and the voice of a loud trumpet.

6. What was the *first* commandment?
   Exodus 20:3
   A. Have no idols.
   B. Have no other gods.
   C. Honor the sabbath day.
   D. Honor your parents.

7. What was the *second* commandment?
   Exodus 20:4–6
   A. Do not covet
   B. Do not steal
   C. Have no idols.
   D. Honor your parents.

8. What was the *third* commandment?
   Exodus 20:7
   A. Honor God's name.
   B. Honor the sabbath day.
   C. Honor your country.
   D. Honor your parents.

9. What was the *fourth* commandment?
   Exodus 20:8–11
   A. Do not commit adultery.
   B. Do not perjure yourself.
   C. Honor the sabbath day.
   D. Honor your parents.

10. What was the *fifth* commandment?
Exodus 20:12
    A. Do not steal.
    B. Have no idols.
    C. Have no other gods.
    D. Honor your parents.

11. What was the *sixth* commandment?
Exodus 20:13
    A. Do not covet.
    B. Do not murder.
    C. Have no other gods.
    D. Honor the sabbath day.

12. What was the *seventh* commandment?
Exodus 20:14
    A. Do not commit adultery.
    B. Do not covet.
    C. Do not murder.
    D. Do not steal.

13. What was the *eighth* commandment?
Exodus 20:15
    A. Do not murder.
    B. Do not steal.
    C. Honor God's name.
    D. Honor the sabbath day.

14. What was the *ninth* commandment?
Exodus 20:16
    A. Do not commit adultery.
    B. Do not murder.
    C. Do not perjure yourself.
    D. Do not steal.

15. What was the *tenth* commandment?
Exodus 20:17
    A. Do not covet.
    B. Have no idols.
    C. Honor God's name.
    D. Honor the sabbath day.

16. After how many years was a master required to set a Hebrew servant free?
Exodus 21:2
    A. 3
    B. 6
    C. 25
    D. 50

17. What could a maidservant do if her betrothed husband took another wife and diminished the maidservant of food, clothes, or sex?
Exodus 21:10–11
    A. She shall be allowed to leave, but without any money.
    B. She shall receive half of her husband's fortune and land.
    C. She shall spit on her husband three times, and then be divorced.
    D. She shall take off her shoe and give it to the elders.

18. What was the penalty for kidnapping?
Exodus 21:16
    A. 10 years of prison
    B. 39 lashes across the back with a whip
    C. 40 lashes across the lower legs with a rod
    D. Death

19. What was the penalty if a person cursed his father or mother?
Exodus 21:17
    A. 1 year of hard labor
    B. 39 lashes across the back with a whip
    C. 40 lashes across the lower legs with a rod
    D. Death

20. What right did a servant have if his master smote the servant's eye causing permanent blindness to the eye?
Exodus 21:26
    A. The master's eye must be put out.
    B. The master must pay the servant ten talents of gold.
    C. The servant must be set free.
    D. The servant must be set free along with his family.

*Answers on page 752

JANUARY 25

Lesson 25
Today's Reading: *Exodus 22–24*
Period of Time: 1491 BC
Author: Moses

1. How many oxen must a thief restore to the owner for killing or selling the owner's ox?
   Exodus 22:1
   A. 2
   B. 3
   C. 5
   D. 7

2. How many oxen would a man, who was safekeeping his neighbor's ox, have to restore to the owner if the ox was stolen?
   Exodus 22:10–12
   A. 0
   B. 1
   C. 4
   D. 7

3. What was the penalty for practicing witchcraft?
   Exodus 22:18
   A. 10 years in jail
   B. 39 stripes across the back
   C. 40 stripes across the back
   D. Death

4. How much interest could an Israelite charge a poor Israelite who borrowed money?
   Exodus 22:25
   A. 0%
   B. 6%
   C. 10%
   D. 21%

5. What must an Israelite do with his firstborn male ox or sheep?
   Exodus 22:29–30
   A. Give it to the LORD.
   B. Never let it do any servile work.
   C. Set it free.
   D. Use it for a burnt offering.

6. What must an Israelite do with the remains of one of his animals killed by beasts?
   Exodus 22:31
   A. Bury the remains before sunset.
   B. Cook and eat what is salvageable.
   C. Give it to the dogs.
   D. Use it for a burnt offering.

7. What was an Israelite to do if he found his enemy's ox or donkey?
   Exodus 23:4
   A. Give it to the priests.
   B. Kill it.
   C. Offer it as a burnt offering.
   D. Return it to the enemy.

8. How many years were the Israelites to work their land before allowing it one year of rest?
   Exodus 23:10–11
   A. 3
   B. 5
   C. 6
   D. 7

9. How many days during the week could an Israelite work?
   Exodus 23:12
   A. 1
   B. 2
   C. 5
   D. 6

10. How many feasts were the Israelites to celebrate every year?
    Exodus 23:14
    A. 3
    B. 5
    C. 7
    D. 12

11. During which month were the Israelites to celebrate the feast of unleavened bread?
    Exodus 23:15
    A. Ab
    B. Abib
    C. Adar
    D. Shebat

12. What did the LORD say he would use to drive out the Hivite, Canaanite, and Hittite?
    Exodus 23:28
    A. Eagles
    B. Hornets
    C. Lions
    D. Serpents

13. What would be the nation of Israel's boundaries?
    Exodus 23:31
    A. Brasen sea to the sea of Galilee, from the desert to the river of Pison
    B. Great sea to the Red sea, from the wilderness to the river of Hiddekel
    C. Red sea to the sea of the Philistines, from the desert to the river of Euphrates
    D. Sea of Joppa to the sea of glass, from desert to the river of Gihon

14. Who went with Moses to worship the LORD?
    Exodus 24:1
    A. Aaron, Nadab, Abihu, and 70 elders
    B. Caleb, Nun, Ehud, and 10 chiefs
    C. Dathan, Raham, Shimri, and 12 princes
    D. Joshua, Balaam, Balak, and 40 priests

15. Which book did Moses read to the people?
    Exodus 24:7
    A. The Book of the Covenant
    B. The Book of the Kings
    C. The Book of the Prophets
    D. The Book of the Revelation

16. What type of stone did the paved work look like under the feet of the God of Israel?
    Exodus 24:10
    A. Emerald
    B. Onyx
    C. Ruby
    D. Sapphire

17. Who went up the mount of God with Moses?
    Exodus 24:13
    A. Abihu
    B. Dathan
    C. Joshua
    D. Samuel

18. Whom did Moses leave in charge of the Israelites while he was away?
    Exodus 24:14
    A. Asa and Asaph
    B. Hur and Aaron
    C. Iob and Caleb
    D. Nun and Serug

19. What did the glory of the LORD look like on the top of the mountain?
    Exodus 24:16–17
    A. A beaming sun
    B. A devouring fire
    C. A looking glass
    D. A rushing waterfall

20. How many days and nights was Moses on the mountain?
    Exodus 24:18
    A. 10
    B. 20
    C. 30
    D. 40

*Answers on page 753

JANUARY 26

Lesson 26
Today's Reading: *Exodus 25–27*
Period of Time: 1491 BC
Author: Moses

1. What did God require of each Israelite in order to build the tabernacle?
   Exodus 25:2
   A. A 10-pound donation of gold
   B. A tithe
   C. A vow to complete the project
   D. An offering made from the heart

2. Which animals' skins were dyed red?
   Exodus 25:5
   A. Badgers' skins
   B. Cows' skins
   C. Rams' skins
   D. Seals' skins

3. What type of wood was used to build the tabernacle?
   Exodus 25:5
   A. Almug wood
   B. Gopher wood
   C. Shittim wood
   D. Thyine wood

4. Why did the Israelites need spices for the tabernacle?
   Exodus 25:6
   A. To make perfumes and colognes for the priests
   B. To use as an anointing oil and for sweet incense
   C. To use as barter to pay the Philistines for swords
   D. To ward off evil spirits and to mask odors from dead bodies

5. Which of the following contained onyx and other precious stones?
   Exodus 25:7
   A. The ark of the covenant and candlestick
   B. The ephod and breastplate
   C. The mercy seat and golden table
   D. The priest's holy rings and bracelets

6. What was to be placed inside the ark of the covenant?
   Exodus 25:16
   A. God's testimony
   B. Joseph's bones
   C. Moses' rod
   D. Pharaoh's crown

7. How many cherubim of gold were on the mercy seat?
   Exodus 25:18
   A. 2
   B. 7
   C. 10
   D. 12

8. What was always present on the golden table?
   Exodus 25:30
   A. Angel food cake
   B. Firstfruits
   C. Red wine
   D. Shewbread

9. How many lamps were on the golden candlestick?
   Exodus 25:31–37
   A. 2
   B. 3
   C. 6
   D. 7

10. How much gold was used to make the golden candlestick and vessels?
    Exodus 25:37–39
    A. 1 talent
    B. 10 minas
    C. 50 shekels
    D. 100 gerahs

11. How many linen curtains were needed for the tabernacle?

    Exodus 26:1

    A. 3
    B. 7
    C. 10
    D. 12

12. How many curtains of goats' hair were needed for the tabernacle?

    Exodus 26:7

    A. 3
    B. 7
    C. 11
    D. 13

13. What was the *inner covering* of the tent covering made of?

    Exodus 26:14

    A. Deer skins
    B. Horsehide
    C. Leather
    D. Rams' skins

14. What was the *outer covering* of the tent covering made of?

    Exodus 26:14

    A. Badgers' skins
    B. Deer skins
    C. Rams' skins
    D. Seals' skins

15. What did the inner vail divide?

    Exodus 26:33

    A. Golden table and altar of incense
    B. Holy place and most holy place
    C. Jews and Gentiles
    D. Men and women

16. Toward which side of the tabernacle was the golden candlestick placed?

    Exodus 26:35

    A. North
    B. South
    C. East
    D. West

17. On which side of the tabernacle was the golden table placed?

    Exodus 26:35

    A. North
    B. South
    C. East
    D. West

18. Which metal did the Israelites use to make the altar for burnt offerings?

    Exodus 27:1–8

    A. Antimony
    B. Brass
    C. Gold
    D. Silver

19. Which oil did the Israelites use for the lamp?

    Exodus 27:20

    A. Coconut oil
    B. Corn oil
    C. Olive oil
    D. Whale oil

20. Which statement is true concerning the lamp?

    Exodus 27:20

    A. It burned from dawn to dusk 7 days a week.
    B. It burned from dusk to dawn 7 days a week.
    C. It burned from dusk to dawn on the sabbath days.
    D. It stayed lit continuously.

*Answers on page 753

JANUARY 27

Lesson 27
Today's Reading: *Exodus 28–29*
Period of Time: 1491 BC
Author: Moses

1. Who were Aaron's sons?
   Exodus 28:1
   A. Felix, Darius, Jabez, and Helem
   B. Melchi, Perez, Claudius, and Korah
   C. Nadab, Abihu, Eleazar, and Ithamar
   D. Saul, Paul, Mered, and Dathan

2. What did the holy garments represent?
   Exodus 28:2
   A. Eternity and forgiveness
   B. Glory and beauty
   C. Protection and security
   D. Superiority and godliness

3. Who made the holy garments?
   Exodus 28:3
   A. The priestly family of Korah
   B. The tribe of Gad
   C. The wise hearted and Spirit filled
   D. The wives of the seventy elders

4. Which four colors were included in the holy garments?
   Exodus 28:5
   A. Blue, gold, purple, and scarlet
   B. Blue, red, white, and green
   C. Gold, green, white, and purple
   D. Maroon, yellow, black, and white

5. What was wrote upon the onyx stones?
   Exodus 28:9
   A. Almighty Father
   B. Father, Son, and Holy Spirit
   C. Names of the children of Israel
   D. The ten commandments

6. What part of the holy garments consisted of 12 precious stones?
   Exodus 28:15–21
   A. Breastplate
   B. Coat
   C. Crown
   D. Necklace

7. Where were the Urim and Thummim placed on the holy garments?
   Exodus 28:30
   A. Breastplate
   B. Coat
   C. Crown
   D. Miter

8. What color was the robe of the ephod?
   Exodus 28:31
   A. Black
   B. Blue
   C. Maroon
   D. White

9. What was similar to the robe of the ephod?
   Exodus 28:32
   A. A cassock
   B. A habergeon
   C. A toga
   D. A tunic

10. Which of the following were located at the bottom hem of the robe of the ephod?
    Exodus 28:33
    A. Apples and silver stars
    B. God's commandments and rams
    C. Golden crosses and sheep
    D. Pomegranates and gold bells

11. What was engraved upon the mitre?
    Exodus 28:36
    A. ABBA FATHER
    B. ALMIGHTY GOD
    C. HOLINESS TO THE LORD
    D. KING OF KINGS

12. Which animals were used to hallow the priests?
    Exodus 29:1
    A. 1 young bullock and 1 dove
    B. 1 young bullock and 2 rams
    C. 2 young bullocks and 1 pigeon
    D. 2 young bullocks and 2 goats

13. Which type of flour was used to make the bread, cakes, and wafers for the priest's basket?

    Exodus 29:2
    A. Corn
    B. Oat
    C. Rice
    D. Wheat

14. What did the priests do before putting on their holy garments?

    Exodus 29:4
    A. Fasted for 24 hours
    B. Gave a tithe
    C. Sacrificed a dove
    D. Washed their bodies

15. Which sacrificial animal was killed first during the consecration of the priests?

    Exodus 29:9–11
    A. A bullock
    B. A dove
    C. A goat
    D. A ram

16. What did the priests do with the blood from the first sacrificed animal?

    Exodus 29:12
    A. Collected it in bowls and took it outside the camp to burn at a place called Gehenna
    B. Placed part of it on the horns of the altar and the rest beside the bottom of the altar
    C. Poured it into silver bowls and then tossed it upon the ground outside the camp
    D. Sprinkled it upon the scapegoat and then set the goat free the next day

17. What was the name of the first offering?

    Exodus 29:14
    A. The heave Offering
    B. The meal Offering
    C. The peace Offering
    D. The sin Offering

18. What parts of the sacrificial animal were burned outside the camp?

    Exodus 29:14
    A. Brain, heart, and kidneys
    B. Dung, heart, and hoofs
    C. Entrails, hoofs, and head
    D. Flesh, skin, and dung

19. Which parts of the ram of consecration belonged to Aaron and his sons?

    Exodus 29:26
    A. Breast and shoulder
    B. Foreshank and hindshank
    C. Leg and neck
    D. Sirloin and ribs

20. What was the continual offering?

    Exodus 29:38–39
    A. A daily sin offering consisting of flour and wine
    B. A daily wave offering consisting of bread and parts of the sacrificial goat
    C. A lamb offered in the morning and another one offered in the evening
    D. A tube filled with oil to create an eternal flame that kept the golden lamp burning

*Answers on page 753

Lesson 28
Today's Reading: *Exodus 30–32*
Period of Time: 1491 BC
Author: Moses

1. Which materials were used to build the altar of incense?
   Exodus 30:1–5
   A. Bronze and gopher wood
   B. Gold and shittim wood
   C. Iron and walnut wood
   D. Silver and maple wood

2. Where was the altar of incense to be located?
   Exodus 30:1–6
   A. Before the vail
   B. Behind the vail
   C. To the left of the ark of the covenant
   D. To the right of the ark of the covenant

3. How often was the high priest to burn incense upon the altar of incense?
   Exodus 30:7–8
   A. Every morning and evening
   B. On sabbath days
   C. Once a year
   D. Three times a year

4. How often was the high priest to make atonement upon the altar of incense?
   Exodus 30:10
   A. Every evening
   B. Every morning
   C. Once a year
   D. Three times a year

5. What was the minimum age in years in order for an Israelite to be numbered among the people?
   Exodus 30:14
   A. 12
   B. 15
   C. 18
   D. 20

6. How much of a shekel was an Israelite required to give to make an atonement for his soul?
   Exodus 30:13–15
   A. ¼ of a shekel
   B. ½ of a shekel
   C. ¾ of a shekel
   D. 1 shekel

7. What was the atonement money used for?
   Exodus 30:16
   A. To educate the young
   B. To feed the military
   C. To house the priests
   D. To maintain the tabernacle

8. What was the purpose of the laver of brass?
   Exodus 30:18–21
   A. For Israelites to bathe in
   B. For priests to wash their hands and feet
   C. To baptize newborns
   D. To wash sacrificial animals

9. Which of the following items were used to make the holy anointing oil?
   Exodus 30:23–25
   A. Aloe, lavender, rose, lily, and honeysuckle
   B. Frankincense, lilac, wormwood, spearmint, and vanilla
   C. Myrrh, cinnamon, calamus, cassia, and olive oil
   D. Sage, bee balm, phlox, tea olive, and silverberry

10. Which of the following items were used to make the holy perfume?
    Exodus 30:34–38
    A. Citrus, anise, hemlock, vinegar, and cassia
    B. Myrrh, camphire, calamus, honey, and saffron
    C. Olive oil, bdellium, coriander, terebinth, and spikenard
    D. Stacte, onycha, galbanum, and frankincense

11. Who was the father of Bezaleel?

    Exodus 31:2

    A. Amasai
    B. Philetus
    C. Shimri
    D. Uri

12. Which tribe was Bezaleel a member of?

    Exodus 31:2

    A. Tribe of Gad
    B. Tribe of Issachar
    C. Tribe of Judah
    D. Tribe of Simeon

13. Who was the father of Aholiab?

    Exodus 31:6

    A. Ahisamach
    B. Dodo
    C. Nathanael
    D. Othni

14. Which tribe was Aholiab a member of?

    Exodus 31:6

    A. Tribe of Asher
    B. Tribe of Benjamin
    C. Tribe of Dan
    D. Tribe of Ephraim

15. What was the penalty for working on the sabbath day?

    Exodus 31:14–15

    A. 39 lashes across the back
    B. 40 days in jail
    C. Banishment to the wilderness
    D. Death

16. How long did God take to make the heaven and the earth?

    Exodus 31:17

    A. 6 days
    B. 40 days
    C. 1.5 million years
    D. 10 billion years

17. Upon which mountain did Moses receive the tables of stone written by the finger of God?

    Exodus 31:18

    A. Mount Pisgah
    B. Mount Sinai
    C. Mount Tabor
    D. Mount Zion

18. Who made the golden calf?

    Exodus 32:1–5, 32:35

    A. Aaron
    B. Caleb
    C. Hur
    D. Joshua

19. What did God call the Israelites who worshiped the golden calf?

    Exodus 32:9

    A. Backsliders
    B. Hardheaded
    C. Stiffnecked
    D. Tarheels

20. Approximately how many men did the children of Levi kill who were **not** on the LORD's side?

    Exodus 32:28

    A. 70
    B. 3,000
    C. 4,500
    D. 10,000

Answers on page 753

JANUARY 29

Lesson 29
Today's Reading: *Exodus 33–35*
Period of Time: 1491 BC
Author: Moses

1. What did God say would lead the Israelites against their enemies?
   Exodus 33:2
   A. A leper
   B. A priest
   C. A prophet
   D. An angel

2. Which nation did God **not** mention he would drive out?
   Exodus 33:2
   A. The Amorites
   B. The Edomites
   C. The Jebusites
   D. The Perizzites

3. How did God describe the land he was giving to the Israelites?
   Exodus 33:3
   A. Flowing with milk and honey
   B. Full of lush trees and fertile fields
   C. Rich in gold and silver
   D. Waves of amber grain and fruited plains

4. What did the Israelites do by mount Horeb?
   Exodus 33:6
   A. Offered a burnt offering unto the LORD
   B. Rent their clothes and washed in a creek
   C. Sang songs and worshipped God
   D. Stripped off their ornaments

5. What descended and stood at the door when Moses entered the tabernacle?
   Exodus 33:9
   A. A pillar of fire
   B. An angel
   C. The cloudy pillar
   D. Winged creatures

6. Who was at the tabernacle with Moses when he spoke with the LORD?
   Exodus 33:11
   A. Aaron
   B. Joshua
   C. Nun
   D. Satan

7. What did Moses see from the clift of the rock?
   Exodus 33:18–23
   A. God's back
   B. Satan
   C. The 12 tribes of Israel
   D. The golden calf

8. What did Moses take with him when he went up mount Sinai?
   Exodus 34:4
   A. A blue robe
   B. A bow and arrows
   C. Extra clothing
   D. Two tables of stone

9. How many generations does God punish children for the sin of their fathers?
   Exodus 34:7
   A. First to second
   B. Third to fourth
   C. Fifth to sixth
   D. Seventh to eighth

10. What did the LORD **not** command the Israelites to do in the land of their enemies?
    Exodus 34:13
    A. Break their idols
    B. Cut down their groves
    C. Destroy their altars
    D. Seek peace treaties

11. During which month were the Israelites to celebrate the feast of unleavened bread?
    Exodus 34:18
    A. Ab
    B. Abib
    C. Elul
    D. Tishri

12. What was required if the owner of a firstling ass did **not** redeem it?
    Exodus 34:20
    A. Break the ass' neck
    B. Fine the owner 10 shekels
    C. Set the donkey free
    D. Stone the owner

13. Which one of the following was **not** part of the annual feasts?
    Exodus 34:22
    A. Feast of ingathering
    B. Feast of weeks
    C. Feast of lights
    D. Firstfruits of the wheat harvest

14. How many days and nights was Moses on mount Sinai?
    Exodus 34:28
    A. 40
    B. 60
    C. 80
    D. 90

15. What change in Moses did the Israelites notice when he returned from mount Sinai?
    Exodus 34:29–30
    A. He was blind.
    B. He was mute.
    C. His face shined.
    D. His hair turned white.

16. What did Moses wear in the presence of the Israelites?
    Exodus 34:33–34
    A. A crown
    B. A hat
    C. A mask
    D. A vail

17. Which type of offering did the Israelites give to build the tabernacle, for all its service, and to make the holy garments?
    Exodus 35:21–29
    A. A burnt offering
    B. A free will offering
    C. A sin offering
    D. A trespass offering

18. Who was the father of Uri?
    Exodus 35:30
    A. David
    B. Goliath
    C. Hur
    D. Michael

19. Which tribe did Uri belong to?
    Exodus 35:30
    A. Tribe of Eli
    B. Tribe of Gamaliel
    C. Tribe of Judah
    D. Tribe of Laban

20. Which tribe did Ahisamach belong to?
    Exodus 35:34
    A. Tribe of Dan
    B. Tribe of Levi
    C. Tribe of Naphtali
    D. Tribe of Reuben

*Answers on page 753

JANUARY 30

Lesson 30
Today's Reading: *Exodus 36–38*
Period of Time: 1491 BC
Author: Moses

1. Which two of the following oversaw the construction of the tabernacle?
   Exodus 36:1–2
   A. Aaron and Nadab
   B. Bezaleel and Aholiab
   C. Ithamar and Eleazar
   D. Nun and Abihu

2. Which type of offering did the Israelites give to construct the tabernacle?
   Exodus 36:3
   A. A burnt offering
   B. A free will offering
   C. A sin offering
   D. A trespass offering

3. What did the workers tell Moses regarding the people and their giving?
   Exodus 36:4–5
   A. Tell the foreigners to give.
   B. Tell the people to stop giving.
   C. The poor should not give anything.
   D. The rich should give more.

4. How many curtains were made of fine twined linen?
   Exodus 36:8
   A. 10
   B. 11
   C. 12
   D. 20

5. What did the fine twined linen curtains look like?
   Exodus 36:8
   A. Blue, purple, scarlet, with cherubims
   B. Blue with pomegranates and bells
   C. White with a crest of each tribe
   D. White with the ten plagues upon Egypt

6. How many curtains were made of goats' hair?
   Exodus 36:14
   A. 10
   B. 11
   C. 12
   D. 20

7. What did the Israelites use for the *inner* covering of the tent covering?
   Exodus 36:19
   A. Badgers' skins
   B. Deer skins
   C. Horses' skins
   D. Rams' skins

8. What did the Israelites use for the *outer* covering of the tent covering?
   Exodus 36:19
   A. Badgers' skins
   B. Deer skins
   C. Horses' skins
   D. Rams' skins

9. What type of wood did the Israelites use to build the tabernacle?
   Exodus 36:20
   A. Cedar wood
   B. Gopher wood
   C. Shittim wood
   D. Walnut wood

10. What type of metal did the Israelites use to make the sockets for the boards?
    Exodus 36:24–30
    A. Brass
    B. Gold
    C. Iron
    D. Silver

11. Which items were made of gold?
    Exodus 37:1–29
    A. Altar of burnt offering, cherubim, staves, and mercy seat
    B. Altar of incense, candlestick, the table, and the laver
    C. Laver, staves, ark of the covenant, and cherubim
    D. The table, ark of the covenant, mercy seat, and the candlestick

12. How many cherubims were on the mercy seat?
    Exodus 37:6–9
    A. 2
    B. 3
    C. 4
    D. 7

13. How many lamps did the candlestick contain?
    Exodus 37:23
    A. 3
    B. 6
    C. 7
    D. 12

14. What was the length in cubits of the tabernacle on the north and south sides?
    Exodus 38:9–11
    A. 20
    B. 30
    C. 50
    D. 100

15. What was the length in cubits of the tabernacle on the east and west sides?
    Exodus 38:12–13
    A. 20
    B. 30
    C. 50
    D. 100

16. Who recorded the inventory of materials used to build the tabernacle?
    Exodus 38:21
    A. Abihu
    B. Eleazar
    C. Ithamar
    D. Nadab

17. How much gold did the Israelites use to build the tabernacle?
    Exodus 38:24
    A. 12 talents and 549 shekels
    B. 29 talents and 730 shekels
    C. 54 talents and 987 shekels
    D. 100 talents and 1,000 shekels

18. How much silver did the Israelites use to build the tabernacle?
    Exodus 38:25
    A. 5 talents and 1,000 shekels
    B. 20 talents and 1,250 shekels
    C. 50 talents and 1,550 shekels
    D. 100 talents and 1,775 shekels

19. How much is a bekah?
    Exodus 38:26
    A. 1/2 shekel
    B. 1/2 talent
    C. 1 1/2 shekels
    D. 1 1/2 talents

20. How many men gave a bekah?
    Exodus 38:26
    A. 175,392
    B. 550,007
    C. 603,550
    D. 1,453,273

*Answers on page 753

JANUARY 31

Lesson 31
Today's Reading: *Exodus 39–40*
Period of Time: 1491–1490 BC
Author: Moses

1. What was woven into the linen of Aaron's holy garments?
   Exodus 39:1–3
   A. Goats' hair
   B. Gold wires
   C. Scenes of the 10 plagues
   D. The ten commandments

2. Which type of stones contained the names of the 12 tribes of Israel?
   Exodus 39:6
   A. Diamonds
   B. Emeralds
   C. Onyxes
   D. Sapphires

3. Which stones were placed on the *first* row of the breastplate?
   Exodus 39:10
   A. Beryl, onyx, jasper
   B. Emerald, sapphire, diamond
   C. Ligure, agate, amethyst
   D. Sardius, topaz, carbuncle

4. Which stones were placed on the *second* row of the breastplate?
   Exodus 39:11
   A. Beryl, onyx, jasper
   B. Emerald, sapphire, diamond
   C. Ligure, agate, amethyst
   D. Sardius, topaz, carbuncle

5. Which stones were placed on the *third* row of the breastplate?
   Exodus 39:12
   A. Beryl, onyx, jasper
   B. Emerald, sapphire, diamond
   C. Ligure, agate, amethyst
   D. Sardius, topaz, carbuncle

6. Which color was the robe of the ephod?
   Exodus 39:22
   A. Blue
   B. Gold
   C. Purple
   D. Scarlet

7. Which of the following were attached to the bottom hem of the robe?
   Exodus 39:24–26
   A. Bells and pomegranates
   B. Crosses and nails
   C. Scrolls and boxes
   D. Stars and shepherd's hooks

8. What was wrote upon the plate of the holy crown of pure gold?
   Exodus 39:30
   A. ALMIGHTY GOD
   B. ALPHA AND OMEGA
   C. EL SHADDAI
   D. HOLINESS TO THE LORD

9. Which color were the rams' skins dyed?
   Exodus 39:34
   A. Blue
   B. Gold
   C. Green
   D. Red

10. When did the Israelites set up the tabernacle?
    Exodus 40:17
    A. 1st day, 1st month, 1st year
    B. 6th day, 7th month, 1st year
    C. 1st day, 1st month, 2nd year
    D. 6th day, 7th month, 3rd year

11. What was placed *inside* the ark of the covenant?
    Exodus 40:20
    A. High priests' clothing
    B. Joseph's bones
    C. Moses' rod
    D. Testimony of God

12. What was placed *upon* the ark of the covenant?

    Exodus 40:20

    A. Fresh flowers
    B. Golden candlestick
    C. Mercy seat
    D. Shewbread

13. Which direction was the table in the tent of the congregation located?

    Exodus 40:22

    A. North
    B. South
    C. East
    D. West

14. Which direction was the golden candlestick located in the tent of the congregation?

    Exodus 40:24

    A. North
    B. South
    C. East
    D. West

15. What was located by the door of the tabernacle?

    Exodus 40:29

    A. Altar of burnt offering
    B. Altar of incense
    C. Ark of the covenant
    D. The vail

16. Between which two objects was the laver located?

    Exodus 40:30

    A. Altar of burnt offering and the golden candlestick
    B. Altar of incense and table of shewbread
    C. The holy of holies and most holy
    D. Tent of the congregation and the altar of burnt offering

17. What was the purpose of the laver?

    Exodus 40:30–32

    A. For collecting the blood of sacrificed animals
    B. For the Israelites to bathe in
    C. For the priests to wash their hands and feet in
    D. For washing the holy instruments

18. What prevented Moses from entering the tent of the congregation when the glory of the LORD filled the tabernacle?

    Exodus 40:34–35

    A. A cloud
    B. Angel of the LORD
    C. Cherubim
    D. Flaming swords

19. What was over the tabernacle during the day?

    Exodus 40:38

    A. Angel of the LORD
    B. Cloud of the LORD
    C. The flag of Israel
    D. The flags of the 12 tribes

20. What was over the tabernacle by night?

    Exodus 40:38

    A. A special star
    B. Fire
    C. The angel of death
    D. The angel of the LORD

Answers on page 753

FEBRUARY 1

Lesson 32
Today's Reading: *Leviticus 1–4*
Period of Time: 1490 BC
Author: Moses

1. Which animals without blemish could be offered as a burnt sacrifice?
   Leviticus 1:2–9
   A. Male asses
   B. Male bullocks
   C. Female goats
   D. Female sheep

2. On which side of the altar is a sheep or goat to be killed if it is going to be a burnt sacrifice?
   Leviticus 1:10–11
   A. North
   B. South
   C. East
   D. West

3. Which statement is true concerning a burnt sacrifice?
   Leviticus 1:10–13
   A. It must be an unblemished female goat.
   B. It must be an unblemished female sheep.
   C. The owner lays the pieces upon the altar.
   D. The priest sprinkles the blood upon the altar.

4. Which statement is true concerning a burnt sacrifice?
   Leviticus 1:14–17
   A. The fowl must be duck or goose.
   B. The owner must wring off its head.
   C. The priest plucks its crop and feathers.
   D. The priest releases a rooster at sunrise.

5. Which statement is true concerning a meat offering?
   Leviticus 2:1–3
   A. The offering must consist of fine flour with oil and frankincense poured upon it.
   B. The owner of the bull must kill it and sprinkle its ashes upon the ground.
   C. The owner of the female sheep must sprinkle its ashes upon the ground.
   D. The priests must sprinkle the blood upon the west side of the altar.

6. Which statement is true concerning an oblation of a meat offering baked in an oven?
   Leviticus 2:4
   A. The bull must be less than one year old without blemish.
   B. The cakes or wafers must be unleavened and anointed with oil.
   C. The cakes or wafers must be unleavened and anointed with raw honey.
   D. The meat must be pink with no blood present when it comes off the altar.

7. Which statement is true concerning an oblation of a meat offering baked in a pan?
   Leviticus 2:5–6
   A. The cake must be broken into pieces and oil poured upon it.
   B. The cake must remain whole and anointed with honey.
   C. The owner must give the leftover meat of the fowl to the priest.
   D. The priest must sprinkle the blood eastward.

8. Which statement is true concerning an oblation of a meat offering cooked in a frying pan?
   Leviticus 2:7–11
   A. The bull must be without blemish.
   B. The cake must contain leaven.
   C. The leftovers shall belong to the priests.
   D. The wafer must contain honey.

9. Which one of the following is added to oblations of meat offerings?
   Leviticus 2:13
   A. Cinnamon
   B. Honey
   C. Salt
   D. Water

10. Which two items must be added if the meal offering contains corn?
    Leviticus 2:12–16
    A. Butter and salt
    B. Herbs and water
    C. Honey and cinnamon
    D. Oil and frankincense

11. Which statement is true concerning a peace offering?
    Leviticus 3:1–5
    A. It can be a blind male if it is less than a year old.
    B. It can be either a male or female without blemish.
    C. It must be a female without blemish.
    D. It must be a three-year old male without blemish.

12. Which of the following may **not** be used as a peace offering?
    Leviticus 3:1–17
    A. Cows
    B. Goats
    C. Lambs
    D. Pigs

13. Which part of a cow was an Israelite forbidden to eat?
    Leviticus 3:17
    A. Brisket
    B. Chuck
    C. Fat
    D. Round

14. Which young animal without blemish would a priest offer for his own sin?
    Leviticus 4:3
    A. A bullock
    B. A goat
    C. A lamb
    D. A ram

15. How many times shall the anointed priest sprinkle the blood before the LORD for the priest's own sin offering?
    Leviticus 4:1–6
    A. 3
    B. 7
    C. 10
    D. 12

16. Which unblemished animal would be offered for a sin offering for the whole congregation?
    Leviticus 4:13–21
    A. A female goat
    B. A female sheep
    C. A ram
    D. A young bullock

17. Which unblemished animal would be offered for a sin offering for a ruler?
    Leviticus 4:22–23
    A. A bullock less than a year old
    B. A female goat less than a year old
    C. A female lamb of the sheep
    D. A male kid of the goats

18. What must a priest do with part of the blood of a sin offering offered by a ruler?
    Leviticus 4:25
    A. Collect the blood and burn it in the fires of Gehenna, located outside the camp.
    B. Pour half the blood upon the altar and the rest on the ground outside the camp.
    C. Use his finger and put it upon the horns of the altar of burnt offering.
    D. Use his staff and dab one drop of blood on each shoulder of the ruler.

19. Which unblemished animal would be offered for a sin offering for a commoner?
    Leviticus 4:27–35
    A. A female ass
    B. A female kid of the goats
    C. A male ass
    D. A male kid of the goats

20. What must the priest do with part of the blood of a sin offering offered by a commoner?
    Leviticus 4:30–34
    A. Put it upon the horns of the altar.
    B. Put it upon the owner's earlobes.
    C. Sprinkle it seven times upon the altar.
    D. Sprinkle it upon the ground seven times.

Answers on page 753

FEBRUARY 2

Lesson 33
Today's Reading: *Leviticus 5–7*
Period of Time: 1490 BC
Author: Moses

1. What did an Israelite need to offer for being an unfaithful witness to a crime?
   Leviticus 5:1–6
   A. 1/10th part of an ephah of fine flour
   B. 1 female lamb or a kid of the goats
   C. 1 young bullock
   D. 2 turtledoves or 2 young pigeons

2. What did an Israelite need to offer for touching anything ceremonially unclean?
   Leviticus 5:1–6
   A. 1/10th part of an ephah of fine flour
   B. 1 female lamb or a kid of the goats
   C. 1 young bull
   D. 2 turtledoves or 2 young pigeons

3. What did an Israelite need to offer for forgiveness of a sinful oath?
   Leviticus 5:1–6
   A. 1/10th part of an ephah of fine flour
   B. 1 female lamb or a kid of the goats
   C. 1 young bull
   D. 2 turtledoves or 2 young pigeons

4. What did a *poor* Israelite need to offer for being an unfaithful witness to a crime?
   Leviticus 5:1–10
   A. 1/10th part of an ephah of fine flour
   B. 1 female lamb or a kid of the goats
   C. 1 young bull
   D. 2 turtledoves or 2 young pigeons

5. What did a *poor* Israelite need to offer for touching anything ceremonially unclean?
   Leviticus 5:1–10
   A. 1/10th part of an ephah of fine flour
   B. 1 female lamb or a kid of the goats
   C. 1 young bull
   D. 2 turtledoves or 2 young pigeons

6. What did a *poor* Israelite need to offer for forgiveness of a sinful oath?
   Leviticus 5:1–10
   A. 1/10th part of an ephah of fine flour
   B. 1 female lamb or a kid of the goats
   C. 1 young bull
   D. 2 turtledoves or 2 young pigeons

7. What did a *very poor* Israelite need to offer for being an unfaithful witness to a crime?
   Leviticus 5:1–13
   A. 1/10th part of an ephah of fine flour
   B. 1 female lamb or a kid of the goats
   C. 1 young bull
   D. 2 turtledoves or 2 young pigeons

8. What did a *very poor* Israelite need to offer for touching anything ceremonially unclean?
   Leviticus 5:1–13
   A. 1/10th part of an ephah of fine flour
   B. 1 female lamb or a kid of the goats
   C. 1 young bull
   D. 2 turtledoves or 2 young pigeons

9. What did a *very poor* Israelite need to offer for forgiveness of a sinful oath?
   Leviticus 5:1–13
   A. 1/10th part of an ephah of fine flour
   B. 1 female lamb or a kid of the goats
   C. 1 young bull
   D. 2 turtledoves or 2 young pigeons

10. Which animal without blemish would be offered for unintentional sin involving the holy things of the LORD?
    Leviticus 5:14–19
    A. A female goat
    B. A lamb
    C. A ram
    D. A young bullock

11. What was the penalty if an Israelite stole from his neighbor and lied about it?
    Leviticus 6:1–7
    A. Offer a lamb for his trespass offering
    B. Offer a ram for his trespass offering
    C. Pay in full, add 20%, and offer a ram on the day of his trespass offering
    D. Restore 5 times the amount and offer a lamb on the day of his trespass offering

12. Which statement is true concerning the law of the burnt offering?
    Leviticus 6:9–13
    A. There was no particular order as to how the offerings were offered.
    B. Oak wood must be used for the fire.
    C. The fire must never go out.
    D. The priest must wear the holy garments and carry the ashes outside of the camp.

13. What was to be included in a meat offering?
    Leviticus 6:14–15
    A. A young bull
    B. Fine flour, olive oil, and frankincense
    C. Male goat
    D. Ram

14. What was God's portion of a meat offering offered by a common Israelite?
    Leviticus 6:15
    A. A handful the flour mixed with olive oil and frankincense
    B. The kidneys and fat of the male goat
    C. The rump of the young bull
    D. The shank bone of the ram

15. What were Aaron and his sons to eat with any remainder of a meat offering offered by a common Israelite?
    Leviticus 6:16
    A. A hardboiled egg
    B. Fruits, nuts, and honey
    C. Horseradish
    D. Unleavened bread

16. Where were Aaron and his sons to eat any remainder of a meat offering offered by an Israelite?
    Leviticus 6:16
    A. At the golden table inside the tent of the tabernacle
    B. Behind the tent of the tabernacle
    C. In the court of the tabernacle of the congregation
    D. Inside their own homes

17. Who could eat one of the heave offering cakes prepared for a peace offering?
    Leviticus 7:11–14
    A. The person who paid the temple tax during the passover
    B. The person who baked the cake and poured oil upon it
    C. The priest who blew one of the silver trumpets
    D. The priest who sprinkled the blood of the peace offerings

18. Which part of the wave offering belonged to Aaron and his sons?
    Leviticus 7:30–31
    A. Breast
    B. Left shoulder
    C. Right shoulder
    D. Rump

19. Which part of the heave offering belonged to the priests?
    Leviticus 7:32
    A. Breast
    B. Left shoulder
    C. Right shoulder
    D. Rump

20. Upon which mountain did the LORD give Moses the instructions for the offerings?
    Leviticus 7:37–38
    A. Mount Nebo
    B. Mount Sinai
    C. Mount Sodom
    D. Mount Tabor

Answers on page 753

FEBRUARY 3

Lesson 34
Today's Reading: *Leviticus 8–9*
Period of Time: 1490 BC
Author: Moses

1. What was Moses to bring to the door of the tabernacle of the congregation?
   Leviticus 8:2–3
   A. 1 bull and 1 lamb
   B. 1 bull, 2 rams, and unleavened bread
   C. 2 bulls and 2 lambs
   D. 2 bulls, 2 rams, and unleavened bread

2. Which part of the high priest's clothes contained the Urim and Thummim?
   Leviticus 8:8
   A. The breastplate
   B. The ephod
   C. The mitre
   D. The robe

3. Which one of the following was sacrificed for the sin offering for the priests?
   Leviticus 8:14–17
   A. A bullock
   B. A goat
   C. A lamb
   D. A ram

4. Which part of the sin offering was **not** burned outside of the camp?
   Leviticus 8:14–17
   A. The dung
   B. The flesh
   C. The hide
   D. The kidneys

5. Which one of the following was sacrificed for the burnt offering?
   Leviticus 8:18–21
   A. A bullock
   B. A goat
   C. A lamb
   D. A ram

6. Which parts of the burnt sacrifice did Moses wash?
   Leviticus 8:21
   A. The breast and thighs
   B. The head and shoulders
   C. The inwards and legs
   D. The rump and liver

7. Which part of Aaron and his son's bodies did Moses **not** put any blood upon?
   Leviticus 8:23–24
   A. Right ear
   B. Right great toe
   C. Right thigh
   D. Right thumb

8. Which part of the wave offering did Moses keep?
   Leviticus 8:29
   A. The breast
   B. The flank
   C. The liver
   D. The rump

9. What did Moses use to sanctify Aaron and his son's garments?
   Leviticus 8:30
   A. Ashes and holy water
   B. Blood and anointing oil
   C. Flour mingled with oil and frankincense
   D. Olive oil and holy water

10. What did Moses tell Aaron and his sons to eat at the door of the tabernacle of the congregation?
    Leviticus 8:21, 8:31
    A. Boiled fish and unleavened bread
    B. Boiled flesh with unleavened bread
    C. Broiled fish with leavened bread
    D. Broiled flesh with leavened bread

11. How many days did it take to consecrate the priests?

    Leviticus 8:33–36

    A. 3
    B. 5
    C. 6
    D. 7

12. What young animal did Aaron offer as a sin offering for his own sin?

    Leviticus 9:2, 9:8

    A. A beaver of the wild
    B. A calf of the herd
    C. A kid of the goats
    D. A lamb of the sheep

13. Which parts of the sin offering offered for Aaron's sins did he burn outside the camp?

    Leviticus 9:11

    A. Caul above the liver and kidneys
    B. Dung and head
    C. Hide and flesh
    D. Liver and kidneys

14. What did Aaron offer as a burnt offering for himself?

    Leviticus 9:2, 9:12–14

    A. A bullock
    B. A goat
    C. A lamb
    D. A ram

15. Which young animal was offered as a sin offering for the people?

    Leviticus 9:3, 9:15

    A. A kid of the goats
    B. A lamb of the sheep
    C. A piglet of the swine
    D. A ram of the flock

16. What was offered as a burnt offering for the people?

    Leviticus 9:1–7, 9:16

    A. A bullock and a goat
    B. A bullock and a ram
    C. A calf and a lamb
    D. A lamb and a ram

17. Which offering came after the burnt offering for the people?

    Leviticus 9:15–17

    A. The drink offering
    B. The meat offering
    C. The peace offering
    D. The wave offering

18. Which of the following were offered as a peace offering for the people?

    Leviticus 9:4, 9:18

    A. A bullock and a lamb
    B. A calf and a goat
    C. A goat and a lamb
    D. A ram and a bullock

19. What did Aaron wave for the wave offering?

    Leviticus 9:21

    A. A leavened cake
    B. An unleavened wafer
    C. The breasts and right shoulder
    D. The unleavened bread and right shoulder

20. In addition to the fat, which offering did the LORD consume?

    Leviticus 9:23–24

    A. The burnt offering
    B. The meat offering
    C. The peace offering
    D. The sin offering

*Answers on page 753

FEBRUARY 4

Lesson 35
Today's Reading: *Leviticus 10–12*
Period of Time: 1490 BC
Author: Moses

1. Who were two of Aaron's sons?
   Leviticus 10:1
   A. Didymus and Festus
   B. Ishbak and Peruda
   C. Nadab and Abihu
   D. Sadoc and Hosea

2. Why did God kill two of Aaron's sons?
   Leviticus 10:1–2
   A. They offered strange fire before the LORD.
   B. They prepared a chamber for an Ammonite in the courts of the house of God.
   C. They slept with women at the door of the tabernacle of the congregation.
   D. They worshipped an idol.

3. What did Aaron do after the LORD slew two of his sons?
   Leviticus 10:3
   A. Cursed God
   B. Held his peace
   C. Rent his clothes
   D. Wore sackcloth and ashes

4. Who carried the dead bodies out of the camp?
   Leviticus 10:4–5
   A. Aaron and Moses
   B. Lemek and Kelita
   C. Mishael and Elzaphan
   D. Samson and Delilah

5. Who was Aaron's uncle?
   Leviticus 10:4
   A. Eli
   B. Hophni
   C. Phinehas
   D. Uzziel

6. Who were Aaron's two other sons?
   Leviticus 10:6
   A. Eleazar and Ithamar
   B. Gaius and Jether
   C. Ophir and Blastus
   D. Rhesa and Hophra

7. What were Aaron and his sons forbidden to do whenever they went into the tabernacle of the congregation?
   Leviticus 10:9
   A. Bathe in water
   B. Drink liquor
   C. Eat meat
   D. Offer a sacrifice

8. Where were Aaron and his sons to eat the meat offering?
   Leviticus 10:12
   A. Beside the altar
   B. In the Tent of Meeting
   C. In their homes
   D. Upon the golden table

9. Which parts of a peace offering belonged to Aaron, his sons, and daughters?
   Leviticus 10:14
   A. Caul and fatty portions
   B. Kidneys and other organ meats
   C. Salted rib eye and t-bone steaks
   D. Wave breast and heave shoulder

10. Why didn't Aaron's sons eat the goat from the sin offering?
    Leviticus 10:16–20
    A. They had offered their sin offering and burnt offering.
    B. They had sprinkled salt on the goat meat.
    C. They were fasting.
    D. They were forbidden to eat goat under the Mosaic dietary laws.

11. Which one of the following could an Israelite consume?
    Leviticus 11:1–19
    A. Camel
    B. Coney
    C. Cow
    D. Cuckow

12. Which one of the following could an Israelite consume?
    Leviticus 11:9–12
    A. Eel
    B. Lobster
    C. Shrimp
    D. Trout

13. Which one of the following could an Israelite consume?
    Leviticus 11:13–19
    A. Bat
    B. Chicken
    C. Eagle
    D. Raven

14. Which one of the following could an Israelite consume?
    Leviticus 11:20–28
    A. Bear
    B. Beetle
    C. Chameleon
    D. Mouse

15. Which one of the following could an Israelite consume?
    Leviticus 11:20–47
    A. Centipede
    B. Locust
    C. Snake
    D. Tortoise

16. How many days was a mother of a newborn male considered unclean?
    Leviticus 12:1–2
    A. 7
    B. 14
    C. 21
    D. 28

17. How many days after birth was a newborn male to be circumcised?
    Leviticus 12:3
    A. 1
    B. 3
    C. 4
    D. 8

18. How many days of purification were required for a mother who delivered a son?
    Leviticus 12:1–4
    A. 0
    B. 20
    C. 40
    D. 80

19. How many days of purification were required for a mother who delivered a daughter?
    Leviticus 12:1–5
    A. 20
    B. 40
    C. 60
    D. 80

20. After the days of purification, which of the following did a mother offer for a burnt offering and a sin offering?
    Leviticus 12:6–8
    A. A bullock and a ram
    B. A goat and a bullock
    C. A young lamb, and a turtledove or pigeon
    D. A young ram, and a turtledove or pigeon

*Answers on page 753

FEBRUARY 5

Lesson 36
Today's Reading: *Leviticus 13*
Period of Time: 1490 BC
Author: Moses

1. Which of the following was a plague of leprosy?
   Leviticus 13:1–4
   A. A sore deep in the flesh with white hairs
   B. A sore elevated in the flesh with no hair
   C. A sore elevated in the flesh with red hairs
   D. A sore level in the flesh with red hairs

2. Initially, how many days was an infected person isolated?
   Leviticus 13:1–4
   A. 3
   B. 7
   C. 14
   D. 30

3. Which of the following are signs of an old leprosy in the skin of the flesh?
   Leviticus 13:9–11
   A. Dry, flaky skin with fluid-filled blisters
   B. Purple spots beneath the skin
   C. Raw flesh in the raised skin, white hair
   D. Yellow skin from head to toe

4. What did the priest do if the leprosy was old?
   Leviticus 13:9–11
   A. Announce he is clean, but no isolation
   B. Announce he is clean and isolate
   C. Announce he is unclean and isolate
   D. Announce he is unclean, but no isolation

5. What would a priest do if the leprosy on the skin turned white from head to toe?
   Leviticus 13:12–13
   A. Announce he is clean
   B. Have him live outside the camp
   C. Have him wear a mask in public
   D. Place him in isolation for 7 days

6. What would a priest do if he saw raw flesh on a person?
   Leviticus 13:12–15
   A. Announce he is clean
   B. Announce he is unclean
   C. Send him to the enemy's camp
   D. Wash him in the river of Jordan

7. What would a priest do if the raw flesh was no longer present from head to toe?
   Leviticus 13:16–17
   A. Announce he is clean
   B. Isolate 7 days
   C. Isolate for 14 days
   D. Wash him in the river of Jordan

8. Which of the following were signs of a plague of leprosy broken out of a boil?
   Leviticus 13:18–20
   A. Sore even with skin and no hair
   B. Sore higher than skin and no hair
   C. Sore lower than skin with white hair
   D. Sore lower than skin with no hair

9. Which of the following were signs of a plague from a boil?
   Leviticus 13:18–22
   A. Sore higher than skin, no black hairs
   B. Sore level with skin, hair red
   C. Sore lower than skin, hair white
   D. Sore spreading, no white hairs

10. Which of the following were signs of a burning boil?
    Leviticus 13:24–28
    A. Bright spot red, higher than the skin, spreading, and hair has turned white
    B. Bright spot somewhat higher than the skin and spreading abroad
    C. Bright spot somewhat dark, not lower than the skin, not spreading, and no white hairs
    D. Bright spot somewhat redder than the skin and spreading, and hair remains black

11. Which one of the following is a dry scall, leprosy upon the head or beard?
    Leviticus 13:29–30
    A. Sore deeper than the skin with yellow thin hair present
    B. Sore elevated than the skin with no hair present
    C. Sore level with the skin with thick gray hair present
    D. Sore level with the skin with wispy black hair present

12. Which of the following would be considered clean after 14 days?
    Leviticus 13:29–34
    A. The scall has spread on the skin, and pus is draining from raw flesh.
    B. The scall has spread on the skin and the hair is black.
    C. The scall has spread on the skin with the presence of thin yellow hairs.
    D. The scall has not spread on the skin, nor is it deeper than the skin.

13. What was a person to do after being pronounced clean of a scall on the head?
    Leviticus 13:34
    A. Decontaminate the room he was in
    B. Wash his clothes
    C. Wear a linen cloth over his mouth
    D. Wear a white linen robe for 14 days

14. Which patient would be considered unclean after his cleansing?
    Leviticus 13:35–36
    A. A patient suffering hair loss
    B. A patient suffering from blindness
    C. A patient with a scall that has spread
    D. A patient with scars on his arms and face

15. Which patient would be considered clean?
    Leviticus 13:37
    A. A patient who has a scall on his bald head that is spreading.
    B. A patient whose skin contains areas with raw flesh.
    C. A patient with a scall that contains hair that has turned thin and yellow.
    D. A patient with a scall that is unchanged and black hair has grown in it.

16. Which person would be considered unclean?
    Leviticus 13:38–42
    A. A teenage boy with a sore in his beard
    B. A teenage girl covered in freckles
    C. An elderly man with a receding hairline
    D. An elderly woman going bald

17. What must a leper do if he is pronounced unclean of the head?
    Leviticus 13:42–46
    A. Bathe, shave all his hair, be isolated for 7 days
    B. Rent his clothes; cover his upper lip, live outside the camp
    C. Shave off all of the hair on his body, be isolated for 14 days
    D. Wear sackcloth and ashes whenever he leaves his house

18. How many days must a leper dwell outside of the camp?
    Leviticus 13:46
    A. 7
    B. 14
    C. 21
    D. As long as he has the plague

19. Which one of the following must be done if the plague of leprosy has spread on a garment after seven days?
    Leviticus 13:47–52
    A. Apply anointment to it
    B. Burn it
    C. Cut out the damaged parts
    D. Wash it

20. Which one of the following must be done to a washed garment that no longer contains a plague?
    Leviticus 13:53–58
    A. Burn it
    B. Dye it red
    C. Wash it a second time
    D. Wash it four more times

Answers on page 753

FEBRUARY 6

Lesson 37
Today's Reading: *Leviticus 14–15*
Period of Time: 1490 BC
Author: Moses

1. Where was the priest to meet the leper?
   Leviticus 14:1–3
   A. Inside the tent of the congregation
   B. Outside the camp
   C. The Holy Place
   D. The Most Holy Place

2. Which items did the priest need in order to perform a purification ceremony for a leper?
   Leviticus 14:4
   A. 2 asses, wine, bread, and ½ shekel
   B. 2 birds, cedar wood, scarlet, and hyssop
   C. 2 bulls, flour mixed with 1 log of oil
   D. 2 goats, frankincense, 1 kab of fine flour

3. What happened to the animals used for the purification ceremony of a leper?
   Leviticus 14:5–7
   A. Kill one, set the other one free
   B. Offer both as a trespass offering
   C. Offer them as sin and burnt offerings
   D. Set them both free after the ceremony

4. What did the leper need to do to be cleansed?
   Leviticus 14:8
   A. Bathe in still water, wash his clothes, and scrub the walls in his home
   B. Bathe, wash his clothes, and be unclean until the evening
   C. Shave his head, offer incense upon the altar, and be unclean until the evening
   D. Wash his clothes, shave off all his hair, and bathe in water

5. What did a cleansed leper do on the 7th day?
   Leviticus 14:9
   A. Bathe in sand, put on clean clothes, and offer a peace offering
   B. Shave his head, burn his clothes, and burn incense upon the altar
   C. Wash his clothes, shave off all his hair, and bathe in water
   D. Wash the walls to his home, bathe in water, and wash his clothes

6. What did the leper need to offer on the 8th day, after being pronounced clean?
   Leviticus 14:10
   A. 1/10 deals of flour mingled with oil, 1 he goat, 1 shekel, and 1 kab of oil
   B. 2/10 deals of flour mingled with oil, 2 rams, 1 shekel, and 1 hin of wine
   C. 3/10 deals of flour mingled with oil, 2 he lambs, 1 ewe lamb, and 1 log of oil
   D. 4/10 deals of flour mingled with oil, 2 rams, 1 he lamb, and 1 log of wine

7. What did the leper need for the trespass offering?
   Leviticus 14:12
   A. 1 he lamb
   B. 1 she lamb
   C. 2 lambs
   D. 2 rams

8. What was the wave offering?
   Leviticus 14:12
   A. 1 he goat and a kab of oil
   B. 1 he goat and a shekel
   C. 1 he lamb and a bath of wine
   D. 1 he lamb and a log of oil

9. Which offerings belonged to the priest?
   Leviticus 14:13
   A. Grain and sin offerings
   B. Peace and drink offerings
   C. Sin and trespass offerings
   D. Wave and burnt offerings

10. What was the correct sequence of the offerings for a leper who was pronounced clean?
    Leviticus 14:12–20
    A. Burnt, meat, sin, and trespass
    B. Meat, burnt, trespass, and sin
    C. Sin, burnt, meat, and trespass
    D. Trespass, sin, burnt, and meat

11. Which substitutions did God allow the poor to fulfill the ritual for a cleansed leper?
    Leviticus 14:21–32
    A. 1 calf, 1 goat, 1 hin of red wine, and 1 shekel
    B. 1 lamb, fine flour mingled with oil, and 2 turtledoves or 2 young pigeons
    C. 2 rams, 2 goats, 1 young lamb, and 1 bath of wine
    D. 2 rams, 2 turtledoves, 2 shekels, and 2 hins of wine

12. What did a priest search for to determine if a house contained the plague of leprosy?
    Leviticus 14:33–38
    A. Black insects in the cupboards and in flour containers
    B. Green or red strakes deeper than the surface of the wall
    C. Mouse droppings in cracks along the floors
    D. The lack of cedar odor from the walls and beams

13. What was to be done to the house if the leprosy inside was a fretting leprosy?
    Leviticus 14:44–45
    A. Burn a fire in the fireplace for 7 days
    B. Remove all the stones, wood, and mortar
    C. Sanitize and isolate the house for 7 days
    D. Sterilize the house a second time

14. Which items were needed to cleanse the house if the plague had **not** spread in the house?
    Leviticus 14:48–49
    A. 1 lamb, boiling water, and cedar brushes
    B. 1 young calf, myrrh, and scalding water
    C. 2 birds, cedar wood, scarlet, and hyssop
    D. 2 young bulls and holy water

15. What did the priest do to the animals used for the purification ceremony of a house?
    Leviticus 14:48–53
    A. Killed one and freed the other one
    B. Offered both animals as a burnt offering
    C. Offered one for a sin offering and the other one for a burnt offering
    D. Offered one for his own sin and the second one for the sin of the home owner

16. Which would be considered clean?
    Leviticus 15:1–12
    A. Eating from a sterilized bowl used for bathing
    B. Lying down on a bed that contains a discharge from a man
    C. Shaking a man's unwashed hand who has the common cold
    D. Sitting on a chair that has a drop of blood on the seat

17. How many days after a man is cleansed from his issue does he need to wait to be clean?
    Leviticus 15:13
    A. 7
    B. 10
    C. 14
    D. 28

18. What did a cleansed person need to offer for a sin and burnt offering?
    Leviticus 15:14
    A. 1 he goat
    B. 1 young bull
    C. 2 rams and 1 lamb
    D. 2 turtledoves or 2 young pigeons

19. How many days did a woman need to wait after being cleansed of her issue?
    Leviticus 15:28
    A. 3
    B. 5
    C. 7
    D. 8

20. What did a woman need to offer after being cleansed of her issue?
    Leviticus 15:29–30
    A. 1 she goat
    B. 1 young bull
    C. 2 rams and 1 lamb
    D. 2 turtledoves or 2 young pigeons

*Answers on page 754

FEBRUARY 7

Lesson 38
Today's Reading: *Leviticus 16–18*
Period of Time: 1490 BC
Author: Moses

1. What did Aaron offer for a sin offering and a burnt offering?
   Leviticus 16:1–3
   A. A goat and a lamb
   B. A lamb and a bullock
   C. A ram and a young goat
   D. A young bullock and a ram

2. Which was **not** a part of the high priest's holy linen garments?
   Leviticus 16:4
   A. Breeches
   B. Coat
   C. Earrings
   D. Girdle

3. How did Aaron determine which goat would be the scapegoat?
   Leviticus 16:8
   A. By age
   B. By casting lots
   C. By color
   D. By gender

4. What happened to the scapegoat?
   Leviticus 16:10, 16:21
   A. It became the burnt offering
   B. It became the meat offering
   C. It became the sin offering
   D. It was released into the wilderness

5. What did Aaron do with the censor of burning coals?
   Leviticus 16:12–13
   A. He burned incense beaten small upon the coals.
   B. He made sinners walk barefoot upon the coals.
   C. He poured the coals upon the altar to light the wood.
   D. He used it as a light at night in the tabernacle.

6. Which direction did Aaron sprinkle the blood upon the mercy seat?
   Leviticus 16:14
   A. North
   B. South
   C. East
   D. West

7. How many persons, besides Aaron, were to make an atonement in the holy place?
   Leviticus 16:17
   A. 0
   B. 2
   C. 3
   D. 7

8. Which day of the year was the day of atonement?
   Leviticus 16:29
   A. 1st day, 1st month
   B. 10th day, 7th month
   C. 12th day, 4th month
   D. 31st day, 12th month

9. What was the penalty for killing an ox, goat, or lamb and **not** bringing an offering to the LORD?
   Leviticus 17:1–4
   A. 36 months of hard labor in prison
   B. 39 lashes across the back
   C. Banishment from the camp
   D. Death

10. What type of offering was an Israelite to give if he killed an ox, goat, or lamb in a field?
    Leviticus 17:5
    A. Burnt
    B. Peace
    C. Sin
    D. Trespass

11. What was the penalty for making a burnt offering or sacrifice unto devils?
    Leviticus 17:7–9
    A. 6 years of hard labor in prison
    B. 39 lashes across the back
    C. Crucifixion
    D. Death

12. Where in the body was the life of the flesh located?
    Leviticus 17:11
    A. Blood
    B. Heart
    C. Liver
    D. Spleen

13. What was an Israelite to cover with dust?
    Leviticus 17:12–13
    A. Blood from a hunted animal
    B. Dead bodies to dry out the body fluids
    C. Leftover food after the third day
    D. Sin offerings and burnt offerings

14. What did an Israelite need to do if he ate an animal that died of natural causes?
    Leviticus 17:15–16
    A. Bathe in water, shave all of his hair, and change his clothes
    B. Change his clothes, wash his hands and feet, and drink a log of wine
    C. Wash his clothes, bathe in water, and be unclean until the evening
    D. Wash his hands, wash his eating utensils, and drink a log of wine

15. Which two nations did the LORD mention when he warned the Israelites **not** to walk in their ordinances?
    Leviticus 18:1–3
    A. The Amalekites and Hittites
    B. The Egyptians and Canaanites
    C. The Greeks and Romans
    D. The Ninevites and Babylonians

16. Whom could an Israelite have sexual intercourse with and still be clean?
    Leviticus 18:6–18
    A. His brother's wife
    B. His daughter-in-law
    C. His wife
    D. His wife's sister

17. What did God claim is an Israelite's own nakedness?
    Leviticus 18:10
    A. A brother's wife
    B. A temple prostitute
    C. Their father's sister
    D. Their grandchildren

18. What type of sex did God call *wickedness* in Leviticus 18:17?
    Leviticus 18:17
    A. A man with a female cousin
    B. A man with a female servant
    C. A man with a woman and her daughter
    D. A man with a woman twice his age

19. Which warning did God give to the Israelites concerning Molech?
    Leviticus 18:21
    A. Not to sacrifice their children to the fires of Molech
    B. Not to seek a peace treaty with the people of Molech
    C. Not to spare the women and children of Molech
    D. Not to take any spoil from the city of Molech

20. What would happen if the Israelites followed the sexual impurities and idol worship of other nations?
    Leviticus 18:24–30
    A. The Israelites would avoid wars with their new neighbors.
    B. The land would spue the Israelites out.
    C. The monarchs of other nations would call the Israelites politically correct.
    D. The other nations would teach the Israelites how to heal their new diseases.

*Answers on page 754

FEBRUARY 8

Lesson 39
Today's Reading: *Leviticus 19–21*
Period of Time: 1490 BC
Author: Moses

1. Which one of the following were the Israelites to do?
   Leviticus 19:1–3
   A. Honor their parents and keep the sabbaths
   B. Learn astrology and respect wizards
   C. Make idols of silver, gold, and wood
   D. Worship and honor Ashtoreth

2. What were the Israelites to do with leftover meat from a peace offering on the third day?
   Leviticus 19:5–8
   A. Burn it in the fire
   B. Bury it in the ground
   C. Finish eating it
   D. Pour dust upon it

3. Which statement is true concerning treatment of the poor?
   Leviticus 19:9–10
   A. The farmer was not to gather the gleanings of their harvest.
   B. The king was to set aside 10,000 bushels of corn each year for the poor.
   C. The merchant was to give a 10% discount to the poor.
   D. The physicians were to give the poor free health care.

4. When was an Israelite to pay a person whom he had hired?
   Leviticus 19:13
   A. End of the day
   B. End of the week
   C. End of two weeks
   D. End of the month

5. What could an Israelite do to an unjust neighbor?
   Leviticus 19:15–18
   A. Get revenge
   B. Hold a grudge
   C. Rebuke him
   D. Slay him

6. How did God say we should treat a neighbor?
   Leviticus 19:18
   A. Love them as yourself
   B. With great suspicion in your heart
   C. The way a wife treats a husband
   D. The way the Egyptians treated them as slaves

7. What was to happen to a betrothed bondmaid who had sexual intercourse with another man?
   Leviticus 19:20
   A. She was to be hung.
   B. She was to be scourged.
   C. She was to be set free from her betrothal.
   D. She was to be stoned to death.

8. In how many years would an Israelite be able to eat the fruit from a newly planted fruit tree?
   Leviticus 19:23–25
   A. 1
   B. 3
   C. 5
   D. 6

9. What was an Israelite to do when an elderly person entered the room?
   Leviticus 19:32
   A. Leave the room immediately unless asked to stay
   B. Redirect the elderly man back to his bedroom
   C. Shout so the elderly person could hear better
   D. Stand up

10. How was an Israelite to treat a stranger?
    Leviticus 19:33–34
    A. Like a slave
    B. Like a son or daughter
    C. Like an employee
    D. Like an enemy

11. Why did God want to drive out the nations in Canaan?

    Leviticus 20:1–26
    A. They had overpopulated the land.
    B. They were giants.
    C. They were uncircumcised.
    D. They worshipped idols.

12. How was a parent to be put to death if he offered his child to the fires of Molech?

    Leviticus 20:2
    A. By drowning
    B. By fire
    C. By hanging
    D. By stoning

13. What punishment did a son receive for cursing his mother or father?

    Leviticus 20:9
    A. He was placed in a labor camp.
    B. He was put to death.
    C. He was scourged.
    D. He was sold as a slave.

14. How was a man to be put to death if he married his wife and mother-in-law?

    Leviticus 20:14
    A. By drowning
    B. By fire
    C. By hanging
    D. By stoning

15. What was the punishment if a man had sexual intercourse with an animal?

    Leviticus 20:15
    A. Only the beast was killed
    B. Only the man was killed
    C. The man and beast were killed
    D. The man was flogged

16. What was the penalty for practicing witchcraft?

    Leviticus 20:27
    A. Death by drowning
    B. Death by fire
    C. Death by hanging
    D. Death by stoning

17. Whom could a priest marry?

    Leviticus 21:7
    A. A divorced woman
    B. A priestess
    C. A temple prostitute
    D. A virgin woman

18. What was the penalty if the daughter of a priest became a prostitute?

    Leviticus 21:9
    A. Death by drowning
    B. Death by fire
    C. Death by hanging
    D. Death by stoning

19. Whom could a high priest marry?

    Leviticus 21:13–15
    A. A divorced woman
    B. A temple prostitute
    C. A virgin woman
    D. A widow

20. Who could come near the altar to give an offering?

    Leviticus 21:16–23
    A. A blind man
    B. A dwarf
    C. A priest with no blemish
    D. A woman with a crooked back

Answers on page 754

FEBRUARY 9

Lesson 40
Today's Reading: *Leviticus 22–23*
Period of Time: 1490 BC
Author: Moses

1. What would a priest who touched an unclean thing need to do to eat of the holy things?
   Leviticus 22:1–7
   A. Bathe in water and wait for the sun to go down
   B. Shave his beard and all of the hair on his head, and wait 7 days
   C. Wash his clothes, shave off all of the hair on his body, and wait 14 days
   D. Wash his face and hands, bathe in water, and offer incense upon the altar

2. Which one of the following could an Israelite consume and still be clean?
   Leviticus 22:5–8
   A. A centipede
   B. A cow that died of natural causes
   C. An antelope torn in pieces by tigers
   D. An ox seethed in boiling water

3. Who could eat of the holy thing?
   Leviticus 22:10–13
   A. A foreigner
   B. A hired servant
   C. A priest's slave
   D. An astrologer

4. What did a man have to do if he unknowingly ate of the holy thing?
   Leviticus 22:14
   A. Be put to death by stoning
   B. Make restitution to the priest for the offering and add a fifth of the value to it
   C. Repent of his sin and offer a bullock less than one year old for a sin offering
   D. Wash his clothes, bathe in water, and be quarantined for 7 days

5. What could be used for a burnt offering?
   Leviticus 22:18–20
   A. A boar
   B. A bullock
   C. A cow
   D. A ewe

6. How many days must a bull, sheep, or a goat remain under the dam before it could be used as an offering?
   Leviticus 22:27
   A. 7
   B. 10
   C. 12
   D. 40

7. In which nation were the Israelites slaves?
   Leviticus 22:33
   A. Babylon
   B. Egypt
   C. Libya
   D. Syria

8. Which day of the week was the sabbath of rest?
   Leviticus 23:1–3
   A. 1st day
   B. 3rd day
   C. 6th day
   D. 7th day

9. Which date during the year was the LORD's passover?
   Leviticus 23:5
   A. 1st day, 7th month
   B. 14th day, 1st month
   C. 15th day, 1st month
   D. 15th day, 7th month

10. When was the feast of unleavened bread?
    Leviticus 23:6
    A. 1st day, 7th month
    B. 14th day, 1st month
    C. 15th day, 1st month
    D. 15th day, 7th month

11. How many days did the Israelites eat unleavened bread during the feast of unleavened bread?
    Leviticus 23:6
    A. 3
    B. 6
    C. 7
    D. 13

12. What was offered as a drink offering?
    Leviticus 23:13
    A. Beer
    B. Milk
    C. Water
    D. Wine

13. Which foods were mentioned that an Israelite was forbidden to eat during the feast of firstfruits until he brought an offering?
    Leviticus 23:10–14
    A. Beets, pumpkins, or any kind of squash
    B. Green beans, kidney beans, or white beans
    C. Horseradish, leeks, or ripe melons from the vine
    D. Parched corn, bread, or corn with green ears

14. How many days did the Israelites need to wait after waving the sheaf offering before they could offer the two wave loaves?
    Leviticus 23:15–22
    A. 30
    B. 40
    C. 50
    D. 60

15. How many bullocks were offered with the two wave loaves?
    Leviticus 23:17–18
    A. 1
    B. 2
    C. 6
    D. 7

16. How many rams were offered with the two wave loaves?
    Leviticus 23:17–18
    A. 1
    B. 2
    C. 6
    D. 7

17. Which date during the year was the annual memorial for the blowing of trumpets?
    Leviticus 23:24
    A. 1st day, 7th month
    B. 14th day, 1st month
    C. 15th day, 1st month
    D. 15th day, 7th month

18. Which one of the following followed the annual memorial for the blowing of trumpets?
    Leviticus 23:27
    A. Day of atonement
    B. Feast of tabernacles
    C. Firstfruits
    D. LORD's passover

19. Which date during the year was the feast of tabernacles?
    Leviticus 23:34
    A. 1st day, 7th month
    B. 14th day, 1st month
    C. 15th day, 1st month
    D. 15th day, 7th month

20. How many days during the feast of tabernacles were the Israelites to live in booths?
    Leviticus 23:33–43
    A. 3
    B. 6
    C. 7
    D. 12

Answers on page 754

FEBRUARY 10

Lesson 41
Today's Reading: *Leviticus 24–25*
Period of Time: 1490 BC
Author: Moses

1. How long were the lamps to burn in the tabernacle of the congregation?
   Leviticus 24:1–4
   A. Daily from dusk to dawn
   B. From dusk to dawn on the sabbath day
   C. From the first to the last day of the feasts
   D. They were to burn continually

2. How many holy cakes of bread were placed upon the pure table every sabbath?
   Leviticus 24:5–8
   A. 7
   B. 12
   C. 30
   D. 40

3. What was placed upon the holy cakes for a memorial?
   Leviticus 24:7
   A. Cinnamon
   B. Flour
   C. Frankincense
   D. Olive oil

4. Where were Aaron and his sons to eat the holy cakes?
   Leviticus 24:9
   A. In their homes
   B. Outside of the camp
   C. The Holy Place
   D. The Most Holy Place

5. Who was the mother of the son guilty of blasphemy?
   Leviticus 24:10–11
   A. Ashtoreth
   B. Bashemath
   C. Mahalath
   D. Shelomith

6. What was the penalty for someone who blasphemed the name of the LORD?
   Leviticus 24:10–16
   A. Death by drowning
   B. Death by fire
   C. Death by hanging
   D. Death by stoning

7. What was the penalty for someone who blinded somebody?
   Leviticus 24:17–22
   A. An eye for an eye
   B. Death by hanging
   C. Restitution of 10 talents of gold
   D. Ten years in jail for each blind eye

8. Upon which mountain did the LORD speak to Moses?
   Leviticus 25:1
   A. Mount Ararat
   B. Mount Carmel
   C. Mount Sinai
   D. Mount Tabor

9. When was the sabbath of rest for the land?
   Leviticus 25:1–7
   A. Every 6 years
   B. Every 7 years
   C. Every 18 years
   D. Every 49 years

10. When was the annual day of atonement?
    Leviticus 25:9
    A. 1st day, 1st month
    B. 7th day, 4th month
    C. 10th day, 7th month
    D. 25th day, 12th month

11. When were the years of a jubile?
    Leviticus 25:8–12
    A. Every 7 years
    B. Every 50 years
    C. Every 100 years
    D. Every 1000 years

12. Which statement is true concerning a year of jubile?
    Leviticus 25:10–17
    A. All possessions were returned to the original owners.
    B. It was a memorial to the Israelites' independence from Egyptian tyranny.
    C. Men could redeem their divorced wives if they could afford to buy them back.
    D. No Israelite labored for one year, but slaves continued to work.

13. Which statement is true concerning the seventh sabbatical year and the year of a jubile?
    Leviticus 25:18–22
    A. God would bless the 6th year to sustain the Israelites for 3 years.
    B. Israelite men from age 18-21 were required to complete military training.
    C. Israelite women who had faithfully served in the military were set free.
    D. Israelites were to use this time to expand their nation's borders.

14. Which of the following was the law if an Israelite sold his possessions?
    Leviticus 25:25–28
    A. A relative or friend could not redeem an item for another man.
    B. Land considered prime real estate could only be sold at an auction.
    C. Livestock could only be sold at an auction to another Israelite.
    D. Possessions had to be returned to the owner during the year of Jubilee.

15. Which statement is true concerning a house sold in a walled city?
    Leviticus 25:29–30
    A. It could never be sold.
    B. It could not be redeemed.
    C. It may be redeemed at any time.
    D. It must be redeemed in the first year.

16. Which statement is true concerning a house sold in a village with no walls around it?
    Leviticus 25:31
    A. It could never be sold.
    B. It could not be redeemed.
    C. It may be redeemed at any time.
    D. It must be redeemed in the first year.

17. Which statement is true concerning the sale of a house owned by a Levite in a city?
    Leviticus 25:32–33
    A. It could be redeemed at any time.
    B. It could never be sold.
    C. It must be redeemed within one year.
    D. It must be sold for twice its value.

18. Which statement is true concerning the fields of the suburbs of the Levites?
    Leviticus 25:34
    A. It could be redeemed at any time.
    B. It could never be sold.
    C. It must be redeemed within one year.
    D. It must be sold for twice its value.

19. How much interest could an Israelite charge a poor Israelite on a loan?
    Leviticus 25:35–37
    A. 0%
    B. 7%
    C. 14%
    D. 21%

20. Which statement is true concerning bondservants?
    Leviticus 25:39–55
    A. All slaves had dark skin.
    B. An Israelite could redeem himself.
    C. Israelites used slaves in gladiator games.
    D. Slaves paid taxes for being slaves.

*Answers on page 754

FEBRUARY 11

Lesson 42
Today's Reading: *Leviticus 26–27*
Period of Time: 1490 BC
Author: Moses

1. Which statement is true concerning idols and the law of Moses?
   Leviticus 26:1
   A. Idol destroyers were to be stoned
   B. Idols were to be bowed to
   C. Israelites were not to make idols
   D. Silver was to be used for lesser gods

2. What were the conditions to receive God's blessings?
   Leviticus 26:3
   A. Be open-minded to homosexuality
   B. Don't say, "God bless" in public
   C. Honor other people's beliefs
   D. Obey God's commandments

3. What was the first conditional blessing God promised the Israelites?
   Leviticus 26:4
   A. Rain in due season
   B. Rid the land of evil beasts
   C. Safety from their enemies
   D. Trees shall yield their fruit

4. How many of their enemies did God say five Israelites would drive from the land?
   Leviticus 26:8
   A. 10
   B. 100
   C. 1,000
   D. 10,000

5. How many of their enemies did God say one hundred Israelites would drive from the land?
   Leviticus 26:8
   A. 10
   B. 100
   C. 1,000
   D. 10,000

6. Which chastisements did God list in the first wave of curses?
   Leviticus 26:16–17
   A. Drought and dried up fields
   B. Famine and their cities destroyed
   C. Terror, consumption, and burning ague
   D. Wild beasts would attack them

7. Which chastisements did God list in the second wave of curses?
   Leviticus 26:18–20
   A. Drought and dried up fields
   B. Famine and their cities destroyed
   C. Terror, consumption, and burning ague
   D. Wild beasts would attack them

8. Which chastisements did God list in the third wave of curses?
   Leviticus 26:21–22
   A. Drought and dried up fields
   B. Famine and their cities destroyed
   C. Terror, consumption, and burning ague
   D. Wild beasts would attack them

9. Which chastisements did God list in the fourth wave of curses?
   Leviticus 26:23–26
   A. Drought and dried up fields
   B. Sword and pestilence
   C. Terror, consumption, and burning ague
   D. Wild beasts would attack them

10. How many women would bake bread in one oven during the fourth wave of curses?
    Leviticus 26:26
    A. 3
    B. 7
    C. 10
    D. 12

11. Which chastisement did God list in the fifth wave of curses?
    Leviticus 26:27–33
    A. Famine and their cities destroyed
    B. Sword and pestilence
    C. Terror, consumption, and burning ague
    D. Wild beasts would attack them

12. What did God say would enjoy her sabbaths after He scatters the Israelites?
    Leviticus 26:34
    A. The beasts
    B. The land
    C. The priests
    D. The temple

13. What sound did God say would strike fear in an Israelite?
    Leviticus 26:36
    A. A horse's gallop
    B. A shaken leaf
    C. A viper's rattler
    D. An enemy's shout

14. What did God say He would remember when the Israelites were living in foreign lands?
    Leviticus 26:40–46
    A. His covenant with Jacob, Isaac, and Abraham
    B. His great flood upon the earth and Noah
    C. His ten commandments
    D. His ten plagues upon Egypt

15. How many shekels of silver was the estimation for a male from 20-60 years old?
    Leviticus 27:1–3
    A. 10
    B. 15
    C. 20
    D. 50

16. How many shekels of silver was the estimation for a male 5-20 years old?
    Leviticus 27:5
    A. 10
    B. 15
    C. 20
    D. 50

17. How many shekels of silver was the estimation for a male 60 years old or older?
    Leviticus 27:7
    A. 10
    B. 15
    C. 20
    D. 50

18. If a man wanted to redeem a beast, a house, or a field how much did he have to add to its estimation?
    Leviticus 27:9–21
    A. A fifth
    B. A sixth
    C. A seventh
    D. An eighth

19. How many shekels of silver was a homer of barley seed worth?
    Leviticus 27:16
    A. 10
    B. 25
    C. 50
    D. 60

20. Upon which mountain did Moses receive God's commandments?
    Leviticus 27:34
    A. Mount Carmel
    B. Mount Ebal
    C. Mount Mariah
    D. Mount Sinai

Answers on page 754

Lesson 43
Today's Reading: *Numbers 1–2*
Period of Time: 1490 BC
Author: Moses

FEBRUARY 12

1. When did God speak to Moses in the wilderness of Sinai?
   Numbers 1:1
   A. 1st day, 1st month, 1st year
   B. 1st day, 2nd month, 2nd year
   C. 7th day, 1st month, 1st year
   D. 7th day, 7th month, 3rd year

2. Who was included in the census if they were able to go to war?
   Numbers 1:2–3
   A. Men 18 years old or older
   B. Men 20 years old or older
   C. Men and women 18 years old or older
   D. Men and women 21 years old or older

3. What was the total number of tribes?
   Numbers 1:5–15
   A. 12
   B. 31
   C. 52
   D. 100

4. Who was the prince of the tribe of Reuben?
   Numbers 1:5
   A. Eliab
   B. Eliasaph
   C. Elishama
   D. Elizur

5. Who was the prince of the tribe of Judah?
   Numbers 1:7
   A. Abidan
   B. Gamaliel
   C. Nahshon
   D. Pagiel

6. Who was the prince of the tribe of Zebulun?
   Numbers 1:9
   A. Aholiab
   B. Ben-abinadab
   C. Chileab
   D. Eliab

7. Who was the prince of the tribe of Manasseh?
   Numbers 1:10
   A. Ahira
   B. Gamaliel
   C. Nethaneel
   D. Shelumiel

8. Who was the prince of the tribe of Benjamin?
   Numbers 1:11
   A. Abidan
   B. Gamaliel
   C. Nethaneel
   D. Pagiel

9. Which tribe had the most members?
   Numbers 1:18–43
   A. Tribe of Benjamin
   B. Tribe of Dan
   C. Tribe of Judah
   D. Tribe of Simeon

10. Which tribe had the least members?
    Numbers 1:18–43
    A. Tribe of Gad
    B. Tribe of Judah
    C. Tribe of Levi
    D. Tribe of Manasseh

11. What was the total membership of all the tribes?
    Numbers 1:44–46
    A. 603,550
    B. 779,834
    C. 981,999
    D. 1,300,256

12. Which tribe was **not** included in the census?
    Numbers 1:47–49
    A. Tribe of Dan
    B. Tribe of Levi
    C. Tribe of Reuben
    D. Tribe of Simeon

13. What was the penalty if a stranger came near the tabernacle?

    Numbers 1:51

    A. He had to hew wood for seven years.
    B. He had to remain unclean until evening.
    C. He was jailed for seven years.
    D. He was put to death.

14. What item did an Israelite tribe use to identify its tribe?

    Numbers 2:2

    A. A banner with an animal printed on it
    B. A wooden crest
    C. An ensign of their father's house
    D. Totem poles with historical carvings

15. Which tribes camped *east* of the tabernacle?

    Numbers 2:3–9

    A. Tribes of Dan, Asher, and Naphtali
    B. Tribes of Ephraim, Manasseh, and Benjamin
    C. Tribes of Judah, Issachar, and Zebulun
    D. Tribes of Reuben, Levi, and Gad

16. Which tribes camped *south* of the tabernacle?

    Numbers 2:10–16

    A. Tribes of Dan, Levi, and Naphtali
    B. Tribes of Ephraim, Manasseh, and Benjamin
    C. Tribes of Judah, Issachar, and Zebulun
    D. Tribes of Reuben, Simeon, and Gad

17. Which tribe camped in the *center* of the camp?

    Numbers 2:17

    A. Tribe of Dan
    B. Tribe of Ephraim
    C. Tribe of Levi
    D. Tribe of Reuben

18. Which tribes camped *west* of the tabernacle?

    Numbers 2:18–24

    A. Tribes of Dan, Asher, and Naphtali
    B. Tribes of Ephraim, Manasseh, and Benjamin
    C. Tribes of Judah, Levi, and Zebulun
    D. Tribes of Reuben, Simeon, and Gad

19. Which tribes camped *north* of the tabernacle?

    Numbers 2:25–31

    A. Tribes of Dan, Asher, and Naphtali
    B. Tribes of Ephraim, Manasseh, and Levi
    C. Tribes of Judah, Issachar, and Zebulun
    D. Tribes of Reuben, Simeon, and Gad

20. Which standard of the camp had the most members?

    Numbers 2:3–31

    A. 1st standard (East side)
    B. 2nd standard (South side)
    C. 3rd standard (West side)
    D. 4th standard (North side)

Answers on page 754

Lesson 44
Today's Reading: *Numbers 3–4*
Period of Time: 1490 BC
Author: Moses

FEBRUARY 13

1. Which of Aaron's two sons died because they offered strange fire before the LORD?
   Numbers 3:1–4
   A. Amram and Kohath
   B. Hebron and Uzziel
   C. Isaac and Esau
   D. Nadab and Abihu

2. Which two of Aaron's sons ministered in the priest's office after the LORD slew their other two brothers?
   Numbers 3:4
   A. Eleazar and Ithamar
   B. Elijah and Elisha
   C. Ephraim and Manasseh
   D. Ezekiel and Ethan

3. Which tribe was responsible for the service of the tabernacle?
   Numbers 3:5–10
   A. Tribe of Asher
   B. Tribe of Levi
   C. Tribe of Reuben
   D. Tribe of Simeon

4. In which nation did God smite all the firstborn sons?
   Numbers 3:11–13
   A. Assyria
   B. Canaan
   C. Egypt
   D. Israel

5. Which group pitched their tents *west* of the tabernacle?
   Numbers 3:23
   A. Gershonites
   B. Kohathites
   C. Merarites
   D. Moses, and Aaron and his sons

6. Which group pitched their tents *south* of the tabernacle?
   Numbers 3:29
   A. Gershonites
   B. Kohathites
   C. Merarites
   D. Moses, and Aaron and his sons

7. Which group pitched their tents *north* of the tabernacle?
   Numbers 3:35
   A. Gershonites
   B. Kohathites
   C. Merarites
   D. Moses, and Aaron and his sons

8. Which group pitched their tents *east* of the tabernacle?
   Numbers 3:38
   A. Gershonites
   B. Kohathites
   C. Merarites
   D. Moses, and Aaron and his sons

9. What was the number of male Levites one-month old and older?
   Numbers 3:39
   A. 10,823
   B. 12,565
   C. 17,249
   D. 22,000

10. What was the number of firstborn males from the children of Israel one-month old and older?
    Numbers 3:40–43
    A. 22,273
    B. 34,568
    C. 41,222
    D. 52,416

11. How many shekels were collected to redeem the 273 firstborn Israelite males?

    Numbers 3:44–49

    A. 666
    B. 1,365
    C. 2,345
    D. 3,375

12. Which age group of the Kohathites was required to work in the tabernacle?

    Numbers 4:1–3

    A. 18-65 years old
    B. 21-65 years old
    C. 30-50 years old
    D. 40-70 years old

13. What color was the cloth used to cover the ark of the testimony when the camp moved forward?

    Numbers 4:5–6

    A. Blue
    B. Purple
    C. Scarlet
    D. White

14. Which colors were the cloths that were used to cover the table of shewbread when the camp moved forward?

    Numbers 4:7–8

    A. Green and orange
    B. Purple and gold
    C. Scarlet and blue
    D. White and red

15. What color was the cloth used to cover the altar of burnt offering when the camp moved forward?

    Numbers 4:13–14

    A. Blue
    B. Purple
    C. Scarlet
    D. White

16. Which family was responsible for carrying the sanctuary parts and vessels?

    Numbers 4:15

    A. The Gershonites
    B. The Kohathites
    C. The Merarites
    D. The Shelanites

17. Who was responsible for the oil for the light, the sweet incense, daily meat offerings, anointing oil, and oversight of the tabernacle?

    Numbers 4:16

    A. Amminadab
    B. Cornelius
    C. Dedan
    D. Eleazar

18. Which family was responsible for the curtains and hangings of the tabernacle?

    Numbers 4:21–28

    A. The Gershonites
    B. The Kohathites
    C. The Merarites
    D. The Shelanites

19. Which family was responsible for the tabernacle boards, bars, pillars, sockets, pins, and cords?

    Numbers 4:29–33

    A. The Gershonites
    B. The Kohathites
    C. The Merarites
    D. The Shelanites

20. What was the total number of the workers who entered into the service of the tabernacle?

    Numbers 4:34–49

    A. 5,210
    B. 6,239
    C. 7,567
    D. 8,580

*Answers on page 754

FEBRUARY 14

Lesson 45
Today's Reading: *Numbers 5–6*
Period of Time: 1490 BC
Author: Moses

1. Who had to live outside of the camp?
   Numbers 5:1–4
   A. People with blindness
   B. People who were cripples
   C. People who were deaf
   D. People who were lepers

2. What did a person have to give the person he trespassed against?
   Numbers 5:5–7
   A. One-tenth of his profits from crops at the end of the year
   B. Full restitution and a fifth part
   C. Full restitution and an ephah of wheat
   D. The use of 1/4 of his field until the debt was paid

3. How much would the priest receive of the trespass offering if there was no kinsman to recompense for the trespass?
   Numbers 5:8–10
   A. 10%
   B. 20%
   C. 50%
   D. 100%

4. In addition to the trespass offering, what else did the sinner need to offer for atonement?
   Numbers 5:8–10
   A. A bull
   B. A goat
   C. A lamb
   D. A ram

5. What did the jealousy offering consist of?
   Numbers 5:11–18
   A. 1/10 part of an ephah of barley meal
   B. 1 young ram less than a year old
   C. 2 turtledoves or 2 young pigeons
   D. 5 shekels of silver

6. What did the priest place in an earthen vessel to determine if a wife had committed adultery?
   Numbers 5:17
   A. Holy water and dust from the floor of the tabernacle
   B. Holy water and frankincense
   C. Wine and a handful of ashes from the burnt offering
   D. Wine and anointing oil

7. What did the priest place in an alleged adulterous woman's hand?
   Numbers 5:18
   A. A lock cut from her hair
   B. Ashes from the altar
   C. Olive oil
   D. The jealousy offering

8. What did the priest use to blot out the curses he wrote in a book?
   Numbers 5:18–23
   A. A knife to cut it out
   B. Ashes from the altar
   C. Bitter water
   D. Goat's blood

9. What did the priest do with the jealousy offering?
   Numbers 5:25–26
   A. Gave it to the woman's husband
   B. Kept it for himself
   C. Kept if for the high priest
   D. Offered it upon the altar

10. What would happen if a wife was guilty of adultery?
    Numbers 5:26–27
    A. All of her hair would fall out.
    B. Her belly would swell and her thigh would rot.
    C. She would become a leper from her head to her toe.
    D. She would suddenly choke and then die.

11. What was a Nazarite forbidden to drink?
    Numbers 6:1–3
    A. Any type of wine
    B. Coffee with milk
    C. Orange juice
    D. Tea with honey

12. What was a Nazarite forbidden to eat?
    Numbers 6:1–3
    A. Bread made with honey
    B. Grapefruit
    C. Raisins
    D. White cheeses

13. How was a Nazarite to wear his hair?
    Numbers 6:5
    A. Any way he wanted to wear it.
    B. He could not cut his hair.
    C. He was to shave all of his hair.
    D. It was to remain shoulder length.

14. What was a Nazarite to do if a family member died?
    Numbers 6:7
    A. Anoint the body with nard
    B. Bow down over the body 7 times
    C. Stay away from the body
    D. Wrap the body in white linen cloths

15. What was a Nazarite to do if a person near him suddenly died?
    Numbers 6:9–12
    A. Burn white candles for 7 days
    B. Place a lock of his hair on the body
    C. Shave his head on the 7th day
    D. Transport the body to a priest

16. What did a Nazarite need to offer for atonement if he touched a dead body?
    Numbers 6:10–11
    A. 1 lamb
    B. 1 ram
    C. 2 turtledoves or young pigeons
    D. 2 young goats and a drink offering

17. What did a Nazarite need to offer for a trespass offering?
    Numbers 6:12
    A. 1 year-old male lamb
    B. 1 young male ram, 1 male sheep, and 2 male goats
    C. 2 turtledoves or young pigeons
    D. 3 rams, 1 young lamb, and wine for the drink offering

18. What did a Nazarite offer for a burnt offering when the days of his separation had ended?
    Numbers 6:13–14
    A. 1 year-old male lamb
    B. 1 young ram
    C. 2 rams and 2 lambs
    D. 2 turtledoves or young pigeons

19. Which parts of a Nazarite's peace offering belonged to the priest?
    Numbers 6:14–20
    A. The lamb's right leg and breast
    B. The wave breast and heave shoulder
    C. The whole ram and lamb
    D. The young goat's right leg and wattles

20. What would shine upon the Israelites when God blessed them?
    Numbers 6:22–25
    A. The lights from heaven
    B. The LORD's face
    C. The Spirit of light
    D. The sun and stars

*Answers on page 754

FEBRUARY 15

Lesson 46
Today's Reading: *Numbers 7*
Period of Time: 1490 BC
Author: Moses

1. How many wagons were brought to the tabernacle?
   Numbers 7:3
   A. 2
   B. 3
   C. 6
   D. 12

2. How many oxen were brought to the tabernacle?
   Numbers 7:3
   A. 4
   B. 6
   C. 12
   D. 24

3. How many wagons did the sons of Gershon receive?
   Numbers 7:7
   A. 2
   B. 4
   C. 8
   D. 10

4. How many wagons did the sons of Merari receive?
   Numbers 7:8
   A. 2
   B. 4
   C. 8
   D. 10

5. Which group of Levites carried the sanctuary holy vessels upon their shoulders?
   Numbers 7:9
   A. The Caananites
   B. The Beerothites
   C. The Gibeonites
   D. The Kohathites

6. Which tribe gave their offering the first day?
   Numbers 7:12
   A. Tribe of Benjamin
   B. Tribe of Judah
   C. Tribe of Reuben
   D. Tribe of Zebulun

7. How much in shekels did one silver charger weigh?
   Numbers 7:13
   A. 10
   B. 70
   C. 100
   D. 130

8. How much in shekels did one silver bowl weigh?
   Numbers 7:13
   A. 10
   B. 70
   C. 100
   D. 130

9. What did the silver chargers and bowls contain?
   Numbers 7:13
   A. Fine flour mingled with oil
   B. Frankincense mingled with myrrh
   C. Shewbread and bitter water
   D. Wine and bread

10. How much in shekels of gold did one spoon weigh?
    Numbers 7:14
    A. 10
    B. 70
    C. 100
    D. 130

11. Which of the following items were used for the burnt offerings?

    Numbers 7:15–45

    A. 1 male goat, 1 ewe of the sheep, and 2 rams
    B. 1 female goat, 1 ewe of the sheep, and 2 rams
    C. 1 young bullock, 1 ram, 1 lamb of the first year
    D. 1 young male goat, 1 bull, 2 turtledoves or 2 young pigeons

12. What was used for the sin offering?

    Numbers 7:16–46

    A. 1 bull
    B. 1 calf
    C. 1 eight-days-old ewe
    D. 1 kid of the goats

13. Which of the following items were used for the peace offerings?

    Numbers 7:17–47

    A. 1 ox, 1 ram, 1 male goat, 1 one-year old lamb
    B. 2 oxen, 2 rams, 2 male goats, 2 one-year old lambs
    C. 2 oxen, 5 rams, 5 male goats, 5 one-year old lambs
    D. 5 oxen, 5 rams, 5 male goats, 5 one-year old lambs

14. Which tribe gave their offering the third day?

    Numbers 7:24

    A. Tribe of Asher
    B. Tribe of Issachar
    C. Tribe of Naphtali
    D. Tribe of Zebulun

15. Who was the prince of the tribe of Ephraim?

    Numbers 7:48

    A. Ahira
    B. Elishama
    C. Nahshon
    D. Shelumiel

16. What did the silver spoons contain?

    Numbers 7:86

    A. Ashes
    B. Honey
    C. Incense
    D. Olive oil

17. What was the total number of golden spoons offered?

    Numbers 7:86

    A. 12
    B. 24
    C. 36
    D. 60

18. What was the total number of oxen offered for the peace offerings?

    Numbers 7:88

    A. 12
    B. 24
    C. 36
    D. 60

19. What was the total number of rams offered for the peace offerings?

    Numbers 7:88

    A. 12
    B. 24
    C. 36
    D. 60

20. Where did God speak to Moses after the dedication of the altar?

    Numbers 7:89

    A. From the mercy seat
    B. In a pillar of a cloud
    C. In the wilderness of Sin
    D. On top of mount Sinai

*Answers on page 754

Lesson 47
Today's Reading: *Numbers 8–10*
Period of Time: 1490 BC
Author: Moses

FEBRUARY 16

1. How many lamps were on the candlestick?
   Numbers 8:1–4
   A. 7
   B. 10
   C. 12
   D. 40

2. Which of the following was **not** a requirement to make the Levites ceremonially clean?
   Numbers 8:5–7
   A. Have holy water sprinkled on them
   B. Shave all of their hair
   C. Wash their clothes
   D. Widen the borders of their garments

3. What was offered as a sin offering to make atonement for the Levites?
   Numbers 8:8–12
   A. A goat
   B. A lamb
   C. A ram
   D. A young bullock

4. What was offered as a burnt offering to make atonement for the Levites?
   Numbers 8:8–12
   A. A kid from the goats
   B. A one-year old lamb
   C. A male ram
   D. A young bullock

5. What gift did God give Aaron and his sons?
   Numbers 8:19
   A. The fruit of the Holy Spirit
   B. The gift of speaking in tongues
   C. The Levites
   D. The Spirit of hope

6. Which age group of the Levites was required to take part in the work of the tabernacle?
   Numbers 8:23–26
   A. 18-65 years old
   B. 21-65 years old
   C. 25-50 years old
   D. 30-50 years old

7. In which year after leaving Egypt did the LORD speak to Moses in the wilderness of Sinai?
   Numbers 9:1
   A. 1st
   B. 2nd
   C. 3rd
   D. 4th

8. When was the LORD's passover to be celebrated?
   Numbers 9:1–5
   A. 1st day, 1st month
   B. 14th day, 1st month
   C. 7th day, 7th month
   D. 21st day, 7th month

9. When was an Israelite to celebrate the LORD's passover if he was unclean for touching a dead body?
   Numbers 9:6–11
   A. 14th day, 2nd month
   B. 21st day, 8th month
   C. 28th day, 1st month
   D. 30th day, 7th month

10. Which of the following were part of the LORD's passover meal?
    Numbers 9:11
    A. Applesauce and pork chops
    B. Lobster and beef steak
    C. Unleavened bread and bitter herbs
    D. Wine and a goat boiled in its mother's milk

11. Who could **not** eat the LORD's passover meal even if he was ceremonially clean?

    Numbers 9:6–14

    A. A Levite
    B. A seven-year-old child
    C. A stranger
    D. Anyone who did not bring an offering

12. What was the punishment if a man that was ceremonially clean refused to keep the LORD's passover?

    Numbers 9:13

    A. Banishment from the camp
    B. Death
    C. Forty stripes, minus one, across the back
    D. Seven years of hard labor

13. What covered the tabernacle during the day?

    Numbers 9:15–16

    A. A band of angels
    B. A cloud
    C. A rainbow
    D. An eclipse

14. What covered the tabernacle during the night?

    Numbers 9:15–16

    A. A special comet
    B. Michael the archangel
    C. The appearance of fire
    D. The Star of David

15. How many silver trumpets did the LORD tell Moses to make?

    Numbers 10:1–2

    A. 2
    B. 7
    C. 12
    D. 24

16. What did it mean if only one trumpet was blown?

    Numbers 10:4

    A. Princes over the tribes needed to meet.
    B. Soldiers needed to grab their swords and spears.
    C. Someone in the camp had died.
    D. The congregation needed to hear an important announcement.

17. During which one of the following were the silver trumpets **not** to be blown?

    Numbers 10:8–10

    A. At the beginning of each month
    B. During solemn days
    C. When it was time to go to war
    D. When the national flag was raised

18. Where did the Israelites go after leaving the wilderness of Sinai?

    Numbers 10:11–15

    A. Wilderness of Egypt
    B. Wilderness of Paran
    C. Wilderness of Shur
    D. Wilderness of Zin

19. What was the correct order of the armies of the Israelites when they traveled?

    Numbers 10:14–28

    A. Dan, Judah, Reuben, and then Ephraim
    B. Ephraim, Dan, Judah, and then Reuben
    C. Judah, Reuben, Ephraim, and then Dan
    D. Reuben, Ephraim, Dan, and then Judah

20. Who was Moses' brother-in-law?

    Numbers 10:29

    A. Hobab
    B. Jobab
    C. Shobab
    D. Zobab

Answers on page 754

FEBRUARY 17

Lesson 48
Today's Reading: *Numbers 11–13*
Period of Time: 1490 BC
Author: Moses

1. Where did God consume with fire the Israelites who had complained to Moses?
   Numbers 11:1–3
   A. Giloh
   B. Joppa
   C. Taberah
   D. Ulai

2. Which food was **not** one of the foods mentioned that the Israelites ate while in Egypt?
   Numbers 11:4–5
   A. Cucumbers
   B. Fish
   C. Melons
   D. Tomatoes

3. What color was the manna?
   Numbers 11:7
   A. Bdellium
   B. Scarlet
   C. Vermilion
   D. White

4. What did the manna taste like?
   Numbers 11:8
   A. Almond nuts
   B. Fresh oil
   C. Naughty figs
   D. Stacte spice

5. Upon how many elders did God place the Spirit?
   Numbers 11:16–25
   A. 7
   B. 10
   C. 12
   D. 70

6. Which of the following individuals prophesied in the camp?
   Numbers 11:26–30
   A. Almodad and Bildad
   B. Henadad and Ben-ha'dad
   C. Eldad and Medad
   D. Zelophehad and Hadad

7. How many homers of quail did the person who gathered the least gather?
   Numbers 11:31–32
   A. 10
   B. 30
   C. 75
   D. 90

8. What did the LORD call the place where he smote the people with a very great plague?
   Numbers 11:33–34
   A. Hadadrimmon
   B. Kibroth-hatta'avah
   C. Metheg-ammah
   D. Zareth-shahar

9. Whom did Moses marry?
   Numbers 12:1
   A. A Canaanite mid-wife
   B. A Hittite slave woman
   C. An Egyptian queen
   D. An Ethiopian woman

10. How did God say he would speak to Moses?
    Numbers 12:6–8
    A. In dreams
    B. Mouth-to-mouth
    C. Through visions
    D. With dark speeches

11. Who became a leper for angering God?
    Numbers 12:9–10
    A. Aaron
    B. Jethro
    C. Miriam
    D. Zipporah

12. How many days was the leper isolated from the camp?

    Numbers 12:14–15

    A. 7
    B. 10
    C. 14
    D. 21

13. Which wilderness did the Israelites travel to after leaving Hazeroth?

    Numbers 12:16

    A. Wilderness of Egypt
    B. Wilderness of Paran
    C. Wilderness of Shur
    D. Wilderness of Sin

14. How many spies did Moses send into Canaan?

    Numbers 13:1–16

    A. 2
    B. 7
    C. 12
    D. 40

15. What did Moses call Oshea?

    Numbers 13:16

    A. Abishua
    B. Elishua
    C. Ishua
    D. Jehoshua

16. When was Hebron built?

    Numbers 13:22

    A. 7 years before Zoan in Egypt
    B. 10 years before the Phoenician city of Tyre
    C. 20 years before the Phoenician city of Sidon
    D. 25 years before Nineveh in Assyria

17. How large was the branch that contained one cluster of grapes?

    Numbers 13:23

    A. Equal in size to a kid from the goats
    B. It required two men to carry it
    C. The size of a shepherd's staff
    D. The weight of one iron chariot

18. How many days were the spies in Canaan?

    Numbers 13:25

    A. 10
    B. 14
    C. 21
    D. 40

19. Which spy had no fear of the people of Canaan?

    Numbers 13:30

    A. Caleb
    B. Gaddiel
    C. Nahbi
    D. Palti

20. Which statement best describes the sons of Anak?

    Numbers 13:28–33

    A. They were carpenters.
    B. They were dwarfs.
    C. They were giants.
    D. They were warlocks.

*Answers on page 754

FEBRUARY 18

Lesson 49
Today's Reading: *Numbers 14–15*
Period of Time: 1490–1489 BC
Author: Moses

1. What did the Israelites want to do after hearing the spies' reports?
   Numbers 14:1–4
   A. Choose a captain and return to Egypt.
   B. Hire mercenaries to kill the Egyptians.
   C. Make Moses their king and invade Egypt.
   D. Send spies into Egypt.

2. What did Moses and Aaron do after the people murmured against them?
   Numbers 14:5
   A. Fell on their faces
   B. Resigned their positions
   C. Sliced off Malchus' ear in anger
   D. Tied torches to 300 foxes' tails

3. Which two spies told the people **not** to rebel?
   Numbers 14:6–10
   A. Ammiel and Palti
   B. Geuel and Sethur
   C. Joshua and Caleb
   D. Shammua and Shaphat

4. What did the two spies say the people of the Promised Land were compared to God and them?
   Numbers 14:9
   A. Ants
   B. Babies
   C. Bread
   D. Grasshoppers

5. What did the Israelites want to do with the two spies?
   Numbers 14:10
   A. Burn them to death
   B. Give them medals for their valor
   C. Make them their kings
   D. Stone them to death

6. How many generations does the iniquity of the fathers last upon their children?
   Numbers 14:18
   A. First–second
   B. Second–third
   C. Third–fourth
   D. Fourth–fifth

7. How many times did the Israelites tempt God?
   Numbers 14:20–22
   A. 6
   B. 10
   C. 12
   D. 17

8. Who dwelled in the valley?
   Numbers 14:25
   A. Amalekites and Canaanites
   B. Assyrians and Persians
   C. Babylonians and Chaldeans
   D. Greeks and Romans

9. Which age group did the LORD say would **not** enter the Promised Land?
   Numbers 14:26–32
   A. 18 years old and above
   B. 20 years old and above
   C. 25–50 years old
   D. 35–50 years old

10. How many years did God say the Israelites' children would wander in the wilderness?
    Numbers 14:33
    A. 10
    B. 20
    C. 30
    D. 40

11. What happened to the ten spies who gave an evil report?

    Numbers 14:36–37
    A. They became double agents.
    B. They died from the plague.
    C. They disappeared in the night.
    D. They were captured by the enemy.

12. What did the Israelites need to offer with the burnt offering of one lamb?

    Numbers 15:1–5
    A. One-tenth deals of flour mingled with 1/4 of a hin of oil and 1/4 of a hin of wine
    B. Two-tenth deals of flour mingled with 1/3 of a hin of oil and 1/3 of a hin of wine
    C. Three-tenth deals of flour mingled with 1/2 of a hin of oil and 1/2 of a hin of wine
    D. Four-tenth deals of flour mingled with 1/5 of a hin of oil and 1/5 of a hin of wine

13. What did the Israelites need to offer with the burnt offering of one ram?

    Numbers 15:6–7
    A. One-tenth deals of flour mingled with 1/4 of a hin of oil and 1/4 of a hin of wine
    B. Two-tenth deals of flour mingled with 1/3 of a hin of oil and 1/3 of a hin of wine
    C. Three-tenth deals of flour mingled with 1/2 of a hin of oil and 1/2 of a hin of wine
    D. Four-tenth deals of flour mingled with 1/5 of a hin of oil and 1/5 of a hin of wine

14. What did the Israelites need to offer with the burnt offering of one bull?

    Numbers 15:8–11
    A. One-tenth deals of flour mingled with 1/4 of a hin of oil and 1/4 of a hin of wine
    B. Two-tenth deals of flour mingled with 1/3 of a hin of oil and 1/3 of a hin of wine
    C. Three-tenth deals of flour mingled with 1/2 of a hin of oil and 1/2 of a hin of wine
    D. Four-tenth deals of flour mingled with 1/5 of a hin of oil and 1/5 of a hin of wine

15. What type of offering was made with the first dough from the Promised Land?

    Numbers 15:17–21
    A. Burnt offering
    B. Heave offering
    C. Sin offering
    D. Wave offering

16. What was the congregation to offer as a *burnt offering* for their unintentional sin?

    Numbers 15:22–24
    A. A male ram
    B. A one-year-old lamb
    C. One kid of the goats
    D. One young bullock

17. What was the congregation to offer as a *sin offering* for their unintentional sin?

    Numbers 15:22–24
    A. A ewe from the flock
    B. A one-year-old lamb
    C. One kid of the goats
    D. One male ram

18. What was an individual to offer as a *sin offering* for unintentional sin?

    Numbers 15:27–29
    A. A bullock without blemish
    B. A he ram of the first year
    C. A kid of the goats
    D. A she goat of the first year

19. What happened to the man who gathered sticks on the sabbath day?

    Numbers 15:32–36
    A. He was honored for his work.
    B. He was hung from a tree.
    C. He was put in jail.
    D. He was stoned to death.

20. What were the Israelites to put upon the fringes of the borders of their garments?

    Numbers 15:37–40
    A. A blue ribbon
    B. A gold star
    C. A red whistle
    D. A silver bell

Answers on page 755

Lesson 50
Today's Reading: *Numbers 16–18*
Period of Time: 1489 BC
Author: Moses

1. Who was the ringleader of the rebellion?
   Numbers 16:1–5
   A. Kadmiel
   B. Kohath
   C. Korah
   D. Koz

2. How many princes joined the rebellion?
   Numbers 16:2
   A. 12
   B. 70
   C. 100
   D. 250

3. Who were Eliab's sons?
   Numbers 16:12
   A. Amram and Judas
   B. Benjamin and Simon
   C. Caleb and James
   D. Dathan and Abiram

4. What happened to the three leaders who led the rebellion and their families?
   Numbers 16:23–33
   A. They were banished from the camp.
   B. They were forced to drink poison.
   C. They were hung for treason.
   D. They were swallowed by the earth.

5. What happened to the men who offered incense?
   Numbers 16:35
   A. Fire from the LORD consumed them.
   B. Snakes struck and killed them.
   C. They died from hail from heaven.
   D. They died from the plague.

6. Who scattered the fire from the censers because they were holy?
   Numbers 16:37
   A. Elam
   B. Eleazar
   C. Ephron
   D. Ezekiel

7. What did the priest do with the censers?
   Numbers 16:38
   A. Buried them outside the camp
   B. Filled them with frankincense in the Holy Place
   C. Made broad plates from them for a covering of the altar
   D. Melted them down into statues for the tabernacle of the congregation

8. What were the censers made of?
   Numbers 16:39
   A. Aluminum
   B. Brass
   C. Copper
   D. Nickel

9. Who placed fire from the altar into a censer to stop the plague?
   Numbers 16:46–48
   A. Aaron
   B. Caleb
   C. Joshua
   D. Moses

10. How many people died from the plague?
    Numbers 16:49
    A. 1,470
    B. 14,700
    C. 147,000
    D. 1,470,000

11. How many rods did the LORD tell Moses to make?
    Numbers 17:1–2
    A. 12
    B. 24
    C. 50
    D. 70

12. What were the Israelites to write upon the rods?

    Numbers 17:1–2

    A. The Jewish calendar
    B. The names of their princes
    C. The ten commandments
    D. The ten Plagues of Egypt

13. Where did Moses place the rods?

    Numbers 17:7

    A. Inside the holy place
    B. Inside the most holy place
    C. Inside the tabernacle of Witness
    D. Upon the golden table

14. Which rod produced buds, blossoms, and yielded almonds?

    Numbers 17:8

    A. Aaron's rod
    B. Abiram's rod
    C. Dathan's rod
    D. Korah's rod

15. Who was to bear the iniquity of the sanctuary and priesthood?

    Numbers 18:1

    A. Aaron and his sons
    B. Abiram and his family
    C. Dathan and Caleb's children
    D. Korah and the tribal chiefs

16. Which tribe was responsible to do the work of the tabernacle of the congregation?

    Numbers 18:6

    A. Tribe of Benjamin
    B. Tribe of Judah
    C. Tribe of Levi
    D. Tribe of Naphtali

17. Where were the priests to eat their portions of the sacred offerings?

    Numbers 18:8–10

    A. Holy Place
    B. Most Holy Place
    C. Tabernacle of Witness
    D. The Golden Table

18. Which of the following of the firstborn were to be redeemed?

    Numbers 18:15–17

    A. All cows
    B. All goats
    C. All sheep
    D. All unclean beasts

19. Which tribe did the LORD give the tithes from the Israelites to?

    Numbers 18:21–24

    A. Tribe of Asher
    B. Tribe of Issachar
    C. Tribe of Judah
    D. Tribe of Levi

20. Which tribe was responsible for paying their tithes to the high priest?

    Numbers 18:25–32

    A. Tribe of Dan
    B. Tribe of Gad
    C. Tribe of Levi
    D. Tribe of Simeon

*Answers on page 755

Lesson 51
Today's Reading: *Numbers 19–21*
Period of Time: 1489–1452 BC
Author: Moses

FEBRUARY 20

1. Which color was the heifer the LORD told Moses to bring to the priest?
   Numbers 19:1–2
   A. Black
   B. Pale
   C. Red
   D. White

2. How many times was the priest to sprinkle the blood from the heifer before the tabernacle?
   Numbers 19:4
   A. 7
   B. 10
   C. 12
   D. 21

3. Which of the following items was the priest to cast into the middle of the burning heifer?
   Numbers 19:6
   A. Anise, fine flour, and olive oil
   B. Cedar wood, hyssop, and scarlet
   C. Gold, frankincense, and myrrh
   D. Thieves, robbers, and sabbath breakers

4. What were the ashes from the burned heifer mixed with water called?
   Numbers 19:9
   A. Ashes to Ashes
   B. Dust to Dust
   C. Sin Remover
   D. Water of Separation

5. How many days was a person unclean if they touched a dead body?
   Numbers 19:11
   A. 7
   B. 10
   C. 12
   D. 40

6. Who died during the first month in the desert of Zin?
   Numbers 20:1
   A. Bathsheba
   B. Candace
   C. Miriam
   D. Phebe

7. What was Moses' sin?
   Numbers 20:7–12
   A. He entered the Most Holy Place.
   B. He offered strange fire.
   C. He smote the rock twice.
   D. He spoiled a Canaanite camp

8. What did the LORD name the place where Moses gave the Israelites water to drink?
   Numbers 20:13
   A. Water of Life
   B. Water of Meribah
   C. Water of Purification
   D. Water of Tears

9. Which nation refused to allow the Israelites to pass through their land?
   Numbers 20:14–21
   A. Edom
   B. Midian
   C. Moab
   D. Syria

10. Which mountain did the Israelites travel to from Kadesh?
    Numbers 20:22
    A. Mount Hazor
    B. Mount Herman
    C. Mount Hor
    D. Mount Horeb

11. How many days did the Israelites mourn after Aaron died?

    Numbers 20:29

    A. 30
    B. 40
    C. 60
    D. 90

12. Who was the Canaanite king that fought against the Israelites?

    Numbers 21:1

    A. Ahab
    B. Arad
    C. Herod
    D. Nadab

13. What did the LORD send to punish the Israelites for their sins?

    Numbers 21:6

    A. Dragons
    B. Locusts
    C. Rats
    D. Serpents

14. What did Moses make to save the Israelites?

    Numbers 21:9

    A. A calf of gold
    B. A cat of silver
    C. A horse of copper
    D. A serpent of brass

15. Which book records what the LORD did in the Red sea, at the brooks of Arnon, and at the stream that goes down to the dwelling of Ar, and lieth upon the border of Moab?

    Numbers 21:14–15

    A. Book of the covenant
    B. Book of the dead
    C. Book of the law of Moses
    D. Book of the wars of the LORD

16. Which song did the Israelites sing at Beer, where they dug a well?

    Numbers 21:16–17

    A. At the Springs of Living Water
    B. As the Deer Pants for Water
    C. Spring Up, O Well
    D. We Shall Gather at the River

17. Who was the Amorite king that fought against the Israelites?

    Numbers 21:21

    A. King Salmon
    B. King Sihon
    C. King Simon
    D. King Solomon

18. Where did the king of the Amorites fight against the Israelites?

    Numbers 21:23

    A. Jabez
    B. Jahaz
    C. Janum
    D. Javan

19. Which Amorite city did the Israelites capture?

    Numbers 21:25–30

    A. Heshbon
    B. Kishon
    C. Lebanon
    D. Sidon

20. Who was the king of Bashan?

    Numbers 21:33

    A. King Agag
    B. King Gog
    C. King Magog
    D. King Og

Answers on page 755

FEBRUARY 21

Lesson 52
Today's Reading: *Numbers 22–24*
Period of Time: 1452 BC
Author: Moses

1. On which plains did the Israelites pitch their tents east of the river of Jordan?
   Numbers 22:1
   A. Plains of Mamre
   B. Plains of Midian
   C. Plains of Moab
   D. Plains of Moreh

2. Who was Balak's father?
   Numbers 22:2
   A. Ziphah
   B. Zippor
   C. Zithri
   D. Ziza

3. Who was Balaam's father?
   Numbers 22:5
   A. Beor
   B. Jotham
   C. Publius
   D. Quirinius

4. Where did Balaam live?
   Numbers 22:5
   A. Padan-aram
   B. Palestine
   C. Penuel
   D. Pethor

5. Which two nations formed a coalition against the Israelites?
   Numbers 22:7
   A. Ammon and Amalek
   B. Edom and Asshur
   C. Moab and Midian
   D. Tyre and Sidon

6. What stood in the path of Balaam?
   Numbers 22:22
   A. A flooded stream
   B. A rockslide
   C. King Magog's soldiers
   D. The angel of the LORD

7. Who asked Balaam why he struck her three times?
   Numbers 22:28
   A. A rock in the desert
   B. Balaam's ass
   C. Cornelius's concubine
   D. Rahab the prostitute

8. Where did Balak take Balaam the first time to curse the Israelites?
   Numbers 22:41
   A. The high places of Baal
   B. The mount of Olives
   C. The top of Peor
   D. The top of Pisgah

9. Which of the following items did Balaam use to offer burnt offerings to the LORD?
   Numbers 23:1–6
   A. 1 altar, 2 goats, and 1 lamb
   B. 2 altars, 2 rams, and 1 goat
   C. 7 altars, 7 oxen, 7 rams
   D. 12 altars, 12 rams, and 12 sheep

10. Where did Balaam say Balak brought him from?
    Numbers 23:7
    A. Aram
    B. Elam
    C. Helam
    D. Jokneam

11. Where did Balak take Balaam the second time to curse the Israelites?
    Numbers 23:14
    A. The high places of Baal
    B. The mount of Olives
    C. The top of Peor
    D. The top of Pisgah

12. What did Balaam say God's strength for the Israelites was similar to?

    Numbers 23:22

    A. A donkey
    B. A horse
    C. A lion
    D. A unicorn

13. What did Balaam say the Israelites would rise like?

    Numbers 23:24

    A. A blazing sun
    B. A great lion
    C. A king cobra
    D. A mountainous phoenix

14. Where did Balak take Balaam the third time to curse the Israelites?

    Numbers 23:28

    A. The high places of Baal
    B. The mount of Olives
    C. The top of Peor
    D. The top of Pisgah

15. Which spirit came upon Balaam when he saw the Israelites abiding in their tents?

    Numbers 24:2

    A. Spirit of Antichrist
    B. Spirit of God
    C. Spirit of Sin
    D. Spirit of Terror

16. Which king did Balaam say the Israelites would be higher than?

    Numbers 24:7

    A. King Agag
    B. King Magog
    C. King Og
    D. King Sihon

17. How many times did Balaam bless the Israelites?

    Numbers 24:10

    A. 3
    B. 7
    C. 10
    D. 12

18. What did Balaam say would come out of Jacob?

    Numbers 24:17

    A. A deliverer
    B. A fountain
    C. A prophet
    D. A star

19. Whom did Balaam say Asshur would carry away captive?

    Numbers 24:21–22

    A. The Hittites
    B. The Kenites
    C. The Perizzites
    D. The Tekonites

20. Which coast did Balaam say ships would come from and afflict Asshur and Eber?

    Numbers 24:24

    A. Coast of Adummim
    B. Coast of Betonim
    C. Coast of Chittim
    D. Coast of Dedanim

Answers on page 755

FEBRUARY 22

Lesson 53
Today's Reading: *Numbers 25–26*
Period of Time: 1452 BC
Author: Moses

1. Where did the Israelites commit whoredom with the daughters of Moab?
   Numbers 25:1
   A. Bezer
   B. Heshbon
   C. Medeba
   D. Shittim

2. Which idol were the Israelites guilty of worshipping?
   Numbers 25:3
   A. Asherah
   B. Baalpeor
   C. Chemosh
   D. Dagon

3. Which one of Eleazar's sons killed an Israelite man and a Midianitish woman?
   Numbers 25:7
   A. Philip
   B. Phinehas
   C. Phlegon
   D. Phygellus

4. What did Eleazar's son use to kill the Israelite man and the Midianitish woman?
   Numbers 25:7
   A. A javelin
   B. A jawbone
   C. A slingshot
   D. A tent peg

5. How many Israelites died from the plague?
   Numbers 25:9
   A. 24,000
   B. 34,233
   C. 45,987
   D. 61,075

6. What did the LORD give to Eleazar's son who killed the Israelite man and the Midianitish woman?
   Numbers 25:13
   A. 10 more years of life
   B. 1,000 acres of land near the river of Jordan
   C. The covenant of an everlasting priesthood
   D. The gift of prophecy

7. What was the name of the Israelite man whom Eleazar's son slew?
   Numbers 25:14
   A. Ezri
   B. Omri
   C. Shimri
   D. Zimri

8. Which tribe did the slain Israelite man belong to?
   Numbers 25:14
   A. Tribe of Gad
   B. Tribe of Levi
   C. Tribe of Simeon
   D. Tribe of Zebulun

9. What was the name of the slain Midianitish woman whom Eleazar's son slew?
   Numbers 25:15
   A. Cozbi
   B. Hazelelponi
   C. Naomi
   D. Vashti

10. Which age group of Israelite males was included in the census?
    Numbers 26:2
    A. 18 years old and above
    B. 20 years old and above
    C. 21 years old and above
    D. 25 years old and above

11. Which of Eliab's sons were swallowed by the earth?

    Numbers 26:9–10

    A. Dathan and Abiram
    B. Korah and Izhar
    C. Nemuel and Hebron
    D. Nepheg and Zichri

12. Which tribe had the most males?

    Numbers 26:5–50

    A. Tribe of Dan
    B. Tribe of Issachar
    C. Tribe of Judah
    D. Tribe of Naftali

13. Which tribe had the least number of males?

    Numbers 26:5–50

    A. Tribe of Asher
    B. Tribe of Gad
    C. Tribe of Reuben
    D. Tribe of Simeon

14. What was the total number of Israelite males, **not** counting the Levites, according to the census?

    Numbers 26:51

    A. 300,716
    B. 601,730
    C. 761,300
    D. 917,017

15. How were the Israelites to divide the land?

    Numbers 26:52–56

    A. By alphabetical order
    B. By auctioning to the highest bidder
    C. By casting lots
    D. By holding a race for the free land

16. Who was Moses' mother?

    Numbers 26:59

    A. Jael
    B. Jezebel
    C. Jochebed
    D. Judith

17. Who was Moses' father?

    Numbers 26:59

    A. Amram
    B. Eliam
    C. Misham
    D. Rehoboam

18. Which of Aaron's sons offered strange fire before the LORD?

    Numbers 26:61

    A. David and Pallu
    B. Eleazar and Tohu
    C. Ithamar and Raphu
    D. Nadab and Abihu

19. What was the total number of Levite males?

    Numbers 26:62

    A. 5,320
    B. 10,046
    C. 21,510
    D. 23,000

20. Which two males were included in the first and second censuses of the Israelite males?

    Numbers 26:63–65

    A. Aaron and Moses
    B. Caleb and Joshua
    C. Eleazar and Phinehas
    D. Ishmael and Puah

*Answers on page 755

FEBRUARY 23

Lesson 54
Today's Reading: *Numbers 27–29*
Period of Time: 1452 BC
Author: Moses

1. Which one of the following was **not** a daughter of Zelophehad?
   Numbers 27:1
   A. Bilhah
   B. Hoglah
   C. Mahlah
   D. Noah

2. Which tribe did Zelophehad belong to?
   Numbers 27:1
   A. Tribe of Judah
   B. Tribe of Levi
   C. Tribe of Manasseh
   D. Tribe of Simeon

3. Why did the daughters of Zelophehad come to Moses?
   Numbers 27:1–5
   A. To lease land west of the river of Jordan
   B. To purchase land east of the river of Jordan
   C. To request their late father's inheritance
   D. To sell their inheritance to a foreigner

4. Who would inherit a deceased man's land if he had no living children?
   Numbers 27:6–11
   A. His brother
   B. His father
   C. His father's brother
   D. His wife

5. Which mountain did God tell Moses to climb to see the land the Israelites would inherit?
   Numbers 27:12
   A. Mount Abarim
   B. Mount Carmel
   C. Mount Hermon
   D. Mount Lebanon

6. In which desert did Moses sin against God when he gave water to the Israelites?
   Numbers 27:14
   A. Desert of Paran
   B. Desert of Shur
   C. Desert of Sinai
   D. Desert of Zin

7. What was the name of the place in Kadesh where Moses gave the Israelites water?
   Numbers 27:14
   A. Jacob's Well
   B. Lake of Gennesaret
   C. The brook Cherith
   D. Water of Meribah

8. Who was to succeed Moses?
   Numbers 27:18–23
   A. Caleb
   B. Jephunneh
   C. Joshua
   D. Nun

9. What did the priest use to make decisions in the LORD's presence regarding Moses' successor?
   Numbers 27:21
   A. A crystal ball
   B. Astrology
   C. Tarot cards
   D. The Urim

10. Upon which mountain did the LORD ordain the continual burnt offering?
    Numbers 28:6
    A. Mount Ebal
    B. Mount Sinai
    C. Mount Sodom
    D. Mount Tabor

11. What did the continual burnt offering include?
    Numbers 28:1–8
    A. 2 bullocks
    B. 2 goats
    C. 2 lambs
    D. 2 rams

12. In addition to the daily sacrifices, what else was offered on the sabbath day?
    Numbers 28:9–10
    A. 1 lamb and its drink offering, and one tenth deals of flour mingled with oil
    B. 2 lambs and their drink offerings, and two tenth deals of flour mingled with oil
    C. 3 lambs and their drink offerings, and three tenth deals of flour mingled with oil
    D. 4 lambs and their drink offerings, and four tenth deals of flour mingled with oil

13. How many animals were used for a burnt offering at the beginning of each month?
    Numbers 28:11–14
    A. 7
    B. 10
    C. 13
    D. 30

14. What is the date for the passover of the LORD?
    Numbers 28:16
    A. 1st day, 1st month
    B. 7th day, 7th month
    C. 14th day, 1st month
    D. 21st day, 7th month

15. What is the date for the feast of unleavened bread?
    Numbers 28:17
    A. 1st day, 1st month
    B. 15th day, 1st month
    C. 21st day, 7th month
    D. 30th day, 12th month

16. How many animals were used for the burnt offering on the day of firstfruits?
    Numbers 28:26–29
    A. 7
    B. 10
    C. 13
    D. 30

17. What is the date for the feast of trumpets?
    Numbers 29:1
    A. 1st day, 7th month
    B. 7th day, 7th month
    C. 8th day, 12th month
    D. 30th day, 12th month

18. What is the date for the day of atonement?
    Numbers 29:7–11
    A. 1st day, 1st month
    B. 7th day, 1st month
    C. 7th day, 7th month
    D. 10th day, 7th month

19. How many animals were used for a burnt offering on the first day of the feast of tabernacles?
    Numbers 29:12–16
    A. 2
    B. 13
    C. 14
    D. 29

20. How many animals were used for a burnt offering on the eighth day of the feast of tabernacles?
    Numbers 29:35–40
    A. 9
    B. 19
    C. 29
    D. 39

Answers on page 755

FEBRUARY 24

Lesson 55
Today's Reading: *Numbers 30–31*
Period of Time: 1452 BC
Author: Moses

1. Which statement is true concerning vows?
   Numbers 30:1–16
   A. A father could revoke an unmarried teenage daughter's vow still living in his house.
   B. A husband could not revoke a wife's vow.
   C. A widow could not make a vow.
   D. A young man going to war could not make a vow.

2. Whom did the Israelites go to war against?
   Numbers 31:2
   A. The Edomites
   B. The Hittites
   C. The Midianites
   D. The Philistines

3. How many Israelites went to war?
   Numbers 31:5
   A. 10,000
   B. 12,000
   C. 36,000
   D. 60,000

4. Who went to war with the army of the Israelites?
   Numbers 31:6
   A. Evil-merodach
   B. Goliath
   C. Nebuchadnezzar
   D. Phinehas

5. How many of the kings that the Israelites slew are named in Numbers 31:8?
   Numbers 31:8
   A. 3
   B. 5
   C. 10
   D. 12

6. Which prophet was killed by the Israelites during the war?
   Numbers 31:8
   A. Amos
   B. Balaam
   C. Malachi
   D. Obadiah

7. Where did the Israelite army take the captives, prey, and the spoil from the war?
   Numbers 31:12
   A. Along the banks of the Red sea
   B. Jericho
   C. Plains of Moab
   D. Wilderness of Judah

8. Why was Moses angry with the officers of the Israelite army?
   Numbers 31:13–20
   A. They allowed the enemy to escape on foot.
   B. They had killed a prophet of God.
   C. They spared the enemy women and children.
   D. They trimmed the corners of their beards.

9. What did Moses tell the Israelites to do with the male children that were prisoners of war?
   Numbers 31:17
   A. Kill them
   B. Make them slaves
   C. Send them away
   D. Train them to be soldiers

10. What did Moses tell the Israelites to do with the female prisoners of war?
    Numbers 31:17
    A. Kill all of them except the virgins
    B. Make them slaves
    C. Send them away
    D. Take them as concubines

11. How many days were the Israelite army to abide outside of the camp in order to become clean?
    Numbers 31:19
    A. 3
    B. 6
    C. 7
    D. 10

12. What was Eleazar's occupation?
    Numbers 31:21
    A. Executioner
    B. Interpreter
    C. Metal forger
    D. Priest

13. What did the Israelites use to purify the precious metals?
    Numbers 31:23
    A. Blood from turtledoves
    B. Olive oil
    C. Water of separation
    D. Wax from beehives

14. How much from their portion did the soldiers have to give as tribute to the LORD?
    Numbers 31:25–29
    A. 1 of every 100
    B. 1 of every 500
    C. 1 of every 1,000
    D. 1 of every 2,000

15. How much from their portion did the rest of the Israelites have to give as tribute to the LORD?
    Numbers 31:25–30
    A. 1 of every 50
    B. 1 of every 100
    C. 1 of every 500
    D. 1 of every 1,000

16. Who was to make a heave offering on behalf of the soldiers?
    Numbers 31:29
    A. Aaron
    B. Eleazar
    C. Joshua
    D. Moses

17. Who was to receive an offering from the rest of the Israelites from the booty?
    Numbers 31:30
    A. The captains
    B. The generals
    C. The high priest
    D. The Levites

18. How many female prisoners of war did the Israelites spare?
    Numbers 31:35
    A. 5,000
    B. 16,000
    C. 24,000
    D. 32,000

19. How many casualties did the Israelite army suffer during the war?
    Numbers 31:48–49
    A. 0
    B. 14
    C. 77
    D. 100

20. What was the total amount in shekels of the soldiers' oblation?
    Numbers 31:50–52
    A. 507
    B. 1,675
    C. 5,761
    D. 16,750

Answers on page 755

Lesson 56
Today's Reading: *Numbers 32–33*
Period of Time: 1451 BC
Author: Moses

FEBRUARY 25

1. Which tribes wanted to settle east of the river of Jordan?
   Numbers 32:1–5
   A. Tribes of Manasseh and Benjamin
   B. Tribes of Reuben and Gad
   C. Tribes of Simeon and Naftali
   D. Tribes of Zebulun and Judah

2. Where did the two tribes with the large herds of cattle want to settle?
   Numbers 32:1
   A. Jazer and Gilead
   B. Lachish and Hebron
   C. Sidon and Tyre
   D. Ziklag and Bethlehem

3. Where were the Israelites when Moses sent the spies into Canaan?
   Numbers 32:8
   A. Eziongeber
   B. Hormah
   C. Kadesh-barnea
   D. Pi-hahiroth

4. Where did the spies go to search out the land?
   Numbers 32:9
   A. Dibon
   B. Kir
   C. The King's Highway
   D. Valley of Eshcol

5. Which of the following men entered the Promised Land?
   Numbers 32:12
   A. Caleb and Joshua
   B. Dathan and Abiram
   C. Jephunneh and Nun
   D. Moses and Aaron

6. How many years did the Israelites wander in the desert?
   Numbers 32:13
   A. 10
   B. 20
   C. 30
   D. 40

7. What did the tribes that wanted to settle east of the river of Jordan want to build before helping the rest of the tribes receive their inheritances?
   Numbers 32:16–19
   A. Dams and irrigation ditches
   B. Log cabins and trading posts
   C. Sheepfolds and fenced cities
   D. Wells and barns

8. What did Moses tell the leaders of the tribes that wanted to settle east of the river of Jordan regarding sin?
   Numbers 32:20–23
   A. Go and sin no more.
   B. Sin is knocking at your door.
   C. The wages of sin is death.
   D. Your sin will find you out.

9. Which tribes settled east of the river of Jordan?
   Numbers 32:33
   A. Tribes of Ephraim, Judah, and ½ of the tribe of Naftali
   B. Tribes of Reuben, Gad, and ½ of the tribe of Manasseh
   C. Tribes of Simeon, Benjamin, and ½ of the tribe of Dan
   D. Tribes of Zebulun, Issachar, and ½ of the tribe of Asher

10. Who was the king of the Amorites?
    Numbers 32:33
    A. King Amraphel
    B. King Arioch
    C. King Sihon
    D. King Tidal

11. Who was the king of Bashan?
    Numbers 32:33
    A. King Heth
    B. King Og
    C. King Sidon
    D. King Xerxes

12. Which tribe built the fenced city Dibon?
    Numbers 32:34–36
    A. Tribe of Gad
    B. Tribe of Issachar
    C. Tribe of Judah
    D. Tribe of Reuben

13. Who kept a journal of the Israelites' journeys?
    Numbers 33:1–2
    A. Caleb
    B. Joshua
    C. Moses
    D. Phinehas

14. When did the Israelites depart Ramses?
    Numbers 33:3
    A. 1st month, 1st day
    B. 1st month, 15th day
    C. 7th month, 1st day
    D. 7th month, 15th day

15. How many fountains of water and palm trees were there in Elim?
    Numbers 33:9
    A. 3 fountains and 10 palm trees
    B. 6 fountains and 30 palm trees
    C. 9 fountains and 50 palm trees
    D. 12 fountains and 70 palm trees

16. Upon which mountain did Aaron die?
    Numbers 33:38
    A. Mount Hor
    B. Mount Moriah
    C. Mount Nebo
    D. Mount Pisgah

17. How many years had the Israelites been wandering in the desert when Aaron died?
    Numbers 33:38
    A. 12
    B. 22
    C. 36
    D. 40

18. When did Aaron die?
    Numbers 33:38
    A. 1st day, 1st month
    B. 1st day, 5th month
    C. 7th day, 7th month
    D. 11th day, 10th month

19. How old was Aaron when he died?
    Numbers 33:39
    A. 65 years old
    B. 93 years old
    C. 123 years old
    D. 145 years old

20. Which Canaanite king lived in the south?
    Numbers 33:40
    A. King Arad
    B. King Necho
    C. King Rezin
    D. King Saul

Answers on page 755

FEBRUARY 26

Lesson 57
Today's Reading: *Numbers 34–36*
Period of Time: 1451 BC
Author: Moses

1. What was the *southern* border of the Promised Land?
   Numbers 34:3–5
   A. Coast along the great sea to mount Hor
   B. Hazar-enan to the banks of the river of Jordan to the salt sea
   C. Mount Hor to Hazarenan
   D. Wilderness of Zin to the river of Egypt to the great sea

2. What was the *western* border of the Promised Land?
   Numbers 34:6
   A. Coast along the great sea to mount Hor
   B. Hazar-enan to the banks of the river of Jordan to the salt sea
   C. Mount Hor to Hazarenan
   D. Wilderness of Zin to the river of Egypt to the great sea

3. What was the *northern* border of the Promised Land?
   Numbers 34:7–9
   A. Coast along the great sea to mount Hor
   B. Hazar-enan to the banks of the river of Jordan to the salt sea
   C. Mount Hor to Hazarenan
   D. Wilderness of Zin to the river of Egypt to the great sea

4. What was the *eastern* border of the Promised Land?
   Numbers 34:10–12
   A. Coast along the great sea to mount Hor
   B. Hazar-enan to the banks of the river of Jordan to the salt sea
   C. Mount Hor to Hazar-enan
   D. Wilderness of Zin to the river of Egypt to the great sea

5. How was the land to be divided?
   Numbers 34:13
   A. By auction
   B. By casting lots
   C. From eldest to youngest tribes
   D. From youngest to eldest tribes

6. How many tribes were to settle *west* of the river of Jordan?
   Numbers 34:13–15
   A. 3 1/2
   B. 5 1/2
   C. 7 1/2
   D. 9 1/2

7. Which tribe did **not** settle *west* of the river of Jordan?
   Numbers 34:14–15
   A. Tribe of Dan
   B. Tribe of Naftali
   C. Tribe of Reuben
   D. Tribe of Zebulun

8. Who was responsible for dividing the land?
   Numbers 34:17
   A. Eleazar and Joshua
   B. Jephunneh and Nun
   C. Moses and Caleb
   D. Phinehas and Nadab

9. Which prince represented the tribe of Judah?
   Numbers 34:19
   A. Cain
   B. Caleb
   C. Carmi
   D. Castor

10. How many cubits did the Levites' suburbs extend to from the wall of each Levite city?
    Numbers 35:4
    A. 1,000
    B. 2,000
    C. 3,000
    D. 4,000

11. How many cities did the Levites receive?
    Numbers 35:6–7
    A. 3
    B. 6
    C. 42
    D. 48

12. How many cities of refuge were *east* of the river of Jordan?
    Numbers 35:14–15
    A. 3
    B. 6
    C. 42
    D. 48

13. How many cities of refuge were *west* of the river of Jordan?
    Numbers 35:14–15
    A. 3
    B. 6
    C. 42
    D. 48

14. What was the penalty for murder?
    Numbers 35:16–21
    A. 40 lashes across the back with a whip
    B. 40 years in prison
    C. Death
    D. Life in prison

15. When could an avenger of a loved one whom was murdered kill the murderer?
    Numbers 35:19–21
    A. During the gladiator games
    B. Inside the city of refuge
    C. Never
    D. When he meets him

16. How long was a person found guilty of involuntary manslaughter required to stay inside a city of refuge?
    Numbers 35:22–25
    A. 7 years
    B. 50 years
    C. Until the high priest dies
    D. Until the next new moon

17. What was the penalty for an avenger if he killed the slayer who left the city of refuge?
    Numbers 35:26–28
    A. He would be stoned to death.
    B. He would get 10 years in prison.
    C. He would get life in prison.
    D. He would receive no penalty.

18. Who was the patriarchal father of the children of Gilead?
    Numbers 36:1
    A. Asher
    B. Manasseh
    C. Reuben
    D. Simeon

19. What is the law concerning a daughter who has inherited her father's land?
    Numbers 36:1–9
    A. Her husband must keep the land within his tribe.
    B. Her husband must return the land to her tribe during the Jubilee.
    C. She must marry someone in her father's tribe.
    D. She must sell the land to her closest relative.

20. Which one of the following was **not** a daughter of Zelophehad?
    Numbers 36:10–12
    A. Hoglah
    B. Leah
    C. Mahlah
    D. Noah

*Answers on page 755

FEBRUARY 27

Lesson 58
Today's Reading: *Deuteronomy 1–2*
Period of Time: 1490–1452 BC
Author: Moses

1. How many days did it take to go from Horeb by way of mount Seir to Kadesh-barnea?
   Deuteronomy 1:2
   A. 3
   B. 7
   C. 11
   D. 12

2. When did Moses speak to the children of Israel in the land of Moab concerning the Israelites' failures at Kadesh-barnea?
   Deuteronomy 1:3
   A. 1st day, 1st month
   B. 1st day, 7th month
   C. 1st day, 11th month
   D. 7th day, 1st month

3. Where did Og, the king of Bashan, reign?
   Deuteronomy 1:4
   A. Anathoth
   B. Astaroth
   C. Rehoboth
   D. Siphmoth

4. What did Moses tell the Israelites **not** to fear when facing one of their judges?
   Deuteronomy 1:17
   A. The face of man
   B. The hand of man
   C. The heart of man
   D. The lips of man

5. How many spies did Moses send into Canaan?
   Deuteronomy 1:22–23
   A. 3
   B. 7
   C. 9
   D. 12

6. Which giants did the spies see in Canaan?
   Deuteronomy 1:28
   A. The Anakims
   B. The Hivites
   C. The Philistines
   D. The Sidonians

7. Who came out like a swarm of bees and chased the rebellious Israelites?
   Deuteronomy 1:41–44
   A. The Adullamites
   B. The Amorites
   C. The Arabians
   D. The Athenians

8. Whose descendants dwelled in Seir?
   Deuteronomy 2:4
   A. Cush's descendants
   B. Dodo's descendants
   C. Esau's descendants
   D. Moab's descendants

9. Whom did the LORD tell the Israelites **not** to go to war against?
   Deuteronomy 2:9–20
   A. Amalekites and Naamites
   B. Gadarenes and Oznites
   C. Hagrites and Cicilians
   D. Moabites and Ammonites

10. What did the Moabites call the giants that dwelled in the wilderness of Moab?
    Deuteronomy 2:8–11
    A. Amalekites
    B. Emim
    C. Horims
    D. Manassites

11. Which ethnic group dwelled in Seir before being destroyed?
    Deuteronomy 2:12
    A. Avims
    B. Chemarims
    C. Gammadims
    D. Horims

12. How many years had passed from the time the Israelites left Kadesh-barnea until they crossed the brook Zered?
    Deuteronomy 2:13–14
    A. 12
    B. 21
    C. 38
    D. 40

13. What did the Ammonites call the people who once lived in the land of the giants?
    Deuteronomy 2:20
    A. Dinohummims
    B. Gammadims
    C. Sukkims
    D. Zamzummims

14. Who dwelt in Hazerim and as far away as Azzah?
    Deuteronomy 2:23
    A. The Avims
    B. The Emims
    C. The Horims
    D. The Lubims

15. Where were the Caphtorims from?
    Deuteronomy 2:23
    A. Capernaum
    B. Caphtor
    C. Cappadocia
    D. Cappopolis

16. Which river did the Israelites cross to battle the Amorite king?
    Deuteronomy 2:24
    A. River Arnon
    B. River Gozan
    C. River Jabbok
    D. River Kishon

17. Which wilderness were the Israelites dwelling in when Moses sent messengers to the king of Heshbon?
    Deuteronomy 2:26
    A. Wilderness of Beersheba
    B. Wilderness of Etham
    C. Wilderness of Gibeon
    D. Wilderness of Kedemoth

18. Where did the Israelites battle against Sihon?
    Deuteronomy 2:32
    A. Jaazer
    B. Jagur
    C. Jahaz
    D. Japho

19. How many prisoners of war did the Israelites allow to live from Aroer to Gilead?
    Deuteronomy 2:32–34
    A. 0
    B. 451
    C. 970
    D. 1,512

20. The nations along which river did the LORD tell the Israelites to spare?
    Deuteronomy 2:37
    A. River Euphrates
    B. River Jabbok
    C. River Pison
    D. River Ulai

*Answers on page 755

FEBRUARY 28

Lesson 59
Today's Reading: *Deuteronomy 3–4*
Period of Time: 1452–1451 BC
Author: Moses

1. At which battle did the Israelites defeat the king of Bashan?
   Deuteronomy 3:1
   A. Battle of Ai
   B. Battle of Edrei
   C. Battle of Lehi
   D. Battle of Minni

2. Which king dwelled at Heshbon?
   Deuteronomy 3:2
   A. King Basha
   B. King Omri
   C. King Sihon
   D. King Uzziah

3. How many prisoners of war did the Israelites allow to live?
   Deuteronomy 3:3–6
   A. 0
   B. 100
   C. 853
   D. 10,358

4. How many cities did the Israelites capture in the region of Argob?
   Deuteronomy 3:4
   A. 60
   B. 101
   C. 165
   D. 214

5. What did the Sidonians call mount Hermon?
   Deuteronomy 3:9
   A. Raamah
   B. Sirion
   C. Tabor
   D. Ulai

6. What did the Amorites call mount Hermon?
   Deuteronomy 3:9
   A. Carmel
   B. Gaash
   C. Olives
   D. Shenir

7. In which city was the king of Bashan's bed located?
   Deuteronomy 3:11
   A. Rabbath
   B. Salem
   C. Tiberius
   D. Uz

8. What was the size in cubits of the king of Bashan's bed?
   Deuteronomy 3:11
   A. 6 x 4
   B. 9 x 4
   C. 10 x 6
   D. 18 x 8

9. Which tribes were given the land that once belonged to the king of Bashan?
   Deuteronomy 3:12–13
   A. Tribes of Benjamin, Dan, and ½ of the tribe of Ephraim
   B. Tribes of Issachar, Asher, and ½ of the tribe of Joseph
   C. Tribes of Judah, Naphtali, and ½ of the tribe of Levi
   D. Tribes of Reuben, Gad, and ½ of the tribe of Manasseh

10. Who took the region of Argob?
    Deuteronomy 3:14
    A. Debir
    B. Endor
    C. Jair
    D. Pharpar

11. Who was given Gilead?
    Deuteronomy 3:15
    A. Amalek
    B. Jabez
    C. Machir
    D. Tartan

12. Where did Moses go to see the land that was beyond the river of Jordan?
    Deuteronomy 3:23–27
    A. Ebal
    B. Moriah
    C. Pisgah
    D. Seir

13. Who was to succeed Moses?
    Deuteronomy 3:28
    A. Gog
    B. Hezekiah
    C. Ishmael
    D. Joshua

14. Which city was adjacent to the valley where the Israelites abode to receive Moses' final instructions?
    Deuteronomy 3:29
    A. Bethpeor
    B. Eschol
    C. Kidron
    D. Siddim

15. Which idol were the Israelite men guilty of worshipping?
    Deuteronomy 4:3
    A. Ashtaroth
    B. Baal-peor
    C. Nebo
    D. Tammuz

16. Upon which mountain did Moses receive the ten commandments?
    Deuteronomy 4:10–13
    A. Mount Ararat
    B. Mount Bezetha
    C. Mount Gilboa
    D. Mount Horeb

17. Which words did Moses use to describe God?
    Deuteronomy 4:24, 4:31
    A. Almighty and dayspring
    B. Deliverer and father
    C. Jealous and merciful
    D. Wonderful and savior

18. What was the name of the city of refuge located in the plain country of the Reubenites?
    Deuteronomy 4:41–43
    A. Bezer
    B. Eder
    C. Gath-hepher
    D. Gezer

19. What was the name of the city of refuge located in Gilead?
    Deuteronomy 4:41–43
    A. Caphtor
    B. Gilboa
    C. Ishtob
    D. Ramoth

20. What was the name of the city of refuge located in Bashan?
    Deuteronomy 4:41–43
    A. Cushan
    B. Golan
    C. Haran
    D. Javan

*Answers on page 755

MARCH 1

Lesson 60
Today's Reading: *Deuteronomy 5–7*
Period of Time: 1451 BC
Author: Moses

1. Upon which mountain did God make a covenant with the Israelites?
   Deuteronomy 5:1–2
   A. Mount Ararat
   B. Mount Carmel
   C. Mount Horeb
   D. Mount Nebo

2. Which type of house did God deliver the Israelites from in Egypt?
   Deuteronomy 5:6
   A. House of bondage
   B. House of insanity
   C. House of love
   D. House of peace

3. What is the *first* commandment?
   Deuteronomy 5:7
   A. Do not covet.
   B. Honor your parents.
   C. You shall have no other Gods.
   D. You shall not murder.

4. What is the *second* commandment?
   Deuteronomy 5:8–10
   A. Do not covet.
   B. Do not make thee any graven image.
   C. Do not steal.
   D. Do not use the LORD's name in vain.

5. How many generations do the children suffer from the sins of their fathers?
   Deuteronomy 5:9
   A. 1st to 2nd
   B. 3rd to 4th
   C. 5th to 6th
   D. 7th to 8th

6. What is the *third* commandment?
   Deuteronomy 5:11
   A. Do not bear false witness.
   B. Do not commit adultery.
   C. Do not make thee any graven image.
   D. Do not use the LORD's name in vain.

7. What is the *fourth* commandment?
   Deuteronomy 5:12–15
   A. Do not commit adultery.
   B. Honor your parents.
   C. Keep holy the sabbath day.
   D. You shall not murder.

8. What is the *fifth* commandment?
   Deuteronomy 5:16
   A. Do not commit adultery.
   B. Honor your parents.
   C. Keep holy the sabbath day.
   D. You shall not murder.

9. What is the *sixth* commandment?
   Deuteronomy 5:17
   A. Do not bear false witness.
   B. Do not make thee any graven image.
   C. Keep holy the sabbath day.
   D. You shall not murder.

10. What is the *seventh* commandment?
    Deuteronomy 5:18
    A. Do not commit adultery.
    B. Do not make thee any graven image.
    C. Do not steal.
    D. Do not use the LORD's name in vain.

11. What is the *eighth* commandment?
    Deuteronomy 5:19
    A. Do not bear false witness.
    B. Do not commit adultery.
    C. Do not make thee any graven image.
    D. Do not steal.

12. What is the *ninth* commandment?
    Deuteronomy 5:20
    A. Do not bear false witness.
    B. Do not covet.
    C. You shall have no other Gods.
    D. You shall not murder.

13. What is the *tenth* commandment?
    Deuteronomy 5:21
    A. Do not bear false witness.
    B. Do not covet.
    C. Honor your parents.
    D. Keep holy the sabbath day.

14. How many Lords is the LORD our God?
    Deuteronomy 6:4
    A. 1
    B. 2
    C. 3
    D. 4

15. What is the essence of the law?
    Deuteronomy 6:5
    A. Do unto others as you would have them do unto you.
    B. God works in mysterious ways.
    C. Love the LORD your God with all of your heart, soul, and might.
    D. Once saved, always saved.

16. Where did the Israelites tempt God during the Exodus?
    Deuteronomy 6:16
    A. Bethlehem
    B. Jerusalem
    C. Luz
    D. Massah

17. Which nation was **not** one of the seven nations Moses said God would cast from the land?
    Deuteronomy 7:1
    A. The Cushites
    B. The Hivites
    C. The Jebusites
    D. The Perizzites

18. What did Moses say the LORD would send among the Israelites' enemies?
    Deuteronomy 7:20
    A. Bolts of lightning
    B. Fire from heaven
    C. Paid mercenaries
    D. The hornet

19. Why did the LORD say he would slowly put out the other nations instead of all at once?
    Deuteronomy 7:22
    A. He knew the Israelite army marched on its stomach and would need food.
    B. He wanted the Israelites to offer peace treaties first.
    C. The beasts of the wild would become a danger to the Israelites.
    D. The Israelite army needed time to form a coalition with Egypt.

20. What did Moses tell the Israelites to do with the graven images of their enemies?
    Deuteronomy 7:25
    A. Admire them in their homes.
    B. Burn them with fire.
    C. Display them in the tabernacle.
    D. Trade them to pay for food and water.

*Answers on page 755

MARCH 2

Lesson 61
Today's Reading: *Deuteronomy 8–10*
Period of Time: 1451 BC
Author: Moses

1. How many years did the LORD lead the Israelites in the desert?
   Deuteronomy 8:2
   A. 40
   B. 50
   C. 60
   D. 70

2. Which lesson did the LORD want the Israelites to learn when he fed them manna?
   Deuteronomy 8:3
   A. All things are possible with God.
   B. Jesus is the bread of life.
   C. Man does not live by bread alone.
   D. There is no god but God.

3. What did the Israelites do for clothing while wandering in the wilderness?
   Deuteronomy 8:4
   A. They learned how to make cloth from cotton and flax.
   B. They purchased clothes from traveling caravans.
   C. They used the skins from their livestock and captured game.
   D. They wore the same clothes and shoes they wore when they left Egypt.

4. Which miracle did the LORD do to give the Israelites water in the desert?
   Deuteronomy 8:15
   A. He filled a dry brook with running water.
   B. He sent a flood during a long drought.
   C. He made water come out of a rock.
   D. He told Moses where to dig a well.

5. Which giants did the Israelites fear?
   Deuteronomy 9:2
   A. The Alexandrians
   B. The Anakims
   C. The Edomites
   D. The Moabites

6. Which term did the LORD use to describe the Israelites?
   Deuteronomy 9:6–13, 10:16
   A. Hardheaded
   B. Heavyhearted
   C. Leadfooted
   D. Stiffnecked

7. Upon which mountain did Moses receive the ten commandments?
   Deuteronomy 9:8–11
   A. Mount Ararat
   B. Mount Horeb
   C. Mount Moriah
   D. Mount Pisgah

8. What did Moses drink while upon the mountain for 40 days and 40 nights?
   Deuteronomy 9:9
   A. Beer
   B. Water
   C. Wine
   D. Nothing

9. Which molten object did the Israelites worship while Moses was away from the camp?
   Deuteronomy 9:16
   A. A calf
   B. A lion
   C. A snake
   D. An eagle

10. What did Moses do with the first tablets of stone containing the ten commandments?
    Deuteronomy 9:16–17
    A. He nailed them to the Tabernacle door.
    B. He smashed them on the ground.
    C. He threw them into the river of Jordan.
    D. He tossed them into the Gehenna fire.

11. Whom did God want to destroy?
    Deuteronomy 9:20
    A. Aaron
    B. Caleb
    C. Joshua
    D. Moses

12. Which place was one of the many places where the Israelites made the LORD angry?
    Deuteronomy 9:22
    A. Antioch
    B. Damascus
    C. Iconium
    D. Massah

13. Where were the Israelites when the spies entered the Promised Land?
    Deuteronomy 9:23
    A. Beth-anoth
    B. Hazor-hadattah
    C. Kadesh-barnea
    D. Migdal-Edar

14. What type of wood was used to build the ark of the covenant?
    Deuteronomy 10:3
    A. Cedar
    B. Gopher
    C. Shittim
    D. Willow

15. What was placed inside the ark of the covenant?
    Deuteronomy 10:4–5
    A. Aaron's priestly garments
    B. Bars of gold, silver, and bronze
    C. Noah's rod that budded
    D. The ten commandments

16. Where did Aaron die?
    Deuteronomy 10:6
    A. Mamre
    B. Mizar
    C. Mosera
    D. Mozah

17. Who succeeded Aaron as high priest?
    Deuteronomy 10:6
    A. Eleazar
    B. Felix
    C. Hezekiah
    D. Jairus

18. Which one of the following places was a land of rivers and waters?
    Deuteronomy 10:7
    A. Gudgodah
    B. Jotbath
    C. Megiddo
    D. Zin

19. Which tribe received no inheritance?
    Deuteronomy 10:9
    A. Tribe of Benjamin
    B. Tribe of Levi
    C. Tribe of Reuben
    D. Tribe of Simeon

20. How many family members went with Jacob to Egypt?
    Deuteronomy 10:22
    A. 70
    B. 700
    C. 7,000
    D. 70,000

*Answers on page 756

Lesson 62
Today's Reading: *Deuteronomy 11–13*
Period of Time: 1451 BC
Author: Moses

1. Which sea did the Israelites cross to escape Pharaoh's army?
   Deuteronomy 11:4
   A. Brasen sea
   B. Red sea
   C. Sea of Galilee
   D. Sea of Joppa

2. What happened to Dathan and Abiram?
   Deuteronomy 11:6
   A. The angel of God slew them.
   B. The earth swallowed them.
   C. The fiery serpents bit them.
   D. The Moabites stoned them.

3. Who was Dathan and Abiram's father?
   Deuteronomy 11:6
   A. Eliab
   B. Festus
   C. Perida
   D. Samuel

4. Which tribe did Dathan and Abiram belong to?
   Deuteronomy 11:6
   A. Tribe of Dan
   B. Tribe of Gad
   C. Tribe of Issachar
   D. Tribe of Reuben

5. How did Moses describe the land of Egypt?
   Deuteronomy 11:10
   A. As a garden in Eden
   B. As tending to a garden of herbs
   C. Mountainous and filled with streams
   D. Wooded and full of rivers

6. How did Moses describe the Promised Land?
   Deuteronomy 11:11
   A. Arid and rich in minerals
   B. Dry and dusty
   C. Filled with hills and valleys
   D. Swampy and mosquito-infested

7. What did God promise to give the Israelites if they obeyed him?
   Deuteronomy 11:13–17
   A. A king to rule over them
   B. Freedom of religion
   C. Horses from Egypt
   D. Rain for their crops

8. Who was primarily responsible for teaching children about God and his laws?
   Deuteronomy 11:18–19
   A. The communities
   B. The parents
   C. The rabbis
   D. The schools

9. Upon which mountain were the Israelites to put God's *blessing*?
   Deuteronomy 11:29
   A. Mount Gerizim
   B. Mount Hazor
   C. Mount Tabor
   D. Mount Zion

10. Upon which mountain were the Israelites to put God's *curse*?
    Deuteronomy 11:29
    A. Mount Ararat
    B. Mount Carmel
    C. Mount Ebal
    D. Mount Gilboa

11. What were the Israelites to do regarding idol worship?
    Deuteronomy 12:1–3
    A. Abstain from meats not offered to idols in temples.
    B. Be tolerant of those who worship other gods.
    C. Destroy the places where idols are worshipped.
    D. Make separation of church and state a law.

12. Which river were the Israelites to cross to enter the Promised Land?

    Deuteronomy 12:10

    A. River of Chebar
    B. River of Egypt
    C. River of Jordan
    D. River of Ulai

13. Which tribe received no inheritance?

    Deuteronomy 12:12

    A. Tribe of Levi
    B. Tribe of Manasseh
    C. Tribe of Simeon
    D. Tribe of Zebulun

14. Where were the Israelites to offer their burnt offerings in the Promised Land?

    Deuteronomy 12:11–15

    A. At their city gates
    B. In a place the LORD would choose
    C. Outside their synagogues
    D. Upon the mountains

15. Which one of the following were the Israelites forbidden to eat?

    Deuteronomy 12:16, 12:23–25

    A. Blood
    B. Broiled fish
    C. Salted meat
    D. Wild honey

16. Where was an Israelite to eat his tithe?

    Deuteronomy 12:17–18

    A. At his home
    B. At the city gates
    C. In the most holy place
    D. In the place God would choose

17. What abomination were the other nations guilty of doing?

    Deuteronomy 12:31

    A. Arranging marriages for their sons
    B. Drinking wine on the sabbath day
    C. Putting to death those guilty of murder
    D. Sacrificing their children to other gods

18. Which one of the following was a sign of a false prophet?

    Deuteronomy 13:1–5

    A. He accurately predicts future events.
    B. He can perform signs and wonders.
    C. He entices others to go after other gods.
    D. He relies on God to supply his needs.

19. What must a relative do to another relative who desires to worship other gods?

    Deuteronomy 13:6–11

    A. Be the first to cast a stone at him
    B. Be the last to cast a stone at him
    C. Keep his brother's sin a secret
    D. Nothing

20. When were the Israelites to kill everyone and burn everything in an Israelite town?

    Deuteronomy 13:12–16

    A. If they refused to go to war
    B. If they refused to pay taxes
    C. If they were all ill
    D. If they were guilty of idol worship

*Answers on page 756

Lesson 63
Today's Reading: *Deuteronomy 14–17*
Period of Time: 1451 BC
Author: Moses

MARCH 4

1. What were the Israelites prohibited from doing when a loved one died?
   Deuteronomy 14:1
   A. Fast more than 7 days
   B. Grieve more than 30 days
   C. Paint a picture of the loved one
   D. Shave their heads between their eyes

2. Which one of the following could an Israelite eat?
   Deuteronomy 14:3–8
   A. Camel
   B. Coney
   C. Goat
   D. Swine

3. Which one of the following was an Israelite forbidden to eat?
   Deuteronomy 14:3–8
   A. Beef jerky
   B. Cow tongue
   C. Grilled pygarg
   D. Pork chops

4. Which one of the following could an Israelite eat?
   Deuteronomy 14:9–10
   A. Cod
   B. Crab
   C. Lobster
   D. Shrimp

5. Which one of the following was an Israelite forbidden to eat?
   Deuteronomy 14:11–20
   A. Chicken
   B. Duck
   C. Owl
   D. Pigeon

6. What could an Israelite do with meat from a cow that died on its own?
   Deuteronomy 14:21
   A. Eat it
   B. Give it to a brother
   C. Sell it to a stranger
   D. Use it for a burnt offering

7. What did an Israelite do if he lived too far from the place designated by God to bring the tithe?
   Deuteronomy 14:22–26
   A. Convert it to money and purchase goods at the designated site.
   B. Offer the sacrifices at the gates of the town.
   C. Send it by caravan down the King's Highway to the Levites.
   D. Transport it by barge down the river of Jordan.

8. Which statement means to cancel a person's debt during the sabbatical year?
   Deuteronomy 15:1–2
   A. The Borrower's Amnesty
   B. The LORD's Release
   C. The Nation's Relief
   D. The Samaritan's Purse

9. What did Moses say would always be in the land?
   Deuteronomy 15:11
   A. Gold seekers
   B. Poor people
   C. Rainfall
   D. Weeds

10. After how many years was a Hebrew servant set free from his bond?
    Deuteronomy 15:12
    A. 3
    B. 6
    C. 10
    D. 12

11. What did a Hebrew servant need to do if he did **not** want to be free from his bond?

    Deuteronomy 15:16–17
    - A. Brand his forearm
    - B. Insert a ring through his nose
    - C. Tattoo his forearm
    - D. Thrust an awl through his ear

12. Which animal could be sacrificed to the LORD?

    Deuteronomy 15:21–22
    - A. A blind calf
    - B. A dove with a broken wing
    - C. A goat less than a year old
    - D. A maimed bullock

13. During which month did the Israelites celebrate the LORD's passover?

    Deuteronomy 16:1
    - A. Abib
    - B. Chislev
    - C. Shebat
    - D. Tebeth

14. How many days was it unlawful to eat leavened bread during the feast of unleavened bread?

    Deuteronomy 16:3
    - A. 3
    - B. 7
    - C. 10
    - D. 12

15. How many times during a year were the men to appear before the LORD in the place God would choose?

    Deuteronomy 16:16
    - A. 3
    - B. 7
    - C. 10
    - D. 12

16. Which one of the following feasts was **not** an Israelite holiday?

    Deuteronomy 16:16
    - A. Feast of all hallows eve
    - B. Feast of tabernacles
    - C. Feast of unleavened bread
    - D. Feast of weeks

17. Which one of the following plants would the Israelites **not** be allowed to plant near the altar of the LORD?

    Deuteronomy 16:21
    - A. A fruit-bearing bush
    - B. A grove of any trees
    - C. A patch of poinsettias
    - D. A row of Easter lilies

18. How was a person guilty of worshipping other gods to be put to death?

    Deuteronomy 17:2–7
    - A. By fire
    - B. Drowning
    - C. Hanging
    - D. Stoning

19. What was a king required to do?

    Deuteronomy 17:14–20
    - A. Buy more horses
    - B. Have many wives
    - C. Invest in silver, gold, and real estate
    - D. Lift not up his heart above his brethren

20. What was a king required to copy?

    Deuteronomy 17:18
    - A. His daily journal for future kings
    - B. His inaugural address
    - C. The laws instituted by Moses
    - D. The oath he took to be the king

*Answers on page 756

Lesson 64
Today's Reading: *Deuteronomy 18–20*
Period of Time: 1451 BC
Author: Moses

1. Which tribe received no inheritance?
   Deuteronomy 18:1–2
   A. Tribe of Levi
   B. Tribe of Naphtali
   C. Tribe of Reuben
   D. Tribe of Zebulun

2. Whom did the cheeks, maw, and shoulder of the sacrifice belong to?
   Deuteronomy 18:3
   A. The priests
   B. The queens
   C. The scribes
   D. The widows

3. What was **not** to be included among the firstfruit offerings?
   Deuteronomy 18:4
   A. Corn
   B. Fleece
   C. Oil
   D. Tares

4. Which one of the following did **not** belong to the priest?
   Deuteronomy 18:4
   A. The first fleece of the sheep
   B. The first oil of the harvest
   C. The first wine of the harvest
   D. The firstborn daughter of a slave

5. What does the term patrimony mean?
   Deuteronomy 18:8
   A. A person who is the head of a clan or tribe
   B. A settlement given to a woman in a divorce
   C. One who zealously supports his own country
   D. Property inherited from one's father or male ancestor

6. What is a necromancer?
   Deuteronomy 18:11
   A. A person that burns dead bodies
   B. A person that keeps records of the dead
   C. A person that uses divination to communicate with the dead
   D. A person that uses embalming fluids to preserve a dead body

7. What did Moses promise would come from one of their tribes and be like him?
   Deuteronomy 18:15–19
   A. A charmer
   B. A necromancer
   C. A prophet
   D. A wizard

8. Upon which mountain did the Israelites tell Moses they no longer wanted to hear the voice of God?
   Deuteronomy 18:16
   A. Mount Ararat
   B. Mount Horeb
   C. Mount Pisgah
   D. Mount Tabor

9. How accurate did a true prophet have to be?
   Deuteronomy 18:22
   A. 10%
   B. 50%
   C. 75%
   D. 100%

10. How many cities of refuge were to be east of the river of Jordan?
    Deuteronomy 19:1–3
    A. 2
    B. 3
    C. 5
    D. 7

11. What was the punishment for a false witness?
    Deuteronomy 19:16–21
    A. The hands and feet were amputated.
    B. The penalty he desired for the accused.
    C. The tongue was cut from his mouth.
    D. The sinner was hanged in public.

12. Who was to speak to the soldiers before going into battle?
    Deuteronomy 20:2
    A. The King
    B. The Parents
    C. The Priest
    D. The Scribe

13. Who was **not** exempt from going to war?
    Deuteronomy 20:5–8
    A. He who had four children
    B. He who had not dedicated his house
    C. He who was engaged to be married
    D. He who was too frightened to fight

14. Who was exempt from going to war?
    Deuteronomy 20:5–8
    A. A man opposed to the war, so that he may speak to the elders
    B. A man who had planted a new vineyard, and hath not eaten of it
    C. A man who recently divorced his wife, so that he may find a new wife
    D. A man with no living brothers, and hath no living sisters

15. What must the Israelite army do before attacking cities that were **not** part of their inheritance?
    Deuteronomy 20:10–13
    A. Build a bulwark high enough to climb over the walls
    B. Give everyone in the city the opportunity to surrender
    C. Give only the elderly, sick, women, and children the opportunity to surrender
    D. March around the city 7 times and then blow their trumpets

16. What were the Israelites to do with the captured women from cities that were **not** part of their inheritance?
    Deuteronomy 20:14–15
    A. Allow all of them to live
    B. Kill all of them
    C. Spare only the ancient ones
    D. Spare only the virgins

17. What were the Israelites to do when going to war against cities that God gave them for an inheritance?
    Deuteronomy 20:16–18
    A. Kill everybody
    B. Spare only the old and young
    C. Spare only the virgin girls
    D. Spare only the women and children

18. Which one of the following nations was **not** one of the nations that Moses told the Israelites to destroy?
    Deuteronomy 20:17
    A. The Amorites
    B. The Canaanites
    C. The Merarites
    D. The Perizzites

19. Which trees were the Israelite army *permitted* to cut down while besieging a city?
    Deuteronomy 20:19–20
    A. Almond trees
    B. Fig trees
    C. Olive trees
    D. Pine trees

20. Which trees were the Israelite army *forbidden* to cut down while besieging a city?
    Deuteronomy 20:19–20
    A. Elm trees
    B. Oak trees
    C. Pomegranate trees
    D. Poplar trees

*Answers on page 756

Lesson 65
Today's Reading: *Deuteronomy 21–23*
Period of Time: 1451 BC
Author: Moses

MARCH 6

1. What did the nearest city need to sacrifice if an unsolved murder occurred in a nearby field?
   Deuteronomy 21:1–9
   A. A goat
   B. A heifer
   C. A ram
   D. A sheep

2. How many months did a man need to wait before he could marry a woman captured in battle?
   Deuteronomy 21:10–14
   A. 1
   B. 3
   C. 6
   D. 12

3. How much inheritance was the oldest son to receive if the father had two wives?
   Deuteronomy 21:15–17
   A. A double-portion
   B. All of it
   C. It depended on the father
   D. None of it

4. How long could the body of a man found guilty of a crime worthy of death hang from a tree?
   Deuteronomy 21:22–23
   A. Before nightfall it must be removed
   B. No more than 30 days
   C. Until the bones fall off
   D. Until the eve of the sabbath day

5. Which statement is true regarding clothing?
   Deuteronomy 22:5
   A. Men may wear women's cloaks
   B. Men may wear women's tunics
   C. Women may wear men's sandals
   D. Women were not to wear men's clothes

6. What must a man do if he builds a new house?
   Deuteronomy 22:8
   A. Place a railing along the roof
   B. Plant a grove of trees near the house
   C. Run the downspouts to a garden
   D. The door must face south

7. Which statement is true regarding farming?
   Deuteronomy 22:9–10
   A. Do not give the firstfruits to the Levites
   B. Do not plow with asses yoked together
   C. Do not sow a vineyard with divers seeds
   D. Do not use cow dung for fertilizer

8. Which statement is true regarding clothing?
   Deuteronomy 22:11–12
   A. Do not wear fleece from a young sheep.
   B. Do not wear linen and wool together.
   C. Do not wear robes dipped in purple.
   D. Do not wear tunics outside of the home.

9. How could parents prove their daughter was a virgin?
   Deuteronomy 22:13–18
   A. Have a doctor do a vaginal exam.
   B. Have her former boyfriends give an oath.
   C. Show the city elders her chastity ring.
   D. Show the city elders the tokens of her virginity.

10. How many shekels of silver did a new son-in-law have to pay his father-in-law if the father-in-law proved his daughter was a virgin?
    Deuteronomy 22:13–19
    A. 1
    B. 10
    C. 100
    D. 1,000

11. What was the punishment if a man found a virgin woman, betrothed to another man, in the city and lie with her?
    Deuteronomy 22:23–24
    A. The man must die.
    B. The woman must die.
    C. The man and woman must die.
    D. Neither one must die.

12. What was the penalty if a man lies with a virgin woman, **not** betrothed to another man?
    Deuteronomy 22:28–29
    A. The man must die.
    B. The woman must die.
    C. They must marry and never divorce.
    D. They shall be stoned to death.

13. Who could **not** enter into the congregation of the LORD?
    Deuteronomy 23:1–2
    A. He who accidently killed his neighbor
    B. He who has put away his wife
    C. He whose child is missing
    D. He whose testicles are deformed

14. Who could **not** enter into the congregation of the LORD even to the 10th generation?
    Deuteronomy 23:3
    A. A Levite or a Reubenite
    B. An Ammonite or a Moabite
    C. An Asherite or a Gadite
    D. An Issacharite or a Simeonite

15. Who could **not** enter into the congregation of the LORD until the 3rd generation?
    Deuteronomy 23:7–8
    A. A Benjamite or Zebulunite
    B. A Gadite or Danite
    C. An Edomite or Egyptian
    D. An Ephraimite or Levite

16. Which statement is true concerning cleanliness?
    Deuteronomy 23:12–14
    A. Burn garbage in the midst of the camp
    B. Drink water from streams that look and smell clean
    C. Sanitize used bandages with pots used for cooking
    D. Use the restroom away from camp and cover the excrement with dirt.

17. Which statement is true regarding servants?
    Deuteronomy 23:15–16
    A. Runaway servants must be put to death.
    B. Runaway servants must not be returned.
    C. Servants were not to ride horses.
    D. Servants were not to wed a master.

18. Which statement was part of the law?
    Deuteronomy 23:17–18
    A. Daughters were to remain silent in public.
    B. Daughters were to serve in the temple for two years.
    C. Sons must be circumcised upon their eighth birthday.
    D. Sons were not to become sodomites.

19. How much interest could an Israelite charge another Israelite?
    Deuteronomy 23:19–20
    A. 0%
    B. 7%
    C. 10%
    D. 12%

20. Which statement is true regarding an Israelite vineyard?
    Deuteronomy 23:24–25
    A. A person must not eat grapes that have fallen to the ground.
    B. A poor person could eat from the vineyard but not carry away any grapes.
    C. The vineyard owner must not give fermented wine to young children.
    D. The vineyard owner must tithe his firstfruits to the Nazarenes.

*Answers on page 756

Lesson 66
Today's Reading: *Deuteronomy 24–26*
Period of Time: 1451 BC
Author: Moses

MARCH 7

1. What did a man give his wife if he wanted a divorce?
   Deuteronomy 24:1–4
   A. A Bill of Divorcement
   B. A Bill of Separation
   C. An Annulment
   D. The Articles for an Open Marriage

2. Which statement is true regarding the law when a man divorces his wife?
   Deuteronomy 24:1–4
   A. The ex-husband must pay alimony until the woman remarries.
   B. The ex-wife is granted custody of any young children.
   C. The ex-wife must marry one of her ex-husband's brothers.
   D. The two of them may not remarry each other.

3. How long did a new husband have to wait after the wedding before he could be sent to war?
   Deuteronomy 24:5
   A. 3 months
   B. 6 months
   C. 1 year
   D. 1.5 years

4. What could **not** be taken as a pledge?
   Deuteronomy 24:6
   A. A bullock
   B. A cloak
   C. A horse
   D. A millstone

5. What was the penalty for kidnapping someone?
   Deuteronomy 24:7
   A. 10 years in jail
   B. 40 lashes across the back
   C. Death
   D. Jail and compensation to the victim

6. Who became a leper after the Israelites left Egypt?
   Deuteronomy 24:8–9
   A. Leah
   B. Miriam
   C. Rachel
   D. Rebekah

7. Which statement is true concerning wages?
   Deuteronomy 24:14–15
   A. A poor man had to be paid on the same day he worked.
   B. A stranger had to be paid with the first fruit from the harvest.
   C. An employer had to pay each employee at the same time.
   D. An Israelite had to be paid weekly.

8. Who was to be put to death if a father murdered someone?
   Deuteronomy 24:16
   A. The father
   B. The father and his family
   C. The father and his sons
   D. The father and his wife

9. What could **not** be taken as collateral from a widow?
   Deuteronomy 24:17
   A. Her clothing
   B. Her cow
   C. Her horse
   D. Her son

10. What was a farmer forbidden to do?
    Deuteronomy 24:19–22
    A. Borrow money to purchase a field
    B. Burn down a vineyard
    C. Cut down an olive grove
    D. Glean a field after the harvest

151

11. What was the maximum number of stripes a guilty man could receive?
    Deuteronomy 25:1–3
    A. 21
    B. 39
    C. 40
    D. 100

12. What was a farmer prohibited to do?
    Deuteronomy 25:4
    A. Buy seed from a foreigner.
    B. Irrigate crops with spring water.
    C. Muzzle an ox that treads corn.
    D. Use compost in his garden.

13. What was a childless widow to do if her late husband's brother refused to marry her?
    Deuteronomy 25:5–10
    A. Call him, "The man of constant shame" in front of the city elders.
    B. Loose his shoe from his foot and spit in his face in front of the city elders.
    C. Report it to the elders so that they will force the brother to marry her.
    D. Take him to the city elders and fine him 100 shekels of silver.

14. What was the punishment if a woman grabbed a man's testicles while he fought her husband?
    Deuteronomy 25:11–12
    A. Beat her with 21 lashes.
    B. Cut off her hand.
    C. Shave all of her hair.
    D. Tar and feather her.

15. Which nation did God say to blot out their memory?
    Deuteronomy 25:17–19
    A. Amalek
    B. Edom
    C. Egypt
    D. Moab

16. Which feast recognizes God's bountiful supply?
    Deuteronomy 26:1–11
    A. Feast of breads
    B. Feast of firstfruits
    C. Feast of tabernacles
    D. Feast of trumpets

17. What did Moses call Jacob?
    Deuteronomy 26:5
    A. A Canaanite
    B. A Galilean
    C. A Nazarene
    D. A Syrian

18. Which year was the year of tithing?
    Deuteronomy 26:12–15
    A. 1st
    B. 2nd
    C. 3rd
    D. 4th

19. How did Moses describe the Promised Land?
    Deuteronomy 26:9, 26:15
    A. A land of abundant riches and wealth
    B. A land that flows with milk and honey
    C. The land of endless blessings
    D. The land of iron and brass

20. What did Moses call the Israelites?
    Deuteronomy 26:16–19
    A. A God-fearing race
    B. A kingdom of God
    C. A nation of priests
    D. A peculiar people

Answers on page 756

Lesson 67
Today's Reading: *Deuteronomy 27–28*
Period of Time: 1451 BC
Author: Moses

MARCH 8

1. Upon which mountain were the Israelites to set up stones and write all the words of the law?
   Deuteronomy 27:4–8
   A. Mount Ebal
   B. Mount Gaash
   C. Mount Nebo
   D. Mount Zion

2. Which material did the Israelites use to make the altar in the mountain?
   Deuteronomy 27:6–7
   A. Brass
   B. Gold
   C. Iron
   D. Stones

3. Upon which mountain were the Israelites to be blessed?
   Deuteronomy 27:11–12
   A. Mount Gerizim
   B. Mount Hor
   C. Mount Sinai
   D. Mount Tabor

4. Which tribe was **not** sent to bless the people?
   Deuteronomy 27:12
   A. Tribe of Benjamin
   B. Tribe of Judah
   C. Tribe of Levi
   D. Tribe of Zebulun

5. Which tribe was **not** sent to curse the people?
   Deuteronomy 27:13
   A. Tribe of Asher
   B. Tribe of Gad
   C. Tribe of Issachar
   D. Tribe of Reuben

6. What would **not** bring curses upon the Israelites?
   Deuteronomy 27:15–18
   A. Making a molten image
   B. Making the blind to wander
   C. Removing a neighbor's landmarks
   D. Trusting in God

7. Which one of the following is **not** a crime?
   Deuteronomy 27:19
   A. A foreigner who committed adultery with his neighbor's wife
   B. A poor man who ate grapes in his neighbor's vineyard
   C. A widow who abducted her neighbor's newborn son
   D. An orphan who raped his neighbor's daughter

8. Whom could an Israelite have sexual intercourse with?
   Deuteronomy 27:20–23
   A. His father's wife
   B. His horse
   C. His mother-in-law
   D. His wife

9. Which one of the following would **not** bring a curse upon the people?
   Deuteronomy 27:16, 27:24–26
   A. Disobeying parents
   B. Murdering another person secretly
   C. Obeying the Mosaic Law
   D. Taking a reward to slay the innocent

10. How many directions did Moses say the Israelites' enemies would flee if the Israelites remained faithful to the LORD?
    Deuteronomy 28:7
    A. 3
    B. 7
    C. 8
    D. 10

11. What did Moses say the sky and earth would be like if the Israelites turned away from the LORD?
    Deuteronomy 28:23
    A. Brass and iron
    B. Crooked and narrow
    C. Dark and smoky
    D. Fire and brimstone

12. Which one of the following did Moses **not** say to describe what the Israelites would become to other nations if they turned away from the LORD?
    Deuteronomy 28:37
    A. A byword
    B. A proverb
    C. An astonishment
    D. An exalted people

13. What did Moses say would eat the Israelites' crops if they turned away from the LORD?
    Deuteronomy 28:38
    A. Beetles
    B. Caterpillars
    C. Locusts
    D. Weevils

14. What did Moses say would destroy the Israelites' vineyards if the Israelites turned away from the LORD?
    Deuteronomy 28:39
    A. Bears
    B. Foxes
    C. Worms
    D. Wrens

15. What did Moses say the Israelites' enemy would place in Israel if the Israelites turned away from the LORD?
    Deuteronomy 28:48
    A. A chain of iron
    B. A yoke of iron
    C. An iron furnace
    D. An iron maiden

16. What did Moses compare the nation to that would come from afar and overthrow the Israelites for turning away from the LORD?
    Deuteronomy 28:49
    A. A bear
    B. A lion
    C. An eagle
    D. An Ostrich

17. What did Moses say the Israelites would become when their enemies besieged their cities for turning away from the LORD?
    Deuteronomy 28:52–57
    A. Cannibals
    B. Heroes
    C. Martyrs
    D. Saints

18. What name did Moses use for the glorious and fearful name of the LORD?
    Deuteronomy 28:58
    A. THE EVERLASTING GOD
    B. THE LORD THY GOD
    C. THE MIGHTY GOD
    D. THE UNKNOWN GOD

19. What did Moses say would eventually happen to the Israelites for turning away from the LORD?
    Deuteronomy 28:63–68
    A. They would be dispersed worldwide.
    B. They would be the head of other nations.
    C. They would become extinct as a people.
    D. They would overtake their enemies.

20. Which country would the Israelites be taken to by ship for turning away from the LORD?
    Deuteronomy 28:68
    A. Cush
    B. Egypt
    C. Midian
    D. Persia

Answers on page 756

Lesson 68
Today's Reading: *Deuteronomy 29–31*
Period of Time: 1451 BC
Author: Moses

1. Where did God make a covenant with the Israelites?
   Deuteronomy 29:1
   A. Amana
   B. Kishon
   C. Moab
   D. Salem

2. Upon which mountain did God make a covenant with the Israelites?
   Deuteronomy 29:1
   A. Mount Ebal
   B. Mount Horeb
   C. Mount Jearim
   D. Mount Moriah

3. Which nation did Pharaoh rule over?
   Deuteronomy 29:2–4
   A. Egypt
   B. Elam
   C. Endor
   D. Ethiopia

4. How many years did the Israelites wander in the wilderness?
   Deuteronomy 29:5
   A. 10
   B. 20
   C. 30
   D. 40

5. Which statement is true concerning the years of wandering in the wilderness?
   Deuteronomy 29:5
   A. Moses was a tyrant and evil leader.
   B. None of the Israelites died from war, disease, or accidents.
   C. The Israelites clothes and shoes did not age.
   D. The Israelites survived on a diet of locusts and wild honey.

6. Which one of the following did the Israelites **not** consume while wandering in the wilderness?
   Deuteronomy 29:6
   A. Beef
   B. Milk
   C. Quail
   D. Wine

7. Who was the king of Heshbon?
   Deuteronomy 29:7
   A. King Sidon
   B. King Sihon
   C. King Simeon
   D. King Simon

8. Who was the king of Bashan?
   Deuteronomy 29:7
   A. King Og
   B. King Omar
   C. King Onan
   D. King Othni

9. Which tribes inherited the land of Heshbon and Bashan?
   Deuteronomy 29:8
   A. Tribes of Benjamin, Judah, and ½ tribe of Zebulun
   B. Tribes of Issachar, Dan, and ½ tribe of Asher
   C. Tribes of Naphtali, Simeon, ½ tribe of Ephraim
   D. Tribes of Reuben, Gad, and ½ tribe of Manasseh

10. Who were the patriarchs of the Israelites?
    Deuteronomy 29:13
    A. Aaron, Moses, and Joshua
    B. Abraham, Isaac, and Jacob
    C. Adam, Moses, and Phinehas
    D. Annas, Herod, and Felix

11. What did Moses say would happen to a person who turned away from the LORD?
    Deuteronomy 29:18–21
    A. He would become a vagabond and thief.
    B. He would cry for his barren wives and lost sons.
    C. He would die without a soul.
    D. He would receive all of the curses written in the book of the law.

12. Which city did God **not** destroy by fire?
    Deuteronomy 29:23
    A. Admah
    B. Gomorrah
    C. Shiloh
    D. Sodom

13. Which prophecy did Moses prophecy to Israel?
    Deuteronomy 29:25–30:8
    A. A man named Jonah would one day save Nineveh from destruction.
    B. God would one day scatter the Israelites throughout the world.
    C. The Israelites would build a great temple one day in Jerusalem.
    D. The LORD would one day send them a saviour born of a virgin.

14. Where were the Israelites to find God's commandment?
    Deuteronomy 30:11–14
    A. In a cave
    B. In the heavens
    C. In the ocean
    D. In their hearts

15. What did Moses tell the Israelites?
    Deuteronomy 30:19
    A. Abortion is good.
    B. Avoid overpopulation.
    C. Choose life.
    D. Life begins at birth.

16. How old was Moses when he died?
    Deuteronomy 31:2
    A. 120 years old
    B. 130 years old
    C. 140 years old
    D. 150 years old

17. Who succeeded Moses?
    Deuteronomy 31:3
    A. Caleb
    B. Joshua
    C. Phinehas
    D. Samuel

18. When was the book of the law to be read to the Israelites?
    Deuteronomy 31:9–13
    A. Every 7 years during the feast of tabernacles
    B. Every morning
    C. Every sabbath day
    D. Every year during the day of atonement

19. How did the LORD appear over the door of the tabernacle before Moses' death?
    Deuteronomy 31:15
    A. In a bolt of lightning
    B. In a burning bush
    C. In a pillar of a cloud
    D. In a vision

20. What was the book of the law stored in?
    Deuteronomy 31:24–26
    A. The ark of the covenant
    B. The high priest's tent
    C. The leader of Israel's tent
    D. The tent of the scribes

*Answers on page 756

Lesson 69
Today's Reading: *Deuteronomy 32–34*
Period of Time: 1451 BC
Author: Moses

1. In the *Song of Moses*, what will drop like rain?
   Deuteronomy 32:2
   A. Angels from heaven
   B. God's doctrine
   C. Manna from above
   D. Meteors

2. In the *Song of Moses*, which two names for God are mentioned?
   Deuteronomy 32:4–8
   A. Adonai and El-Shaddai
   B. Bread and Door
   C. Rock and Most High
   D. Yahweh and Jehovah

3. In the *Song of Moses*, where did the LORD find Jacob?
   Deuteronomy 32:10
   A. In a crowded prison
   B. In a mountain cave
   C. In his father Isaac's home
   D. In the desert

4. In the *Song of Moses*, what did God make Jacob suck out of a rock?
   Deuteronomy 32:13
   A. Honey
   B. Milk
   C. Water
   D. Wine

5. Which two cities are mentioned in the *Song of Moses*?
   Deuteronomy 32:32
   A. Admah and Zeboiim
   B. Bashan and Heshbon
   C. Jericho and Jerusalem
   D. Sodom and Gomorrah

6. What is the enemies' wine the poison of in the *Song of Moses*?
   Deuteronomy 32:33
   A. Bees
   B. Dragons
   C. Scorpions
   D. Spiders

7. In the *Song of Moses*, what did the LORD say he would do to his arrows?
   Deuteronomy 32:42
   A. Break them in two
   B. Cast them into the fire
   C. Make them drunk with blood
   D. Shoot out the lights of heaven

8. Who accompanied Moses when he came to recite the *Song of Moses* to the people?
   Deuteronomy 32:44
   A. Asaph
   B. Hoshea
   C. Jeduthun
   D. Jubal

9. Which title does Moses use for himself as he blesses the tribes?
   Deuteronomy 33:5
   A. King in Jeshurun
   B. King of the Beasts
   C. Moses Our Teacher
   D. Moses the Lawgiver

10. Which tribe did Moses say, "The beloved of the LORD shall dwell in safety by him"?
    Deuteronomy 33:12
    A. Tribe of Benjamin
    B. Tribe of Gad
    C. Tribe of Judah
    D. Tribe of Levi

11. Which horns does Moses say the horns of Joseph are similar to?

    Deuteronomy 33:17

    A. Bull horns
    B. Deer horns
    C. Ram horns
    D. Unicorn horns

12. Which tribes did Moses say would suck the abundance of the seas and the treasures hid in the sand?

    Deuteronomy 33:18–19

    A. Tribes of Asher and Gad
    B. Tribes of Dan and Judah
    C. Tribes of Issachar and Zebulun
    D. Tribes of Simeon and Naphtali

13. Which tribe did Moses say dwells like a lion?

    Deuteronomy 33:20–21

    A. Tribe of Ephraim
    B. Tribe of Gad
    C. Tribe of Naphtali
    D. Tribe of Zebulun

14. Which tribe did Moses call a lion's whelp?

    Deuteronomy 33:22

    A. Tribe of Dan
    B. Tribe of Judah
    C. Tribe of Levi
    D. Tribe of Manasseh

15. Which mountain did Moses climb to see the Promised Land?

    Deuteronomy 34:1–4

    A. Mount Ararat
    B. Mount Mariah
    C. Mount Nebo
    D. Mount Tabor

16. Where did Moses die?

    Deuteronomy 34:5–6

    A. Edom
    B. Egypt
    C. Midian
    D. Moab

17. How old was Moses when he died?

    Deuteronomy 34:7

    A. 80 years old
    B. 90 years old
    C. 120 years old
    D. 150 years old

18. Which statement is true concerning Moses' vision before he died?

    Deuteronomy 34:7

    A. He did not have any blurry vision
    B. He had partial vision in both eyes
    C. He was blind in one eye
    D. He was completely blind

19. How many days did the Israelites mourn after Moses died?

    Deuteronomy 34:8

    A. 20
    B. 30
    C. 60
    D. 90

20. What was Joshua filled with after Moses laid his hands on him?

    Deuteronomy 34:9

    A. A double portion of Moses' spirit
    B. A familiar spirit
    C. An unclean spirit
    D. The spirit of wisdom

Answers on page 756

Lesson 70
Today's Reading: *Joshua 1–4*
Period of Time: 1451 BC
Author: Joshua

MARCH 11

1. Which book were the Israelites to meditate on day and night?
   Joshua 1:8
   A. Book of Jasher
   B. Book of the covenant
   C. Book of the law
   D. Book of the wars of the LORD

2. How many days did the Israelites prepare before entering the Promised Land?
   Joshua 1:11
   A. 2
   B. 3
   C. 7
   D. 10

3. Where did Joshua command the spies to enter the Promised Land?
   Joshua 2:1
   A. Adam
   B. Beth-aram
   C. Shittim
   D. Sidon

4. How many spies went into the Promised Land?
   Joshua 2:1
   A. 2
   B. 4
   C. 6
   D. 8

5. Which city did the spies enter?
   Joshua 2:1
   A. Armageddon
   B. Hamath-zobah
   C. Jericho
   D. Nazareth

6. Which prostitute hid the spies?
   Joshua 2:1
   A. Gomer
   B. Oholah
   C. Rahab
   D. Tamar

7. Where did the prostitute hide the spies?
   Joshua 2:6
   A. Beneath a trap door leading to a cellar
   B. Down a well in the courtyard
   C. Inside a barn under horse manure
   D. Under stalks of flax upon the roof

8. Which sea did the LORD divide so the Israelites could cross on dry land when they came out of Egypt?
   Joshua 2:10
   A. Brasen sea
   B. Great sea
   C. Molten sea
   D. Red sea

9. Which kings were Amorite kings?
   Joshua 2:10
   A. Artaxerxes I and Cambysses
   B. Sihon and Og
   C. Tiberius and Claudius
   D. Tilgath-pileser and Pul

10. How many days did the spies hide in the mountains?
    Joshua 2:16–22
    A. 2
    B. 3
    C. 6
    D. 10

11. Which signal did the harlot need to give to protect her and her family?

    Joshua 2:18

    A. Bind a scarlet line in the window
    B. Paint her doorpost red with sheep's blood
    C. Shoot three blue arrows over the east wall
    D. Wave a white flag from the tower

12. What was the signal for the Israelites to pack up and move from the camp?

    Joshua 3:3–6

    A. Ark of the covenant being carried by the priests
    B. One long blast from the two silver trumpets
    C. The pillar of fire moving by night and the cloud by day
    D. The sound from the ram's horn

13. Which nation was **not** mentioned to drive from the Promised Land?

    Joshua 3:10

    A. The Amorites
    B. The Cushites
    C. The Girgashites
    D. The Hittites

14. How many men from each tribe were to lead the Israelites across the river?

    Joshua 3:12

    A. 1
    B. 3
    C. 6
    D. 12

15. Which river did the Israelites cross to enter the Promised Land?

    Joshua 3:14–17

    A. River of Arnon
    B. River of Jordan
    C. River of Kanah
    D. River of Pison

16. Which city was near Zaretan?

    Joshua 3:16

    A. Adam
    B. Galilee
    C. Luz
    D. Syracuse

17. How many stones were used to build the memorial?

    Joshua 4:3–24

    A. 3
    B. 6
    C. 9
    D. 12

18. Approximately how many Israelite men were prepared to go to war?

    Joshua 4:13

    A. 10,000
    B. 20,000
    C. 30,000
    D. 40,000

19. When did the Israelites enter the Promised Land?

    Joshua 4:19

    A. 1st day, 1st month
    B. 7th day, 1st month
    C. 10th day, 1st month
    D. 7th day, 7th month

20. Where did the Israelites pitch camp after entering the Promised Land?

    Joshua 4:19

    A. Ai
    B. Bethlehem
    C. Cana
    D. Gilgal

*Answers on page 756

Lesson 71
Today's Reading: *Joshua 5–7*
Period of Time: 1451 BC
Author: Joshua

MARCH 12

1. What did Joshua do to the Israelite males?
   Joshua 5:2–8
   A. Circumcised them
   B. Gave them tattoos
   C. Inspected their weapons
   D. Made a pact with them

2. What is the name of the place where the Israelites camped?
   Joshua 5:9–10
   A. Elim
   B. Gilgal
   C. Kadesh-Barnea
   D. Succoth

3. What was the first feast the Israelites celebrated in the Promised Land?
   Joshua 5:10
   A. Day of atonement
   B. Feast of firstfruits
   C. Feast of tabernacles
   D. The passover

4. What was the name of the bread from heaven?
   Joshua 5:12
   A. Bread of life
   B. Ezekiel's bread
   C. Homer
   D. Manna

5. Which messenger met Joshua before the battle of Jericho?
   Joshua 5:13–15
   A. The angel Gabriel
   B. The angel of death
   C. The archangel Michael
   D. The captain of the host of the LORD

6. Which order did the messenger give to Joshua?
   Joshua 5:15
   A. Hide the women and children
   B. Offer a lamb
   C. Sharpen his sword
   D. Take off his shoes

7. How many times were the Israelites to march around the walls of Jericho the first six days?
   Joshua 6:1–3
   A. 1
   B. 6
   C. 7
   D. 12

8. How many priests were to bear ram's horns and march with the army around Jericho?
   Joshua 6:4
   A. 2
   B. 6
   C. 7
   D. 12

9. How many times were the Israelites to march around the walls of Jericho on the seventh day?
   Joshua 6:4
   A. 1
   B. 6
   C. 7
   D. 12

10. What did the Israelite army do to cause the walls of Jericho to fall?
    Joshua 6:5–20
    A. Gave a loud shout
    B. Hurled boulders from war machines
    C. Tunneled trenches beneath the walls
    D. Used battering rams against the wall

11. Who was the harlot that rescued the two spies?
    Joshua 6:17
    A. Gomer
    B. Oholah
    C. Rahab
    D. Tamar

12. Which future curse would happen with the rebuilding of Jericho?

    Joshua 6:26
    A. A great earthquake would occur 100 years after Jericho was rebuilt.
    B. It would cost the builder the lives of his first and last sons.
    C. The builder would die a horrible death caused by a plague.
    D. The new residents would all die within the first year from the drinking water.

13. Who was guilty of taking spoil from Jericho?

    Joshua 7:1
    A. Achan
    B. Caleb
    C. Piram
    D. Tobiah

14. How many soldiers were sent to destroy Ai?

    Joshua 7:4
    A. 2,000
    B. 3,000
    C. 4,000
    D. 5,000

15. Approximately how many soldiers died in the battle of Ai?

    Joshua 7:5
    A. 18
    B. 36
    C. 54
    D. 72

16. What did the LORD say to Joshua after the Israelites were defeated at Ai?

    Joshua 7:10
    A. Find five smooth stones and then go slay the giant.
    B. Get up; why are you lying upon your face?
    C. Place Uriah the Hittite in front of the battle.
    D. Take only the men who lap water like a dog.

17. Which tribe did the guilty person belong to?

    Joshua 7:1, 7:17–18
    A. Tribe of Asher
    B. Tribe of Benjamin
    C. Tribe of Judah
    D. Tribe of Reuben

18. How many shekels of silver did the soldier take from the spoil?

    Joshua 7:21
    A. 50
    B. 100
    C. 150
    D. 200

19. In which valley did the Israelites kill the guilty soldier and his family?

    Joshua 7:24–26
    A. Valley of Achor
    B. Valley of Gehenna
    C. Valley of Kidron
    D. Valley of Siddim

20. How did the Israelites kill the guilty soldier and his family?

    Joshua 7:25
    A. Drowned them in a river
    B. Hung them from trees
    C. Stoned and burned them
    D. Used swords to lop off their heads

Answers on page 756

MARCH 13

Lesson 72
Today's Reading: *Joshua 8–9*
Period of Time: 1451 BC
Author: Joshua

1. How many soldiers did Joshua dispatch the night before the second battle of Ai?
   Joshua 8:3
   A. 10,000
   B. 20,000
   C. 30,000
   D. 40,000

2. What was to be the signal that Ai had fallen to the Israelites?
   Joshua 8:8
   A. A flag was to be raised in the guard tower
   B. A rider on a black horse was to bring Joshua the message
   C. The ambushers were to give a long blast from the ram's horns
   D. The city was to be set on fire.

3. Between which two cities did Joshua send the soldiers involved in the ambush?
   Joshua 8:9
   A. Bethel and Ai
   B. Damascus and Ai
   C. Hazor and Ai
   D. Megiddo and Ai

4. In which direction of Ai did Joshua and the rest of his army set up camp?
   Joshua 8:10–11
   A. North
   B. South
   C. East
   D. West

5. How many soldiers did Joshua use for the ambush?
   Joshua 8:12
   A. 2,000
   B. 3,000
   C. 4,000
   D. 5,000

6. How many soldiers did the king of Ai leave to defend the city?
   Joshua 8:17
   A. 0
   B. 50
   C. 100
   D. 1,000

7. What did Joshua use to signal to his soldiers lying in wait to ambush the city of Ai?
   Joshua 8:18
   A. A fire
   B. A flag
   C. A spear
   D. A trumpet

8. After the second battle of Ai, how many soldiers from Ai survived?
   Joshua 8:22
   A. 0
   B. 32
   C. 43
   D. 56

9. How many people from Ai died in the second battle of Ai?
   Joshua 8:25
   A. 2,000
   B. 4,000
   C. 8,000
   D. 12,000

10. What did Joshua do to the king of Ai?
    Joshua 8:29
    A. Gouged out his eyes and placed him in a large bird cage
    B. Hung him on a tree
    C. Let him go free
    D. Tied him to a stake and burned him to death

11. Upon which mountain did Joshua build an altar?

    Joshua 8:30

    A. Mount Ebal
    B. Mount Nebo
    C. Mount Sinai
    D. Mount Tabor

12. In front of which two mountains did Joshua divide the people?

    Joshua 8:33

    A. Mount Carmel and mount Tabor
    B. Mount Ebal and mount Gerizim
    C. Mount Nebo and mount Mariah
    D. Mount Sinai and mount Pisgah

13. Which book did Joshua read to the Israelites?

    Joshua 8:34–35

    A. Book of Jasher
    B. Book of the covenant
    C. Book of the law
    D. Book of the wars of the LORD

14. Which nation did **not** form an alliance against the Israelites?

    Joshua 9:1–2

    A. The Hittites
    B. The Jebusites
    C. The Perizzites
    D. The Tishbites

15. The inhabitants from which city tricked the Israelites into forming a league with them?

    Joshua 9:3–15

    A. Adam
    B. Cesarea
    C. Gibeon
    D. Palastine

16. Where did Joshua set up camp?

    Joshua 9:6

    A. Arpad
    B. Gilgal
    C. Migdal
    D. Ummah

17. Which nation did the men who beguiled the Israelites belong to?

    Joshua 9:7

    A. The Hittites
    B. The Hivites
    C. The Horites
    D. The Horonites

18. How many days did it take the Israelites before they realized they had been tricked?

    Joshua 9:16

    A. 2
    B. 3
    C. 12
    D. 21

19. Which city did **not** belong to the nation that beguiled the Israelites?

    Joshua 9:17

    A. Beeroth
    B. Chephirah
    C. Damascus
    D. Kirjath-je'arim

20. What did the Israelites do with the people who beguiled them?

    Joshua 9:21–27

    A. Forced the men to become soldiers in Israel's army
    B. Killed all of the men, but spared the women and children
    C. Killed all of them
    D. Made them hewers of wood and drawers of water

Answers on page 756

Lesson 73
Today's Reading: *Joshua 10–11*
Period of Time: 1451–1450 BC
Author: Joshua

MARCH 14

1. Who was the king of Jerusalem?
   Joshua 10:1
   A. King Adonizedek
   B. King Ben-ha'dad
   C. King Ebed-melech
   D. King Ir-nahash

2. Who was the king of Hebron?
   Joshua 10:3
   A. King Ahab
   B. King Elab
   C. King Hoham
   D. King Nadab

3. Who was the king of Jarmuth?
   Joshua 10:3
   A. King Ahaziah
   B. King Baasha
   C. King Omri
   D. King Piram

4. Who was the king of Lachish?
   Joshua 10:3
   A. King Asa
   B. King Japhia
   C. King Pekah
   D. King Zedekiah

5. Who was the king of Eglon?
   Joshua 10:3
   A. King Amon
   B. King Baasha
   C. King Cyrus
   D. King Debir

6. Whom did the five kings of the Amorites wage war against?
   Joshua 10:4–5
   A. Ai
   B. Bashan
   C. Gibeon
   D. Kadesh

7. Where was Joshua when the five kings waged war?
   Joshua 10:6
   A. Gebal
   B. Gilgal
   C. Mashal
   D. Mishal

8. What did the LORD use to slay the Amorite soldiers?
   Joshua 10:11
   A. Hailstones
   B. Lions
   C. Plagues
   D. Serpents

9. What miraculous event took place until the Israelites avenged themselves upon their enemies?
   Joshua 10:13
   A. An angel of the LORD cornered the Amorite armies.
   B. Chariots of fire cut off the escape route of the Amorite armies.
   C. God fed Joshua's starving army with water and quails.
   D. The sun and the moon stood still.

10. Which book records Joshua's defeat of the five Amorite kings?
    Joshua 10:13
    A. Book of Esther
    B. Book of Jasher
    C. Book of Jether
    D. Book of Zacher

11. Where did the Amorite kings hide?
    Joshua 10:16
    A. Among the baggage of the army of Israel in Mizpah
    B. At a prostitute's house in the country of Jericho
    C. In a cave at Makkedah
    D. Inside the tent of Jael

12. How did Joshua kill the five Amorite kings?

    Joshua 10:26

    A. Dragged them across the desert behind horses.
    B. Slew them and hung their bodies on trees.
    C. Stoned them to death inside a pit.
    D. Tied them to stakes and burned them alive.

13. After slaying the five Amorite kings, where did Joshua go for his next battle?

    Joshua 10:29–30

    A. Libnah
    B. Mizzah
    C. Potipherah
    D. Ziphah

14. After defeating Hebron, where did Joshua go for his next battle?

    Joshua 10:36–38

    A. Athens
    B. Boaz
    C. Debir
    D. Eglon

15. Who was the king of Hazor?

    Joshua 11:1

    A. King Jabin
    B. King Jachin
    C. King Jehoiachin
    D. King Jehonathan

16. Who was the king of Madon?

    Joshua 11:1

    A. King Joab
    B. King Job
    C. King Jobab
    D. King Jonadab

17. Where did the kings from the north join forces to fight against the Israelites?

    Joshua 11:5

    A. Waters of Makheloth
    B. Waters of Marah
    C. Waters of Meribah
    D. Waters of Merom

18. What did Joshua do to the horses of the army of the north?

    Joshua 11:9

    A. Fed them to his army
    B. Houghed them
    C. Sold them to Egypt
    D. Used them in his cavalry

19. Who dwelled in Gibeon?

    Joshua 11:19

    A. Hivites
    B. Jebusites
    C. Moabites
    D. Perezzites

20. In which city were there **no** remaining Anakim?

    Joshua 11:21–22

    A. Ashdod
    B. Gath
    C. Gaza
    D. Hebron

*Answers on page 757

Lesson 74
Today's Reading: *Joshua 12–14*
Period of Time: 1450–1445 BC
Author: Joshua

MARCH 15

1. What were the borders for the tribes that did **not** inherit land *west* of the river of Jordan?
   Joshua 12:1
   A. Brasen sea on the west, wilderness to the east, brook Zered to the south, and mount Nebo to the north
   B. River of Jordan on the west, Arabah to the east, river of Kishon to the south, and mount Tabor to the north
   C. River of Jordan on the west, the plain on the east, Arnon to the south, and mount Hermon to the north
   D. Sea of Chinnereth on the west, Bashan on the east, river Jabbok to the south, and mount Lebanon to the north

2. Who was the king of the Amorites?
   Joshua 12:2
   A. King Ahab
   B. King Joram
   C. King Manasseh
   D. King Sihon

3. Who was the king of Bashan?
   Joshua 12:4
   A. King Og
   B. King Magog
   C. King Raamah
   D. King Shimeah

4. Which tribe settled *east* of the river of Jordan?
   Joshua 12:4–6
   A. Tribe of Benjamin
   B. Tribe of Reuben
   C. Tribe of Simeon
   D. Tribe of Zebulun

5. Which nation did **not** fight against Joshua?
   Joshua 12:7–8
   A. Hittites
   B. Hivites
   C. Jebusites
   D. Ninevites

6. How many kings did the Israelites conquer *west* of the river of Jordan?
   Joshua 12:7–24
   A. 27
   B. 31
   C. 49
   D. 65

7. How many tribes settled *west* of the river of Jordan?
   Joshua 13:1–7
   A. 3½
   B. 7½
   C. 9½
   D. 10½

8. Where did the king of the Amorites reign before being driven out by the Israelites?
   Joshua 13:10
   A. Heshbon
   B. Heshmon
   C. Hethlon
   D. Hezron

9. Which nations dwelled among the Israelites during the days of Joshua?
   Joshua 13:13
   A. Babylonians and Iconians
   B. Egyptians and Syrians
   C. Grecians and Romans
   D. Maacathites and Geshurites

10. Which tribe received no inheritance?
    Joshua 13:14
    A. Tribe of Asher
    B. Tribe of Levi
    C. Tribe of Naphtali
    D. Tribe of Reuben

11. Who was a soothsayer and the son of Beor?
    Joshua 13:22
    A. Balaam
    B. Rabshakeh
    C. Simon the sorcerer
    D. The witch of Endor

12. Who was the high priest when Joshua was the Israelites' leader?
    Joshua 14:1
    A. Annas
    B. Caiphas
    C. Eleazar
    D. Joiada

13. How was the land divided among the Israelites?
    Joshua 14:2
    A. An auction was held
    B. By casting lots
    C. From oldest to youngest tribe
    D. From youngest to oldest tribe

14. Which children of Joseph formed two tribes?
    Joshua 14:4
    A. Asher and Issachar
    B. Benjamin and Simeon
    C. Dan and Gad
    D. Ephraim and Manasseh

15. Which tribe did Caleb belong to?
    Joshua 14:6
    A. Tribe of Dan
    B. Tribe of Issachar
    C. Tribe of Judah
    D. Tribe of Naphtali

16. How old was Caleb when he spied out the Promised Land?
    Joshua 14:7
    A. 40 years old
    B. 50 years old
    C. 60 years old
    D. 70 years old

17. How old was Caleb when he asked Joshua for his inheritance?
    Joshua 14:10
    A. 80 years old
    B. 85 years old
    C. 90 years old
    D. 95 years old

18. Who dwelled in the Promised Land when Moses sent in the 12 spies?
    Joshua 14:12
    A. The Anakims
    B. The Greeks
    C. The Persians
    D. The Romans

19. Which city did Caleb inherit?
    Joshua 14:13
    A. Ai
    B. Bethlehem
    C. Damascus
    D. Hebron

20. Who was Arba?
    Joshua 14:15
    A. A famous Israelite warrior from the tribe of Benjamin.
    B. An Israelite high priest who rebelled against Joshua.
    C. He was once a great man among the Anakim.
    D. The author of the *book of the wars of the LORD*.

*Answers on page 757

Lesson 75
Today's Reading: *Joshua 15–17*
Period of Time: 1445 BC
Author: Joshua

1. Which wilderness was Judah's *southern* border?
   Joshua 15:1
   A. Wilderness of Beersheba
   B. Wilderness of Paran
   C. Wilderness of Sinai
   D. Wilderness of Zin

2. Which sea was part of Judah's *eastern* border?
   Joshua 15:5
   A. Molten sea to the end of the river of Egypt
   B. Salt sea to the end of the river of Jordan
   C. Sea of Galilee to the end of the river Pison
   D. Sea of Tiberius to the end of the river Gihon

3. What was Judah's *western* border?
   Joshua 15:12
   A. Great sea
   B. Salt sea
   C. Sea of Chinnereth
   D. Sea of the plain

4. Who was Caleb's father?
   Joshua 15:13
   A. Jabel
   B. Japheth
   C. Jephunneh
   D. Jubal

5. Which city was known as the city of Arba?
   Joshua 15:13
   A. Hebron
   B. Laodicea
   C. Shushan
   D. Thyatira

6. Who was **not** a descendant of Anak?
   Joshua 15:14
   A. Ahiman
   B. Sheshai
   C. Talmai
   D. Vaizatha

7. What is the other name for the city called Kirjathsepher?
   Joshua 15:15
   A. Ai
   B. Beersheba
   C. Debir
   D. Eglon

8. Who was Caleb's daughter?
   Joshua 15:16
   A. Abigail
   B. Achsah
   C. Ada
   D. Anna

9. Who became Caleb's son-in-law?
   Joshua 15:17
   A. Obadiah
   B. Omri
   C. Othniel
   D. Ozni

10. In addition to land in the south, what else did Caleb give to his daughter?
    Joshua 15:19
    A. Arabian horses
    B. Herds of cattle
    C. Male and female slaves
    D. Springs of water

11. Who inhabited Jerusalem?
    Joshua 15:63
    A. Hittites
    B. Jebusites
    C. Midianites
    D. Perizzites

12. Which mountain was part of Ephraim's inheritance?
    Joshua 16:1–10
    A. Mount Bethel
    B. Mount Hermon
    C. Mount Nebo
    D. Mount Zion

13. Which river passed through Ephraim's inheritance?

    Joshua 16:8

    A. River Arnon
    B. River Euphrates
    C. River Gozan
    D. River Kanah

14. Which ethnic group was Judah unable to drive out of Gezer?

    Joshua 16:10

    A. Canaanites
    B. Gibeonites
    C. Hivites
    D. Ninevites

15. Which tribe received an inheritance on both sides of the river of Jordan?

    Joshua 17:1–18

    A. Tribe of Issachar
    B. Tribe of Judah
    C. Tribe of Manasseh
    D. Tribe of Simeon

16. Who was Gilead's father?

    Joshua 17:1

    A. Jair
    B. Machir
    C. Ophir
    D. Shamir

17. How many daughters did Zelophehad have?

    Joshua 17:3

    A. 5
    B. 7
    C. 12
    D. 26

18. Who was the high priest when Joshua ruled Israel?

    Joshua 17:4

    A. Anna
    B. Eleazar
    C. Hilkiah
    D. Josedech

19. Whom did Joshua tell Ephraim and Manasseh to drive from the land?

    Joshua 17:15

    A. The Ammonites
    B. The Girgashites
    C. The Jebusites
    D. The Perizzites

20. What metal did the Canaanites use to build their chariots?

    Joshua 17:16

    A. Brass
    B. Copper
    C. Iron
    D. Steel

*Answers on page 757

MARCH 17

Lesson 76
Today's Reading: *Joshua 18–20*
Period of Time: 1445–1444 BC
Author: Joshua

1. Where did the Israelites gather and set up the tabernacle of the congregation?
   Joshua 18:1
   A. Bethlehem
   B. Jericho
   C. Jerusalem
   D. Shiloh

2. How many tribes had **not** received their inheritance?
   Joshua 18:2
   A. 3
   B. 5
   C. 7
   D. 9

3. How many men from each tribe did Joshua send to survey the land?
   Joshua 18:4
   A. 3
   B. 6
   C. 9
   D. 12

4. Which tribe *west* of the river of Jordan lived on the southern border of the Promised Land?
   Joshua 18:5
   A. Tribe of Asher
   B. Tribe of Issachar
   C. Tribe of Judah
   D. Tribe of Naphtali

5. Which tribes, *west* of the river of Jordan, formed the northern border?
   Joshua 18:5
   A. Tribe of Asher and ½ tribe of Simeon
   B. Tribe of Ephraim and ½ tribe of Manasseh
   C. Tribe of Issachar and ½ tribe of Reuben
   D. Tribe of Judah and ½ tribe of Gad

6. How was the land to be divided?
   Joshua 18:6
   A. By auction
   B. By casting lots
   C. From oldest tribes to youngest
   D. From youngest tribes to oldest

7. Which tribe received no inheritance among their brethren?
   Joshua 18:7
   A. Tribe of Levi
   B. Tribe of Naphtali
   C. Tribe of Simeon
   D. Tribe of Zebulun

8. Which tribes, besides half the tribe of Manasseh, settled *east* of the river of Jordan?
   Joshua 18:7
   A. Tribes of Dan and Naphtali
   B. Tribes of Ephraim and Benjamin
   C. Tribes of Issachar and Judah
   D. Tribes of Reuben and Gad

9. Which tribe inherited the city of Jericho?
   Joshua 18:21
   A. Tribe of Benjamin
   B. Tribe of Gad
   C. Tribe of Judah
   D. Tribe of Naphtali

10. What is another name for Jerusalem?
    Joshua 18:28
    A. Antioch
    B. Ekron
    C. Ijon
    D. Jebusi

11. Which tribe's land surrounded the land inherited by Simeon?
    Joshua 19:1, 19:9
    A. Tribe of Dan
    B. Tribe of Issachar
    C. Tribe of Judah
    D. Tribe of Reuben

12. Which tribe inherited the city of Bethlehem?

    Joshua 19:10–16

    A. Tribe of Naphtali
    B. Tribe of Reuben
    C. Tribe of Simeon
    D. Tribe of Zebulun

13. Which tribe inherited mount Tabor?

    Joshua 19:17–23

    A. Tribe of Gad
    B. Tribe of Issachar
    C. Tribe of Judah
    D. Tribe of Simeon

14. Which tribe inherited the cities of Tyre and Zidon?

    Joshua 19:24–31

    A. Tribe of Asher
    B. Tribe of Gad
    C. Tribe of Judah
    D. Tribe of Zebulun

15. Which tribe was bordered by Zebulun and Asher?

    Joshua 19:32–39

    A. Tribe of Benjamin
    B. Tribe of Issachar
    C. Tribe of Naphtali
    D. Tribe of Simeon

16. Which tribe attacked Leshem?

    Joshua 19:47

    A. Tribe of Benjamin
    B. Tribe of Dan
    C. Tribe of Gad
    D. Tribe of Issachar

17. Which city did the Israelites give to Joshua?

    Joshua 19:49–50

    A. Capernaum
    B. Gennesaret
    C. Nazareth
    D. Timnathserah

18. Which city became a place of refuge in Galilee?

    Joshua 20:6–7

    A. Bethsaida
    B. Kedesh
    C. Merom
    D. Shunem

19. Which city is also known as Hebron?

    Joshua 20:6–7

    A. Kirjath-arba
    B. Kirjath-huzoth
    C. Kirjath-je'arim
    D. Kirjath-sepher

20. Which city became a place of refuge in Gilead?

    Joshua 20:6–8

    A. Bezer
    B. Golan
    C. Ramoth
    D. Shechem

Answers on page 757

Lesson 77
Today's Reading: *Joshua 21–22*
Period of Time: 1444 BC
Author: Joshua

MARCH 18

1. How many towns were given to the Kohathites?
   Joshua 21:4–5
   A. 9
   B. 14
   C. 23
   D. 30

2. How many towns were given to the Gershonites?
   Joshua 21:6
   A. 6
   B. 7
   C. 13
   D. 27

3. How many towns were given to the Merarites?
   Joshua 21:7
   A. 12
   B. 24
   C. 36
   D. 48

4. Which tribe did **not** give a town to the Kohathites?
   Joshua 21:1–26
   A. Tribe of Dan
   B. Tribe of Gad
   C. Tribe of Judah
   D. Tribe of Simeon

5. Who was the father of Anak?
   Joshua 21:11
   A. Aaron
   B. Abram
   C. Andrew
   D. Arba

6. What was the name of the city of refuge located in the hill country of Judah?
   Joshua 21:11–13
   A. Golan
   B. Hebron
   C. Kedesh
   D. Shechem

7. Which tribes gave nine cities to the Kohathites?
   Joshua 21:9–16
   A. Tribes of Asher and Naphtali
   B. Tribes of Gad and Reuben
   C. Tribes of Judah and Simeon
   D. Tribes Zebulun and Dan

8. Which tribe did **not** give a city to the Gershonites?
   Joshua 21:27–33
   A. Half of the tribe of Manasseh
   B. Tribe of Asher
   C. Tribe of Issachar
   D. Tribe of Simeon

9. Which tribe did **not** give a city to the Merarites?
   Joshua 21:34–40
   A. Tribe of Gad
   B. Tribe of Naphtali
   C. Tribe of Reuben
   D. Tribe of Zebulun

10. Which city of refuge was located in mount Ephraim?
    Joshua 21:21
    A. Bezer
    B. Golan
    C. Ramoth
    D. Shechem

11. Which city of refuge was located in Bashan?

    Joshua 21:27

    A. Bezer
    B. Golan
    C. Hebron
    D. Ramoth

12. Which city of refuge was located in Galilee?

    Joshua 21:32

    A. Bezer
    B. Golan
    C. Hebron
    D. Kedesh

13. Which city of refuge was located in the land Reuben inherited?

    Joshua 21:36

    A. Bezer
    B. Hebron
    C. Kedesh
    D. Shechem

14. Which city of refuge was located in Gilead?

    Joshua 21:38

    A. Golan
    B. Kedesh
    C. Ramoth
    D. Shechem

15. What was the total number of towns the Levites received?

    Joshua 21:41

    A. 48
    B. 60
    C. 72
    D. 84

16. Which tribes built an altar by the river of Jordan?

    Joshua 22:10–12

    A. Tribes of Asher, Issachar, ½ tribe of Zebulun
    B. Tribes of Ephraim, Dan, and ½ tribe of Judah
    C. Tribes of Reuben, Gad, and ½ tribe of Manasseh
    D. Tribes of Simeon, Benjamin, and ½ tribe of Naphtali

17. Who was Phinehas' father?

    Joshua 22:13

    A. Azariah
    B. Eleazar
    C. Jehoiada
    D. Zadok

18. What did God send to punish the Israelites for the iniquity of Peor?

    Joshua 22:17

    A. A plague
    B. An earthquake
    C. Hailstones
    D. Serpents

19. Which son of Zerah perished for taking from the plunder of Jericho?

    Joshua 22:20

    A. Achan
    B. Ananias
    C. Gehazi
    D. Judas

20. What was the name of the altar the tribes built east of the river of Jordan?

    Joshua 22:34

    A. Al
    B. Bob
    C. Cal
    D. Ed

*Answers on page 757

Lesson 78
Today's Reading: *Joshua 23–24*
Period of Time: 1443 BC
Author: Joshua

1. Which book did Joshua tell the Israelites to obey?
   Joshua 23:6
   A. Book of Jasher
   B. Book of remembrance
   C. Book of the law of Moses
   D. Book of the wars of the LORD

2. What could an Israelite do regarding foreign gods?
   Joshua 23:7
   A. Bow to them
   B. Mention their names
   C. Swear by them
   D. Tear them down

3. How many men did Joshua say one Israelite would drive away if they obeyed the LORD?
   Joshua 23:10
   A. 10
   B. 100
   C. 1,000
   D. 10,000

4. What did Joshua say the other nations would become to the Israelites if they followed their gods?
   Joshua 23:13
   A. Darts in their hearts
   B. Cankers in their mouths
   C. Pains in their necks
   D. Thorns in their eyes

5. In which city did Joshua and the tribes meet?
   Joshua 24:1
   A. Salem
   B. Shechem
   C. Sidon
   D. Sodom

6. Who was Abraham's father?
   Joshua 24:2
   A. Terah
   B. Tibni
   C. Titus
   D. Tubal

7. Who was Abraham's son?
   Joshua 24:3
   A. Esau
   B. Isaac
   C. Jacob
   D. Lot

8. Which mountain did the LORD give to Esau?
   Joshua 24:4
   A. Mount Seir
   B. Mount Sinai
   C. Mount Tabor
   D. Mount Zion

9. Where did Jacob and his children go to dwell?
   Joshua 24:4
   A. Assyria
   B. Babylon
   C. Egypt
   D. Lebanon

10. Which prophet did Balak hire to curse Israel?
    Joshua 24:9
    A. Balaam
    B. Isaiah
    C. Malachi
    D. Nathan

11. Which nation was **not** one of the nations the LORD delivered into the Israelites' hands?
    Joshua 24:11
    A. The Amorites
    B. The Girgashites
    C. The Jebusites
    D. The Simeonites

12. What did the LORD use to drive the Israelites' enemies from the land?

    Joshua 24:12

    A. The hornet
    B. The lion
    C. The serpent
    D. The unicorn

13. Which quote did Joshua speak?

    Joshua 24:15

    A. "As for me and my house, we will serve the LORD."
    B. "Hear, O Israel: The LORD our God is one LORD."
    C. "Love the LORD your God with all your heart."
    D. "The LORD is my strength and my shield."

14. In which book did Joshua record the decrees and laws?

    Joshua 24:26

    A. Book of the kings of Israel
    B. Book of the law of God
    C. Book of the prophet Iddo
    D. Book of the wars of the LORD

15. What did Joshua use as a witness to the covenant he made with the Israelites?

    Joshua 24:26–27

    A. A book in the ark of the covenant
    B. A great stone
    C. An elder from the tribe of Judah
    D. An officer from the high priest's office

16. How old was Joshua when he died?

    Joshua 24:29

    A. 96 years old
    B. 100 years old
    C. 110 years old
    D. 156 years old

17. Where was Joshua's body laid to rest?

    Joshua 24:30

    A. Hamathzobah
    B. Kirjath-arba
    C. Ramoth-gilead
    D. Timnathserah

18. Where were the bones of Joseph buried?

    Joshua 24:32

    A. Bezek
    B. Gezer
    C. Hebron
    D. Shechem

19. How many pieces of silver did Jacob spend for the parcel of ground to bury his children?

    Joshua 24:32

    A. 50
    B. 100
    C. 500
    D. 1,000

20. Which high priest's body was laid to rest in a hill on mount Ephraim?

    Joshua 24:33

    A. Annas' body
    B. Caiaphas' body
    C. Eleazar's body
    D. Zadok's body

*Answers on page 757

Lesson 79
Today's Reading: *Judges 1–3*
Period of Time: 1443–1325 BC
Author: Unknown

1. Which tribe joined Judah to fight the Canaanites?

   Judges 1:1–3

   A. Tribe of Dan
   B. Tribe of Naphtali
   C. Tribe of Reuben
   D. Tribe of Simeon

2. How many men did Judah and its ally slay in Bezek?

   Judges 1:4

   A. 100
   B. 1,000
   C. 10,000
   D. 100,000

3. Who was a Canaanite king?

   Judges 1:1–6

   A. King Adonibezek
   B. King Karibezek
   C. King Nebebezek
   D. King Tigabezek III

4. How many kings had their thumbs and great toes cut off by the wicked Canaanite king?

   Judges 1:7

   A. 17
   B. 70
   C. 81
   D. 101

5. Where did the Israelites take the Canaanite king after they removed his thumbs and great toes?

   Judges 1:7

   A. Bethlehem
   B. Hebron
   C. Jerusalem
   D. Shiloh

6. What was Moses' father-in-law's ethnicity?

   Judges 1:16

   A. Ammonite
   B. Jebusite
   C. Kenite
   D. Tishbite

7. What did the Israelites name the city of Zephath?

   Judges 1:17

   A. Bethel
   B. Hormah
   C. Sidon
   D. Tyre

8. Which city did Judah capture?

   Judges 1:18

   A. Gaza
   B. Hazor
   C. Sidon
   D. Tyre

9. Which metal did the inhabitants of the valley use to build their chariots?

   Judges 1:19

   A. Brass
   B. Copper
   C. Gold
   D. Iron

10. Who were the inhabitants of Jerusalem?

    Judges 1:21

    A. Jebusites
    B. Kenites
    C. Ninevites
    D. Perizzites

11. What was the former name of the city of Bethel?

    Judges 1:23

    A. Ava
    B. Luz
    C. Ono
    D. Pau

12. Whom did the Israelites meet in Bochim?

    Judges 2:1–5

    A. An angel of the LORD
    B. An escaped fugitive from Egypt
    C. The general of the Syrian army
    D. The prophet Samuel

13. How old was Joshua when he died?

    Judges 2:8

    A. 90 years old
    B. 100 years old
    C. 110 years old
    D. 135 years old

14. Which two deities did the Israelites serve?

    Judges 2:13

    A. Baal and Ashtaroth
    B. Castor and Pollux
    C. Dagon and Tartak
    D. Diana and Zeus

15. Which Mesopotamian king did the Israelites serve for eight years?

    Judges 3:8

    A. King Belshazzar
    B. King Cushan-rishatha'im
    C. King Nebuchadnezzar II
    D. King Pul

16. Who was the first Israelite judge?

    Judges 3:9–10

    A. Barak
    B. Deborah
    C. Gideon
    D. Othniel

17. How does the Bible describe Eglon?

    Judges 3:17

    A. A giant over nine feet tall
    B. A very fat man
    C. Ruddy, with a fine appearance and handsome features
    D. Six fingers on each hand and six toes on each foot

18. How was Eglon killed?

    Judges 3:17–25

    A. He was choked to death.
    B. He was drowned in a pool.
    C. He was poisoned with arsenic.
    D. He was stabbed with a knife.

19. How many Moabites did the Israelites slay?

    Judges 3:29

    A. 10
    B. 100
    C. 1,000
    D. 10,000

20. How many years of peace did the Israelites enjoy after Moab was subdued?

    Judges 3:30

    A. 40
    B. 60
    C. 80
    D. 100

*Answers on page 757

MARCH 21

Lesson 80
Today's Reading: *Judges 4–6*
Period of Time: 1285–1245 BC
Author: Unknown

1. Which Canaanite king did God sell the Israelites to?
   Judges 4:2
   A. King Jabin
   B. King Mamre
   C. King Og
   D. King Sidon

2. Who was the captain of Canaan's army?
   Judges 4:2
   A. Cornelius
   B. Jehu
   C. Sargon
   D. Sisera

3. What weapons did the king of Canaan possess?
   Judges 4:3
   A. 200 fortified military posts
   B. 750 naval ships
   C. 900 chariots of iron
   D. 1,000 warriors in his cavalry

4. How many years did Canaan oppress the Israelites?
   Judges 4:3
   A. 10
   B. 20
   C. 30
   D. 40

5. Where did Deborah meet with her people?
   Judges 4:4–5
   A. At her home
   B. Inside her diner
   C. Near the river of Jordan
   D. Under a palm tree

6. How many men did Barak gather to fight the Canaanites?
   Judges 4:10
   A. 100
   B. 1,000
   C. 10,000
   D. 100,000

7. Who was Heber's wife?
   Judges 4:17
   A. Hannah
   B. Jael
   C. Kezia
   D. Mara

8. What did Heber's wife use to kill the Canaanite soldier?
   Judges 4:21
   A. A knife with two edges
   B. A tent nail
   C. An ox goad
   D. The jawbone of an ass

9. In the *Song of Deborah and Barak*, how many men in Israel had no shield or spear?
   Judges 5:8
   A. 40,000
   B. 80,000
   C. 120,000
   D. 160,000

10. In the *Song of Deborah and Barak*, what color were the asses the nobility rode upon?
    Judges 5:10
    A. Black
    B. Tan
    C. White
    D. Yellow

11. What did Heber's wife give the Canaanite soldier to drink?

    Judges 5:25

    A. Beer
    B. Herbal tea
    C. Milk
    D. Wine

12. In the *Song of Deborah and Barak*, who waits for the Canaanite soldier to return?

    Judges 5:28–30

    A. His children
    B. His mistress
    C. His mother
    D. His wife

13. Who oppressed Israel for seven years?

    Judges 6:1

    A. Edom
    B. Midian
    C. Moab
    D. Philistia

14. What was Gideon hiding from the enemy when an angel of the LORD appeared?

    Judges 6:11

    A. Barley
    B. Corn
    C. Flax
    D. Wheat

15. What did the angel of the LORD use to consume Gideon's offering?

    Judges 6:21

    A. A bolt of lightning
    B. A flock of seagulls
    C. The sparks from his flint
    D. The tip of his staff

16. What did Gideon do at night that angered the men of the city?

    Judges 6:25–30

    A. Destroyed his father's altar to Baal
    B. Escaped to the enemy's camp
    C. Stole the town's prize racehorse
    D. Switched his dead son for a live one

17. Who was Gideon's father?

    Judges 6:30

    A. Joash
    B. Job
    C. Joelah
    D. Joiada

18. What did Gideon's father name him after the men in the city became angry with Gideon?

    Judges 6:30–32

    A. Jerubbaal
    B. Meribaal
    C. Shobal
    D. Zerubbabel

19. In which valley did Israel's enemies gather together?

    Judges 6:33

    A. Valley of Achor
    B. Valley of Elah
    C. Valley of Gehenna
    D. Valley of Jezreel

20. What was the first sign Gideon asked the LORD to show him?

    Judges 6:37–38

    A. The fleece would be dry and the ground wet.
    B. The fleece would be wet and the ground dry.
    C. The water served at the wedding would turn into wine.
    D. The wine served at the wedding would turn into water.

Answers on page 757

Lesson 81
Today's Reading: *Judges 7–8*
Period of Time: 1245–1236 BC
Author: Unknown

MARCH 22

1. What was Gideon's other name?
   Judges 7:1
   A. Ethbaal
   B. Jerubbaal
   C. Meribaal
   D. Zerubbabel

2. At which well did the army of Gideon meet?
   Judges 7:1
   A. Well of Beerlahairoi
   B. Well of Esek
   C. Well of Harod
   D. Well of Sechu

3. How many men left Gideon's army because they were too afraid to fight?
   Judges 7:3
   A. 11,000
   B. 22,000
   C. 33,000
   D. 44,000

4. How many men remained in Gideon's army after those who were afraid left?
   Judges 7:3
   A. 10,000
   B. 20,000
   C. 30,000
   D. 40,000

5. How many of Gideon's men lapped water like dogs?
   Judges 7:6
   A. 30
   B. 300
   C. 3,000
   D. 30,000

6. Who was Gideon's servant?
   Judges 7:10
   A. Mizzah
   B. Nedabiah
   C. Obadiah
   D. Phurah

7. What did the Midianite soldier dream?
   Judges 7:13
   A. A battalion of Midianite soldiers marched over a steep cliff.
   B. A bear from the wilderness destroyed a Midianite chariot and its men.
   C. A cake of barley bread crushed a Midianite tent.
   D. A dappled horse and its pale rider set the Midianite camp on fire.

8. What did Gideon give his soldiers to confuse the Midianites?
   Judges 7:16
   A. A hornet's nest and a river
   B. Boulders and a wooden bridge
   C. Fake maps and road signs
   D. Trumpets and pitchers containing lamps

9. What did Gideon's men shout outside the Midianite camp?
   Judges 7:17–20
   A. "Charge."
   B. "Don't stop until we've run every last Midianite through with the sword."
   C. "Onward to victory and to God be the glory."
   D. "The sword of the LORD, and of Gideon."

10. Who were the two Midianite princes?
    Judges 7:25
    A. Elidad and Zabad
    B. Gareb and Heleb
    C. Oreb and Zeeb
    D. Pedaiah and Raamiah

11. Which two cities refused to give bread to Gideon and his men?
    Judges 8:4–9
    A. Succoth and Penuel
    B. Taberah and Jagur
    C. Uzza and Cappadocia
    D. Ziphron and Gittaim

12. Who were the two Midianite kings?

    Judges 8:5

    A. Ahirah and Ara
    B. Jaalah and Jarha
    C. Timnah and Tola
    D. Zebah and Zalmunna

13. Approximately how many Midianite soldiers fled to Karkor?

    Judges 8:10

    A. 15,000
    B. 40,000
    C. 75,000
    D. 90,000

14. Near which two cities was the Midianite army overtaken?

    Judges 8:11

    A. Beth-shean and Maon
    B. Nobah and Jogbehah
    C. Ramoth-gilead and Edrei
    D. Tob and Kamon

15. How many princes and elders lived in Succoth?

    Judges 8:14

    A. 77
    B. 88
    C. 99
    D. 111

16. What did Gideon make from the golden earrings?

    Judges 8:24–27

    A. A chariot
    B. A throne
    C. An ephod
    D. An urn

17. How many sons did Gideon have?

    Judges 8:30

    A. 7
    B. 12
    C. 71
    D. 88

18. Who was a son of Gideon?

    Judges 8:31

    A. Abimelech
    B. Elimelech
    C. Hammelech
    D. Regem-melech

19. In which city was Gideon's body laid to rest?

    Judges 8:32

    A. Adamah
    B. Jotbah
    C. Mizpah
    D. Ophrah

20. Whom did Israel make their god after Gideon died?

    Judges 8:33

    A. Amon
    B. Baalberith
    C. Chemosh
    D. Dagon

*Answers on page 757

MARCH 23

Lesson 82
Today's Reading: *Judges 9–10*
Period of Time: 1236–1188 BC
Author: Unknown

1. Who was Abimelech's father?
   Judges 9:1
   A. Conaniah
   B. Hanoch
   C. Jerubbaal
   D. Putiel

2. In which city did Abimelech persuade his relatives to make him ruler over them?
   Judges 9:1–2
   A. Alexandrium
   B. Gadara
   C. Phasaelis
   D. Shechem

3. How many brothers did Abimelech have?
   Judges 9:2
   A. 40
   B. 70
   C. 80
   D. 100

4. How many pieces of silver did Abimelech's relatives give him?
   Judges 9:4
   A. 70
   B. 100
   C. 250
   D. 300

5. Where did Abimelech's relatives obtain the pieces of silver to give to Abimelech?
   Judges 9:4
   A. From the army of the Midianites
   B. From the caves of the Moabites
   C. From the house of Baalberith
   D. From the temple of Dagon

6. What type of men did Abimelech hire?
   Judges 9:4
   A. Humble and daring
   B. Modest and fearless
   C. Solid and unmovable
   D. Vain and light

7. In which city did Abimelech slay his brothers?
   Judges 9:5
   A. Hebron
   B. Ophrah
   C. Punon
   D. Rabbah

8. Which brother escaped from Abimelech and his men?
   Judges 9:5
   A. Jotham
   B. Mibsam
   C. Raham
   D. Zetham

9. Where did Abimelech's brother flee to?
   Judges 9:21
   A. Arad
   B. Beer
   C. Dion
   D. Gaza

10. Who was Abimelech's officer?
    Judges 9:28
    A. Elzabad
    B. Joash
    C. Maaseiah
    D. Zebul

11. Who led a rebellion against Abimelech?
    Judges 9:28–39
    A. Gaal
    B. Gideon
    C. Gog
    D. Goliath

12. What did Abimelech do to the city of Shechem?
    Judges 9:41–45
    A. Built a strong fence around it
    B. Made it his headquarters
    C. Sowed it with salt
    D. Traded it to the Philistines for Gaza

13. Upon which mountain did Abimelech gather boughs from trees?

    Judges 9:46–49

    A. Mount Carmel
    B. Mount Hermon
    C. Mount Tabor
    D. Mount Zalmon

14. How many people perished in the tower of Shechem?

    Judges 9:49

    A. 1,000
    B. 2,000
    C. 3,000
    D. 4,000

15. Which city did Abimelech attack after he destroyed the tower in Shechem?

    Judges 9:50

    A. Jahaz
    B. Meroz
    C. Thebez
    D. Uz

16. What did the woman use to crack Abimelech's skull?

    Judges 9:53

    A. A hammer
    B. A piece of a millstone
    C. An anchor from a fisherman's boat
    D. An anvil from the blacksmith's shop

17. Who judged Israel for 23 years after Abimelech died?

    Judges 10:1–2

    A. Hophni
    B. Tola
    C. Vaniah
    D. Zelek

18. How many years did Jair judge Israel?

    Judges 10:3

    A. 22
    B. 35
    C. 40
    D. 51

19. How many sons did Jair have?

    Judges 10:3–4

    A. 7
    B. 12
    C. 30
    D. 40

20. Which two nations did the LORD sell the children of Israel to after Jair died?

    Judges 10:6–7

    A. The Canaanites and Perizzites
    B. The Hittites and Hivites
    C. The Moabites and Edomites
    D. The Philistines and Ammonites

Answers on page 757

MARCH 24

Lesson 83
Today's Reading: *Judges 11–13*
Period of Time: 1188–1155 BC
Author: Unknown

1. Who was Jephthah's father?
   Judges 11:1
   A. Gilead
   B. Jethro
   C. Nethaneel
   D. Tahrea

2. Where did Jephthah go to when he fled from his brothers?
   Judges 11:3
   A. Land of Ashtaroth
   B. Land of Edrei
   C. Land of Tob
   D. Land of Zaphon

3. Who waged war against Israel?
   Judges 11:4
   A. The Ammonites
   B. The Babylonians
   C. The Chaldeans
   D. The Persians

4. Who was the former king of Heshbon?
   Judges 11:19
   A. King Cyrus
   B. King Og
   C. King Magog
   D. King Sihon

5. Where did the former king of Heshbon pitch his tents to fight against Israel?
   Judges 11:20
   A. Jabneel
   B. Jahaz
   C. Jericho
   D. Jerusalem

6. Which god did Jephthah tell his enemy to turn to for help?
   Judges 11:24
   A. Amon
   B. Chemosh
   C. Dagon
   D. Nergal

7. Who was the son of Zippor?
   Judges 11:25
   A. Balaam
   B. Balak
   C. Barabbas
   D. Bariah

8. How many years had Israel dwelled in Heshbon, Aroer, and the cities along the coasts of Arnon?
   Judges 11:26
   A. 50
   B. 100
   C. 200
   D. 300

9. How many days each year did the daughters of Israel lament the daughter of Jephthah?
   Judges 11:39–40
   A. 2
   B. 3
   C. 4
   D. 5

10. What word did the Gileadites have the captured men pronounce?
    Judges 12:5–6
    A. Hauran
    B. Kadesh
    C. Michmash
    D. Shibboleth

11. How many Ephraimites did Jephthah and his men slay at the passages of the river of Jordan?
    Judges 12:6
    A. 42,000
    B. 61,000
    C. 83,000
    D. 96,000

12. How many sons and daughters did Ibzan have?

    Judges 12:8–9

    A. 30
    B. 60
    C. 80
    D. 90

13. How many years did Ibzan judge Israel?

    Judges 12:8–9

    A. 3
    B. 5
    C. 7
    D. 9

14. Who judged Israel after Ibzan died?

    Judges 12:11

    A. Elon
    B. Gideon
    C. Jair
    D. Shamgar

15. Which Pirathonite judged Israel for eight years?

    Judges 12:13–15

    A. Abdon
    B. Allon
    C. Ammon
    D. Amnon

16. Who ruled over Israel for forty years?

    Judges 13:1

    A. The Edomites
    B. The Kenites
    C. The Moabites
    D. The Philistines

17. Which man of Zorah had no children?

    Judges 13:2

    A. Ahoah
    B. Joah
    C. Manoah
    D. Noah

18. Who told the wife of the man of Zorah she was going to have a son?

    Judges 13:2–3

    A. A priest
    B. A prophet
    C. A witch
    D. An angel

19. What was the man of Zorah's future son going to be?

    Judges 13:5

    A. A Levite
    B. A Nazarite
    C. A Punite
    D. An Oznite

20. What did the man of Zorah's wife name their son?

    Judges 13:24

    A. Sachon
    B. Salmon
    C. Samson
    D. Sargon

Answers on page 757

Lesson 84
Today's Reading: *Judges 14–16*
Period of Time: 1155–1117 BC
Author: Unknown

1. Where did Samson fall in love?
   Judges 14:1–2
   A. Ramath
   B. Seirath
   C. Timnath
   D. Zephath

2. Which animal did Samson kill with his bare hands?
   Judges 14:5–6
   A. A bear
   B. A camel
   C. A dragon
   D. A lion

3. What did Samson later find inside the carcass of the animal he slew?
   Judges 14:8
   A. Bees and honey
   B. Diamonds and rubies
   C. Fish and bread
   D. Gold and silver

4. How many days did Samson's wedding feast last?
   Judges 14:12
   A. 3
   B. 7
   C. 10
   D. 14

5. How many changes of garments did Samson promise the Philistines if they solved his riddle?
   Judges 14:12
   A. 10
   B. 15
   C. 20
   D. 30

6. What did Samson tell the Philistines after they solved his riddle?
   Judges 14:18
   A. "Had ye not gotten me drunk, ye would have not solved my riddle."
   B. "If ye had not plowed with my heifer, ye had not found out my riddle."
   C. "Let me tell ye another riddle: run and hide."
   D. "Ye men of Philistia are cunning indeed, but twain can play that game."

7. What did Samson do to get revenge on the Philistines?
   Judges 15:1–5
   A. He burned down their crops by tying torches to the tails of 300 foxes.
   B. He caused a stampede of cattle to crush their tents in Ashkelon.
   C. He poisoned all of their drinking wells.
   D. He stole their horses and released them into the desert.

8. How did the Philistines kill Samson's wife and father-in-law?
   Judges 15:6
   A. Burned them
   B. Drowned them
   C. Hung them
   D. Stoned them

9. How many men from Judah went to speak with Samson?
   Judges 15:11
   A. 1,000
   B. 2,000
   C. 3,000
   D. 4,000

10. What did Samson use to slay 1000 Philistines?
    Judges 15:15
    A. A tar pit
    B. An ox goad
    C. Goliath's sword
    D. The jawbone of an ass

11. How many years did Samson judge Israel?
    Judges 15:20, 16:31
    A. 10
    B. 15
    C. 20
    D. 40

12. What did Samson do at Gaza to further anger the Philistines?
    Judges 16:3
    A. Dragged away the gates and doorposts to the city.
    B. Replaced his dead child with a live child at night.
    C. Smashed their beer kegs and broke their bottles of wine.
    D. Stole their temple idols and later sold the gold and silver from them.

13. How many pieces of silver did each lord of the Philistines promise to give Delilah?
    Judges 16:5
    A. 1,000
    B. 1,100
    C. 1,200
    D. 1,300

14. How many times did Samson trick Delilah?
    Judges 16:15
    A. 2
    B. 3
    C. 4
    D. 5

15. What was Samson called?
    Judges 16:17
    A. A Hittite
    B. A Hivite
    C. A Nazarite
    D. A Perizzite

16. What did the Philistines do to Samson to make him weak?
    Judges 16:19–21
    A. Shaved the seven locks from his head
    B. Tied him up with new ropes
    C. Tied him up with seven green cords
    D. Took away his wife and son

17. What did the Philistines do to Samson after they captured him?
    Judges 16:21
    A. Applied honey and ants to his skin
    B. Blinded him
    C. Cut off his thumbs and great toes
    D. Murdered his parents

18. Who was the god of the Philistines?
    Judges 16:23
    A. Baal
    B. Chemosh
    C. Dagon
    D. Merodach

19. How did Samson kill the 3,000 Philistines?
    Judges 16:25–30
    A. He boiled them in hot oil.
    B. He burned down their homes while they slept.
    C. He caused cattle to stampede through their camp.
    D. He crushed them with a building.

20. Who was Samson's father?
    Judges 15:20, 16:31
    A. Gershon
    B. Ishbak
    C. Jonathan
    D. Manoah

Answers on page 757

Lesson 85
Today's Reading: *Judges 17–19*
Period of Time: 1413–1405 BC
Author: Unknown

MARCH 26

1. Upon which mountain did Micah dwell?
   Judges 17:1
   A. Mount Carmel
   B. Mount Ephraim
   C. Mount Moriah
   D. Mount Nebo

2. How many shekels of silver did Micah take from his mother?
   Judges 17:2
   A. 100
   B. 500
   C. 1,000
   D. 1,100

3. Whom did Micah's mother give 200 shekels of silver to?
   Judges 17:4
   A. The baker
   B. The butcher
   C. The founder
   D. The priest

4. Which one of the following did Micah **not** do?
   Judges 17:5
   A. He consecrated one of his sons.
   B. He made a teraphim.
   C. He made an ephod.
   D. He tore down his groves.

5. Who was the king of Israel in those days?
   Judges 17:6, 18:1
   A. King David
   B. King Samson
   C. King Saul
   D. There was no king.

6. Where was the Levite from?
   Judges 17:7–8
   A. Bethlehemgalilee
   B. Bethlehemjudah
   C. Ramathlehi
   D. Ramathmizpeh

7. How many shekels of silver did Micah agree to pay the Levite annually?
   Judges 17:10
   A. 10
   B. 50
   C. 100
   D. 500

8. How many men did the Danites send to search the land?
   Judges 18:2
   A. 2
   B. 3
   C. 5
   D. 7

9. Where did the Danite men go after departing Micah's house?
   Judges 18:7
   A. Ashtaroth
   B. Damascus
   C. Laish
   D. Tob

10. How many Danites went to war?
    Judges 18:11
    A. 600
    B. 6,000
    C. 60,000
    D. 600,000

11. What did the Danites steal from Micah?
    Judges 18:14–24
    A. His daughters
    B. His idols
    C. His slaves
    D. His wives

12. How many Danites did Micah and his neighbors slay?

    Judges 18:22–26

    A. 0
    B. 100
    C. 200
    D. 300

13. What did the Danites name the city they captured near Bethrehob?

    Judges 18:27–29

    A. Dan
    B. Lod
    C. Nob
    D. Ono

14. Who was a Danite priest?

    Judges 18:30

    A. Abishua
    B. Hilkiah
    C. Jonathan
    D. Zerahiah

15. Which city was the concubine from?

    Judges 19:1

    A. Bethlehem Ephratah
    B. Bethlehemjudah
    C. Ramathlehi
    D. Ramath-mizpeh

16. On which day did the Levite and his concubine leave his father-in-law's house?

    Judges 19:3–10

    A. 3rd
    B. 4th
    C. 5th
    D. 6th

17. What is another name for Jebus?

    Judges 19:10

    A. Jahaz
    B. Jerusalem
    C. Joppa
    D. Jotbah

18. Where did the Levite and his concubine stop to spend the night?

    Judges 19:11–15

    A. Adamah
    B. Baalah
    C. Calah
    D. Gibeah

19. Whom did the sons of Belial want to have sex with?

    Judges 19:22

    A. The Levite
    B. The Levite's concubine
    C. The Levite's servant
    D. The old man

20. What did the Levite do with his concubine's dead body?

    Judges 19:29

    A. He ate it in order to survive in the barren desert.
    B. He buried it in the cave where Rachel and Rebekah were buried.
    C. He burned it upon hot coals as an offering to the god Baal.
    D. He divided the body into 12 pieces and sent a part to each tribe of Israel.

Answers on page 758

Lesson 86
Today's Reading: *Judges 20–21*
Period of Time: 1413–1405 BC
Author: Unknown

MARCH 27

1. Where did the Israelites gather to judge the Benjamites?
   Judges 20:1
   A. Hadasha
   B. Keilah
   C. Mizpeh
   D. Saba

2. How many Israelite footmen were ready to go to war against Benjamin?
   Judges 20:2
   A. 100,000
   B. 400,000
   C. 800,000
   D. 1,000,000

3. In which city was the concubine murdered?
   Judges 20:4
   A. Gibeah
   B. Maachah
   C. Parah
   D. Riblah

4. Who divided the concubine's body into 12 pieces?
   Judges 20:3–6
   A. A judge over Israel
   B. A man from the tribe of Benjamin
   C. The chief priest
   D. The Levite

5. What did the Israelites call the Benjamites who murdered the concubine?
   Judges 20:13
   A. Angels from Hell
   B. Children of Belial
   C. Devil Dogs
   D. Satan's Soldiers

6. How many Benjamites were ready to go to war against Israel?
   Judges 20:15
   A. 10,300
   B. 17,500
   C. 26,700
   D. 70,900

7. How many left-handed Benjamites were experts at slinging stones?
   Judges 20:16
   A. 700
   B. 1,700
   C. 23,000
   D. 25,400

8. Which tribe went in first to fight the Benjamites?
   Judges 20:18
   A. Tribe of Dan
   B. Tribe of Gad
   C. Tribe of Judah
   D. Tribe of Reuben

9. How many Israelites died on the first day of battle?
   Judges 20:18–21
   A. 10,000
   B. 22,000
   C. 34,000
   D. 66,000

10. How many Israelites died on the second day of battle?
    Judges 20:25
    A. 18,000
    B. 27,000
    C. 33,000
    D. 42,000

11. Who was the high priest?

    Judges 20:27–28

    A. Azariah
    B. Eleazar
    C. Jehoiada
    D. Phinehas

12. How many Israelites died on the third day of battle?

    Judges 20:31

    A. 15
    B. 30
    C. 45
    D. 60

13. Where did the Israelites set up an ambush?

    Judges 20:33

    A. Baaltamar
    B. Laish
    C. Oboth
    D. Taanach

14. What was the sign the city had been captured?

    Judges 20:38

    A. Smoke coming from within the city
    B. The city walls crumbling to the ground
    C. The flag of Israel blowing in the wind
    D. Trumpet blasts from the city towers

15. Approximately how many Benjamites died on the third day of battle?

    Judges 20:46

    A. 10,000
    B. 13,000
    C. 18,000
    D. 25,000

16. How many Benjamites fled to the rock of Rimmon?

    Judges 20:45–47

    A. 100
    B. 600
    C. 900
    D. 1,200

17. How many Israelites were sent to punish the city of Jabesh-gilead?

    Judges 21:10

    A. 6,000
    B. 9,000
    C. 12,000
    D. 15,000

18. How many young virgins were spared at Jabesh-gilead?

    Judges 21:12

    A. 40
    B. 360
    C. 400
    D. 720

19. Which city were the young virgins from Jabesh-gilead taken to?

    Judges 21:12

    A. Gazara
    B. Marisa
    C. Nob
    D. Shiloh

20. Who was the king of Israel in those days?

    Judges 21:25

    A. King David
    B. King Saul
    C. King Solomon
    D. There was no king.

Answers on page 758

Lesson 87
Today's Reading: *Ruth 1–4*
Period of Time: 1405–1095 BC
Author: Unknown

MARCH 28

1. Who was Naomi's husband?
   Ruth 1:1–2
   A. Eliashib
   B. Elimelech
   C. Elioenai
   D. Eliphalet

2. Where did Naomi and her family move to?
   Ruth 1:1–2
   A. Babylon
   B. Edom
   C. Moab
   D. Tarsus

3. Who were Naomi's sons?
   Ruth 1:1–2
   A. Andrew and Peter
   B. Cain and Abel
   C. Esau and Jacob
   D. Mahlon and Chilion

4. Where was Naomi's family from?
   Ruth 1:1–2
   A. Bethlehemjudah
   B. Jegarsahadutha
   C. Maalehacrabbim
   D. Ramathaimzophim

5. What happened to Naomi's husband?
   Ruth 1:3
   A. He abandoned the family.
   B. He became a leper.
   C. He died.
   D. He was cast into prison.

6. Who married one of Naomi's sons?
   Ruth 1:4
   A. Orpah
   B. Puah
   C. Rahab
   D. Timna

7. Who married Naomi's other son?
   Ruth 1:4
   A. Delilah
   B. Esther
   C. Ruth
   D. Vashti

8. Approximately how many years did Naomi live in the foreign land?
   Ruth 1:4
   A. 10
   B. 12
   C. 15
   D. 20

9. Where did Naomi and her daughter-in-law move to?
   Ruth 1:19
   A. Aleppo
   B. Bethlehem
   C. Golan
   D. Paneas

10. What did Naomi want to be called?
    Ruth 1:20
    A. Ada
    B. Mara
    C. Sara
    D. Tirzah

11. Who owned the field Naomi's daughter-in-law gleaned in?
    Ruth 2:1–3
    A. Amaziah
    B. Boaz
    C. Laban
    D. Simon

12. What did the daughter-in-law glean?
    Ruth 2:23
    A. Flax
    B. Grapes
    C. Olives
    D. Wheat

13. Which word describes the daughter-in-law that remained with Naomi?

    Ruth 3:11

    A. Monstrous
    B. Scandalous
    C. Tempestuous
    D. Virtuous

14. How many elders met at the city gate to hear Naomi's case?

    Ruth 4:1–5

    A. 10
    B. 12
    C. 16
    D. 18

15. What did the relative do as a sign he did **not** want to redeem Naomi's land or raise up the name of one of her dead sons?

    Ruth 4:7–8

    A. Gave his shoe to his neighbor
    B. Left a homer of barley at the city gate
    C. Paid his neighbor 30 shekels of silver
    D. Signed a contract

16. Who were known as the women who built the house of Israel?

    Ruth 4:11–12

    A. Dinah and Martha
    B. Esther and Syntyche
    C. Rachel and Leah
    D. Tabitha and Joanna

17. Who was Pharez's mother?

    Ruth 4:12

    A. Bath-sheba
    B. Julia
    C. Sarai
    D. Tamar

18. Who was Naomi's grandson?

    Ruth 4:13–21

    A. Agag
    B. Jude
    C. Mark
    D. Obed

19. Who was Ram's father?

    Ruth 4:18–19

    A. Benjamin
    B. Caleb
    C. Hezron
    D. Samuel

20. Who was David's father?

    Ruth 4:17–22

    A. Gabriel
    B. Jesse
    C. Michael
    D. Vaniah

*Answers on page 758

MARCH 29

Lesson 88
Today's Reading: *I Samuel 1–3*
Period of Time: 1137–1125 BC
Author: Unknown

1. Where was Elkanah from?
   I Samuel 1:1
   A. Bethlehem-galilee
   B. Chushan-rishathaim
   C. Ramatha'im-zophim
   D. Zaphnath-paaneah

2. Who was Elkanah's father?
   I Samuel 1:1
   A. Jehoram
   B. Jeroham
   C. Joab
   D. Jobab

3. What was Zuph's ethnicity?
   I Samuel 1:1
   A. Ephrathite
   B. Ishmaelite
   C. Oznite
   D. Uzzielite

4. Who was one of Elkanah's wives?
   I Samuel 1:2
   A. Eunice
   B. Gomer
   C. Kezia
   D. Peninnah

5. Where did Elkanah go annually to sacrifice unto the LORD?
   I Samuel 1:3
   A. Gilgal
   B. Jerusalem
   C. Kirjath-jearim
   D. Shiloh

6. Who were Eli's sons?
   I Samuel 1:3
   A. Eleazar and Ithamar
   B. Elishama and Jehoram
   C. Hophni and Phinehas
   D. Nadab and Abihu

7. What did Elkanah's wife do to Hannah?
   I Samuel 1:5–7
   A. Made fun of her for being overweight
   B. Made sport of her because she was a foreigner
   C. Mocked her for having dark skin
   D. Ridiculed her for not having any children

8. What did Eli accuse Hannah of?
   I Samuel 1:9–14
   A. Drunkenness
   B. Gluttony
   C. Prostitution
   D. Spying

9. How many bullocks did Hannah bring to the house of the LORD in Shiloh?
   I Samuel 1:24
   A. 2
   B. 3
   C. 5
   D. 7

10. What happened to Samuel?
    I Samuel 1:24–28
    A. Eli removed him from Hannah's care.
    B. Hannah gave him to Eli to raise.
    C. He became Eli's stepson.
    D. He ran away from home.

11. What did Hannah say in her prayer was nothing like God?
    I Samuel 2:2
    A. Any door
    B. Any fountain
    C. Any rock
    D. Any shepherd

12. Which statement describes Eli's sons?
    I Samuel 2:12
    A. Sons of Belial
    B. Sons of Confusion
    C. Sons of Righteousness
    D. Sons of Thunder

13. Which part of a sacrifice seethed in a pot belonged to the priest?

    I Samuel 2:12–14

    A. All of it unless it was a peace offering
    B. The tenderloin and the left shoulder
    C. Whatever was collected with a fleshhook
    D. Whatever was leftover after the meal

14. What did Samuel wear when he ministered before the LORD?

    I Samuel 2:18

    A. A linen ephod
    B. A mitre upon his head
    C. A purple girdle
    D. A skirt with pomegranates and bells

15. What did Hannah give to Samuel every year?

    I Samuel 2:19

    A. A coat
    B. A pair of shoes
    C. A shekel of gold
    D. A shekel of silver

16. Besides Samuel, how many other sons and daughters did Hannah have?

    I Samuel 2:21

    A. 2 daughters and 1 son
    B. 2 daughters and 2 sons
    C. 3 sons and 1 daughter
    D. 3 sons and 2 daughters

17. Why did Eli rebuke his sons?

    I Samuel 2:22

    A. They accepted bribes while acting as judges over Israel.
    B. They had been having sex with male shrine prostitutes of the pagan nations.
    C. They had been having sex with the women who had assembled at the tabernacle.
    D. They stole 1,000 shekels of gold from the temple treasury during the annual sacrifices.

18. Which prophetic statement did the man of God tell Eli?

    I Samuel 2:27–34

    A. A great tempest would flood Israel.
    B. Both of Eli's sons were going to die on the same day.
    C. If the Ninevites did not repent, God would destroy their city.
    D. Not one arrow from the Babylonian army would enter into Israel.

19. How many times during the night did the LORD call out to Samuel?

    I Samuel 3:2–10

    A. 2
    B. 4
    C. 6
    D. 8

20. Where did the LORD reveal himself again to Samuel?

    I Samuel 3:21

    A. Bethel
    B. Jerusalem
    C. Nazareth
    D. Shiloh

*Answers on page 758

MARCH 30

Lesson 89
Today's Reading: *I Samuel 4–7*
Period of Time: 1117–1055 BC
Author: Unknown

1. Approximately how many Israelite soldiers did the Philistines slay in the first battle?
   I Samuel 4:2
   A. 2,000
   B. 4,000
   C. 6,000
   D. 8,000

2. Where was the ark of the covenant located when the Israelite army came to get it?
   I Samuel 4:3–4
   A. Bethel
   B. Hebron
   C. Jerusalem
   D. Shiloh

3. What did the Philistines call the Israelites?
   I Samuel 4:6
   A. Hebrews
   B. Jews
   C. The circumcised
   D. Semites

4. How many Israelite footmen were slain when the Philistines captured the ark of the covenant?
   I Samuel 4:10–11
   A. 300
   B. 3,000
   C. 30,000
   D. 300,000

5. Which two men were Eli's sons?
   I Samuel 4:11
   A. Abihu and Nadab
   B. Elishama and Jehoram
   C. Hophni and Phinehas
   D. Shelemiah and Zadok

6. Which tribe was the messenger from who told Eli his sons were dead?
   I Samuel 4:12–17
   A. Tribe of Benjamin
   B. Tribe of Issachar
   C. Tribe of Judah
   D. Tribe of Reuben

7. How old was Eli when he died?
   I Samuel 4:15–18
   A. 79 years old
   B. 98 years old
   C. 100 years old
   D. 120 years old

8. How many years did Eli judge Israel?
   I Samuel 4:18
   A. 20
   B. 30
   C. 40
   D. 50

9. What did Eli's daughter-in-law name her child?
   I Samuel 4:21
   A. Gilalai
   B. Habaiah
   C. Ichabod
   D. Japhlet

10. What was the name of the Philistine god?
    I Samuel 5:3
    A. Dagon
    B. Merodach
    C. Molech
    D. Nisroch

11. What did the god of the Philistines look like on the second morning?

    I Samuel 5:4
    A. It had blood running from its eyes and down both cheeks.
    B. Its head and both palms of its hands had been cut off.
    C. It was shattered into hundreds of pieces.
    D. I was standing on its head

12. What happened to the Philistines after they captured the ark of the covenant?

    I Samuel 5:6–12
    A. God brought a great famine upon their land.
    B. God brought pestilence and disease upon their crops and livestock.
    C. God closed the wombs of their women.
    D. God struck them with emerods in their secret places.

13. How many months did the ark of the covenant stay in the land of the Philistines?

    I Samuel 6:1
    A. 7
    B. 8
    C. 10
    D. 11

14. How many men of Beth-she'mesh did the LORD smite for looking into the ark of the covenant?

    I Samuel 6:19
    A. 22,350
    B. 38,090
    C. 46,700
    D. 50,070

15. How many years did the ark of the covenant stay in Kirjath-je'arim?

    I Samuel 7:2
    A. 10
    B. 20
    C. 30
    D. 40

16. Which two gods were Israel guilty of worshiping?

    I Samuel 7:4
    A. Baalim and Ashtaroth
    B. Chemosh and Hermes
    C. Rimmon and Beelzebub
    D. Tartak and Nibhaz

17. Where did Samuel meet with the Israelites?

    I Samuel 7:5–6
    A. Arumah
    B. Gibeah
    C. Mizpeh
    D. Secacah

18. What did the LORD use to terrorize the Philistine army?

    I Samuel 7:10
    A. An earthquake
    B. Swarms of mice
    C. The angel of the LORD
    D. Thunder

19. What did Samuel name the place where he set up a memorial stone?

    I Samuel 7:12
    A. Benjamin
    B. Ebenezer
    C. Jennings
    D. Prentice

20. Where was Samuel's house located?

    I Samuel 7:17
    A. Bethel
    B. Gilgal
    C. Mizpah
    D. Ramah

Answers on page 758

Lesson 90
Today's Reading: *I Samuel 8–10*
Period of Time: 1117–1095 BC
Author: Unknown

1. Who was Samuel's oldest son?
   I Samuel 8:2
   A. Anan
   B. Boaz
   C. Joel
   D. Mash

2. Who was Samuel's other son?
   I Samuel 8:2
   A. Abiah
   B. Conaniah
   C. Gemariah
   D. Ishmaiah

3. Where did Samuel's sons judge the people?
   I Samuel 8:2
   A. Baalah
   B. Baalpeor
   C. Beersheba
   D. Bethany

4. What were Samuel's sons guilty of?
   I Samuel 8:3
   A. Having sex inside the tabernacle
   B. Having sex with male prostitutes
   C. Stealing from the tabernacle
   D. Taking bribes and perverting judgments

5. Which tribe did Saul belong to?
   I Samuel 9:1–2
   A. Tribe of Asher
   B. Tribe of Benjamin
   C. Tribe of Dan
   D. Tribe of Gad

6. How does the Bible describe Saul?
   I Samuel 9:2
   A. Brilliant and gallant
   B. Dashing and heroic
   C. Suave and debonair
   D. Tall and handsome

7. Who was Saul's father?
   I Samuel 9:3
   A. Kadmiel
   B. Kenaz
   C. Kish
   D. Kore

8. What was Saul searching for?
   I Samuel 9:3
   A. Asses
   B. Camels
   C. Cattle
   D. Sheep

9. How much of a shekel of silver was Saul going to give the man of God?
   I Samuel 9:8–10
   A. 1/4
   B. 1/2
   C. 2/3
   D. 3/4

10. What was a prophet of Israel called before the days of Saul?
    I Samuel 9:9
    A. A necromancer
    B. A seer
    C. A warlock
    D. A witch

11. Approximately how many persons had gathered in Samuel's parlor by the time Saul arrived?
    I Samuel 9:22
    A. 7
    B. 15
    C. 21
    D. 30

12. In which part of the house did Samuel commune with Saul at dawn?

    I Samuel 9:25–26

    A. Beside the kitchen stove
    B. Inside the den
    C. Near the fireplace in the living room
    D. Upon the top of the house

13. Where was Saul to meet two men after he left Samuel's house?

    I Samuel 10:2

    A. Jacob's well
    B. Naboth's garden
    C. Rachel's sepulcher
    D. Tower in Shiloh

14. Where were the three men going that Saul met on the plain of Tabor?

    I Samuel 10:3

    A. Bethel
    B. Gibeah
    C. Hazor
    D. Tekoa

15. How many loaves of bread were the three men Saul was to meet on the plain of Tabor suppose to give him?

    I Samuel 10:4

    A. 2
    B. 3
    C. 5
    D. 7

16. What were the prophets carrying when Saul met them?

    I Samuel 10:5

    A. A scroll of the book of Deuteronomy
    B. Baskets of fruit
    C. Musical instruments
    D. Smoked fish

17. Where was Saul to meet Samuel to make offerings to the LORD?

    I Samuel 10:8

    A. Bethel
    B. Gilgal
    C. Phasaelis
    D. Thamna

18. Where did Samuel gather the tribes of Israel to install their new king?

    I Samuel 10:17

    A. Maacah
    B. Madmannah
    C. Meribah
    D. Mizpeh

19. Where did Saul hide?

    I Samuel 10:22

    A. Among the bushes
    B. Among the stuff
    C. Among the trees
    D. Among the unicorns

20. What did the people shout when Samuel introduced Saul as their king?

    I Samuel 10:24

    A. "Away with him, away with him, crucify him."
    B. "God save the king."
    C. "Let us pick our own king."
    D. "We have no king but Caesar."

*Answers on page 758

APRIL 1

Lesson 91
Today's Reading: *I Samuel 11–13*
Period of Time: 1095–1093 BC
Author: Unknown

1. Which Ammonite king waged war against Jabesh-gilead?
   I Samuel 11:1
   A. King Naaman
   B. King Naarai
   C. King Nahash
   D. King Nathan

2. Which body parts did the Ammonite king want to remove from the inhabitants of Jabesh-gilead?
   I Samuel 11:2
   A. Both great toes
   B. Both thumbs
   C. Their right eyes
   D. Their right hands

3. What did King Saul tell the Israelites he would do to them if they did **not** join him in the fight against the Ammonite king?
   I Samuel 11:7
   A. He would burn their fields.
   B. He would demolish their homes.
   C. He would kill their firstborn sons.
   D. He would slaughter their oxen.

4. How many men gathered in Bezek to fight against Ammon?
   I Samuel 11:8
   A. 3,000
   B. 30,000
   C. 300,000
   D. 3,000,000

5. How many men gathered in Judah to fight against Ammon?
   I Samuel 11:8
   A. 3,000
   B. 30,000
   C. 300,000
   D. 3,000,000

6. What did King Saul do to the men who had refused to accept him as their king?
   I Samuel 11:12–13
   A. Burned them with fire
   B. Crushed them with stones
   C. Hung them from trees
   D. Pardoned them

7. In which city did Samuel and the Israelites meet to renew the kingdom?
   I Samuel 11:14–15
   A. Gilgal
   B. Mishal
   C. Rachal
   D. Tidal

8. Who was captain of the host of Hazor?
   I Samuel 12:9
   A. Perida
   B. Sisera
   C. Tirza
   D. Zereda

9. Which pagan gods was Israel guilty of worshipping?
   I Samuel 12:10
   A. Baalim and Ashtaroth
   B. Chemosh and Rimmon
   C. Dagon and Nisroch
   D. Moloch and Tammuz

10. Who was a judge in Israel?
    I Samuel 12:11
    A. Baalpeor
    B. Bamothbaal
    C. Eshbaal
    D. Jerubbaal

11. How did the LORD punish Israel for asking for a king?
    I Samuel 12:17–19
    A. He caused a famine in Israel for seven years.
    B. He destroyed their wheat fields with thunder and rain.
    C. He made Israel a failure in warfare for three months.
    D. He sent a plague throughout Israel for three days.

12. How old was King Saul when he had reigned two years over Israel?
    I Samuel 13:1
    A. 20 years old
    B. 30 years old
    C. 40 years old
    D. Unknown

13. How many Israelite men were with King Saul in Michmash and in mount Bethel?
    I Samuel 13:2
    A. 2,000
    B. 20,000
    C. 200,000
    D. 2,000,000

14. How many Israelite men were with Jonathan in Gibeah?
    I Samuel 13:2
    A. 1,000
    B. 2,000
    C. 3,000
    D. 4,000

15. How many chariots and horsemen did the Philistines use to fight against Israel?
    I Samuel 13:5
    A. 20,000 chariots and 5,000 horsemen
    B. 30,000 chariots and 6,000 horsemen
    C. 40,000 chariots and 7,000 horsemen
    D. 50,000 chariots and 8,000 horsemen

16. Why did God refuse to establish Saul's kingdom upon Israel forever?
    I Samuel 13:8–14
    A. Saul committed adultery.
    B. Saul intruded into the priest's office.
    C. Saul murdered his brothers.
    D. Saul numbered the people.

17. Who was King Saul's son?
    I Samuel 13:16
    A. Elnathan
    B. Herodian
    C. Jonathan
    D. Shiphtan

18. Where did the Philistines establish their camp to fight against Israel?
    I Samuel 13:16
    A. Ashkelon
    B. Caesarea
    C. Michmash
    D. Neballat

19. Who sharpened Israel's farm equipment since there was no blacksmith in Israel?
    I Samuel 13:19–21
    A. The Ammonites
    B. The Egyptians
    C. The Moabites
    D. The Philistines

20. How many swords and spears, **not** counting King Saul's and Jonathan's, did the Israelite army have to fight against the Philistines?
    I Samuel 13:19–22
    A. 0
    B. 100
    C. 1,000
    D. 10,000

*Answers on page 758

APRIL 2

Lesson 92
Today's Reading: *I Samuel 14–15*
Period of Time: 1093–1063 BC
Author: Unknown

1. Approximately how many men were with King Saul at Migron?
   I Samuel 14:2
   A. 6
   B. 60
   C. 600
   D. 6,000

2. Which priest was with King Saul at Migron?
   I Samuel 14:3
   A. Ahiah
   B. Amariah
   C. Amaziah
   D. Azariah

3. What were the names of the two sharp rocks?
   I Samuel 14:4
   A. Abarim and Tabor
   B. Bozez and Seneh
   C. Carmel and Nebo
   D. Ebal and Zion

4. How many Philistines did Jonathan and his armourbearer slay on the top of the hill?
   I Samuel 14:14
   A. 2
   B. 20
   C. 200
   D. 2,000

5. What did King Saul command the priest to bring him?
   I Samuel 14:18
   A. A translator
   B. An ephod
   C. His armor
   D. The ark of God

6. Why was the army of Israel distressed on the day of battle?
   I Samuel 14:24
   A. Saul had forbidden them to eat any food.
   B. They feared the giant named Goliath.
   C. They were outnumbered 10:1 against the Philistines.
   D. When they awoke, Saul was nowhere to be found.

7. What did Jonathan eat?
   I Samuel 14:25–29, 14:43
   A. Apples
   B. Beetles
   C. Honey
   D. Mushrooms

8. What were the Israelite men guilty of doing?
   I Samuel 14:32–33
   A. Eating the blood from slain animals
   B. Killing innocent women and children
   C. Raping the Philistine women
   D. Taking the Philistine idols

9. Whom did King Saul order to be killed?
   I Samuel 14:36–44
   A. Ichabod
   B. Jonathan
   C. Nebaioth
   D. Tobijah

10. Which nation did King Saul **not** fight against?
    I Samuel 14:47–48
    A. Ammon
    B. Edom
    C. Egypt
    D. Zobah

11. Which one of the following men was **not** one of King Saul's sons?

    I Samuel 14:49

    A. Ishui
    B. Ithamar
    C. Jonathan
    D. Melchishua

12. Who were King Saul's daughters?

    I Samuel 14:49

    A. Leah and Rachel
    B. Merab and Michal
    C. Sarah and Zipporah
    D. Tamar and Dinah

13. Who was King Saul's wife?

    I Samuel 14:50

    A. Abigail
    B. Abishag
    C. Ahinoam
    D. Aholibah

14. Who was the captain of the army of Israel?

    I Samuel 14:50

    A. Abner
    B. Heber
    C. Jether
    D. Peter

15. Who was King Saul's father?

    I Samuel 14:51

    A. Kadmiel
    B. Kareah
    C. Kenaz
    D. Kish

16. What was the total number of men who gathered in Telaim to fight against the Philistines?

    I Samuel 15:4

    A. 21
    B. 210
    C. 21,000
    D. 210,000

17. Whom did the army of Israel spare in an Amalek city?

    I Samuel 15:5–6

    A. The Ammonites
    B. The Buzites
    C. The Kenites
    D. The Moabites

18. Who was the king of the Amalekites?

    I Samuel 15:8–20, 15:32–33

    A. King Agag
    B. King Doeg
    C. King Peleg
    D. King Serug

19. Who ordered Israel to spare the Amalekite livestock?

    I Samuel 15:9–26

    A. Captain of the host
    B. God
    C. Samuel
    D. Saul

20. Where did Samuel slay the king of the Amalekites?

    I Samuel 15:33

    A. Gerar
    B. Gezer
    C. Gibeah
    D. Gilgal

*Answers on page 758

Lesson 93
Today's Reading: *I Samuel 16–17*
Period of Time: 1063 BC
Author: Unknown

1. What did Samuel tell King Saul when he asked him why he was going to Bethlehem?
   I Samuel 16:1–4
   A. He did not tell him anything.
   B. He told him to mind his own business.
   C. He was going there to anoint Israel's next king.
   D. He was taking a heifer there to make a sacrifice to the LORD.

2. How many sons did Jesse have?
   I Samuel 16:10–11, 17:12
   A. 7
   B. 8
   C. 10
   D. 12

3. How does the Bible describe David?
   I Samuel 16:12
   A. Confident, proud, and athletic
   B. Creative, slow to anger, and agile
   C. Pale, tall, and muscular
   D. Ruddy, beautiful, and handsome

4. How does one of King Saul's servants describe David?
   I Samuel 16:18
   A. Brilliant, talented, and stocky
   B. Colossal, quick-tempered, and honest
   C. Mighty, valiant, and prudent
   D. Tall, dark, and handsome

5. Which one of the following did Jesse send as a gift to King Saul?
   I Samuel 16:20
   A. Almonds
   B. Bread
   C. Dates
   D. Figs

6. What job did King Saul give to David?
   I Samuel 16:21
   A. Armourbearer
   B. Captain of the host
   C. Orchestra conductor
   D. Stable hand

7. What musical instrument did David play to calm King Saul?
   I Samuel 16:23
   A. Flute
   B. Harp
   C. Lyre
   D. Trumpet

8. Which city was Goliath from?
   I Samuel 17:4
   A. Baalath
   B. Gath
   C. Hamath
   D. Naarath

9. How tall was Goliath?
   I Samuel 17:4
   A. 4 cubits and 1 span
   B. 5 cubits and 2 spans
   C. 6 cubits and 1 span
   D. 7 cubits and 2 spans

10. How many shekels of brass did Goliath's coat of mail weigh?
    I Samuel 17:5
    A. 2,000
    B. 3,000
    C. 4,000
    D. 5,000

11. How many shekels of iron did the head of Goliath's spear weigh?
    I Samuel 17:7
    A. 100
    B. 300
    C. 600
    D. 1,000

12. Which of Jesse's sons were in King Saul's army?
    I Samuel 17:13
    A. Eliab, Abinadab, and Shammah
    B. Nethaneel, Hobab, and Gershon
    C. Ozem, Joash, and Jobab
    D. Raddai, Shimri, and Chileab

13. How many days did Goliath challenge the army of Israel?
    I Samuel 17:16
    A. 10
    B. 20
    C. 30
    D. 40

14. How many loaves of bread and cheeses did David take to his brothers and their captain?
    I Samuel 17:17–18
    A. 3 loaves of bread and 6 cheeses
    B. 5 loaves of bread and 5 cheeses
    C. 7 loaves of bread and 3 cheeses
    D. 10 loaves of bread and 10 cheeses

15. In which valley did the armies of Israel and the Philistines do battle?
    I Samuel 17:19
    A. Valley of Elah
    B. Valley of Jehoshaphat
    C. Valley of Rephaim
    D. Valley of Shaveh

16. Which one of David's brothers rebuked him?
    I Samuel 17:28
    A. Chileab
    B. Eliab
    C. Hobab
    D. Jobab

17. Which wild animal—besides a bear—did David kill?
    I Samuel 17:34–36
    A. A boar
    B. A leopard
    C. A lion
    D. A wolf

18. How many stones did David place in his bag?
    I Samuel 17:40
    A. 5
    B. 6
    C. 7
    D. 8

19. Where did David take the head of Goliath?
    I Samuel 17:54
    A. Jagur
    B. Jericho
    C. Jerusalem
    D. Jethlah

20. Who was the captain of the army of Israel?
    I Samuel 17:55
    A. Abner
    B. Eber
    C. Hepher
    D. Jesher

Answers on page 758

APRIL 4

Lesson 94
Today's Reading: *I Samuel 18–20*
Period of Time: 1063–1060 BC
Author: Unknown

1. What was one of the items Jonathan gave to David?
   I Samuel 18:4
   - **A.** A chariot
   - **B.** A harp
   - **C.** A pigeon
   - **D.** A sword

2. Which musical instrument—mentioned in I Samuel 18:6—did the women play for David?
   I Samuel 18:6
   - **A.** Cornets
   - **B.** Drums
   - **C.** Psalteries
   - **D.** Tabrets

3. How many Philistines did the women claim David slew?
   I Samuel 18:7
   - **A.** Hundreds
   - **B.** Thousands
   - **C.** Ten thousands
   - **D.** Hundred thousands

4. How many times did King Saul try to kill David with a javelin?
   I Samuel 18:10–11, 19:10
   - **A.** 2
   - **B.** 3
   - **C.** 4
   - **D.** 5

5. How many men did King Saul put under David's command?
   I Samuel 18:12–13
   - **A.** 600
   - **B.** 1,000
   - **C.** 1,200
   - **D.** 2,000

6. Who was King Saul's oldest daughter?
   I Samuel 18:17
   - **A.** Mahalath
   - **B.** Mara
   - **C.** Merab
   - **D.** Miriam

7. What was Adriel's surname?
   I Samuel 18:19
   - **A.** The Meholathite
   - **B.** The Naamathite
   - **C.** The Phoenician
   - **D.** The Sidonian

8. How many Philistine foreskins did King Saul demand from David?
   I Samuel 18:25
   - **A.** 100
   - **B.** 200
   - **C.** 500
   - **D.** 1,000

9. How many Philistine foreskins did David bring to King Saul?
   I Samuel 18:26–27
   - **A.** 100
   - **B.** 200
   - **C.** 500
   - **D.** 1,000

10. Who was David's first wife?
    I Samuel 18:27
    - **A.** Abigail
    - **B.** Bathsheba
    - **C.** Haggith
    - **D.** Michal

11. Who told David that King Saul wanted to kill him?
    I Samuel 19:1–2
    - **A.** Abinadab
    - **B.** Jonathan
    - **C.** Malchishua
    - **D.** Mephibosheth

12. In which city did David find Samuel?
    I Samuel 19:18
    A. Nobah
    B. Parah
    C. Ramah
    D. Salcah

13. Where did David and Samuel go to dwell?
    I Samuel 19:18
    A. Bealoth
    B. Kedemoth
    C. Naioth
    D. Ramoth

14. What happened when King Saul's men came upon the company of prophets?
    I Samuel 19:19–21
    A. The prophets killed them.
    B. They cut out the prophet's tongues.
    C. They murdered the prophets.
    D. They prophesied alongside the prophets.

15. What did the town of Sechu contain?
    I Samuel 19:22
    A. A deep tar pit
    B. A fine winery
    C. A great well
    D. A secret tunnel

16. What did King Saul do when he came to the place Samuel was in?
    I Samuel 19:23–24
    A. He paid the town witch to cast a spell on David and Samuel.
    B. He stripped off all of his clothes and prophesied.
    C. He tortured Samuel throughout the night.
    D. He was duped by the people into believing that Saul and David had already fled.

17. How many days did David hide in a field to avoid capture by Saul?
    I Samuel 20:5–35
    A. 1
    B. 3
    C. 5
    D. 7

18. Where did Jonathan tell King Saul that David had traveled to?
    I Samuel 20:6, 20:28
    A. Bethlehem
    B. Gibeon
    C. Jericho
    D. Mizpah

19. Who sat at King Saul's dinner table?
    I Samuel 20:24–25
    A. Abner
    B. Becher
    C. Hepher
    D. Shemer

20. Which signal did Jonathan use to inform David that King Saul still wanted to kill him?
    I Samuel 20:19–39
    A. He blew a ram's horn.
    B. He dropped a note on a trail.
    C. He lit torches on the castle wall.
    D. He shot arrows into a field.

*Answers on page 758

APRIL 5

Lesson 95
Today's Reading: *I Samuel 21–24*
Period of Time: 1060–1057 BC
Author: Unknown

1. In which city did David speak with Ahimelech?
   I Samuel 21:1
   A. Dor
   B. Gog
   C. Nob
   D. Tob

2. What type of bread did Ahimelech give to David?
   I Samuel 21:2–6
   A. Cornbread
   B. Shewbread
   C. Toasted Bread
   D. Zopf Bread

3. What was Doeg's title?
   I Samuel 21:7
   A. Captain of the guard
   B. Chariot driver
   C. Chief of Saul's herdsmen
   D. Commander of the horsemen

4. What did Ahimelech give David?
   I Samuel 21:9
   A. David's slingshot
   B. Goliath's sword
   C. Jonathan's bow
   D. Saul's javelin

5. Who was the king of Gath?
   I Samuel 21:10
   A. King Achish
   B. King Ben-ha'dad
   C. King Sennacherib
   D. King Xerxes

6. What did the king of Gath call David?
   I Samuel 21:10–15
   A. A brave warrior
   B. A mad man
   C. A military genius
   D. A talented musician

7. Where did David go after he left Gath?
   I Samuel 22:1
   A. The cave Adullam
   B. The house of Dagon
   C. The valley of Megiddo
   D. The witch of Endor's home

8. Approximately how many men joined David before he traveled to Mizpeh?
   I Samuel 22:1–3
   A. 100
   B. 200
   C. 400
   D. 800

9. Which nation was the king from that gave David's parents asylum?
   I Samuel 22:3–4
   A. Ammon
   B. Edom
   C. Midian
   D. Moab

10. Who told David to go to Judah?
    I Samuel 22:5
    A. Eldad
    B. Gad
    C. Medad
    D. Oded

11. Where was Doeg from?
    I Samuel 22:9, 22:18
    A. Edom
    B. Midian
    C. Philistia
    D. Sinai

12. How many priests did Doeg slay?
    I Samuel 22:18
    A. 12
    B. 58
    C. 60
    D. 85

13. Who informed David of the slaughter of the priests?

    I Samuel 22:20–21

    A. Abiathar
    B. Eleazar
    C. Ibhar
    D. Kedar

14. Which town did David deliver from the Philistines?

    I Samuel 23:1–5

    A. Iphtah
    B. Juttah
    C. Keilah
    D. Lebonah

15. Which wilderness did David flee to?

    I Samuel 23:13–15

    A. Wilderness of Beersheba
    B. Wilderness of Paran
    C. Wilderness of Shur
    D. Wilderness of Ziph

16. Who visited David while he was hiding in the wilderness?

    I Samuel 23:16–18

    A. Ahitub
    B. Jonathan
    C. Michal
    D. Samuel

17. Where is the hill of Hachilah located?

    I Samuel 23:19

    A. East of Eden
    B. North of Betharabah
    C. South of Jeshimon
    D. West of Debir

18. Who invaded Israel, delaying King Saul's hunt for David?

    I Samuel 23:27–28

    A. The Gadarenes
    B. The Hagarenes
    C. The Libertines
    D. The Philistines

19. What did David do to King Saul while he slept in a cave?

    I Samuel 24:1–5

    A. Cut off a piece of his robe
    B. Placed a goat's head in his bed
    C. Removed the tips to his arrows
    D. Stole his sword

20. What did King Saul do after David told him he had spared his life?

    I Samuel 24:16

    A. Called David a liar and a dog
    B. Cursed God
    C. Vowed to one day kill David
    D. Wept

*Answers on page 758

APRIL 6

Lesson 96
Today's Reading: *I Samuel 25–27*
Period of Time: 1057 BC
Author: Unknown

1. In which city was Samuel's body laid to rest?
   I Samuel 25:1
   - **A.** Baalah
   - **B.** Parah
   - **C.** Ramah
   - **D.** Saqqarah

2. Where was Nabal shearing his sheep?
   I Samuel 25:2–3
   - **A.** Bethel
   - **B.** Carmel
   - **C.** Neiel
   - **D.** Peniel

3. How many sheep did Nabal own?
   I Samuel 25:2–3
   - **A.** 1,000
   - **B.** 2,000
   - **C.** 3,000
   - **D.** 4,000

4. How many goats did Nabal own?
   I Samuel 25:2–3
   - **A.** 1,000
   - **B.** 2,000
   - **C.** 3,000
   - **D.** 4,000

5. Who was Nabal's wife?
   I Samuel 25:3
   - **A.** Abigail
   - **B.** Abihail
   - **C.** Abijah
   - **D.** Abital

6. How many men did David send to Nabal?
   I Samuel 25:5
   - **A.** 2
   - **B.** 3
   - **C.** 7
   - **D.** 10

7. What did Nabal give to David's men?
   I Samuel 25:10–11
   - **A.** 10 loaves of bread
   - **B.** 20 bottles of wine
   - **C.** 300 young chickens
   - **D.** Nothing

8. Approximately how many men went with David to kill Nabal?
   I Samuel 25:13
   - **A.** 200
   - **B.** 400
   - **C.** 600
   - **D.** 800

9. How does the Bible describe Nabal's character?
   I Samuel 25:3, 25:17
   - **A.** Anxious and jumpy
   - **B.** Charming and humble
   - **C.** Depressed and forgetful
   - **D.** Evil and churlish

10. What did Nabal's wife give to David and his men?
    I Samuel 25:18–35
    - **A.** 3 kegs of beer
    - **B.** 5 dressed sheep
    - **C.** 100 clusters of grapes
    - **D.** Nothing

11. What name did David use when referring to God?
    I Samuel 25:32
    - **A.** El Shaddai
    - **B.** Jehovah
    - **C.** LORD God of Israel
    - **D.** Yahweh

12. Who were David's wives?

    I Samuel 25:39–43

    A. Abigail and Ahinoam
    B. Adah and Aholibamah
    C. Mary and Martha
    D. Rachel and Leah

13. Whom did King Saul give David's wife, Michal, to?

    I Samuel 25:44

    A. Phalee
    B. Phallu
    C. Phalti
    D. Pharaoh

14. How many men accompanied King Saul into the wilderness of Ziph?

    I Samuel 26:1–2

    A. 1,000
    B. 3,000
    C. 6,000
    D. 8,000

15. Who sneaked into King Saul's camp at night with David?

    I Samuel 26:6–12

    A. Abishai
    B. Ahimelech
    C. Asaph
    D. Attai

16. What did David steal from King Saul in the middle of the night?

    I Samuel 26:11–12

    A. His armor and a basket of fruit
    B. His blanket and lyre
    C. His cloak and dagger
    D. His spear and a cruse of water

17. Who was the king of Gath?

    I Samuel 27:2

    A. King Achish
    B. King Gibbar
    C. King Japhia
    D. King Mattan

18. Which town did the king of Gath give to David?

    I Samuel 27:6

    A. Bethlehem
    B. Jerusalem
    C. Tyre
    D. Ziklag

19. How many months did David dwell in the country of the Philistines?

    I Samuel 27:7

    A. 8
    B. 16
    C. 18
    D. 26

20. Which one of the following is one of the three nations that David invaded?

    I Samuel 27:8–9

    A. The Ashurites
    B. The Berites
    C. The Gezrites
    D. The Hagarites

*Answers on page 758

Lesson 97
Today's Reading: *I Samuel 28–31*
Period of Time: 1056–1055 BC
Author: Unknown

APRIL 7

1. Whom did King Saul expel from the land?
   I Samuel 28:3
   A. Giants
   B. Hittites
   C. Prophets
   D. Wizards

2. In which town did King Saul visit a witch?
   I Samuel 28:7–8
   A. Abdon
   B. Endor
   C. Gibeah
   D. Hebron

3. What did the witch tell King Saul?
   I Samuel 28:13
   A. Saul's army would destroy the Philistine army.
   B. She observed Rachel weeping for her slaughtered children.
   C. She saw gods ascending out of the earth.
   D. The youngest son of Saul would overthrow him.

4. Who was to become king of Israel after King Saul died?
   I Samuel 28:17
   A. David
   B. Jonathan
   C. Rehoboam
   D. Solomon

5. Why did God take the kingdom away from King Saul?
   I Samuel 28:18
   A. He did not build a temple unto God in the holy city.
   B. He failed to capture and execute the son of Jesse.
   C. He had too many wives, horses, and taxed the people too much.
   D. He refused to execute God's wrath upon the Amalekites.

6. Which type of meat did King Saul eat for his last supper?
   I Samuel 28:22–25
   A. Beef
   B. Chicken
   C. Fish
   D. Lamb

7. Which name did the Philistines use when referring to the Israelites?
   I Samuel 29:3
   A. Circumcised people
   B. Hebrews
   C. Israelites
   D. Jews

8. Who did **not** trust David and refused to let him go with them into battle?
   I Samuel 29:1–7
   A. Achish, the king of Gath
   B. Saul and his sons
   C. The princes of the Philistines
   D. The Roman soldiers under Augustus

9. Who burned Ziklag to the ground?
   I Samuel 30:1–2
   A. The Amalekites
   B. The Edomites
   C. The Moabites
   D. The Philistines

10. Who were David's wives?
    I Samuel 30:5
    A. Ahinoam and Abigail
    B. Gomer and Eunice
    C. Orpah and Jezebel
    D. Vashti and Naomi

11. Which one of the following was a priest?
    I Samuel 30:7
    A. Abiathar
    B. Barabbas
    C. Naphtali
    D. Philemon

12. What did David use to determine whether it was God's will to pursue those guilty of destroying Ziklag?
    I Samuel 30:7–8
    A. A crystal ball
    B. Astrology
    C. Tarot cards
    D. The ephod

13. Where did David leave 200 of his men who were too weak to continue?
    I Samuel 30:9–10
    A. The armory in Nob
    B. The brook Besor
    C. The cave of Adullam
    D. The house of Dagon

14. Who led David to the enemy's location?
    I Samuel 30:11–16
    A. A Kenite
    B. A Moabite
    C. An Egyptian
    D. An Ishmaelite

15. Upon which mountain was Saul and his army defeated by the Philistines?
    I Samuel 31:1–8
    A. Mount Ararat
    B. Mount Baalah
    C. Mount Carmel
    D. Mount Gilboa

16. Which one of the following was **not** King Saul's son?
    I Samuel 31:2
    A. Abinadab
    B. Habakkuk
    C. Jonathan
    D. Melchishua

17. Where did the Philistines place King Saul's armor?
    I Samuel 31:10
    A. House of Artemis
    B. House of Ashtaroth
    C. House of Gilgal
    D. House of Haman

18. What was the name of the city where the Philistines hung King Saul's body on a wall?
    I Samuel 31:10
    A. Baris
    B. Bashan
    C. Bethshan
    D. Bethzur

19. In which town did the Israelites cremate the bodies of King Saul and his sons?
    I Samuel 31:11–12
    A. Bethlehemjudah
    B. Gibeah
    C. Hebron
    D. Jabesh-gilead

20. How many days did the Israelites fast after burying the remains of King Saul and his sons?
    I Samuel 31:13
    A. 3
    B. 6
    C. 7
    D. 10

*Answers on page 759

APRIL 8

Lesson 98
Today's Reading: *II Samuel 1–3*
Period of Time: 1055–1048 BC
Author: Unknown

1. What did the man—who claimed he killed King Saul—state that he was?
   II Samuel 1:1–13

   A. A Hittite
   B. A Moabite
   C. An Amalekite
   D. An Egyptian

2. Upon which mountain was King Saul killed?
   II Samuel 1:6

   A. Mount Carmel
   B. Mount Gilboa
   C. Mount Mariah
   D. Mount Sinai

3. What did the man—who claimed he killed King Saul—take from him?
   II Samuel 1:10

   A. His armor and spear
   B. His bow and robe
   C. His crown and bracelet
   D. His sword and shield

4. What did David do to the man who claimed he had killed King Saul?
   II Samuel 1:13–16

   A. Banished him from the land
   B. Killed him
   C. Made him an officer in David's army
   D. Paid him 30 pieces of silver

5. Which book contains instructions on how to use a bow?
   II Samuel 1:18

   A. Book of Jasher
   B. Book of life
   C. Book of the wars of the LORD
   D. Book of wars

6. How old was Ishbosheth when he became king over the northern tribes?
   II Samuel 2:8–10

   A. 25 years old
   B. 30 years old
   C. 35 years old
   D. 40 years old

7. How long did Ishbosheth rule as king over the northern tribes?
   II Samuel 2:10

   A. 2 years
   B. 5 years and 3 months
   C. 7 years
   D. 12 years and 7 months

8. How many years did King David rule in Hebron over the house of Judah?
   II Samuel 2:10–11

   A. 2 years
   B. 3 years and 5 months
   C. 5 years
   D. 7 years and 6 months

9. Which one of the following men was **not** one of Zeruiah's sons?
   II Samuel 2:18

   A. Abishai
   B. Asahel
   C. Joab
   D. Joel

10. Which one of Zeruiah's sons did Abner kill?
    II Samuel 2:19–23

    A. Abishai
    B. Asahel
    C. Joab
    D. Joel

11. How many of King David's men did Abner and his men kill?

    II Samuel 2:30

    A. 20
    B. 40
    C. 200
    D. 400

12. How many of Abner's men did King David's men kill?

    II Samuel 2:31

    A. 60
    B. 260
    C. 360
    D. 460

13. Who was King David's firstborn son?

    II Samuel 3:2

    A. Amnon
    B. Chileab
    C. Ithream
    D. Shephatiah

14. Who was King David's secondborn son?

    II Samuel 3:3

    A. Amnon
    B. Chileab
    C. Ithream
    D. Shephatiah

15. Who was King David's fifthborn son?

    II Samuel 3:4

    A. Amnon
    B. Chileab
    C. Ithream
    D. Shephatiah

16. Who was King David's sixthborn son?

    II Samuel 3:5

    A. Amnon
    B. Chileab
    C. Ithream
    D. Shephatiah

17. Which of King Saul's concubines was Abner accused of having sex with?

    II Samuel 3:7

    A. Peninnah
    B. Rizpah
    C. Sarah
    D. Tabitha

18. Which wife did King David want back from Phaltiel?

    II Samuel 3:13–15

    A. Abigail
    B. Ahinoam
    C. Maacah
    D. Michal

19. Which two brothers killed Abner?

    II Samuel 3:27–30

    A. Abishai and Joab
    B. Absalom and Ithream
    C. Adonijah and Shephatiah
    D. Asahel and Joel

20. In which city was Abner's body laid to rest?

    II Samuel 3:32

    A. Bethlehem
    B. Gibeon
    C. Hebron
    D. Mahanaim

*Answers on page 759

APRIL 9

Lesson 99
Today's Reading: *II Samuel 4–7*
Period of Time: 1048–1044 BC
Author: Unknown

1. Where did the Beerothites flee to?
   II Samuel 4:2–3
   A. Adithaim
   B. Gittaim
   C. Mahanaim
   D. Zemaraim

2. Who became lame when his nurse dropped him as a child?
   II Samuel 4:4
   A. Mattaniah
   B. Melchizedek
   C. Mephibosheth
   D. Merodach-baladan

3. Who killed Ishbosheth?
   II Samuel 4:5–6
   A. Baanah and Rechab
   B. Mark and Barnabas
   C. Paul and Silas
   D. Trophimus and Tychicus

4. Where did King David hang the dead bodies of the men who killed Ishbosheth?
   II Samuel 4:12
   A. Bethlehem
   B. Hebron
   C. Sidon
   D. Tyre

5. Where was the head of Ishbosheth buried?
   II Samuel 4:12
   A. In the sepulcher of Abner
   B. In the valley of Rephaim
   C. Near the pool of Siloam
   D. Under the palm tree of Deborah

6. Where was King David anointed king over all of Israel?
   II Samuel 5:3
   A. Gibeah
   B. Hebron
   C. Jerusalem
   D. Mahanaim

7. Who occupied Jerusalem before being overthrown by King David?
   II Samuel 5:6
   A. The Ammonites
   B. The Gibeonites
   C. The Jebusites
   D. The Perizzites

8. How did King David's army capture Jerusalem?
   II Samuel 5:7–8
   A. They besieged the city and forced its occupants to surrender.
   B. They blew their trumpets on the seventh day and the walls fell down.
   C. They built a machine to knock down the walls.
   D. They entered the city through a gutter.

9. What did King David call Jerusalem after he captured it?
   II Samuel 5:9
   A. The city of David
   B. The city on a hill
   C. The holy city
   D. The new Jerusalem

10. Who was the king of Tyre?
    II Samuel 5:11
    A. King Cyrus
    B. King Darius
    C. King Hiram
    D. King Joram

11. Which one of the following was **not** King David's son?
    II Samuel 5:13–16
    A. Eliada
    B. Nathan
    C. Solomon
    D. Timothy

12. Who attacked Israel when it learned King David had become the king of Israel?

    II Samuel 5:17

    A. The Assyrians
    B. The Egyptians
    C. The Philistines
    D. The Sabeans

13. Where was the ark of the covenant being kept before King David brought it to Jerusalem?

    II Samuel 6:3

    A. House of Abinadab
    B. House of Dagon
    C. House of Micah
    D. House of Rimmon

14. Whom did God smite for touching the ark of the covenant?

    II Samuel 6:6–7

    A. Ahioh
    B. Dumah
    C. Terah
    D. Uzzah

15. How long did the ark of the covenant stay in the house of Obededom?

    II Samuel 6:11

    A. 2 months
    B. 2 months and 3 days
    C. 3 months
    D. 3 months and 2 days

16. Which one of King David's wives despised him when she saw him dancing before the LORD?

    II Samuel 6:16

    A. Abigail
    B. Michal
    C. Rizpah
    D. Zillah

17. What was **not** given to each person when the ark of the covenant was brought to Jerusalem?

    II Samuel 6:19

    A. A cake of bread
    B. A flagon of wine
    C. A portion of meat
    D. A wedge of cheese

18. What was the total number of children Michal bore to King David and Phaltiel?

    II Samuel 6:23

    A. 0
    B. 7
    C. 11
    D. 12

19. Which prophet advised King David?

    II Samuel 7:2

    A. Elijah
    B. Nathan
    C. Phinehas
    D. Samuel

20. What did God promise King David?

    II Samuel 7:16

    A. David would live to a ripe old age.
    B. David would one day build the LORD a great temple.
    C. David's army would have victory over the Egyptians.
    D. David's throne would be established forever.

Answers on page 759

APRIL 10

Lesson 100
Today's Reading: *II Samuel 8–11*
Period of Time: 1044–1035 BC
Author: Unknown

1. Whom did King David conquer and divide?
   II Samuel 8:2
   A. The Ammonites
   B. The Edomites
   C. The Hittites
   D. The Moabites

2. Who was the king of Zobah?
   II Samuel 8:3
   A. King Hadadezer
   B. King Immer
   C. King Jesher
   D. King Sopater

3. How many chariots did King David take from the king of Zobah?
   II Samuel 8:4
   A. 10
   B. 100
   C. 1,000
   D. 10,000

4. What did King David take from the king of Zobah's men?
   II Samuel 8:7
   A. Arrows of silver
   B. Shields of gold
   C. Spears of brass
   D. Vessels of iron

5. Who was the king of Hamath?
   II Samuel 8:9
   A. King Ard
   B. King Buz
   C. King Rei
   D. King Toi

6. Which gifts did the king of Hamath send to King David?
   II Samuel 8:10
   A. Cattle, sheep, and bottles of wine
   B. Chariots made of iron and 100 horses
   C. Loaves of bread to feed David's army
   D. Vessels of gold, silver, and brass

7. In which valley did King David kill 18,000 Syrian men?
   II Samuel 8:13
   A. Valley of Achor
   B. Valley of Lebanon
   C. Valley of salt
   D. Valley of Zared

8. Who was the commander of King David's army?
   II Samuel 8:16
   A. Abinadab
   B. Joab
   C. Mezahab
   D. Nadab

9. Who were the priests during King David's reign?
   II Samuel 8:17
   A. Ahimelech and Zadok
   B. Eleazar and Uzzi
   C. Johanan and Azariah
   D. Phinehas and Hilkiah

10. Who was the scribe during King David's reign?
    II Samuel 8:17
    A. Nedabiah
    B. Obadiah
    C. Raamiah
    D. Seraiah

11. Who was Jonathan's son?
    II Samuel 9:6
    A. Heth
    B. Japheth
    C. Mephibosheth
    D. Peleth

12. Who was Jonathan's grandson?

    II Samuel 9:12

    A. Micah
    B. Micaiah
    C. Micha
    D. Michael

13. Who was the king of Ammon?

    II Samuel 10:1

    A. King Beanun
    B. King Hanun
    C. King Jeduthun
    D. King Nun

14. What did the king of Ammon do to King David's messengers?

    II Samuel 10:4–5

    A. Flogged them across their backs and threw them into jail
    B. Paid them 100 pieces of gold to assassinate David and his general
    C. Shaved half of their beards and cut off half of their clothes
    D. Sold them 100 lame horses and 50 iron chariots with faulty wheels

15. Who was Joab's brother?

    II Samuel 10:10

    A. Abishai
    B. Naarai
    C. Sheshai
    D. Zabbai

16. Which army did Joab fight against while his brother fought against another army?

    II Samuel 10:11

    A. The Ammonite army
    B. The Egyptian army
    C. The Midianite army
    D. The Syrian army

17. Which army did Joab's brother fight against while Joab fought against another army?

    II Samuel 10:11

    A. The Ammonite army
    B. The Egyptian army
    C. The Midianite army
    D. The Syrian army

18. Who was Uriah's wife?

    II Samuel 11:3

    A. Bathsheba
    B. Elisheba
    C. Jehosheba
    D. Shelomith

19. What was Uriah's surname?

    II Samuel 11:3

    A. The Ammonite
    B. The Hittite
    C. The Moabite
    D. The Perizzite

20. How did King David kill Uriah?

    II Samuel 11:15–17

    A. He fed Uriah toxic mushrooms.
    B. He placed Uriah in the heat of a battle.
    C. He poisoned Uriah's wine.
    D. He smote Uriah under the fifth rib.

*Answers on page 759

APRIL 11

Lesson 101
Today's Reading: *II Samuel 12–13*
Period of Time: 1034–1030 BC
Author: Unknown

1. Who told King David, "Thou art the man"?
   II Samuel 12:1–7
   A. Absalom
   B. Jesse
   C. Nathan
   D. Uriah

2. How did King David kill Uriah?
   II Samuel 12:9
   A. He drowned him in a pool.
   B. He poisoned him with mushrooms.
   C. He sent him into a deadly battle.
   D. He shot him with an arrow in the chest.

3. What was Uriah's surname?
   II Samuel 12:9
   A. The Ammonite
   B. The Hittite
   C. The Midianite
   D. The Perizzite

4. Who told King David the sword would never depart from his house?
   II Samuel 12:7–10
   A. Absalom
   B. Jesse
   C. Nathan
   D. Uriah

5. Who told King David his wives would one day be raped in public?
   II Samuel 12:7–11
   A. Abinadab
   B. Eliab
   C. Ibhar
   D. Nathan

6. How many days did King David and Bathsheba's first child live?
   II Samuel 12:18
   A. 2
   B. 3
   C. 5
   D. 7

7. What did King David say after his child died?
   II Samuel 12:23
   A. "He's in a better place now."
   B. "I shall go to him, but he shall not return to me."
   C. "I shall slay my enemies' sons before his eyes."
   D. "The LORD giveth, and the LORD taketh away."

8. What did King David name his and Bathsheba's second child?
   II Samuel 12:24
   A. Sargon
   B. Shimea
   C. Shobab
   D. Solomon

9. What did Nathan the prophet call King David and Bathsheba's second child?
   II Samuel 12:25
   A. Jedidiah
   B. Jeduthun
   C. Joab
   D. Jonadab

10. Who told King David to come and capture the royal city of Rabbah?
    II Samuel 12:26–28
    A. Absalom
    B. Doeg
    C. Eliam
    D. Joab

11. How many talents of gold did the king of Rabbah's crown weigh with its precious stones?
    II Samuel 12:26–30
    A. 1
    B. 2
    C. 3
    D. 4

12. Who was King David's daughter?

    II Samuel 13:1

    A. Tabitha
    B. Tamar
    C. Tryphena
    D. Tryphosa

13. Who was King David's nephew?

    II Samuel 13:3

    A. Jobab
    B. Jonadab
    C. Jonah
    D. Jozabad

14. Who was King David's brother?

    II Samuel 13:3

    A. Adonijah
    B. Ithream
    C. Shimeah
    D. Uriah

15. Who was in love with his sister?

    II Samuel 13:1–13

    A. Amnon
    B. Chilion
    C. Eglon
    D. Gershon

16. What did a daughter of King David wear if she was still a virgin?

    II Samuel 13:18

    A. A chastity belt
    B. A cover over her face
    C. A garment of divers colours
    D. A long white dress

17. How many years after King David's son raped his sister was he murdered?

    II Samuel 13:23–29

    A. 2
    B. 3
    C. 5
    D. 7

18. Which of King David's sons murdered his brother?

    II Samuel 13:28–29

    A. Absalom
    B. Nethanel
    C. Raddai
    D. Shimea

19. Who was the king of Geshur?

    II Samuel 13:37

    A. King Abishai
    B. King Barzillai
    C. King Hushai
    D. King Talmai

20. Which one of King David's sons lived in Geshur for 3 years?

    II Samuel 13:37–38

    A. Abner
    B. Absalom
    C. Adonijah
    D. Amnon

*Answers on page 759

APRIL 12

Lesson 102
Today's Reading: *II Samuel 14–15*
Period of Time: 1027–1023 BC
Author: Unknown

1. Who was Joab's father?
   II Samuel 14:1
   A. Chenaniah
   B. Kareah
   C. Telah
   D. Zeruiah

2. Where was the woman from that Joab sent to speak with King David?
   II Samuel 14:2–20
   A. Eshtemoa
   B. Gilboa
   C. Koa
   D. Tekoah

3. Where was Absalom living before Joab brought him back to Jerusalem?
   II Samuel 14:23
   A. Gath
   B. Geshur
   C. Gibeah
   D. Gozan

4. How much in shekels did Absalom's hair weigh after it was cut?
   II Samuel 14:26
   A. 100
   B. 200
   C. 300
   D. 400

5. How many sons and daughters did Absalom have?
   II Samuel 14:27
   A. 1 son and 2 daughters
   B. 2 sons and 4 daughters
   C. 3 sons and 1 daughter
   D. 4 sons and 3 daughters

6. How many years did Absalom dwell in Jerusalem—after his return—before he saw King David again?
   II Samuel 14:28
   A. 2
   B. 4
   C. 6
   D. 8

7. What did Absalom do to Joab for ignoring him?
   II Samuel 14:30
   A. Burned his barley fields
   B. Murdered his sons and brothers
   C. Raped his concubines
   D. Stole his idols

8. How many men ran in front of Absalom's chariot?
   II Samuel 15:1
   A. 20
   B. 30
   C. 40
   D. 50

9. Where did Absalom tell King David he wanted to go to pay his vows?
   II Samuel 15:7–9
   A. Ekron
   B. Hebron
   C. Migron
   D. Shimron

10. How many men from Jerusalem did Absalom invite to join him in his conspiracy against King David?
    II Samuel 15:11–12
    A. 100
    B. 150
    C. 200
    D. 250

11. Which one of King David's counselors joined the confederacy?

    II Samuel 15:12, 15:31

    A. Ahithophel
    B. Bethuel
    C. Mehujael
    D. Shebuel

12. Which city was King David's counselor from?

    II Samuel 15:12

    A. Aleppo
    B. Giloh
    C. Megiddo
    D. Shiloh

13. How many concubines did King David leave in Jerusalem?

    II Samuel 15:16

    A. 10
    B. 20
    C. 30
    D. 40

14. How many men from Gath joined King David?

    II Samuel 15:18

    A. 300
    B. 400
    C. 500
    D. 600

15. Who was the Gittite who refused to leave King David behind?

    II Samuel 15:19

    A. Amasai
    B. Dodai
    C. Ittai
    D. Maadai

16. Which brook did King David cross when he fled Jerusalem?

    II Samuel 15:23

    A. Brook Besor
    B. Brook Eschol
    C. Brook Kidron
    D. Brook Zered

17. Who was Zadok's son?

    II Samuel 15:27

    A. Ahimaaz
    B. Boaz
    C. Eliphaz
    D. Joahaz

18. Who was Abiathar's son?

    II Samuel 15:27

    A. Abidan
    B. Jonathan
    C. Ladan
    D. Shiphtan

19. Upon which mountain did King David weep?

    II Samuel 15:30

    A. Mount Carmel
    B. Mount Mariah
    C. Mount Nebo
    D. Mount Olivet

20. Whom did King David send back to Jerusalem to spy on Absalom?

    II Samuel 15:32–37

    A. Ezbai
    B. Gilalai
    C. Hushai
    D. Zillethai

*Answers on page 759

APRIL 13

Lesson 103
Today's Reading: *II Samuel 16–17*
Period of Time: 1023 BC
Author: Unknown

1. Who was Ziba's master?
   II Samuel 16:1
   A. Malachi
   B. Manasseh
   C. Melchizedek
   D. Mephibosheth

2. How many bottles of wine did Ziba bring to King David?
   II Samuel 16:1
   A. 1
   B. 10
   C. 100
   D. 1,000

3. How many loaves of bread did Ziba bring King David?
   II Samuel 16:1
   A. 200
   B. 400
   C. 600
   D. 800

4. Where did a man throw stones at King David?
   II Samuel 16:5
   A. Adithaim
   B. Bahurim
   C. Ephraim
   D. Mahanaim

5. Who threw stones at King David?
   II Samuel 16:5–14
   A. Haggai
   B. Michri
   C. Phalti
   D. Shimei

6. Who offered to take off the man's head who threw the stones at King David?
   II Samuel 16:9
   A. Abishai
   B. Jaanai
   C. Mebunnai
   D. Salmai

7. Which tribe did the man who threw the stones at King David belong to?
   II Samuel 16:11
   A. Tribe of Asher
   B. Tribe of Benjamin
   C. Tribe of Judah
   D. Tribe of Naphtali

8. Who was King David's friend—although he swore allegiance to Absalom?
   II Samuel 16:16–17:15
   A. Amasai
   B. Dodai
   C. Hushai
   D. Maasai

9. Who was a counselor to Absalom?
   II Samuel 16:20–21
   A. Adonizedek
   B. Ahithophel
   C. Andronicus
   D. Artaxerxes

10. Which lewd act did Absalom commit?
    II Samuel 16:21–22
    A. He married David's daughter.
    B. He murdered David's priests.
    C. He raped David's concubines.
    D. He set the City of David on fire.

11. Who convinced Absalom **not** to attack King David?
    II Samuel 17:6–14
    A. Amasai
    B. Dodai
    C. Hushai
    D. Maasai

12. Who were priests during King David's reign?
    II Samuel 17:15–16
    A. Abiathar and Zadok
    B. Caiaphas and Theophilus
    C. Eleazar and Joiada
    D. Phinehas and Abishua

13. Where did a lad see Jonathan and Ahimaaz talking to a woman?

    II Samuel 17:17–18

    A. Endor
    B. Engedi
    C. Enrogel
    D. Enshemesh

14. Where did Jonathan and Ahimaaz flee to after being seen by the lad?

    II Samuel 17:18

    A. Abronah
    B. Bahurim
    C. Cinnereth
    D. Dophkah

15. Where did the woman hide Jonathan and Ahimaaz?

    II Samuel 17:18–21

    A. Beneath the floor
    B. Down a well
    C. In the barn
    D. Upon the roof

16. Which river did King David and his people cross when they fled from Absalom?

    II Samuel 17:22

    A. River of Ahava
    B. River of Gihon
    C. River of Hiddekel
    D. River of Jordan

17. How did Ahithophel die?

    II Samuel 17:23

    A. Absalom poisoned him.
    B. David burned him at the stake.
    C. He died in battle.
    D. He hung himself.

18. Whom did Absalom make captain of the army?

    II Samuel 17:25

    A. Amasa
    B. Ethan
    C. Jubal
    D. Mamre

19. Where did Absalom pitch his tent?

    II Samuel 17:26

    A. Ammon
    B. Bashan
    C. Gilead
    D. Syria

20. Which of the following greeted King David in Mahanaim with many gifts?

    II Samuel 17:27–29

    A. Cain, Abel, Seth
    B. Eliphaz, Zophar, Bildad
    C. Mishael, Azariah, Hananiah
    D. Shobi, Machir, Barzillai

Answers on page 759

APRIL 14

Lesson 104
Today's Reading: *II Samuel 18–19*
Period of Time: 1023 BC
Author: Unknown

1. Who was Joab's brother?
   II Samuel 18:2
   A. Abishai
   B. Shobai
   C. Talmai
   D. Zabbai

2. Which one of King David's generals was a Gittite?
   II Samuel 18:2
   A. Ittai
   B. Paarai
   C. Shimshai
   D. Tattenai

3. Which small wooded area was the battle site between King David's army and Absalom's army?
   II Samuel 18:6–8
   A. Wood of Ararat
   B. Wood of Carmel
   C. Wood of Ephraim
   D. Wood of Nebo

4. How many of Absalom's men were slaughtered by the army of King David?
   II Samuel 18:7
   A. 10,000
   B. 20,000
   C. 30,000
   D. 40,000

5. Which statement is true concerning Absalom?
   II Samuel 18:9–10
   A. His bull rammed him in the lower back, severing his spinal cord.
   B. His camel kicked him in the head, rendering him unconscious.
   C. His horse bucked him, breaking his hip.
   D. His mule left him wedged in the branches of a tree.

6. How many shekels of silver did Joab tell a man he would have paid him if he had killed Absalom?
   II Samuel 18:10–11
   A. 5
   B. 10
   C. 15
   D. 20

7. What did Joab do to Absalom?
   II Samuel 18:14
   A. He placed an asp in Absalom's bed.
   B. He sent an arrow into Absalom's back.
   C. He stoned Absalom to death.
   D. He thrust 3 darts into Absalom's chest.

8. How many men helped Joab slay Absalom?
   II Samuel 18:15
   A. 2
   B. 3
   C. 10
   D. 12

9. What did Joab do with Absalom's dead body?
   II Samuel 18:17
   A. Buried it under stones
   B. Cremated it
   C. Fed it to dogs
   D. Hung it on a wall

10. Who erected a monument to himself in the king's dale because he had no sons to carry on his name?
    II Samuel 18:18
    A. Absalom
    B. David
    C. Joab
    D. Zadok

11. Who was Ahimaaz's father?

    II Samuel 18:19

    A. Bakbuk
    B. Ishbak
    C. Lemek
    D. Zadok

12. Whom did Ahimaaz outrun?

    II Samuel 18:19–32

    A. Aran
    B. Cushi
    C. Jogli
    D. Pildash

13. Who rebuked King David for mourning the death of Absalom?

    II Samuel 19:1–7

    A. Abda
    B. Heli
    C. Iddo
    D. Joab

14. Whom did King David appoint to replace Joab as commander of Israel's army?

    II Samuel 19:13

    A. Amariah
    B. Amasa
    C. Amasai
    D. Amashsai

15. Which tribe was Shimei a member of?

    II Samuel 19:16

    A. Tribe of Asher
    B. Tribe of Benjamin
    C. Tribe of Levi
    D. Tribe of Judah

16. How many of Ziba's sons and servants came with him to meet King David?

    II Samuel 19:17

    A. 5 sons and 10 servants
    B. 10 sons and 15 servants
    C. 15 sons and 20 servants
    D. 20 sons and 25 servants

17. Who wanted Shimei put to death for cursing the LORD's anointed?

    II Samuel 19:21

    A. Abishai
    B. Abishalom
    C. Abishua
    D. Abishur

18. Who was one of King Saul's sons?

    II Samuel 19:24

    A. Azmaveth
    B. Ishbosheth
    C. Jetheth
    D. Mephibosheth

19. How old was Barzillai when he declined King David's offer to go with him to Jerusalem?

    II Samuel 19:32–37

    A. 40 years old
    B. 60 years old
    C. 80 years old
    D. 100 years old

20. Who took Barzillai's place and went to Jerusalem with King David?

    II Samuel 19:37–40

    A. Azrikam
    B. Bishlam
    C. Chimham
    D. Hoham

Answers on page 759

APRIL 15

Lesson 105
Today's Reading: *II Samuel 20–22*
Period of Time: 1023–1018 BC
Author: Unknown

1. How many of King David's concubines lived as widows after he returned to Jerusalem?
   II Samuel 20:3
   A. 4
   B. 6
   C. 8
   D. 10

2. Who killed Amasa?
   II Samuel 20:8–10
   A. Ahab
   B. Eliab
   C. Joab
   D. Moab

3. In which city was Sheba's head thrown over a wall?
   II Samuel 20:14–22
   A. Abel of Beth-ma'achah
   B. Abelmeholah
   C. Abelmizraim
   D. Abelshittim

4. Who was the commander of the Cherethites and the Pelethites?
   II Samuel 20:23
   A. Ahiezer
   B. Benaiah
   C. Nahshon
   D. Phicol

5. Who was over the tribute?
   II Samuel 20:24
   A. Adoram
   B. Hadoram
   C. Jehoram
   D. Zimran

6. Who was the recorder?
   II Samuel 20:24
   A. Jehoram
   B. Jehoshaphat
   C. Jehosheba
   D. Jehozabad

7. Who was King David's scribe?
   II Samuel 20:25
   A. Aaron
   B. Jacob
   C. Maoch
   D. Sheva

8. Who were the priests when King David ruled over Israel?
   II Samuel 20:25
   A. Ahimelech and Jahaziel
   B. Eleazar and Ithamar
   C. Nadab and Abihu
   D. Zadok and Abiathar

9. Who was a chief ruler to King David?
   II Samuel 20:26
   A. Eli
   B. Hur
   C. Ira
   D. Lud

10. How many years was there a famine in Israel because King Saul slew the Gibeonites?
    II Samuel 21:1
    A. 2
    B. 3
    C. 6
    D. 7

11. Whom were the Gibeonites remnants of?
    II Samuel 21:2
    A. The Amorites
    B. The Benjamites
    C. The Cushites
    D. The Danites

12. How many of King Saul's descendants did the Gibeonites hang?
    II Samuel 21:3–9
    A. 2
    B. 3
    C. 7
    D. 9

13. Which city were the bones of King Saul, his sons, and those who were hanged buried in?
    II Samuel 21:12–14
    A. Rabbah
    B. Salcah
    C. Ummah
    D. Zelah

14. Who were sons of the giant Goliath?
    II Samuel 21:16–18
    A. Adonizedek and Jabin
    B. Ishbibenob and Saph
    C. Og and Magog
    D. Talmai and Sheshai

15. Who was a son of Zeruiah—King David's sister?
    II Samuel 21:17
    A. Abishai
    B. Arisai
    C. Athlai
    D. Attai

16. Who slew one of Goliath's sons?
    II Samuel 21:18
    A. Jehdeiah
    B. Potiphar
    C. Sibbechai
    D. Togarmah

17. Who slew Goliath's brother?
    II Samuel 21:19
    A. Elhanan
    B. Jokshan
    C. Memucan
    D. Shaphan

18. Who killed the giant who had six fingers upon each hand and six toes upon each foot?
    II Samuel 21:20–21
    A. Jokshan
    B. Jonathan
    C. Jotham
    D. Jozabad

19. How many sons of Goliath did Israel slay?
    II Samuel 21:22
    A. 2
    B. 3
    C. 4
    D. 5

20. What did King David do to thank God for delivering him from his enemies?
    II Samuel 22:1–51
    A. Built a temple
    B. Offered 1,000 bulls
    C. Planted a vineyard
    D. Sang a song

*Answers on page 759

APRIL 16

Lesson 106
Today's Reading: *II Samuel 23–24*
Period of Time: 1017 BC
Author: Unknown

1. Who was King David's father?
   II Samuel 23:1
   A. James
   B. Jesse
   C. Jonah
   D. Juniah

2. Who was a Tachmonite?
   II Samuel 23:8
   A. Adino the Eznite
   B. Elijah the Tishbite
   C. Eliphaz the Temanite
   D. Hamor the Hivite

3. Who was the son of Dodo?
   II Samuel 23:9
   A. Abiathar
   B. Eleazar
   C. Jozachar
   D. Mibhar

4. Who slew the Philistines in a field full of lentils?
   II Samuel 23:11–12
   A. Hashubah
   B. Iphdeiah
   C. Jaakobah
   D. Shammah

5. How many men risked their lives to bring King David water from the well of Bethlehem?
   II Samuel 23:13–16
   A. 2
   B. 3
   C. 10
   D. 12

6. Which brother of Joab became famous after he slew 300 men?
   II Samuel 23:18
   A. Abishai
   B. Barzillai
   C. Chelubai
   D. Dodai

7. Who slew a lion in a pit on a snowy day?
   II Samuel 23:20
   A. Azariah
   B. Benaiah
   C. Conaniah
   D. Delaiah

8. Who was Joab's brother?
   II Samuel 23:24
   A. Asahel
   B. Hillel
   C. Uzziel
   D. Zuriel

9. Who was Joab's armourbearer?
   II Samuel 23:37
   A. Kareah
   B. Laadan
   C. Mishma
   D. Nahari

10. Which one of King David's mighty men was a Hittite?
    II Samuel 23:39
    A. Ucal
    B. Unni
    C. Uriah
    D. Uriel

11. What was the total number of King David's mighty men?
    II Samuel 23:39
    A. 12
    B. 21
    C. 37
    D. 43

12. How long did it take to complete the census?
    II Samuel 24:1–8
    A. 3 months and 10 days
    B. 5 months and 17 days
    C. 6 months and 14 days
    D. 9 months and 20 days

13. How many valiant men lived in Israel?

    II Samuel 24:9

    A. 20,000
    B. 90,000
    C. 350,000
    D. 800,000

14. How many valiant men lived in Judah?

    II Samuel 24:9

    A. 80,000
    B. 100,000
    C. 500,000
    D. 1,000,000

15. Which prophet did the LORD send to King David after the census was completed?

    II Samuel 24:11–12

    A. Gad
    B. Ham
    C. Ira
    D. Koz

16. How many choices did the LORD offer King David as punishment for conducting the census?

    II Samuel 24:12–13

    A. 2
    B. 3
    C. 5
    D. 7

17. Which punishment did King David receive?

    II Samuel 24:12–15

    A. Famine for 7 years
    B. Flee 3 months from his enemies
    C. Heavy rainfall for 7 days
    D. Pestilence in the land for 3 days

18. How many men died because of King David's sin in numbering the people?

    II Samuel 24:15

    A. 30,000
    B. 60,000
    C. 70,000
    D. 90,000

19. What did King David see at the threshing floor of Araunah?

    II Samuel 24:16–17

    A. The angel of the LORD
    B. The ghost of Goliath
    C. The prince of the devils
    D. The spirit of Samuel

20. How many shekels of silver did King David pay Araunah for the threshing floor and oxen?

    II Samuel 24:24

    A. 25
    B. 40
    C. 50
    D. 75

Answers on page 759

Lesson 107

Today's Reading: *I Kings 1*
Period of Time: 1017–1015 BC
Author: Unknown

1. Who kept King David warm and cared for him during his last days?
   I Kings 1:1–4
   A. Abigail
   B. Abihail
   C. Abijah
   D. Abishag

2. Who was Adonijah's mother?
   I Kings 1:5
   A. Hagar
   B. Haggith
   C. Hannah
   D. Hazzelelponi

3. How many men ran in front of Adonijah's chariot?
   I Kings 1:5
   A. 30
   B. 40
   C. 50
   D. 60

4. Who was Adonijah's brother?
   I Kings 1:6
   A. Absalom
   B. Benaiah
   C. Joab
   D. Nathan

5. Who was Joab's mother?
   I Kings 1:7
   A. Abigail
   B. Bathsheba
   C. Michal
   D. Zeruiah

6. Who were the priests during the days of Adonijah?
   I Kings 1:7–8
   A. Abiathar and Zadok
   B. Eleazar and Ithamar
   C. Hophni and Phinehas
   D. Nadab and Abihu

7. Who was invited to Adonijah's feast?
   I Kings 1:7–10, 1:19
   A. Abiathar
   B. Benaiah
   C. Nathan
   D. Solomon

8. Who was Benaiah's father?
   I Kings 1:8
   A. Jehoiada
   B. Jehoiakim
   C. Jehonathan
   D. Jehoshaphat

9. Near which place did Adonijah hold his great feast?
   I Kings 1:9
   A. Endor
   B. Engedi
   C. Enrogel
   D. Enshemesh

10. Which one of the following was a prophet?
    I Kings 1:10
    A. Benaiah
    B. Nathan
    C. Solomon
    D. Zadok

11. Who was also Adonijah's brother?
    I Kings 1:10
    A. Esarhaddon
    B. Gideon
    C. Jalon
    D. Solomon

12. Who was Bathsheba's son?
    I Kings 1:11
    A. Benaiah
    B. Jonathan
    C. Rei
    D. Solomon

13. Which woman was a Shunammite?

    I Kings 1:15

    A. Abishag
    B. Bathsheba
    C. Candace
    D. Deborah

14. Who was captain of the host?

    I Kings 1:19

    A. Ahab
    B. Iddo
    C. Joab
    D. Nero

15. Who went with Bathsheba to discuss with King David which son should be the next king?

    I Kings 1:15–22

    A. Johanan
    B. Nathan
    C. Ornan
    D. Shalman

16. What did Solomon use that belonged to King David to ride to the place he was to be anointed?

    I Kings 1:33–39

    A. His chariot
    B. His horse
    C. His litter
    D. His mule

17. Where was Solomon anointed king of Israel?

    I Kings 1:33–39

    A. Aenon
    B. Gihon
    C. Pison
    D. Sidon

18. Who informed Adonijah that Solomon had been anointed king of Israel?

    I Kings 1:41–48

    A. Johanan
    B. Jonathan
    C. Joram
    D. Joshua

19. Where did Adonijah flee to?

    I Kings 1:50

    A. A Canaanite king
    B. One of the cities of refuge
    C. The horns of the altar
    D. The wilderness

20. What did Solomon do to Adonijah for trying to steal the kingdom from him?

    I Kings 1:50–53

    A. Burned him
    B. Hung him
    C. Spared him
    D. Stoned him

Answers on page 759

APRIL 18

Lesson 108
Today's Reading: *I Kings 2–3*
Period of Time: 1015–1013 BC
Author: Unknown

1. Which law did King David tell Solomon to obey?
   I Kings 2:3
   A. Law of Draco
   B. Law of Hammurabi
   C. Law of Moses
   D. Law of Solon

2. Who killed Abner and Amasa?
   I Kings 2:5
   A. Abiathar
   B. Benaiah
   C. Gera
   D. Joab

3. Whose sons did King David tell Solomon to treat with kindness?
   I Kings 2:7
   A. Abiathar's sons
   B. Absalom's sons
   C. Barzillai's sons
   D. Benaiah's sons

4. Who was Solomon's brother?
   I Kings 2:7
   A. Absalom
   B. Barzillai
   C. Joab
   D. Nathan

5. What was the total number of years David ruled in Hebron and Jerusalem?
   I Kings 2:11
   A. 10
   B. 20
   C. 30
   D. 40

6. Who was Adonijah's mother?
   I Kings 2:13
   A. Abigail
   B. Bathsheba
   C. Eglah
   D. Haggith

7. Whom did Adonijah want to marry?
   I Kings 2:17
   A. Abijah
   B. Abishag
   C. Abital
   D. Azubah

8. Who was King Solomon's mother?
   I Kings 2:13, 2:19
   A. Abigail
   B. Bathsheba
   C. Eglah
   D. Michal

9. Who slew Adonijah?
   I Kings 2:19–25
   A. Abner
   B. Absalom
   C. Benaiah
   D. Boanerges

10. Which city did King Solomon banish Abiathar to?
    I Kings 2:26
    A. Anathoth
    B. Berothai
    C. Damascus
    D. Ecbatana

11. Who slew Joab?
    I Kings 2:28–34
    A. Abiathar
    B. Benaiah
    C. Cornelius
    D. Dathan

12. Who replaced Joab as captain of the host?
    I Kings 2:35
    A. Abner
    B. Absalom
    C. Benaiah
    D. Benjamin

13. Who replaced Abiathar as high priest?
    I Kings 2:35
    A. Azariah
    B. Eliashib
    C. Jehoiada
    D. Zadok

14. How many years did Shimei live in Jerusalem before disobeying King Solomon's order **not** to leave the city?
    I Kings 2:39–40
    A. 2
    B. 3
    C. 5
    D. 7

15. Who was the king of Gath?
    I Kings 2:39
    A. King Achish
    B. King Eglon
    C. King Mesha
    D. King Rezin

16. Who slew Shimei?
    I Kings 2:41–46
    A. Abiathar
    B. Benaiah
    C. Joab
    D. Nathan

17. Which one of the following did King Solomon **not** build?
    I Kings 3:1
    A. The hanging gardens of Babylon
    B. The house of the LORD
    C. The palace in Jerusalem
    D. The wall of Jerusalem

18. Where did King Solomon offer a thousand burnt offerings?
    I Kings 3:4
    A. Gath
    B. Gerar
    C. Gibeon
    D. Gittaim

19. What did King Solomon ask from God?
    I Kings 3:11
    A. To become the wealthiest man ever
    B. To defeat all of his enemies
    C. To give him a long and peaceful life
    D. To give him wisdom to rule wisely

20. Which decision did King Solomon make regarding custody of a baby?
    I Kings 3:16–27
    A. Divide it in half with a sword
    B. Give it to the high priest to rear as his own son
    C. Place it in foster care until the child was older
    D. Put it up for adoption

Answers on page 759

APRIL 19

Lesson 109
Today's Reading: *I Kings 4–6*
Period of Time: 1015–1005 BC
Author: Unknown

1. Who was Zadok's son?
   I Kings 4:2
   - **A.** Azariah
   - **B.** Berechiah
   - **C.** Chenaiah
   - **D.** Delaiah

2. Who were Shisha's sons?
   I Kings 4:3
   - **A.** Apollos and Jonathan
   - **B.** Elihoreph and Ahiah
   - **C.** Jehoshaphat and Ahilud
   - **D.** Shemaiah and Ezra

3. Who were Nathan's sons?
   I Kings 4:5
   - **A.** Azariah and Zabud
   - **B.** Gaddiel and Rehum
   - **C.** Harbonah and Sallu
   - **D.** Kadmiel and Maath

4. How many sheep were provided to King Solomon each day?
   I Kings 4:22–23
   - **A.** 1
   - **B.** 10
   - **C.** 100
   - **D.** 1,000

5. How many horse stalls did King Solomon own?
   I Kings 4:26
   - **A.** 400
   - **B.** 4,000
   - **C.** 40,000
   - **D.** 400,000

6. How many proverbs did King Solomon speak?
   I Kings 4:32
   - **A.** 95
   - **B.** 1,005
   - **C.** 2,000
   - **D.** 3,000

7. How many songs did King Solomon write?
   I Kings 4:32
   - **A.** 95
   - **B.** 1,005
   - **C.** 2,000
   - **D.** 3,000

8. Who was the king of Tyre?
   I Kings 5:1
   - **A.** King Abiram
   - **B.** King Ahira
   - **C.** King Hiram
   - **D.** King Ira

9. Which type of trees did King Solomon receive from Lebanon?
   I Kings 5:6
   - **A.** Ashe trees
   - **B.** Cedar trees
   - **C.** Oak trees
   - **D.** Walnut trees

10. What skill were the Sidonians famous for?
    I Kings 5:6
    - **A.** Accounting
    - **B.** Cooking
    - **C.** Metalworking
    - **D.** Woodcutting

11. How many measures of wheat did King Solomon pay each year for the trees?
    I Kings 5:11
    - **A.** 20
    - **B.** 200
    - **C.** 2,000
    - **D.** 20,000

12. How many measures of pure oil did King Solomon pay each year for the trees?
    I Kings 5:11
    - **A.** 20
    - **B.** 200
    - **C.** 2,000
    - **D.** 20,000

13. How many foremen supervised the construction of King Solomon's temple?

    I Kings 5:16

    A. 1,500
    B. 2,400
    C. 3,300
    D. 4,200

14. How many years after Israel came out of Egypt did the construction of King Solomon's temple begin?

    I Kings 6:1

    A. 480
    B. 635
    C. 814
    D. 973

15. During which month did the work on King Solomon's temple begin?

    I Kings 6:1

    A. Abib
    B. Bul
    C. Ethanim
    D. Zif

16. What was the length in cubits of King Solomon's temple?

    I Kings 6:2

    A. 30
    B. 40
    C. 50
    D. 60

17. What was the width in cubits of King Solomon's temple?

    I Kings 6:2

    A. 20
    B. 30
    C. 40
    D. 50

18. What was the height in cubits of King Solomon's temple?

    I Kings 6:2

    A. 20
    B. 30
    C. 40
    D. 50

19. During which month was the work on King Solomon's temple completed?

    I Kings 6:38

    A. Abib
    B. Bul
    C. Ethanim
    D. Zif

20. How many years did it take to build King Solomon's temple?

    I Kings 6:38

    A. 3
    B. 5
    C. 7
    D. 10

Answers on page 760

APRIL 20

Lesson 110
Today's Reading: *I Kings 7*
Period of Time: 1013–992 BC
Author: Unknown

1. How many years did it take to build King Solomon's palace?
   I Kings 7:1
   A. 7
   B. 9
   C. 13
   D. 21

2. How many cubits was the length of the house of the forest of Lebanon?
   I Kings 7:2
   A. 40
   B. 60
   C. 80
   D. 100

3. How many cubits was the breadth of the house of the forest of Lebanon?
   I Kings 7:2
   A. 30
   B. 40
   C. 50
   D. 60

4. How many cubits was the height of the house of the forest of Lebanon?
   I Kings 7:2
   A. 20
   B. 30
   C. 40
   D. 50

5. What type of wood was used for the pillars and beams in the house of the forest of Lebanon?
   I Kings 7:2
   A. Ash
   B. Cedar
   C. Pine
   D. Walnut

6. Whom did King Solomon build a house for?
   I Kings 7:8
   A. His mother
   B. His mother-in-law
   C. King Hiram
   D. Pharaoh's daughter

7. Which tribe was Hiram the artificer's mother from?
   I Kings 7:13–14
   A. Tribe of Naphtali
   B. Tribe of Reuben
   C. Tribe of Simeon
   D. Tribe of Zebulun

8. Which city was Hiram the artificer's father from?
   I Kings 7:13–14
   A. Anab
   B. Gaza
   C. Tyre
   D. Zion

9. What was the name of the pillar on the right side of the temple?
   I Kings 7:21
   A. Faith
   B. Jachin
   C. Manoah
   D. Peace

10. What was the name of the pillar on the left side of the temple?
    I Kings 7:21
    A. Boaz
    B. Hope
    C. Love
    D. Ruth

11. What was the diameter in cubits of the molten sea?

    I Kings 7:23

    A. 10
    B. 20
    C. 30
    D. 40

12. How many brass oxen did the molten sea rest upon?

    I Kings 7:25

    A. 6
    B. 8
    C. 12
    D. 16

13. What was the volume in baths of the molten sea?

    I Kings 7:26

    A. 500
    B. 1,000
    C. 1,500
    D. 2,000

14. What was the number of movable bases?

    I Kings 7:27–37

    A. 10
    B. 12
    C. 14
    D. 16

15. Which design was **not** on the panel of the movable bases?

    I Kings 7:29

    A. Cherubims
    B. Lions
    C. Oxen
    D. Rams

16. What was the number of brass lavers?

    I Kings 7:38

    A. 10
    B. 20
    C. 30
    D. 40

17. How many baths did each brass laver contain?

    I Kings 7:38

    A. 20
    B. 40
    C. 60
    D. 80

18. How many pomegranates were on the two network pillars?

    I Kings 7:42

    A. 100
    B. 200
    C. 300
    D. 400

19. Between which two towns were the tools and equipment for the temple cast?

    I Kings 7:46

    A. Ashdod and Ashkelon
    B. Jerusalem and Bethlehem
    C. Succoth and Zarthan
    D. Zorah and Beth-shemeth

20. Which type of metal was used to make the temple's altar, candlesticks, and table?

    I Kings 7:48–50

    A. Brass
    B. Gold
    C. Iron
    D. Silver

*Answers on page 760

Lesson 111
Today's Reading: *I Kings 8*
Period of Time: 1004 BC
Author: Unknown

1. Which city was also called the City of David?
   I Kings 8:1
   A. Bethel
   B. Gilgal
   C. Nazareth
   D. Zion

2. What is the name of the seventh month in the Jewish calendar?
   I Kings 8:2
   A. Abib
   B. Bul
   C. Ethanim
   D. Ziv

3. Where was the ark of the covenant placed inside the temple?
   I Kings 8:6
   A. Courtyard
   B. Holy place
   C. Most holy place
   D. Porch

4. What stood above the ark of the covenant?
   I Kings 8:6–7
   A. A crystal ceiling
   B. The shadow of the Almighty
   C. Solomon's throne
   D. Wings of the cherubims

5. Upon which mountain did Moses receive the ten commandments?
   I Kings 8:9
   A. Mount Ararat
   B. Mount Horeb
   C. Mount Mariah
   D. Mount Tabor

6. What was placed inside the ark of the covenant?
   I Kings 8:9
   A. Moses' rod that budded
   B. Royal jewels
   C. The High priest's garments
   D. Two tables of stone

7. From which nation did God deliver Israel from slavery?
   I Kings 8:9–21, 8:51–53
   A. Egypt
   B. Greece
   C. Rome
   D. Syria

8. Who was King Solomon's father?
   I Kings 8:15
   A. Adonijah
   B. David
   C. Jesse
   D. Rehoboam

9. What was the purpose for building the temple?
   I Kings 8:21
   A. To allow Solomon to flaunt his empire
   B. To give the high priest a place to dwell
   C. To house the ark of the covenant
   D. To make other nations jealous

10. Which name did King Solomon use for God in his prayer?
    I Kings 8:23
    A. Almighty God
    B. El Shaddai
    C. Jehovah
    D. LORD God of Israel

11. What did God promise King David?

    I Kings 8:25

    A. He would have peace from all of his enemies once he became king.
    B. His family would set the example of what an ideal family should be like.
    C. Nations from afar would come to David's temple to destroy it.
    D. One of his descendants would always sit on the throne of Israel if they obeyed God.

12. What was a person to do in order for God to forgive him of his sin?

    I Kings 8:30–34

    A. Ask God humbly for forgiveness and make supplication in the LORD's House
    B. Offer a burnt offering consisting of one bull
    C. Offer a peace offering consisting of two rams
    D. Pay the sin penalty according to the weight of the temple shekel

13. Why does God sometimes allow famines, pestilences, and droughts?

    I Kings 8:35–40

    A. To allow nature to run its course
    B. To discipline sinners
    C. To prevent overpopulation
    D. To promote evolution

14. What did King Solomon pray for concerning foreigners?

    I Kings 8:41–43

    A. All foreigners would come to know the LORD
    B. Foreign women would not turn Israel from the LORD
    C. The LORD would condemn the foreigners for their wickedness
    D. The LORD would purge the foreigners from among God's people

15. What did King Solomon mention in his prayer during the dedication of the temple?

    I Kings 8:46

    A. "All men are sinners."
    B. "Be sure your sin will find you out."
    C. "Go and sin no more."
    D. "Sin shall not have dominion over you."

16. What was included in King Solomon's benediction during the dedication of the temple?

    I Kings 8:61

    A. "A merry heart doeth good like medicine."
    B. "Let your heart be perfect with the LORD."
    C. "The heart knoweth its own bitterness."
    D. "The heart of kings is unsearchable."

17. How many oxen were offered during the dedication of the temple?

    I Kings 8:63

    A. 22,000
    B. 98,000
    C. 120,000
    D. 218,000

18. How many sheep were offered during the dedication of the temple?

    I Kings 8:63

    A. 22,000
    B. 98,000
    C. 120,000
    D. 218,000

19. What was consecrated because the bronze altar was too small for the number of offerings during the dedication of the temple?

    I Kings 8:64

    A. The holy place
    B. The middle of the court
    C. The most holy place
    D. The porch

20. How many days did the children of Israel celebrate the dedication of the temple?

    I Kings 8:65

    A. 3
    B. 7
    C. 14
    D. 28

*Answers on page 760

Lesson 112
Today's Reading: *I Kings 9–10*
Period of Time: 992–975 BC
Author: Unknown

1. Where did God appear to King Solomon the first time?
   I Kings 9:2
   A. Gibeon
   B. Makkedah
   C. Ramoth-gilead
   D. Ziph

2. How many years did it take to complete the house of the LORD and the king's house?
   I Kings 9:10
   A. 10
   B. 20
   C. 30
   D. 40

3. Who was the king of Tyre?
   I Kings 9:11
   A. King Balak
   B. King Eglon
   C. King Hiram
   D. King Rezin

4. What was **not** furnished to King Solomon by the king of Tyre?
   I Kings 9:11
   A. Cedar trees
   B. Fir trees
   C. Gold
   D. Silk

5. How many cities did King Solomon give to the king of Tyre?
   I Kings 9:11
   A. 10
   B. 20
   C. 30
   D. 40

6. In which place were the cities that King Solomon gave the king of Tyre located?
   I Kings 9:11
   A. Auranitis
   B. Batanaea
   C. Galilee
   D. Ituraea

7. What did the king of Tyre call the cities King Solomon gave him?
   I Kings 9:13
   A. Land of Cabul
   B. Land of Egypt
   C. Land of Gilead
   D. Land of Shinar

8. What was the name of the city Pharaoh captured and gave to his daughter?
   I Kings 9:16
   A. Gebal
   B. Gedor
   C. Gerar
   D. Gezer

9. How many supervisors worked for King Solomon?
   I Kings 9:23
   A. 290
   B. 370
   C. 550
   D. 910

10. How many times during a year did King Solomon offer burnt and peace offerings upon the altar he built unto the LORD?
    I Kings 9:25
    A. 2
    B. 3
    C. 7
    D. 12

11. Where was King Solomon's naval base located?

    I Kings 9:26

    A. Eziongeber
    B. Hierapolis
    C. Pihahiroth
    D. Trogyllium

12. How many talents of gold did King Solomon's navy collect from Ophir?

    I Kings 9:28

    A. 150
    B. 290
    C. 370
    D. 420

13. Which queen gave King Solomon 120 talents of gold?

    I Kings 10:1–10

    A. Queen of Babylon
    B. Queen of England
    C. Queen of Nineveh
    D. Queen of Sheba

14. Which type of trees did the king of Tyre bring to King Solomon?

    I Kings 10:11

    A. Almug trees
    B. Chestnut trees
    C. Palm trees
    D. Tamarisk trees

15. How many talents of gold did King Solomon collect in one year?

    I Kings 10:14

    A. 222
    B. 444
    C. 666
    D. 888

16. In which house did King Solomon place 200 targets and 300 shields made of gold?

    I Kings 10:16–17

    A. House of the forest of Hebron
    B. House of the forest of Lebanon
    C. House of the forest of Madon
    D. House of the forest of Zion

17. What was used in addition to gold to build King Solomon's throne?

    I Kings 10:18

    A. Diamonds
    B. Ivory
    C. Pearls
    D. Silver

18. How many steps did King Solomon's throne contain?

    I Kings 10:19

    A. 6
    B. 7
    C. 10
    D. 12

19. Which navy arrived every three years with goods for King Solomon?

    I Kings 10:22

    A. Navy of Carchemish
    B. Navy of Kithlish
    C. Navy of Lachish
    D. Navy of Tarshish

20. How many chariots did King Solomon own?

    I Kings 10:26

    A. 600
    B. 1,000
    C. 1,400
    D. 20,000

Answers on page 760

APRIL 23

Lesson 113
Today's Reading: *I Kings 11–12*
Period of Time: 992–975 BC
Author: Unknown

1. How many wives did King Solomon have?
   I Kings 11:3
   A. 100
   B. 700
   C. 900
   D. 1,400

2. How many concubines did King Solomon have?
   I Kings 11:3, 11:33
   A. 100
   B. 200
   C. 300
   D. 400

3. Who was the goddess of the Zidonians?
   I Kings 11:5, 11:33
   A. Ashtoreth
   B. Baal
   C. Diana
   D. Nergal

4. Who was the god of the Ammonites?
   I Kings 11:5, 11:33
   A. Amon
   B. Dagon
   C. Jupiter
   D. Milcom

5. Who was the god of Moab?
   I Kings 11:7, 11:33
   A. Anammelech
   B. Chemosh
   C. Mercurius
   D. Nibhaz

6. How many times did God appear to King Solomon?
   I Kings 11:9
   A. 2
   B. 4
   C. 7
   D. 8

7. Who was the Edomite adversary sent by God to chasten King Solomon?
   I Kings 11:14
   A. Bela
   B. Esau
   C. Hadad
   D. Jobab

8. Which Israelite military commander slaughtered many Edomites?
   I Kings 11:15–16
   A. Asahel
   B. Benaiah
   C. Helez
   D. Joab

9. Which queen was Pharaoh's wife?
   I Kings 11:19
   A. Queen Esther
   B. Queen Sheba
   C. Queen Tahpenes
   D. Queen Vashti

10. Who was also an adversary to King Solomon?
    I Kings 11:23–25
    A. Adoram
    B. Benhesed
    C. Jehoshaphat
    D. Rezon

11. Who was the king of Zobah?
    I Kings 11:23
    A. King Agag
    B. King Hadadezer
    C. King Nahash
    D. King Sennacherib

12. Who was the Shilonite prophet?
    I Kings 11:29
    A. Ahijah
    B. Hilkiah
    C. Obadiah
    D. Zebadiah

13. Who ruled Egypt during King Solomon's reign?

    I Kings 11:40

    A. King Hophra
    B. King Necho II
    C. King Shishak
    D. King Tirhakah

14. Which book contained the recorded acts and wisdom of King Solomon?

    I Kings 11:41

    A. Book of the acts of Solomon
    B. Book of wisdom
    C. Chronicles of King Solomon
    D. Journal of the wisest king ever

15. How many years did King Solomon rule over Israel?

    I Kings 11:42

    A. 10
    B. 12
    C. 28
    D. 40

16. What did Rehoboam say he would use to chastise the people?

    I Kings 12:11–14

    A. Fire
    B. Scorpions
    C. Snakes
    D. Whips

17. Which tribe continued to follow the house of David after the kingdom was divided?

    I Kings 12:20

    A. Tribe of Asher
    B. Tribe of Judah
    C. Tribe of Naphtali
    D. Tribe of Reuben

18. Who told King Rehoboam **not** to go to war against Israel?

    I Kings 12:21–24

    A. Adoram
    B. Kemuel
    C. Parshandatha
    D. Shemaiah

19. Which two cities contained King Jeroboam's calves of gold?

    I Kings 12:25–33

    A. Bethel and Dan
    B. Cana and Zoar
    C. Eziongeber and Ramah
    D. Gibeon and Mizpah

20. During which month did King Jeroboam ordain a feast to replace the annual feast in Israel?

    I Kings 12:32–33

    A. Third month
    B. Sixth month
    C. Eighth month
    D. Twelfth month

*Answers on page 760

Lesson 114
Today's Reading: *I Kings 13–14*
Period of Time: 975–958 BC
Author: Unknown

APRIL 24

1. Where was the man of God from that came to see King Jeroboam in Bethel?
   I Kings 13:1
   A. Ammon
   B. Judah
   C. Moab
   D. Sidon

2. Who would one day burn men's bones upon King Jeroboam's altar?
   I Kings 13:2
   A. Benaiah
   B. Elijah
   C. Josiah
   D. Nehemiah

3. What happened to King Jeroboam when he ordered his men to seize the man of God?
   I Kings 13:4
   A. His ears became deaf.
   B. His eyes became blind.
   C. His foot became hot.
   D. His hand became lame.

4. Who lied to the man of God and invited him to his home?
   I Kings 13:11–19
   A. A blacksmith
   B. A jailer
   C. A lawyer
   D. A prophet

5. How did the man of God die?
   I Kings 13:24
   A. A lion attacked and killed him.
   B. An angel of the LORD struck him.
   C. His ass threw him, breaking his neck.
   D. Jeroboam hung him from a tree.

6. Who was King Jeroboam's son?
   I Kings 14:1
   A. Abijah
   B. Ahijah
   C. Elijah
   D. Hodijah

7. Which town did King Jeroboam send his wife to?
   I Kings 14:2
   A. Cyrene
   B. Keilah
   C. Shiloh
   D. Tadmor

8. Which prophet spoke to King Jeroboam's wife?
   I Kings 14:2–16
   A. Abijah
   B. Ahijah
   C. Elijah
   D. Hodijah

9. What did the prophet say would eat the remains of King Jeroboam's family in the city?
   I Kings 14:11
   A. Birds
   B. Dogs
   C. Lions
   D. Worms

10. What did the prophet say would eat the remains of King Jeroboam's family in the field?
    I Kings 14:11
    A. Birds
    B. Dogs
    C. Lions
    D. Worms

11. Where was King Jeroboam's wife when her son died?

    I Kings 14:17

    A. Tadmor
    B. Tekoa
    C. Tirzah
    D. Tjaru

12. Which book contains the acts of King Jeroboam?

    I Kings 14:19

    A. Book of Jeroboam
    B. Book of kings and their holy wars
    C. Book of the acts of Jeroboam
    D. Book of the chronicles of the kings of Israel

13. How many years did King Jeroboam reign?

    I Kings 14:20

    A. 10
    B. 13
    C. 17
    D. 22

14. Who was King Jeroboam's son?

    I Kings 14:20

    A. Abinadab
    B. Jobab
    C. Nadab
    D. Shobab

15. How many years did King Rehoboam rule in Jerusalem?

    I Kings 14:21

    A. 17
    B. 25
    C. 33
    D. 41

16. Who was King Rehoboam's mother?

    I Kings 14:21

    A. Maachah
    B. Naamah
    C. Peninnah
    D. Tehinnah

17. Who lived in Judah and committed abominations against the LORD, according to I Kings 14:24?

    I Kings 14:24

    A. The Ammonites
    B. The Edomites
    C. The Midianites
    D. The Sodomites

18. Which king of Egypt waged war against King Rehoboam?

    I Kings 14:25

    A. King Osiris
    B. King Ramses
    C. King Shishak
    D. King Tutankhamun

19. Which book contains the acts of King Rehoboam?

    I Kings 14:29

    A. Book of the chronicles of the kings of Judah
    B. Book of the covenant
    C. Book of the lords and their holy wars
    D. Book of the wars of the LORD

20. Who succeeded King Rehoboam?

    I Kings 14:31

    A. King Abijah
    B. King Abijam
    C. King Abimael
    D. King Abimelech

*Answers on page 760

APRIL 25

Lesson 115
Today's Reading: *I Kings 15–17*
Period of Time: 958–901 BC
Author: Unknown

1. Who was King Jeroboam's father?
   I Kings 15:1
   A. Nabal
   B. Nebat
   C. Niger
   D. Nogah

2. Which one of the following was a Hittite?
   I Kings 15:5
   A. Benaiah
   B. Jedaiah
   C. Tobiah
   D. Uriah

3. Where was King Abijam buried after he died?
   I Kings 15:8
   A. Abilene
   B. Bethlehem
   C. City of David
   D. Damascus

4. Whom did King Asa remove from the land?
   I Kings 15:12
   A. The Hittites
   B. The Perizzites
   C. The Sodomites
   D. The Tekonites

5. Who was the king of Syria?
   I Kings 15:18
   A. King Ben-ha'dad
   B. King Claudius
   C. King Rehoboam
   D. King Thutmose I

6. Which cities were built using the stones and timber from Ramah?
   I Kings 15:22
   A. Arad and Tekoa
   B. Beer and Tappuah
   C. Elon and Eshtemoa
   D. Geba and Mizpah

7. Which king of Judah—in his old age—was diseased in his feet?
   I Kings 15:23
   A. King Asa
   B. King Ater
   C. King Augustus
   D. King Azariah

8. How many years did King Nadab rule over Israel?
   I Kings 15:25
   A. 2
   B. 4
   C. 8
   D. 16

9. Who killed King Nadab?
   I Kings 15:27
   A. Ahijah
   B. Baasha
   C. Eldaah
   D. Shavsha

10. Where was King Nadab assassinated?
    I Kings 15:27
    A. Babylon
    B. Gibbethon
    C. Hannathon
    D. Pirathon

11. What was Ahijah's surname?
    I Kings 15:29
    A. The Gibeonite
    B. The Ninevite
    C. The Shilonite
    D. The Tekoite

12. Who was King Baasha's father?
    I Kings 15:33
    A. Ahijah
    B. Elijah
    C. Hodijah
    D. Zidkijah

13. In whose house was King Elah slain?

    I Kings 16:8–10

    A. Abdi's house
    B. Ahab's house
    C. Arza's house
    D. Azor's house

14. How many days did King Zimri rule Israel?

    I Kings 16:15–19

    A. 3
    B. 7
    C. 10
    D. 12

15. Who rivaled King Omri over who should be king of Israel?

    I Kings 16:21–22

    A. Bani
    B. Hanani
    C. Libni
    D. Tibni

16. Where did King Omri rule for six years before moving his capital to Samaria?

    I Kings 16:23–24

    A. Bozrah
    B. Mozah
    C. Tirzah
    D. Zanoah

17. Who was King Ahab's wife?

    I Kings 16:28–31

    A. Queen Bithiah
    B. Queen Delilah
    C. Queen Hamutal
    D. Queen Jezebel

18. Which two sons of Hiel died when he rebuilt Jericho?

    I Kings 16:34

    A. Abiram and Segub
    B. Amnon and Absalom
    C. Esau and Jacob
    D. Perez and Zerah

19. Which type of birds did God send to feed Elijah?

    I Kings 17:4–6

    A. Cuckoos
    B. Doves
    C. Ossifrages
    D. Ravens

20. How many times did Elijah lay across the widow's son to bring him back to life?

    I Kings 17:21

    A. 2
    B. 3
    C. 7
    D. 12

Answers on page 760

Lesson 116
Today's Reading: *I Kings 18–19*
Period of Time: 958–901 BC
Author: Unknown

APRIL 26

1. Who was the governor of King Ahab's house?
   I Kings 18:3
   A. Obadiah
   B. Olympas
   C. Onesimus
   D. Othniel

2. Upon which mountain did Elijah challenge the prophets of Baal?
   I Kings 18:20
   A. Mount Ararat
   B. Mount Carmel
   C. Mount Gilboa
   D. Mount Moriah

3. How many prophets of Baal did Elijah challenge?
   I Kings 18:22
   A. 300
   B. 350
   C. 400
   D. 450

4. How long did the prophets of Baal call upon their god?
   I Kings 18:26–29
   A. From morning until noon
   B. From morning until mid afternoon
   C. From morning until evening
   D. From morning until midnight

5. How many stones did Elijah use to build an altar?
   I Kings 18:31–32
   A. 12
   B. 24
   C. 50
   D. 100

6. How many barrels of water did Elijah pour upon his sacrifice?
   I Kings 18:33–34
   A. 6
   B. 12
   C. 18
   D. 24

7. At which brook did Elijah slay the prophets of Baal?
   I Kings 18:40
   A. Brook Besor
   B. Brook Cedron
   C. Brook Eschol
   D. Brook Kishon

8. What was the total number of times Elijah's servant looked toward the sea?
   I Kings 18:43–44
   A. 3
   B. 5
   C. 7
   D. 9

9. What did Elijah's servant say the cloud resembled?
   I Kings 18:44
   A. A bull's head
   B. A man's hand
   C. A musician's harp
   D. A shepherd's hook

10. Where did King Ahab drive his chariot when the rain fell?
    I Kings 18:45
    A. Jabneel
    B. Jeruel
    C. Jezreel
    D. Joktheel

11. Where did Elijah leave his servant after Queen Jezebel threatened to kill him?

    I Kings 19:3

    A. Beersheba
    B. Gaza
    C. Joppa
    D. Samosata

12. Which type of tree did Elijah sleep under?

    I Kings 19:5

    A. A birch tree
    B. A cedar tree
    C. A fig tree
    D. A juniper tree

13. What did the angel bring Elijah?

    I Kings 19:6

    A. A cake and a cruse of water
    B. A loaf of bread and a bottle of milk
    C. A piece of fish and a flask of beer
    D. A wedge of cheese and a carafe of wine

14. How many days and nights did Elijah go without eating?

    I Kings 19:8

    A. 20
    B. 40
    C. 60
    D. 80

15. Which mountain is called the mount of God?

    I Kings 19:8

    A. Mount Ararat
    B. Mount Carmel
    C. Mount Horeb
    D. Mount Nebo

16. What is the sequence of events that occurred when the LORD passed by Elijah?

    I Kings 19:11–12

    A. A still, small voice; wind, earthquake, and fire
    B. Earthquake, fire, wind; and a still, small voice
    C. Fire; a still, small voice; wind, and an earthquake
    D. Wind, earthquake, fire; and a still, small voice

17. Whom did the LORD tell Elijah to anoint as king of Syria?

    I Kings 19:15

    A. Ben-ha'dad I
    B. Ben-ha'dad II
    C. Hazael
    D. Rezin

18. Whom did the LORD tell Elijah to anoint as king of Israel?

    I Kings 19:16

    A. Ahab
    B. Jehu
    C. Omri
    D. Zimri

19. How many prophets of the LORD did the LORD tell Elijah remained in Israel?

    I Kings 19:18

    A. 1,000
    B. 3,000
    C. 5,000
    D. 7,000

20. How many yoke of oxen was Elisha using to plow with?

    I Kings 19:19

    A. 12
    B. 24
    C. 50
    D. 100

Answers on page 760

APRIL 27

Lesson 117
Today's Reading: *I Kings 20–22*
Period of Time: 901–897 BC
Author: Unknown

1. Who was the king of Syria?
   I Kings 20:1
   A. King Ahab
   B. King Ben-ha'dad
   C. King Nadab
   D. King Shinab

2. How many kings allied with the king of Syria?
   I Kings 20:1
   A. 32
   B. 40
   C. 66
   D. 99

3. How many young men of the princes of the provinces did King Ahab number?
   I Kings 20:15
   A. 33
   B. 123
   C. 232
   D. 323

4. Where did the king of Syria and his allies fight King Ahab in the first campaign?
   I Kings 20:1–23
   A. The bitter springs
   B. The crooked valley
   C. The hill country
   D. The mountain of God

5. How many Syrian footmen did King Ahab's army slay in one day during the second campaign?
   I Kings 20:29
   A. 1,000
   B. 10,000
   C. 100,000
   D. 1,000,000

6. How were the remaining 27,000 Syrian soldiers that fled to Aphek killed?
   I Kings 20:30
   A. A wall fell on them
   B. An angel of the LORD slew them
   C. They died of plague
   D. They fought against each other

7. What did King Ahab do to the king of Syria after capturing him?
   I Kings 20:31–34
   A. Hung him from a tree
   B. Nailed him to a wall
   C. Sent him away
   D. Stoned him

8. What happened to the first man that refused to smite the prophet of God with a sword?
   I Kings 20:35–36
   A. A lion slew him
   B. Ahab's men stoned him to death
   C. Ahab's wife fed him to dogs
   D. Syrian soldiers drowned him

9. Why did Naboth refuse to sell King Ahab his vineyard?
   I Kings 21:3
   A. Ahab's offer was too low.
   B. He was too proud of it to sell it.
   C. It was part of his inheritance.
   D. Naboth had already sold it.

10. Who was King Ahab's wife?
    I Kings 21:5
    A. Queen Jedidah
    B. Queen Jerioth
    C. Queen Jerusha
    D. Queen Jezebel

11. What was Naboth falsely accused of?

    I Kings 21:13

    A. Blaspheming God and the king
    B. Murdering the king's son
    C. Stealing from God and the king
    D. Raping the king's daughter

12. How was Naboth put to death?

    I Kings 21:13

    A. He was castrated and hung to a wall.
    B. He was placed in a den full of lions.
    C. He was stabbed by Nadab.
    D. He was stoned to death.

13. Whom did God send to tell King Ahab he was going to die?

    I Kings 21:17–29

    A. Eli
    B. Elijah
    C. Elika
    D. Elisha

14. Which king of Judah became an ally to King Ahab?

    I Kings 22:1–4

    A. King Jehoahaz
    B. King Jehoash
    C. King Jehoram
    D. King Jehoshaphat

15. Approximately how many prophets served King Ahab?

    I Kings 22:6

    A. 200
    B. 400
    C. 600
    D. 800

16. Which prop did Zedekiah use to try to convince King Ahab he would have victory over the Syrians?

    I Kings 22:11

    A. A sword dredged in blood
    B. Birds in a cage
    C. Dry bones
    D. Horns of iron

17. Who was a prophet of God?

    I Kings 22:13–28

    A. Maachah
    B. Micaiah
    C. Mordecai
    D. Mushi

18. Where did King Ahab and the king of Judah go to battle the king of Syria?

    I Kings 22:29

    A. Gilgal
    B. Keilah
    C. Mizpah
    D. Ramoth-gilead

19. Where were King Jehoshaphat's ships broken?

    I Kings 22:48

    A. Alexandria
    B. Eziongeber
    C. Sidon
    D. Tyre

20. Who succeeded King Ahab?

    I Kings 22:51

    A. King Ahaziah
    B. King Hezekiah
    C. King Malchiah
    D. King Shemariah

Answers on page 760

Lesson 118
Today's Reading: *II Kings 1–2*
Period of Time: 897–896 BC
Author: Unknown

APRIL 28

1. Which nation rebelled against Israel after King Ahab died?
   II Kings 1:1
   A. Ammon
   B. Edom
   C. Moab
   D. Syria

2. How was King Ahaziah injured?
   II Kings 1:2
   A. He fell from his horse.
   B. He fell in front of a chariot.
   C. He fell into a well.
   D. He fell through a lattice.

3. Who was the god of Ekron?
   II Kings 1:2–3
   A. Baalzebub
   B. Chemosh
   C. Nisroch
   D. Tartak

4. What was Elijah's surname?
   II Kings 1:3
   A. The Naamite
   B. The Ramathite
   C. The Shulamite
   D. The Tishbite

5. How does the Bible describe Elijah?
   II Kings 1:8
   A. A giant with a nine-foot spear
   B. A man with six fingers and six toes
   C. Hairy and wearing a girdle of leather
   D. Thin with a ruddy complexion

6. What happened to the first two captains, and their men, sent to fetch Elijah?
   II Kings 1:9–12
   A. An angel of the LORD slew them.
   B. Fire from heaven consumed them.
   C. The earth swallowed them whole.
   D. They drowned in the Red sea.

7. Who succeeded King Ahaziah as king of Israel?
   II Kings 1:17
   A. King Agag
   B. King Hanun
   C. King Jehoram
   D. King Rezin

8. Who succeeded King Jehoshaphat as king of Judah?
   II Kings 1:17
   A. King Agag
   B. King Eglon
   C. King Hanun
   D. King Jehoram

9. Where was Elisha from?
   II Kings 2:1
   A. Gath
   B. Gaza
   C. Gibeon
   D. Gilgal

10. Which is the correct sequence for the path Elijah and Elisha traveled?
    II Kings 2:2–7
    A. Ashdod, Ashkelon, and Gaza
    B. Beer, Hammath, sea of Chinnereth
    C. Bethel, Jericho, river of Jordan
    D. Dibon, mount Nebo, Jericho

11. Who told Elisha that Elijah would die that day?
    II Kings 2:3–5
    A. The sons of the prophets
    B. The tormented man from Gadarene
    C. The twelve virgin prophets
    D. The witch of Endor

12. What did Elijah use to divide the river of Jordan?

    II Kings 2:8

    A. His finger
    B. His mantle
    C. His sandal
    D. His staff

13. What did Elisha ask from God?

    II Kings 2:9

    A. A double portion of Elijah's spirit
    B. A talking donkey
    C. The king's daughter for a wife
    D. Twelve yoke of oxen

14. What happened to Elijah?

    II Kings 2:11

    A. He was slain by two she-lions.
    B. He was taken to heaven in a chariot of fire.
    C. The king of Syria hung him from a tree.
    D. The virgin daughters of Absalom poisoned him.

15. How many men searched for Elijah's body?

    II Kings 2:15–17

    A. 30
    B. 40
    C. 50
    D. 60

16. How many days did the men search for Elijah's body?

    II Kings 2:17

    A. 2
    B. 3
    C. 6
    D. 7

17. What did Elisha do to heal the waters of Jericho?

    II Kings 2:19–21

    A. Cast salt upon the water
    B. Mingled goat blood with the water
    C. Tossed a tree into the water
    D. Used a stick to strike the water

18. Where did Elisha travel to after leaving Jericho?

    II Kings 2:23

    A. Ashdod
    B. Bethel
    C. Gallim
    D. Kedesh

19. How does the Bible describe Elisha?

    II Kings 2:23

    A. Bald
    B. Hairy
    C. Short
    D. Tall

20. What happened to the 42 children that mocked Elisha?

    II Kings 2:23–24

    A. Their parents beat them with cords.
    B. Their tongues went numb.
    C. They were attacked by asps.
    D. They were attacked by two she bears.

*Answers on page 760

Lesson 119
Today's Reading: *II Kings 3–4*
Period of Time: 896–895 BC
Author: Unknown

APRIL 29

1. Who was the king of Israel?
   II Kings 3:1
   A. King Jehoram
   B. King Jehoshaphat
   C. King Jeroboam
   D. King Jeroham

2. Who was the king of Judah?
   II Kings 3:1
   A. King Jehoram
   B. King Jehoshaphat
   C. King Jeroboam
   D. King Jeroham

3. Who was the son of Nebat?
   II Kings 3:3
   A. Jehoram
   B. Jehoshaphat
   C. Jeroboam
   D. Jeroham

4. Who was the king of Moab?
   II Kings 3:4
   A. King Madai
   B. King Magog
   C. King Meres
   D. King Mesha

5. Which king joined the kings of Judah and Israel to go to war against Moab?
   II Kings 3:9
   A. King of Edom
   B. King of Gath
   C. King of Seba
   D. King of Tyre

6. Who was Elisha's father?
   II Kings 3:11
   A. Shapham
   B. Shaphat
   C. Sharai
   D. Sharezer

7. What did Elisha prophesy?
   II Kings 3:16–20
   A. Israel would flee for 3 months from its enemies.
   B. Pestilence would cover the land for 3 days.
   C. The country would be filled with water.
   D. The famine would last seven years.

8. Why did the Moabites think the armies of the three kings had killed each other?
   II Kings 3:21–24
   A. The enemy camps were deserted.
   B. The soldiers appeared to be dead.
   C. There was great chaos within the three camps.
   D. They mistook water on the ground for blood.

9. Which part of the Israelite army destroyed Kir-haresheth?
   II Kings 3:25
   A. The archers
   B. The cavalry
   C. The footmen
   D. The slingers

10. What did the king of Moab offer for a burnt offering?
    II Kings 3:27
    A. 700 of his soldiers
    B. 1000 bullocks
    C. His eldest son
    D. The captain of his host

11. How many sons did the widow have?
    II Kings 4:1
    A. 2
    B. 3
    C. 6
    D. 7

12. What did Elisha tell the widow to borrow from her neighbors?

    II Kings 4:3

    A. Honey
    B. Vessels
    C. Wine
    D. Wood

13. What did the widow sell to pay off her debt?

    II Kings 4:7

    A. Garments
    B. Oil
    C. Oxen
    D. Sons

14. Where did Elisha stop to eat bread regularly with a woman and her husband?

    II Kings 4:8–9

    A. Salcah
    B. Saphir
    C. Shiloh
    D. Shunem

15. Who was Elisha's servant?

    II Kings 4:12

    A. Gaius
    B. Gallio
    C. Gehazi
    D. Gideon

16. What did Elisha tell the charitable woman?

    II Kings 4:16–17

    A. She needed to flee the city.
    B. She was going to have a son.
    C. She would be consumed by dogs.
    D. She would find honey in a dead lion.

17. What happened to the boy when he went among the reapers?

    II Kings 4:18–21

    A. He suffered a head wound.
    B. He was sorely burned from the fire.
    C. His brother attacked him in the field.
    D. His horse threw him.

18. Where was Elisha when he was informed of the injured boy?

    II Kings 4:22–25

    A. Mount Carmel
    B. Mount Gilboa
    C. Mount Moriah
    D. Mount Pisgah

19. What did Elisha give his servant to heal the injured boy?

    II Kings 4:29

    A. His cloak
    B. His ephod
    C. His mantle
    D. His staff

20. Where was the man from who brought Elisha the firstfruits?

    II Kings 4:42

    A. Baalperazim
    B. Baalgad
    C. Baalshalisha
    D. Baaltamar

*Answers on page 760

Lesson 120
Today's Reading: *II Kings 5–7*
Period of Time: 895–892 BC
Author: Unknown

APRIL 30

1. What was Naaman's occupation?
   II Kings 5:1
   A. Blacksmith
   B. Carpenter
   C. Sheepherder
   D. Soldier

2. What disease did Naaman have?
   II Kings 5:1
   A. Ague
   B. Blindness
   C. Emerods
   D. Leprosy

3. Who told Naaman's wife that the prophet in Samaria could heal Naaman?
   II Kings 5:2–4
   A. Her butler
   B. Her doctor
   C. Her maid
   D. Her nurse

4. What did Naaman take with him to Samaria?
   II Kings 5:5
   A. 10 talents of gold, 10 changes of raiment, and 1000 pieces of silver
   B. 10 talents of silver, 10 changes of raiment, and 6000 pieces of gold
   C. 100 pieces of silver, 100 talents of gold, and 100 changes of raiment
   D. 6000 pieces of gold, 100 talents of silver, and 2 changes of raiment

5. What did the king of Israel do after reading the letter Naaman brought him?
   II Kings 5:7
   A. Fled to Egypt
   B. Paid tribute to the king of Syria
   C. Rent his clothes
   D. Surrendered

6. Who was the man of God living in Samaria?
   II Kings 5:3, 5:8
   A. Elijah
   B. Elisha
   C. Jehoshaphat
   D. Shaphat

7. What did the prophet tell Naaman to do to be healed?
   II Kings 5:10
   A. Ask the king of Israel for forgiveness
   B. Offer a burnt offering to the LORD
   C. Wash in the river of Jordan seven times
   D. Wrestle an angel from dusk to dawn

8. Where are the Abana and Pharpar rivers located?
   II Kings 5:12
   A. Damascus
   B. Egypt
   C. Greece
   D. Israel

9. What did Naaman offer the man of God for healing him?
   II Kings 5:17
   A. 2 mules
   B. 4 talents of gold
   C. 10 changes of raiment
   D. 100 pieces of silver

10. Who was the servant of the man of God?
    II Kings 5:20
    A. Gallio
    B. Gehazi
    C. Geshem
    D. Goliath

11. What did Naaman give to the man of God's servant?

    II Kings 5:23

    A. 2 talents of silver and 2 changes of garments
    B. 4 talents of gold and 4 changes of garments
    C. 6 talents of silver and 10 changes of garments
    D. 8 talents of gold and 100 changes of garments

12. What disease did the man of God's servant receive?

    II Kings 5:27

    A. Ague
    B. Blindness
    C. Emerods
    D. Leprosy

13. Which miracle did the man of God do?

    II Kings 6:5–6

    A. He allowed a cruse of oil to remain full.
    B. He brought a dead doctor back to life.
    C. He divided the river of Jordan.
    D. He made an axe head swim.

14. In which city did the king of Syria's spies find the man of God?

    II Kings 6:8–13

    A. Ajalon
    B. Dothan
    C. Goshen
    D. Middin

15. What happened to the Syrian soldiers sent to fetch the man of God?

    II Kings 6:18

    A. An angel of the LORD slew them.
    B. The armies of Israel destroyed them.
    C. The LORD smote them with blindness.
    D. They starved to death during the famine.

16. Which one of the following was a Syrian king?

    II Kings 6:24

    A. King Ben-ha'dad
    B. King Darius the Great
    C. King Nahash
    D. King Sargon II

17. How many pieces of silver did 1/4 of a cab of dove's dung cost during the famine?

    II Kings 6:25

    A. 1
    B. 3
    C. 5
    D. 7

18. How many lepers entered the Syrian camp?

    II Kings 7:3–5

    A. 2
    B. 4
    C. 8
    D. 10

19. How many shekels did a measure of fine flour cost after the Syrian army fled?

    II Kings 7:16

    A. 1
    B. 10
    C. 100
    D. 1,000

20. How did the lord on whose hand the king of Israel leaned on die?

    II Kings 7:17–20

    A. A millstone crushed him.
    B. An angel smote him.
    C. He was stoned to death.
    D. He was trod upon.

Answers on page 760

Lesson 121
Today's Reading: *II Kings 8–9*
Period of Time: 892–884 BC
Author: Unknown

1. How many years did the famine last?
   II Kings 8:1–2
   A. 2
   B. 3
   C. 5
   D. 7

2. Where did the woman, whose son Elijah brought back to life, and her family go during the famine?
   II Kings 8:2
   A. Land of the Gadarenes
   B. Land of the Libertines
   C. Land of the Nazarenes
   D. Land of the Philistines

3. Who was Elisha's servant?
   II Kings 8:4
   A. Gehazi
   B. Haggai
   C. Jehudi
   D. Zichri

4. Who was the king of Syria?
   II Kings 8:7
   A. King Ben-ha'dad
   B. King Hezekiah
   C. King Joash
   D. King Shallum

5. Whom did the king of Syria send to Elisha?
   II Kings 8:8
   A. Asahel
   B. Daniel
   C. Hazael
   D. Jehiel

6. How many camels did the king of Syria give to Elisha?
   II Kings 8:9
   A. 7
   B. 25
   C. 40
   D. 62

7. How was the king of Syria murdered?
   II Kings 8:12–15
   A. He was poisoned.
   B. He was pushed down a well.
   C. He was smothered.
   D. He was stabbed with a sword.

8. Who was King Ahab's son?
   II Kings 8:16
   A. Joash
   B. Joram
   C. Josiah
   D. Jotham

9. How old was King Jehoram when he became king of Judah?
   II Kings 8:16–17
   A. 12 years old
   B. 27 years old
   C. 32 years old
   D. 40 years old

10. Who revolted against Judah?
    II Kings 8:20–22
    A. Cush and Thyatira
    B. Edom and Libnah
    C. Moab and Nineveh
    D. Syria and Shema

11. Which book contains the acts of King Joram of Judah?
    II Kings 8:23
    A. Chronicles of the kings and their wars
    B. Chronicles of the kings of Judah
    C. Words of Shemaiah the prophet
    D. Words of the kings of Israel

12. How many years did King Ahaziah reign in Jerusalem?
    II Kings 8:26
    A. 1
    B. 2
    C. 3
    D. 4

13. Which king was wounded in a battle against the Syrians?

    II Kings 8:26–28

    A. King Joram
    B. King Malchiram
    C. King Piram
    D. King Ram

14. Who was King Jehoshaphat's father?

    II Kings 9:2

    A. Nadab
    B. Nahash
    C. Nimrod
    D. Nimshi

15. Where was King Jehu anointed king of Israel?

    II Kings 9:4–6

    A. Beth-hanan
    B. Beth-haram
    C. Jabesh-gilead
    D. Ramoth-gilead

16. How many men on horseback were sent to meet King Jehu?

    II Kings 9:17–19

    A. 1
    B. 2
    C. 3
    D. 4

17. How did King Jehu kill King Joram (Jehoram)?

    II Kings 9:24

    A. He shot him with an arrow.
    B. He slashed his throat with a knife.
    C. He smashed his body against the rocks.
    D. He stabbed him in the bowels with a spear.

18. Which field was King Joram's (Jehoram) dead body cast into?

    II Kings 9:25–26

    A. Field of Jehu
    B. Field of Naboth
    C. The Pauper's Field
    D. The Potter's Field

19. Where did King Ahaziah die?

    II Kings 9:27

    A. Gimzo
    B. Jericho
    C. Megiddo
    D. Shocho

20. Whose dead body did the dogs in Jezreel eat?

    II Kings 9:30–37

    A. Jecoliah's dead body
    B. Jedidah's dead body
    C. Jerusha's dead body
    D. Jezebel's dead body

*Answers on page 761

MAY 2

Lesson 122
Today's Reading: *II Kings 10–12*
Period of Time: 884–839 BC
Author: Unknown

1. How many of King Ahab's sons lived in Samaria?
   II Kings 10:1
   A. 7
   B. 70
   C. 700
   D. 7,000

2. How many of King Ahaziah's brethrens did King Jehu slay?
   II Kings 10:14
   A. 17
   B. 25
   C. 38
   D. 42

3. Who was Jehonadab's father?
   II Kings 10:15
   A. Aminadab
   B. Hobab
   C. Rechab
   D. Shobab

4. Who was King Jeroboam's father?
   II Kings 10:29
   A. Nebat
   B. Necho II
   C. Nero
   D. Neziah

5. Which two cities contained King Jeroboam's golden calves?
   II Kings 10:29
   A. Bethel and Dan
   B. Debir and Ziklag
   C. Michmash and Socoh
   D. Pirathon and Eglon

6. How many generations of King Jehu would sit on the throne?
   II Kings 10:30
   A. 2
   B. 4
   C. 7
   D. 10

7. Who was King Jehu's son?
   II Kings 10:35
   A. Jehdeiah
   B. Jehiel
   C. Jehizkiah
   D. Jehoahaz

8. How many years did King Jehu rule over Israel?
   II Kings 10:36
   A. 7
   B. 16
   C. 28
   D. 33

9. Who was King Ahaziah's mother?
   II Kings 11:1
   A. Abijah
   B. Aholah
   C. Athaliah
   D. Azubah

10. Who was King Ahaziah's sister?
    II Kings 11:2
    A. Bathsheba
    B. Elisheba
    C. Jehosheba
    D. Sheba

11. Who was King Ahaziah's son?
    II Kings 11:2
    A. Geber
    B. Joash
    C. Titus
    D. Zadok

12. Which one of the following was a priest?

    II Kings 11:4–9

    A. Elishua
    B. Jehoiada
    C. Peruda
    D. Shimea

13. Who was a priest of Baal?

    II Kings 11:18

    A. Mattan
    B. Nadab
    C. Phinehas
    D. Zadok

14. How old was King Jehoash when he became king of Judah?

    II Kings 11:21

    A. 5 years old
    B. 7 years old
    C. 10 years old
    D. 14 years old

15. How many years did King Jehoash rule over Judah?

    II Kings 12:1

    A. 10
    B. 20
    C. 30
    D. 40

16. Who was King Jehoash's mother?

    II Kings 12:1

    A. Abijah
    B. Jedidah
    C. Keturah
    D. Zibiah

17. What did the high priest do to collect money to repair the temple?

    II Kings 12:9–10

    A. Held a chariot wash
    B. Hired more temple prostitutes
    C. Raised the temple tax
    D. Set a chest beside the altar

18. Who was the king of Syria?

    II Kings 12:17

    A. King Hazael
    B. King Hezekiah
    C. King Hiram
    D. King Hoshea

19. Who slew King Joash?

    II Kings 12:20–21

    A. Jannes and Jambres
    B. Jehohanan and Jabez
    C. Jozachar and Jehozabad
    D. Julius and Junia

20. Who was King Joash's son?

    II Kings 12:21

    A. Amaziah
    B. Jeshaiah
    C. Uriah
    D. Zebediah

Answers on page 761

Lesson 123

Today's Reading: *II Kings 13–14*
Period of Time: 839–810 BC
Author: Unknown

1. Who was King Joash's father?
   II Kings 13:1
   A. Ahaziah
   B. Hezekiah
   C. Jeremiah
   D. Uzziah

2. How many years did King Jehoahaz reign over Samaria?
   II Kings 13:1
   A. 17
   B. 25
   C. 33
   D. 41

3. Who was King Jeroboam's father?
   II Kings 13:2
   A. Naboth
   B. Nebat
   C. Niger
   D. Nun

4. Who was the king of Syria?
   II Kings 13:3
   A. King Barachel
   B. King Gamaliel
   C. King Hazael
   D. King Pethuel

5. How many years did King Jehoash reign over Samaria?
   II Kings 13:10
   A. 4
   B. 8
   C. 16
   D. 32

6. Who invaded the land of Judah after Elisha died?
   II Kings 13:20
   A. The Moabites
   B. The Nazarites
   C. The Oznites
   D. The Perizzites

7. How did the dead man come back to life?
   II Kings 13:21
   A. Amaziah took the dead man's hand and said, "Arise."
   B. His body touched the bones of Elisha as they buried him.
   C. Jehoash came to the sepulcher and shouted, "Come forth."
   D. Pethuel touched the body with Elisha's handkerchief.

8. How many times did King Jehoash defeat King Ben-ha'dad?
   II Kings 13:25
   A. 3
   B. 7
   C. 9
   D. 11

9. How old was King Amaziah when he began to reign?
   II Kings 14:1–2
   A. 15 years old
   B. 25 years old
   C. 35 years old
   D. 45 years old

10. How many years did King Amaziah reign in Jerusalem?
    II Kings 14:1–2
    A. 17
    B. 29
    C. 36
    D. 40

11. How many Edomites did King Amaziah slay in the valley of salt?
    II Kings 14:7
    A. 1,000
    B. 3,000
    C. 6,000
    D. 10,000

12. What did King Amaziah rename Selah?

    II Kings 14:7

    A. Jabneel
    B. Jezreel
    C. Joktheel
    D. Kabzeel

13. Where did King Amaziah and King Jehoash meet?

    II Kings 14:11–14

    A. Bethesda
    B. Bethlehem
    C. Bethphage
    D. Beth-she'mesh

14. Where did King Amaziah flee to?

    II Kings 14:17–19

    A. Charchemish
    B. Kithlish
    C. Lachish
    D. Tarshish

15. Who succeeded King Amaziah?

    II Kings 14:21

    A. King Adaiah
    B. King Ahaziah
    C. King Azariah
    D. King Azaziah

16. Who was King Jeroboam's father?

    II Kings 14:23

    A. Joab
    B. Joah
    C. Joahaz
    D. Joash

17. How many years did King Jeroboam reign in Samaria?

    II Kings 14:23

    A. 15
    B. 29
    C. 37
    D. 41

18. Who was Jonah's father?

    II Kings 14:25

    A. Amittai
    B. Jaazeil
    C. Rephael
    D. Shemaah

19. Where was Jonah from?

    II Kings 14:25

    A. Damascus
    B. Gath-hepher
    C. Nineveh
    D. Tarshish

20. Who succeeded King Jeroboam?

    II Kings 14:29

    A. King Harhaiah
    B. King Maaseiah
    C. King Raamiah
    D. King Zachariah

*Answers on page 761

Lesson 124
Today's Reading: *II Kings 15–16*
Period of Time: 810–726 BC
Author: Unknown

1. Who was King Azariah's father?
   II Kings 15:1
   A. Amaziah
   B. Conaniah
   C. Hizkiah
   D. Jehizkiah

2. How old was King Azariah when he began to reign?
   II Kings 15:2
   A. 8 years old
   B. 16 years old
   C. 32 years old
   D. 64 years old

3. How many years did King Azariah reign?
   II Kings 15:2
   A. 2
   B. 32
   C. 52
   D. 62

4. Who was King Azariah's mother?
   II Kings 15:2
   A. Gedaliah
   B. Hananiah
   C. Ishmaiah
   D. Jecholiah

5. Which disease did the LORD smite King Azariah with?
   II Kings 15:5
   A. Blains
   B. Dysentery
   C. Emerods
   D. Leprosy

6. How many months did King Zachariah rule over Samaria?
   II Kings 15:8
   A. 3
   B. 6
   C. 9
   D. 12

7. Who killed King Zachariah?
   II Kings 15:10
   A. Shabbthai
   B. Shadrach
   C. Shallum
   D. Shalman

8. Who was King Menahem's father?
   II Kings 15:14
   A. Gadi
   B. Joel
   C. Naam
   D. Puah

9. Who was the king of Assyria?
   II Kings 15:19
   A. King Buz
   B. King Lud
   C. King Nun
   D. King Pul

10. Who was King Menahem's son?
    II Kings 15:22
    A. Jonathan
    B. Meremoth
    C. Pekahiah
    D. Sherezer

11. How many years did King Pekah reign?
    II Kings 15:27
    A. 10
    B. 20
    C. 30
    D. 40

12. Who was King Jotham's father?
    II Kings 15:32
    A. Uzziah
    B. Uzziel
    C. Zatthu
    D. Zattu

13. Who was King Jotham's mother?

    II Kings 15:33
    - **A.** Bernice
    - **B.** Jerusha
    - **C.** Maachah
    - **D.** Rebecca

14. Who was the king of Syria?

    II Kings 15:37
    - **A.** King Cain
    - **B.** King Jachin
    - **C.** King Miamin
    - **D.** King Rezin

15. Which city did the king of Syria capture?

    II Kings 16:6
    - **A.** Bethanath
    - **B.** Daberath
    - **C.** Elath
    - **D.** Hamath

16. Which king of Assyria did King Ahaz seek help from?

    II Kings 16:7
    - **A.** King Asnappar
    - **B.** King Esarhaddon
    - **C.** King Sennacherib
    - **D.** King Tiglath-pileser

17. Which Syrian city did the king of Assyria capture?

    II Kings 16:9
    - **A.** Damascus
    - **B.** Lebanon
    - **C.** Sidon
    - **D.** Tyre

18. Where did the king of Assyria take the Syrian captives?

    II Kings 16:9
    - **A.** Gur
    - **B.** Iim
    - **C.** Kir
    - **D.** Luz

19. Which priest built an altar for King Ahaz?

    II Kings 16:10–11
    - **A.** Uriah
    - **B.** Urijah
    - **C.** Uzzah
    - **D.** Uzziah

20. Who was King Ahaz's son?

    II Kings 16:20
    - **A.** Hezekiah
    - **B.** Iphedeiah
    - **C.** Jaazaniah
    - **D.** Maaseiah

*Answers on page 761

Lesson 125
Today's Reading: *II Kings 17–18*
Period of Time: 739–710 BC
Author: Unknown

1. Who was King Hoshea's father?
   II Kings 17:1
   A. Amos
   B. Elah
   C. Gera
   D. Hazo

2. How many years did King Hoshea reign in Samaria?
   II Kings 17:1
   A. 3
   B. 9
   C. 12
   D. 15

3. Which king of Assyria cast King Hoshea into prison?
   II Kings 17:3–4
   A. King Asnappar
   B. King Esarhaddon
   C. King Shalmaneser
   D. King Tiglath-pileser

4. Who was the king of Egypt?
   II Kings 17:4
   A. King Er
   B. King Og
   C. King So
   D. King Uz

5. Which two cities were the captured Samarians relocated to in Assyria?
   II Kings 17:6
   A. Alexandria and Thebez
   B. Halah and Habor
   C. Sodom and Gomorrah
   D. Tyre and Sidon

6. How many priests did the king of Assyria send back to Samaria?
   II Kings 17:27–28
   A. 1
   B. 3
   C. 7
   D. 12

7. What was the name given to the new and mixed inhabitants of Samaria?
   II Kings 17:29
   A. Manhattans
   B. Nehushtans
   C. Puritans
   D. Samaritans

8. Which god did the men of Babylon worship?
   II Kings 17:30
   A. Baal
   B. Dagon
   C. Rimmon
   D. Succothbenoth

9. Which god did the men of Cuth worship?
   II Kings 17:30
   A. Beelzebub
   B. Chemosh
   C. Nergal
   D. Queen of Heaven

10. Which god did the men of Hamath worship?
    II Kings 17:30
    A. Amon
    B. Aquarius
    C. Ashima
    D. Ashtoreth

11. Which two gods did the Avites worship?
    II Kings 17:31
    A. Diana and Hermes
    B. Merodach and Nebo
    C. Nergal and Dagon
    D. Nibhaz and Tartak

12. Which two gods did the Sepharvites worship?

    II Kings 17:31

    A. Adrammelech and Anammelech
    B. Ashima and Ashtoreth
    C. Castor and Pollux
    D. Milcom and Molech

13. Who was King Hezekiah's father?

    II Kings 18:1

    A. Ahaz
    B. Amoz
    C. Boaz
    D. Buz

14. How old was King Hezekiah when he became king of Judah?

    II Kings 18:2

    A. 25 years old
    B. 37 years old
    C. 49 years old
    D. 51 years old

15. How many years did King Hezekiah reign over Judah?

    II Kings 18:2

    A. 2
    B. 12
    C. 22
    D. 29

16. Who was King Hezekiah's mother?

    II Kings 18:2

    A. Abi
    B. Eve
    C. Ova
    D. Zoe

17. What did King Hezekiah name the brasen serpent that Moses had made?

    II Kings 18:4

    A. Charlatan
    B. Harmattan
    C. Nehushtan
    D. Orangutan

18. Who was over King Hezekiah's household?

    II Kings 18:18

    A. Eliadah
    B. Eliakim
    C. Eliashib
    D. Eliathah

19. Which one of the following was a scribe?

    II Kings 18:18

    A. Adina
    B. Harbona
    C. Janna
    D. Shebna

20. How many horses did the Rabshakeh offer to Judah?

    II Kings 18:19–23

    A. 1,000
    B. 2,000
    C. 3,000
    D. 4,000

*Answers on page 761

MAY 6

Lesson 126
Today's Reading: *II Kings 19–21*
Period of Time: 710–649 BC
Author: Unknown

1. Who was Isaiah's father?
   II Kings 19:2
   A. Amnon
   B. Amon
   C. Amos
   D. Amoz

2. Which nation did Assyria go to war against?
   II Kings 19:8
   A. Ebronah
   B. Kinah
   C. Libnah
   D. Mattanah

3. Who was the king of Ethiopia?
   II Kings 19:9
   A. King Balak
   B. King Hiram
   C. King Sargon
   D. King Tirhakah

4. What did King Hezekiah do with the letter from Sennacherib?
   II Kings 19:14
   A. Burned it on top of the guard tower
   B. Nailed it to the temple door
   C. Spread it before the LORD
   D. Wrote "Nuts" on it and sent it back

5. How many Assyrian soldiers did the angel of the LORD slay?
   II Kings 19:35
   A. 64,000
   B. 93,000
   C. 185,000
   D. 250,000

6. Where did King Sennacherib go after he left Judah?
   II Kings 19:36
   A. Asshur
   B. Babylon
   C. Libya
   D. Nineveh

7. Which god did King Sennacherib worship?
   II Kings 19:37
   A. Nebo
   B. Nergal
   C. Nibhaz
   D. Nisroch

8. Which two of King Sennacherib's sons murdered him?
   II Kings 19:37
   A. Abimelech and Shimri
   B. Adrammelech and Sharezer
   C. Ahimelech and Shobal
   D. Ebed-melech and Shemaah

9. Where did King Sennacherib's sons flee to after murdering their father?
   II Kings 19:37
   A. Arabian desert
   B. Cappadocia
   C. Land of Armenia
   D. Nabataean kingdom

10. Who succeeded King Sennacherib on the throne?
    II Kings 19:37
    A. King Chilion
    B. King Esarhaddon
    C. King Talmon
    D. King Zibeon

11. How many years did God promise to add to King Hezekiah's life?
    II Kings 20:6
    A. 15
    B. 25
    C. 35
    D. 45

12. Which one of the following foods did Isaiah use to cure King Hezekiah's illness?

    II Kings 20:7

    A. Cucumbers
    B. Figs
    C. Honey
    D. Wine

13. Which sign did God send to show he would extend King Hezekiah's life?

    II Kings 20:10–11

    A. He brought the shadow ten degrees backward.
    B. He caused the earth to shake and the mountains to fall.
    C. He divided the river of Jordan during the time of the flood.
    D. He sent dew upon the ground but the fleece remained dry.

14. Who was King Berodachbaladan's father?

    II Kings 20:12

    A. Baladan
    B. Dan
    C. Merodach-baladan
    D. Nebuzaradan

15. What did Isaiah say would happen to some of King Hezekiah's sons?

    II Kings 20:18

    A. They would become eunuchs in Babylon.
    B. They would die from the plague in Egypt.
    C. They would marry women from Eden.
    D. They would overthrow him at Hena.

16. How old was King Manasseh when he began to reign?

    II Kings 21:1

    A. 6 years old
    B. 12 years old
    C. 18 years old
    D. 24 years old

17. How many years did King Manasseh reign in Jerusalem?

    II Kings 21:1

    A. 13
    B. 29
    C. 36
    D. 55

18. Who was King Manasseh's mother?

    II Kings 21:1

    A. Hephzibah
    B. Reumah
    C. Shiphrah
    D. Tirzah

19. Who murdered King Amon?

    II Kings 21:23

    A. His brothers
    B. His servants
    C. His soldiers
    D. His wives

20. Who was King Amon's son?

    II Kings 21:26

    A. Hezekiah
    B. Isaiah
    C. Josiah
    D. Micaiah

Answers on page 761

Lesson 127
Today's Reading: *II Kings 22–25*
Period of Time: 649–588 BC
Author: Unknown

1. How old was King Josiah when he began to reign in Jerusalem?
   II Kings 22:1
   A. 8 years old
   B. 16 years old
   C. 24 years old
   D. 32 years old

2. How many years did King Josiah reign in Jerusalem?
   II Kings 22:1
   A. 14
   B. 29
   C. 31
   D. 55

3. Which high priest found the book of the law inside the temple?
   II Kings 22:8
   A. Eli
   B. Hilkiah
   C. Jahaziel
   D. Pashur

4. Who was a prophetess?
   II Kings 22:14
   A. Hadassah
   B. Helah
   C. Hoglah
   D. Huldah

5. Whose houses did King Josiah destroy?
   II Kings 23:7
   A. The Canaanites' houses
   B. The Jebusites' houses
   C. The Pharzites' houses
   D. The Sodomites' houses

6. Which king built high places to honor Ashtoreth the abomination of the Zidonians?
   II Kings 23:13
   A. King David
   B. King Hezekiah
   C. King Solomon
   D. King Zechariah

7. Which deity was the abomination of the Moabites?
   II Kings 23:13
   A. Chemosh
   B. Dagon
   C. Mercurius
   D. Rimmon

8. Which deity was the abomination of the Ammonites?
   II Kings 23:13
   A. Ashima
   B. Milcom
   C. Nergal
   D. Tartak

9. Which pharaoh slew King Josiah?
   II Kings 23:29
   A. Pharaoh-hophra
   B. Pharaoh-nechoh
   C. Pharaoh So
   D. Pharaoh Thutmosis

10. Where was King Josiah slain?
    II Kings 23:29
    A. Ai
    B. Jericho
    C. Megiddo
    D. Shittim

11. How many months did King Jehoahaz reign in Jerusalem?

    II Kings 23:31
    A. 3
    B. 5
    C. 8
    D. 10

12. Whose name did the Pharaoh of Egypt change to Jehoiakim?

    II Kings 23:34
    A. Ahab's name
    B. Baasha's name
    C. Eliakim's name
    D. Hoshea's name

13. Who was the king of Babylon?

    II Kings 24:1
    A. King Adonizedek
    B. King Esarhaddon
    C. King Hazael
    D. King Nebuchadnezzar

14. How many months did King Jehoiachin reign in Jerusalem?

    II Kings 24:8
    A. 3
    B. 5
    C. 7
    D. 10

15. Who was the mother of King Jehoahaz and King Zedekiah?

    II Kings 23:31, 24:18
    A. Abihail
    B. Hamutal
    C. Jezebel
    D. Michal

16. Which Babylonian captain of the guard destroyed Jerusalem?

    II Kings 25:8–10
    A. Nebuchadnezzar
    B. Nebuchadrezzar
    C. Nebushasban
    D. Nebuzaradan

17. Who was the chief priest when Jerusalem was destroyed?

    II Kings 25:18
    A. Meshelemiah
    B. Nethaniah
    C. Pethahiah
    D. Seraiah

18. Who was the Babylonian governor of Judah?

    II Kings 25:22–23
    A. Gedaliah
    B. Hananiah
    C. Iphedeiah
    D. Jaazaniah

19. Who killed the Babylonian governor of Judah?

    II Kings 25:25
    A. Ishbak
    B. Ishbibenob
    C. Ishmael
    D. Ishmaiah

20. Which Babylonian king released King Jehoiachin from prison?

    II Kings 25:27
    A. King Belshazzar
    B. King Evilmerodach
    C. King Merodach-baladan
    D. King Nebuchadnezzar

Answers on page 761

Lesson 128
Today's Reading: *I Chronicles 1*
Period of Time: 4004–1716 BC
Author: Unknown

MAY 8

1. Who was the first man?
   I Chronicles 1:1

   A. Adam
   B. Cain
   C. Jehu
   D. Seth

2. Who was Noah's father?
   I Chronicles 1:3–4

   A. Baruch
   B. Henoch
   C. Lamech
   D. Meshach

3. Which one of the following was **not** one of Noah's sons?
   I Chronicles 1:4

   A. Gomer
   B. Ham
   C. Japheth
   D. Shem

4. Who began to be *mighty upon the earth*?
   I Chronicles 1:10

   A. Naaman
   B. Nehemiah
   C. Nimrod
   D. Nymphas

5. Whom are the Philistines descendants of?
   I Chronicles 1:12

   A. Caiaphas
   B. Calcol
   C. Carmi
   D. Casluhim

6. During whose days was the earth divided?
   I Chronicles 1:19

   A. Pekah
   B. Peleg
   C. Perez
   D. Peter

7. Who was Abraham's father?
   I Chronicles 1:26–27

   A. Adaiah
   B. Pekah
   C. Terah
   D. Zebah

8. Which one of the following was one of Abraham's sons?
   I Chronicles 1:28

   A. Eliphaz
   B. Gaddiel
   C. Hizkiah
   D. Ishmael

9. Who was Abraham's concubine?
   I Chronicles 1:32

   A. Keturah
   B. Maachah
   C. Sarah
   D. Zilpah

10. Who was Teman's father?
    I Chronicles 1:36

    A. Ahimaaz
    B. Eliphaz
    C. Jehoahaz
    D. Kenaz

11. Who was Nahath's father?
    I Chronicles 1:37

    A. Immanuel
    B. Jeuel
    C. Reuel
    D. Samuel

12. Who was Lotan's father?
    I Chronicles 1:38

    A. Hezir
    B. Jair
    C. Ophir
    D. Seir

13. Who was Lotan's sister?

    I Chronicles 1:39

    A. Ahlai
    B. Chloe
    C. Rhoda
    D. Timna

14. Who were Zibeon's sons?

    I Chronicles 1:40

    A. Aiah and Anah
    B. Bariah and Bealiah
    C. Chenaanah and Conaniah
    D. Delaiah and Dumah

15. Who was Bilhan's father?

    I Chronicles 1:42

    A. Doeg
    B. Ezer
    C. Gaal
    D. Heli

16. Who were Dishan's sons?

    I Chronicles 1:42

    A. Cain and Abel
    B. Esau and Isaac
    C. Peter and Paul
    D. Uz and Aran

17. Who was Bela's father?

    I Chronicles 1:43

    A. Anak
    B. Beor
    C. Cush
    D. Dodo

18. Where was Husham from?

    I Chronicles 1:45

    A. Land of the Punites
    B. Land of the Sodomites
    C. Land of the Temanites
    D. Land of the Uzzielites

19. What was the name of Hadad's city?

    I Chronicles 1:50

    A. Ai
    B. Pai
    C. Sinai
    D. Ulai

20. Who was Hadad's wife?

    I Chronicles 1:50

    A. Mehetabel
    B. Nehushta
    C. Peninnah
    D. Zeresh

*Answers on page 761

Lesson 129
Today's Reading: *I Chronicles 2–4*
Period of Time: 1758–588 BC
Author: Unknown

MAY 9

1. How many sons did Israel have?
   I Chronicles 2:1–2
   A. 3
   B. 5
   C. 7
   D. 12

2. Who was Judah's firstborn son?
   I Chronicles 2:3
   A. Er
   B. Og
   C. So
   D. Uz

3. Who was Judah's daughter-in-law?
   I Chronicles 2:3–4
   A. Esther
   B. Gomer
   C. Hagar
   D. Tamar

4. How many sons did Judah have?
   I Chronicles 2:4
   A. 3
   B. 5
   C. 7
   D. 12

5. Who was called *the troubler of Israel*?
   I Chronicles 2:7
   A. Achar
   B. Debir
   C. Ornan
   D. Sceva

6. How many sons did Jesse have?
   I Chronicles 2:13–15
   A. 3
   B. 5
   C. 7
   D. 12

7. What was the name of Sheshan's Egyptian servant?
   I Chronicles 2:34
   A. Jambres
   B. Jannes
   C. Japhia
   D. Jarha

8. Who was Caleb's concubine?
   I Chronicles 2:46
   A. Eglah
   B. Elisabeth
   C. Ephah
   D. Eunice

9. Who was the father of Bethlehem?
   I Chronicles 2:51
   A. Elishama
   B. Mishma
   C. Salma
   D. Tema

10. How many years did King David reign in Hebron?
    I Chronicles 3:4
    A. 5 years and 3 months
    B. 7 years and 6 months
    C. 9 years and 9 months
    D. 12 years and 11 months

11. Who was King David's daughter?
    I Chronicles 3:9
    A. Damaris
    B. Rahab
    C. Sarah
    D. Tamar

12. Who was King Solomon's son?
    I Chronicles 3:10
    A. Raamah
    B. Rehabiah
    C. Rehoboam
    D. Romamtiezer

13. Who was Ephrathah's firstborn?

I Chronicles 4:4

   A. Ara
   B. Hur
   C. Put
   D. Toi

14. Why did Jabez's mother name him Jabez?

I Chronicles 4:9

   A. His name means forerunner.
   B. She bore him in her old age.
   C. She bore him with sorrow.
   D. That was her father's name.

15. Who was Chelub's brother?

I Chronicles 4:11

   A. Beriah
   B. Josiah
   C. Mizzah
   D. Shuah

16. What was the trade of the men in the valley of Charashim?

I Chronicles 4:14

   A. They were brickmakers.
   B. They were craftsmen.
   C. They were fishermen.
   D. They were stonemasons.

17. Who was Pharaoh's daughter?

I Chronicles 4:18

   A. Bithiah
   B. Jecoliah
   C. Michaiah
   D. Zeruiah

18. Which family was known for making fine linen?

I Chronicles 4:21

   A. House of Ashbea
   B. House of Caleb
   C. House of Micah
   D. House of Pharez

19. Whose descendants dwelled in Gedor long ago?

I Chronicles 4:39–40

   A. Ham's descendants
   B. Japheth's descendants
   C. Shem's descendants
   D. Tubal's descendants

20. How many Simeonites went to mount Seir to smite the rest of the Amalekites?

I Chronicles 4:42–43

   A. 50
   B. 500
   C. 5,000
   D. 50,000

Answers on page 761

Lesson 130

Today's Reading: *I Chronicles 5–6*
Period of Time: 1758–1145 BC
Author: Unknown

1. Who was Israel's firstborn?
   I Chronicles 5:1
   A. Benjamin
   B. Levi
   C. Reuben
   D. Zebulun

2. Who prevailed above his brethren?
   I Chronicles 5:2
   A. Asher
   B. Gad
   C. Issachar
   D. Judah

3. Whom did the birthright belong to?
   I Chronicles 5:2
   A. Dan
   B. Joseph
   C. Naphtali
   D. Simeon

4. Which one of the following was an Assyrian king?
   I Chronicles 5:6
   A. King Belshazzar
   B. King Evil-merodach
   C. King Shishak
   D. King Tilgath-pilneser

5. Which tribe settled in the land of Gilead?
   I Chronicles 5:1–9
   A. Tribe of Naphtali
   B. Tribe of Reuben
   C. Tribe of Simeon
   D. Tribe of Zebulun

6. Who did King Saul make war with in the land of Gilead?
   I Chronicles 5:10
   A. The Hagarites
   B. The Heberites
   C. The Hittites
   D. The Horites

7. Which tribe settled in the land of Bashan?
   I Chronicles 5:11
   A. Tribe of Dan
   B. Tribe of Gad
   C. Tribe of Judah
   D. Tribe of Levi

8. Who was the king of Judah?
   I Chronicles 5:17
   A. King Jabin
   B. King Jehoahaz
   C. King Jotham
   D. King Julius

9. Who was the king of Israel?
   I Chronicles 5:17
   A. King Amaziah
   B. King Azariah
   C. King Jeroboam
   D. King Rehoboam

10. How many men went to war from the tribes that settled east of the river of Jordan?
    I Chronicles 5:18
    A. 11,380
    B. 22,450
    C. 33,290
    D. 44,760

11. How many camels did the tribes east of the river of Jordan take from the spoils of war?
    I Chronicles 5:21
    A. 2,000
    B. 50,000
    C. 100,000
    D. 250,000

12. Which one of the following men was an Assyrian king?
    I Chronicles 5:26
    A. King Asa
    B. King Koz
    C. King Ner
    D. King Pul

13. Who was Moses' father?

I Chronicles 6:3

- **A.** Amram
- **B.** Hiram
- **C.** Iram
- **D.** Joram

14. Which one of the following men was one of Aaron's sons?

I Chronicles 6:3

- **A.** Amminadab
- **B.** Jehonadab
- **C.** Jonadab
- **D.** Nadab

15. Who executed the high priest's office in the temple that Solomon built?

I Chronicles 6:10

- **A.** Azariah
- **B.** Coniah
- **C.** Gemariah
- **D.** Isaiah

16. Which Babylonian king conquered Jerusalem?

I Chronicles 6:15

- **A.** King Asnappar
- **B.** King Esarhaddon
- **C.** King Nebuchadnezzar
- **D.** King Sennacherib

17. Who was **not** a son of Levi?

I Chronicles 6:16

- **A.** Epher
- **B.** Gershom
- **C.** Kohath
- **D.** Merari

18. Who was a singer?

I Chronicles 6:33

- **A.** Heman
- **B.** Mehuman
- **C.** Naaman
- **D.** Shalman

19. Which Levite family received the first lot?

I Chronicles 6:54

- **A.** The Epherites
- **B.** The Gershomites
- **C.** The Kohathites
- **D.** The Mararites

20. Who was Caleb's father?

I Chronicles 6:56

- **A.** Elipheleh
- **B.** Jephunneh
- **C.** Manasseh
- **D.** Rabshakeh

Answers on page 761

Lesson 131

Today's Reading: *I Chronicles 7–9*
Period of Time: 1745–588 BC
Author: Unknown

MAY 11

1. How many sons did Issachar have?
   I Chronicles 7:1
   A. 2
   B. 3
   C. 4
   D. 5

2. What was the total number of valiant men among the families of Issachar?
   I Chronicles 7:5
   A. 21,000
   B. 45,000
   C. 63,000
   D. 87,000

3. How many sons did Benjamin have, according to I Chronicles 7:6?
   I Chronicles 7:6
   A. 2
   B. 3
   C. 4
   D. 5

4. Who is the father of Gilead?
   I Chronicles 7:14
   A. Debir
   B. Jair
   C. Machir
   D. Seir

5. Which one of Ephraim's descendants was slain by the men of Gath?
   I Chronicles 7:20–22
   A. Eglon
   B. Elead
   C. Enoch
   D. Ethan

6. Who was Jehoshua's father?
   I Chronicles 7:27
   A. Dan
   B. Gad
   C. Non
   D. Rei

7. What was the total number of mighty men of valor among the families of Asher?
   I Chronicles 7:40
   A. 20,000
   B. 22,000
   C. 24,000
   D. 26,000

8. Who was Benjamin's firstborn?
   I Chronicles 8:1
   A. Bela
   B. Juda
   C. Reba
   D. Tola

9. How many sons did Benjamin have, according to I Chronicles 8:1-2?
   I Chronicles 8:1–2
   A. 2
   B. 3
   C. 4
   D. 5

10. Which two cities did Shamed build?
    I Chronicles 8:12
    A. Ain and Nod
    B. Ono and Lod
    C. Sin and Gog
    D. Tob and Pul

11. Who was the father of Kish?
    I Chronicles 8:33
    A. Asa
    B. Eli
    C. Ner
    D. Pul

12. Who was King Saul's son?
    I Chronicles 8:33
    A. Heman
    B. Jonathan
    C. Medan
    D. Shaphan

13. How many sons did Azel have?

    I Chronicles 8:38, 9:44

    A. 6
    B. 9
    C. 12
    D. 15

14. What were the sons of Ulam known for in battle?

    I Chronicles 8:40

    A. Being archers
    B. Being chariot drivers
    C. Being horsemen
    D. Being swordsmen

15. Where was Judah taken for their transgression?

    I Chronicles 9:1

    A. Babylon
    B. Egypt
    C. Libya
    D. Syria

16. Who was responsible for preparing the shewbread every sabbath?

    I Chronicles 9:32

    A. The Gershonites
    B. The Jebusites
    C. The Kohathites
    D. The Mararites

17. Who was Jehiel's wife?

    I Chronicles 8:29, 9:35

    A. Jecoliah
    B. Keturah
    C. Loruhammah
    D. Maachah

18. Who was Jehiel's firstborn son?

    I Chronicles 9:35–36

    A. Abdon
    B. Eglon
    C. Gershon
    D. Helon

19. Who was Jonathan's son?

    I Chronicles 9:40

    A. Eshbaal
    B. Ethbaal
    C. Jerubbaal
    D. Meribbaal

20. Who was Azel's father?

    I Chronicles 9:43

    A. Eldaah
    B. Eleasah
    C. Eliezer
    D. Elijah

Answers on page 761

MAY 12

Lesson 132
Today's Reading: *I Chronicles 10–12*
Period of Time: 1055–1048 BC
Author: Unknown

1. How many of King Saul's sons died with him in battle?
   I Chronicles 10:6
   A. 3
   B. 7
   C. 12
   D. 28

2. Upon which mountain were King Saul and his sons slain?
   I Chronicles 10:8
   A. Mount Ebal
   B. Mount Gilboa
   C. Mount Horeb
   D. Mount Jearim

3. Inside which temple did the Philistines place King Saul's head?
   I Chronicles 10:10
   A. Ashtoreth
   B. Chemosh
   C. Dagon
   D. Jupiter

4. In which city were King Saul and his son's dead bodies laid to rest?
   I Chronicles 10:11–12
   A. Geshur
   B. Jabesh
   C. Kadesh
   D. Leshem

5. How many days did the Israelites fast after King Saul and his sons were slain?
   I Chronicles 10:12
   A. 3
   B. 7
   C. 12
   D. 28

6. Who was David's father?
   I Chronicles 10:14
   A. Abinadab
   B. Eliab
   C. Jesse
   D. Shammah

7. Where was David anointed king of Israel?
   I Chronicles 11:1–3
   A. Gibeon
   B. Hebron
   C. Jerusalem
   D. Mizpah

8. What is another name for Jerusalem?
   I Chronicles 11:4
   A. Debir
   B. Ebenezer
   C. Gebal
   D. Jebus

9. Who was Joab's father?
   I Chronicles 11:6
   A. Berechiah
   B. Hezekiah
   C. Jaazaniah
   D. Zeruiah

10. How many men did Jashobeam kill at one time?
    I Chronicles 11:11
    A. 3
    B. 30
    C. 300
    D. 3,000

11. Which one of the following cities contained a Philistine garrison?
    I Chronicles 11:16
    A. Bethlehem
    B. Cyrene
    C. Damascus
    D. Ephron

12. Who was chief of the three men who brought King David water from the Philistine well?

    I Chronicles 11:15–21

    A. Abishai
    B. Jeaterai
    C. Maadai
    D. Zophai

13. Who went down into a pit to slay a lion on a snowy day?

    I Chronicles 11:22

    A. Ahaziah
    B. Benaiah
    C. Chenaniah
    D. Dalaiah

14. Which one of King David's mighty men was a Hittite?

    I Chronicles 11:41

    A. Ahiah
    B. Eliah
    C. Neziah
    D. Uriah

15. Which tribe is described as having the faces of lions and was as swift as roes?

    I Chronicles 12:8

    A. Tribe of Benjamin
    B. Tribe of Dan
    C. Tribe of Gad
    D. Tribe of Reuben

16. Who told King David, "Thy God helpeth thee"?

    I Chronicles 12:18

    A. Amasai
    B. Gabbai
    C. Shobai
    D. Talmai

17. Who was the leader of the Aaronites?

    I Chronicles 12:27

    A. Darda
    B. Eliada
    C. Jehoiada
    D. Shemida

18. Which tribe was King Saul a kindred of?

    I Chronicles 12:29

    A. Tribe of Benjamin
    B. Tribe of Ephraim
    C. Tribe of Issachar
    D. Tribe of Naphtali

19. Which tribe is described as **not** being of a double heart?

    I Chronicles 12:33

    A. Tribe of Asher
    B. Tribe of Manasseh
    C. Tribe of Simeon
    D. Tribe of Zebulun

20. What was the total number of men of war from the Reubenites, Gadites, and the half tribe of Manasseh?

    I Chronicles 12:37

    A. 30,000
    B. 60,000
    C. 90,000
    D. 120,000

Answers on page 761

Lesson 133
Today's Reading: *I Chronicles 13–16*
Period of Time: 1045 BC
Author: Unknown

1. Where is Shihor located?
   I Chronicles 13:5
   A. Assyria
   B. Egypt
   C. Moab
   D. Syria

2. What is another name for Kirjath-jearim?
   I Chronicles 13:6
   A. Baalah
   B. Galeed
   C. Madon
   D. Tirzah

3. In whose house was the ark of God being kept?
   I Chronicles 13:7
   A. Abi-albon's house
   B. Abiasaph's house
   C. Abiathar's house
   D. Abinadab's house

4. Who died because he touched the ark of God?
   I Chronicles 13:9–10
   A. Ebed
   B. Iddo
   C. Mash
   D. Uzza

5. Which one of the following men was a Gittite?
   I Chronicles 13:13
   A. Belteshazzar
   B. Jesharelah
   C. Obededom
   D. Shethar-boznai

6. Who was the king of Tyre?
   I Chronicles 14:1
   A. King Amram
   B. King Hiram
   C. King Joram
   D. King Piram

7. Which one of the following was one of King David's sons?
   I Chronicles 14:3–4
   A. Philemon
   B. Rimmon
   C. Solomon
   D. Talmon

8. Where did King David smite the host of the Philistines the first time?
   I Chronicles 14:8–11
   A. Baalperazim
   B. Chephirah
   C. Dalmanutha
   D. Gath-hepher

9. What did King David do with the gods the Philistines left behind?
   I Chronicles 14:12
   A. Burned them
   B. Hid them
   C. Kept them
   D. Sold them

10. From the tops of which kind of trees did King David hear the marching of the Philistines?
    I Chronicles 14:13–16
    A. Algum trees
    B. Cedar trees
    C. Mulberry trees
    D. Sycamore trees

11. Where did King David smite the host of the Philistines the second time?
    I Chronicles 14:16–17
    A. From Bethpeor to Penuel
    B. From Gibeon to Gazer
    C. From Hebron to Jerusalem
    D. From Jericho to Ai

12. Where was the ark of God to be placed in the City of David?

    I Chronicles 15:1

    A. Inside a tent
    B. Inside David's palace
    C. Inside the temple
    D. Inside Uriel's house

13. How many sons belonged to the family of the Merarites?

    I Chronicles 15:6

    A. 120
    B. 220
    C. 320
    D. 420

14. Who were the priests?

    I Chronicles 15:11

    A. Abdon and Jephthah
    B. Elon and Gideon
    C. Othniel and Shamgar
    D. Zadok and Abiathar

15. Which tribe bore the ark of God upon their shoulders with staves?

    I Chronicles 15:15

    A. Tribe of Benjamin
    B. Tribe of Levi
    C. Tribe of Naphtali
    D. Tribe of Reuben

16. Which skilful chief of the Levites taught song to others?

    I Chronicles 15:22, 15:27

    A. Amasiah
    B. Berechiah
    C. Chenaniah
    D. Delaiah

17. Who despised King David in her heart?

    I Chronicles 15:29

    A. Abital
    B. Bathsheba
    C. Haggith
    D. Michal

18. Who made a sound with cymbals?

    I Chronicles 16:5

    A. Asaph
    B. Perez
    C. Sheva
    D. Zabud

19. Where was the high place located?

    I Chronicles 16:39

    A. Galeed
    B. Gennesaret
    C. Gibeon
    D. Gurbaal

20. Whose sons were porters?

    I Chronicles 16:42

    A. Jedaiah's sons
    B. Jediael's sons
    C. Jedidiah's sons
    D. Jeduthun's sons

*Answers on page 762

Lesson 134
Today's Reading: *I Chronicles 17–19*
Period of Time: 1044–1036 BC
Author: Unknown

MAY 14

1. Who told King David that God did **not** want him to build him a house to dwell in?
   I Chronicles 17:3–15
   A. Nathan
   B. Samuel
   C. Zechariah
   D. Zephaniah

2. What was King David's occupation before becoming a king?
   I Chronicles 17:7
   A. Blacksmith
   B. Carpenter
   C. Rancher
   D. Shepherd

3. Which town did King David take from the Philistines?
   I Chronicles 18:1
   A. Cush
   B. Gath
   C. Ivah
   D. Noph

4. Who was Hadarezer the king of?
   I Chronicles 18:3
   A. Rumah
   B. Selah
   C. Tarah
   D. Zobah

5. How many chariots did King David take from Hadarezer?
   I Chronicles 18:3–4
   A. 10
   B. 100
   C. 1,000
   D. 10,000

6. How many Syrian soldiers did King David slay?
   I Chronicles 18:5
   A. 22,000
   B. 44,000
   C. 66,000
   D. 88,000

7. Which two cities of Hadarezer contained a lot of brass?
   I Chronicles 18:8
   A. Manahath and Eber
   B. Mephaath and Seir
   C. Tibhath and Chun
   D. Zarephath and Aija

8. Who was the king of Hamath?
   I Chronicles 18:9
   A. King Lou
   B. King Mou
   C. King Tou
   D. King You

9. Who was the king of Hamath's son?
   I Chronicles 18:9–10
   A. Adoniram
   B. Hadoram
   C. Iram
   D. Jehoram

10. Who slew 18,000 Edomites in the valley of salt?
    I Chronicles 18:12
    A. Abishai
    B. Ahasbai
    C. Amashai
    D. Amittai

11. Who was over the host of Israel?
    I Chronicles 18:15
    A. Er
    B. Huz
    C. Joab
    D. Lahmi

12. Who was King David's recorder?

    I Chronicles 18:15

    A. Jehoshaphat
    B. Melchizedek
    C. Onesiphorus
    D. Tobadonijah

13. Which two men were priests?

    I Chronicles 18:16

    A. Cyrus and Darius
    B. Jeroboam and Rehoboam
    C. Peter and Paul
    D. Zadok and Abimelech

14. Which one of the following was a scribe?

    I Chronicles 18:16

    A. Shapham
    B. Shashai
    C. Shashak
    D. Shavsha

15. Who was over the Cherethites and the Pelethites?

    I Chronicles 18:17

    A. Amariah
    B. Benaiah
    C. Chenaniah
    D. Dalaiah

16. Who was the king of Ammon?

    I Chronicles 19:1

    A. King Machir
    B. King Nahash
    C. King Pagiel
    D. King Raddai

17. Who was the king of Ammon's son?

    I Chronicles 19:2

    A. Hanun
    B. Heber
    C. Hiram
    D. Hobab

18. Which king formed an alliance with the Ammonites to fight against King David?

    I Chronicles 19:6–7

    A. King of Baalah
    B. King of Maachah
    C. King of Naamah
    D. King of Raamaah

19. Who was the captain of the host of Hadarezer?

    I Chronicles 19:16

    A. Hatach
    B. Meshach
    C. Parnach
    D. Shophach

20. How many Syrians fighting in chariots did King David slay?

    I Chronicles 19:18

    A. 3,000
    B. 5,000
    C. 7,000
    D. 9,000

*Answers on page 762

Lesson 135
Today's Reading: *I Chronicles 20–23*
Period of Time: 1035–1014 BC
Author: Unknown

1. Which king's crown did King David take for himself?
   I Chronicles 20:1–2
   A. The king of Hukkok's crown
   B. The king of Naamah's crown
   C. The king of Rabbah's crown
   D. The king of Ziddim's crown

2. How many talents of gold did King David's crown weigh?
   I Chronicles 20:2
   A. 1
   B. 3
   C. 5
   D. 7

3. What did King David do to the captured Ammonites?
   I Chronicles 20:1–3
   A. Enslaved them
   B. Executed them
   C. Set them free
   D. Sold them

4. Where did King David go to war against the Philistines?
   I Chronicles 20:4
   A. Bezer
   B. Ether
   C. Gezer
   D. Immer

5. Which one of the following men was a Hushathite?
   I Chronicles 20:4
   A. Bigthana
   B. Hizkijah
   C. Mikneiah
   D. Sibbechai

6. Who was Goliath's son?
   I Chronicles 20:4
   A. Samson
   B. Semachiah
   C. Sippai
   D. Sosthenes

7. Who was Goliath's brother?
   I Chronicles 20:5
   A. Hurai
   B. Lahmi
   C. Othni
   D. Tibni

8. Who slew the son of Goliath who had twelve fingers and twelve toes?
   I Chronicles 20:6–7
   A. Jonathan
   B. Naaman
   C. Ornan
   D. Zethan

9. Who enticed King David to number Israel?
   I Chronicles 21:1
   A. Elhanan
   B. Joab
   C. Phlegon
   D. Satan

10. How many men drew the sword in Israel?
    I Chronicles 21:5
    A. 1,000
    B. 10,000
    C. 100,000
    D. 1,100,000

11. How many men drew the sword in Judah?
    I Chronicles 21:5
    A. 470
    B. 4,700
    C. 47,000
    D. 470,000

12. Which two tribes were excluded in the census?
    I Chronicles 21:6
    A. Tribes of Judah and Dan
    B. Tribes of Levi and Benjamin
    C. Tribes of Simeon and Manasseh
    D. Tribes of Zebulun and Gad

13. Who was King David's seer?
    I Chronicles 21:9
    A. Gad
    B. Non
    C. Sem
    D. Uri

14. How many Israelites died from the pestilence?
    I Chronicles 21:14
    A. 20,000
    B. 50,000
    C. 70,000
    D. 100,000

15. Who owned a threshing floor?
    I Chronicles 21:15–18
    A. Ophir
    B. Ornan
    C. Oshea
    D. Othni

16. What did the Zidonians and the people of Tyre bring to King David?
    I Chronicles 22:4
    A. Cedar wood
    B. Gold pieces
    C. Oak wood
    D. Silver pieces

17. Which one of the following men was one of King David's sons?
    I Chronicles 22:6, 23:1
    A. Abner
    B. Joab
    C. Nethaniah
    D. Solomon

18. Who were Moses' sons?
    I Chronicles 23:15
    A. Gershom and Eliezer
    B. Ithream and Daniel
    C. Nathan and Japhia
    D. Shephatiah and Adonijah

19. Which man had many sons?
    I Chronicles 23:17
    A. Jephthah
    B. Lot
    C. Rehabiah
    D. Zelophehad

20. Which tribe had been responsible for carrying the tabernacle and its vessels?
    I Chronicles 23:26
    A. Tribe of Dan
    B. Tribe of Levi
    C. Tribe of Naphtali
    D. Tribe of Reuben

*Answers on page 762

Lesson 136
Today's Reading: *I Chronicles 24–26*
Period of Time: 1035–1014 BC
Author: Unknown

1. How many sons did Aaron have?
   I Chronicles 24:1
   A. 4
   B. 7
   C. 10
   D. 11

2. Which two of Aaron's sons had no children?
   I Chronicles 24:2
   A. Eliab and Elihu
   B. Hobab and Raphu
   C. Jobab and Sallu
   D. Nadab and Abihu

3. Which two of Aaron's sons executed the priest's office?
   I Chronicles 24:2
   A. Eladah and Ithai
   B. Eleazar and Ithamar
   C. Elhanan and Ithiel
   D. Eliadah and Ithmah

4. Whom was Zadok a descendant of?
   I Chronicles 24:3
   A. Eladah
   B. Eleazar
   C. Elhanan
   D. Eliadah

5. Whom was Ahimelech a descendant of?
   I Chronicles 24:3
   A. Ithai
   B. Ithamar
   C. Ithiel
   D. Ithmah

6. Which of Aaron's sons had the most chief men?
   I Chronicles 24:4
   A. Eladah
   B. Eleazar
   C. Elhanan
   D. Eliadah

7. Which of Aaron's sons had eight chief men?
   I Chronicles 24:4
   A. Ithai
   B. Ithamar
   C. Ithiel
   D. Ithmah

8. Which Levite was a scribe?
   I Chronicles 24:6
   A. Pelaliah
   B. Rehabiah
   C. Shemaiah
   D. Tebaliah

9. How many priestly divisions were there?
   I Chronicles 24:7–18
   A. 24
   B. 48
   C. 62
   D. 86

10. Whom did the first lot fall upon concerning the priestly divisions?
    I Chronicles 24:7
    A. Jehoiarib
    B. Jehonadab
    C. Jehonathan
    D. Jehoram

11. Whom did the last lot fall upon concerning the priestly divisions?
    I Chronicles 24:18
    A. Jaalam
    B. Laadan
    C. Maaziah
    D. Naashon

12. Which one of the following men was a musician?
    I Chronicles 25:1
    A. Asaph
    B. Barak
    C. Cushi
    D. Deuel

13. How many sons did Heman have?
    I Chronicles 25:5
    A. 7
    B. 10
    C. 12
    D. 14

14. How many men were instructed in the songs of the LORD?
    I Chronicles 25:7
    A. 122
    B. 166
    C. 244
    D. 288

15. Whom did the lot to guard the *east* gate fall to?
    I Chronicles 26:14
    A. Nicodemus
    B. Prochorus
    C. Shelemiah
    D. Tanhumeth

16. Whom did the lot to guard the *north* gate fall to?
    I Chronicles 26:14
    A. Benaiah
    B. Jekamiah
    C. Pekahiah
    D. Zechariah

17. Whom did the lot to guard the *south* gate fall to?
    I Chronicles 26:15
    A. Jekameam
    B. Nahamani
    C. Obededom
    D. Shammoth

18. Which two men did the lot to guard the *west* gate and the Shallecheth gate fall to?
    I Chronicles 26:16
    A. Ephraim and Manasseh
    B. Jannes and Jambres
    C. Moab and Benammi
    D. Shuppim and Hosah

19. Which Levite was over the treasures of the house of God and the dedicated things?
    I Chronicles 26:20
    A. Ahijah
    B. Joelah
    C. Tikvah
    D. Zanoah

20. How many Hebronites ruled over the Reubenites, Gadites, and the half tribe of Manasseh for every matter pertaining to God and the affairs of the king?
    I Chronicles 26:31–32
    A. 72
    B. 120
    C. 2,700
    D. 17,200

*Answers on page 762

Lesson 137

Today's Reading: *I Chronicles 27–29*
Period of Time: 1015 BC
Author: Unknown

1. How many people served the king during one course of the year?
   I Chronicles 27:1
   A. 12,000
   B. 24,000
   C. 36,000
   D. 48,000

2. Who was the eighth captain for the eighth month?
   I Chronicles 27:11
   A. Benaiah
   B. Dodai
   C. Jashobeam
   D. Sibbecai

3. Who was the prince of the Aaronites?
   I Chronicles 27:17
   A. Zadok
   B. Zaham
   C. Zarah
   D. Zavan

4. Which age group was **not** included in the census?
   I Chronicles 27:23
   A. Those twelve years old and under
   B. Those eighteen years old and under
   C. Those twenty years old and under
   D. Those thirty years old and under

5. Who was over the king's treasures?
   I Chronicles 27:25
   A. Azmaveth
   B. Genubath
   C. Jeremoth
   D. Manahath

6. Who was over those that did the work of the field for tillage of the ground?
   I Chronicles 27:26
   A. Buzi
   B. Ezri
   C. Gadi
   D. Hori

7. Who was over King David's wine cellars?
   I Chronicles 27:27
   A. Habaziniah
   B. Nabal
   C. Tabeel
   D. Zabdi

8. Who was over the king's cellars of oils?
   I Chronicles 27:28
   A. Joah
   B. Joahaz
   C. Joash
   D. Joatham

9. Who was over the king's camels?
   I Chronicles 27:30
   A. Asahel
   B. Dodai
   C. Obil
   D. Shamhuth

10. Who was King David's uncle?
    I Chronicles 27:32
    A. Joahaz
    B. Jonathan
    C. Josiah
    D. Jozadak

11. Who was the general over King David's army?
    I Chronicles 27:34
    A. Joab
    B. Kish
    C. Luke
    D. Moza

12. Which one of King David's sons would one day build the temple?
    I Chronicles 28:6
    A. Absalom
    B. Chileab
    C. Nathan
    D. Solomon

13. How many talents of gold did King David give from his personal account to build the temple?
    I Chronicles 29:3–4
    A. 3
    B. 30
    C. 300
    D. 3,000

14. How many talents of silver did King David give from his personal account to build the temple?
    I Chronicles 29:3–4
    A. 3,000
    B. 5,000
    C. 7,000
    D. 10,000

15. How many bullocks were sacrificed unto the LORD?
    I Chronicles 29:21
    A. 500
    B. 1,000
    C. 1,500
    D. 2,000

16. How many rams were sacrificed unto the LORD?
    I Chronicles 29:21
    A. 1,000
    B. 2,000
    C. 3,000
    D. 4,000

17. How many lambs were sacrificed unto the LORD?
    I Chronicles 29:21
    A. 500
    B. 1,000
    C. 6,000
    D. 12,000

18. Who was King David's father?
    I Chronicles 29:26
    A. Jeiel
    B. Jered
    C. Jesse
    D. Jezer

19. How many years did King David reign over Israel?
    I Chronicles 29:27
    A. 10
    B. 20
    C. 30
    D. 40

20. Which book was **not** mentioned as a book about the acts of David the king?
    I Chronicles 29:29–30
    A. Book of David the king
    B. Book of Gad the seer
    C. Book of Nathan the prophet
    D. Book of Samuel the seer

*Answers on page 762

Lesson 138

Today's Reading: *II Chronicles 1–4*
Period of Time: 1015–1012 BC
Author: Unknown

MAY 18

1. Who was King Solomon's father?
   II Chronicles 1:1
   A. Aaron
   B. David
   C. Gaham
   D. Jacob

2. Where was the high place King Solomon visited?
   II Chronicles 1:3
   A. Calneh
   B. Dimnah
   C. Gibeon
   D. Ibleam

3. Who made the brasen altar?
   II Chronicles 1:5
   A. Bezaleel
   B. Hanameel
   C. Jezreel
   D. Maleleel

4. What did King Solomon ask from God?
   II Chronicles 1:7–12
   A. Fame and fortune
   B. Good health and wealth
   C. Victory over enemies and long life
   D. Wisdom and knowledge

5. How many chariots did King Solomon own?
   II Chronicles 1:14
   A. 350
   B. 700
   C. 1,050
   D. 1,400

6. Who was the king of Tyre?
   II Chronicles 2:3
   A. King Hanun
   B. King Herod
   C. King Hophra
   D. King Huram

7. Where did the lumber come from to build the temple?
   II Chronicles 2:16
   A. Alexandria
   B. Lebanon
   C. Makkedah
   D. Trachonitis

8. How many supervisors did King Solomon hire to oversee the work on the temple?
   II Chronicles 2:18
   A. 3,600
   B. 7,200
   C. 10,800
   D. 14,400

9. Upon which mountain was the temple built?
   II Chronicles 3:1
   A. Mount Abarim
   B. Mount Carmel
   C. Mount Moriah
   D. Mount Olivet

10. When did the work on the temple begin?
    II Chronicles 3:2
    A. 1st day of the 1st month
    B. 2nd day of the 2nd month
    C. 3rd day of the 3rd month
    D. 4th day of the 4th month

11. What was the length in cubits of the temple?
    II Chronicles 3:3
    A. 20
    B. 40
    C. 60
    D. 80

12. What was the breadth in cubits of the temple?
    II Chronicles 3:3
    A. 20
    B. 40
    C. 60
    D. 80

13. Where did King Solomon get the gold used for the temple?

    II Chronicles 3:6
    - **A.** Havilah
    - **B.** Midas
    - **C.** Ophir
    - **D.** Parvaim

14. What were the dimensions in cubits of the most holy house?

    II Chronicles 3:8
    - **A.** 10 x 10
    - **B.** 20 x 20
    - **C.** 30 x 30
    - **D.** 40 x 40

15. Which colors were used to make the vail?

    II Chronicles 3:14
    - **A.** Blue, purple, crimson
    - **B.** Gold, silver, and crimson
    - **C.** Red, white, and blue
    - **D.** Scarlet, purple, and green

16. What was the name of the pillar on the right?

    II Chronicles 3:17
    - **A.** Jaalam
    - **B.** Jabesh
    - **C.** Jachin
    - **D.** Jaddua

17. What was the name of the pillar on the left?

    II Chronicles 3:17
    - **A.** Bani
    - **B.** Beor
    - **C.** Boaz
    - **D.** Buzi

18. What was used to make the altar for the burnt offerings?

    II Chronicles 4:1
    - **A.** Brass
    - **B.** Gold
    - **C.** Iron
    - **D.** Silver

19. Which 12 images held up the molten sea?

    II Chronicles 4:2–5
    - **A.** Angels
    - **B.** Horses
    - **C.** Men
    - **D.** Oxen

20. What was used to make the vessels for the house of God?

    II Chronicles 4:19–22
    - **A.** Brass
    - **B.** Gold
    - **C.** Iron
    - **D.** Silver

Answers on page 762

Lesson 139
Today's Reading: *II Chronicles 5–7*
Period of Time: 1012–1004 BC
Author: Unknown

1. What is another name for the City of David?
   II Chronicles 5:2
   A. Cush
   B. Eden
   C. Rome
   D. Zion

2. During which month did the men of Israel assemble for the feast?
   II Chronicles 5:3
   A. 4th
   B. 5th
   C. 6th
   D. 7th

3. Who carried the ark, the tabernacle, and the holy vessels?
   II Chronicles 5:4–5
   A. The Danites
   B. The Gadites
   C. The Levites
   D. The Reubenites

4. The wings of which creatures covered the ark?
   II Chronicles 5:7–8
   A. Cherubims
   B. Dragons
   C. Seraphims
   D. Unicorns

5. How many tables were inside the ark?
   II Chronicles 5:10
   A. 1
   B. 2
   C. 3
   D. 4

6. Upon which mountain did Moses receive the tables?
   II Chronicles 5:10
   A. Mount Ararat
   B. Mount Gilead
   C. Mount Horeb
   D. Mount Jearim

7. On which end of the altar did the singers stand?
   II Chronicles 5:12
   A. North
   B. South
   C. East
   D. West

8. How many priests sounded the trumpets?
   II Chronicles 5:12
   A. 120
   B. 240
   C. 360
   D. 480

9. Which words did the singers sing?
   II Chronicles 5:13
   A. "Amazing grace"
   B. "For he is good"
   C. "Just as I am"
   D. "Sweet Beulah land"

10. What is God's chosen city?
    II Chronicles 6:6
    A. Ephesus
    B. Jerusalem
    C. Laodicea
    D. Philadelphia

11. Whom did the LORD choose to be over his people?
    II Chronicles 6:6
    A. David
    B. Elymas
    C. Nahash
    D. Pilate

12. What were the measurements in cubits to the brasen scaffold?
    II Chronicles 6:13
    A. 2 x 2 x 4
    B. 3 x 3 x 5
    C. 4 x 4 x 2
    D. 5 x 5 x 3

13. What happened after King Solomon finished praying?
    II Chronicles 7:1
    A. Fire came down from heaven
    B. God sent a pestilence
    C. Israel's enemies invaded the land
    D. Locusts devoured the crops

14. How many *oxen* did King Solomon sacrifice during the dedication of the temple?
    II Chronicles 7:5
    A. 22,000
    B. 44,000
    C. 66,000
    D. 88,000

15. How many *sheep* did King Solomon sacrifice during the dedication of the temple?
    II Chronicles 7:5
    A. 100,000
    B. 110,000
    C. 120,000
    D. 130,000

16. Which area of the temple did King Solomon make hallow for the abundant number of sacrificial offerings?
    II Chronicles 7:7
    A. The holy place
    B. The middle of the court
    C. The most holy place
    D. The wailing wall

17. How many days did Israel spend dedicating the altar?
    II Chronicles 7:9
    A. 2
    B. 3
    C. 6
    D. 7

18. How many days were the days of the feast?
    II Chronicles 7:9
    A. 2
    B. 3
    C. 6
    D. 7

19. On which day of the month did King Solomon send the people away?
    II Chronicles 7:10
    A. 1st day
    B. 2nd day
    C. 23rd day
    D. 30th day

20. From which land did the LORD rescue his people?
    II Chronicles 7:22
    A. Asia
    B. Egypt
    C. India
    D. Spain

*Answers on page 762

Lesson 140

Today's Reading: *II Chronicles 8–10*
Period of Time: 992–975 BC
Author: Unknown

1. Which city did King Solomon conquer?
   II Chronicles 8:3
   A. Hamathzobah
   B. Jabeshgilead
   C. Thessalonica
   D. Zarethshahar

2. Which city did King Solomon build in the wilderness?
   II Chronicles 8:4
   A. Humtah
   B. Jotbah
   C. Tadmor
   D. Zereda

3. How many officers served under King Solomon?
   II Chronicles 8:10
   A. 250
   B. 500
   C. 750
   D. 1,000

4. Which two cities were located in Edom?
   II Chronicles 8:17
   A. Eziongeber and Eloth
   B. Fair Havens and Salmone
   C. Joppa and Tarshish
   D. Sidon and Alexandria

5. Where did King Solomon send ships for its gold?
   II Chronicles 8:18
   A. Golan
   B. Halah
   C. Ophir
   D. Troas

6. Where was the queen from that visited King Solomon?
   II Chronicles 9:1–12
   A. Berea
   B. India
   C. Sheba
   D. Tekoa

7. What type of wood did King Solomon use to make terraces, harps, and psalteries?
   II Chronicles 9:11
   A. Algum
   B. Chestnut
   C. Hazel
   D. Poplar

8. What was the weight of gold measured in talents that came to King Solomon in one year?
   II Chronicles 9:13
   A. 222
   B. 444
   C. 666
   D. 888

9. How many *targets* of beaten gold did King Solomon make?
   II Chronicles 9:15
   A. 100
   B. 200
   C. 300
   D. 400

10. How many shekels of beaten gold went to one *target*?
    II Chronicles 9:15
    A. 6
    B. 60
    C. 600
    D. 6,000

11. How many *shields* of beaten gold did King Solomon make?

    II Chronicles 9:16

    A. 150
    B. 200
    C. 250
    D. 300

12. Where did King Solomon place the golden shields and targets?

    II Chronicles 9:16

    A. House of the forest of Arabia
    B. House of the forest of Hareth
    C. House of the forest of Jerusalem
    D. House of the forest of Lebanon

13. Which two materials were used to build King Solomon's throne?

    II Chronicles 9:17

    A. Brass and gems
    B. Ivory and gold
    C. Rubies and wood
    D. Silver and leather

14. How many steps were there to King Solomon's throne?

    II Chronicles 9:18

    A. 3
    B. 6
    C. 9
    D. 12

15. What was the total number of lion images located on the steps to King Solomon's throne?

    II Chronicles 9:19

    A. 12
    B. 18
    C. 20
    D. 28

16. How many stalls did King Solomon have for his horses and chariots?

    II Chronicles 9:25

    A. 1,000
    B. 2,000
    C. 3,000
    D. 4,000

17. How many years did King Solomon rule over Israel?

    II Chronicles 9:30

    A. 10
    B. 20
    C. 30
    D. 40

18. Who was King Solomon's son?

    II Chronicles 9:31

    A. Abinoam
    B. Jeroboam
    C. Jorkoam
    D. Rehoboam

19. Who returned from Egypt after King Solomon died?

    II Chronicles 10:2

    A. Abinoam
    B. Jeroboam
    C. Jorkoam
    D. Rehoboam

20. Who was stoned to death by the children of Israel?

    II Chronicles 10:18

    A. Ahijah
    B. Hadoram
    C. Jesse
    D. Nebat

Answers on page 762

Lesson 141
Today's Reading: *II Chronicles 11–14*
Period of Time: 975–951 BC
Author: Unknown

1. How many warriors did King Rehoboam gather to fight against Israel?
   II Chronicles 11:1
   A. 180,000
   B. 240,000
   C. 300,000
   D. 360,000

2. Whom did God send to King Rehoboam?
   II Chronicles 11:2–4
   A. Shemaah
   B. Shemaiah
   C. Shemida
   D. Shemuel

3. Which city is one of the many cities King Rehoboam fortified?
   II Chronicles 11:6
   A. Bethlehem
   B. Jericho
   C. Megiddo
   D. Shiloh

4. Which two tribes sided with King Rehoboam?
   II Chronicles 11:12
   A. Tribes of Asher and Issachar
   B. Tribes of Judah and Benjamin
   C. Tribes of Reuben and Gad
   D. Tribes of Zebulun and Manasseh

5. Who was Absalom's daughter?
   II Chronicles 11:21
   A. Keturah
   B. Loruhamah
   C. Maachah
   D. Peninnah

6. Who was the king of Egypt?
   II Chronicles 12:2
   A. King Belshazzar
   B. King Darius
   C. King Rezin
   D. King Shishak

7. What was one of the three nations that joined Egypt in its fight against King Rehoboam?
   II Chronicles 12:3
   A. The Greeks
   B. The Naamathites
   C. The Philippians
   D. The Sukkiims

8. Which king had made the shields of gold the king of Egypt took from Judah?
   II Chronicles 12:9–10
   A. King David
   B. King Rehoboam
   C. King Solomon
   D. King Tut

9. How old was King Rehoboam when he began to reign?
   II Chronicles 12:13
   A. 21 years old
   B. 41 years old
   C. 61 years old
   D. 81 years old

10. What was Naamah?
    II Chronicles 12:13
    A. A Carmelitess
    B. A Moabitess
    C. An Ammonitess
    D. An Edomitess

11. How many men did King Abijah have to fight against King Jeroboam's 800,000 men?
    II Chronicles 13:3
    A. 200,000
    B. 400,000
    C. 600,000
    D. 800,000

12. Upon which mountain did King Abijah address King Jeroboam and all of Israel?
    II Chronicles 13:4
    A. Mount Ephraim
    B. Mount Lebanon
    C. Mount Tabor
    D. Mount Zemaraim

13. Which golden images did King Jeroboam make for the people to worship?
    II Chronicles 13:8
    A. Calves
    B. Eagles
    C. Goats
    D. Snakes

14. Which book contained the acts of King Abijah, his ways, and sayings?
    II Chronicles 13:22
    A. The book of Jehu
    B. The chronicles of Samuel the seer
    C. The life and times of Abijah the king
    D. The story of the prophet Iddo

15. How many years of peace occurred during the time of King Asa?
    II Chronicles 14:1
    A. 10
    B. 20
    C. 30
    D. 40

16. Who was the Ethiopian that came against King Asa?
    II Chronicles 14:9
    A. Jerah
    B. Serah
    C. Terah
    D. Zerah

17. How many warriors were in the Ethiopian army?
    II Chronicles 14:9
    A. 1,000,000
    B. 2,000,000
    C. 3,000,000
    D. 4,000,000

18. How many chariots did the Ethiopian army have?
    II Chronicles 14:9
    A. 100
    B. 200
    C. 300
    D. 400

19. Where did King Asa and the people who were with him go to battle the Ethiopian army?
    II Chronicles 14:10
    A. Cuthah
    B. Jogbehah
    C. Mareshah
    D. Netophah

20. How far did King Asa and the people who were with him pursue the Ethiopian army?
    II Chronicles 14:13
    A. Unto Chebar
    B. Unto Gerar
    C. Unto Lodebar
    D. Unto Sephar

*Answers on page 762

Lesson 142
Today's Reading: *II Chronicles 15–18*
Period of Time: 951–897 BC
Author: Unknown

MAY 22

1. Whom did the Spirit of God come upon?
   II Chronicles 15:1
   A. Azariah
   B. Jeriah
   C. Neariah
   D. Sheriah

2. During which year in his reign did King Asa hold a meeting in Jerusalem?
   II Chronicles 15:10
   A. 15th year
   B. 23rd year
   C. 36th year
   D. 41st year

3. How many *oxen* were offered to the LORD during the meeting in Jerusalem?
   II Chronicles 15:11
   A. 7
   B. 70
   C. 700
   D. 7,000

4. How many *sheep* were offered to the LORD during the meeting in Jerusalem?
   II Chronicles 15:11
   A. 7
   B. 70
   C. 700
   D. 7,000

5. Who was King Asa's mother?
   II Chronicles 15:16
   A. Baarah
   B. Maachah
   C. Naamah
   D. Naarah

6. Who was the king of Israel during the thirty-sixth year of King Asa's reign?
   II Chronicles 16:1
   A. King Ahaz
   B. King Baasha
   C. King Hezekiah
   D. King Manasseh

7. Who was the king of Syria?
   II Chronicles 16:2
   A. King Ahasuerus
   B. King Ben-ha'dad
   C. King Cyrus the Great
   D. King Darius

8. Which seer rebuked King Asa for turning to the king of Syria for help against the king of Israel?
   II Chronicles 16:7
   A. Amos
   B. Gad
   C. Hanani
   D. Iddo

9. Which part of King Asa's body became diseased during the thirty-ninth year of his reign?
   II Chronicles 16:12
   A. His arms
   B. His buttocks
   C. His feet
   D. His hands

10. During which year of his reign did King Asa die?
    II Chronicles 16:13
    A. 23rd year
    B. 36th year
    C. 41st year
    D. 55th year

11. Who brought King Jehoshaphat presents and tribute silver?

    II Chronicles 17:11

    A. The Hagarenes
    B. The Libertines
    C. The Nazarenes
    D. The Philistines

12. Who brought King Jehoshaphat rams and he goats?

    II Chronicles 17:11

    A. The Arabians
    B. The Cretians
    C. The Grecians
    D. The Persians

13. How many men served under *Adnah*?

    II Chronicles 17:14

    A. 180,000
    B. 200,000
    C. 280,000
    D. 300,000

14. How many men served under *Jehohanan*?

    II Chronicles 17:15

    A. 180,000
    B. 200,000
    C. 280,000
    D. 300,000

15. How many men served under *Eliada*?

    II Chronicles 17:17

    A. 180,000
    B. 200,000
    C. 280,000
    D. 300,000

16. How many men served under *Jehozabad*?

    II Chronicles 17:18

    A. 180,000
    B. 200,000
    C. 280,000
    D. 300,000

17. How many false prophets served King Ahab?

    II Chronicles 18:5

    A. 400
    B. 800
    C. 1200
    D. 1600

18. Which one of the following was a prophet of the LORD?

    II Chronicles 18:7

    A. Hananiah
    B. Micaiah
    C. Noadiah
    D. Zedekiah

19. Which object made of iron did the false prophets present to King Ahab and King Jehoshaphat?

    II Chronicles 18:10

    A. Axes
    B. Birdcages
    C. Daggers
    D. Horns

20. Where did King Ahab and King Jehoshaphat battle the king of Syria?

    II Chronicles 18:28–34

    A. Ai
    B. Jericho
    C. Michmash
    D. Ramoth-gilead

*Answers on page 762

Lesson 143

Today's Reading: *II Chronicles 19–22*
Period of Time: 897–884 BC
Author: Unknown

1. Which seer told King Jehoshaphat that wrath was upon him from the LORD for helping the ungodly?

    II Chronicles 19:2

    A. Gad
    B. Hanani
    C. Iddo
    D. Jehu

2. What is another name for Hazazon-tamar?

    II Chronicles 20:2

    A. Athens
    B. Cyprus
    C. Engedi
    D. Geshur

3. Whom did the Spirit of the LORD come upon?

    II Chronicles 20:14

    A. Jahath
    B. Jahaziel
    C. Jahdai
    D. Jahdiel

4. How many days did Judah gather the spoil of the children of Ammon, Moab, and mount Seir?

    II Chronicles 20:22–25

    A. 3
    B. 5
    C. 7
    D. 9

5. In which valley did Judah assemble to bless the LORD?

    II Chronicles 20:26

    A. Valley of Achor
    B. Valley of Berachah
    C. Valley of Eshcol
    D. Valley of Gerar

6. Who was King Jehoshaphat's mother?

    II Chronicles 20:31

    A. Azubah
    B. Hadassah
    C. Iscah
    D. Jecoliah

7. Who was King Jehoshaphat's father?

    II Chronicles 20:32

    A. Asa
    B. Ira
    C. Pua
    D. Zia

8. Who was the king of Israel?

    II Chronicles 20:35

    A. King Ahaziah
    B. King Hezekiah
    C. King Uzziah
    D. King Zedekiah

9. Where did King Jehoshaphat and the king of Israel build ships?

    II Chronicles 20:36

    A. Cypress
    B. Eziongeber
    C. Rhodes
    D. Tyre

10. Who prophesied the ships King Jehoshaphat and the king of Israel built would be destroyed?

    II Chronicles 20:37

    A. Abiezer
    B. Bezer
    C. Eliezer
    D. Hadadezer

11. Which two nations revolted against King Jehoram?

    II Chronicles 21:8–10

    A. Assyria and Egypt
    B. Babylon and Syria
    C. Edom and Libnah
    D. Greece and Ethiopia

12. Who prophesied against King Jehoram?

    II Chronicles 21:12–15

    A. Abijah
    B. Elijah
    C. Irijah
    D. Urijah

13. Which part of King Jehoram's body became diseased?

    II Chronicles 21:15, 21:18–19

    A. His arms
    B. His bowels
    C. His feet
    D. His gums

14. Who was King Jehoram's youngest son?

    II Chronicles 21:17

    A. Achaz
    B. Ahaz
    C. Eliphaz
    D. Jehoahaz

15. How old was King Ahaziah when he began to reign over Judah?

    II Chronicles 22:2

    A. 12 years old
    B. 22 years old
    C. 32 years old
    D. 42 years old

16. How many years did King Ahaziah reign over Jerusalem?

    II Chronicles 22:2

    A. 1
    B. 11
    C. 21
    D. 31

17. Who was King Ahaziah's mother?

    II Chronicles 22:2

    A. Abigail
    B. Anna
    C. Asenath
    D. Athaliah

18. Who was King Ahab's son?

    II Chronicles 22:5

    A. Abiram
    B. Hiram
    C. Jehoram
    D. Piram

19. Who was the king of Syria?

    II Chronicles 22:5

    A. King Abimael
    B. King Azarael
    C. King Hazael
    D. King Ishmael

20. Who hid King Ahaziah's son for six years?

    II Chronicles 22:11–12

    A. Ephrath
    B. Goliath
    C. Hemath
    D. Jehoshabeath

**Answers on page 762*

Lesson 144
Today's Reading: *II Chronicles 23–25*
Period of Time: 878–810 BC
Author: Unknown

1. How many captains of hundreds conspired with Jehoiada?
   II Chronicles 23:1
   A. 2
   B. 3
   C. 4
   D. 5

2. Where were King David's spears, bucklers, and shields being stored?
   II Chronicles 23:9
   A. The armory in Hebron
   B. The house of God
   C. The king's house
   D. The tower in Jerusalem

3. Who cried out, "Treason, Treason"?
   II Chronicles 23:12–13
   A. Athaliah
   B. Bathsheba
   C. Esther
   D. Vashti

4. Who was the priest of Baal?
   II Chronicles 23:17
   A. Joktan
   B. Lotan
   C. Mattan
   D. Tartan

5. How old was King Joash when he began to reign over Judah?
   II Chronicles 24:1
   A. 7 years old
   B. 12 years old
   C. 28 years old
   D. 35 years old

6. What did King Joash order to be placed at the gate of the house of the LORD?
   II Chronicles 24:8
   A. A chest
   B. A moat
   C. A palm tree
   D. A statue of Joash

7. How old was Jehoiada when he died?
   II Chronicles 24:15
   A. 70 years old
   B. 90 years old
   C. 110 years old
   D. 130 years old

8. Whom did the Spirit of God come upon?
   II Chronicles 24:20
   A. Beriah
   B. Jeriah
   C. Shemariah
   D. Zechariah

9. Which two men slew King Joash?
   II Chronicles 24:24–26
   A. Ammizabad and Jozabad
   B. Elzabad and Abaddon
   C. Sinbad and Hashbadana
   D. Zabad and Jehozabad

10. How old was King Amaziah when he began to reign over Judah?
    II Chronicles 25:1
    A. 18 years old
    B. 25 years old
    C. 32 years old
    D. 41 years old

11. Who was King Amaziah's mother?
    II Chronicles 25:1
    A. Bashemath
    B. Elisabeth
    C. Jehoaddan
    D. Sophereth

12. How many men from Judah did King Amaziah gather for his army?

    II Chronicles 25:5

    A. 100,000
    B. 200,000
    C. 300,000
    D. 400,000

13. How many talents of silver did King Amaziah pay the mighty men of valour from Israel?

    II Chronicles 25:6

    A. 100
    B. 1,000
    C. 10,000
    D. 100,000

14. In which valley did King Amaziah smite the Edomites?

    II Chronicles 25:11–14

    A. Valley of craftsmen
    B. Valley of Hamongog
    C. Valley of salt
    D. Valley of vision

15. How many of the Edomites were cast down from the top of the rock?

    II Chronicles 25:11–14

    A. 100
    B. 1,000
    C. 10,000
    D. 100,000

16. Who was the king of Israel?

    II Chronicles 25:17

    A. King Joash
    B. King Jonah
    C. King Joram
    D. King Joses

17. Where did King Amaziah battle the king of Israel?

    II Chronicles 25:21

    A. Abelbethmaachah
    B. Beth-she'mesh
    C. Elonbethhanan
    D. Gibbethon

18. Whom did the king of Israel take back with him to Samaria?

    II Chronicles 25:24

    A. Abednego
    B. Bedeiah
    C. Jochebed
    D. Obededom

19. In which book are the acts of King Amaziah written?

    II Chronicles 25:26

    A. Book of the acts of King Amaziah
    B. Book of the kings of Judah and Israel
    C. Book of the law of Moses
    D. Book of the wars of the LORD

20. In which city was King Amaziah slain?

    II Chronicles 25:27

    A. Achish
    B. Lachish
    C. Magbish
    D. Tarshish

*Answers on page 762

Lesson 145
Today's Reading: *II Chronicles 26–28*
Period of Time: 810–726 BC
Author: Unknown

1. How old was King Uzziah when he became king of Judah?
   II Chronicles 26:1
   A. 8 years old
   B. 16 years old
   C. 24 years old
   D. 32 years old

2. Who was King Uzziah's father?
   II Chronicles 26:1
   A. Amaziah
   B. Jahaziah
   C. Maaziah
   D. Neziah

3. What city did King Uzziah build and restore to Judah?
   II Chronicles 26:2
   A. Eloth
   B. Kerioth
   C. Ramoth
   D. Succoth

4. How many years did King Uzziah reign over Judah?
   II Chronicles 26:3
   A. 41
   B. 52
   C. 63
   D. 74

5. Who was King Uzziah's mother?
   II Chronicles 26:3
   A. Hodiah
   B. Jecoliah
   C. Michaiah
   D. Noadiah

6. Who was a prophet of God?
   II Chronicles 26:5
   A. Beriah
   B. Gemariah
   C. Shemariah
   D. Zechariah

7. Who was one of King Uzziah's captains?
   II Chronicles 26:11
   A. Ananiah
   B. Chenaniah
   C. Conaniah
   D. Hananiah

8. Which sin was King Uzziah guilty of?
   II Chronicles 26:16
   A. Adultery with Bathsheba
   B. Burning incense upon the altar
   C. Murdering his children
   D. Numbering the people

9. Who was chief priest during King Uzziah's reign?
   II Chronicles 26:17–20
   A. Azariah
   B. Gemariah
   C. Neariah
   D. Sheariah

10. How did God punish King Uzziah?
    II Chronicles 26:19
    A. He caused seven years of famine.
    B. He made Uzziah flee for three months.
    C. He sent a pestilence upon Judah.
    D. He turned Uzziah into a leper.

11. Who wrote about the acts of King Uzziah?
    II Chronicles 26:22
    A. Adaiah
    B. Benaiah
    C. Isaiah
    D. Reaiah

12. How old was King Jotham when he became king of Judah?
    II Chronicles 27:1
    A. 25 years old
    B. 37 years old
    C. 41 years old
    D. 59 years old

13. How many years did King Jotham reign over Judah?

    II Chronicles 27:1

    A. 16
    B. 24
    C. 32
    D. 48

14. Who was King Jotham's mother?

    II Chronicles 27:1

    A. Bilhah
    B. Ephah
    C. Jerushah
    D. Maachah

15. Which sin was King Ahaz guilty of?

    II Chronicles 28:3

    A. Adultery with Bathsheba
    B. Burning incense upon the altar
    C. Murdering his children
    D. Numbering the people

16. Who was the king of Israel during King Ahaz's reign?

    II Chronicles 28:6

    A. King Achish
    B. King Josiah
    C. King Nahash
    D. King Pekah

17. Who was a mighty man of Ephraim?

    II Chronicles 28:7

    A. Bichri
    B. Michri
    C. Zichri
    D. Zithri

18. Who was a prophet of the LORD?

    II Chronicles 28:9

    A. Er
    B. Lot
    C. Oded
    D. Padon

19. Who was the king of Assyria?

    II Chronicles 28:20

    A. King Ben-ha'dad
    B. King Evil-merodach
    C. King Merodach-baladan
    D. King Tilgath-pilneser

20. Who was King Ahaz's son?

    II Chronicles 28:27

    A. Ahaziah
    B. Hezekiah
    C. Pekahiah
    D. Zechariah

*Answers on page 763

Lesson 146
Today's Reading: *II Chronicles 29–30*
Period of Time: 726 BC
Author: Unknown

1. How old was King Hezekiah when he began to reign?
   II Chronicles 29:1
   A. 15 years old
   B. 25 years old
   C. 35 years old
   D. 45 years old

2. How many years did King Hezekiah reign over Judah?
   II Chronicles 29:1
   A. 29
   B. 39
   C. 40
   D. 41

3. Who was King Hezekiah's mother?
   II Chronicles 29:1
   A. Abijah
   B. Huldah
   C. Naarah
   D. Reumah

4. What did King Hezekiah do the first month of his reign?
   II Chronicles 29:3
   A. He defended Judah from Egypt.
   B. He invaded Lebanon.
   C. He murdered all of his brothers.
   D. He repaired the doors to the temple.

5. Which two men were Kohathites?
   II Chronicles 29:12
   A. Joah and Eden
   B. Kish and Azariah
   C. Mahath and Joel
   D. Shimri and Jeiel

6. Which two men were Heman's sons?
   II Chronicles 29:14
   A. Abdi and Jehalelel
   B. Amasai and Azariah
   C. Jehiel and Shimei
   D. Zimmah and Joah

7. Into which brook did the Levites cast the uncleanness found in the house of the LORD?
   II Chronicles 29:16
   A. Brook Besor
   B. Brook Cherith
   C. Brook Eshcol
   D. Brook Kidron

8. When did the Levites begin to sanctify the house of the LORD?
   II Chronicles 29:17
   A. 1st day of 1st month
   B. 7th day of 2nd month
   C. 14th day of the 5th month
   D. 21st day of 7th month

9. How many days did it take to sanctify the house of the LORD?
   II Chronicles 29:17
   A. 8
   B. 21
   C. 39
   D. 40

10. Which king in his transgression cast away the temple vessels?
    II Chronicles 29:19
    A. King Ahab
    B. King Ahaz
    C. King Aher
    D. King Ahio

11. Which offering were the seven he goats used for?
    II Chronicles 29:21
    A. The burnt offering
    B. The drink offering
    C. The meat offering
    D. The sin offering

12. Who was a prophet of the LORD?
II Chronicles 29:25
   A. Azur
   B. Barjesus
   C. Nathan
   D. Zedekiah

13. Who played the cymbals, psalteries, and harps?
II Chronicles 29:25–26
   A. The Benjamites
   B. The Gadites
   C. The Levites
   D. The Simeonites

14. Who played the trumpets?
II Chronicles 29:25–26
   A. The bishops
   B. The deacons
   C. The elders
   D. The priests

15. Which one of the following men was a seer?
II Chronicles 29:30
   A. Asaph
   B. Jidlaph
   C. Saraph
   D. Zalaph

16. Where was the passover to be held?
II Chronicles 30:5
   A. Bethlehem
   B. Damascus
   C. Jerusalem
   D. Samaria

17. How did the people of Ephraim and Manasseh react to the king's and prince's decree?
II Chronicles 30:1–10
   A. They destroyed their idols and groves.
   B. They laughed and mocked them.
   C. They offered tithes and gifts.
   D. They repented and sanctified themselves.

18. When was the passover killed?
II Chronicles 30:15
   A. 7th day of 1st month
   B. 14th day of 2nd month
   C. 21st day of 3rd month
   D. 28th day of 4th month

19. How many days did the children of Israel keep the feast of unleavened bread?
II Chronicles 30:21
   A. 6
   B. 7
   C. 8
   D. 9

20. How many sheep did the princes give to the congregation?
II Chronicles 30:24
   A. 1,000
   B. 3,000
   C. 7,000
   D. 10,000

*Answers on page 763

Lesson 147

Today's Reading: *II Chronicles 31–33*
Period of Time: 726–641 BC
Author: Unknown

1. Which Levite was over the dedicated things?
   II Chronicles 31:12
   A. Berechiah
   B. Cononiah
   C. Remaliah
   D. Vaniah

2. Who was ruler of the house of God?
   II Chronicles 31:13
   A. Azariah
   B. Beriah
   C. Gemariah
   D. Neariah

3. Who was the Assyrian king during King Hezekiah's reign?
   II Chronicles 32:1
   A. King Sargon
   B. King Saul
   C. King Sennacherib
   D. King Shishak

4. What did King Hezekiah do to frustrate the king of Assyria?
   II Chronicles 32:3
   A. Sent his army to the capital of Assyria
   B. Stole his spear at night
   C. Stopped the fountains without the city
   D. Surrounded his army

5. Which fortification did King Hezekiah repair?
   II Chronicles 32:5
   A. Accho
   B. Calno
   C. Millo
   D. Shoco

6. Which city did the king of Assyria besiege?
   II Chronicles 32:9
   A. Achish
   B. Lachish
   C. Magbish
   D. Tarshish

7. Who was Isaiah's father?
   II Chronicles 32:20
   A. Amok
   B. Amon
   C. Amos
   D. Amoz

8. What did God use to defeat the Assyrian army?
   II Chronicles 32:21
   A. An angel
   B. An earthquake
   C. Great hailstones
   D. Swarms of bees

9. Who killed the king of Assyria in the house of his god?
   II Chronicles 32:21
   A. His servants
   B. His slaves
   C. His soldiers
   D. His sons

10. Where was the watercourse King Hezekiah closed to bring water to Jerusalem?
    II Chronicles 32:30
    A. Eglon
    B. Gihon
    C. Madon
    D. Punon

11. Which book—besides the book of the kings of Judah and Israel—contains the acts of King Hezekiah?
    II Chronicles 32:32
    A. The book of Isaiah the seer
    B. The chronicles of Isaiah the seer
    C. The prophecy of Isaiah the prophet
    D. The vision of Isaiah the prophet

12. How old was King Manasseh when he began to reign?

    II Chronicles 33:1

    A. 2 years old
    B. 12 years old
    C. 22 years old
    D. 55 years old

13. How many years did King Manasseh reign in Jerusalem?

    II Chronicles 33:1

    A. 2
    B. 12
    C. 22
    D. 55

14. Whom did King Manasseh build altars for?

    II Chronicles 33:3

    A. Adrammelech
    B. Baalim
    C. Chemosh
    D. Dagon

15. Where did King Manasseh burn his children?

    II Chronicles 33:1–6

    A. Valley of the giants
    B. Valley of the kings
    C. Valley of the passengers
    D. Valley of the son of Hinnom

16. What did King Manasseh do to the house of God?

    II Chronicles 33:7

    A. Cleansed it of all uncleanness
    B. Had the doors repaired
    C. Placed an idol inside it
    D. Sacrificed a pig to Jupiter

17. Which nation bound King Manasseh with fetters?

    II Chronicles 33:11

    A. Assyria
    B. Cush
    C. Egypt
    D. Persia

18. How old was King Amon when he began to reign in Jerusalem?

    II Chronicles 33:21

    A. 22 years old
    B. 33 years old
    C. 44 years old
    D. 55 years old

19. Who slew King Amon in King Amon's house?

    II Chronicles 33:24

    A. His servants
    B. His slaves
    C. His soldiers
    D. His sons

20. Who was King Amon's son?

    II Chronicles 33:25

    A. Amasiah
    B. Gemariah
    C. Josiah
    D. Pethahiah

*Answers on page 763

Lesson 148
Today's Reading: *II Chronicles 34–36*
Period of Time: 641–537 BC
Author: Unknown

1. Hold many years old was King Josiah when he began to reign over Jerusalem?
   II Chronicles 34:1
   A. 3
   B. 8
   C. 11
   D. 21

2. Who found a book of the law of the LORD given by Moses?
   II Chronicles 34:14
   A. Bakbukiah
   B. Hilkiah
   C. Jehizkiah
   D. Zedekiah

3. Who delivered the book of the law of the LORD given by Moses to King Josiah?
   II Chronicles 34:16
   A. Elhanan
   B. Jokshan
   C. Matthan
   D. Shaphan

4. Who was a prophetess?
   II Chronicles 34:22
   A. Adah
   B. Huldah
   C. Jedidah
   D. Zebudah

5. On which day of the first month did they kill the passover?
   II Chronicles 35:1
   A. 1st day
   B. 7th day
   C. 14th day
   D. 21st day

6. Who was the king of Egypt?
   II Chronicles 35:20
   A. King Ginnetho
   B. King Necho
   C. King Socho
   D. King Zepho

7. Whom did the king of Egypt fight against?
   II Chronicles 35:20
   A. Charchemish
   B. Kithlish
   C. Lachish
   D. Tarshish

8. In which valley did the king of Egypt mortally wound King Josiah?
   II Chronicles 35:22–23
   A. Valley of Ajalon
   B. Valley of Jezreel
   C. Valley of Lebanon
   D. Valley of Megiddo

9. Who lamented for King Josiah?
   II Chronicles 35:25
   A. Daniel
   B. Ezekiel
   C. Isaiah
   D. Jeremiah

10. How old was King Jehoahaz when he began to reign in Jerusalem?
    II Chronicles 36:1–2
    A. 13 years old
    B. 15 years old
    C. 23 years old
    D. 25 years old

11. How many months did King Jehoahaz reign in Jerusalem?
    II Chronicles 36:1–2
    A. 3 months
    B. 6 months
    C. 9 months
    D. 11 months

12. Which name did the king of Egypt change King Eliakim's name to?

    II Chronicles 36:4

    A. Jabin
    B. Jehoahaz
    C. Jehoiakim
    D. Jehoram

13. How old was King Eliahim when he began to reign in Jerusalem?

    II Chronicles 36:4–5

    A. 25 years old
    B. 35 years old
    C. 45 years old
    D. 55 years old

14. How many years did King Eliakim reign in Jerusalem?

    II Chronicles 36:4–5

    A. 3
    B. 8
    C. 11
    D. 21

15. How old was King Jehoiachin when he began to reign in Jerusalem?

    II Chronicles 36:9

    A. 3 years old
    B. 8 years old
    C. 11 years old
    D. 21 years old

16. How old was King Zedekiah when he began to reign in Jerusalem?

    II Chronicles 36:11

    A. 21 years old
    B. 39 years old
    C. 44 years old
    D. 56 years old

17. Which prophet warned King Zedekiah to turn from his evil ways?

    II Chronicles 36:12

    A. Daniel
    B. Ezekiel
    C. Isaiah
    D. Jeremiah

18. Which Chaldean king destroyed Jerusalem?

    II Chronicles 36:6–20

    A. Belshazzar
    B. Evil-merodach
    C. Merodach-baladan
    D. Nebuchadnezzar

19. How many years was the land of Israel desolate?

    II Chronicles 36:21

    A. 6
    B. 40
    C. 70
    D. 100

20. Who was the king of Persia?

    II Chronicles 36:22–23

    A. King Cyrus
    B. King Jairus
    C. King Lazarus
    D. King Onesiphorus

*Answers on page 763

Lesson 149
Today's Reading: *Ezra 1–2*
Period of Time: 537–536 BC
Author: Ezra

MAY 29

1. Who was the king of Persia?
   Ezra 1:1
   A. King Cyrus
   B. King Hiram
   C. King Necho
   D. King Pekah

2. Who prophesied the king of Persia would rebuild the temple in Jerusalem?
   Ezra 1:1–2
   A. Jeremiah
   B. Micaiah
   C. Obadiah
   D. Shemaiah

3. What did the king of Persia call the LORD?
   Ezra 1:2
   A. LORD God of David
   B. LORD God of gods
   C. LORD God of heaven
   D. LORD God of Israel

4. Which Babylonian king placed the temple vessels in the house of his gods?
   Ezra 1:7
   A. King Asnappar
   B. King Esarhaddon
   C. King Nebuchadnezzar
   D. King Shalmaneser

5. Who was the treasurer?
   Ezra 1:8
   A. Fortunatus
   B. Mithredath
   C. Potipherah
   D. Zerubbabel

6. Who was the prince of Judah?
   Ezra 1:8
   A. Belteshazzar
   B. Eleazar
   C. Nebuchadnezzar
   D. Sheshbazzar

7. What was the total number of vessels of gold and of silver?
   Ezra 1:11
   A. 4,289
   B. 5,400
   C. 6,720
   D. 7,564

8. What was the total number of priests that returned to Jerusalem?
   Ezra 2:36–39
   A. 4,289
   B. 5,400
   C. 6,720
   D. 7,564

9. What was the total number of Levites that returned to Jerusalem?
   Ezra 2:40
   A. 31
   B. 55
   C. 74
   D. 93

10. Whose family did the singers belong to?
    Ezra 2:41
    A. Asaph
    B. Bezaleel
    C. Gabriel
    D. Jubal

11. What was one of the five cities some of the families came from that could **not** prove they were from Israel?
    Ezra 2:59
    A. Telabib
    B. Telassar
    C. Telem
    D. Telmelah

12. What was Barzillai's surname?

    Ezra 2:61

    A. The Gileadite
    B. The Judahite
    C. The Phoenician
    D. The Samarian

13. Who told the priests—who had no proof of being of Israel—that they could **not** eat the most holy things?

    Ezra 2:63

    A. The Rabmag
    B. The Rabshakeh
    C. The Tartan
    D. The Tirshatha

14. How many *horses* were brought to Jerusalem?

    Ezra 2:66

    A. 625
    B. 736
    C. 847
    D. 978

15. How many *mules* were brought to Jerusalem?

    Ezra 2:66

    A. 167
    B. 245
    C. 398
    D. 474

16. How many *camels* were brought to Jerusalem?

    Ezra 2:67

    A. 118
    B. 221
    C. 387
    D. 435

17. How many *asses* were brought to Jerusalem?

    Ezra 2:67

    A. 4,289
    B. 5,400
    C. 6,720
    D. 7,564

18. How many drams of gold did some of the chief of the fathers offer for the house of the LORD?

    Ezra 2:68–69

    A. 23,000
    B. 48,000
    C. 61,000
    D. 87,000

19. How many pounds of silver did some of the chief of the fathers offer for the house of the LORD?

    Ezra 2:68–69

    A. 3,000
    B. 5,000
    C. 7,000
    D. 9,000

20. How many priests' garments did the chief of the fathers offer for the house of the LORD?

    Ezra 2:68–69

    A. 40
    B. 60
    C. 80
    D. 100

*Answers on page 763

Lesson 150
Today's Reading: *Ezra 3–5*
Period of Time: 536–519 BC
Author: Ezra

1. During which month did the children of Israel gather in Jerusalem?
   Ezra 3:1
   A. 1st month
   B. 3rd month
   C. 7th month
   D. 10th month

2. Who was Jeshua's father?
   Ezra 3:2
   A. Elijah
   B. Jozadak
   C. Lazarus
   D. Matthew

3. Who was Zerubbabel's father?
   Ezra 3:2
   A. Ezekiel
   B. Gamaliel
   C. Phaltiel
   D. Shealtiel

4. Which feast did the children of Israel keep?
   Ezra 3:4
   A. Feast of alms
   B. Feast of ingathering
   C. Feast of tabernacles
   D. Feast of unleavened bread

5. During which cycle of the moon did the children of Israel give offerings?
   Ezra 3:5
   A. Crescent moons
   B. Full moons
   C. Half moons
   D. New moons

6. Which sea was used to float logs from Lebanon to Israel?
   Ezra 3:7
   A. Sea of Chinnereth
   B. Sea of glass
   C. Sea of Joppa
   D. Sea of the plain

7. Which musical instruments did the priests play?
   Ezra 3:10
   A. Cymbals
   B. Harps
   C. Psalteries
   D. Trumpets

8. Which musical instruments did the Levites play?
   Ezra 3:10
   A. Cymbals
   B. Harps
   C. Psalteries
   D. Trumpets

9. Which Assyrian king transplanted the adversaries of Judah and Benjamin to Israel?
   Ezra 4:1–2
   A. King Abimelech
   B. King Esarhaddon
   C. King Rameses
   D. King Shalmaneser

10. Which king of Persia did Bishlam and his companions write to in the Syrian tongue?
    Ezra 4:7
    A. King Artaxerxes
    B. King Belshazzar
    C. King Evilmerodach
    D. King Merodach-baladan

11. Who was the adversaries' chancellor?
    Ezra 4:8
    A. Ahumai
    B. Nahum
    C. Rehum
    D. Tanhumeth

12. Who was the adversaries' scribe?

    Ezra 4:8

    A. Sherezer
    B. Shimshai
    C. Shiphtan
    D. Shophach

13. Which Assyrian king transplanted nations to cities in Samaria?

    Ezra 4:10

    A. King Asnappar
    B. King Belshazzar
    C. King Ithamar
    D. King Shenazar

14. During which year of King Darius' reign did work on the temple continue?

    Ezra 4:24

    A. 1st year
    B. 2nd year
    C. 3rd year
    D. 4th year

15. Which prophets helped to rebuild the temple?

    Ezra 5:1–2

    A. Balaam and Balak
    B. Haggai and Zechariah
    C. Jeremiah and Isaiah
    D. Malachi and Zedekiah

16. Who was the governor *west* of the river of Jordan?

    Ezra 5:3

    A. Anaiah
    B. Benaiah
    C. Elienai
    D. Tatnai

17. Who joined the governor in sending a letter of complaint against Israel to King Darius?

    Ezra 5:6

    A. The Apharsachites
    B. The Jerahmeelites
    C. The Mecherathites
    D. The Netophathites

18. Which Babylonian king destroyed the house of God?

    Ezra 5:12

    A. King Berodachbaladan
    B. King Magormissabib
    C. King Nebuchadnezzar
    D. King Tiglath-pileser

19. During which year of King Cyrus' reign did he make a decree to rebuild the house of God?

    Ezra 5:13

    A. 1st year
    B. 2nd year
    C. 3rd year
    D. 4th year

20. Whom did the king of Babylon make governor of Judah?

    Ezra 5:14

    A. Belteshazzar
    B. Eleazar
    C. Melzar
    D. Sheshbazzar

*Answers on page 763

Lesson 151
Today's Reading: *Ezra 6–8*
Period of Time: 519–467 BC
Author: Ezra

1. Which king ordered the search for the record to rebuild the house of God?
   Ezra 6:1
   A. King Ahasuerus
   B. King Artaxerxes
   C. King Cyrus
   D. King Darius

2. In which city was the record found?
   Ezra 6:2
   A. Achmetha
   B. Bethshemeth
   C. Methegammah
   D. Remmonmethoar

3. Which Persian king ordered that the house of God be rebuilt?
   Ezra 6:3
   A. King Ahasuerus
   B. King Artaxerxes
   C. King Cyrus
   D. King Darius

4. What was the height of the house of God measured in cubits?
   Ezra 6:3
   A. 30
   B. 60
   C. 90
   D. 120

5. What was the breadth of the house of God measured in cubits?
   Ezra 6:3
   A. 30
   B. 60
   C. 90
   D. 120

6. How many rows of great stones did the house of God contain?
   Ezra 6:4
   A. 1
   B. 2
   C. 3
   D. 4

7. How many rows of new timber did the house of God contain?
   Ezra 6:4
   A. 1
   B. 2
   C. 3
   D. 4

8. How was a person to be put to death for interfering with the work of the house of God?
   Ezra 6:11
   A. Burning
   B. Drowning
   C. Hanging
   D. Stoning

9. Who was Zechariah's father?
   Ezra 6:14
   A. Beno
   B. Dodo
   C. Hazo
   D. Iddo

10. In which month was the house of God completed?
    Ezra 6:15
    A. Adar
    B. Elul
    C. Nisan
    D. Sebat

11. How many rams were offered at the dedication of the house of God?

    Ezra 6:17

    A. 100
    B. 200
    C. 300
    D. 400

12. Who was Ezra's father?

    Ezra 7:1

    A. Kelaiah
    B. Meraiah
    C. Pelaiah
    D. Seraiah

13. How many months did it take for Ezra to travel from Babylon to Jerusalem?

    Ezra 7:9

    A. 3
    B. 5
    C. 7
    D. 9

14. How many counselors advised the Persian king?

    Ezra 7:14

    A. 3
    B. 5
    C. 7
    D. 9

15. How many baths of oil did the king of Persia give Ezra?

    Ezra 7:22

    A. 100
    B. 200
    C. 300
    D. 400

16. Near which river did Ezra meet with other Jews for three days?

    Ezra 8:15

    A. River of Ahava
    B. River of Gihon
    C. River of Jabbok
    D. River of Kanah

17. Where did the ministers for the house of God come from?

    Ezra 8:17–20

    A. Armenia
    B. Bithynia
    C. Casiphia
    D. Dalmatia

18. How many talents of silver did Ezra weigh for the freewill offering?

    Ezra 8:26–28

    A. 350
    B. 450
    C. 550
    D. 650

19. Who was Phinehas' son?

    Ezra 8:33

    A. Bilshan
    B. Chislon
    C. Dodavah
    D. Eleazar

20. How many he goats did those returning from the captivity offer for a sin offering?

    Ezra 8:35

    A. 6
    B. 12
    C. 18
    D. 24

*Answers on page 763

Lesson 152
Today's Reading: *Ezra 9–10*
Period of Time: 467–466 BC
Author: Ezra

1. Which one of the following nations did the Jews take strange wives from?
   Ezra 9:1–2
   A. Assyrians
   B. Greeks
   C. Hittites
   D. Romans

2. Which group of Jews married the most foreign women?
   Ezra 9:2
   A. The princes and rulers
   B. The middle class
   C. The lower class
   D. The peasants

3. What did Ezra do when he found out the Jews were taking strange wives?
   Ezra 9:3
   A. Beat them with cords
   B. Drowned them
   C. Made their homes dung hills
   D. Rent his garment

4. How long did Ezra remain astonied?
   Ezra 9:4
   A. Until the Day of Atonement
   B. Until the evening sacrifice
   C. Until the new moon feast
   D. Until the morning sacrifice

5. The kings from which nation released the Jews to rebuild the house of God?
   Ezra 9:9
   A. Ammon
   B. Canaan
   C. Moab
   D. Persia

6. What else was repaired in Jerusalem besides the house of God?
   Ezra 9:9
   A. The amphitheater
   B. The forum
   C. The palace
   D. The wall

7. Who spoke on behalf of the Jews, desiring a covenant to put away their strange wives and any children born of them?
   Ezra 10:2–3
   A. Conaniah
   B. Hananiah
   C. Shechaniah
   D. Zephaniah

8. Who was Eliashib's son?
   Ezra 10:6
   A. Eliphaz
   B. Johanan
   C. Phanuel
   D. Timothy

9. How many days were the Jews—who had married strange women—given to come back to Jerusalem?
   Ezra 10:8
   A. 3
   B. 10
   C. 21
   D. 40

10. During which month did the Jews guilty of marrying strange women come to Jerusalem?
    Ezra 10:9
    A. 1st month
    B. 9th month
    C. 10th month
    D. 11th month

11. What was Ezra's title?

    Ezra 10:10

    A. Governor
    B. Levite
    C. Priest
    D. Satrap

12. During what time of the year did the Jews meet in Jerusalem to separate themselves from the strange wives?

    Ezra 10:9–13

    A. The dry season
    B. The harvest season
    C. The planting season
    D. The rainy season

13. Which two men were employed to examine the matter of Jews marrying strange women?

    Ezra 10:15

    A. Jonathan and Jahaziah
    B. Manasseh and Mordecai
    C. Phinehas and Philetus
    D. Tychicus and Tyrannus

14. Who were the Levites that helped to examine the Jews guilty of marrying strange women?

    Ezra 10:15

    A. Bishlam and Shashai
    B. Elam and Sibbechai
    C. Jaalam and Shimshai
    D. Meshullam and Shabbethai

15. During which month did the examinations begin?

    Ezra 10:16

    A. 1st month
    B. 9th month
    C. 10th month
    D. 11th month

16. During which month did the examinations end?

    Ezra 10:17

    A. 1st month
    B. 9th month
    C. 10th month
    D. 11th month

17. Who was Jozadak's son?

    Ezra 10:18

    A. Jemuel
    B. Jeshua
    C. Jethro
    D. Jeziah

18. What was offered for a trespass offering?

    Ezra 10:19

    A. A goat
    B. A pigeon
    C. A ram
    D. A sheep

19. What is the same name as Kelita?

    Ezra 10:23

    A. Kareah
    B. Kelaiah
    C. Kittim
    D. Kohath

20. Who was a singer?

    Ezra 10:24

    A. Eliashib
    B. Eliathah
    C. Elioenai
    D. Elishama

*Answers on page 763

Lesson 153
Today's Reading: *Nehemiah 1–3*
Period of Time: 455–454 BC
Author: Nehemiah

JUNE 2

1. Who was Nehemiah's father?
   Nehemiah 1:1
   A. Azaliah
   B. Hachaliah
   C. Pelaliah
   D. Tebaliah

2. During which month did Nehemiah learn about the sad condition of Jerusalem?
   Nehemiah 1:1
   A. Chisleu
   B. Elul
   C. Sebat
   D. Zif

3. Where was the Persian palace located?
   Nehemiah 1:1
   A. Cushan
   B. Dothan
   C. Nibshan
   D. Shushan

4. Who informed Nehemiah about the sad condition of Jerusalem?
   Nehemiah 1:2
   A. Aquila
   B. Hanani
   C. Jotham
   D. Raguel

5. What was Nehemiah's job?
   Nehemiah 1:11
   A. Cupbearer
   B. Gardener
   C. Mason
   D. Physician

6. During which month did Nehemiah ask the king for permission to visit Jerusalem?
   Nehemiah 2:1
   A. Bul
   B. Ethanim
   C. Nisan
   D. Sivan

7. Who was the king of Persia?
   Nehemiah 2:1
   A. King Artaxerxes
   B. King Baasha
   C. King Claudius
   D. King David

8. Who sat next to the king?
   Nehemiah 2:6
   A. The duke
   B. The queen
   C. The rabbi
   D. The scribe

9. How many days was Nehemiah in Jerusalem before he secretly went out at night to inspect the walls?
   Nehemiah 2:11–12
   A. 2
   B. 3
   C. 4
   D. 5

10. Who was the Horonite that laughed with scorn at Nehemiah and the Jews?
    Nehemiah 2:19
    A. Jeroboam
    B. Quartus
    C. Rehoboam
    D. Sanballat

11. Who was the Arabian that laughed with scorn at Nehemiah and the Jews?
    Nehemiah 2:19
    A. Geshem
    B. Hashem
    C. Menahem
    D. Shechem

12. Who was the high priest?

    Nehemiah 3:1

    A. Eli
    B. Eliadah
    C. Eliashib
    D. Elijah

13. Who repaired the *dung gate*?

    Nehemiah 3:14

    A. Malachi
    B. Malcham
    C. Malchiah
    D. Malchus

14. Who repaired the *gate of the fountain*?

    Nehemiah 3:15

    A. Gallio
    B. Kallai
    C. Phallu
    D. Shallun

15. Who ruled half of Keilah?

    Nehemiah 3:17

    A. Abiah
    B. Hashabiah
    C. Sherebiah
    D. Tobiah

16. Who ruled the other half of Keilah?

    Nehemiah 3:17–18

    A. Bavai
    B. Ephai
    C. Nebai
    D. Sotai

17. Who dwelled in Ophel?

    Nehemiah 3:26

    A. The artificers in brass
    B. The drawers of water
    C. The keepers of flocks
    D. The Nethinims

18. Who repaired the *horse gate*?

    Nehemiah 3:28

    A. The Levites
    B. The musicians
    C. The priests
    D. The singers

19. Who repaired the *east gate*?

    Nehemiah 3:29

    A. Ishmaiah
    B. Kushaiah
    C. Rephaiah
    D. Shemaiah

20. Who helped the merchants repair the *sheep gate*?

    Nehemiah 3:32

    A. The blacksmiths
    B. The coppersmiths
    C. The goldsmiths
    D. The silversmiths

*Answers on page 763

Lesson 154
Today's Reading: *Nehemiah 4–6*
Period of Time: 454 BC
Author: Nehemiah

1. Whose army did Sanballat speak to?
   Nehemiah 4:1–2
   A. Ammon's army
   B. Assyria's army
   C. Philistia's army
   D. Samaria's army

2. What was Tobiah?
   Nehemiah 4:3
   A. A Philistine
   B. A Samarian
   C. An Ammonite
   D. An Assyrian

3. Who became wroth with the Jews?
   Nehemiah 4:7
   A. The Ashdodites
   B. The Gadites
   C. The Hanochites
   D. The Sardites

4. What was used to warn the people?
   Nehemiah 4:20
   A. A bell
   B. A fire
   C. A flag
   D. A trumpet

5. Who was exacting usury from the people?
   Nehemiah 5:7
   A. Arabians
   B. Babylonians
   C. Ephesians
   D. Other Jews

6. Who was the king of Persia?
   Nehemiah 5:14
   A. King Artaxerxes
   B. King Esarhaddon
   C. King Hophra
   D. King Shalmaneser

7. How many years had Nehemiah been a governor?
   Nehemiah 5:14
   A. 1
   B. 6
   C. 12
   D. 40

8. How many shekels of silver had the former governors taken from the people?
   Nehemiah 5:15
   A. 1
   B. 6
   C. 12
   D. 40

9. How many people sat at Nehemiah's table each day?
   Nehemiah 5:17
   A. 50
   B. 100
   C. 150
   D. 200

10. How many oxen were prepared daily for Nehemiah?
    Nehemiah 5:18
    A. 1
    B. 6
    C. 12
    D. 40

11. How many sheep were prepared daily for Nehemiah?
    Nehemiah 5:18
    A. 1
    B. 6
    C. 12
    D. 40

12. Where did Sanballat want to meet Nehemiah?
    Nehemiah 6:1–2
    A. Plain of Jordan
    B. Plain of Ono
    C. Plain of the Vineyards
    D. Plain of Zaanaim

13. How many times did Sanballat send a messenger to Nehemiah?
    Nehemiah 6:2–5
    A. 5
    B. 7
    C. 10
    D. 12

14. Who made a false report claiming Nehemiah was plotting to be Judah's next king?
    Nehemiah 6:6
    A. Gabbai
    B. Gallio
    C. Gashmu
    D. Gazzam

15. Whom did Sanballat and Tobiah hire to try and trick Nehemiah into sinning?
    Nehemiah 6:10–13
    A. Jeshaiah
    B. Kushaiah
    C. Rephaiah
    D. Shemaiah

16. Who was a prophetess?
    Nehemiah 6:14
    A. Naomi
    B. Noadiah
    C. Noah
    D. Nymphas

17. During which month was the wall completed?
    Nehemiah 6:15
    A. Elul
    B. Nisan
    C. Sebat
    D. Tebeth

18. How many days did it take to complete the wall?
    Nehemiah 6:15
    A. 48
    B. 52
    C. 66
    D. 74

19. Who was Tobiah's father-in-law?
    Nehemiah 6:17–18
    A. Chenaniah
    B. Hashabniah
    C. Shechaniah
    D. Zephaniah

20. Who was Tobiah's son?
    Nehemiah 6:18
    A. Joatham
    B. Johanan
    C. Joiarib
    D. Josabad

Answers on page 763

Lesson 155
Today's Reading: *Nehemiah 7–8*
Period of Time: 454 BC
Author: Nehemiah

JUNE 4

1. Who was Nehemiah's brother?
   Nehemiah 7:2
   A. Anani
   B. Bani
   C. Chenani
   D. Hanani

2. Who was the ruler of the palace?
   Nehemiah 7:2
   A. Cononiah
   B. Hananiah
   C. Jezaniah
   D. Vaniah

3. Who was a Babylonian king?
   Nehemiah 7:6
   A. King Nadab
   B. King Nahash
   C. King Nebuchadnezzar
   D. King Nero

4. What was the total number of the congregation?
   Nehemiah 7:66
   A. 23,460
   B. 34,603
   C. 42,360
   D. 60,234

5. What was the total number of the servants?
   Nehemiah 7:67
   A. 3,377
   B. 7,337
   C. 7,373
   D. 7,733

6. What was the total number of the singers?
   Nehemiah 7:67
   A. 245
   B. 435
   C. 736
   D. 1,000

7. What was the total number of *horses*?
   Nehemiah 7:68
   A. 245
   B. 435
   C. 736
   D. 1,000

8. What was the total number of *mules*?
   Nehemiah 7:68
   A. 245
   B. 435
   C. 736
   D. 1,000

9. What was the total number of *camels*?
   Nehemiah 7:69
   A. 245
   B. 435
   C. 736
   D. 1,000

10. What was the total number of *asses*?
    Nehemiah 7:69
    A. 2,670
    B. 4,560
    C. 5,640
    D. 6,720

11. How many drams of gold did the Tirshatha give to the treasurer of the work?
    Nehemiah 7:70
    A. 245
    B. 435
    C. 736
    D. 1,000

12. How many drams of gold did the chief fathers give to the treasurer of the work?
    Nehemiah 7:71
    A. 5,000
    B. 10,000
    C. 15,000
    D. 20,000

13. How many drams of gold did the people give?
    Nehemiah 7:72
    A. 10,000
    B. 20,000
    C. 30,000
    D. 40,000

14. At which gate did the people meet?
    Nehemiah 8:1
    A. Horse gate
    B. King's gate
    C. Valley gate
    D. Water gate

15. Which book was read to the people?
    Nehemiah 8:1
    A. Book of the covenant
    B. Book of the law of Moses
    C. Book of the kings of Israel and Judah
    D. Book of the wars of the LORD

16. On which day of the seventh month did the people meet?
    Nehemiah 8:2
    A. 1st day
    B. 7th day
    C. 14th day
    D. 21st day

17. Who read the book to the people?
    Nehemiah 8:4–8
    A. Ezra
    B. Gera
    C. Jada
    D. Moza

18. Who was the Tirshatha?
    Nehemiah 8:9
    A. Jeremiah
    B. Meshelemiah
    C. Nehemiah
    D. Shelemiah

19. What were the people to do during the feast of the seventh month?
    Nehemiah 8:14
    A. Dwell in booths
    B. Eat unleavened bread
    C. Give the firstfruits
    D. Kill the passover

20. Who was Jeshua's father?
    Nehemiah 8:17
    A. Bunni
    B. Guni
    C. Nun
    D. Unni

*Answers on page 763

JUNE 5

Lesson 156
Today's Reading: *Nehemiah 9–10*
Period of Time: 454 BC
Author: Nehemiah

1. On which day of the seventh month did the people assemble dressed in sackcloth?
   Nehemiah 9:1
   A. 6th day
   B. 12th day
   C. 18th day
   D. 24th day

2. What portion of the day did people spend reading the book of the law of the LORD?
   Nehemiah 9:3
   A. 1/4
   B. 1/2
   C. 2/3
   D. 3/4

3. What portion of the day did people spend making confessions and worshipping the LORD?
   Nehemiah 9:3
   A. 1/4
   B. 1/2
   C. 2/3
   D. 3/4

4. In which city of the Chaldees did Abraham live?
   Nehemiah 9:7
   A. Ai
   B. No
   C. Ur
   D. Uz

5. Which sea was parted so the children of Israel could escape from Pharaoh?
   Nehemiah 9:9–11
   A. Great sea
   B. Molten sea
   C. Red sea
   D. Salt sea

6. Upon which mountain did the children of Israel receive the LORD's commandments?
   Nehemiah 9:13
   A. Mount Hor
   B. Mount Lebanon
   C. Mount Tabor
   D. Mount Sinai

7. Whom did God use to teach his commandments to the people in the desert?
   Nehemiah 9:14
   A. Hosea
   B. Moses
   C. Ophir
   D. Uriah

8. Where did the people miraculously receive water in the desert?
   Nehemiah 9:15
   A. From a rock
   B. From a stream
   C. From a tree
   D. From a waterfall

9. Which idol did the children of Israel worship in the desert?
   Nehemiah 9:18
   A. A cave drawing
   B. A molten calf
   C. A star in the sky
   D. A wooden doll

10. What type of bread did God give the people to eat in the desert?
    Nehemiah 9:20
    A. Ezekiel
    B. Leavened
    C. Manna
    D. Wheat

11. What did the people do for clothing while in the desert?
    Nehemiah 9:21
    A. They did not wear clothes.
    B. They made them from animal hides.
    C. They bought them from the Philistines.
    D. They wore the same clothes for 40 years.

12. Who was the king of Bashan?
    Nehemiah 9:22
    A. King Ir
    B. King Og
    C. King On
    D. King So

13. Which one of the following nations was inhabiting the Promised Land?
    Nehemiah 9:24
    A. The Canaanites
    B. The Greeks
    C. The Libyans
    D. The Romans

14. What are God's ways?
    Nehemiah 9:33
    A. Accursed
    B. Blasphemous
    C. Evil
    D. Just

15. What was Nehemiah's official title?
    Nehemiah 10:1
    A. Judge
    B. Rabshakeh
    C. Tirshatha
    D. Watchman

16. Who was Nehemiah's father?
    Nehemiah 10:1
    A. Azaliah
    B. Hachaliah
    C. Igdaliah
    D. Pelaliah

17. What did the people promise **not** to do on the sabbath or on any holy days?
    Nehemiah 10:31
    A. Buy, trade, or sell merchandise
    B. Eat meat of any animal
    C. Have sexual relations with their wives
    D. Walk more than one mile

18. Upon which year were debts forgiven?
    Nehemiah 10:31
    A. 3rd year
    B. 7th year
    C. 10th year
    D. 12th year

19. How much of a shekel did the Jews charge themselves annually for the house of God?
    Nehemiah 10:32
    A. 1/8
    B. 1/4
    C. 1/3
    D. 1/2

20. Which tribe was responsible for bringing the tithe of the tithe into the house of God?
    Nehemiah 10:38
    A. Tribe of Asher
    B. Tribe of Dan
    C. Tribe of Gad
    D. Tribe of Levi

Answers on page 763

Lesson 157
Today's Reading: *Nehemiah 11–13*
Period of Time: 454–442 BC
Author: Nehemiah

JUNE 6

1. What was the ratio of men living in Jerusalem to those living outside the city?
   Nehemiah 11:1
   A. 1:10
   B. 2:10
   C. 3:10
   D. 4:10

2. How many Levites lived in the holy city?
   Nehemiah 11:18
   A. 215
   B. 263
   C. 284
   D. 297

3. What was the total number of porters?
   Nehemiah 11:19
   A. 101
   B. 136
   C. 154
   D. 172

4. Where did the Nethinims dwell?
   Nehemiah 11:21
   A. Oboth
   B. Ophel
   C. Ophir
   D. Ophni

5. Who was the overseer of the Levites in Jerusalem?
   Nehemiah 11:22
   A. Amzi
   B. Buzi
   C. Uzzi
   D. Zimri

6. What were the sons of Asaph?
   Nehemiah 11:22
   A. Creditors
   B. Exchangers of money
   C. Singers
   D. Tax collectors

7. Who was a Persian king?
   Nehemiah 12:22
   A. King Achish
   B. King Darius
   C. King Hiram
   D. King Pekah

8. What was Nehemiah's official title?
   Nehemiah 12:26
   A. Doorkeeper
   B. Governor
   C. Interpreter
   D. Post

9. Which priest was a scribe?
   Nehemiah 12:26
   A. Ezra
   B. Izri
   C. Ozni
   D. Uzzi

10. What was Jezrahiah overseer of?
    Nehemiah 12:42
    A. Creditors
    B. Exchangers of money
    C. Singers
    D. Tax collectors

11. Which two nations were to never enter into the congregation?
    Nehemiah 13:1
    A. Ammonites and Moabites
    B. Ekronites and Heberites
    C. Jebusites and Ninevites
    D. Temanites and Dehavites

12. Which prophet was hired to curse Israel?
    Nehemiah 13:2
    A. Abiram
    B. Balaam
    C. Elnaam
    D. Gazzam

13. Which high priest gave Tobiah a room in the temple?

    Nehemiah 13:4–5

    A. Azariah
    B. Eliashib
    C. Hophni
    D. Phinehas

14. Who was the king of Babylon?

    Nehemiah 13:6

    A. King Artaxerxes
    B. King Hezekiah
    C. King Jeroboam
    D. King Rehoboam

15. Which priest was a treasurer?

    Nehemiah 13:13

    A. Jeremiah
    B. Meshelemiah
    C. Raamiah
    D. Shelemiah

16. Which scribe was a treasurer?

    Nehemiah 13:13

    A. Amok
    B. Jokshan
    C. Joktan
    D. Zadok

17. Merchants from which nation came to Jerusalem to trade on the sabbath day?

    Nehemiah 13:16

    A. Cyprus
    B. Lycia
    C. Myra
    D. Tyre

18. What was one of the nations the Jews married strange women from?

    Nehemiah 13:23

    A. Ashdod
    B. Gudgodah
    C. Sodom
    D. Tahtimhodshi

19. Which king of Israel sinned because of outlandish women?

    Nehemiah 13:26

    A. King Abimelech
    B. King Ben-ha'dad
    C. King Claudius
    D. King Solomon

20. What was Sanballat's surname?

    Nehemiah 13:28

    A. The Benjamite
    B. The Gibeonite
    C. The Horonite
    D. The Levite

*Answers on page 764

Lesson 158
Today's Reading: *Esther 1–3*
Period of Time: 518–510 BC
Author: Esther

1. Approximately how many provinces did Ahasuerus rule over?
   Esther 1:1
   A. 127
   B. 259
   C. 345
   D. 444

2. Where was Ahasuerus' palace located?
   Esther 1:2
   A. Bethshan
   B. Nibshan
   C. Shushan
   D. Zarthan

3. Who was the queen who refused Ahasuerus' order?
   Esther 1:9–12
   A. Bernice
   B. Michal
   C. Rizpah
   D. Vashti

4. Whose idea was it to replace the queen?
   Esther 1:16–22
   A. Memucan
   B. Nicanor
   C. Shecaniah
   D. Toucan

5. What is the other name for Hegai?
   Esther 2:3–8
   A. Hazo
   B. Hege
   C. Hori
   D. Huri

6. What was Hegai's title?
   Esther 2:3–8
   A. Keeper of the books
   B. Keeper of the doors
   C. Keeper of the women
   D. Keeper of the zoos

7. Who had been the king of Judah?
   Esther 2:6
   A. King Jeberechiah
   B. King Jeconiah
   C. King Jedidiah
   D. King Jehizkiah

8. What was Esther's Jewish name?
   Esther 2:7
   A. Ephratah
   B. Hadassah
   C. Jehudijah
   D. Shiphrah

9. How many maidens were given to Esther?
   Esther 2:9
   A. 2
   B. 3
   C. 5
   D. 7

10. How many months did it take to complete purification?
    Esther 2:9–12
    A. 3
    B. 6
    C. 9
    D. 12

11. Who was keeper of the concubines?
    Esther 2:14
    A. Jaazaniah
    B. Raamah
    C. Shaashgaz
    D. Zaavan

12. Who was Mordecai's uncle?
    Esther 2:15
    A. Abihail
    B. Abner
    C. Abraham
    D. Absalom

13. What was the name of the tenth month?
    Esther 2:16

    A. Adar
    B. Elul
    C. Nisan
    D. Tebeth

14. At which gate did Mordecai wait to see Esther?
    Esther 2:19–21

    A. Dung gate
    B. Fish gate
    C. Horse gate
    D. King's gate

15. Which two men sought to lay hand on the king?
    Esther 2:21

    A. Achan and Jabesh
    B. Bigthan and Teresh
    C. Elhanan and Shelesh
    D. Johanan and Heresh

16. How were the two conspirators put to death?
    Esther 2:23

    A. Burned
    B. Drowned
    C. Hanged
    D. Stoned

17. What was Haman's surname?
    Esther 3:1

    A. The Agagite
    B. The Benjamite
    C. The Moabite
    D. The Tishbite

18. What is the name of the first month?
    Esther 3:7

    A. Adar
    B. Elul
    C. Nisan
    D. Tebeth

19. What is the name of the twelfth month?
    Esther 3:7, 3:13

    A. Adar
    B. Elul
    C. Nisan
    D. Tebeth

20. On which day of the twelfth month were all Jews to be slaughtered?
    Esther 3:13

    A. 7th day
    B. 13th day
    C. 20th day
    D. 28th day

Answers on page 764

Lesson 159
Today's Reading: *Esther 4–7*
Period of Time: 510 BC
Author: Esther

JUNE 8

1. At which gate did Mordecai cry a loud and bitter cry?
   Esther 4:1–2
   A. Dung gate
   B. Golden gate
   C. King's gate
   D. Queen's gate

2. What did Esther send Mordecai?
   Esther 4:4
   A. A book
   B. A camel
   C. Raiment
   D. Swords

3. Who was one of the king's chamberlains?
   Esther 4:5
   A. Hatach
   B. Mahath
   C. Parnach
   D. Tahath

4. Where was the decree to exterminate all Jews given?
   Esther 4:8
   A. Chorashan
   B. Elonbethhanan
   C. Nibshan
   D. Shushan

5. What could save a person from death?
   Esther 4:11
   A. The entrails of a dove
   B. The golden scepter
   C. The thumb pointing downward
   D. The white feather

6. How many days had passed since Esther had been called to come in unto the king?
   Esther 4:11
   A. 10
   B. 20
   C. 30
   D. 40

7. What did Mordecai tell Esther?
   Esther 4:14
   A. Be sure your sin will find you out.
   B. Do not weep for me for I am old.
   C. Flee the city at once before they kill you.
   D. Perhaps God sent you for a time like this.

8. How many days did the Jews neither eat nor drink?
   Esther 4:16–5:1
   A. 2
   B. 3
   C. 4
   D. 5

9. Where did the king hold court?
   Esther 4:11, 5:1
   A. Beneath the palm tree
   B. Inner court of the king's house
   C. Near the great gate to the city
   D. Upon the temple steps

10. Who was Haman's wife?
    Esther 5:10–14, 6:13
    A. Elisheba
    B. Hodesh
    C. Shelomith
    D. Zeresh

11. How many cubits high were the gallows?
    Esther 5:14, 7:9
    A. 20
    B. 30
    C. 40
    D. 50

12. Which book did the king send for?
    Esther 6:1
    A. The book of records of the chronicles
    B. The chronicles of the seers
    C. The seven-sealed book
    D. The vision of Isaiah the prophet

337

13. Who warned the king about a conspiracy against him?

    Esther 6:2

    A. Esther
    B. Haman
    C. Hammedatha
    D. Mordecai

14. Who conspired against the king?

    Esther 6:2

    A. Bigthana and Teresh
    B. Jannes and Jambres
    C. Nadab and Abihu
    D. Peter and Paul

15. What did Haman bring to Mordecai?

    Esther 6:11

    A. King's apparel and a horse
    B. Prisoner's raiment and paper
    C. Rope and chains
    D. Sackcloth and ashes

16. On which day of the banquet did Esther plea for her people and herself?

    Esther 7:2–4

    A. 2nd day
    B. 3rd day
    C. 4th day
    D. 5th day

17. Where did the king go in anger?

    Esther 7:7

    A. The horse stalls
    B. The palace garden
    C. The queen's bedroom
    D. The wine cellar

18. Where did the king find Haman?

    Esther 7:8

    A. At the gallows
    B. Underneath the banquet table
    C. Upon Esther's bed
    D. Wedged inside a chimney

19. Who was also one of the king's chamberlains?

    Esther 7:9

    A. Haran
    B. Harbonah
    C. Harnepher
    D. Harumaph

20. How was Haman put to death?

    Esther 7:10

    A. He was burned.
    B. He was drowned.
    C. He was hanged.
    D. He was poisoned.

*Answers on page 764

Lesson 160
Today's Reading: *Esther 8–10*
Period of Time: 510–509 BC
Author: Esther

1. Who was the king of Persia?
   Esther 8:1
   A. King Ahasuerus
   B. King Claudius
   C. King Nero
   D. King Tiberius

2. What did the king give to Mordecai that he took from Haman?
   Esther 8:2
   A. A cloke
   B. A house
   C. A mule
   D. A ring

3. Which name was attached to Haman?
   Esther 8:3
   A. The Agagite
   B. The Elonite
   C. The Heberite
   D. The Nemuelite

4. What did the king use to spare a person's life and allow them to speak?
   Esther 8:4–6
   A. A goat
   B. A maze
   C. A ring
   D. A sceptre

5. Who was Haman's father?
   Esther 8:5
   A. Abraham
   B. Chimham
   C. Gaham
   D. Hammedatha

6. How was Haman put to death?
   Esther 8:7
   A. Beheaded
   B. Hanged
   C. Poisoned
   D. Stoned

7. What is the name of the third month?
   Esther 8:9
   A. Adar
   B. Elul
   C. Sivan
   D. Zif

8. Where were the king's provinces located?
   Esther 8:9
   A. From Assyria unto Babylon
   B. From Greece unto Persia
   C. From India unto Ethiopia
   D. From Syria unto Africa

9. On which day of the twelfth month were the Jews to be exterminated?
   Esther 8:7–12
   A. 2nd day
   B. 13th day
   C. 23rd day
   D. 31st day

10. What is the name of the twelfth month?
    Esther 8:12
    A. Adar
    B. Elul
    C. Sivan
    D. Zif

11. What colors were in the royal apparel?
    Esther 8:15
    A. Blue and white
    B. Gold and black
    C. Orange and green
    D. Red and yellow

12. What color was the garment of fine linen?
    Esther 8:15
    A. Black
    B. Gold
    C. Purple
    D. White

13. How many men did the Jews kill at the palace on the first day?

    Esther 9:6

    A. 200
    B. 300
    C. 400
    D. 500

14. How many sons did Haman have?

    Esther 9:10–12

    A. 7
    B. 10
    C. 12
    D. 21

15. What happened to Haman's sons?

    Esther 9:13–14

    A. They were dragged through the streets.
    B. They were fed to vicious dogs.
    C. They were hung upon the gallows.
    D. They were nailed to the city walls.

16. How many men did the Jews kill on the second day in Shushan?

    Esther 9:15

    A. 100
    B. 200
    C. 300
    D. 400

17. How many men did the Jews kill in the provinces on the second day?

    Esther 9:16

    A. 30,000
    B. 45,000
    C. 50,000
    D. 75,000

18. What is the name of the annual festival to commemorate how Esther helped to save her people?

    Esther 9:26

    A. Chanukkah
    B. Purim
    C. Rosh Hashanah
    D. Yom Kippur

19. Who was Esther's father?

    Esther 9:29

    A. Abihail
    B. Kelaiah
    C. Malcham
    D. Theudas

20. Which book contains the acts of Mordecai?

    Esther 10:2

    A. Book of remembrance of the acts of Mordecai the Jew
    B. Book of the chronicles of the kings of Media and Persia
    C. Chronicles of the Jews in Persia and their war against anti-Jews
    D. Record and chronicles of the Jews and their queen Esther

Answers on page 764

Lesson 161
Today's Reading: *Job 1–5*
Period of Time: Unknown
Author: Unknown

1. Where did Job live?
   Job 1:1
   A. Land of Ai
   B. Land of Ar
   C. Land of Ur
   D. Land of Uz

2. How many sons did Job have?
   Job 1:2
   A. 3
   B. 5
   C. 7
   D. 10

3. How many daughters did Job have?
   Job 1:2
   A. 2
   B. 3
   C. 4
   D. 2

4. How many sheep did Job own?
   Job 1:3
   A. 7
   B. 70
   C. 700
   D. 7,000

5. How many camels did Job own?
   Job 1:3
   A. 1,000
   B. 3,000
   C. 5,000
   D. 7,000

6. How many yoke of oxen did Job own?
   Job 1:3
   A. 5
   B. 50
   C. 500
   D. 5,000

7. How many she asses did Job own?
   Job 1:3
   A. 5
   B. 50
   C. 500
   D. 5,000

8. Who stole Job's oxen and asses?
   Job 1:14–15
   A. Romans
   B. Sabeans
   C. Syrians
   D. Thessalonians

9. Who stole Job's camels?
   Job 1:17
   A. The Chaldeans
   B. The Ethiopians
   C. The Galileans
   D. The Sidonians

10. What killed Job's children?
    Job 1:19
    A. A great earthquake
    B. A great fire
    C. A great flood
    D. A great wind

11. What did Satan use to torment Job's body?
    Job 2:7
    A. Boils
    B. Emerods
    C. Hornets
    D. Lice

12. What was Eliphaz's surname?
    Job 2:11
    A. The Agagite
    B. The Naamathite
    C. The Shuhite
    D. The Temanite

13. What was Bildad's surname?

    Job 2:11

    A. The Agagite
    B. The Naamathite
    C. The Shuhite
    D. The Temanite

14. What was Zophar's surname?

    Job 2:11

    A. The Agagite
    B. The Naamathite
    C. The Shuhite
    D. The Temanite

15. How many days and nights passed before Job's friends spoke a word to him?

    Job 2:13

    A. 7
    B. 14
    C. 21
    D. 28

16. What did Job curse?

    Job 3:1–3

    A. His birth
    B. His body
    C. His family
    D. His marriage

17. Whose teeth did Eliphaz say were broken?

    Job 4:10

    A. The bears' teeth
    B. The cows' teeth
    C. The horses' teeth
    D. The lions' teeth

18. What did Eliphaz say made the hair of his flesh stand up?

    Job 4:15

    A. A dragon
    B. A giant
    C. A spirit
    D. A tempest

19. What did Eliphaz say slays the silly one?

    Job 5:2

    A. Envy
    B. Kindness
    C. Trust
    D. Virtue

20. According to Eliphaz, what makes a man happy?

    Job 5:17

    A. He that findeth a virtuous wife
    B. He that God correcteth
    C. He that has close friends
    D. He that Satan cannot harm

Answers on page 764

JUNE 11

Lesson 162
Today's Reading: *Job 6–10*
Period of Time: Unknown
Author: Unknown

1. What—of the sea—does Job say his grief and calamity are heavier than?
   Job 6:3
   A. Leviathan
   B. Sand
   C. Ships
   D. Whales

2. Whose arrows does Job say are within him?
   Job 6:4
   A. The Almighty's arrows
   B. The Chaldeans' arrows
   C. The Devil's arrows
   D. The Sabeans' arrows

3. What question does Job use as a comparison to the things he longs for?
   Job 6:5
   A. "Doth the wild ass bray when he hath grass?"
   B. "Doth the duck quack when he has water?"
   C. "Doth the lion roar when he hath prey?"
   D. "Doth the swine grunt when he hath mud?"

4. What does Job ask if it has any taste?
   Job 6:6
   A. The dew of the ground
   B. The holes of the bread
   C. The salt of the earth
   D. The white of an egg

5. What does Job say should be shown to the afflicted?
   Job 6:14
   A. Hurt
   B. Pity
   C. Rigor
   D. Woe

6. What does Job compare his friends to?
   Job 6:15–18
   A. A dry brook during the summer
   B. A hungry suckling with no mother
   C. A poor man begging for food
   D. An evil thief robbing a house

7. Whose troops looked in hopes of being refreshed?
   Job 6:19
   A. Dumah's troops
   B. Hadad's troops
   C. Massa's troops
   D. Tema's troops

8. What does Job compare the days of man to?
   Job 7:1
   A. The days of a hireling
   B. The days of a woman in travail
   C. The days of spring
   D. The days of youth

9. What does Job say his flesh is clothed with?
   Job 7:5
   A. Feathers and tears he has wept
   B. Rags and blood stained bandages
   C. Sweat and a leather girdle
   D. Worms and clods of dust

10. What does Job say his days are swifter than?
    Job 7:6
    A. A fowler's snare
    B. A slinger's stone
    C. A weaver's shuttle
    D. An archer's arrow

11. What does Job call his life?
    Job 7:7
    A. Fire
    B. Hail
    C. Rain
    D. Wind

343

12. What does Job call his days?

    Job 7:16

    A. Death
    B. Snow
    C. Vanity
    D. Wickedness

13. What does Bildad say Job's words are like?

    Job 8:2

    A. A continual dropping
    B. A horse's bit
    C. A strong wind
    D. A terrible famine

14. What does Bildad call our days upon the earth?

    Job 8:9

    A. A journey
    B. A leaf
    C. A shadow
    D. A trial

15. Which one of the stars does Job mention?

    Job 9:9

    A. Aries
    B. Orion
    C. Pisces
    D. Sagittarius

16. What does Job say God breaks him with?

    Job 9:17

    A. A cord
    B. A horse
    C. A rod
    D. A tempest

17. What else does Job say his days are swifter than?

    Job 9:25

    A. A horse
    B. A post
    C. A river
    D. A viper

18. Which bird does Job say his days are as swift as?

    Job 9:26

    A. A dove
    B. A raven
    C. An eagle
    D. An owl

19. What does Job feel he has been poured out like?

    Job 10:10

    A. Milk
    B. Strong drink
    C. Water
    D. Wine

20. Where does Job say he will go after he dies?

    Job 10:21

    A. The eternal fires of hell
    B. The land of darkness
    C. The place of eternal bliss
    D. The tunnel of light

Answers on page 764

Lesson 163
Today's Reading: *Job 11–15*
Period of Time: Unknown
Author: Unknown

JUNE 12

1. What was Zophar's surname?
   Job 11:1
   A. The Agagite
   B. The Naamathite
   C. The Shuhite
   D. The Temanite

2. What does Zophar state a vain man's birth is like?
   Job 11:12
   A. A bastard child
   B. A rich man's son
   C. A stillborn child
   D. A wild ass's colt

3. Whose tabernacles does Job state will prosper?
   Job 12:6
   A. Tabernacles of Ancients
   B. Tabernacles of Orphans
   C. Tabernacles of Robbers
   D. Tabernacles of Widows

4. What does Job state the ancients have?
   Job 12:12
   A. Fame
   B. Power
   C. Riches
   D. Wisdom

5. What does Job state are found in length of days?
   Job 12:12
   A. Confusion
   B. Honor
   C. Losses
   D. Understanding

6. Whom does Job claim God makes into fools?
   Job 12:17
   A. Judges
   B. Lawyers
   C. Students
   D. Teachers

7. What—of the people—does Job claim God causes to stagger like a drunken man?
   Job 12:24–25
   A. The brave
   B. The chief
   C. The poor
   D. The sick

8. What does Job call his friends?
   Job 13:4
   A. Clouds without rain
   B. Physicians of no value
   C. Sails that lack wind
   D. Wagons with precarious wheels

9. What does Job call his friends' bodies?
   Job 13:12
   A. Bodies of clay
   B. Houses of misery
   C. Temples of doom
   D. Vessels of shame

10. What does Job state his misery is like?
    Job 13:28
    A. A bottle that has cracks
    B. A desert that has no oasis
    C. A garment that has been moth eaten
    D. A wound that has been filled with salt

11. Which plants—when cut—does Job state are similar to the days of man?
    Job 14:2
    A. Cornstalks
    B. Flowers
    C. Grass
    D. Trees

12. Which plants does Job state have hope even though they have been cut?
    Job 14:7–9
    A. Cornstalks
    B. Flowers
    C. Grass
    D. Trees

13. What was Eliphaz's surname?

    Job 15:1

    A. The Agagite
    B. The Naamathite
    C. The Shuhite
    D. The Temanite

14. Which wind does Eliphaz ask if a wise man should fill his belly with it?

    Job 15:2

    A. The north wind
    B. The south wind
    C. The east wind
    D. The west wind

15. What condemns Job, according to Eliphaz?

    Job 15:6

    A. Job's brother
    B. Job's heart
    C. Job's mouth
    D. Job's wife

16. What does Eliphaz claim is on his—and Job's friends'—side?

    Job 15:10

    A. The gray headed and very aged men
    B. The judges and the people
    C. The prophets and priests
    D. The world and nature itself

17. According to Eliphaz, where on his body does the wicked man maketh collops of fat?

    Job 15:20–27

    A. On his brains
    B. On his calves
    C. On his flanks
    D. On his kidneys

18. According to Eliphaz, where do the wicked dwell?

    Job 15:20–28

    A. In desolate cities
    B. In fox's dens
    C. In hidden caves
    D. In widow's houses

19. According to Eliphaz, what shall be the wicked man's recompence?

    Job 15:20–31

    A. Vanity
    B. Vengeance
    C. Vitality
    D. Vomit

20. According to Eliphaz, which plant shakes off its flower?

    Job 15:33

    A. The oak
    B. The olive
    C. The onion
    D. The orange

*Answers on page 764

Lesson 164
Today's Reading: *Job 16–21*
Period of Time: Unknown
Author: Unknown

1. What did Job say he would do if his friends' souls were in his soul's stead?
   Job 16:1–5

   A. Asswage their grief
   B. Exacerbate their affliction
   C. Heighten their misery
   D. Intensify their terror

2. What does Job state his friends have filled him with?
   Job 16:8

   A. Gravel
   B. Irony
   C. Lead
   D. Wrinkles

3. What does Job state God has done to him?
   Job 16:13

   A. Covered him with his hand
   B. Filled him with pride
   C. Poured his gall upon the ground
   D. Sifted him as with the sieve of vanity

4. What does Job state God is like?
   Job 16:14

   A. A comforter
   B. A giant
   C. A physician
   D. A rock

5. What does Job state is corrupt?
   Job 17:1

   A. His breath
   B. His eye
   C. His foot
   D. His hand

6. What does Job state he was like before he lost everything?
   Job 17:6

   A. A cornet
   B. A harp
   C. A psaltery
   D. A tabret

7. What does Job call his father?
   Job 17:14

   A. Benevolent
   B. Corruption
   C. Temperate
   D. Sober

8. What does Job call his mother and sister?
   Job 17:14

   A. The butterfly
   B. The caterpillar
   C. The snake
   D. The worm

9. What was Bildad's surname?
   Job 18:1

   A. The Agagite
   B. The Naamathite
   C. The Shuhite
   D. The Temanite

10. What does Bildad state will take Job by the heel?
    Job 18:9

    A. The archer
    B. The devil
    C. The gin
    D. The viper

11. What does Bildad state will prevail against Job?
    Job 18:9

    A. The avenger
    B. The plague
    C. The robber
    D. The scales

12. What does Bildad state will be hungerbitten?
    Job 18:12

    A. Job's belly
    B. Job's heel
    C. Job's pride
    D. Job's strength

13. What does Bildad state Job's confidence will bring him to?

    Job 18:14

    A. The king of clubs
    B. The king of hearts
    C. The king of spades
    D. The king of terrors

14. How many times does Job claim his friends have reproached him?

    Job 19:3

    A. 10
    B. 20
    C. 30
    D. 40

15. How does Job state he escaped from total calamity?

    Job 19:20

    A. By the hair of his chin
    B. By the skin of his teeth
    C. By the touch of an angel
    D. By the will of God

16. How will Job see God after worms eat his body?

    Job 19:26

    A. He shall see God as an angel.
    B. He shall see God in the flesh.
    C. He shall see God in the spirit.
    D. He will never see God.

17. What was Zophar's surname?

    Job 20:1

    A. The Agagite
    B. The Naamathite
    C. The Shuhite
    D. The Temanite

18. What does Zophar state will slay Job?

    Job 20:16

    A. The executioner's axe
    B. The sword of the LORD
    C. The viper's tongue
    D. The word of God

19. What does Job claim the wicked are like?

    Job 21:17–18

    A. Stubble before the wind
    B. Traps before the beast
    C. Wicks before the wax
    D. Wood before the fire

20. What of the valley does Job state shall be sweet to the wicked?

    Job 21:33

    A. The clods
    B. The grass
    C. The lily
    D. The oak

*Answers on page 764

Lesson 165
Today's Reading: *Job 22–28*
Period of Time: Unknown
Author: Unknown

1. What is Eliphaz's surname?
   Job 22:1
   A. The Agagite
   B. The Naamathite
   C. The Shuhite
   D. The Temanite

2. Whom does Eliphaz accuse Job of breaking the arms of?
   Job 22:9
   A. The ancients
   B. The fatherless
   C. The invalid
   D. The widows

3. What does Job state God would put in him if he could find God?
   Job 23:6
   A. Bread
   B. Faith
   C. Strength
   D. Water

4. What does Job state the way the wicked go about their business is like?
   Job 24:5
   A. Crooked serpents in the hole
   B. Fatted calves in the pasture
   C. Wild asses in the desert
   D. Young lions in secret places

5. What does Job claim the morning is to the murderer, thief, and adulterer?
   Job 24:14–17
   A. The dawn of a new day
   B. The light of the world
   C. The mother of darkness
   D. The shadow of death

6. What does Job state the wicked person is as swift as?
   Job 24:18
   A. The cloud
   B. The dromedary
   C. The roes
   D. The waters

7. What does Job say the wicked shall be cut off like?
   Job 24:24
   A. The branches of the vine
   B. The foreskin of the man child
   C. The tops of the ears of corn
   D. The waters of a flood

8. What was Bildad's surname?
   Job 25:1
   A. The Agagite
   B. The Naamathite
   C. The Shuhite
   D. The Temanite

9. What does Bildad call man?
   Job 25:6
   A. A worm
   B. A young whelp
   C. An ass
   D. An odious son

10. According to Job, what is found in heaven that trembles and are astonished at God's reproof?
    Job 26:11
    A. The gates
    B. The pillars
    C. The streets
    D. The windows

11. Where is the spirit of God in Job's parable?
    Job 27:3
    A. Inside Job's nostrils
    B. Riding upon the wind
    C. Sitting upon his throne
    D. Waiting at the gates of hell

12. Whose cry does Job state God will **not** hear?

    Job 27:8–9

    A. The fatherless
    B. The hypocrite
    C. The prophet
    D. The widow

13. What does Job call God?

    Job 27:10

    A. The Almighty
    B. The Deliverer
    C. The Highest
    D. The Maker

14. According to Job, who shall divide the wicked man's silver when he dies?

    Job 27:17

    A. The exchangers
    B. The innocent
    C. The sons
    D. The widows

15. What does Job say the wicked builds his house like?

    Job 27:18

    A. A bee
    B. A moth
    C. A spider
    D. A viper

16. According to Job, which wind carrieth away the wicked?

    Job 27:21

    A. The east wind
    B. The west wind
    C. The north wind
    D. The south wind

17. Which metal was Ophir known for?

    Job 28:16

    A. Gold
    B. Iron
    C. Silver
    D. Tin

18. Which jewel was Ethiopia known for?

    Job 28:19

    A. Diamond
    B. Onyx
    C. Ruby
    D. Topaz

19. What is the fear of the Lord?

    Job 28:28

    A. Boredom
    B. Knowledge
    C. Understanding
    D. Wisdom

20. According to Job, what will a person receive if he departs from evil?

    Job 28:28

    A. Boredom
    B. Knowledge
    C. Understanding
    D. Wisdom

Answers on page 764

Lesson 166
Today's Reading: *Job 29–33*
Period of Time: Unknown
Author: Unknown

JUNE 15

1. What does Job state was upon his tabernacle?
   Job 29:4
   A. A pillar of a cloud
   B. A pillar of fire
   C. The angel of the LORD
   D. The secret of God

2. What did Job claim he washed his steps with?
   Job 29:6
   A. Butter
   B. Milk
   C. Oil
   D. Water

3. What does Job state poured out of the rock like rivers?
   Job 29:6
   A. Butter
   B. Milk
   C. Oil
   D. Water

4. Whose heart does Job state sang for joy because of his kindness?
   Job 29:13
   A. The orphan's heart
   B. The ruler's heart
   C. The widow's heart
   D. The worlds' heart

5. What was Job's judgment like?
   Job 29:14
   A. A belt and a crown
   B. A cloke and a girdle
   C. A mantel and a garment
   D. A robe and a diadem

6. How does Job state the young men treat him?
   Job 30:1–15
   A. Compassionately
   B. Disrespectfully
   C. Justly
   D. Thankfully

7. What does Job say his welfare passes away like?
   Job 30:15
   A. A bow
   B. A cloud
   C. A flower
   D. A rain

8. What does Job state boiled within him?
   Job 30:27
   A. His blood
   B. His bowels
   C. His heart
   D. His lungs

9. What does Job state he is brother to?
   Job 30:29
   A. Behemoths
   B. Chamois
   C. Dragons
   D. Unicorns

10. What does Job state he is a companion to?
    Job 30:29
    A. Eagles
    B. Hawks
    C. Owls
    D. Peacocks

11. What color is Job's skin?
    Job 30:30
    A. Almond
    B. Black
    C. Tan
    D. White

12. Which musical instrument does Job state has turned to mourning?
    Job 30:31
    A. His dulcimer
    B. His harp
    C. His sackbut
    D. His viol

13. Which musical instrument does Job state has become the voice of them that weep?

    Job 30:31

    A. His cymbals
    B. His flute
    C. His harp
    D. His trumpet

14. Who tried to cover his transgressions by hiding from God?

    Job 31:33

    A. Adam
    B. Iram
    C. Onam
    D. Ulam

15. What does Job say thistles should grow instead of?

    Job 31:40

    A. Barley
    B. Hay
    C. Oats
    D. Wheat

16. What does Job say cockles should grow instead of?

    Job 31:40

    A. Barley
    B. Hay
    C. Oats
    D. Wheat

17. What was Barachel's surname?

    Job 32:2

    A. The Buzite
    B. The Naamathite
    C. The Shuhite
    D. The Temanite

18. Why did Elihu speak last?

    Job 32:4

    A. He was the oldest.
    B. He was the richest.
    C. He was the wisest.
    D. He was the youngest.

19. What does Elihu state his desire to speak is like?

    Job 32:19

    A. A bottle bursting with wine
    B. A general marching into battle
    C. A horse delivering a colt
    D. A rose blooming in snow

20. What does Elihu call the place in the afterlife?

    Job 33:18–30

    A. The eternity
    B. The fire
    C. The grave
    D. The pit

*Answers on page 764

Lesson 167
Today's Reading: *Job 34–37*
Period of Time: Unknown
Author: Unknown

JUNE 16

1. According to Elihu, Job drinks up scorning like what?
   Job 34:7
   A. Gall
   B. Milk
   C. Wine
   D. Water

2. According to Elihu, what are the eyes of God upon?
   Job 34:21
   A. The channel of the river
   B. The path of the meek
   C. The road of glory
   D. The ways of man

3. According to Elihu, the people become ensnared when who reigns?
   Job 34:30
   A. The hypocrite
   B. The innocent
   C. The just
   D. The righteous

4. What kind of a man does Elihu want to listen to him?
   Job 34:34
   A. A rich man
   B. A simple man
   C. A tired man
   D. A wise man

5. What does Elihu state Job addeth to his sin?
   Job 34:37
   A. Knowledge
   B. Rebellion
   C. Understanding
   D. Wisdom

6. What does Elihu claim that Job believes he is more than God?
   Job 35:2
   A. Omnipotent
   B. Omniscient
   C. Righteous
   D. Wise

7. What does Elihu state God will **not** hear?
   Job 35:13
   A. Cries
   B. Praise
   C. Prayer
   D. Vanity

8. Which name does Elihu use for God?
   Job 36:3
   A. Alpha
   B. Elohim
   C. Maker
   D. Omega

9. What does Elihu claim righteous kings receive?
   Job 36:7–11
   A. Betrayal and death
   B. Hardship and wives
   C. Misery and rebellion
   D. Prosperity and pleasures

10. According to Elihu, what do kings that disobey God die without?
    Job 36:7–12
    A. Knowledge
    B. Rebellion
    C. Understanding
    D. Wisdom

11. What word besides *mighty* does Elihu use to describe God?
    Job 36:26
    A. Great
    B. Joy
    C. Love
    D. Patient

12. Elihu states man cannot search out what about God?

    Job 36:26

    A. If he is truly the creator
    B. The number of his years
    C. Who sits at his right side
    D. Why he sent his son to die

13. What does Elihu state God makes small?

    Job 36:27

    A. Ants
    B. Mustard seed
    C. Raindrops
    D. Sin

14. Elihu states the whirlwind comes from which direction?

    Job 37:9

    A. North
    B. South
    C. East
    D. West

15. Elihu states the cold air comes from which direction?

    Job 37:9

    A. North
    B. South
    C. East
    D. West

16. According to Elihu, what is given by the breath of God?

    Job 37:10

    A. Dust
    B. Frost
    C. Heat
    D. Salt

17. According to Elihu, what does God wearieth by watering?

    Job 37:11

    A. The desert floor
    B. The river bed
    C. The thick cloud
    D. The wiry vine

18. According to Elihu, hot air comes from which direction?

    Job 37:17

    A. North
    B. South
    C. East
    D. West

19. What does Elihu call the sky?

    Job 37:18

    A. A brassy firmament
    B. A canopy of heaven
    C. A molten looking glass
    D. A starry expanse

20. According to Elihu, fair weather comes from which direction?

    Job 37:22

    A. North
    B. South
    C. East
    D. West

Answers on page 764

Lesson 168
Today's Reading: *Job 38–42*
Period of Time: Unknown
Author: Unknown

1. Where did God speak to Job?
   Job 38:1

   A. From a burning bush
   B. From a cloud
   C. From a rock
   D. From a whirlwind

2. Which constellation is mentioned?
   Job 38:31–32

   A. Arcturus
   B. Capricorn
   C. Sagittarius
   D. Taurus

3. Which animal with his band in his furrow does God ask Job if he can bind?
   Job 39:9–12

   A. Behemoth
   B. Cormorant
   C. Leviathan
   D. Unicorn

4. Which bird treats her young as if they are **not** hers?
   Job 39:13–18

   A. Eagle
   B. Hawk
   C. Ostrich
   D. Raven

5. Which animal eats grass like an ox?
   Job 40:15–24

   A. Behemoth
   B. Bittern
   C. Cockatrice
   D. Cormorant

6. Which animal has a flame going out of its mouth?
   Job 41:1–34

   A. Bittern
   B. Cuckow
   C. Leviathan
   D. Unicorn

7. What was Eliphaz's surname?
   Job 42:9

   A. The Agagite
   B. The Naamathite
   C. The Shuhite
   D. The Temanite

8. What was Bildad's surname?
   Job 42:9

   A. The Agagite
   B. The Naamathite
   C. The Shuhite
   D. The Temanite

9. What was Zophar's surname?
   Job 42:9

   A. The Agagite
   B. The Naamathite
   C. The Shuhite
   D. The Temanite

10. Besides a piece of money, what else did every man give to Job?
    Job 42:11

    A. A change of raiment
    B. A he goat
    C. A young bullock
    D. An earring of gold

11. How many sheep did the LORD give to Job?
    Job 42:12

    A. 1,000
    B. 6,000
    C. 14,000
    D. 25,000

12. How many camels did the LORD give to Job?
    Job 42:12

    A. 1,000
    B. 6,000
    C. 14,000
    D. 25,000

13. How many yoke of oxen did the LORD give to Job?

    Job 42:12

    A. 1,000
    B. 6,000
    C. 14,000
    D. 25,000

14. How many she asses did the LORD give to Job?

    Job 42:12

    A. 1,000
    B. 6,000
    C. 14,000
    D. 25,000

15. How many sons did the LORD give to Job?

    Job 42:13

    A. 3
    B. 7
    C. 10
    D. 12

16. What was the name of Job's *first* daughter?

    Job 42:14

    A. Jehoshabeath
    B. Jemima
    C. Kerenhappuch
    D. Kezia

17. What was the name of Job's *second* daughter?

    Job 42:14

    A. Jehoshabeath
    B. Jemima
    C. Kerenhappuch
    D. Kezia

18. What was the name of Job's *third* daughter?

    Job 42:14

    A. Jehoshabeath
    B. Jemima
    C. Kerenhappuch
    D. Kezia

19. How many more years did Job live after God restored him?

    Job 42:16

    A. 140
    B. 150
    C. 160
    D. 170

20. How many generations of sons did Job see before he died?

    Job 42:16

    A. 3
    B. 4
    C. 5
    D. 6

*Answers on page 764

JUNE 18

Lesson 169
Today's Reading: *Psalms 1–9*
Period of Time: Various Dates
Authors: David, Unknown

1. In Psalm 1, how often doth the blessed man meditate upon the law of the LORD?
   Psalm 1:1–2
   A. Every day and night
   B. Every Sunday morning and evening
   C. Every Sunday and Wednesday
   D. Every Christmas and Easter

2. In Psalm 1, what shall the blessed man be like?
   Psalm 1:3
   A. A pale rider upon a pale horse
   B. A tree planted by the rivers
   C. A world without end
   D. A young lamb without blemish

3. In Psalm 1, what are the ungodly like?
   Psalm 1:4
   A. Altars which burneth the daily offerings
   B. Chaff which the wind driveth away
   C. Millstones which grind the meal
   D. Spears which pierceth Leviathan

4. In Psalm 2, where has God placed his King?
   Psalm 2:6
   A. Holy hill of Zion
   B. Mount Olympus
   C. Temple of Dagon
   D. Valley of the kings

5. In Psalm 2, what shall God give the righteous for an inheritance?
   Psalm 2:8
   A. The heathen
   B. The hen
   C. The horse
   D. The husbandmen

6. In Psalm 2, what shall God give the righteous for a possession?
   Psalm 2:8
   A. The Greek isles
   B. The mines of Solomon
   C. The rivers of Egypt
   D. The uttermost parts of the earth

7. In Psalm 2, what does God use to break the ungodly?
   Psalm 2:9
   A. A carpenter's square
   B. A horse's whip
   C. A miry pit
   D. A rod of iron

8. In Psalm 2, what is the dashing in pieces of the ungodly like?
   Psalm 2:9
   A. A miller's stone
   B. A potter's vessel
   C. A refiner's fire
   D. A silversmith's hammer

9. In Psalm 2, whom does God command us to kiss?
   Psalm 2:12
   A. The Child
   B. The Father
   C. The Mother
   D. The Son

10. In Psalm 3, what has God broken of the ungodly?
    Psalm 3:7
    A. Their arms
    B. Their backs
    C. Their legs
    D. Their teeth

11. In Psalm 4, what do the unrighteous seek?
    Psalm 4:2
    A. Honesty
    B. Leasing
    C. Trustworthiness
    D. Uprightness

12. In Psalm 5, what is the throat of the wicked?

    Psalm 5:9

    A. An open sepulcher
    B. Empty graves
    C. Hot air from the south
    D. The well of wisdom

13. In Psalm 6, what does the psalmist water with his tears?

    Psalm 6:6

    A. His beard
    B. His couch
    C. His garden
    D. His grass

14. In Psalm 7, what animal is similar to the person who persecutes the psalmist?

    Psalm 7:1–2

    A. A bear
    B. A goat
    C. A lion
    D. A wolf

15. In Psalm 7, what will the violent dealings of the wicked man come down upon?

    Psalm 7:16

    A. His home
    B. His orchard
    C. His pate
    D. His vineyard

16. In Psalm 8, what has God ordained to give strength to overcome the enemies?

    Psalm 8:2

    A. The chief of the princes
    B. The gift of compromise
    C. The mouth of babes and sucklings
    D. The thirty mighties

17. In Psalm 8, whom did God give dominion over the works of his hands?

    Psalm 8:4–8

    A. Angels
    B. Lions
    C. Man
    D. Satan

18. In Psalm 9, which name does the psalmist use for God?

    Psalm 9:2

    A. Most High
    B. Prince of Life
    C. Son of the Father
    D. The Word of God

19. In Psalm 9, what does the psalmist call God in times of trouble?

    Psalm 9:9

    A. A bulwark
    B. A flag
    C. A pit
    D. A refuge

20. Which word is found in Psalm 9:16 before the word Selah?

    Psalm 9:16

    A. Amen
    B. Easter
    C. Higgaion
    D. JEHOVAH

*Answers on page 765

Lesson 170
Today's Reading: *Psalms 10–17*
Period of Time: Various Dates
Authors: Unknown, David

JUNE 19

1. In Psalm 10, what question does the psalmist ask God?
   Psalm 10:1
   A. What blessing will you give me today?
   B. Where can I hide from my enemies?
   C. Who is my real father in heaven?
   D. Why do you hide in times of trouble?

2. In Psalm 10, what are the ways of the wicked?
   Psalm 10:4–5
   A. Grievous
   B. Pious
   C. Religious
   D. Righteous

3. In Psalm 10, what does the wicked do to his enemies?
   Psalm 10:5
   A. He maketh peace with them.
   B. He pardoneth them.
   C. He puffeth at them.
   D. He setteth them free.

4. In Psalm 10, what is under the tongue of the wicked?
   Psalm 10:7
   A. Goodness and mercy
   B. Honesty and integrity
   C. Mischief and vanity
   D. Wisdom and reason

5. In Psalm 10, how do the wicked catch the poor?
   Psalm 10:9
   A. As a bird hasteneth to the snare
   B. As a fisher's net in the seas
   C. As a king bringeth the wheel over them
   D. As a lion in his den

6. In Psalm 10, how long will the LORD be King?
   Psalm 10:16
   A. For ever and ever
   B. Until the cows come home
   C. Until the end of the world
   D. Until the fat lady sings

7. In Psalm 11, what does the person tell the psalmist's soul to do?
   Psalm 11:1
   A. Fight like a man
   B. Flee like a bird
   C. Hide like an outcast
   D. Run like the lightning

8. In Psalm 11, what shall God send upon the wicked?
   Psalm 11:6
   A. Fire and brimstone
   B. Love and kindness
   C. Peace and joy
   D. Water and blessings

9. In Psalm 12, how were the men speaking to their neighbors?
   Psalm 12:2
   A. With constructive criticism
   B. With flattering lips
   C. With honest words
   D. With uprightness

10. In Psalm 12, how many times was the silver purified in the furnace?
    Psalm 12:6
    A. 7
    B. 10
    C. 21
    D. 40

11. In Psalm 12, when who is exalted do the wicked walk on every side?

    Psalm 12:8

    A. The Godliest of men
    B. The strongest of men
    C. The vilest of men
    D. The wisest of men

12. In Psalm 13, what fills the psalmist's heart daily?

    Psalm 13:2

    A. Cheer
    B. Peace
    C. Sorrow
    D. Truth

13. In Psalm 14, what does the fool say in his heart?

    Psalm 14:1

    A. There is a heaven.
    B. There is a hell.
    C. There is a Messiah.
    D. There is no God.

14. In Psalm 14, who shall rejoice when the LORD bringeth back the captivity of his people?

    Psalm 14:7

    A. Ahab
    B. Eliashib
    C. Jacob
    D. Segub

15. In Psalm 15, who shall never be moved?

    Psalm 15:1–5

    A. He that is cruel to his parents.
    B. He that murders his brother.
    C. He that sinneth against God.
    D. He that walketh uprightly.

16. In Psalm 16, what does the psalmist state he will never speak?

    Psalm 16:4

    A. The language of another nation
    B. The name of another god
    C. The truth if it hurts Israel
    D. The words of the prophets

17. In Psalm 16, where will the LORD **not** leave the soul of the righteous?

    Psalm 16:10

    A. In heaven
    B. In hell
    C. In paradise
    D. In the better country

18. In Psalm 16, what will the LORD show the righteous?

    Psalm 16:11

    A. The path of life
    B. The rocky road
    C. The trail of sorrow
    D. The way of the Buddha

19. In Psalm 17, where does the psalmist ask the LORD to hide him?

    Psalm 17:8

    A. Along the banks of the river of Jordan
    B. Beneath the holy city of Jerusalem
    C. In the cave of Machpelah
    D. Under the shadow of his wings

20. In Psalm 17, what are the wicked enclosed in?

    Psalm 17:10

    A. Their own bones
    B. Their own fat
    C. Their own muscles
    D. Their own sinews

*Answers on page 765

Lesson 171
Today's Reading: *Psalms 18–22*
Period of Time: Various Dates
Author: David

1. In Psalm 18, where did the smoke come from?
   Psalm 18:8
   A. The chariot wheels
   B. The dragon's mouth
   C. The fiery furnace
   D. The nostrils of God

2. In Psalm 18, what did the LORD ride upon?
   Psalm 18:10
   A. A black horse
   B. A cherub
   C. A lightning bolt
   D. A pale horse

3. In Psalm 18, what did God make his secret place?
   Psalm 18:11
   A. Darkness
   B. Heaven
   C. Jerusalem
   D. Zion

4. In Psalm 18, what name does the psalmist use for God?
   Psalm 18:13
   A. The Highest
   B. The Judge
   C. The Messiah
   D. The Spirit

5. In Psalm 18, where was the psalmist when the LORD took him?
   Psalm 18:16
   A. At the temple
   B. Behind a bush
   C. In many waters
   D. Upon mount Zion

6. In Psalm 18, what does the psalmist state his feet are like?
   Psalm 18:33
   A. Crows' feet
   B. Hinds' feet
   C. Rabbits' feet
   D. Tortoises' feet

7. In Psalm 19, what is the law of the LORD?
   Psalm 19:7
   A. Crude
   B. Lacking
   C. Perfect
   D. Scanty

8. In Psalm 19, what are the statutes of the LORD?
   Psalm 19:8
   A. Right
   B. Sin
   C. Transgression
   D. Unfair

9. In Psalm 19, what is the fear of the LORD?
   Psalm 19:9
   A. Base
   B. Clean
   C. Degraded
   D. Filthy

10. In Psalm 20, what name does the psalmist use for God?
    Psalm 20:1
    A. God of hosts
    B. God of Israel
    C. God of Jacob
    D. God of peace

11. In Psalm 21, what name does the psalmist use for God?

    Psalm 21:7

    A. Most High
    B. Our Father
    C. The Apostle
    D. Wonderful

12. In Psalm 21, what will happen when a righteous king is disobeyed?

    Psalm 21:9

    A. Enemies shall seize him
    B. Fire shall devour his enemies
    C. Revolutions shall erupt
    D. Young people shall die

13. In Psalm 22, what question does the psalmist ask God?

    Psalm 22:1

    A. "What hast thou done?"
    B. "Where art thou?"
    C. "Who art thou?"
    D. "Why hast thou forsaken me?"

14. In Psalm 22, what does the psalmist call himself?

    Psalm 22:6

    A. A child
    B. A dog
    C. A lion
    D. A worm

15. In Psalm 22, what does the psalmist state he is being poured out like?

    Psalm 22:14

    A. Gall
    B. Milk
    C. Water
    D. Wine

16. In Psalm 22, what does the psalmist state his heart is like?

    Psalm 22:14

    A. Cheese
    B. Dust
    C. Fire
    D. Wax

17. In Psalm 22, what does the psalmist state his strength is dried up like?

    Psalm 22:15

    A. A desert
    B. A potsherd
    C. A river
    D. An empty bottle

18. In Psalm 22, what has the wicked done to the psalmist?

    Psalm 22:16

    A. They cut off the waters to his field
    B. They made his children bondservants
    C. They pierced his hands and feet
    D. They ravished his wife

19. In Psalm 22, what does the psalmist say the wicked did with his clothes?

    Psalm 22:18

    A. Cast lots for them
    B. Gave them to the poor
    C. Made torches from them
    D. Traded them for bread

20. In Psalm 22, from the horns of which animals did the LORD hear the psalmist's pleas?

    Psalm 22:21

    A. The bullocks' horns
    B. The calves' horns
    C. The rams' horns
    D. The unicorns' horns

*Answers on page 765

JUNE 21

Lesson 172
Today's Reading: *Psalms 23–31*
Period of Time: Various Dates
Author: David

1. In Psalm 23, what does the psalmist call the LORD?
   Psalm 23:1
   A. His lord
   B. His redeemer
   C. His shepherd
   D. His teacher

2. In Psalm 23, where does the psalmist state the LORD makes him lie down?
   Psalm 23:2
   A. Along the trails
   B. In green pastures
   C. On floors of straw
   D. Upon his bed

3. In Psalm 23, what does the LORD prepare for the psalmist before his enemies?
   Psalm 23:5
   A. A bow
   B. A horse
   C. A sword
   D. A table

4. In Psalm 24, what name does the psalmist use for the LORD?
   Psalm 24:7
   A. Father of glory
   B. God of glory
   C. King of glory
   D. Lord of glory

5. In Psalm 25, whom will the LORD guide in judgment?
   Psalm 25:9
   A. The dead
   B. The meek
   C. The poor
   D. The rich

6. In Psalm 26, whom does the psalmist state he will **not** go in with?
   Psalm 26:4
   A. Dissemblers
   B. Millers
   C. Travelers
   D. Victualers

7. In Psalm 26, what does the psalmist state is in the right hand of the bloody man?
   Psalm 26:9–10
   A. Arrows
   B. Bribes
   C. Knives
   D. Spears

8. In Psalm 27, what does the psalmist call the LORD?
   Psalm 27:1
   A. His compass
   B. His hope
   C. His light
   D. His map

9. In Psalm 27, where does the psalmist state the LORD will hide him?
   Psalm 27:5
   A. In his cave
   B. In his garden
   C. In his lodge
   D. In his pavilion

10. In Psalm 27, where does the LORD place the psalmist?
    Psalm 27:5
    A. Beneath his wing
    B. In a large room
    C. Near his throne
    D. Upon a rock

11. In Psalm 27, what does the psalmist ask the LORD to lead him down?

    Psalm 27:11

    A. A plain path
    B. A rocky road
    C. A seductive street
    D. An endless trail

12. In Psalm 28, what does the psalmist call the LORD?

    Psalm 28:1

    A. His God
    B. His King
    C. His Rock
    D. His Shepherd

13. In Psalm 28, what does the psalmist give to the LORD?

    Psalm 28:7

    A. His lamb
    B. His prayer
    C. His song
    D. His works

14. In Psalm 29, what name does the psalmist use for God?

    Psalm 29:3

    A. Father of glory
    B. God of glory
    C. King of glory
    D. Lord of glory

15. In Psalm 29, which trees shall skip like a calf?

    Psalm 29:5–6

    A. The cedar trees
    B. The elm trees
    C. The oak trees
    D. The sycamine trees

16. In Psalm 29, which wilderness is mentioned?

    Psalm 29:8

    A. Wilderness of Beersheba
    B. Wilderness of Gibeon
    C. Wilderness of Judaea
    D. Wilderness of Kadesh

17. In Psalm 30, how long does the LORD's anger endureth?

    Psalm 30:5

    A. For a moment
    B. For a season
    C. For years
    D. For eternity

18. In Psalm 30, what cometh in the morning?

    Psalm 30:5

    A. Joy
    B. Light
    C. Tears
    D. War

19. In Psalm 31, what did the LORD do to the psalmist?

    Psalm 31:5

    A. Beat him
    B. Cursed him
    C. Excommunicated him
    D. Redeemed him

20. In Psalm 31, what does the psalmist state the LORD placed him in?

    Psalm 31:8

    A. A barren desert
    B. A large room
    C. An empty cave
    D. An open sepulcher

Answers on page 765

Lesson 173
Today's Reading: *Psalms 32–37*
Period of Time: Various Dates
Authors: David, Unknown

JUNE 22

1. In Psalm 32, what happened when the psalmist kept silent?
   Psalm 32:3
   A. His army besieged Jerusalem.
   B. His bones waxed old.
   C. His field grew thorns and thistles.
   D. His neighbor murdered a man.

2. In Psalm 32, what does the psalmist state his moisture is like?
   Psalm 32:4
   A. The brooks of Arnon
   B. The cup of iniquity
   C. The drought of summer
   D. The water drops of spring

3. In Psalm 32, which animals does the psalmist use as an illustration?
   Psalm 32:9
   A. Dog and cat
   B. Horse and mule
   C. Mouse and pig
   D. Roe and unicorn

4. In Psalm 33, how many strings does the psalmist state the musical instrument has?
   Psalm 33:2
   A. 2
   B. 5
   C. 7
   D. 10

5. According to Psalm 33, how was the earth created?
   Psalm 33:6–9
   A. A big bang happened 60 billion years ago.
   B. An asteroid collided with a planet.
   C. Cold dust particles formed clay.
   D. God spoke it, and it was done.

6. In Psalm 33, which nations are blessed?
   Psalm 33:12
   A. Those who are politically correct.
   B. Those who sacrifice their children
   C. Those whose armies are the largest
   D. Those whose God is the LORD

7. In Psalm 34, what happened to those who looked upon the LORD?
   Psalm 34:5
   A. They were ashamed.
   B. They were blinded.
   C. They were lightened.
   D. They were subdued.

8. In Psalm 34, what kind of a man does the psalmist claim to be?
   Psalm 34:6
   A. A giant man
   B. A little man
   C. A poor man
   D. A rich man

9. In Psalm 34, which animals lack and suffer hunger?
   Psalm 34:10
   A. The female lions
   B. The male lions
   C. The old lions
   D. The young lions

10. What does Psalm 34, state our lips should **not** speak?
    Psalm 34:13
    A. Frankness
    B. Guile
    C. Plainly
    D. Simplicity

11. According to Psalm 34, how many afflictions does the LORD deliver the righteous from?

    Psalm 34:19

    A. A few of them
    B. All of them
    C. Many of them
    D. None of them

12. In Psalm 35, what does the psalmist want to chase those who persecute him?

    Psalm 35:5

    A. A bear
    B. A demon
    C. A lion
    D. An angel

13. In Psalm 35, how had the psalmist treated those who were now rising up against him?

    Psalm 35:14

    A. As a friend
    B. As a lover
    C. As a master
    D. As a thief

14. In Psalm 35, what does the psalmist call those who joined them who were persecuting him?

    Psalm 35:16

    A. Brothers of low degree
    B. Demons from hell
    C. Hypocritical mockers
    D. Sons of thunder

15. In Psalm 35, what does the psalmist ask the LORD to rescue from the lions?

    Psalm 35:17

    A. His brother
    B. His darling
    C. His foal
    D. His servant

16. In Psalm 36, how high does the LORD's faithfulness reach

    Psalm 36:5

    A. The clouds
    B. The hills
    C. The mountains
    D. The valleys

17. In Psalm 36, what is the LORD's righteousness like?

    Psalm 36:6

    A. Great mountains
    B. Little rainbows
    C. Small streams
    D. Tall trees

18. According to Psalm 37, what shall the meek inherit?

    Psalm 37:11

    A. The earth
    B. The moon
    C. The stars
    D. The sun

19. In Psalm 37, what has the psalmist never seen the righteous do?

    Psalm 37:25

    A. Have their seed beg for bread
    B. Help a husbandman to plant seed
    C. Sell seed to the husbandman
    D. Sow seed in the spring

20. In Psalm 37, what type of tree does the wicked spread himself like?

    Psalm 37:35

    A. A black walnut tree
    B. A blue spruce tree
    C. A green bay tree
    D. A red elm tree

Answers on page 765

JUNE 23

Lesson 174
Today's Reading: *Psalms 38–44*
Period of Time: Various Dates
Authors: David, Unknown

1. In Psalm 38, what does the psalmist state God has rebuked him with?
   Psalm 38:1–2
   A. Arrows
   B. Clubs
   C. Spears
   D. Swords

2. In Psalm 38, what does the psalmist state stinks because of his foolishness?
   Psalm 38:5
   A. His bones
   B. His heart
   C. His loins
   D. His wounds

3. In Psalm 38, what does the psalmist state is filled with a loathsome disease?
   Psalm 38:7
   A. His bones
   B. His heart
   C. His loins
   D. His wounds

4. In Psalm 38, what does the psalmist state he is like?
   Psalm 38:13
   A. A dead dog and a flea
   B. A deaf and dumb man
   C. A horse and its rider
   D. An ox and an ass

5. In Psalm 39, what does the psalmist state was hot within him?
   Psalm 39:3
   A. His bones
   B. His heart
   C. His loins
   D. His wounds

6. In Psalm 39, what does the psalmist state he is consumed by?
   Psalm 39:10
   A. The blow of God's hand
   B. The disease in his liver
   C. The heat from the sun
   D. The sword of his enemy

7. In Psalm 39, what does the psalmist state something that loses its beauty is like?
   Psalm 39:11
   A. A goat
   B. A hart
   C. A moth
   D. A seal

8. In Psalm 39, what does the psalmist state his fathers were?
   Psalm 39:12
   A. Bondservants
   B. Husbandmen
   C. Mercenaries
   D. Sojourners

9. In Psalm 40, what does the psalmist state he has done?
   Psalm 40:9
   A. Confounded the wise
   B. Lifted the veil
   C. Preached righteousness
   D. Walked with vanity

10. In Psalm 40, what does the psalmist state has taken hold of him?
    Psalm 40:12
    A. His enemies
    B. His iniquities
    C. His masters
    D. His servants

11. In Psalm 41, where will the LORD strengthen the psalmist?

    Psalm 41:3

    A. Along the banks of the river of Jordan
    B. In the wilderness of Beersheba
    C. Near the everlasting mercy seat
    D. Upon the bed of languishing

12. In Psalm 41, who has lifted his heel against the psalmist?

    Psalm 41:9

    A. His brother
    B. His father
    C. His friend
    D. His son

13. What does the psalmist want to do to his enemies in Psalm 41?

    Psalm 41:10

    A. Rearm them
    B. Replenish them
    C. Requite them
    D. Revive them

14. In Psalm 41, which name does the psalmist use for God?

    Psalm 41:13

    A. LORD God of Israel
    B. LORD JEHOVAH
    C. LORD of heaven
    D. LORD thy God

15. In Psalm 42, what animal panteth for water?

    Psalm 42:1

    A. The hart
    B. The lamb
    C. The mule
    D. The wolf

16. Upon which hill in Psalm 42 does the psalmist state he will remember the LORD?

    Psalm 42:6

    A. Hill Aeropagus
    B. Hill Gareb
    C. Hill Hachilah
    D. Hill Mizar

17. In Psalm 42, the psalmist states his enemies reproach him like a sword stuck where in his body?

    Psalm 42:10

    A. His bones
    B. His heart
    C. His loins
    D. His shoulder

18. Upon which musical instrument does the psalmist state he will praise the LORD in Psalm 43?

    Psalm 43:4

    A. Coronet
    B. Harp
    C. Sackbut
    D. Trumpet

19. In Psalm 44, where did God break his people?

    Psalm 44:19

    A. The house of mourning
    B. The place of dragons
    C. The valley of the shadow of death
    D. The wilderness of Zin

20. In Psalm 44, which animals—counted for the slaughter—does the psalmist state Israel's death is similar to?

    Psalm 44:22

    A. Death of bulls
    B. Death of goats
    C. Death of pigeons
    D. Death of sheep

*Answers on page 765

Lesson 175
Today's Reading: *Psalms 45–51*
Period of Time: Various Dates
Authors: Unknown, David, Asaph

1. In Psalm 45, what is the psalmist's heart doing?

    Psalm 45:1

    A. Inditing a good matter
    B. Leaping toward heaven
    C. Reciting spiritual songs
    D. Waxing confidently

2. In Psalm 45, what does the psalmist call his tongue?

    Psalm 45:1

    A. The frame of a deceitful man
    B. The pen of a ready writer
    C. The sword of a warrior
    D. The window of a lost soul

3. In Psalm 45, whom does the psalmist say God is fairer than?

    Psalm 45:2

    A. The children of men
    B. The lilies of the valley
    C. The rose of Sharon
    D. The virgins of Shushan

4. In Psalm 45, what does the psalmist state will teach men terrible things?

    Psalm 45:4

    A. God's angels
    B. God's cherubims
    C. God's right hand
    D. God's sore troops

5. In Psalm 45, who stood next to the king?

    Psalm 45:9

    A. The captain
    B. The duke
    C. The general
    D. The queen

6. In Psalm 45, who shall be waiting for the king with a gift?

    Psalm 45:12

    A. The city of Babylon
    B. The daughter of Tyre
    C. The king of Canaan
    D. The queen of Sheba

7. In Psalm 46, what shall make the city of God glad?

    Psalm 46:4

    A. A bay
    B. A lake
    C. A river
    D. A waterfall

8. In Psalm 46, who is in the midst of the city of God?

    Psalm 46:5

    A. Abraham
    B. God
    C. Isaac
    D. Jacob

9. In Psalm 46, which name does the psalmist use for God?

    Psalm 46:7

    A. God of Abraham
    B. God of David
    C. God of Isaac
    D. God of Jacob

10. In Psalm 47, which musical instrument is played when God goes up with a shout?

    Psalm 47:5

    A. Cornet
    B. Dulcimer
    C. Psaltery
    D. Trumpet

11. In Psalm 47, which name does the psalmist use for God?

    Psalm 47:9

    A. God of Abraham
    B. God of David
    C. God of Isaac
    D. God of Jacob

12. In Psalm 48, which side is mount Zion located?

    Psalm 48:2

    A. North
    B. South
    C. East
    D. West

13. In Psalm 48, the wind from which direction destroyed the ships of Tarshish?

    Psalm 48:7

    A. North
    B. South
    C. East
    D. West

14. In Psalm 48, what is in God's right hand?

    Psalm 48:10

    A. Arrows
    B. Lightning
    C. Righteousness
    D. Stars

15. In Psalm 48, the daughters from which nation will be glad?

    Psalm 48:11

    A. Egypt
    B. Judah
    C. Sidon
    D. Tyre

16. In Psalm 49, which musical instrument does the psalmist use to tell his parable?

    Psalm 49:4

    A. The cymbals
    B. The harp
    C. The trumpet
    D. The viol

17. In Psalm 49, what does the psalmist state death is like?

    Psalm 49:14

    A. David dying upon his bed
    B. Rachel weeping for her children
    C. Sheep lying in the grave
    D. Walking in darkness

18. In Psalm 50, which name does the psalmist use for God?

    Psalm 50:1

    A. Almighty God
    B. Everlasting God
    C. Jealous God
    D. Mighty God

19. In Psalm 50, who owns the cattle upon a thousand hills?

    Psalm 50:10

    A. God
    B. Job
    C. Lot
    D. Nun

20. In Psalm 51, what does the psalmist state he will be if God washes him?

    Psalm 51:2–7

    A. Clean as a whistle
    B. Dirty as a dog
    C. Smooth as silk
    D. Whiter than snow

Answers on page 765

Lesson 176
Today's Reading: *Psalms 52–59*
Period of Time: Various Dates
Author: David

JUNE 25

1. In Psalm 52, what does the psalmist state the tongue is like?
   Psalm 52:2
   A. A devouring fire
   B. A sharp razor
   C. A tree of life
   D. A writer's pen

2. In Psalm 52, what will the psalmist do when God punishes the wicked?
   Psalm 52:6
   A. Hiss at him
   B. Laugh at him
   C. Puff at him
   D. Shoot at him

3. In Psalm 52, which kind of green tree does the psalmist state he is like?
   Psalm 52:8
   A. An apple tree
   B. An elm tree
   C. An olive tree
   D. An orange tree

4. In Psalm 53, how many people were seeking God?
   Psalm 53:1–3
   A. 0
   B. 10
   C. 30
   D. 50

5. In Psalm 54, what does the psalmist call God?
   Psalm 54:4
   A. His deliverer
   B. His father
   C. His helper
   D. His maker

6. In Psalm 55, what does the psalmist ask God **not** to ignore?
   Psalm 55:1
   A. His deeds
   B. His family
   C. His offering
   D. His supplication

7. In Psalm 55, which bird does the psalmist wish he had the wings of?
   Psalm 55:6
   A. Cuckow
   B. Dove
   C. Eagle
   D. Quail

8. In Psalm 55, who reproached the psalmist?
   Psalm 55:12–13
   A. His acquaintance
   B. His betrothed
   C. His son
   D. His wife

9. In Psalm 55, what were the words of the wicked smoother than?
   Psalm 55:21
   A. Butter
   B. Glass
   C. Ice
   D. Silk

10. In Psalm 55, what were the words of the wicked softer than?
    Psalm 55:21
    A. Feathers
    B. Oil
    C. Pillows
    D. Sheets

11. In Psalm 56, what do the psalmist's enemies do to him?

    Psalm 56:5

    A. Besiege his city
    B. Close his wells
    C. Shoot arrows at him
    D. Wrest his words

12. In Psalm 56, what does the psalmist ask if it has been recorded in God's book?

    Psalm 56:8

    A. His blood
    B. His deeds
    C. His sweat
    D. His tears

13. In Psalm 57, what does the psalmist state he will make his refuge?

    Psalm 57:1

    A. The cave of Adullam
    B. The hills of Judea
    C. The midst of the temple
    D. The shadow of God's wings

14. In Psalm 57, what is the psalmist's soul among?

    Psalm 57:4

    A. Asps
    B. Kine
    C. Lions
    D. Worms

15. In Psalm 58, which poison is similar to the poison of the wicked?

    Psalm 58:1–4

    A. A dragon's poison
    B. A scorpion's poison
    C. A serpent's poison
    D. A spider's poison

16. In Psalm 58, what does the psalmist want the wicked to melt like?

    Psalm 58:1–8

    A. A beetle
    B. A gnat
    C. A snail
    D. An ant

17. In Psalm 58, which metaphor does the psalmist use for something God suddenly takes away?

    Psalm 58:9

    A. Before their pots can feel the thorns
    B. Faster than the LORD's arrow
    C. Passing quickly like the wheels of justice
    D. Suddenly as the wintry forest of life

18. In Psalm 59, which name does the psalmist use for God?

    Psalm 59:5

    A. LORD God almighty
    B. LORD God of David
    C. LORD God of gods
    D. LORD God of hosts

19. In Psalm 59, the noise from which animal is similar to the noise of the psalmist's enemies?

    Psalm 59:1–14

    A. A bull
    B. A dog
    C. A satyr
    D. A wolf

20. In Psalm 59, during which part of the day will the psalmist sing God's praises?

    Psalm 59:16

    A. Morning
    B. Noon
    C. Evening
    D. Midnight

*Answers on page 765

Lesson 177
Today's Reading: *Psalms 60–67*
Period of Time: Various Dates
Authors: David, Unknown

JUNE 26

1. In Psalm 60, what did God cause the earth to do?
   Psalm 60:2
   A. Burn
   B. Flood
   C. Freeze
   D. Tremble

2. In Psalm 60, which kind of wine did God make the people drink?
   Psalm 60:3
   A. Wine of astonishment
   B. Wine of condemnation
   C. Wine of vengeance
   D. Wine of wrath

3. In Psalm 60, which city will God divide?
   Psalm 60:6
   A. Pisidia
   B. Raamaah
   C. Shechem
   D. Telabib

4. In Psalm 60, which valley will God mete out?
   Psalm 60:6
   A. Valley of craftsmen
   B. Valley of Jehoshaphat
   C. Valley of Mizpeh
   D. Valley of Succoth

5. In Psalm 60, who is God's lawgiver?
   Psalm 60:7
   A. Benjamin
   B. Ephraim
   C. Judah
   D. Manasseh

6. In Psalm 60, what is God's washpot?
   Psalm 60:8
   A. Edom
   B. Moab
   C. Syria
   D. Tyre

7. In Psalm 61, where does the psalmist state he will abide forever?
   Psalm 61:4
   A. In God's tabernacle
   B. On the north side of Jerusalem
   C. Upon mount Sion
   D. Within the land of eternal light

8. In Psalm 62, what does the psalmist state his enemies shall fall like?
   Psalm 62:3
   A. A decaying gate
   B. A rotting tower
   C. A tottering fence
   D. A vanquishing bridge

9. In Psalm 62, what does the psalmist call men of low degree?
   Psalm 62:9
   A. Honorable
   B. Robbers
   C. Thieves
   D. Vanity

10. In Psalm 62, what does the psalmist call men of high degree?
    Psalm 62:9
    A. A blessing
    B. A lie
    C. A reviving
    D. A spirit

11. In Psalm 62, how many times has the psalmist heard that power belongeth unto God?
    Psalm 62:11
    A. 2
    B. 6
    C. 12
    D. 24

12. In Psalm 63, what does the psalmist state is better than life?

    Psalm 63:3

    A. A filled belly
    B. God's lovingkindness
    C. Mercy from an enemy
    D. Victory over one's enemy

13. In Psalm 63, what will the psalmist do in God's name?

    Psalm 63:4

    A. Lift up his hands
    B. Move a mountain
    C. Offer his prayer
    D. Sing a song

14. In Psalm 63, what does the psalmist state will eat his enemies' dead bodies?

    Psalm 63:10

    A. Bears
    B. Dogs
    C. Foxes
    D. Lions

15. In Psalm 64, what shall God do to the psalmist's enemies?

    Psalm 64:7

    A. Gnash at them with his teeth
    B. Laugh at them with a terror
    C. Run at them with a spear
    D. Shoot at them with an arrow

16. In Psalm 65, what are they that wait in the uttermost parts of the earth afraid of?

    Psalm 65:8

    A. Beasts of the earth
    B. God's tokens
    C. Pharaoh's chariots
    D. The face of man

17. In Psalm 65, what does the psalmist call the water that nourishes the earth?

    Psalm 65:9

    A. Firmament of heaven
    B. Mountain of dew
    C. River of God
    D. Stream of rain

18. In Psalm 65, what are the valleys covered with?

    Psalm 65:13

    A. Barley
    B. Corn
    C. Grapes
    D. Wheat

19. In Psalm 66, what did God's people go through to reach a wealthy place?

    Psalm 66:12

    A. Fire and water
    B. Hell and back
    C. Snow and ice
    D. War and peace

20. According to Psalm 67, God will bless all of the people when what happens?

    Psalm 67:5–7

    A. All the children praise God
    B. All the leaders praise God
    C. All the men praise God
    D. All the people praise God

*Answers on page 765

Lesson 178
Today's Reading: *Psalms 68–71*
Period of Time: Various Dates
Authors: David, Unknown

JUNE 27

1. In Psalm 68, how does the psalmist want God to scatter his enemies?
   Psalm 68:1–2
   A. As smoke is driven away
   B. As the sun chases the moon
   C. As wolves divide the flock
   D. As wounded men flee the battle

2. In Psalm 68, how does the psalmist want the wicked to perish?
   Psalm 68:2
   A. As fire burneth wood
   B. As fire consumeth chaff
   C. As fire melteth wax
   D. As fire vanisheth vapor

3. In Psalm 68, which name does the psalmist use for God?
   Psalm 68:4
   A. I AM
   B. JAH
   C. JEHOVAH
   D. THE UNKNOWN GOD

4. In Psalm 68, what was moved at the presence of God?
   Psalm 68:8
   A. Mount Carmel
   B. Mount Horeb
   C. Mount of Olives
   D. Mount Sinai

5. In Psalm 68, which bird covered in silver and gold does the psalmist refer to?
   Psalm 68:13
   A. A dove
   B. A raven
   C. An eagle
   D. An ostrich

6. In Psalm 68, which place contained snow?
   Psalm 68:14
   A. Dimon
   B. Heshmon
   C. Salmon
   D. Zaphon

7. In Psalm 68, what is the hill of God like?
   Psalm 68:15
   A. Hill of Ammah
   B. Hill of Bashan
   C. Hill of Hachilah
   D. Hill of Moreh

8. In Psalm 68, how many chariots does God have?
   Psalm 68:17
   A. 20
   B. 200
   C. 2,000
   D. 20,000

9. In Psalm 68, which name is used for God?
   Psalm 68:20
   A. God of glory
   B. God of heaven and earth
   C. God of salvation
   D. God of the armies of Israel

10. In Psalm 68, which musical instruments did the damsels play?
    Psalm 68:25
    A. Cymbals
    B. Flutes
    C. Harps
    D. Timbrels

11. In Psalm 68, which nation is mentioned that would soon stretch out her hands to God?
    Psalm 68:31
    A. Bithynia
    B. Ethiopia
    C. Phenicia
    D. Seleucia

12. In Psalm 69, which name is used for God?

    Psalm 69:6

    A. God of Israel
    B. God of Jacob
    C. God of peace
    D. God of salvation

13. In Psalm 69, which song does the psalmist state he was?

    Psalm 69:12

    A. Song of the drunkards
    B. Song of the lovers
    C. Song of the necromancers
    D. Song of the south

14. In Psalm 69, what does the psalmist want to be rescued from?

    Psalm 69:14

    A. The hail
    B. The mire
    C. The tempest
    D. The sword

15. In Psalm 69, what did the psalmist's adversaries give him to eat?

    Psalm 69:21

    A. Bread
    B. Fish
    C. Gall
    D. Pulse

16. In Psalm 69, what did the psalmist's adversaries give him to drink?

    Psalm 69:21

    A. Milk
    B. Vinegar
    C. Water
    D. Wine

17. In Psalm 69, which book is mentioned?

    Psalm 69:28

    A. Book of the dead
    B. Book of the kings
    C. Book of the living
    D. Book of the prophets

18. In Psalm 70, what are they that love God's salvation to say continually?

    Psalm 70:4

    A. Let God be magnified.
    B. Praise him, all ye people.
    C. Rejoice! Rejoice! Emmanuel!
    D. Worthy is the lamb.

19. In Psalm 71, what does the psalmist call God?

    Psalm 71:3

    A. His compass and map
    B. His deliverer and fenced city
    C. His hammer and saw
    D. His rock and fortress

20. In Psalm 71, which two musical instruments will the psalmist praise God with?

    Psalm 71:22

    A. Bells and viol
    B. Dulcimer and trumpet
    C. Organ and tabret
    D. Psaltery and harp

Answers on page 765

Lesson 179
Today's Reading: *Psalms 72–77*
Period of Time: Various Dates
Authors: Solomon, Asaph

JUNE 28

1. In Psalm 72, what shall bring peace to the people by righteousness?
   Psalm 72:3
   A. The heavens
   B. The mountains
   C. The seas
   D. The trees

2. In Psalm 72, how will God come according to the psalmist?
   Psalm 72:6
   A. Like clouds across the sunny sky
   B. Like rain upon the mown grass
   C. Like snow upon the mountain top
   D. Like wind across the barren land

3. In Psalm 72, where will the kings bringing presents come from?
   Psalm 72:10
   A. Achish
   B. Lachish
   C. Magbish
   D. Tarshish

4. In Psalm 72, which place was known for its gold?
   Psalm 72:15
   A. Chozeba
   B. Geba
   C. Medeba
   D. Sheba

5. In Psalm 72, which place was shaken?
   Psalm 72:16
   A. Babylon
   B. Heshbon
   C. Lebanon
   D. Shimron

6. In Psalm 72, how shall the city flourish?
   Psalm 72:16
   A. Like a branch on a dry tree
   B. Like flowers in the desert
   C. Like grass of the earth
   D. Like the palm tree

7. In Psalm 72, who was David's father?
   Psalm 72:20
   A. Jesse
   B. Massa
   C. Pallu
   D. Uzzah

8. In Psalm 73, how does pride compasseth them about?
   Psalm 73:6
   A. As a chain
   B. As a fortress
   C. As a moat
   D. As an army

9. In Psalm 73, how does violence covereth them?
   Psalm 73:6
   A. As a buckler
   B. As a garment
   C. As the rain
   D. As the snow

10. In Psalm 73, what does the psalmist state he was foolish and ignorant like?
    Psalm 73:22
    A. A beast
    B. A dragon
    C. A serpent
    D. A worm

11. In Psalm 74, what does the psalmist state there are no more of?

    Psalm 74:9

    A. Houses
    B. Prophets
    C. Rivers
    D. Victuals

12. In Psalm 74, what does the psalmist call God?

    Psalm 74:12

    A. His Judge of old
    B. His King of old
    C. His Priest of old
    D. His Saviour of old

13. In Psalm 74, whose heads does God break into pieces?

    Psalm 74:14

    A. The behemoth's heads
    B. The devil's heads
    C. The leviathan's heads
    D. The unicorn's heads

14. In Psalm 74, what does the psalmist call himself?

    Psalm 74:19

    A. A bittern
    B. A cuckow
    C. A kite
    D. A turtledove

15. In Psalm 75, what is in God's cup?

    Psalm 75:8

    A. Red wine
    B. White wine
    C. Wine of astonishment
    D. Wine of salvation

16. In Psalm 75, which name does the psalmist use for God?

    Psalm 75:9

    A. God of David
    B. God of Isaac
    C. God of Jacob
    D. God of Moses

17. In Psalm 76, where is God's tabernacle?

    Psalm 76:2

    A. Ai
    B. Bethlehem
    C. Damascus
    D. Salem

18. In Psalm 76, what are cast into a deep sleep?

    Psalm 76:6

    A. The chariot and horse
    B. The husbandman and plow
    C. The poor and hungry
    D. The seed and ground

19. In Psalm 77, what saw God and was afraid?

    Psalm 77:16

    A. The flowers
    B. The grass
    C. The trees
    D. The waters

20. In Psalm 77, which two men led God's people by the hand like a flock?

    Psalm 77:20

    A. Abraham and Lot
    B. David and Jonathan
    C. Moses and Aaron
    D. Peter and Paul

*Answers on page 765

Lesson 180
Today's Reading: *Psalms 78–81*
Period of Time: Various Dates
Author: Asaph

JUNE 29

1. In Psalm 78, which tribe turned back in the day of battle?
   Psalm 78:9
   A. Tribe of Asher
   B. Tribe of Benjamin
   C. Tribe of Dan
   D. Tribe of Ephraim

2. In Psalm 78, in which field did God do marvelous things in the sight of the Israelites?
   Psalm 78:12
   A. Field of Ephron
   B. Field of Joshua
   C. Field of Moab
   D. Field of Zoan

3. In Psalm 78, what is another name for manna?
   Psalm 78:24
   A. Barley of heaven
   B. Corn of heaven
   C. Rye of heaven
   D. Wheat of heaven

4. In Psalm 78, which name does the psalmist use for God?
   Psalm 78:41
   A. God of Israel
   B. Holy One of Israel
   C. LORD God of Israel
   D. Mighty One of Israel

5. In Psalm 78, what did God turn the rivers of Egypt into?
   Psalm 78:43–44
   A. Blood
   B. Boiling pots
   C. Dry gulches
   D. Wine

6. In Psalm 78, what did God send among the Egyptians?
   Psalm 78:45
   A. Dragons
   B. Flies
   C. Lions
   D. Vipers

7. In Psalm 78, what did God send to destroy Egypt's sycamore trees?
   Psalm 78:47
   A. Blight
   B. Drought
   C. Frost
   D. Lightning

8. In Psalm 78, what did God send to destroy Egypt's cattle?
   Psalm 78:48
   A. Drought
   B. Hail
   C. Lions
   D. Wolves

9. In Psalm 78, what did God send to destroy Egypt's flocks?
   Psalm 78:48
   A. Hot thunderbolts
   B. Poisonous vipers
   C. Roaring lions
   D. Tempestuous winds

10. In Psalm 78, what was the final plague upon Egypt?
    Psalm 78:51
    A. God rained down fire.
    B. God sent a great earthquake.
    C. God smote their firstborn sons.
    D. God turned Pharaoh into a pillar of salt.

11. In Psalm 78, whom are the Egyptians descendants of?

    Psalm 78:51

    A. Ham
    B. Japheth
    C. Lucifer
    D. Shem

12. In Psalm 78, what is the name of the tent God placed among men?

    Psalm 78:60

    A. Tabernacle of Beulah
    B. Tabernacle of Consolation
    C. Tabernacle of Hephzibah
    D. Tabernacle of Shiloh

13. In Psalm 78, which tribe did God choose over the tabernacle of Joseph?

    Psalm 78:67–68

    A. Tribe of Issachar
    B. Tribe of Judah
    C. Tribe of Manasseh
    D. Tribe of Naphtali

14. In Psalm 78, what was David's occupation before becoming a king?

    Psalm 78:70

    A. Carpenter
    B. Fisherman
    C. Mason
    D. Shepherd

15. In Psalm 79, how many times does the psalmist ask God to punish his enemies?

    Psalm 79:12

    A. Twofold
    B. Fivefold
    C. Sixfold
    D. Sevenfold

16. In Psalm 80, which name does the psalmist use for God?

    Psalm 80:1

    A. Ancient of days
    B. God of salvation
    C. Shepherd of Israel
    D. Word of life

17. In Psalm 80, what did God give the Israelites to drink?

    Psalm 80:5

    A. Milk
    B. Rain
    C. Tears
    D. Wine

18. In Psalm 80, which animal destroyed the vine out of Egypt?

    Psalm 80:8–13

    A. The boar
    B. The calf
    C. The goat
    D. The mule

19. In Psalm 81, at which body of water did God prove Israel?

    Psalm 81:7

    A. Waters of Megiddo
    B. Waters of Memphis
    C. Waters of Meribah
    D. Waters of Merom

20. In Psalm 81, what would God have given the Israelites to eat if they had obeyed him?

    Psalm 81:16

    A. Honey out of the rock
    B. Grapes from the wild
    C. Olives in winter
    D. Tares for their mills

*Answers on page 765

JUNE 30

Lesson 181
Today's Reading: *Psalms 82–89*
Period of Time: Various Dates
Authors: Asaph, Unknown, David, Ethan

1. In Psalm 82, what does God judge among?
   Psalm 82:1
   A. The angels
   B. The gods
   C. The kings
   D. The lords

2. In Psalm 83, what do the psalmist's enemies make?
   Psalm 83:2
   A. A bulwark
   B. A tower
   C. A tumult
   D. An engine

3. In Psalm 83, what is one of the confederate nations that are mentioned?
   Psalm 83:5–8
   A. Balah
   B. Gebal
   C. Halah
   D. Tubal

4. In Psalm 83, at which brook was Sisera defeated?
   Psalm 83:9
   A. Brook Besor
   B. Brook Cherith
   C. Brook Eshcol
   D. Brook Kison

5. In Psalm 83, where did the fugitives from Sisera's army perish?
   Psalm 83:10
   A. Endor
   B. Gedor
   C. Habor
   D. Nahor

6. In Psalm 83, which nobles are mentioned?
   Psalm 83:11
   A. Ahab and Moab
   B. Joab and Anub
   C. Oreb and Zeeb
   D. Rechab and Hobab

7. In Psalm 83, how does the psalmist want his enemies destroyed?
   Psalm 83:14
   A. As fire burneth wood
   B. As fire consumeth chaff
   C. As fire melteth wax
   D. As fire vanisheth away

8. In Psalm 83, which name does the psalmist use for God?
   Psalm 83:18
   A. I AM
   B. JAH
   C. JEHOVAH
   D. UNKNOWN GOD

9. In Psalm 84, what adjective is used to describe God's tabernacles?
   Psalm 84:1
   A. Amiable
   B. Degenerate
   C. Ragged
   D. Terrible

10. In Psalm 84, in which valley does the rain filleth the pools?
    Psalm 84:6
    A. Valley of Ajalon
    B. Valley of Baca
    C. Valley of Elah
    D. Valley of Solomon

11. In Psalm 84, a day in God's courts is better than how many years?

    Psalm 84:10

    A. 100
    B. 1,000
    C. 10,000
    D. 100,000

12. In Psalm 85, what kissed each other?

    Psalm 85:10

    A. Knowledge and understanding
    B. Mercy and truth
    C. Righteousness and peace
    D. Vanity and pride

13. In Psalm 86, what does the psalmist ask God to do?

    Psalm 86:1

    A. "Bow down thine ear."
    B. "Comfort me with thine arm."
    C. "Guide me with thine hand."
    D. "Kiss me with thine lips."

14. In Psalm 87, which gates does God love more than all the dwellings of Jacob?

    Psalm 87:2

    A. Gates of Elon
    B. Gates of Hebron
    C. Gates of Sidon
    D. Gates of Zion

15. In Psalm 88, whom is the psalmist counted among?

    Psalm 88:4

    A. Those that are numbered for the battle.
    B. Those that carry a heavy burden.
    C. Those that go down into the pit.
    D. Those that have a righteous heart.

16. In Psalm 88, how does the psalmist describe the way his enemy came round about him daily?

    Psalm 88:17

    A. Like frost
    B. Like rain
    C. Like sand
    D. Like water

17. In Psalm 89, what did God break into pieces?

    Psalm 89:10

    A. Kezia
    B. Naomi
    C. Phebe
    D. Rahab

18. In Psalm 89, which mountains shall rejoice in God's name?

    Psalm 89:12

    A. Nebo and Bashan
    B. Pisgah and Ephraim
    C. Sinai and Gilboa
    D. Tabor and Hermon

19. In Psalm 89, which name does the psalmist use for God?

    Psalm 89:18

    A. Creator of the ends of the earth
    B. Holy One of Israel
    C. King of saints
    D. Omega

20. In Psalm 89, whom did God anoint with holy oil?

    Psalm 89:20

    A. David
    B. Jonathan
    C. Levi
    D. Solomon

Answers on page 766

Lesson 182
Today's Reading: *Psalms 90–97*
Period of Time: Various Dates
Authors: Moses, Unknown

JULY 1

1. In Psalm 90, what has the LORD been to all generations?
   Psalm 90:1
   A. Our dwelling place
   B. Our mighty fortress
   C. Our oasis in the desert
   D. Our strong tower

2. In Psalm 90, what are a thousand years with the LORD like?
   Psalm 90:4
   A. A long day
   B. A moment in time
   C. A season
   D. A watch in the night

3. In Psalm 90, how do we spend our years?
   Psalm 90:9
   A. As a journey to a far land
   B. As a mown grass
   C. As a shower that waters the earth
   D. As a tale that is told

4. In Psalm 90, how many years does the average person live?
   Psalm 90:10
   A. 70
   B. 80
   C. 90
   D. 100

5. In Psalm 90, what happens after we die?
   Psalm 90:10
   A. We become food for the worm.
   B. We fly away.
   C. We go to meet the Father.
   D. We turn to dust.

6. In Psalm 90, what are we to number?
   Psalm 90:12
   A. Our children
   B. Our days
   C. Our enemies
   D. Our money

7. In Psalm 91, how many shall fall at the right hand of the righteous?
   Psalm 91:7
   A. 100
   B. 1,000
   C. 10,000
   D. 100,000

8. In Psalm 92, what are the righteous to show in the morning?
   Psalm 92:2
   A. Thy affliction
   B. Thy faithfulness
   C. Thy lovingkindness
   D. Thy mercy

9. In Psalm 92, what are the righteous to show every night?
   Psalm 92:2
   A. Thy affliction
   B. Thy faithfulness
   C. Thy lovingkindness
   D. Thy mercy

10. In Psalm 92, which animal's horn will God exalt the horn of the psalmist like?
    Psalm 92:10
    A. A bull's horn
    B. A deer's horn
    C. A ram's horn
    D. A unicorn's horn

11. In Psalm 92, which tree will the righteous flourish like?
    Psalm 92:12
    A. A cedar tree
    B. A maple tree
    C. A palm tree
    D. A willow tree

12. In Psalm 93, which noise is the LORD mightier than?

    Psalm 93:4

    A. Noise of many chariots
    B. Noise of many lions
    C. Noise of many mountains
    D. Noise of many waters

13. In Psalm 94, what does the psalmist call God?

    Psalm 94:22

    A. The beacon of his hope
    B. The light of his world
    C. The rock of his refuge
    D. The shepherd of his flock

14. In Psalm 95, what are the people to sing to make a joyful noise unto the LORD?

    Psalm 95:2

    A. Hymns
    B. New songs
    C. Old songs
    D. Psalms

15. In Psalm 95, what is in the LORD's hand?

    Psalm 95:4

    A. The deep places of the earth
    B. The evil arrows of famine
    C. The mystery of the seven stars
    D. The tears of the righteousness

16. In Psalm 95, how many years was God grieved with the generation in the wilderness?

    Psalm 95:10

    A. 10
    B. 40
    C. 70
    D. 800

17. In Psalm 96, what does the psalmist state to sing unto the LORD?

    Psalm 96:1

    A. A hymn
    B. A new song
    C. A psalm
    D. An old song

18. In Psalm 97, what surrounds God?

    Psalm 97:2

    A. Clouds and darkness
    B. Lightning and thunder
    C. Peace and angels
    D. Stars and honor

19. In Psalm 97, what melted at the presence of the LORD?

    Psalm 97:5

    A. The hills
    B. The ice
    C. The rivers
    D. The wax

20. In Psalm 97, whose daughter's rejoiced because of the LORD's judgments?

    Psalm 97:8

    A. Asher's daughters
    B. Ephraim's daughters
    C. Judah's daughters
    D. Simeon's daughters

Answers on page 766

JULY 2

Lesson 183
Today's Reading: *Psalms 98–104*
Period of Time: Various Dates
Authors: Unknown, David

1. In Psalm 98, what do the floods do?
   Psalm 98:8
   A. Clap their hands
   B. Drown the horse and rider
   C. Hide a multitude of sins
   D. Quench a thirsty land

2. In Psalm 99, where does the LORD sit?
   Psalm 99:1
   A. Between the cherubims
   B. By the redeemed
   C. Near the anointed
   D. Upon the sea

3. In Psalm 99, who are the LORD's two priests?
   Psalm 99:6
   A. Adam and Methuselah
   B. Moses and Aaron
   C. Noah and Ham
   D. Peter and Paul

4. In Psalm 99, which word is used to describe God?
   Psalm 99:3–9
   A. Almighty
   B. Holy
   C. Lowly
   D. Satisfy

5. In Psalm 100, which metaphor is used for God's people?
   Psalm 100:3
   A. Cattle upon a thousand hills
   B. Lilies of the valley
   C. Sheep of his pasture
   D. Vessels of gold

6. In Psalm 101, what shall the eyes of the psalmist be upon?
   Psalm 101:6
   A. The faithful
   B. The lawful
   C. The peaceful
   D. The sorrowful

7. In Psalm 102, what are the psalmist's days consumed like?
   Psalm 102:3
   A. Bread
   B. Hills
   C. Smoke
   D. Wine

8. In Psalm 102, which bird of the wilderness does the psalmist state he is like?
   Psalm 102:6
   A. The eagle
   B. The falcon
   C. The pelican
   D. The vulture

9. In Psalm 102, which bird of the desert does the psalmist state he is like?
   Psalm 102:6
   A. The hawk
   B. The owl
   C. The pelican
   D. The sparrow

10. In Psalm 102, which bird upon the housetop does the psalmist state he is like?
    Psalm 102:7
    A. The blue jay
    B. The cardinal
    C. The robin
    D. The sparrow

11. In Psalm 103, which bird does the psalmist state his youth has been renewed like?
    Psalm 103:5
    A. The eagle
    B. The falcon
    C. The hawk
    D. The swan

12. In Psalm 103, how does the LORD pitieth them that fear him?

    Psalm 103:13

    A. As a dam pitieth her young
    B. As a father pitieth his children
    C. As a king pitieth a widow
    D. As an ass pitieth her foal

13. In Psalm 104, how does the LORD stretchest out the heavens?

    Psalm 104:2

    A. Like a curtain
    B. Like a desert
    C. Like a hill
    D. Like a sea

14. In Psalm 104, what does the LORD use the clouds for?

    Psalm 104:3

    A. His bucket
    B. His chariot
    C. His horse
    D. His shield

15. In Psalm 104, what are the LORD's ministers?

    Psalm 104:4

    A. A beacon on top of a mountain
    B. A chariot cutting through the enemy
    C. A flaming fire
    D. A poisonous viper

16. In Psalm 104, what are the trees of the LORD full of?

    Psalm 104:16

    A. Apples
    B. Gold
    C. Maple
    D. Sap

17. In Psalm 104, which bird makes the fir trees its house?

    Psalm 104:17

    A. The eagle
    B. The glede
    C. The kite
    D. The stork

18. In Psalm 104, what are the high hills a refuge for?

    Psalm 104:18

    A. Demonic spirits
    B. God's prophets
    C. Leprous people
    D. Wild goats

19. In Psalm 104, what are the rocks a refuge for?

    Psalm 104:18

    A. The adder
    B. The bat
    C. The conies
    D. The dromedary

20. In Psalm 104, what has God made to play in the sea?

    Psalm 104:25–26

    A. Behemoth
    B. Cormorant
    C. Dagon
    D. Leviathan

*Answers on page 766

Lesson 184
Today's Reading: *Psalms 105–107*
Period of Time: Various Dates
Author: Unknown

JULY 3

1. In Psalm 105, what does the psalmist state to sing unto the LORD?
   Psalm 105:2
   A. Hymns
   B. New songs
   C. Old songs
   D. Psalms

2. In Psalm 105, which name does the psalmist use for God?
   Psalm 105:7
   A. LORD my God
   B. LORD our God
   C. LORD their God
   D. LORD your God

3. In Psalm 105, whom did the LORD make a covenant with?
   Psalm 105:9
   A. Abraham
   B. David
   C. Joseph
   D. Solomon

4. In Psalm 105, which land did the LORD promise to give to Israel?
   Psalm 105:11
   A. Land of Canaan
   B. Land of Egypt
   C. Land of Lebanon
   D. Land of Rome

5. In Psalm 105, whom did the LORD command the people **not** to harm?
   Psalm 105:15
   A. His kings
   B. His lawyers
   C. His prophets
   D. His teachers

6. In Psalm 105, who was sold as a servant?
   Psalm 105:17
   A. Aaron
   B. Dathan
   C. Joseph
   D. Moses

7. In Psalm 105, in which land did Jacob sojourn in?
   Psalm 105:23
   A. Land of Ham
   B. Land of Japheth
   C. Land of Nod
   D. Land of Shem

8. In Psalm 105, which two men did the LORD send to show signs and wonders?
   Psalm 105:26–27
   A. Balak and Balaam
   B. Jannes and Jambres
   C. Moses and Aaron
   D. Saul and Barnabbas

9. In Psalm 106, at which sea did the Israelites provoke the LORD?
   Psalm 106:7
   A. Blue sea
   B. Green sea
   C. Red sea
   D. White sea

10. In Psalm 106, who is referred to as the saint of the LORD?
    Psalm 106:16
    A. Aaron
    B. Dathan
    C. Joseph
    D. Moses

11. In Psalm 106, who was swallowed by the earth?

    Psalm 106:17

    A. Aaron
    B. Dathan
    C. Joseph
    D. Moses

12. In Psalm 106, who was buried along with his followers?

    Psalm 106:17

    A. Abiram
    B. Hiram
    C. Joram
    D. Piram

13. In Psalm 106, where did the Israelites make a golden calf?

    Psalm 106:19

    A. Golan
    B. Horeb
    C. Joppa
    D. Socoh

14. In Psalm 106, who turned the LORD's wrath away from the Israelites?

    Psalm 106:23

    A. Aaron
    B. Dathan
    C. Joseph
    D. Moses

15. In Psalm 106, which god did the Israelites turn to?

    Psalm 106:28

    A. Adrammelech
    B. Baalpeor
    C. Merodach
    D. Tartak

16. In Psalm 106, who was responsible for stopping the plague?

    Psalm 106:30

    A. Cleopas
    B. Jeremias
    C. Phinehas
    D. Theudas

17. In Psalm 107, who staggers as a drunken man?

    Psalm 107:23–29

    A. The fool
    B. The husbandman
    C. The king
    D. The sailor

18. In Psalm 107, what does the LORD turn rivers into?

    Psalm 107:33

    A. A brook
    B. A stream
    C. A pool
    D. A wilderness

19. In Psalm 107, what does the LORD turn dry ground into?

    Psalm 107:35

    A. Clay
    B. Dust
    C. Mud
    D. Watersprings

20. In Psalm 107, what does the LORD make families like?

    Psalm 107:41

    A. A colony
    B. A flock
    C. A swarm
    D. A troop

*Answers on page 766

JULY 4

Lesson 185
Today's Reading: *Psalms 108–112*
Period of Time: Various Dates
Authors: David, Unknown

1. In Psalm 108, how high does the truth of God reach?
   Psalm 108:4
   A. The clouds
   B. The hills
   C. The mountains
   D. The valleys

2. In Psalm 108, which place will the LORD divide?
   Psalm 108:7
   A. Bethlehem
   B. Jashubilehem
   C. Leshem
   D. Shechem

3. In Psalm 108, which valley will the LORD mete out?
   Psalm 108:7
   A. Valley of Berachah
   B. Valley of Jezreel
   C. Valley of Megiddo
   D. Valley of Succoth

4. In Psalm 108, who is the strength of God's head?
   Psalm 108:8
   A. Ephraim
   B. Idumaea
   C. Memphis
   D. Raamses

5. In Psalm 108, who is the LORD's lawgiver?
   Psalm 108:8
   A. Issachar
   B. Judah
   C. Manasseh
   D. Naphtali

6. In Psalm 108, who is the LORD's washpot?
   Psalm 108:9
   A. Edom
   B. Gaza
   C. Moab
   D. Rome

7. In Psalm 108, over whom will the LORD cast out his shoe?
   Psalm 108:9
   A. Edom
   B. Gaza
   C. Moab
   D. Rome

8. In Psalm 108, over whom will the LORD triumph?
   Psalm 108:9
   A. Alexandria
   B. Macedonia
   C. Philistia
   D. Samaria

9. In Psalm 109, which name does the psalmist use for God?
   Psalm 109:1
   A. God of my father
   B. God of my praise
   C. God of my righteousness
   D. God of my salvation

10. In Psalm 109, whom does the psalmist want to stand at the right hand of his adversaries?
    Psalm 109:6
    A. Holy Ghost
    B. Jesus
    C. Satan
    D. The LORD

11. In Psalm 109, what does the psalmist ask his adversaries bones and bowels be filled with?
    Psalm 109:18
    A. Cursing
    B. Fat
    C. Oil
    D. Water

12. In Psalm 109, what does the psalmist state he is gone like?
    Psalm 109:23
    A. The dawn
    B. The rain
    C. The shadow
    D. The wind

13. In Psalm 110, from where will the LORD send the rod of his strength?
    Psalm 110:2
    A. Edom
    B. Iron
    C. Moab
    D. Zion

14. In Psalm 110, which priest is mentioned?
    Psalm 110:4
    A. Aaron
    B. Eleazar
    C. Melchizedek
    D. Shelemiah

15. In Psalm 111, what are the works of the LORD's hands?
    Psalm 111:7
    A. Hard and fast
    B. Mercy and sure
    C. Tender and kind
    D. Verity and judgment

16. In Psalm 111, what is the LORD's name?
    Psalm 111:9
    A. Benevolent and strong
    B. Holy and reverend
    C. Justice and weighed
    D. Wonderful and counselor

17. In Psalm 111, what is the beginning of wisdom?
    Psalm 111:10
    A. The Book of Genesis
    B. The fear of the LORD
    C. The mountain of holiness
    D. The school of prophecy

18. In Psalm 112, which man is blessed?
    Psalm 112:1
    A. He that feareth the LORD
    B. He that knoweth the scriptures
    C. He that loveth the poor
    D. He that seeketh the rich

19. In Psalm 112, what shall be in the house of the blessed man?
    Psalm 112:3
    A. Bread and water
    B. Cream and sugar
    C. Milk and honey
    D. Wealth and riches

20. In Psalm 112, what will a good man do?
    Psalm 112:5
    A. Kill
    B. Lend
    C. Steal
    D. Tempt

*Answers on page 766

JULY 5

Lesson 186
Today's Reading: *Psalms 113–118*
Period of Time: Various Dates
Author: Unknown

1. What are the first and last verses in Psalm 113?
   Psalm 113:1, 113:9
   A. Blessed be the name of the LORD.
   B. Glory to God in the highest.
   C. O LORD I give thee praise.
   D. Praise ye the LORD.

2. In Psalm 113, whom does the LORD lift out of the dunghill?
   Psalm 113:7
   A. The diseased
   B. The enemy
   C. The needy
   D. The wise

3. In Psalm 114, which nation did the Israelites come out of?
   Psalm 114:1
   A. Egypt
   B. Greece
   C. Rome
   D. Syria

4. In Psalm 114, which nation was the LORD's sanctuary?
   Psalm 114:2
   A. Assyria
   B. Damascus
   C. Judah
   D. Macedonia

5. In Psalm 114, which nation was the LORD's dominion?
   Psalm 114:2
   A. Babylon
   B. Israel
   C. Libya
   D. Tyre

6. In Psalm 114, what skipped like rams?
   Psalm 114:4
   A. The brooks
   B. The great seas
   C. The little hills
   D. The mountains

7. In Psalm 114, what skipped like lambs?
   Psalm 114:4
   A. The brooks
   B. The great seas
   C. The little hills
   D. The mountains

8. In Psalm 114, which name does the psalmist use for God?
   Psalm 114:7
   A. God of Abraham
   B. God of Jacob
   C. God of Moses
   D. God of Noah

9. In Psalm 115, what is God to Israel?
   Psalm 115:9
   A. Their bow and their arrow
   B. Their help and their shield
   C. Their peace and their joy
   D. Their rock and their defense

10. In Psalm 115, who made heaven and earth?
    Psalm 115:15
    A. Baalpeor
    B. Poseidon
    C. The LORD
    D. Zeus

11. In Psalm 116, what took hold of the psalmist?
    Psalm 116:3
    A. The enemy's chains
    B. The hand of God
    C. The lion's teeth
    D. The pains of hell

12. In Psalm 116, what did the psalmist say in his haste?

    Psalm 116:11

    A. All men are liars.
    B. I am the king of kings.
    C. My hands are clean.
    D. There is no God.

13. In Psalm 116, what is precious in the sight of the LORD?

    Psalm 116:15

    A. The death of his saints
    B. The kiss of charity
    C. The lips of the wise
    D. The sacrifices of his people

14. How does Psalm 117 begin?

    Psalm 117:1

    A. I love the LORD.
    B. Judge me, O LORD.
    C. O praise the LORD.
    D. The LORD said unto my lord.

15. How does Psalm 117 end?

    Psalm 117:2

    A. Bless all the LORD's people.
    B. I salute thee O LORD.
    C. Make a joyful noise unto the LORD.
    D. Praise ye the LORD.

16. How do the first four and last verses of Psalm 118 end?

    Psalm 118:1–4, 118:29

    A. Great and mighty is the LORD our God.
    B. His mercy endureth for ever.
    C. I shall forever praise his holy name.
    D. Thy will be done.

17. In Psalm 118, what did the psalmist's enemies compass him about like?

    Psalm 118:12

    A. Bees
    B. Gnats
    C. Hornets
    D. Locusts

18. In Psalm 118, which simile describes how the psalmist's enemies will be destroyed?

    Psalm 118:12

    A. Quenched as the fire of thorns.
    B. Reviled as a dying dog.
    C. Torn asunder as beasts of the wild.
    D. Whipped as the churning of butter.

19. In Psalm 118, what does the psalmist state the LORD is to him?

    Psalm 118:14

    A. His compass and map
    B. His light and candlestick
    C. His knowledge and understanding
    D. His strength and song

20. In Psalm 118, what did the builders refuse?

    Psalm 118:22

    A. The brass of the doors
    B. The head stone of the corner
    C. The iron nails of the walls
    D. The wood beams of the roof

*Answers on page 766

JULY 6

Lesson 187
Today's Reading: *Psalm 119*
Period of Time: Unknown
Author: Unknown

1. What is the second letter of the Hebrew alphabet?
   Psalm 119:8–9
   A. BETH
   B. HE
   C. SAMECH
   D. TAU

2. What did the psalmist hide in his heart?
   Psalm 119:11
   A. His love for the fair maiden
   B. His plot to overthrow his enemies
   C. The sins he committed since his youth
   D. The word of God

3. What does the psalmist claim are his delight and his counselors?
   Psalm 119:24
   A. The LORD's goodness
   B. The LORD's mercies
   C. The LORD's testimonies
   D. The LORD's vanities

4. What is the fifth letter of the Hebrew alphabet?
   Psalm 119:32–33
   A. BETH
   B. HE
   C. SCHIN
   D. TAU

5. When does the psalmist state he will thank God for his righteous judgments?
   Psalm 119:62
   A. Morning
   B. Noon
   C. Evening
   D. Midnight

6. What is the heart of the wicked as fat as?
   Psalm 119:70
   A. Grease
   B. Oil
   C. Swine
   D. Whales

7. What is the tenth letter of the Hebrew alphabet?
   Psalm 119:72–73
   A. ALPHA
   B. JOD
   C. PE
   D. TETH

8. What does the psalmist state he has become like?
   Psalm 119:83
   A. A bottle in the smoke
   B. A dry river in the desert
   C. A falling star in the night
   D. A lost lamb in the flock

9. What is the twelfth letter of the Hebrew alphabet?
   Psalm 119:88–89
   A. GIMEL
   B. LAMED
   C. SAMECH
   D. TZADDI

10. Who has the LORD made the psalmist wiser than through his commandments?
    Psalm 119:98
    A. All his teachers
    B. His enemies
    C. His judges
    D. The ancients

11. Who has the LORD gave the psalmist more understanding than?

    Psalm 119:99

    A. All his teachers
    B. His enemies
    C. His judges
    D. The ancients

12. Whom does the psalmist have more understanding than because he keeps God's precepts?

    Psalm 119:100

    A. All his teachers
    B. His enemies
    C. His judges
    D. The ancients

13. What is God's word unto the psalmist's feet?

    Psalm 119:105

    A. A carpet
    B. A lamp
    C. A mat
    D. A shoe

14. What is the fifteenth letter of the Hebrew alphabet?

    Psalm 119:112–113

    A. GIMEL
    B. LAMED
    C. SAMECH
    D. TZADDI

15. What is the seventeenth letter of the Hebrew calendar?

    Psalm 119:128–129

    A. ALPHA
    B. JOD
    C. PE
    D. TETH

16. How does the psalmist describe himself?

    Psalm 119:141

    A. Bold and beautiful
    B. Meek and mild
    C. Ruddy and tall
    D. Small and despised

17. How does the psalmist rejoice at God's word?

    Psalm 119:162

    A. As one that findeth great spoil
    B. As one that goeth down into the pit
    C. As the bee seeketh the nectar
    D. As the deer panteth for the water

18. How many times a day does the psalmist praise the LORD?

    Psalm 119:164

    A. 3
    B. 5
    C. 7
    D. 9

19. What is the last letter of the Hebrew alphabet?

    Psalm 119:168–169

    A. BETH
    B. HE
    C. SCHIN
    D. TAU

20. Which animal does the psalmist state he is similar to?

    Psalm 119:176

    A. A blind ox
    B. A dying dog
    C. A lost sheep
    D. An old lion

*Answers on page 766

Lesson 188
Today's Reading: *Psalms 120–135*
Period of Time: Various Dates
Authors: Unknown, David

1. In Psalm 120, what are on the arrows of the mighty?
   Psalm 120:4
   A. Coals of juniper
   B. Flesh of their enemy's sons
   C. Iron mingled with blood
   D. Poison of asps

2. In Psalm 120, where does the psalmist sojourn?
   Psalm 120:5
   A. Athach
   B. Mesech
   C. Sheshach
   D. Taanach

3. In Psalm 120, whose tents does the psalmist dwell in?
   Psalm 120:5
   A. Kedar's tents
   B. Nephilim's tents
   C. Nethinim's tents
   D. Samaritan's tents

4. In Psalm 121, what does the psalmist state God never does?
   Psalm 121:3
   A. Fight
   B. Judge
   C. Love
   D. Slumber

5. In Psalm 121, what does the psalmist call the LORD?
   Psalm 121:5
   A. His father
   B. His keeper
   C. His maker
   D. His writer

6. In Psalm 122, what does the psalmist ask to pray for?
   Psalm 122:6
   A. The children of Manasseh
   B. The fathers of Ephraim
   C. The peace of Jerusalem
   D. The slaves of Babylon

7. In Psalm 123, which name does the psalmist use for God?
   Psalm 123:2
   A. LORD my God
   B. LORD our God
   C. LORD their God
   D. LORD your God

8. In Psalm 124, how did the soul of Israel escape from the wicked?
   Psalm 124:7
   A. As a bird out of the snare
   B. As behemoth crushes the gin
   C. As leviathan breaks the hook
   D. As the blind avoids the stumblingblock

9. In Psalm 125, which mountain shall they that trust in the LORD be like?
   Psalm 125:1
   A. Mount Mariah
   B. Mount Nebo
   C. Mount Sinai
   D. Mount Zion

10. In Psalm 126, where are the streams the psalmist refers to?
    Psalm 126:4
    A. In the east
    B. In the west
    C. In the south
    D. In the north

11. In Psalm 127, what does the LORD give to his beloved?

    Psalm 127:2

    A. Clothing
    B. Meat
    C. Sleep
    D. Water

12. In Psalm 128, what shall be as a fruitful vine?

    Psalm 128:3

    A. Thy beeves
    B. Thy children
    C. Thy sheep
    D. Thy wife

13. In Psalm 128, what shall be like olive plants?

    Psalm 128:3

    A. Thy beeves
    B. Thy children
    C. Thy sheep
    D. Thy wife

14. In Psalm 129, what does the psalmist want his enemies to be like?

    Psalm 129:6

    A. Grass upon the housetops
    B. Ice upon the mountains
    C. Olives upon the vines
    D. Sap upon the trees

15. In Psalm 130, the psalmist's soul waiteth for the LORD more than what?

    Psalm 130:6

    A. They that hunt for meat.
    B. They that labor for freedom.
    C. They that pray for their sick children.
    D. They that watch for the morning.

16. In Psalm 131, what does the psalmist state his soul is like?

    Psalm 131:2

    A. A drunken man
    B. A mother in travail
    C. A rich merchant
    D. A weaned child

17. In Psalm 132, where did Israel learn about the ark?

    Psalm 132:6

    A. Ephratah
    B. Hadattah
    C. Jiphtah
    D. Kartah

18. In Psalm 133, what is similar to brothers dwelling together in unity?

    Psalm 133:1–2

    A. Beaten metal
    B. Old wine
    C. Precious ointment
    D. Young children

19. In Psalm 134, where were the servants of the LORD found at night?

    Psalm 134:1

    A. Among the shepherds
    B. In the house of the LORD
    C. Near the street corners
    D. Upon the walls

20. In Psalm 135, who is the king of Bashan?

    Psalm 135:11

    A. King Agag
    B. King Herod
    C. King Og
    D. King Sihon

*Answers on page 766

Lesson 189
Today's Reading: *Psalms 136–142*
Period of Time: Various Dates
Authors: Unknown, David

JULY 8

1. In Psalm 136, how do all of the verses end?
   Psalm 136:1–26
   A. Amen.
   B. For his mercy endureth for ever.
   C. Praise ye the LORD.
   D. Selah.

2. In Psalm 136, which sea did the LORD divide?
   Psalm 136:13
   A. Brasen sea
   B. Great sea
   C. Molten sea
   D. Red sea

3. In Psalm 136, who was king of the Amorites?
   Psalm 136:19
   A. King Agag
   B. King Cyrus
   C. King Og
   D. King Sihon

4. In Psalm 136, who was the king of Bashan?
   Psalm 136:20
   A. King Agag
   B. King Cyrus
   C. King Og
   D. King Sihon

5. In Psalm 137, by the rivers of which nation did the captives weep?
   Psalm 137:1
   A. Babylon
   B. Egypt
   C. Rome
   D. Syria

6. In Psalm 137, what was hung upon the willows?
   Psalm 137:2
   A. Garments
   B. Harps
   C. Prisoners
   D. Tokens

7. In Psalm 137, which city did the captives grieve for?
   Psalm 137:5–6
   A. Bethlehem
   B. Damascus
   C. Jerusalem
   D. Nineveh

8. In Psalm 137, which nation said, "Rase it, rase it, even to the foundation thereof"?
   Psalm 137:7
   A. Cush
   B. Edom
   C. Moab
   D. Tyre

9. In Psalm 138, whom does the psalmist state he will sing praises unto God before?
   Psalm 138:1
   A. The gods
   B. The kings
   C. The priests
   D. The rabbis

10. In Psalm 138, who shall praise the LORD?
    Psalm 138:4
    A. All the animals
    B. All the children
    C. All the kings
    D. All the lepers

11. In Psalm 138, whom does the LORD respect?
    Psalm 138:6
    A. The bridesmaid
    B. The groom
    C. The lowly
    D. The stranger

12. In Psalm 139, what are both alike to God?
    Psalm 139:12
    A. The cherubim and seraphim
    B. The darkness and the light
    C. The man and the woman
    D. The warmth and the cold

13. In Psalm 140, what have the wicked sharpened their tongues like?

    Psalm 140:3

    A. A hook
    B. A knife
    C. A razor
    D. A serpent

14. In Psalm 140, what did the LORD do to the psalmist in the day of battle?

    Psalm 140:7

    A. Covered his head
    B. Gave him the armor of the LORD
    C. Placed a sword in his hand
    D. Uncovered his nakedness

15. In Psalm 140, what did the psalmist want to use to burn the wicked?

    Psalm 140:10

    A. Coals
    B. Irons
    C. Water
    D. Wood

16. In Psalm 140, what did the psalmist ask the LORD **not** to establish upon the earth?

    Psalm 140:11

    A. A new city in Israel
    B. A river to divide the land
    C. A tree for his enemies
    D. An evil speaker

17. In Psalm 141, what is similar to the psalmist's prayer?

    Psalm 141:2

    A. Burnt offerings
    B. Incense offerings
    C. Sin offerings
    D. Trespass offerings

18. In Psalm 141, which sacrifices are similar to the psalmist lifting up his hands?

    Psalm 141:2

    A. Morning sacrifices
    B. Noon sacrifices
    C. Evening sacrifices
    D. Midnight sacrifices

19. In Psalm 141, how are the bones scattered at the grave's mouth?

    Psalm 141:7

    A. As clouds in the heaven
    B. As dust spread upon the ground
    C. As sand upon the sea
    D. As wood cleaved upon the earth

20. In Psalm 142, what request does the psalmist ask of God?

    Psalm 142:7

    A. Bring his soul out of prison
    B. Feed him manna from heaven
    C. Keep him from temptation
    D. Quench his thirst

*Answers on page 766

JULY 9

Lesson 190
Today's Reading: *Psalms 143–150*
Period of Time: Various Dates
Authors: David, Unknown

1. In Psalm 143, what does the psalmist state has been left desolate?
   Psalm 143:4
   A. His fields
   B. His heart
   C. His people
   D. His wells

2. In Psalm 144, what does the psalmist state the LORD teaches his fingers to do?
   Psalm 144:1
   A. Grow corn
   B. Harvest wheat
   C. Play music
   D. To fight

3. In Psalm 144, what are the days of man similar to?
   Psalm 144:4
   A. A river
   B. A shadow
   C. A tree
   D. A well

4. In Psalm 144, how many strings does the musical instrument contain?
   Psalm 144:9
   A. 5
   B. 7
   C. 10
   D. 12

5. In Psalm 144, whom did the LORD deliver from the hurtful sword?
   Psalm 144:10
   A. David
   B. Jonathan
   C. Saul
   D. Uriah

6. In Psalm 144, what are the sons similar to?
   Psalm 144:12
   A. Corner stones
   B. Dust
   C. Plants
   D. Wine

7. In Psalm 144, what are the daughters similar to?
   Psalm 144:12
   A. Corner stones
   B. Dust
   C. Plants
   D. Wine

8. In Psalm 144, what does the psalmist ask the LORD to do for his people?
   Psalm 144:13
   A. Fill their garners
   B. Lead them to the Promised Land
   C. Send his only begotten son to them
   D. Teach them to pray

9. In Psalm 145, which words does the psalmist use to describe God's kingdom?
   Psalm 145:13
   A. It is an everlasting kingdom.
   B. Jerusalem is the LORD's kingdom.
   C. Sweet Beulah land will be the kingdom.
   D. The LORD shall have no more kingdoms.

10. In Psalm 146, who made heaven, earth, and the sea?
    Psalm 146:5–6
    A. God
    B. Merodach
    C. Rimmon
    D. Tammuz

11. In Psalm 147, what does God know the names of?

    Psalm 147:4

    A. The birds
    B. The fish
    C. The stars
    D. The trees

12. In Psalm 147, which musical instrument does the psalmist state to use to praise God?

    Psalm 147:7

    A. Cornet
    B. Harp
    C. Organ
    D. Viol

13. In Psalm 147, which young birds cried?

    Psalm 147:9

    A. Doves
    B. Eagles
    C. Falcons
    D. Ravens

14. In Psalm 147, what does the LORD give that is white like wool?

    Psalm 147:16

    A. Flour
    B. Milk
    C. Snow
    D. Topaz

15. In Psalm 147, what does the LORD scatter like ashes?

    Psalm 147:16

    A. Bones
    B. Hoarfrost
    C. Manna
    D. Wood

16. In Psalm 147, what does the LORD cast forth like morsels?

    Psalm 147:17

    A. Ants
    B. Ice
    C. Nuts
    D. Seeds

17. In Psalm 148, whose name are the people to praise?

    Psalm 148:13

    A. Abraham's name
    B. David's name
    C. Moses' name
    D. The LORD's name

18. In Psalm 149, which two musical instruments are mentioned?

    Psalm 149:3

    A. Cymbals and viol
    B. Psaltery and bells
    C. Sackbut and flute
    D. Timbrel and harp

19. In Psalm 149, what does the psalmist ask be placed in the hands of God's people?

    Psalm 149:6

    A. A cup of joy
    B. A dish filled with meat
    C. A pot to hold water
    D. A twoedged sword

20. In Psalm 150, what is the last sentence in the final verse?

    Psalm 150:6

    A. Amen.
    B. His truth endureth to all generations.
    C. Praise ye the LORD.
    D. Shout to the LORD.

Answers on page 766

Lesson 191
Today's Reading: *Proverbs 1–4*
Period of Time: 1015-975 BC
Author: Solomon

JULY 10

1. Who was Solomon's father?
   Proverbs 1:1
   A. Absalom
   B. David
   C. Goliath
   D. Saul

2. What do the proverbs give to the simple?
   Proverbs 1:4
   A. Absurdity
   B. Subtilty
   C. Vacuity
   D. Wittiness

3. What do the proverbs give to the young man?
   Proverbs 1:4
   A. Fame and fortune
   B. Glory and honor
   C. Knowledge and discretion
   D. Wisdom and popularity

4. What does the wise man gain from proverbs?
   Proverbs 1:5
   A. More books
   B. More degrees
   C. More learning
   D. More students

5. What is the beginning of knowledge?
   Proverbs 1:7
   A. The awe of creation
   B. The breath of Adam
   C. The day a person is born again
   D. The fear of the LORD

6. What shall destroy fools?
   Proverbs 1:32
   A. Their animals
   B. Their family
   C. Their neighbors
   D. Their prosperity

7. What does Solomon tell his son to apply to his heart?
   Proverbs 2:2
   A. Gambling
   B. Hoarding
   C. Investing
   D. Understanding

8. What is God to those who walk uprightly?
   Proverbs 2:7
   A. A buckler
   B. A cane
   C. A map
   D. A sandal

9. What shall preserve those who follow God's proverbs?
   Proverbs 2:11
   A. Discretion
   B. Imagination
   C. Obligation
   D. Reformation

10. What does the strange woman forsake?
    Proverbs 2:16–17
    A. The guide of her youth
    B. The lessons of vanity
    C. The path of ungodliness
    D. The ways of adulterous women

11. What does Solomon tell his son **not** to forsake?
    Proverbs 3:3
    A. Food and wine
    B. Mercy and truth
    C. Pride and prejudice
    D. Women and song

12. According to Proverbs 3:8, what does wisdom give to those who depart from evil?

    Proverbs 3:7–8

    A. Doors to thy homes
    B. Hulls to thy ships
    C. Marrow to thy bones
    D. Signs to thy paths

13. What is in wisdom's right hand?

    Proverbs 3:16

    A. Darkness of night
    B. Length of days
    C. Mysteries of life
    D. Vanity of vanities

14. What is in wisdom's left hand?

    Proverbs 3:16

    A. Moon and stars
    B. Pain and suffering
    C. Riches and honor
    D. Sickness and death

15. What are wisdom's ways?

    Proverbs 3:17

    A. Darkness
    B. Heaviness
    C. Licentiousness
    D. Pleasantness

16. What shall be sweet for the righteous person?

    Proverbs 3:24

    A. Apples
    B. Kisses
    C. Pies
    D. Sleep

17. What shall wisdom place upon the head of the righteous person?

    Proverbs 4:9

    A. A crown of glory
    B. A hat of honor
    C. A head full of heavy hair
    D. A hundred measures of oil

18. What did Solomon's father tell him to take fast hold of?

    Proverbs 4:13

    A. Instruction
    B. Production
    C. Reproduction
    D. Seduction

19. What does Solomon state the path of the just is like?

    Proverbs 4:18

    A. The beaming moon
    B. The flickering candle
    C. The shining light
    D. The twinkling stars

20. What is the righteous person to put far away from him?

    Proverbs 4:24

    A. Innocent eyes
    B. Perverse lips
    C. Slender hips
    D. Tired hands

Answers on page 766

Lesson 192
Today's Reading: *Proverbs 5–8*
Period of Time: 1015–975 BC
Author: Solomon

JULY 11

1. What do the lips of a strange woman drop like?
   Proverbs 5:3
   A. A honeycomb
   B. A snowflake
   C. An apple
   D. An icicle

2. What is the mouth of a strange woman smoother than?
   Proverbs 5:3
   A. Ice
   B. Oil
   C. Silk
   D. Wax

3. What is as bitter as the end of a strange woman?
   Proverbs 5:4
   A. Blood
   B. Gall
   C. Tears
   D. Wormwood

4. What is a husband to always be satisfied with from his wife?
   Proverbs 5:19
   A. Her breasts
   B. Her cooking
   C. Her family
   D. Her housekeeping

5. Which insect is wise?
   Proverbs 6:6
   A. The ant
   B. The bee
   C. The fly
   D. The grasshopper

6. What is the want of the sluggard similar to?
   Proverbs 6:9–11
   A. A prudent man
   B. A working man
   C. An armed man
   D. An earnest man

7. What does God hate?
   Proverbs 6:16–19
   A. He that careth for orphans and widows.
   B. He that doeth the work of an evangelist.
   C. He that giveth financially to God's church.
   D. He that soweth discord among brethren.

8. Where are we to tie thy father's commandment?
   Proverbs 6:20–21
   A. About thy head
   B. About thy neck
   C. Around thy chest
   D. Around thy tongue

9. What is a commandment to the righteous?
   Proverbs 6:23
   A. A burden
   B. A hurdle
   C. A lamp
   D. A trap

10. How much shall a thief pay back if he steals because he is hungry?
    Proverbs 6:30–31
    A. Twofold
    B. Fivefold
    C. Sevenfold
    D. Tenfold

11. What is the rage of a man?
    Proverbs 6:34
    A. Honesty
    B. Jealousy
    C. Pride
    D. Wealth

12. What are we to say unto wisdom?

    Proverbs 7:4

    A. Thou art my daughter
    B. Thou art my lover
    C. Thou art my mother
    D. Thou art my sister

13. What are we to call understanding?

    Psalms 7:4

    A. Thy kinswoman
    B. Thy redeemer
    C. Thy scribe
    D. Thy thorn

14. When did the author see the young man?

    Psalms 7:6–7

    A. When he fell from his horse
    B. When he looked through his casement
    C. When he strolled along the seashore
    D. When he was at the sheep market

15. Whose attire did the woman's resemble?

    Proverbs 7:10

    A. A harlot's attire
    B. A maid's attire
    C. A princess's attire
    D. A queen's attire

16. What did the woman's face look like as she kissed the young man?

    Proverbs 7:13

    A. Bashful
    B. Fawning
    C. Humble
    D. Impudent

17. Where does the woman's house lead to?

    Proverbs 7:27

    A. Ecstasy
    B. Forests
    C. Gardens
    D. Hell

18. Which gem does the author say wisdom is better than?

    Proverbs 8:11

    A. Bdellium
    B. Diamonds
    C. Rubies
    D. Sapphires

19. What does wisdom dwell with?

    Proverbs 8:12

    A. Folly
    B. Indiscretion
    C. Prudence
    D. Rashness

20. What does a person find if he finds wisdom?

    Proverbs 8:35

    A. Darkness
    B. Life
    C. Pain
    D. Suffering

Answers on page 766

JULY 12

Lesson 193
Today's Reading: *Proverbs 9–13*
Period of Time: 1015–975 BC
Author: Solomon

1. How many pillars did wisdom hewn out?
   Proverbs 9:1
   A. 3
   B. 4
   C. 5
   D. 7

2. What will happen if you rebuke a wise man?
   Proverbs 9:8
   A. He will be none the wiser.
   B. He will love thee.
   C. He will put ye to the question.
   D. He will rebuke thee.

3. What is the knowledge of the holy?
   Proverbs 9:10
   A. Confusing
   B. Erring
   C. Perplexing
   D. Understanding

4. What stolen items does the clamorous woman claim is sweet?
   Proverbs 9:17
   A. Grapes
   B. Raisins
   C. Waters
   D. Wines

5. What does the clamorous woman claim is pleasant while eaten in secret?
   Proverbs 9:17
   A. Bread
   B. Curds
   C. Honey
   D. Quail

6. What is the mouth of a righteous man similar to?
   Proverbs 10:11
   A. A bucket of understanding
   B. A river of knowledge
   C. A stream of wisdom
   D. A well of life

7. What is the tongue of the just like?
   Proverbs 10:20
   A. Choice silver
   B. Fine linen
   C. Precious onyx
   D. Refined gold

8. What does Solomon state a sluggard is like to those who send him?
   Proverbs 10:26
   A. Rottenness to the bones
   B. Swelling to the belly
   C. Vinegar to the teeth
   D. Wantonness to the eyes

9. In Proverbs 11:1 what is delightful to the LORD?
   Proverbs 11:1
   A. A child's smile
   B. A heavy yoke
   C. A just weight
   D. A sharp axe

10. Which type of men retain riches?
    Proverbs 11:16
    A. Frugal men
    B. Strong men
    C. Thrifty men
    D. Vain men

11. What does Solomon state a fair woman who lacks discretion is like?
    Proverbs 11:22
    A. A foot out of joint
    B. A jewel of gold in a swine's snout
    C. A miscarrying womb and dry breasts
    D. A snow in time of harvest

12. What will happen to those who trust in their riches?

    Proverbs 11:28

    A. They will fall.
    B. They will give more to the poor.
    C. They will increase in wisdom.
    D. They will wax richer.

13. What is he that winnest souls?

    Proverbs 11:30

    A. Dull
    B. Keen
    C. Silly
    D. Wise

14. Which type of wife is a crown to her husband?

    Proverbs 12:4

    A. A beautiful woman
    B. A fair woman
    C. A virtuous woman
    D. A whorish woman

15. What are the tender mercies of the wicked like?

    Proverbs 12:10

    A. Cruel
    B. Kind
    C. Prudent
    D. Unselfish

16. Which term describes the tongue of the wise?

    Proverbs 12:18

    A. Corrupt
    B. Health
    C. Rotten
    D. Septic

17. What shall the soul of the diligent be made?

    Proverbs 13:4

    A. Fat
    B. Indigent
    C. Lean
    D. Penniless

18. What causes contention?

    Proverbs 13:10

    A. Humility
    B. Meekness
    C. Pride
    D. Self-denial

19. Who is the wealth of the sinner laid up for?

    Proverbs 13:22

    A. The iniquitous
    B. The just
    C. The knavish
    D. The partial

20. What does he who spares the rod hate?

    Proverbs 13:24

    A. His brother
    B. His grandfather
    C. His father
    D. His son

*Answers on page 767

JULY 13

Lesson 194
Today's Reading: *Proverbs 14–17*
Period of Time: 1015–975 BC
Author: Solomon

1. What knows its own bitterness?
   Proverbs 14:10
   A. The crib
   B. The heart
   C. The lime
   D. The tongue

2. Who has many friends?
   Proverbs 14:20
   A. The clergy
   B. The poor
   C. The rich
   D. The tax collector

3. Who does he that oppresseth the poor reproach?
   Proverbs 14:31
   A. His father
   B. His neighbor
   C. His Maker
   D. His spouse

4. What exalteth a nation?
   Proverbs 14:34
   A. Armies
   B. Borders
   C. Righteousness
   D. Wealth

5. What turneth away wrath?
   Proverbs 15:1
   A. A big stick
   B. A large army
   C. A melodious song
   D. A soft answer

6. Where are the eyes of the LORD?
   Proverbs 15:3
   A. In every place
   B. In heaven
   C. In the discerning heart
   D. In the head of the wise

7. Who is the LORD far from?
   Proverbs 15:29
   A. The wicked
   B. The widow
   C. The wise
   D. The wretched

8. What does a good report make fat?
   Proverbs 15:30
   A. The belly
   B. The bones
   C. The eyes
   D. The heart

9. What will the LORD establish if you commit your works to him?
   Proverbs 16:3
   A. Thy bitterness
   B. Thy greed
   C. Thy strife
   D. Thy thoughts

10. What shall the wise in heart be called?
    Proverbs 16:21
    A. Corrupt
    B. Dull
    C. Foolish
    D. Prudent

11. What increaseth learning?
    Proverbs 16:21
    A. The attributes of the sage
    B. The character of the school
    C. The number of read books
    D. The sweetness of the lips

12. What is a crown of glory?
    Proverbs 16:31
    A. The anointed head
    B. The bald head
    C. The fat head
    D. The hoary head

13. What is better than the mighty?

    Psalms 16:32

    A. He that drinketh from his own fountain
    B. He that is early to rise
    C. He that is slow to anger
    D. He that is swifter than a rabbit

14. What does a liar giveth ear to?

    Psalms 17:4

    A. A lovely damsel
    B. A naughty tongue
    C. A prudent simpleton
    D. A wise fool

15. What is the crown of old men?

    Proverbs 17:6

    A. Their children's children
    B. Their fast horses
    C. Their many doctors
    D. Their young wives

16. What is worse than a man meeting a bear robbed of her whelps?

    Proverbs 17:12

    A. Meeting a fool in his folly
    B. Meeting a maid whose lover left her
    C. Meeting a rich man robbed of his money
    D. Meeting a poor man in need of food

17. What does the father of a fool lack?

    Proverbs 17:21

    A. Friends
    B. Joy
    C. Money
    D. Tears

18. What does good like medicine?

    Proverbs 17:22

    A. A bitter tonic
    B. A merry heart
    C. A sweet song
    D. A warm bed

19. What does a broken spirit drieth?

    Proverbs 17:22

    A. Bones
    B. Hearts
    C. Mouths
    D. Tears

20. A man who shutteth his lips is a man filled with what?

    Proverbs 17:28

    A. Babbling
    B. Fantasizing
    C. Understanding
    D. Wavering

*Answers on page 767

Lesson 195
Today's Reading: *Proverbs 18–21*
Period of Time: 1015–975 BC
Author: Solomon

JULY 14

1. What comes with ignominy?
   Proverbs 18:3
   A. Greatness
   B. Immortality
   C. Popularity
   D. Reproach

2. What is the name of the LORD?
   Proverbs 18:10
   A. A delicate fortress
   B. A feeble buckler
   C. A strong tower
   D. A worn bulwark

3. What comes before honour?
   Proverbs 18:12
   A. Glory
   B. Humility
   C. Praise
   D. Respect

4. What will bring a man before great men?
   Proverbs 18:16
   A. His gift
   B. His legacy
   C. His reputation
   D. His wealth

5. What makes many friends?
   Proverbs 19:4
   A. Fear
   B. Intimidation
   C. Strength
   D. Wealth

6. What are the contentions of a wife?
   Proverbs 19:13
   A. A continual dropping
   B. A frequent treasure
   C. A repeated blessing
   D. An everlasting profit

7. What is a poor man better than?
   Proverbs 19:22
   A. A damsel
   B. A liar
   C. A master
   D. A slave

8. What kind of man is hard to find?
   Proverbs 20:6
   A. A cunning man
   B. A drunken man
   C. A faithful man
   D. A learned man

9. What does a king on a throne of judgment use to scatter away evil?
   Proverbs 20:8
   A. His duke
   B. His eyes
   C. His henchman
   D. His scepter

10. What is a precious jewel?
    Proverbs 20:15
    A. The bride's family heirlooms
    B. The gold in the temple
    C. The king's high tower
    D. The lips of knowledge

11. What is the mouth filled with later after eating the bread of deceit?
    Proverbs 20:17
    A. Gravel
    B. Honey
    C. Water
    D. Satisfaction

12. Who should **not** be meddled with?
    Proverbs 20:19
    A. He that flattereth with his lips
    B. He that goeth about planting crops
    C. He that ploweth with a heifer
    D. He that returneth from a journey

13. What is the candle of the LORD?

    Psalms 20:27

    A. The burning bush
    B. The radiance of the sun
    C. The spirit of man
    D. The umbra of the moon

14. What is the glory of young men?

    Psalms 20:29

    A. Their children
    B. Their fathers
    C. Their strength
    D. Their wisdom

15. What is the beauty of old men?

    Proverbs 20:29

    A. The dim eye
    B. The grey head
    C. The peace of mind
    D. The sound of music

16. What is better than sacrifice to the LORD?

    Proverbs 21:3

    A. Bestowing all goods to feed the poor
    B. Having the gift of prophecy
    C. Speaking with the tongues of angels
    D. To do justice and judgment

17. What is better than dwelling with a brawling woman in a wide house?

    Proverbs 21:9

    A. Beating her with a rod
    B. Dwelling in the corner of the housetop
    C. Giving her a writing of divorce
    D. Tying her up with a cord

18. What pacifieth anger?

    Proverbs 21:14

    A. A gift in secret
    B. Getting revenge
    C. Removing the ancient landmarks
    D. Two birds in a bush

19. What is better than dwelling with a contentious and an angry woman?

    Proverbs 21:19

    A. Dwelling in a narrower house
    B. Dwelling in a wider house
    C. Dwelling in her sister's house
    D. Dwelling in the wilderness

20. Who speaks constantly?

    Proverbs 21:28

    A. The man that beggeth
    B. The man that boasteth
    C. The man that heareth
    D. The man that selleth

*Answers on page 767

Lesson 196
Today's Reading: *Proverbs 22–24*
Period of Time: 1015–975 BC
Author: Solomon

JULY 15

1. What will happen if you train up a child in the way he should go?
   Proverbs 22:6
   A. He will become rebellious as an adult.
   B. He will hate his parents when he is older.
   C. He will lose his way as a child.
   D. He will not depart from it.

2. What type of man will **not** work and lie that there is a lion in the streets?
   Proverbs 22:13
   A. A careful man
   B. A faithful man
   C. A slothful man
   D. A watchful man

3. What is considered a deep pit?
   Proverbs 22:14
   A. The fowler's snare
   B. The mouth of strange women
   C. The opening to a bear's cave
   D. The well without water

4. Whom should man put their trust in?
   Proverbs 22:19
   A. Doctors
   B. God
   C. Lawyers
   D. Preachers

5. Whom should a person **not** have friendship with?
   Proverbs 22:24
   A. An angry man
   B. An eager man
   C. An impotent man
   D. An ugly man

6. Who shall stand before kings?
   Proverbs 22:29
   A. A man diligent in his business
   B. A man often reproved
   C. A man who kicks against the pricks
   D. A man who lacks wisdom

7. What will fly away as an eagle toward heaven?
   Proverbs 23:5
   A. Bread
   B. Dragons
   C. Love
   D. Riches

8. Whom should a person **not** be among?
   Proverbs 23:20
   A. Weepers
   B. Winebibbers
   C. Woodcutters
   D. Worshippers

9. What should be bought and never sold?
   Proverbs 23:23
   A. Gold
   B. Land
   C. Rubies
   D. Truth

10. What is a deep ditch?
    Proverbs 23:27
    A. A cleft
    B. A pit
    C. A rumor
    D. A whore

11. What does wine biteth like?
    Proverbs 23:32
    A. A coney
    B. A lion
    C. A serpent
    D. A wolf

12. What does wine sting like?
    Proverbs 23:32
    A. A bee
    B. A hornet
    C. A scorpion
    D. An adder

13. What does being drunk with wine feel like?

    Proverbs 23:34

    A. Diving into the ocean
    B. Lying upon a ship's mast
    C. Navigating a vessel
    D. Swimming in a sea

14. What does it take to build a house?

    Proverbs 24:3

    A. Knowledge
    B. Understanding
    C. Wisdom
    D. Worry

15. What does it take to establish a house?

    Proverbs 24:3

    A. Knowledge
    B. Understanding
    C. Wisdom
    D. Worry

16. What does it take to fill a house with precious and pleasant riches?

    Proverbs 24:4

    A. Knowledge
    B. Understanding
    C. Wisdom
    D. Worry

17. What does a man of knowledge increase in?

    Proverbs 24:5

    A. Friends
    B. Riches
    C. Strength
    D. Worries

18. What is found in a multitude of counselors?

    Proverbs 24:6

    A. Chaos
    B. Pride
    C. Safety
    D. Tales

19. What does every man do when he giveth a right answer?

    Proverbs 24:26

    A. Kiss his lips
    B. Puff up his pride
    C. Scorn others
    D. Thank her who bore him

20. How shall poverty come upon a lazy man?

    Proverbs 24:34

    A. As a man that travelleth
    B. As a rich man with no heir
    C. As a widow with child
    D. As a woman in great sorrow

*Answers on page 767

JULY 16

Lesson 197
Today's Reading: *Proverbs 25–28*
Period of Time: 1015–975 BC
Author: Solomon

1. Which king wrote most of the proverbs?
    Proverbs 25:1
    A. King Hezekiah
    B. King Jehoshaphat
    C. King Solomon
    D. King Uzziah

2. Whose men copied the proverbs?
    Proverbs 25:1
    A. King Hezekiah's men
    B. King Jehoshaphat's men
    C. King Solomon's men
    D. King Uzziah's men

3. What are the hearts of kings?
    Proverbs 25:3
    A. Conceivable
    B. Irreplaceable
    C. Respectable
    D. Unsearchable

4. What is a word fitly spoken similar to?
    Proverbs 25:11
    A. Apples of gold in pictures of silver
    B. Birds of a feather flocking together
    C. Jewels cast in a crown of glory
    D. Medicine that's good for the soul

5. What is confidence in an unfaithful man in time of trouble similar to?
    Proverbs 25:19
    A. A blueness of a wound
    B. A broken tooth
    C. A compassionate judge
    D. A rod for the back of fools

6. What is he that singeth songs to a heavy heart similar to?
    Proverbs 25:20
    A. Bread upon the waters
    B. Fish upon coals
    C. Honey upon the ground
    D. Vinegar upon nitre

7. Which wind driveth away rain?
    Proverbs 25:23
    A. North wind
    B. South wind
    C. East wind
    D. West wind

8. Which animal returns to its vomit?
    Proverbs 26:11
    A. The cow
    B. The dog
    C. The fox
    D. The hog

9. How many men—that can render a reason—is a sluggard wiser than in his own conceit?
    Proverbs 26:16
    A. 7
    B. 70
    C. 700
    D. 7,000

10. What are burning lips and a wicked heart similar to?
    Proverbs 26:23
    A. A jewel of gold in a swine's snout
    B. A muzzled ox that treadeth out the corn
    C. A potsherd covered with silver dross
    D. A wink of the eye of a whorish woman

11. What is cruel?
    Proverbs 27:4
    A. Bliss
    B. Eden
    C. Roses
    D. Wrath

12. What is better than secret love?
    Proverbs 27:5
    A. Hidden treasure
    B. Open rebuke
    C. Unbridled lust
    D. Veiled pleasure

13. What does the prudent man do when he foreseeth the evil?

    Proverbs 27:12

    A. Becometh part of it
    B. Denieth its existence
    C. Hideth himself
    D. Standeth alone

14. Which are never full?

    Proverbs 27:20

    A. Cups and glasses
    B. Hell and destruction
    C. Mouths and bellies
    D. Pots and pans

15. What is never satisfied?

    Proverbs 27:20

    A. The bones of man
    B. The bowels of man
    C. The eyes of man
    D. The heart of man

16. What is a poor man that oppresseth the poor similar to?

    Proverbs 28:3

    A. A bridesmaid with no oil for her lamp
    B. A cook with no kettle for the meat
    C. A rain which leaveth no food
    D. A soldier with no sharp sword

17. What shall happen to the man that hateth covetousness?

    Proverbs 28:16

    A. He shall become prestigious.
    B. He shall gain in wealth.
    C. He shall live in glory.
    D. He shall prolong his days.

18. What shall a man that tilleth his land have plenty of?

    Proverbs 28:19

    A. Aches
    B. Bread
    C. Calluses
    D. Friends

19. What does a man have that hasteth to be rich?

    Proverbs 28:22

    A. A bold face
    B. A good counselor
    C. A supportive wife
    D. An evil eye

20. What will the LORD do to the man who putteth his trust in the LORD?

    Proverbs 28:25

    A. Make him fat
    B. Make him lean
    C. Make him poor
    D. Make him rich

*Answers on page 767

Lesson 198
Today's Reading: *Proverbs 29–31*
Period of Time: 1015–975 BC
Author: Solomon, Agur, and Lemuel

JULY 17

1. What do the people do when the righteous are in authority?
   Proverbs 29:2
   A. Fret
   B. Rejoice
   C. Tremble
   D. Wince

2. What do the people do when the wicked beareth rule?
   Proverbs 29:2
   A. Cheer
   B. Frolic
   C. Mourn
   D. Revel

3. What happens to the man that keepeth company with harlots?
   Proverbs 29:3
   A. He becometh rich in the LORD.
   B. He forsaketh all other worldly pleasures.
   C. He repenteth of the evil he has done.
   D. He spendeth his substance.

4. If a ruler hearkens to lies, what are his servants?
   Proverbs 29:12
   A. Innocent
   B. Just
   C. Proper
   D. Wicked

5. What will happen if a king faithfully judgeth the poor?
   Proverbs 29:14
   A. His children shall curse him.
   B. His enemies shall destroy him.
   C. His subjects shall rise up against him.
   D. His throne shall be established for ever.

6. What shall the father receive if he corrects his son?
   Proverbs 29:17
   A. Dishonor
   B. Hate
   C. Rest
   D. Stripes

7. What will happen to people if there is no vision?
   Proverbs 29:18
   A. They will blossom.
   B. They will flourish.
   C. They will perish.
   D. They will triumph.

8. Who is the son of Jakeh?
   Proverbs 30:1
   A. Agur
   B. Ahab
   C. Amos
   D. Aram

9. What is every word of God?
   Proverbs 30:5
   A. Erroneous
   B. Froward
   C. Pure
   D. Unsubstantial

10. How many daughters does the horseleach have?
    Proverbs 30:15
    A. 2
    B. 5
    C. 7
    D. 10

11. What can the earth **not** bear?
    Proverbs 30:21–23
    A. A faithful king when he reigns
    B. A laborer when he is filled with meat
    C. An obedient son that is heir to his father
    D. An odious woman when she is married

12. What are **not** strong, yet prepares their meat in the summer?

    Proverbs 30:25

    A. Ants
    B. Conies
    C. Locusts
    D. Spiders

13. Which animal is the strongest among beasts?

    Proverbs 30:30

    A. The lion
    B. The ox
    C. The ram
    D. The unicorn

14. Which one of the following was a king?

    Proverbs 31:1

    A. King Lemuel
    B. King Nemuel
    C. King Penuel
    D. King Shebuel

15. Who should drink strong drink?

    Proverbs 31:6

    A. Him that has a strong stomach
    B. Him that is ready to perish
    C. Him that knows no evil
    D. Him that worships the true God

16. Who should drink wine?

    Proverbs 31:6

    A. Those that are of age to drink
    B. Those that be of heavy hearts
    C. Those that were once soldiers
    D. Those that will do battle

17. What is a virtuous woman like?

    Proverbs 31:14

    A. The finer's silver
    B. The merchant's ships
    C. The potter's clay
    D. The weaver's beam

18. What is the color of the household's clothes?

    Proverbs 31:21

    A. Blue
    B. Scarlet
    C. Violet
    D. White

19. What type of clothing does the virtuous woman wear?

    Proverbs 31:22

    A. Cotton and white
    B. Flax and black
    C. Silk and purple
    D. Wool and blue

20. What is beauty?

    Proverbs 31:30

    A. Diffident
    B. Humble
    C. Meek
    D. Vain

*Answers on page 767

JULY 18

Lesson 199
Today's Reading: *Ecclesiastes 1–6*
Period of Time: 975 BC
Author: Solomon

1. What does the writer call himself?
   Ecclesiastes 1:1
   A. The Evangelist
   B. The Minister
   C. The Preacher
   D. The Teacher

2. Who is the writer's father?
   Ecclesiastes 1:1
   A. David
   B. Jesse
   C. Rehoboam
   D. Solomon

3. In which city does the writer live?
   Ecclesiastes 1:1, 1:12–16
   A. Bethlehem
   B. Jerusalem
   C. Nicopolis
   D. Ptolemais

4. What did the writer say abides forever?
   Ecclesiastes 1:4
   A. The earth
   B. The memory
   C. The pain
   D. The sky

5. What is found in much wisdom?
   Ecclesiastes 1:18
   A. Much apostasy
   B. Much darkness
   C. Much envy
   D. Much grief

6. What did the writer say was mad?
   Ecclesiastes 2:2
   A. Agony
   B. Laughter
   C. Pain
   D. Sorrow

7. Where are the wise man's eyes?
   Ecclesiastes 2:14
   A. In his hair
   B. In his hand
   C. In his head
   D. In his heart

8. What does God give to the sinner?
   Ecclesiastes 2:26
   A. Joy
   B. Knowledge
   C. Travail
   D. Wisdom

9. Which one of the following is part of Ecclesiastes 3:1-8?
   Ecclesiastes 3:1–8
   A. A time to dine
   B. A time to kill
   C. A time to sleep
   D. A time to wed

10. What was found in the place of judgment?
    Ecclesiastes 3:16
    A. Doors
    B. Liberty
    C. Sunshine
    D. Wickedness

11. What was found in the place of righteousness?
    Ecclesiastes 3:16
    A. Brotherhood
    B. Family
    C. Iniquity
    D. Temptation

12. What does the writer claim is better in verse 4:9?
    Ecclesiastes 4:9
    A. Two are better than one
    B. Understanding is better than riches
    C. Victory is better than defeat
    D. Wisdom is better than foolishness

13. What is **not** quickly broken?

    Ecclesiastes 4:12

    A. A fool's arrow
    B. A golden circle
    C. A miller's stone
    D. A threefold cord

14. What is better than an old foolish king?

    Ecclesiastes 4:13

    A. A comely and strong prince
    B. A poor and wise child
    C. A simple and courageous soldier
    D. A virtuous and honest wife

15. What should a person be more ready to do in the house of God?

    Ecclesiastes 5:1

    A. Confess his sins
    B. Give a sacrifice
    C. Hear the Word of God
    D. Partake of the church supper

16. What is found in the multitude of dreams and in many words?

    Ecclesiastes 5:7

    A. Divers vanities
    B. Hidden prophecies
    C. Life's answers
    D. Sweet sleep

17. Whose sleep is sweet?

    Ecclesiastes 5:12

    A. A hungry man's sleep
    B. A labouring man's sleep
    C. A rich man's sleep
    D. A wise man's sleep

18. What is better than living many years, having one hundred children, an evil soul, and no one to bury you?

    Ecclesiastes 6:3

    A. A good name
    B. A vast domain
    C. An empty nest
    D. An untimely birth

19. What of a labouring man is never filled?

    Ecclesiastes 6:7

    A. His appetite
    B. His heart
    C. His purse
    D. His shoes

20. What is better than the wandering of the desire?

    Ecclesiastes 6:9

    A. The dreams of the sojourner
    B. The end of the journey
    C. The lust of the soul
    D. The sight of the eyes

*Answers on page 767

Lesson 200
Today's Reading: *Ecclesiastes 7–12*
Period of Time: 975 BC
Author: Solomon

JULY 19

1. What is better than precious ointment?
   Ecclesiastes 7:1
   A. A good name
   B. A good physician
   C. A good son
   D. A good wife

2. What is better than laughter?
   Ecclesiastes 7:3
   A. Birth
   B. Death
   C. Sleep
   D. Sorrow

3. What destroys the heart?
   Ecclesiastes 7:7
   A. A gift
   B. Exercise
   C. Laziness
   D. Wine

4. What does the author of the Book of Ecclesiastes call himself?
   Ecclesiastes 7:27
   A. The bishop
   B. The evangelist
   C. The preacher
   D. The savior

5. Which war is man destined to lose?
   Ecclesiastes 8:8
   A. War against baal
   B. War against death
   C. War against poverty
   D. War against Satan

6. What can no man fully understand?
   Ecclesiastes 8:17
   A. All the work of God
   B. If there is life after death
   C. The heart of a loving child
   D. Why a mother forgets her pain after birth

7. What are the hearts of the sons of men full of?
   Ecclesiastes 9:3
   A. Courage
   B. Decency
   C. Evil
   D. Virtue

8. How should wine be drunk?
   Ecclesiastes 9:7
   A. Among thy close friends
   B. In a goblet of sorrow
   C. With a merry heart
   D. Under the cloak of darkness

9. Who saved the little city?
   Ecclesiastes 9:14–15
   A. A bright child
   B. A cunning king
   C. A humble slave
   D. A poor wise man

10. What is better than weapons of war?
    Ecclesiastes 9:18
    A. Death
    B. Love
    C. Sickness
    D. Wisdom

11. What causes the apothecary's ointment to stink?
    Ecclesiastes 10:1
    A. Burnt coal
    B. Dead flies
    C. Swine sweat
    D. Too much air

12. Where is a wise man's heart located?
    Ecclesiastes 10:2
    A. At his left hand
    B. At his right hand
    C. In his chest
    D. In his head

13. What will bite a person if he breaks a hedge?

    Ecclesiastes 10:8

    A. A cockatrice
    B. A flea
    C. A lion
    D. A serpent

14. What answereth all things?

    Ecclesiastes 10:19

    A. Birds
    B. Kings
    C. Money
    D. Prophets

15. What shall be found after many days after it is cast upon the water?

    Ecclesiastes 11:1

    A. Bread
    B. Coins
    C. Fishing poles
    D. Nets

16. What should you do in the morning?

    Ecclesiastes 11:6

    A. Be merry
    B. Drink milk
    C. Eat eggs
    D. Sow seed

17. What will be many if a person lives to an old age?

    Ecclesiastes 11:8

    A. Hours of cheerfulness
    B. Days of darkness
    C. Months of joyousness
    D. Years of smoothness

18. When is it most important for a person to remember the Creator?

    Ecclesiastes 12:1

    A. As a father
    B. As a youth
    C. As an educator
    D. As an old man

19. What are the words of the wise like?

    Ecclesiastes 12:11

    A. Books
    B. Fountains
    C. Goads
    D. Honeycombs

20. What is the whole duty of man?

    Ecclesiastes 12:13

    A. To fear God and keep his commandments
    B. To follow the path of riches and honor
    C. To give to the poor and needy
    D. To love thy neighbor and thyself

*Answers on page 767

Lesson 201
Today's Reading: *Song of Solomon 1–8*
Period of Time: 1015–975 BC
Author: Solomon

1. What does Solomon's bride say Solomon's love is better than?
   Song of Solomon 1:2
   A. Gold
   B. Meat
   C. Stars
   D. Wine

2. What color is Solomon's bride's skin?
   Song of Solomon 1:5–6
   A. Black
   B. Chestnut
   C. Mahogany
   D. White

3. What does Solomon say his bride's eyes are similar to?
   Song of Solomon 1:15
   A. Doves' eyes
   B. Eagles' eyes
   C. Sparrows' eyes
   D. Ravens' eyes

4. What does Solomon's bride call herself?
   Song of Solomon 2:1
   A. The daisy of the hills
   B. The lily of the valleys
   C. The rose of the garden
   D. The tulip of the waters

5. Where does Solomon's bride say Solomon took her?
   Song of Solomon 2:4
   A. The banqueting house
   B. The greeting house
   C. The praising house
   D. The teaching house

6. Which animals spoil the grapevines?
   Song of Solomon 2:15
   A. Bears
   B. Dogs
   C. Foxes
   D. Squirrels

7. How many valiant men are about Solomon's bed?
   Song of Solomon 3:7
   A. 20
   B. 40
   C. 60
   D. 80

8. What does Solomon compare his bride's teeth to?
   Song of Solomon 4:2
   A. A flock of geese
   B. A flock of goats
   C. A flock of pigeons
   D. A flock of sheep

9. What does Solomon's bride say her head is filled with?
   Song of Solomon 5:2
   A. Dew
   B. Fluff
   C. Pain
   D. Worries

10. What did the keepers of the wall take from Solomon's bride?
    Song of Solomon 5:7
    A. Her candle
    B. Her purse
    C. Her shoe
    D. Her veil

11. How does Solomon's bride describe Solomon's skin?
    Song of Solomon 5:10
    A. Black and comely
    B. Fuzzy and warm
    C. Pale and pasty
    D. White and ruddy

12. Which city does Solomon say his bride is as beautiful as?
    Song of Solomon 6:4
    A. Jazah
    B. Mozah
    C. Tirzah
    D. Zelzah

13. What does Solomon say his bride's hair is like?
    Song of Solomon 6:5
    A. A flock of geese
    B. A flock of goats
    C. A flock of pigeons
    D. A flock of sheep

14. What do the daughters of Jerusalem call the bride?
    Song of Solomon 6:13
    A. A Rechabite
    B. A Shulamite
    C. A Tishbite
    D. An Uzzielite

15. What does Solomon say his bride's navel is similar to?
    Song of Solomon 7:2
    A. A cup
    B. A dish
    C. A goblet
    D. A ladle

16. What does Solomon say his bride's breasts are similar to?
    Song of Solomon 7:3
    A. Elevated hills
    B. Green trees
    C. Ripe apricots
    D. Young roes

17. What does Solomon say his bride's eyes are like?
    Song of Solomon 7:4
    A. The brooks in Arnon
    B. The fishpools in Heshbon
    C. The ponds in Egypt
    D. The streams in Shem

18. What does Solomon say his bride's nose has the smell of?
    Song of Solomon 7:8
    A. Apples
    B. Berries
    C. Cherries
    D. Pears

19. What does the bride say is as cruel as the grave?
    Song of Solomon 8:6
    A. Discipline
    B. Friendship
    C. Jealousy
    D. Pride

20. Where did Solomon have a vineyard?
    Song of Solomon 8:11
    A. Baalberith
    B. Baalhamon
    C. Baalmeon
    D. Baaltamar

*Answers on page 767

Lesson 202
Today's Reading: *Isaiah 1–4*
Period of Time: 759 BC
Author: Isaiah

1. Who was Isaiah's father?
   Isaiah 1:1
   A. Amoz
   B. Booz
   C. Jeuz
   D. Maaz

2. Who reigned during the days of Isaiah?
   Isaiah 1:1
   A. Coniah
   B. Neriah
   C. Tobiah
   D. Uzziah

3. Which animal knew his master's crib?
   Isaiah 1:3
   A. The ass
   B. The dog
   C. The goat
   D. The swine

4. What is the daughter of Zion?
   Isaiah 1:8
   A. A city in a land of wild beasts
   B. A flower in a snow of white
   C. A lodge in a garden of cucumbers
   D. A river in a mountain rent asunder

5. The rulers of which two cities were told to give ear unto the law of our God?
   Isaiah 1:9–10
   A. Babylon and Nineveh
   B. Jerusalem and Jericho
   C. Sidon and Tyre
   D. Sodom and Gomorrah

6. What had become an abomination to God?
   Isaiah 1:13
   A. Ice
   B. Incense
   C. Isaiah
   D. Ishmaelites

7. What are the people's hands full of?
   Isaiah 1:15
   A. Blood
   B. Mud
   C. Sweat
   D. Tears

8. What shall sin be like though it is red like crimson?
   Isaiah 1:18
   A. Cotton
   B. Flax
   C. Silk
   D. Wool

9. What shall the LORD take away when he purges away the dross?
   Isaiah 1:25
   A. Brass
   B. Lead
   C. Silver
   D. Tin

10. What shall Jerusalem be called once again?
    Isaiah 1:21–26
    A. The city of brotherly love
    B. The faithful city
    C. The new Babylon
    D. The terrible city

11. What shall the people be ashamed of which they desired?
    Isaiah 1:29
    A. The hay
    B. The iron
    C. The oaks
    D. The rubies

12. Which simile does Isaiah use for those who have forsaken God?

    Isaiah 1:30

    A. As a barn that has no roof.
    B. As a flock that has no shepherd.
    C. As a garden that has no water.
    D. As a palace that has no king.

13. What shall the strong be like?

    Isaiah 1:31

    A. Chains
    B. Linen
    C. Tow
    D. Wheat

14. What shall the swords become after the LORD judges the nations?

    Isaiah 2:4

    A. Hammers
    B. Plowshares
    C. Shovels
    D. Vises

15. What shall the spears become after the LORD judges the nations?

    Isaiah 2:4

    A. Axes
    B. Pruning hooks
    C. Reeds
    D. Saws

16. Who does God say Judah is similar to?

    Isaiah 2:6

    A. The Crete soothsayers
    B. The Philistine soothsayers
    C. The Rephaim soothsayers
    D. The Uzzielite soothsayers

17. Which city was mentioned for its ships?

    Isaiah 2:16

    A. Engedi
    B. Joppa
    C. Tarshish
    D. Ummah

18. What type of eyes do the daughters of Zion have?

    Isaiah 3:16

    A. Blind
    B. Innocent
    C. Tired
    D. Wanton

19. How many women shall take hold of one man when the LORD brings judgment upon Zion?

    Isaiah 4:1

    A. 7
    B. 15
    C. 21
    D. 30

20. Which spirits will the LORD use to purge the blood of Jerusalem?

    Isaiah 4:4

    A. Spirit of burning and spirit of judgment
    B. Spirit of evil and spirit of familiar
    C. Spirit of God and spirit of man
    D. Spirit of unclean and spirit of lying

*Answers on page 767

Lesson 203
Today's Reading: *Isaiah 5–8*
Period of Time: 759–742 BC
Author: Isaiah

JULY 22

1. What is the vineyard of the LORD of hosts?
   Isaiah 5:7
   A. House of Assyria
   B. House of Egypt
   C. House of Israel
   D. House of Lebanon

2. What is the pleasant plant of the LORD of the hosts?
   Isaiah 5:7
   A. Men of Benjamin
   B. Men of Issachar
   C. Men of Judah
   D. Men of Levi

3. How many baths will ten acres of a vineyard yield?
   Isaiah 5:10
   A. 1
   B. 3
   C. 7
   D. 10

4. How many ephahs shall the seed of a homer yield?
   Isaiah 5:10
   A. 1
   B. 3
   C. 7
   D. 10

5. What object does Isaiah use for sin?
   Isaiah 5:18
   A. A cart rope
   B. A dry well
   C. A flaming fire
   D. A heavy cloud

6. Which name does Isaiah use for God?
   Isaiah 5:19
   A. Holy One
   B. Holy One of God
   C. Holy One of Israel
   D. Holy One of Jacob

7. How many wings did each seraphim have?
   Isaiah 6:2
   A. 2
   B. 4
   C. 6
   D. 8

8. What did one of the seraphims have in his hand?
   Isaiah 6:6–7
   A. Arrows
   B. Coal
   C. Lightning
   D. Vials

9. Who was the king of Syria?
   Isaiah 7:1
   A. King Balak
   B. King Eglon
   C. King Pekah
   D. King Rezin

10. Who was the king of Israel?
    Isaiah 7:1
    A. King Balak
    B. King Eglon
    C. King Pekah
    D. King Rezin

11. What was the capital of Syria?
    Isaiah 7:8
    A. Babylon
    B. Damascus
    C. Nineveh
    D. Susa

12. In how many years did Isaiah say Ephraim would no longer be a people?
    Isaiah 7:8
    A. 12
    B. 21
    C. 40
    D. 65

13. What was the capital of Ephraim?

    Isaiah 7:9

    A. Cush
    B. Jerusalem
    C. Memphis
    D. Samaria

14. What shall be the name of the virgin's baby?

    Isaiah 7:14

    A. Ezekiel
    B. Immanuel
    C. Jeremiah
    D. Malachi

15. Which two of the following shall the virgin's son eat?

    Isaiah 7:15

    A. Beans and cornbread
    B. Butter and honey
    C. Eggs and bacon
    D. Meat and potatoes

16. What shall the LORD hiss for that is in the uttermost part of the rivers of Egypt?

    Isaiah 7:18

    A. The bee
    B. The fly
    C. The gnat
    D. The mosquito

17. What shall the LORD hiss for that is in the land of Assyria?

    Isaiah 7:18

    A. The bee
    B. The fly
    C. The gnat
    D. The mosquito

18. Who were the two faithful witnesses?

    Isaiah 8:2

    A. Gog and Magog
    B. Jeroboam and Rehoboam
    C. Omri and Zimri
    D. Uriah and Zechariah

19. What was the name of the prophetess' son?

    Isaiah 8:1–3

    A. Chushan-rishathaim
    B. Berodachbaladan
    C. Joshbekashah
    D. Maher-shalal-hashbaz

20. Which nation shall overthrow the kings of Damascus and Samaria?

    Isaiah 8:4

    A. Assyria
    B. Egypt
    C. Greece
    D. Rome

*Answers on page 767

Lesson 204
Today's Reading: *Isaiah 9–12*
Period of Time: 742–740 BC
Author: Isaiah

JULY 23

1. Which name is one of the names that Isaiah mentions for the child that shall be born?
   Isaiah 9:6
   A. Awesome
   B. Counselor
   C. Prince of darkness
   D. The mighty son

2. What will the people use to replace the bricks?
   Isaiah 9:10
   A. Cedar wood
   B. Hewn stones
   C. Precious gems
   D. Shiny brass

3. Which trees will replace the sycamores?
   Isaiah 9:10
   A. Cedar trees
   B. Elm trees
   C. Gopher trees
   D. Pine trees

4. Which two nations will devour Israel with an open mouth?
   Isaiah 9:12
   A. The Arabians and Egyptians
   B. The Hittites and Hivites
   C. The Libyans and Ethiopians
   D. The Syrians and Philistines

5. Which two of the following are Israel's head?
   Isaiah 9:15
   A. The ancient and honorable
   B. The common and poor
   C. The rich and wealthy
   D. The wizards and warlocks

6. What is Israel's tail?
   Isaiah 9:15
   A. The king who loveth pleasures
   B. The prince who killeth his brethren
   C. The prophet that teacheth lies
   D. The ruler that grindeth his teeth

7. Which two nations shall be against Judah?
   Isaiah 9:21
   A. Ephraim and Manasseh
   B. Greece and Rome
   C. Persia and Egypt
   D. Tyre and Sidon

8. What does Isaiah call Assyria?
   Isaiah 10:5
   A. The hammer of justice
   B. The pick of redemption
   C. The rod of God's anger
   D. The sword of the LORD

9. Which city is similar to Carchemish?
   Isaiah 10:9
   A. Calno
   B. Damascus
   C. Hamath
   D. Samaria

10. Which city is similar to Arpad?
    Isaiah 10:9
    A. Calno
    B. Damascus
    C. Hamath
    D. Samaria

11. How many days would God use to destroy Assyria?
    Isaiah 10:17
    A. 1
    B. 3
    C. 7
    D. 12

12. Who was slaughtered at the rock of Oreb?
    Isaiah 10:26
    A. Assyria
    B. Babylon
    C. Ethiopia
    D. Midian

13. Where did the invading army from the north lay up its carriages?

    Isaiah 10:28

    A. Anathoth
    B. Geba
    C. Laish
    D. Michmash

14. Out of whose roots shall the *Branch* come from?

    Isaiah 11:1

    A. Aaron's roots
    B. Jesse's roots
    C. Laban's roots
    D. Simon's roots

15. What shall dwell with the wolf?

    Isaiah 11:6

    A. The asp
    B. The kid
    C. The lamb
    D. The ox

16. What shall lie down with the leopard?

    Isaiah 11:6

    A. The asp
    B. The kid
    C. The lamb
    D. The ox

17. What shall the lion eat?

    Isaiah 11:7

    A. Eggs
    B. Ham
    C. Rocks
    D. Straw

18. Where shall the weaned child place his hand?

    Isaiah 11:8

    A. In the scorpion's hole
    B. Into the fiery furnace
    C. On the cockatrice' den
    D. Upon the bull's mouth

19. Which sea's tongue will the LORD destroy?

    Isaiah 11:15

    A. The brasen sea's tongue
    B. The Egyptian sea's tongue
    C. The great sea's tongue
    D. The molten sea's tongue

20. What name for God does Isaiah use for his strength, song, and salvation?

    Isaiah 12:2

    A. LORD God of David
    B. LORD God of heaven
    C. LORD his God
    D. LORD JEHOVAH

*Answers on page 767

Lesson 205
Today's Reading: *Isaiah 13–16*
Period of Time: 726 BC
Author: Isaiah

JULY 24

1. Who was Isaiah's father?
   Isaiah 13:1
   A. Amoz
   B. Joel
   C. Noah
   D. Obed

2. What shall the faces of the Babylonians be like?
   Isaiah 13:1–8
   A. Dust
   B. Flames
   C. Ice
   D. Snakes

3. What will God make more precious than fine gold?
   Isaiah 13:12
   A. Apples
   B. Camels
   C. Man
   D. Water

4. Whom shall the LORD stir up against the Babylonians?
   Isaiah 13:17
   A. The Assyrians
   B. The Egyptians
   C. The Greeks
   D. The Medes

5. Which two cities did God overthrow?
   Isaiah 13:19
   A. Corinth and Ephesus
   B. Memphis and Thebes
   C. Sodom and Gomorrah
   D. Tyre and Sidon

6. What shall dance in the ruined houses of Babylon?
   Isaiah 13:21
   A. Angels
   B. Dragons
   C. Satyrs
   D. Unicorns

7. What shall cry in Babylon's pleasant palaces?
   Isaiah 13:22
   A. Angels
   B. Dragons
   C. Satyrs
   D. Unicorns

8. What does Isaiah call Babylon?
   Isaiah 14:4
   A. The Emerald City
   B. The Golden City
   C. The Ruby City
   D. The Silver City

9. Whom does Isaiah call the son of the morning?
   Isaiah 14:12
   A. Christopher
   B. Lucifer
   C. Ofer
   D. Shafer

10. After which king died did the burden of Palestina begin?
    Isaiah 14:28–32
    A. King Ahaz
    B. King Booz
    C. King Jeuz
    D. King Maaz

11. What shall come out of the serpent's root?
    Isaiah 14:29
    A. A behemoth
    B. A cankerworm
    C. A cockatrice
    D. A seraphim

12. From which direction will the smoke come from?

    Isaiah 14:31

    A. North
    B. South
    C. East
    D. West

13. What were the two strongholds of Moab?

    Isaiah 15:1

    A. Ai and Gur
    B. Ar and Kir
    C. Ur and Zir
    D. Uz and Dor

14. Where shall the fugitives of Moab flee to?

    Isaiah 15:5

    A. Adar
    B. Jair
    C. Seir
    D. Zoar

15. Which waters shall become desolate?

    Isaiah 15:6

    A. Dimon
    B. Judah
    C. Meribah
    D. Nimrim

16. Which waters shall be filled with blood?

    Isaiah 15:9

    A. Waters of Dimon
    B. Waters of Judah
    C. Waters of Meribah
    D. Waters of Nimrim

17. What shall the LORD send to destroy the remnants of Moab?

    Isaiah 15:9

    A. Dragons
    B. Hornets
    C. Lions
    D. Serpents

18. At which fords shall the daughters of Moab flee like a wandering bird cast out of the net?

    Isaiah 16:2

    A. Fords of Archi
    B. Fords of Argob
    C. Fords of Ariel
    D. Fords of Arnon

19. Which musical instrument shall the LORD's bowels sound like for Moab?

    Isaiah 16:11

    A. A cymbal
    B. A dulcimer
    C. A flute
    D. A harp

20. Within how many years would Moab be contemned?

    Isaiah 16:14

    A. 3
    B. 5
    C. 7
    D. 9

*Answers on page 768

Lesson 206
Today's Reading: *Isaiah 17–21*
Period of Time: 726–710 BC
Author: Isaiah

JULY 25

1. In which cities shall the flocks lie down?
   Isaiah 17:2
   A. Cities of Aroer
   B. Cities of Ether
   C. Cities of Immer
   D. Cities of Jazer

2. Whose glory shall be made thin and the fatness of his flesh shall wax lean?
   Isaiah 17:4
   A. Edom's glory
   B. Jacob's glory
   C. Moab's glory
   D. Syria's glory

3. In which valley does Isaiah mention reapers gathering corn?
   Isaiah 17:5
   A. Valley of Jezreel
   B. Valley of Lebanon
   C. Valley of Megiddo
   D. Valley of Rephaim

4. What name does Isaiah use for God?
   Isaiah 17:7
   A. Creator
   B. Deliverer
   C. Elohim
   D. Maker

5. What shall Israel and Damascus set their pleasant plants with?
   Isaiah 17:10
   A. Iron cages
   B. Mud packs
   C. Strange slips
   D. Trellised wood

6. What does the land beyond the rivers of Ethiopia use to send their ambassadors?
   Isaiah 18:2
   A. Chariots of fire
   B. Coffins filled with bones
   C. Vessels of bulrushes
   D. Wagons laden with gold

7. How many cities in the land of Egypt shall speak the language of Canaan?
   Isaiah 19:18
   A. 5
   B. 10
   C. 15
   D. 20

8. What shall be found in the midst of the land of Egypt?
   Isaiah 19:19
   A. A fountain to the sky
   B. A mountain divided
   C. An altar to the LORD
   D. An oasis in the desert

9. Where will the highway out of Egypt end?
   Isaiah 19:23
   A. In Assyria
   B. In Damascus
   C. In Jerusalem
   D. In Rome

10. Whom will God call his people?
    Isaiah 19:25
    A. Assyria
    B. Babylon
    C. Egypt
    D. Israel

11. Whom will God call the work of his hands?
    Isaiah 19:25
    A. Assyria
    B. Babylon
    C. Egypt
    D. Israel

12. Whom will God call his inheritance?

    Isaiah 19:25

    A. Assyria
    B. Babylon
    C. Egypt
    D. Israel

13. Who fought against Ashdod and took it?

    Isaiah 20:1

    A. Baalis
    B. Nahash
    C. Sargon
    D. Tartan

14. Who was the king of Assyria?

    Isaiah 20:1

    A. King Baalis
    B. King Nahash
    C. King Sargon
    D. King Tartan

15. Who was Isaiah's father?

    Isaiah 20:2

    A. Amoz
    B. Joel
    C. Moses
    D. Noah

16. How many years did Isaiah walk naked and barefoot?

    Isaiah 20:3

    A. 2
    B. 3
    C. 4
    D. 5

17. Whom did the LORD tell to go up and attack the desert of the sea?

    Isaiah 21:1–2

    A. Cush
    B. Elam
    C. Moab
    D. Syria

18. Which nation fell and all of its graven images were destroyed?

    Isaiah 21:9

    A. Assyria
    B. Babylon
    C. Egypt
    D. Israel

19. Where were the people from who brought water to the thirsty?

    Isaiah 21:14

    A. Cabul
    B. Ham
    C. Seir
    D. Tema

20. Which nation would fall within a year?

    Isaiah 21:16

    A. India
    B. Kedar
    C. Libya
    D. Media

*Answers on page 768

JULY 26

Lesson 207
Today's Reading: *Isaiah 22–25*
Period of Time: 726–717 BC
Author: Isaiah

1. Which valley was full of stirs?
   Isaiah 22:1–6
   A. Valley of Hinnom
   B. Valley of Jezreel
   C. Valley of vision
   D. Valley of Zared

2. Who bares the quiver with chariots of men and horsemen?
   Isaiah 22:6
   A. Elam
   B. Gaza
   C. Nain
   D. Seba

3. Who uncovered the shield?
   Isaiah 22:6
   A. Hai
   B. Kir
   C. Pai
   D. Sin

4. Which pool's waters in the City of David were gathered together?
   Isaiah 22:9
   A. The lower pool
   B. The new pool
   C. The old pool
   D. The upper pool

5. What was numbered in Jerusalem?
   Isaiah 22:10
   A. Corpses
   B. Houses
   C. Orphans
   D. Widows

6. For which pool did the people of Jerusalem make a ditch between two walls?
   Isaiah 22:11
   A. The lower pool
   B. The new pool
   C. The old pool
   D. The upper pool

7. Who was the treasurer?
   Isaiah 22:15
   A. Sharar
   B. Shebna
   C. Shilhi
   D. Shobal

8. Who is the son of Hilkiah?
   Isaiah 22:20
   A. Eliadah
   B. Eliakim
   C. Eliezer
   D. Eliphaz

9. Which place was known for its ships?
   Isaiah 23:1–14
   A. Bethaven
   B. Neapolis
   C. Pergamos
   D. Tarshish

10. Which one of the following was a mart of nations?
    Isaiah 23:3
    A. Abana
    B. Gihon
    C. Sihor
    D. Ulai

11. Who destroyed the Chaldeans and their land?
    Isaiah 23:13
    A. The Assyrians
    B. The Egyptians
    C. The Grecians
    D. The Hebrews

12. How many years shall Tyre be forgotten?
    Isaiah 23:15
    A. 70
    B. 100
    C. 250
    D. 400

13. Which musical instrument does God say to use to make music in Tyre?

    Isaiah 23:16

    A. Bell
    B. Harp
    C. Pipe
    D. Viol

14. What does the LORD make empty?

    Isaiah 24:1

    A. Earth
    B. Jupiter
    C. Moon
    D. Sun

15. What shall become bitter?

    Isaiah 24:9

    A. Fruit juice
    B. Goat's milk
    C. River water
    D. Strong drink

16. What shall be confounded?

    Isaiah 24:23

    A. Earth
    B. Jupiter
    C. Moon
    D. Sun

17. What shall be ashamed?

    Isaiah 24:23

    A. Earth
    B. Jupiter
    C. Moon
    D. Sun

18. Which shall be served at the LORD's feast on the mountain?

    Isaiah 25:6

    A. Cakes upon the hearth
    B. Lobster stewed with the crab
    C. Savoury meat with bread
    D. Wines on the lees

19. Which nation shall be trodden down as straw for the dunghill?

    Isaiah 25:10

    A. Cush
    B. Edom
    C. Moab
    D. Tyre

20. How shall the LORD spread his hands?

    Isaiah 25:11

    A. Like a carpenter
    B. Like a fowler
    C. Like a miller
    D. Like a swimmer

*Answers on page 768

JULY 27

Lesson 208
Today's Reading: *Isaiah 26–28*
Period of Time: 717 BC
Author: Isaiah

1. What name does Isaiah use for God?
   Isaiah 26:4
   A. LORD Almighty
   B. LORD God
   C. LORD his God
   D. LORD JEHOVAH

2. What did the people do when God chastened them?
   Isaiah 26:16
   A. Cursed Him
   B. Poured out a prayer
   C. Spoke in tongues
   D. Trusted in their money

3. Which dew is like Judah's dew?
   Isaiah 26:19
   A. Dew of fruits
   B. Dew of grass
   C. Dew of herbs
   D. Dew of nuts

4. What shall the earth no longer do?
   Isaiah 26:21
   A. Cover her slain
   B. Hide the sinner
   C. Mourn for the dead
   D. Rotate like a top

5. Which one of the following is the piercing serpent?
   Isaiah 27:1
   A. Apollyon
   B. Behemoth
   C. Leviathan
   D. Satyr

6. Which nation will fill the face of the world with fruit?
   Isaiah 27:6
   A. Assyria
   B. Babylon
   C. Egypt
   D. Israel

7. What shall the stones of the altar be as?
   Isaiah 27:9
   A. Boulders
   B. Chalkstones
   C. Pebbles
   D. Rubble

8. Which musical instrument shall call the outcasts to come and worship?
   Isaiah 27:13
   A. Cymbals
   B. Dulcimer
   C. Sackbut
   D. Trumpet

9. Where were the people ready to perish?
   Isaiah 27:13
   A. Alexandria
   B. Assyria
   C. Athens
   D. Ava

10. Where shall the outcasts of Egypt go to worship?
    Isaiah 27:13
    A. Ethiopia
    B. Jerusalem
    C. Nineveh
    D. Thebes

11. Whose glorious beauty is a fading flower?
    Isaiah 28:1
    A. Ephraim
    B. Judah
    C. Manasseh
    D. Naphtali

12. What are the tables full of?
    Isaiah 28:8
    A. Bread and meat
    B. Candles and linen
    C. Fruit and nuts
    D. Vomit and filthiness

13. How are we to let the word of God speak to us?

    Isaiah 28:10–13

    A. Day upon day
    B. Mile upon mile
    C. Precept upon precept
    D. Sand upon sand

14. Which adjective does Isaiah use to describe the rulers of Jerusalem?

    Isaiah 28:14

    A. Cheerful
    B. Merciful
    C. Remorseful
    D. Scornful

15. Whom did the rulers of Jerusalem make a covenant with?

    Isaiah 28:15

    A. Death
    B. Egypt
    C. Jacob
    D. Satyr

16. What did the LORD lay in Zion?

    Isaiah 28:16

    A. A corner stone
    B. A foundation of sand
    C. A retaining wall
    D. A window of light

17. What was too short for a man?

    Isaiah 28:20

    A. His bed
    B. His fence
    C. His horse
    D. His shoes

18. Which mount shall the LORD rise up like?

    Isaiah 28:21

    A. Mount Ararat
    B. Mount Carmel
    C. Mount Perazim
    D. Mount Tabor

19. What is **not** threshed with a threshing instrument?

    Isaiah 28:27

    A. Barley
    B. Corn
    C. Fitches
    D. Wheat

20. What is a cart wheel **not** to be turned upon?

    Isaiah 28:27

    A. Apples
    B. Cummin
    C. Grapes
    D. Olives

Answers on page 768

Lesson 209
Today's Reading: *Isaiah 29–31*
Period of Time: 717 BC
Author: Isaiah

JULY 28

1. Who dwelled in the city of Ariel?
   Isaiah 29:1
   A. David
   B. Eglon
   C. Mesha
   D. Rezin

2. What shall the speech of Ariel be like?
   Isaiah 29:4
   A. A clap of thunder
   B. A multitude of chariots
   C. A sea rushing to shore
   D. A whisper out of the dust

3. What shall the multitude of all nations that fight against Ariel be like?
   Isaiah 29:7
   A. A braying of donkeys
   B. A dream of a night vision
   C. A mountain melting
   D. A river overflowing its banks

4. What spirit did the LORD pour upon those who fought against Zion?
   Isaiah 29:10
   A. The spirit of bitter jealousy
   B. The spirit of deep sleep
   C. The spirit of foolish liberalism
   D. The spirit of worldly wisdom

5. How were the people being taught to fear the LORD?
   Isaiah 29:13
   A. By the angel of the LORD
   B. By the foreign servants
   C. By the precept of men
   D. By the strange women

6. What shall the turning of things upside down by Judah be like?
   Isaiah 29:16
   A. The carpenter's wood
   B. The husbandman's plow
   C. The miller's wheel
   D. The potter's clay

7. What shall be turned into a fruitful field?
   Isaiah 29:17
   A. Babylon
   B. Heshbon
   C. Lebanon
   D. Shimron

8. What shall the strength of Egypt be to Judah?
   Isaiah 30:2–3
   A. Their breastplate
   B. Their diadem
   C. Their reed
   D. Their shame

9. Where were Pharaoh's princes?
   Isaiah 30:4
   A. Cush
   B. Etam
   C. Phut
   D. Zoan

10. Where did Pharaoh's ambassadors travel to?
    Isaiah 30:6
    A. Hanes
    B. Italy
    C. Spain
    D. Tekoa

11. How shall the LORD break rebellious Judah?
    Isaiah 30:9–14
    A. Like a potter's vessel
    B. Like a wild ass
    C. Like the fallow ground
    D. Like the miller's corn

12. How many of Judah shall flee at the rebuke of one person?

    Isaiah 30:17

    A. 10
    B. 100
    C. 1,000
    D. 10,000

13. What shall Judah see?

    Isaiah 30:20

    A. Thy ancestors
    B. Thy houses
    C. Thy teachers
    D. Thy vineyards

14. What shall Judah discard like a menstruous cloth?

    Isaiah 30:22

    A. Their bandages
    B. Their idols
    C. Their robes
    D. Their swords

15. What shall cause the nations to err?

    Isaiah 30:28

    A. A bridle in their jaws
    B. A fire in their cities
    C. A hole in their walls
    D. A sieve in their homes

16. Which nation will be beaten down by the voice of the LORD?

    Isaiah 30:31

    A. Assyria
    B. Babylon
    C. Egypt
    D. Greece

17. Who is ordained of old?

    Isaiah 30:33

    A. Ashnah
    B. Naaran
    C. Rhodes
    D. Tophet

18. How will the LORD of hosts defend Jerusalem?

    Isaiah 31:5

    A. As adders waiting
    B. As birds flying
    C. As lions roaring
    D. As wolves deceiving

19. Where is the LORD's fire?

    Isaiah 31:9

    A. Zair
    B. Zeba
    C. Zion
    D. Zuph

20. Where is the LORD's furnace?

    Isaiah 31:9

    A. Bethlehem
    B. Jerusalem
    C. Leshem
    D. Sychem

Answers on page 768

JULY 29

Lesson 210
Today's Reading: *Isaiah 32–35*
Period of Time: 717 BC
Author: Isaiah

1. What shall the vile person no longer be called?
   Isaiah 32:5
   A. Carnal
   B. Egotistical
   C. Liberal
   D. Tyrannical

2. What shall no longer be called bountiful?
   Isaiah 32:5
   A. The churl
   B. The midwife
   C. The orchard
   D. The pantry

3. Which two of the following shall become a joy for wild asses?
   Isaiah 32:14
   A. Barns and pastures
   B. Forts and towers
   C. Hills and mountains
   D. Rivers and streams

4. What did the people ask God to be for them every morning?
   Isaiah 33:2
   A. Their arm
   B. Their foot
   C. Their hand
   D. Their mouth

5. How shall Israel gather the spoil?
   Isaiah 33:4
   A. Like ants and squirrels
   B. Like caterpillars and locusts
   C. Like mice and serpents
   D. Like worms and flies

6. What is ashamed and hewn down?
   Isaiah 33:9
   A. Eltekon
   B. Hethlon
   C. Kishion
   D. Lebanon

7. Which one of the following is like a wilderness?
   Isaiah 33:9
   A. Hezron
   B. Kitron
   C. Migron
   D. Sharon

8. Who shall shake off their fruits?
   Isaiah 33:9
   A. Antioch and Philippi
   B. Bashan and Carmel
   C. Sodom and Gomorrah
   D. Tyre and Sidon

9. What shall Israel conceive?
   Isaiah 33:11
   A. Branches
   B. Chaff
   C. Ice
   D. Mud

10. What shall Israel bring forth?
    Isaiah 33:11
    A. Ashes
    B. Pots
    C. Stubble
    D. Water

11. Which burnings shall the people be like?
    Isaiah 33:12
    A. Burnings of cummin
    B. Burnings of hyssop
    C. Burnings of lime
    D. Burnings of pine

12. What does Isaiah say shall **not** pass by Jerusalem?
    Isaiah 33:21
    A. A bride's family
    B. A foreign trader
    C. A gallant ship
    D. A mass of people

13. Where shall the LORD bathe his sword?

    Isaiah 34:5

    A. Heaven
    B. Hebron
    C. Hell
    D. Hermon

14. Where will there be a great slaughter?

    Isaiah 34:6

    A. Land of Arimathaea
    B. Land of Berea
    C. Land of Chaldea
    D. Land of Idumea

15. What shall possess the land after the great slaughter?

    Isaiah 34:11

    A. The adder and the wolf
    B. The cormorant and bittern
    C. The ox and the hart
    D. The stork and the leopard

16. Which two of the following shall inhabit the destroyed palaces and fortresses?

    Isaiah 34:13

    A. Dragons and owls
    B. Goats and camels
    C. Lions and bears
    D. Sheep and dogs

17. Who shall cry to his fellow?

    Isaiah 34:14

    A. The behemoth
    B. The dromedary
    C. The leviathan
    D. The satyr

18. What flower shall the desert blossom like?

    Isaiah 35:1

    A. The carnation
    B. The daffodil
    C. The lily
    D. The rose

19. What shall the lame man leap like?

    Isaiah 35:6

    A. A hart
    B. A kangaroo
    C. A lion
    D. A rabbit

20. What shall the highway be called?

    Isaiah 35:8

    A. Glory road
    B. Highway to heaven
    C. The way of holiness
    D. Victory lane

*Answers on page 768

Lesson 211
Today's Reading: *Isaiah 36–38*
Period of Time: 713–710 BC
Author: Isaiah

JULY 30

1. Who was the king of Assyria?
   Isaiah 36:1
   A. King Nebushasban
   B. King Onesiphorus
   C. King Romamtiezer
   D. King Sennacherib

2. Where was the Rabshakeh when the king of Assyria sent him to Jerusalem?
   Isaiah 36:2
   A. Armenia
   B. Egypt
   C. Lachish
   D. Telassar

3. Who was Hilkiah's son?
   Isaiah 36:3, 36:22
   A. Eliadah
   B. Eliakim
   C. Eliezer
   D. Eliphaz

4. Who was the scribe?
   Isaiah 36:3, 36:22
   A. Gozan
   B. Haran
   C. Rezeph
   D. Shebna

5. Who was Asaph's son?
   Isaiah 36:3, 36:22
   A. Amoz
   B. Joah
   C. Shebna
   D. Thamah

6. Whom did the Rabshakeh call a broken reed?
   Isaiah 36:6
   A. Egypt
   B. Lebanon
   C. Syria
   D. Tyre

7. How many horses did the Rabshakeh promise to give the men of Jerusalem?
   Isaiah 36:8
   A. 1,000
   B. 2,000
   C. 3,000
   D. 4,000

8. Which language did Hezekiah's men ask the Rabshakeh to use?
   Isaiah 36:11
   A. Egyptian
   B. Hebrew
   C. Lebanese
   D. Syrian

9. Who was Isaiah's father?
   Isaiah 37:2
   A. Amoz
   B. Joah
   C. Shebna
   D. Thamah

10. Who was the king of Assyria warring against?
    Isaiah 37:8
    A. Ashnah
    B. Dimnah
    C. Libnah
    D. Timnah

11. Who was the king of Ethiopia?
    Isaiah 37:9
    A. King Baaseiah
    B. King Jecamiah
    C. King Pekahiah
    D. King Tirhakah

12. Where did the king of Assyria destroy the children of Eden?
    Isaiah 37:12
    A. Armenia
    B. Egypt
    C. Lachish
    D. Telassar

13. How many Assyrian soldiers did the angel of the LORD kill?

    Isaiah 37:36

    A. 113,000
    B. 141,000
    C. 185,000
    D. 197,000

14. Where did the king of Assyria go after his great army was destroyed?

    Isaiah 37:37

    A. Elealeh
    B. Lachish
    C. Nineveh
    D. Rithmah

15. Which god did the king of Assyria worship?

    Isaiah 37:38

    A. Anammelech
    B. Bel
    C. Nisroch
    D. Tartak

16. Who was the king of Assyria's sons?

    Isaiah 37:38

    A. Adrammelech and Sharezer
    B. Elimelech and Romamtiezer
    C. Hammelech and Nergalsharezer
    D. Regemmelech and Hadarezer

17. Which land did the king of Assyria's sons flee to after murdering their father?

    Isaiah 37:38

    A. Land of Armenia
    B. Land of Egypt
    C. Land of Lachish
    D. Land of Telassar

18. Who became the next king of Assyria?

    Isaiah 37:38

    A. King Abaddon
    B. King Esarhaddon
    C. King Padon
    D. King Zidon

19. How many years did the LORD add to Hezekiah's life?

    Isaiah 38:5

    A. 10
    B. 15
    C. 20
    D. 25

20. How many degrees backward did the LORD move the shadow on the sun dial?

    Isaiah 38:8

    A. 10 degrees
    B. 15 degrees
    C. 20 degrees
    D. 25 degrees

*Answers on page 768

JULY 31

Lesson 212
Today's Reading: *Isaiah 39–42*
Period of Time: 710–698 BC
Author: Isaiah

1. Who was the king of Babylon?
   Isaiah 39:1
   A. King Adonizedek
   B. King Ben-ha'dad
   C. King Esarhaddon
   D. King Merodach-baladan

2. Why did the king of Babylon send gifts and a letter to Hezekiah?
   Isaiah 39:1
   A. He had bought horses from Hezekiah.
   B. He owed tribute money to Hezekiah.
   C. Hezekiah had recovered from an illness.
   D. Hezekiah wanted to marry his daughter.

3. Why did Isaiah rebuke Hezekiah?
   Isaiah 39:2–7
   A. He committed adultery.
   B. He gave away the holy vessels.
   C. He married a Babylon princess.
   D. He revealed his dominion treasures.

4. What would Hezekiah's sons become?
   Isaiah 39:7
   A. Eunuchs
   B. Judges
   C. Martyrs
   D. Sailors

5. How much punishment did Jerusalem receive for her sins?
   Isaiah 40:2
   A. Double
   B. Triple
   C. Quadruple
   D. Quintuple

6. Which is part of Isaiah 40:3?
   Isaiah 40:3
   A. Be ye holy, for I am holy.
   B. He shall not cry.
   C. Keep silence before me.
   D. Prepare ye the way of the LORD.

7. What did the voice say in Isaiah 40:6?
   Isaiah 40:6
   A. Beg
   B. Cry
   C. Dig
   D. Run

8. What does God call the people of Jerusalem?
   Isaiah 40:7
   A. Brass
   B. Grass
   C. Strass
   D. Trass

9. What does Isaiah state the nations are like?
   Isaiah 40:15
   A. A bubble in a bottle
   B. A cup in a cabinet
   C. A drop of a bucket
   D. A pie of a baker

10. What was **not** sufficient to burn, nor the beasts thereof for a burnt offering?
    Isaiah 40:16
    A. Damascus
    B. Jerusalem
    C. Lebanon
    D. Samaria

11. What does God sit upon?
    Isaiah 40:22
    A. The circle of the earth
    B. The dark of the moon
    C. The eye of the needle
    D. The hump of the camel

12. What are people compared to God?
    Isaiah 40:22
    A. Ants
    B. Grasshoppers
    C. Kine
    D. Sparrows

13. What shall happen to those who wait upon the LORD?

    Isaiah 40:31

    A. They shall mount up with wings as doves.
    B. They shall renew their strength.
    C. They shall run and grow weary.
    D. They shall walk and faint.

14. Where was the righteous man from?

    Isaiah 41:2

    A. The North
    B. The South
    C. The East
    D. The West

15. Whom did the carpenter encourage?

    Isaiah 41:7

    A. The apothecary
    B. The goldsmith
    C. The mason
    D. The physician

16. What will Israel become?

    Isaiah 41:14–15

    A. A cunning red fox
    B. A fire-breathing dragon
    C. A lion stalking desert prey
    D. A new sharp threshing instrument

17. Where will the king come from who shall come upon princes as upon morter?

    Isaiah 41:25

    A. The North
    B. The South
    C. The East
    D. The West

18. What does God call molten images?

    Isaiah 41:29

    A. Brass and misery
    B. Mud and chaos
    C. Stone and darkness
    D. Wind and confusion

19. What does God promise to give the Gentiles?

    Isaiah 42:6

    A. Chaff
    B. Drink
    C. Light
    D. Wheat

20. What will God magnify and make honorable?

    Isaiah 42:21

    A. The law
    B. The meek
    C. The peacemakers
    D. The widows

Answers on page 768

AUGUST 1

Lesson 213

Today's Reading: *Isaiah 43–47*
Period of Time: 710–698 BC
Author: Isaiah

1. Whom did God give for Israel's ransom?
   Isaiah 43:3
   A. Assyria
   B. Babylon
   C. Egypt
   D. Greece

2. Whose cry is in the ships?
   Isaiah 43:14
   A. The Assyrians' cry
   B. The Chaldeans' cry
   C. The Egyptians' cry
   D. The Grecians' cry

3. What are the chariot and horse quenched as?
   Isaiah 43:17
   A. Lime
   B. Runners
   C. Sponges
   D. Tow

4. What does God say Jacob has **not** bought him?
   Isaiah 43:24
   A. Sweet butter
   B. Sweet cane
   C. Sweet honey
   D. Sweet milk

5. Whom has God chosen?
   Isaiah 44:2
   A. Apollyon
   B. Jesurun
   C. Philemon
   D. Stephen

6. How shall Israel spring up?
   Isaiah 44:4
   A. As cedars in mount Lebanon
   B. As lilies in the valley
   C. As springs by the green fields
   D. As willows by the water courses

7. Who forms idols using tongs, hot coals, and hammers?
   Isaiah 44:12
   A. The carpenter
   B. The mason
   C. The smith
   D. The tanner

8. Who carves idols using rulers, lines, and compasses?
   Isaiah 44:13
   A. The carpenter
   B. The mason
   C. The smith
   D. The tanner

9. Whom has the LORD made mad?
   Isaiah 44:24–25
   A. Apothecaries
   B. Bankers
   C. Diviners
   D. Husbandmen

10. Which statement is true concerning God?
    Isaiah 45:5
    A. God is dead.
    B. God is whatever you want him to be.
    C. There are many Gods.
    D. There is no God, but God.

11. What has God done to the heavens?
    Isaiah 45:12
    A. Blackened it
    B. Froze it
    C. Shrunk it
    D. Stretched it

12. Who shall let God's captives go?
    Isaiah 45:1–13
    A. Cyrus
    B. Festus
    C. Lucius
    D. Marcus

13. Why did God create the earth?

    Isaiah 45:18

    A. So he could destroy it
    B. So it could be inhabited
    C. To show his power
    D. To torment man

14. Which idol boweth down in Isaiah 46:1?

    Isaiah 46:1

    A. Bel
    B. Jupiter
    C. Mercurius
    D. Nebo

15. Which idol stoopeth in Isaiah 46:1?

    Isaiah 46:1

    A. Bel
    B. Jupiter
    C. Mercurius
    D. Nebo

16. From which direction shall the ravenous bird come?

    Isaiah 46:11

    A. North
    B. South
    C. East
    D. West

17. What shall the daughter of the Chaldeans no longer be called?

    Isaiah 47:5

    A. Lady of kingdoms
    B. Madam of the night
    C. Maid of honor
    D. Woman of sorrow

18. Which two things shall come upon the Chaldeans in one day?

    Isaiah 47:9

    A. Loss of children and widowhood
    B. Loss of horses and chariots
    C. Loss of palaces and towers
    D. Loss of spearmen and horsemen

19. Which great wickedness does Isaiah say the Chaldeans practiced?

    Isaiah 47:9

    A. Cannibalism
    B. Sorceries
    C. Temperance
    D. Wife-swapping

20. What shall be like stubble?

    Isaiah 47:13–14

    A. Bishops
    B. Elders
    C. Stargazers
    D. Valleys

*Answers on page 768

AUGUST 2

Lesson 214
Today's Reading: *Isaiah 48–51*
Period of Time: 710–698 BC
Author: Isaiah

1. Which name is synonymous with Israel?
   Isaiah 48:1
   A. Glory of Abraham
   B. House of Jacob
   C. Offspring of Isaac
   D. Sons of David

2. What does God say the neck of Israel is like?
   Isaiah 48:4
   A. An empty cup
   B. An iron sinew
   C. An open sepulcher
   D. An unbroken vessel

3. What does God say the brow of Israel is like?
   Isaiah 48:4
   A. Brass
   B. Gold
   C. Iron
   D. Silver

4. In which furnace does the LORD refine Israel?
   Isaiah 48:10
   A. Furnace of affliction
   B. Furnace of conception
   C. Furnace of deception
   D. Furnace of perdition

5. What has the LORD's right hand done in Isaiah 48:13?
   Isaiah 48:13
   A. Dried Israel's tears
   B. Lifted up the widows
   C. Spanned the heavens
   D. Touched man's lips

6. Whom shall the arm of the LORD be upon?
   Isaiah 48:14
   A. The Assyrians
   B. The Chaldeans
   C. The Egyptians
   D. The Grecians

7. What would Israel's peace be like if they had obeyed the LORD's commands?
   Isaiah 48:18
   A. A brook
   B. A lake
   C. A river
   D. A sea

8. What would Israel's righteousness be like had they obeyed the LORD's commands?
   Isaiah 48:18
   A. The bubbles of the brook
   B. The calmness of the river
   C. The ripples of the lake
   D. The waves of the sea

9. What did the LORD make Isaiah into?
   Isaiah 49:1–2
   A. A broken reed
   B. A polished shaft
   C. A sounding trumpet
   D. A violent wind

10. Where did the LORD hide Isaiah?
    Isaiah 49:2
    A. Among the fold
    B. Beneath the clay
    C. In his quiver
    D. Under his wing

11. From which land shall the people come from besides the north and west?
    Isaiah 49:12
    A. Land of Sinim
    B. Land of Tob
    C. Land of Uz
    D. Land of Zuph

12. Who said, "The LORD hath forsaken me, and my Lord hath forgotten me"?

    Isaiah 49:14

    A. Cush
    B. Elam
    C. Tyre
    D. Zion

13. Where has the LORD engraved the names of his people?

    Isaiah 49:16

    A. At the wall of memory
    B. In the holy city of Jerusalem
    C. Near the pearly gates of heaven
    D. Upon the palms of his hands

14. What shall God use to make those who oppress his children drunk?

    Isaiah 49:26

    A. Blood
    B. Milk
    C. Water
    D. Wine

15. Which relative of Israel did God put away?

    Isaiah 50:1

    A. Their daughter
    B. Their father
    C. Their mother
    D. Their son

16. Who does Isaiah say bore Israel?

    Isaiah 51:2

    A. Sarah
    B. Tamar
    C. Vashti
    D. Zipporah

17. What shall the worm eat the reproach of men like?

    Isaiah 51:7–8

    A. Cotton
    B. Leather
    C. Silk
    D. Wool

18. From which cup has Jerusalem drank the dregs?

    Isaiah 51:17

    A. The cup of giving
    B. The cup of laughing
    C. The cup of praising
    D. The cup of trembling

19. Who fainted in Jerusalem?

    Isaiah 51:20

    A. Daughters
    B. Fathers
    C. Sons
    D. Widows

20. What do the sons of Jerusalem lay in the streets like?

    Isaiah 51:20

    A. A small calf among wolves
    B. A wild bull in a net
    C. A young bird in a snare
    D. An old lion in a pit

*Answers on page 768

AUGUST 3

Lesson 215
Today's Reading: *Isaiah 52–56*
Period of Time: 710–698 BC
Author: Isaiah

1. Where had God's people sojourned?
   Isaiah 52:4
   A. Assyria
   B. Egypt
   C. Greece
   D. Rome

2. Who oppressed God's people without cause?
   Isaiah 52:4
   A. Assyria
   B. Cappadocia
   C. Ethiopia
   D. Persia

3. What has the LORD made bare in the eyes of all the nations?
   Isaiah 52:10
   A. Abraham's bosom
   B. David's seed
   C. God's holy arm
   D. Isaiah's land

4. Whose visage was marred more than any man?
   Isaiah 52:13–14
   A. Abraham's nephew's visage
   B. God's servant's visage
   C. Pharaoh's lieutenant's visage
   D. Tyre's captain's visage

5. How shall God's servant grow up before him?
   Isaiah 53:1–2
   A. As a coursing river
   B. As a leavened cake
   C. As a stubborn child
   D. As a tender plant

6. What shall God's servant be called?
   Isaiah 53:3
   A. A disjointed foot
   B. A man of sorrows
   C. A repentant sinner
   D. A wise merchant

7. Why was God's servant wounded?
   Isaiah 53:5
   A. Because he fell asleep
   B. Because he had no shield
   C. Because of his sins
   D. Because of our transgressions

8. Why was God's servant bruised?
   Isaiah 53:5
   A. Because he killed a lion
   B. Because he lacked meat
   C. Because of his skin condition
   D. Because of our iniquities

9. How are we healed?
   Isaiah 53:5
   A. By abstaining from meat
   B. By drinking animal blood
   C. By God's servant's stripes
   D. By trusting in the physician

10. Whom was God's servant numbered with?
    Isaiah 53:12
    A. Debtors
    B. Slaves
    C. Transgressors
    D. Warriors

11. Who has the most children in Isaiah 54:1?
    Isaiah 54:1
    A. The desolate
    B. The married wife
    C. The virgin bride
    D. The widow

12. What shall no longer go over the earth?
    Isaiah 54:9
    A. The angel of death
    B. The dove of peace
    C. The star of David
    D. The waters of Noah

13. What shall the foundations of Jerusalem be made with?

    Isaiah 54:11

    A. Agates
    B. Carbuncles
    C. Diamonds
    D. Sapphires

14. What shall the windows of Jerusalem be made with?

    Isaiah 54:12

    A. Agates
    B. Carbuncles
    C. Diamonds
    D. Sapphires

15. What shall the gates of Jerusalem be made with?

    Isaiah 54:12

    A. Agates
    B. Carbuncles
    C. Diamonds
    D. Sapphires

16. What has God created to destroy?

    Isaiah 54:16

    A. The crusher
    B. The grinder
    C. The waster
    D. The zapper

17. What shall **not** return to God void?

    Isaiah 55:11

    A. God's tears
    B. God's word
    C. The sun
    D. The wind

18. What kind of tree shall come up instead of the briar?

    Isaiah 55:13

    A. The myrtle tree
    B. The pine tree
    C. The sycamore tree
    D. The willow tree

19. What should the eunuch **not** say?

    Isaiah 56:3

    A. "I am a dry tree."
    B. "Look not upon me."
    C. "My strength is gone."
    D. "Thou art faithful."

20. What shall the LORD's house be called?

    Isaiah 56:7

    A. A cottage of refuge
    B. A den of thieves
    C. A house of prayer
    D. A palace of hope

*Answers on page 768

AUGUST 4

Lesson 216
Today's Reading: *Isaiah 57–59*
Period of Time: 710–698 BC
Author: Isaiah

1. What was slain in the valleys under the clifts of the rock?
   Isaiah 57:5
   A. Children
   B. Kings
   C. Prisoners
   D. Traitors

2. What did the people take to the king?
   Isaiah 57:9
   A. Books
   B. Maps
   C. Ointment
   D. Plants

3. Which name does Isaiah use for God?
   Isaiah 57:15
   A. God of the armies of Israel
   B. High and lofty one
   C. Jealous God
   D. Maker

4. What are the wicked like?
   Isaiah 57:20
   A. A bear robbed of her whelps
   B. Clouds without rain
   C. The troubled sea
   D. Wind in the desert

5. How shall the light break forth?
   Isaiah 58:8
   A. As the candle
   B. As the morning
   C. As the rain
   D. As the star

6. What shall spring forth speedily?
   Isaiah 58:8
   A. Babbling brooks
   B. Green herbs
   C. Noonday sun
   D. Thine health

7. What shall the LORD say when the people cry?
   Isaiah 58:9
   A. "Depart from me"
   B. "Here I am"
   C. "I never knew you"
   D. "Save your tears in a bottle"

8. What shall the people be like if they repent?
   Isaiah 58:11
   A. A cutting knife
   B. A precious stone
   C. A shining star
   D. A watered garden

9. What shall the repentant be called?
   Isaiah 58:12
   A. The nation of prophets
   B. The repairer of the breach
   C. The sheep of the hills
   D. The tribe of Judah

10. What of the LORD's is **not** shortened in Isaiah 59:1?
    Isaiah 59:1
    A. His ear
    B. His feet
    C. His hand
    D. His leg

11. What of the LORD's is **not** heavy in Isaiah 59:1?
    Isaiah 59:1
    A. His ear
    B. His feet
    C. His hand
    D. His leg

12. What has become defiled with blood?
    Isaiah 59:3
    A. Israel's fingers
    B. Israel's gates
    C. Israel's hands
    D. Israel's swords

13. What has become defiled with iniquity?

    Isaiah 59:3

    A. Israel's fingers
    B. Israel's gates
    C. Israel's hands
    D. Israel's swords

14. What has Israel put their trust in?

    Isaiah 59:4

    A. Abraham
    B. Moses
    C. Offerings
    D. Vanity

15. What kind of eggs has Israel hatched?

    Isaiah 59:5

    A. Cockatrice eggs
    B. Eagle eggs
    C. Leviathan eggs
    D. Satyr eggs

16. What does Israel roar like?

    Isaiah 59:11

    A. Bears
    B. Lions
    C. Swine
    D. Wolves

17. What does Israel mourn like?

    Isaiah 59:11

    A. Chicks
    B. Doves
    C. Hawks
    D. Ravens

18. What has fallen in the street?

    Isaiah 59:14

    A. Charity
    B. Love
    C. Mercy
    D. Truth

19. What type of garment did the LORD put upon the man?

    Isaiah 59:17

    A. Garments of praise
    B. Garments of righteousness
    C. Garments of salvation
    D. Garments of vengeance

20. Who does Isaiah say shall come to Zion?

    Isaiah 59:20

    A. The Creator
    B. The Deliverer
    C. The Redeemer
    D. The Word

Answers on page 768

Lesson 217

Today's Reading: *Isaiah 60–63*
Period of Time: 710–698 BC
Author: Isaiah

1. What shall the multitude from Midian, Ephah, and Sheba bring?
   Isaiah 60:6
   A. Brass and camels
   B. Gold and incense
   C. Iron and trees
   D. Silver and myrrh

2. Whose flocks shall be gathered together?
   Isaiah 60:7
   A. Flocks of Kedar
   B. Flocks of Media
   C. Flocks of Ramah
   D. Flocks of Tekoa

3. Whose rams shall minister unto thee?
   Isaiah 60:7
   A. Rams of Jaakobah
   B. Rams of Nebaioth
   C. Rams of Patrobas
   D. Rams of Zalmunna

4. Whose ships will be the first to bring sons, gold, and silver to Israel?
   Isaiah 60:9
   A. Ships of Chittim
   B. Ships of Eziongeber
   C. Ships of Galilee
   D. Ships of Tarshish

5. Who shall send the fir, pine, and box tree to Israel?
   Isaiah 60:13
   A. Lachish
   B. Lebanon
   C. Libnah
   D. Lodebar

6. What will Israel receive instead of brass?
   Isaiah 60:17
   A. Gold
   B. Iron
   C. Silver
   D. Wood

7. What will Israel receive instead of iron?
   Isaiah 60:17
   A. Brass
   B. Gold
   C. Silver
   D. Wood

8. What will Israel receive instead of wood?
   Isaiah 60:17
   A. Brass
   B. Gold
   C. Iron
   D. Silver

9. What will Israel receive instead of stones?
   Isaiah 60:17
   A. Gold
   B. Iron
   C. Silver
   D. Wood

10. What shall Israel call the walls?
    Isaiah 60:18
    A. Boaz
    B. Jachin
    C. Praise
    D. Salvation

11. What shall Israel call the gates?
    Isaiah 60:18
    A. Boaz
    B. Jachin
    C. Praise
    D. Salvation

12. What shall a little one become?
    Isaiah 60:22
    A. 10
    B. 100
    C. 1,000
    D. 10,000

13. Which garment will the LORD give to those who have the spirit of heaviness?

    Isaiah 61:3

    A. Garment of Aaron
    B. Garment of heaviness
    C. Garment of Joseph
    D. Garment of praise

14. What shall those who mourn in Zion be called?

    Isaiah 61:3

    A. Branches of holiness
    B. Leaves of salvation
    C. Seeds of glory
    D. Trees of righteousness

15. What has the LORD clothed Isaiah with?

    Isaiah 61:10

    A. Garments of hope
    B. Garments of mercy
    C. Garments of righteousness
    D. Garments of salvation

16. What shall the righteous of Zion be in the hand of God?

    Isaiah 62:3

    A. A future blessing
    B. A gift of liberty
    C. A royal diadem
    D. A signet of faith

17. What shall the righteous of Zion be called?

    Isaiah 62:4

    A. Doeg
    B. Hephzibah
    C. Lebbaeus
    D. Phicol

18. What shall the land of Zion be called?

    Isaiah 62:4

    A. Beulah
    B. Havilah
    C. Maralah
    D. Telmelah

19. Where did the dyed garments come from that the Edomites wore?

    Isaiah 63:1

    A. Bozrah
    B. Daberah
    C. Gomorrah
    D. Ophrah

20. Which color were the Edomite garments?

    Isaiah 63:2

    A. Blue
    B. Purple
    C. Red
    D. White

*Answers on page 769

AUGUST 6

Lesson 218
Today's Reading: *Isaiah 64–66*
Period of Time: 710–698 BC
Author: Isaiah

1. What does Isaiah say Israel's righteousness is like?
   Isaiah 64:6
   A. Filthy rags
   B. Holy incense
   C. Olive oil
   D. Temple treasures

2. What has Zion become?
   Isaiah 64:10
   A. A desert
   B. A mountain
   C. A stream
   D. A wilderness

3. What was Israel guilty of eating?
   Isaiah 65:4
   A. Leavened bread
   B. Meat offered to idols
   C. Swine's flesh
   D. The ossifrage

4. Who shall be a fold of flocks?
   Isaiah 65:10
   A. Bithron
   B. Sharon
   C. Takeron
   D. Ziphron

5. In which valley shall the herds lie down?
   Isaiah 65:10
   A. Valley of Achor
   B. Valley of Craftsmen
   C. Valley of Salt
   D. Valley of Vision

6. How many years shall the child live?
   Isaiah 65:20
   A. 60
   B. 80
   C. 100
   D. 120

7. What shall the days of God's people be like?
   Isaiah 65:22
   A. The days of a bird
   B. The days of a mountain
   C. The days of a snake
   D. The days of a tree

8. Who does Isaiah say shall feed together?
   Isaiah 65:25
   A. The dog and the cat
   B. The fox and the hen
   C. The ox and the lion
   D. The wolf and the lamb

9. What does Isaiah say shall eat straw like the bullock?
   Isaiah 65:25
   A. The bear
   B. The lion
   C. The swine
   D. The unicorn

10. Which one of the following shall be the serpent's meat?
    Isaiah 65:25
    A. Dust
    B. Eggs
    C. Fruit
    D. Nuts

11. What is God's throne?
    Isaiah 66:1
    A. Heaven
    B. Earth
    C. Jerusalem
    D. Zion

12. What is God's footstool?
    Isaiah 66:1
    A. Heaven
    B. Earth
    C. Jerusalem
    D. Zion

13. What will killing an ox be similar to killing?
    Isaiah 66:3
    A. A boar
    B. A hornet
    C. A man
    D. An eagle

14. What will sacrificing a lamb be similar to?
    Isaiah 66:3
    A. Cutting off a dog's neck
    B. Destroying an enemy
    C. Offering a turtle dove
    D. Slaying a dragon

15. What will offering an oblation be similar to offering?
    Isaiah 66:3
    A. Offering firstfruits
    B. Offering kidneys
    C. Offering swine's blood
    D. Offering young kine

16. What will offering incense be similar to?
    Isaiah 66:3
    A. Aiding an orphan
    B. Blessing an idol
    C. Offering a goat
    D. Sacrificing a ram

17. What will the LORD use to punish the unrighteous?
    Isaiah 66:4
    A. Asps
    B. Delusions
    C. Hornets
    D. Plagues

18. What will the LORD's peace be like for those who love Jerusalem?
    Isaiah 66:12
    A. A horse
    B. A flower
    C. A pasture
    D. A river

19. What shall the glory of the Gentiles be like?
    Isaiah 66:12
    A. A babbling brook
    B. A dark lake
    C. A flowing stream
    D. A swift river

20. How shall the bones of the righteous flourish?
    Isaiah 66:14
    A. Like a field
    B. Like a raven
    C. Like an eagle
    D. Like an herb

*Answers on page 769

Lesson 219
Today's Reading: *Jeremiah 1–3*
Period of Time: 629–610 BC
Author: Jeremiah

AUGUST 7

1. Who was Jeremiah's father?
   Jeremiah 1:1
   A. Benaiah
   B. Hilkiah
   C. Isshiah
   D. Maaziah

2. Who was one of the kings of Judah during the days of Jeremiah?
   Jeremiah 1:2–3
   A. King Baasha
   B. King Jeroboam
   C. King Nadab
   D. King Zedekiah

3. In which month was Jerusalem captured and its people taken away?
   Jeremiah 1:3
   A. 4th
   B. 5th
   C. 6th
   D. 7th

4. From which direction would evil come and break forth upon the inhabitants of the land?
   Jeremiah 1:14
   A. North
   B. South
   C. East
   D. West

5. Who broke the crown of Jerusalem's head?
   Jeremiah 2:16
   A. Core and Sosthenes
   B. Kish and Bethgader
   C. Noph and Tahapanes
   D. Phut and Meshullam

6. What did Jerusalem use in addition to soap to wash with?
   Jeremiah 2:22
   A. Hyssop
   B. Nitre
   C. Slime
   D. Tow

7. What does Jeremiah call the people of Judah?
   Jeremiah 2:23
   A. A blind bear
   B. A loving hind
   C. A swift dromedary
   D. A violent ox

8. Whom did Judah's sword devour like a destroying lion?
   Jeremiah 2:30
   A. Predators
   B. Priests
   C. Princes
   D. Prophets

9. Where was the blood of the poor innocents found?
   Jeremiah 2:34
   A. In bottles
   B. In cisterns
   C. In rivers
   D. In skirts

10. Which nation will Judah be ashamed of?
    Jeremiah 2:36
    A. Egypt
    B. Media
    C. Persia
    D. Rome

11. How has Judah polluted the land?
    Jeremiah 3:2
    A. As the Arabian in the wilderness
    B. As the fiery flying serpent
    C. As the Pharaoh of Egypt
    D. As the thief in the night

12. What did the LORD use to punish Judah?

    Jeremiah 3:3

    A. Droughts
    B. Floods
    C. Locusts
    D. Plagues

13. What did Jeremiah claim Judah had?

    Jeremiah 3:3

    A. A beggar's cup
    B. A cripple's feet
    C. A thief's hand
    D. A whore's forehead

14. Who was a king of Judah?

    Jeremiah 3:6

    A. King Jashen
    B. King Jehudi
    C. King Josiah
    D. King Justus

15. Who played the harlot in addition to Judah?

    Jeremiah 3:8

    A. Egypt
    B. Israel
    C. Libya
    D. Sidon

16. Who shall feed Judah with knowledge and understanding?

    Jeremiah 3:15

    A. Bishops
    B. Lawyers
    C. Pastors
    D. Scribes

17. What shall the people no longer remember?

    Jeremiah 3:16

    A. The ark of the covenant
    B. The book of the law
    C. The sword of the LORD
    D. The tree of knowledge

18. What shall Jerusalem be called?

    Jeremiah 3:17

    A. The bridge to the world
    B. The end of the road
    C. The jackal's den
    D. The throne of the LORD

19. Who shall walk together from the land of the north?

    Jeremiah 3:18

    A. Assyria and Babylon
    B. Judah and Israel
    C. Lebanon and Syria
    D. Tyre and Zidon

20. What covereth Judah?

    Jeremiah 3:25

    A. The hand of the LORD
    B. The wings of an angel
    C. Their confusion
    D. Their sheep

*Answers on page 769

AUGUST 8

Lesson 220
Today's Reading: *Jeremiah 4–6*
Period of Time: 629–610 BC
Author: Jeremiah

1. What are the men of Judah and Jerusalem **not** to sow among?
   Jeremiah 4:3
   A. Corn
   B. Rocks
   C. Thorns
   D. Wheat

2. From which direction shall evil come?
   Jeremiah 4:6
   A. North
   B. South
   C. East
   D. West

3. What has come up from his thicket?
   Jeremiah 4:7
   A. The dragon
   B. The lion
   C. The ox
   D. The ram

4. Who is on his way to Judah and Jerusalem?
   Jeremiah 4:7
   A. The avenger of the Egyptians
   B. The bruiser of the Babylonians
   C. The crusher of the Persians
   D. The destroyer of the Gentiles

5. From where does the voice proclaim that watchers come from a far country?
   Jeremiah 4:15–16
   A. Benjamin
   B. Dan
   C. Sidon
   D. Tyre

6. What does God call the children of Israel and Judah?
   Jeremiah 4:22
   A. Deaf
   B. Green
   C. Sottish
   D. Turbulent

7. What color shall the heavens be?
   Jeremiah 4:28
   A. Black
   B. Crimson
   C. Purple
   D. Red

8. Which color were the clothes of the men of Judah and Jerusalem?
   Jeremiah 4:30
   A. Black
   B. Crimson
   C. Purple
   D. White

9. What shall spoil the people of Jerusalem in the evening?
   Jeremiah 5:6
   A. A bear
   B. A leopard
   C. A pygarg
   D. A wolf

10. What shall watch over the cities of Judah?
    Jeremiah 5:6
    A. A bear
    B. A leopard
    C. A pygarg
    D. A wolf

11. What does God say the men of Judah were like?
    Jeremiah 5:7–8
    A. Fed horses in the morning
    B. Gabby hyenas at noon
    C. Lame goats in the evening
    D. Washed swine at night

12. What does Jeremiah say the men of Judah have done to the LORD?

    Jeremiah 5:12

    A. Belied him
    B. Esteemed him
    C. Praised him
    D. Revered him

13. What shall the prophets become?

    Jeremiah 5:13

    A. Dirt
    B. Fire
    C. Sand
    D. Wind

14. What will God make the people of Jerusalem?

    Jeremiah 5:14

    A. Dust
    B. Grass
    C. Stone
    D. Wood

15. Where is Benjamin to blow the trumpet?

    Jeremiah 6:1

    A. Meroz
    B. Punon
    C. Tekoa
    D. Zimri

16. Where is Benjamin to set up a sign of fire?

    Jeremiah 6:1

    A. Beth-haccerem
    B. Beth-jeshimoth
    C. Beth-shemesh
    D. Beth-tappuah

17. What has the LORD likened the daughter of Zion to?

    Jeremiah 6:2

    A. A bold and beautiful lady
    B. A comely and delicate woman
    C. A little and profane maid
    D. A weak and soft wife

18. What shall happen to the remnant of Israel?

    Jeremiah 6:9

    A. They shall be bruised as bread corn.
    B. They shall be crushed like grapes.
    C. They shall be gleaned as a vine.
    D. They shall be harvested as cane.

19. Where shall Israel find rest for their souls?

    Jeremiah 6:16

    A. On the broad ways
    B. On the new trails
    C. On the old paths
    D. On the rocky roads

20. What shall men call the people of Israel?

    Jeremiah 6:30

    A. Evil brass
    B. Fool's gold
    C. Pig iron
    D. Reprobate silver

*Answers on page 769

Lesson 221
Today's Reading: *Jeremiah 7–9*
Period of Time: 629–610 BC
Author: Jeremiah

AUGUST 9

1. Where did God order Jeremiah to stand?
   Jeremiah 7:2
   A. Along the banks of the river of Jordan
   B. Between the temple altars
   C. In the gate of the LORD's house
   D. Upon the hills of Megiddo

2. Which false god did the people burn incense to?
   Jeremiah 7:9
   A. Baal
   B. Chemosh
   C. Dagon
   D. Nibhaz

3. Whose whole seed did the LORD cast out?
   Jeremiah 7:15
   A. Benjamin's seed
   B. Ephraim's seed
   C. Naphtali's seed
   D. Simeon's seed

4. Which queen did the people of Jerusalem make cakes for?
   Jeremiah 7:18
   A. Queen of Ethiopia
   B. Queen of heaven
   C. Queen of queens
   D. Queen of Sheba

5. What did God order the people of Jerusalem to eat?
   Jeremiah 7:21
   A. Corn
   B. Flesh
   C. Grapes
   D. Pulse

6. What did God order the people of Jerusalem to do?
   Jeremiah 7:29
   A. Buy bread out of the bakers' street
   B. Cut off their hair
   C. Dress in sackcloth
   D. Wash at noon in the river of Jordan

7. What was the name of the high place the people built to worship their false god?
   Jeremiah 7:31
   A. Geshur
   B. Keilah
   C. Tophet
   D. Zanoah

8. In which valley were children sacrificed using fires?
   Jeremiah 7:31
   A. Valley of Achor
   B. Valley of Charashim
   C. Valley of Eshcol
   D. Valley of the son of Hinnom

9. What shall Judah's enemies spread before the sun and moon?
   Jeremiah 8:1–2
   A. Bones
   B. Idols
   C. Rocks
   D. Seeds

10. Which bird is mentioned for knowing her appointed time?
    Jeremiah 8:7
    A. The dove
    B. The eagle
    C. The raven
    D. The stork

11. What did the LORD give the people of Judah to drink?

    Jeremiah 8:14, 9:15

    A. Bitter goat's milk
    B. Sweet wine
    C. Tears of joy
    D. Water of gall

12. Where was the snorting of horses heard from?

    Jeremiah 8:16

    A. Asshur
    B. Dan
    C. Gad
    D. Issachar

13. What will God send among the people of Judah?

    Jeremiah 8:17

    A. Cockatrices and serpents
    B. Dragons and scorpions
    C. Satyrs and bears
    D. Unicorns and lions

14. What color does Jeremiah say he is?

    Jeremiah 8:21

    A. Black
    B. Red
    C. White
    D. Yellow

15. What will every neighbor walk with?

    Jeremiah 9:4

    A. Canes
    B. Merchants
    C. Princes
    D. Slanders

16. What does the LORD say the people of Judah's tongues are like?

    Jeremiah 9:8

    A. An arrow
    B. Good medicine
    C. Poison of vipers
    D. Sweet honeycombs

17. Which city shall become a den of dragons?

    Jeremiah 9:11

    A. Bethlehem
    B. Caesarea
    C. Jerusalem
    D. Samaria

18. Whose ways did the fathers teach their children?

    Jeremiah 9:14

    A. Aaron's ways
    B. Adam's ways
    C. Baalim's ways
    D. Baruch's ways

19. What will God feed the people of Judah?

    Jeremiah 9:15

    A. Bread
    B. Corn
    C. Manna
    D. Wormwood

20. What was one of the uncircumcised nations mentioned in Jeremiah 9:26?

    Jeremiah 9:26

    A. Cush
    B. Eber
    C. Moab
    D. Tyre

Answers on page 769

AUGUST 10

Lesson 222
Today's Reading: *Jeremiah 10–12*
Period of Time: 629–610 BC
Author: Jeremiah

1. What does Jeremiah tell the people **not** to be dismayed at?
   Jeremiah 10:2
   A. The lack of meat
   B. The number of Assyrian horses
   C. The signs of heaven
   D. The way of the LORD

2. Which tree is the carved upright idol like?
   Jeremiah 10:3–5
   A. The cedar tree
   B. The elm tree
   C. The oak tree
   D. The palm tree

3. Where are the plates covered with silver from?
   Jeremiah 10:9
   A. Asia
   B. Corinth
   C. Spain
   D. Tarshish

4. Where is the gold from?
   Jeremiah 10:9
   A. Gaash
   B. Kedar
   C. Paran
   D. Uphaz

5. Which colors are in the clothing of the house of Israel?
   Jeremiah 10:9
   A. Blue and purple
   B. Gold and silver
   C. Orange and yellow
   D. Scarlet and black

6. What did the LORD use to make the earth?
   Jeremiah 10:12
   A. His angel
   B. His discretion
   C. His power
   D. His wisdom

7. What did the LORD use to establish the world?
   Jeremiah 10:12
   A. His angel
   B. His discretion
   C. His power
   D. His wisdom

8. What did the LORD use to stretch out the heavens?
   Jeremiah 10:12
   A. His angel
   B. His discretion
   C. His power
   D. His wisdom

9. Who has become brutish and have **not** sought the LORD?
   Jeremiah 10:21
   A. Bishops
   B. Missionaries
   C. Pastors
   D. Shepherds

10. Which noise has come?
    Jeremiah 10:22
    A. The noise of the bruit
    B. The noise of the furnace
    C. The noise of the rampage
    D. The noise of the waterfall

11. From which country shall a great commotion come?
    Jeremiah 10:22
    A. North country
    B. South country
    C. East country
    D. West country

12. What shall inhabit the cities of Judah?

    Jeremiah 10:22
    A. Bulls
    B. Camels
    C. Dragons
    D. Foxes

13. From which land did God bring Israel out of?

    Jeremiah 11:4
    A. Land of Canaan
    B. Land of Egypt
    C. Land of Lebanon
    D. Land of Macedonia

14. How does God describe the land promised to Israel?

    Jeremiah 11:5
    A. Brimming with drink and meat
    B. Flowing with milk and honey
    C. Spilling with silver and gold
    D. Teaming with horses and grass

15. Whom did Israel burn incense to?

    Jeremiah 11:13, 11:17
    A. Baal
    B. Chemosh
    C. Dagon
    D. Nebo

16. Where were the men from that told Jeremiah **not** to prophesy in the name of the LORD?

    Jeremiah 11:21–23
    A. Anathoth
    B. Manasseh
    C. Syracuse
    D. Thyatira

17. What is Jeremiah's heritage like?

    Jeremiah 12:8–9
    A. A greyhound in the field
    B. A lion in the forest
    C. A raven in the nest
    D. A spider in the palace

18. Which bird are the other birds against?

    Jeremiah 12:9
    A. A black bird
    B. A blue bird
    C. A speckled bird
    D. A white bird

19. Who destroyed the LORD's vineyard?

    Jeremiah 12:10
    A. Many noblemen
    B. Many pastors
    C. Many rulers
    D. Many servants

20. What has Judah sown but reaped thorns instead?

    Jeremiah 12:13
    A. Cucumbers
    B. Garlic
    C. Melons
    D. Wheat

*Answers on page 769

AUGUST 11

Lesson 223
Today's Reading: *Jeremiah 13–15*
Period of Time: 629–610 BC
Author: Jeremiah

1. What did the LORD tell Jeremiah **not** to do with the girdle?
   Jeremiah 13:1
   A. Cast it to the enemy
   B. Get it dirty
   C. Put it into water
   D. Wear it upon his loins

2. Near which river did Jeremiah hide the girdle?
   Jeremiah 13:4–5
   A. River Euphrates
   B. River Jabbok
   C. River Kishon
   D. River Ulai

3. What happened to the girdle?
   Jeremiah 13:7
   A. It became marred.
   B. It shined like lightning.
   C. It turned to stone.
   D. It was stolen.

4. What will fill every bottle?
   Jeremiah 13:12
   A. Honey
   B. Milk
   C. Tears
   D. Wine

5. What will the LORD fill all the inhabitants of Judah with?
   Jeremiah 13:13
   A. Drunkenness
   B. Lies
   C. Pride
   D. Terror

6. What was Jeremiah to tell the king and queen?
   Jeremiah 13:18
   A. "Flee while you can."
   B. "Humble yourselves."
   C. "Lend to the poor."
   D. "Stand and deliver."

7. From which direction shall the armies come to destroy Judah?
   Jeremiah 13:20
   A. North
   B. South
   C. East
   D. West

8. Whom is Jeremiah referring to when he asks if it can change the color of its skin?
   Jeremiah 13:23
   A. The Assyrian
   B. The Ethiopian
   C. The Grecian
   D. The Libyan

9. What was the land of Judah going through?
   Jeremiah 14:1
   A. A bountiful harvest
   B. A dearth
   C. A great earthquake
   D. An eclipse

10. What had become black?
    Jeremiah 14:2
    A. The gates of Judah
    B. The moon at night
    C. The noon day sun
    D. The red heifer

11. What did the nobles send their little ones to find?
    Jeremiah 14:3
    A. Asses
    B. Eggs
    C. Flowers
    D. Water

12. How does the LORD describe the land?
    Jeremiah 14:4
    A. Acrid
    B. Barren
    C. Chapt
    D. Desolate

13. What snuffed up the wind like dragons?

    Jeremiah 14:6

    A. Bear whelps
    B. Old sheep
    C. Wild asses
    D. Young calves

14. Who prophesied lies in the LORD's name?

    Jeremiah 14:14

    A. Astrologers
    B. Magicians
    C. Prophets
    D. Witches

15. Which two people does the LORD say stood before him?

    Jeremiah 15:1

    A. Adam and Eve
    B. Joshua and Caleb
    C. Moses and Samuel
    D. Noah and Ham

16. How many kinds did the LORD say he would send to destroy Judah?

    Jeremiah 15:3

    A. 1
    B. 2
    C. 3
    D. 4

17. Who was the king of Judah?

    Jeremiah 15:4

    A. King Baasha
    B. King Hoshea
    C. King Jehoahaz
    D. King Manasseh

18. Where will the LORD fan them with a fan?

    Jeremiah 15:7

    A. At the coliseum
    B. In the gates of the land
    C. Near the Egyptian sea
    D. Upon mount Pisgah

19. What had increased above the sands of the seas?

    Jeremiah 15:8

    A. Children
    B. Dogs
    C. Horses
    D. Widows

20. What will Jeremiah be to the people of Judah?

    Jeremiah 15:20

    A. A basket filled with fruit
    B. A fenced brasen wall
    C. A light unto their path
    D. A well of fresh water

*Answers on page 769

Lesson 224
Today's Reading: *Jeremiah 16–18*
Period of Time: 629–610 BC
Author: Jeremiah

AUGUST 12

1. What did God forbid Jeremiah to do?
   Jeremiah 16:2
   A. Bathe
   B. Eat
   C. Marry
   D. Speak

2. What was the name of the first house Jeremiah was forbidden to enter?
   Jeremiah 16:5
   A. House of evil
   B. House of joy
   C. House of love
   D. House of mourning

3. Why did some of the people cut themselves and shave their heads bald?
   Jeremiah 16:6
   A. It was part of their lamentation.
   B. The blood foreshadowed Christ.
   C. They were devoted to God.
   D. To prove they could withstand pain.

4. What was the name of the second house Jeremiah was forbidden to enter?
   Jeremiah 16:8
   A. House of feasting
   B. House of laughter
   C. House of pain
   D. House of visions

5. Where did the children of Israel live before entering the Promised Land?
   Jeremiah 16:14
   A. Egypt
   B. Greece
   C. Italy
   D. Spain

6. Which two of the following workers will God send for?
   Jeremiah 16:16
   A. Bakers and stewards
   B. Carpenters and masons
   C. Fishers and hunters
   D. Priests and prophets

7. What type of pen was used to write the sin of Judah?
   Jeremiah 17:1
   A. A pen of blood
   B. A pen of dung
   C. A pen of iron
   D. A pen of mud

8. What was on the point used to write the sin of Judah?
   Jeremiah 17:1
   A. A diamond
   B. A ruby
   C. A sapphire
   D. An emerald

9. What shall a man be like that trusteth in man?
   Jeremiah 17:5–6
   A. The fish in the seas
   B. The heath in the desert
   C. The rams in the mountains
   D. The stars in the heavens

10. What shall a man be like that trusteth in the LORD?
    Jeremiah 17:7–8
    A. A gardener in a meadow
    B. A home built on sand
    C. A strong horse fit for battle
    D. A tree planted by the waters

11. What is deceitful above all things?

    Jeremiah 17:9

    A. The eye
    B. The heart
    C. The lips
    D. The tongue

12. Which bird sitteth on eggs and hatcheth them **not**?

    Jeremiah 17:11

    A. The dove
    B. The eagle
    C. The osprey
    D. The partridge

13. What does Jeremiah call the LORD?

    Jeremiah 17:13

    A. The brook of great peace
    B. The fountain of living waters
    C. The river of abundant joy
    D. The stream of eternal life

14. Where did the LORD tell Jeremiah to stand?

    Jeremiah 17:19

    A. By the pool of Siloam
    B. In all the gates of Jerusalem
    C. Near the mount of Olives
    D. Upon the temple mount

15. Which day was to be hallowed?

    Jeremiah 17:22

    A. Friday
    B. Sabbath
    C. Thursday
    D. Wednesday

16. Whose house did God send Jeremiah to?

    Jeremiah 18:2

    A. The carpenter's house
    B. The king's house
    C. The potter's house
    D. The scribe's house

17. What did the people of Judah say?

    Jeremiah 18:12

    A. God is our hope.
    B. Hope will save us.
    C. No hope, no God.
    D. There is no hope.

18. Which place mentioned in Jeremiah 18:14 contained snow?

    Jeremiah 18:14

    A. Lebanon
    B. Migron
    C. Punon
    D. Sharon

19. How shall the LORD scatter the rebellious people?

    Jeremiah 18:17

    A. Like a north wind
    B. Like a south wind
    C. Like a west wind
    D. Like an east wind

20. Which one of the following statements did Jeremiah say?

    Jeremiah 18:18–20

    A. Forgive them, for they know not what they do.
    B. It is better to give than to receive.
    C. They have digged a pit for my soul.
    D. We shall overcome.

Answers on page 769

August 13

Lesson 225
Today's Reading: *Jeremiah 19–22*
Period of Time: 629–610 BC
Author: Jeremiah

1. What did the LORD tell Jeremiah to get?
   Jeremiah 19:1
   A. A carpenter's plumb line
   B. A miller's stone wheel
   C. A potter's earthen bottle
   D. A scribe's writing tablet

2. Which gate was the valley of the son of Hinnom by?
   Jeremiah 19:2
   A. North gate
   B. South gate
   C. East gate
   D. West gate

3. Which false god did Judah offer their children to?
   Jeremiah 19:5
   A. Baal
   B. Nisroch
   C. Rimmon
   D. Tartak

4. Which one of the following is another name for the valley of the son of Hinnom?
   Jeremiah 19:6
   A. Tob
   B. Tochen
   C. Togarmah
   D. Tophet

5. What would the valley of the son of Hinnom be called?
   Jeremiah 19:6
   A. Valley of dearth
   B. Valley of famine
   C. Valley of peace
   D. Valley of slaughter

6. Who was Pashur's father?
   Jeremiah 20:1
   A. Immer
   B. Nebuchadnezzar
   C. Shallum
   D. Zephaniah

7. What did Pashur do to Jeremiah?
   Jeremiah 20:2
   A. Cut off his foot
   B. Dropped him into a pit
   C. Made him governor
   D. Put him in stocks

8. What would Pashur be called?
   Jeremiah 20:3
   A. Berodachbaladan
   B. Chushan-rishatha'im
   C. Magormissabib
   D. Shethar-boznai

9. What was the word in Jeremiah's heart like?
   Jeremiah 20:9
   A. A burning fire in his bones
   B. A corner stone that was rejected
   C. A lamp unto his feet
   D. A room filled with books

10. Who was Pashur's father?
    Jeremiah 21:1
    A. Malchiah
    B. Melatiah
    C. Melchiah
    D. Mikneiah

11. Who was the son of Maaseiah?
    Jeremiah 21:1
    A. Immer
    B. Nebuchadnezzar
    C. Shallum
    D. Zephaniah

12. Who was the king of Babylon?

    Jeremiah 21:2

    A. King Immer
    B. King Nebuchadnezzar
    C. King Shallum
    D. King Zephaniah

13. What was the king's house of Judah unto the LORD?

    Jeremiah 22:6

    A. Gilead
    B. Lebanon
    C. Michmash
    D. Tahpanhes

14. What was the king's house of Judah the head of?

    Jeremiah 22:6

    A. Gilead
    B. Lebanon
    C. Michmash
    D. Tahpanhes

15. Which choice trees would be cut down and cast into the fire?

    Jeremiah 22:7

    A. Cedars
    B. Oaks
    C. Palms
    D. Sycamores

16. Who was a son of Josiah—king of Judah?

    Jeremiah 22:11

    A. Immer
    B. Nebuchadnezzar
    C. Shallum
    D. Zephaniah

17. What shall the unrighteous paint his house with?

    Jeremiah 22:13–14

    A. Blackberries
    B. Indigo
    C. Juniper
    D. Vermilion

18. Who was also a son of Josiah—king of Judah?

    Jeremiah 22:18

    A. Jehohanan
    B. Jehoiakim
    C. Jehoiarib
    D. Jehonadab

19. Which two places did Jeremiah tell Israel to go to and cry?

    Jeremiah 22:20

    A. Bethlehem and Jerusalem
    B. Lebanon and Bashan
    C. Sodom and Gomorrah
    D. Tyre and Sidon

20. Who was the father of Coniah?

    Jeremiah 22:24

    A. Jehohanan
    B. Jehoiakim
    C. Jehoiarib
    D. Jehonadab

*Answers on page 769

AUGUST 14

Lesson 226
Today's Reading: *Jeremiah 23–24*
Period of Time: 610 BC
Author: Jeremiah

1. Who destroyed and scattered the LORD's sheep?
   Jeremiah 23:1
   A. Bishops
   B. Kings
   C. Pastors
   D. Shepherds

2. Whom shall the LORD set over his sheep?
   Jeremiah 23:4
   A. Bishops
   B. Kings
   C. Pastors
   D. Shepherds

3. Who does the LORD say will execute judgment and justice in the earth?
   Jeremiah 23:5–6
   A. THE ALMIGHTY FATHER
   B. THE LORD OUR RIGHTEOUSNESS
   C. THE PROPHET OF GOD
   D. THE SERVANT OF THE LORD

4. What does Jeremiah say he feels like?
   Jeremiah 23:9
   A. A broken man
   B. A condemned man
   C. A drunken man
   D. An ill man

5. What does Jeremiah say the land is full of?
   Jeremiah 23:10
   A. Adulterers
   B. Blasphemers
   C. Coveters
   D. Murderers

6. Which two of the following are profane?
   Jeremiah 23:11
   A. The butcher and baker
   B. The judge and lawyer
   C. The king and general
   D. The prophet and priest

7. What shall the ways of the wicked be like?
   Jeremiah 23:12
   A. A drop of water in the desert
   B. Raging fires across the land
   C. Slippery ways in the darkness
   D. The bitter taste of wormwood

8. Where has Jeremiah seen folly?
   Jeremiah 23:13
   A. Samaria
   B. Secacah
   C. Sibraim
   D. Succoth

9. Whom did the people prophesy in?
   Jeremiah 23:13
   A. Baal
   B. Nisroch
   C. Rimmon
   D. Tartak

10. Which two cities does the LORD compare the prophets of Jerusalem to?
    Jeremiah 23:14
    A. Alexandria and Memphis
    B. Damascus and Lebanon
    C. Ephesus and Thessalonica
    D. Sodom and Gomorrah

11. What will the LORD feed the prophets of Jerusalem?
    Jeremiah 23:15
    A. Chaff
    B. Manna
    C. Quail
    D. Wormwood

12. Which drink will the LORD give the prophets of Jerusalem?
    Jeremiah 23:15
    A. Juice of limes
    B. Tears of bitterness
    C. Water of gall
    D. Wine of affliction

13. What has gone forth in a fury?

    Jeremiah 23:19

    A. A flood
    B. A pestilence
    C. A whirlwind
    D. An earthquake

14. According to Jeremiah 23:29, what is the word of the LORD like?

    Jeremiah 23:29

    A. A bow and a quiver
    B. A fire and a hammer
    C. A rock and a cup
    D. A sword and a buckler

15. What shall every man's word become?

    Jeremiah 23:36

    A. His bond
    B. His burden
    C. His fruit
    D. His peace

16. How many baskets were set before the temple of the LORD?

    Jeremiah 24:1

    A. 2
    B. 7
    C. 10
    D. 12

17. What did the baskets contain?

    Jeremiah 24:1–2

    A. Bread
    B. Figs
    C. Fish
    D. Money

18. Who was the king of Babylon?

    Jeremiah 24:1

    A. King Nebuchadrezzar
    B. King Nephishesim
    C. King Nergalsharezer
    D. King Nethaneel

19. Who was the son of Jehoiakim?

    Jeremiah 24:1

    A. Jeberechiah
    B. Jeconiah
    C. Jedidiah
    D. Jehizkiah

20. Who was a king of Judah?

    Jeremiah 24:8

    A. King Bakbukiah
    B. King Hilkiah
    C. King Jehizkiah
    D. King Zedekiah

*Answers on page 769

Lesson 227
Today's Reading: *Jeremiah 25–27*
Period of Time: 607 BC
Author: Jeremiah

AUGUST 15

1. During which year of King Jehoiakim's reign did the word come to Jeremiah concerning the people of Judah?
   Jeremiah 25:1
   A. 2nd year
   B. 3rd year
   C. 4th year
   D. 5th year

2. Who was King Jehoiakim's father?
   Jeremiah 25:1
   A. King Isaiah
   B. King Josiah
   C. King Neriah
   D. King Uzziah

3. Who was the king of Babylon?
   Jeremiah 25:1
   A. King Joshbekashah
   B. King Mephibosheth
   C. King Nebuchadrezzar
   D. King Tiglath-pilneser

4. Who was King Amon's son?
   Jeremiah 25:3
   A. King Isaiah
   B. King Josiah
   C. King Neriah
   D. King Uzziah

5. How many years did Jeremiah rise early to speak to the people?
   Jeremiah 25:3
   A. 3
   B. 5
   C. 6
   D. 10

6. How many years would Judah serve the king of Babylon?
   Jeremiah 25:11
   A. 10
   B. 30
   C. 50
   D. 70

7. Whom will the LORD punish?
   Jeremiah 25:12
   A. The Chaldeans
   B. The Egyptians
   C. The Grecians
   D. The Macedonians

8. What did Jeremiah take from the LORD's hand?
   Jeremiah 25:17
   A. A cup
   B. A nail
   C. A rose
   D. A sword

9. Who shall have no way to flee?
   Jeremiah 25:35
   A. The shepherds
   B. The tent makers
   C. The vine dressers
   D. The woodsmen

10. Where did the LORD tell Jeremiah to stand?
    Jeremiah 26:2
    A. The court of the LORD's house
    B. The holiest place in the temple
    C. The most holy place in the temple
    D. The porch of Solomon

11. What will the temple of God become like?
    Jeremiah 26:6, 26:9
    A. Bamoth
    B. Kenath
    C. Pisgah
    D. Shiloh

12. At which gate of the LORD's house did the princes of Judah sit down?

    Jeremiah 26:10

    A. Fish gate
    B. Horse gate
    C. New gate
    D. Old gate

13. What was Micah's surname?

    Jeremiah 26:18

    A. The Gazathite
    B. The Jeezerite
    C. The Morasthite
    D. The Pelethite

14. Who was the king of Judah when Micah prophesied?

    Jeremiah 26:18

    A. King Gemariah
    B. King Hezekiah
    C. King Kushaiah
    D. King Shemaiah

15. Who was Urijah's father?

    Jeremiah 26:20

    A. Gemariah
    B. Hezekiah
    C. Kushaiah
    D. Shemaiah

16. Where did Urijah flee to?

    Jeremiah 26:21

    A. Babylon
    B. Egypt
    C. Greece
    D. Spain

17. Whom did the king of Judah send to fetch Urijah?

    Jeremiah 26:22

    A. Ahikam
    B. Elnathan
    C. Ismachiah
    D. Mehuman

18. Who was the son of Shaphan?

    Jeremiah 26:24

    A. Ahikam
    B. Elnathan
    C. Ismachiah
    D. Mehuman

19. Who was the king of Judah when Jeremiah prophesied yokes would be placed upon the five ungodly kings?

    Jeremiah 27:3–12

    A. King Baaseiah
    B. King Hoshaiah
    C. King Jeconiah
    D. King Zedekiah

20. Which king of Judah did the king of Babylon capture and send to Babylon?

    Jeremiah 27:20

    A. King Baaseiah
    B. King Hoshaiah
    C. King Jeconiah
    D. King Zedekiah

Answers on page 769

AUGUST 16

Lesson 228
Today's Reading: *Jeremiah 28–30*
Period of Time: 607 BC
Author: Jeremiah

1. Who was the king of Judah?
   Jeremiah 28:1
   A. King Balak
   B. King Jeroboam
   C. King Nebuchadnezzar
   D. King Zedekiah

2. Who was Hananiah's father?
   Jeremiah 28:1
   A. Azur
   B. Kish
   C. Luke
   D. Tola

3. Where did Jeremiah speak to the priests and all the people?
   Jeremiah 28:1–11
   A. Along the river of Jordan
   B. Behind the governor's palace
   C. In the house of the LORD
   D. Near the waters of Beersheba

4. Within how many years did Hananiah say the temple vessels would return to Jerusalem?
   Jeremiah 28:3
   A. 1
   B. 2
   C. 3
   D. 4

5. Who was the king of Babylon?
   Jeremiah 28:3
   A. King Balak
   B. King Jeroboam
   C. King Nebuchadnezzar
   D. King Zedekiah

6. Who was King Jehoiakim's son?
   Jeremiah 28:4
   A. King Conaniah
   B. King Jeconiah
   C. King Mattaniah
   D. King Shecaniah

7. What did Hananiah break?
   Jeremiah 28:10
   A. A cup
   B. A hook
   C. A scroll
   D. A yoke

8. During which month did Hananiah die?
   Jeremiah 28:17
   A. 2nd month
   B. 5th month
   C. 7th month
   D. 10th month

9. Who was Elasah's father?
   Jeremiah 29:3
   A. Shadrach
   B. Shamgar
   C. Shammua
   D. Shaphan

10. Who was Gemariah's father?
    Jeremiah 29:3
    A. Hilkiah
    B. Kolaiah
    C. Masseiah
    D. Zephaniah

11. How many years would the people of Judah live in Babylon?
    Jeremiah 29:10
    A. 40
    B. 70
    C. 200
    D. 400

12. Which fruit represented the people in captivity that turned from God?
    Jeremiah 29:17
    A. Vile figs
    B. Vile limes
    C. Vile melons
    D. Vile pomegranates

13. Who was Ahab's father?

    Jeremiah 29:21

    A. Hilkiah
    B. Kolaiah
    C. Masseiah
    D. Zephaniah

14. Who was Zedekiah's father?

    Jeremiah 29:21

    A. Hilkiah
    B. Kolaiah
    C. Masseiah
    D. Zephaniah

15. Which two men did the king of Babylon roast in the fire?

    Jeremiah 29:22

    A. Abednego and Zoar
    B. Barnabas and Paul
    C. Pedahzur and Iddo
    D. Zedekiah and Ahab

16. What was Shemaiah's surname?

    Jeremiah 29:24

    A. The Beerothite
    B. The Ishmaelite
    C. The Nehelamite
    D. The Shillemite

17. Who was Maaseiah's son?

    Jeremiah 29:25

    A. Hilkiah
    B. Kolaiah
    C. Masseiah
    D. Zephaniah

18. Where was Jeremiah from?

    Jeremiah 29:27

    A. Anathoth
    B. Geliloth
    C. Oboth
    D. Succoth

19. What did Jeremiah call the troubling days that Israel and Judah would go through?

    Jeremiah 30:7

    A. The dark perilous days
    B. The time of Jacob's trouble
    C. The vilest days of evil
    D. The world's dying days

20. What will become incurable?

    Jeremiah 30:12

    A. Israel's bruise
    B. Israel's emroids
    C. Israel's tumor
    D. Israel's wound

*Answers on page 769

Lesson 229
Today's Reading: *Jeremiah 31–32*
Period of Time: 607 BC
Author: Jeremiah

1. Where shall Israel plant vines?
   Jeremiah 31:5
   A. Coasts of the great sea
   B. Hills of Galilee
   C. Mountains of Samaria
   D. Wilderness of Zin

2. Whom does God call his firstborn?
   Jeremiah 31:9
   A. Ephraim
   B. Judah
   C. Reuben
   D. Zebulun

3. How shall the LORD gather Israel?
   Jeremiah 31:10
   A. As a fisherman doth his nets
   B. As a gardener doth his garden
   C. As a herdsman doth his herd
   D. As a shepherd doth his flock

4. What shall the soul of Israel be like?
   Jeremiah 31:12
   A. A new honeycomb
   B. A roaring lion
   C. A sour grape
   D. A watered garden

5. Whose souls shall the LORD satiate with fatness?
   Jeremiah 31:14
   A. The captains' souls
   B. The kings' souls
   C. The priests' souls
   D. The shepherds' souls

6. Who wept for her children and refused to be comforted?
   Jeremiah 31:15
   A. Esther
   B. Rahel
   C. Sarah
   D. Vashti

7. What part of his body did Jeremiah smite?
   Jeremiah 31:19
   A. His chest
   B. His hand
   C. His thigh
   D. His waist

8. What did Jeremiah call Israel?
   Jeremiah 31:22
   A. A backsliding daughter
   B. A fattened maid
   C. A negligent mother
   D. A whorish woman

9. What new thing in the earth will the LORD create?
   Jeremiah 31:22
   A. A cow shall jump over the moon.
   B. A donkey shall speak.
   C. A man shall give birth.
   D. A woman shall compass a man.

10. What have the fathers eaten?
    Jeremiah 31:29
    A. A bitter herb
    B. A roasted ear
    C. A sour grape
    D. A vile fig

11. What does Jeremiah say a neighbor will no longer do to his neighbor?
    Jeremiah 31:34
    A. Beat him in the field
    B. Kill him upon the streets
    C. Nurture him as a stranger
    D. Teach him about the LORD

12. Who was the king of Judah?
    Jeremiah 32:1
    A. King Abednego
    B. King Meshach
    C. King Shadrach
    D. King Zedekiah

13. Who was the son of Shallum?
    Jeremiah 32:7
    A. Hanameel
    B. Jahleel
    C. Mahaleel
    D. Tabeel

14. In which country was Anathoth located?
    Jeremiah 32:7–8
    A. Country of Benjamin
    B. Country of Issachar
    C. Country of Manasseh
    D. Country of Naphtali

15. How many shekels of silver did Jeremiah pay for the land?
    Jeremiah 32:9
    A. 7
    B. 17
    C. 27
    D. 37

16. Whom did Jeremiah give the evidence of the purchase of the land to?
    Jeremiah 32:12
    A. Baruch
    B. Lamech
    C. Melech
    D. Saruch

17. Whom would the LORD give Jerusalem to?
    Jeremiah 32:1–2, 32:24–29
    A. The Assyrians
    B. The Chaldeans
    C. The Egyptians
    D. The Libyans

18. Who was the king of Babylon?
    Jeremiah 32:28
    A. King Neariah
    B. King Nebuchadrezzar
    C. King Nephishesim
    D. King Nergalsharezer

19. Where did Israel sacrifice their children?
    Jeremiah 32:35
    A. Valley of the draftsmen
    B. Valley of the dolls
    C. Valley of the son of Hinnom
    D. Valley of the tears

20. Which false god mentioned in Jeremiah 32:35 did Israel sacrifice their children to?
    Jeremiah 32:35
    A. Ashima
    B. Molech
    C. Rimmon
    D. Tartak

Answers on page 770

AUGUST 18

Lesson 230
Today's Reading: *Jeremiah 33–35*
Period of Time: 607 BC
Author: Jeremiah

1. Where was Jeremiah the second time the LORD spoke to him?
   Jeremiah 33:1
   A. At the temple
   B. By the sea of Galilee
   C. In prison
   D. Near the horse gate

2. Who came to fight against Jerusalem?
   Jeremiah 33:5
   A. The Chaldeans
   B. The Ethiopians
   C. The Grecians
   D. The Libyans

3. Which two things did God promise to give to Israel?
   Jeremiah 33:6
   A. Disease and famine
   B. Health and cure
   C. Machines and chariots
   D. Swords and shields

4. What will the people bring to the temple?
   Jeremiah 33:11
   A. The dead men
   B. The golden calf
   C. The pot of silver
   D. The sacrifice of praise

5. Who shall inhabit the desolate land?
   Jeremiah 33:12
   A. Bondmen
   B. Husbandmen
   C. Potters
   D. Shepherds

6. Who shall execute judgment and righteousness in the land?
   Jeremiah 33:15
   A. The Branch of righteousness
   B. The Leaf of freedom
   C. The Root of liberty
   D. The Tree of holiness

7. Which name does Jeremiah use for he who shall sit upon the throne of the house of Israel?
   Jeremiah 33:16–18
   A. The Almighty
   B. The LORD our righteousness
   C. The Rock of my refuge
   D. The Word of life

8. Which tribe was chosen to minister unto the house of the LORD?
   Jeremiah 33:22
   A. Tribe of Benjamin
   B. Tribe of Levi
   C. Tribe of Naphtali
   D. Tribe of Reuben

9. How many families did the people say the LORD has chosen, and even cast them off?
   Jeremiah 33:24
   A. 2
   B. 12
   C. 22
   D. 32

10. Who was the king of Babylon?
    Jeremiah 34:1
    A. King Nebai
    B. King Nebaioth
    C. King Nebat
    D. King Nebuchadnezzar

11. Who did Jeremiah say would die in peace?
    Jeremiah 34:2–5
    A. King Zebadiah
    B. King Zechariah
    C. King Zedekiah
    D. King Zephaniah

12. Which two of the following were the remaining strongholds of Judah?

    Jeremiah 34:7

    A. Bethlehem and Pelusium
    B. El-berith and Horesh
    C. Engedi and Ziph
    D. Lachish and Azekah

13. After how many years was a Hebrew servant to be set free?

    Jeremiah 34:14

    A. 3
    B. 5
    C. 6
    D. 9

14. Who was King Josiah's son?

    Jeremiah 35:1

    A. King Chenaanah
    B. King Hadadezer
    C. King Jehoiakim
    D. King Malchiram

15. Who was Jeremiah's son?

    Jeremiah 35:3

    A. Baaseiah
    B. Eshbaal
    C. Jaazaniah
    D. Raamiah

16. Who was Igdaliah's son?

    Jeremiah 35:4

    A. Arnan
    B. Hanan
    C. Kenan
    D. Ornan

17. Who was Shallum's son?

    Jeremiah 35:4

    A. Maachah
    B. Maadiah
    C. Maai
    D. Maaseiah

18. What were the Rechabites forbidden to do?

    Jeremiah 35:2–10

    A. Drink wine
    B. Eat meat
    C. Live in tents
    D. Ride upon animals

19. Who was Rechab's son?

    Jeremiah 35:6

    A. Jona
    B. Jonadab
    C. Jonan
    D. Jonas

20. Which two armies did the Rechabites fear?

    Jeremiah 35:11

    A. Chaldean and Syrian armies
    B. Ethiopian and Egyptian armies
    C. Grecian and Assyrian armies
    D. Libyan and Phoenician armies

*Answers on page 770

Lesson 231
Today's Reading: *Jeremiah 36–38*
Period of Time: 606–588 BC
Author: Jeremiah

AUGUST 19

1. During which year of Jehoiakim's reign did the LORD tell Jeremiah to write in a roll of a book?
   Jeremiah 36:1–2
   A. 2nd year
   B. 4th year
   C. 6th year
   D. 8th year

2. Who was Baruch's father?
   Jeremiah 36:4–8, 36:32
   A. Delaiah
   B. Josibiah
   C. Neriah
   D. Raamiah

3. During which month was a fast proclaimed?
   Jeremiah 36:9
   A. 3rd month
   B. 5th month
   C. 7th month
   D. 9th month

4. In whose chamber was the scroll read?
   Jeremiah 36:10
   A. Gemariah's chamber
   B. Ishmaiah's chamber
   C. Kolaiah's chamber
   D. Shechaniah's chamber

5. Who told the princes about the scroll?
   Jeremiah 36:11–13
   A. Coniah
   B. Jesaiah
   C. Michaiah
   D. Pethahiah

6. Which one of the following was a scribe?
   Jeremiah 36:12
   A. Azmaveth
   B. Elishama
   C. Ishmerai
   D. Obededom

7. Who was Shemaiah's son?
   Jeremiah 36:12
   A. Delaiah
   B. Josibiah
   C. Neriah
   D. Raamiah

8. Who was Achbor's son?
   Jeremiah 36:12
   A. Elizaphan
   B. Elnathan
   C. Elpalet
   D. Elzaphan

9. Whom did the princes send to fetch Baruch?
   Jeremiah 36:14
   A. Jehubbah
   B. Jehucal
   C. Jehudi
   D. Jehush

10. Who read the words in the scroll to the king?
    Jeremiah 36:21
    A. Cephas
    B. Festus
    C. Hamuel
    D. Jehudi

11. Where was the king staying when the scroll was read to him?
    Jeremiah 36:22
    A. His autumnhouse
    B. His springhouse
    C. His summerhouse
    D. His winterhouse

12. What did the king do after the scroll was read to him?
    Jeremiah 36:23
    A. Burned it
    B. Made copies of it
    C. Posted it on a wall
    D. Wept over it in his chambers

13. Who preceded King Zedekiah as king of Judah?

    Jeremiah 37:1

    A. King Coniah
    B. King Jesaiah
    C. King Michaiah
    D. King Pethahiah

14. Which army fled when they heard Pharaoh's army was headed to Jerusalem?

    Jeremiah 37:5

    A. Assyrian army
    B. Chaldean army
    C. Ethiopian army
    D. Grecian army

15. Who was the captain of the ward?

    Jeremiah 37:13

    A. Ahijah
    B. Elijah
    C. Irijah
    D. Urijah

16. Whose house was made into a prison?

    Jeremiah 37:15

    A. Berachah's house
    B. Gedaliah's house
    C. Hizkijah's house
    D. Jonathan's house

17. Whose dungeon was Jeremiah cast into?

    Jeremiah 38:6

    A. Gedaliah's dungeon
    B. Jezaniah's dungeon
    C. Kushaiah's dungeon
    D. Malchiah's dungeon

18. Who was an Ethiopian?

    Jeremiah 38:7–13

    A. Ebed-melech
    B. Ir-nahash
    C. Joseph-barsabas
    D. Pahath-moab

19. How many men went with the Ethiopian to remove Jeremiah from the pit?

    Jeremiah 38:7–13

    A. 10
    B. 20
    C. 30
    D. 40

20. Where was Jeremiah when Jerusalem was taken?

    Jeremiah 38:28

    A. At the temple
    B. In prison
    C. Near the river of Jordan
    D. Traveling to Egypt

*Answers on page 770

Lesson 232
Today's Reading: *Jeremiah 39–41*
Period of Time: 590–587 BC
Author: Jeremiah

AUGUST 20

1. During which year of King Zedekiah's reign was Jerusalem besieged?
   Jeremiah 39:1
   A. 3rd year
   B. 6th year
   C. 9th year
   D. 12th year

2. Who was the king of Babylon?
   Jeremiah 39:1
   A. King Evilmerodach
   B. King Haahashtari
   C. King Joshbekashah
   D. King Nebuchadrezzar

3. During which year of King Zedekiah's reign was Jerusalem broken up?
   Jeremiah 39:2
   A. 5th year
   B. 8th year
   C. 11th year
   D. 14th year

4. In which place was King Zedekiah captured?
   Jeremiah 39:6
   A. Baalah
   B. Idalah
   C. Keilah
   D. Riblah

5. What did the king of Babylon do to King Zedekiah when he captured him?
   Jeremiah 39:7
   A. Branded him with fire
   B. Cut out his tongue
   C. Hung him from a tree
   D. Put out his eyes

6. Who was the captain of the guard?
   Jeremiah 39:9–13, 40:1
   A. Adrammelech
   B. Jehoshaphat
   C. Nebuzaradan
   D. Sheshbazzar

7. Who was released from prison?
   Jeremiah 39:14
   A. Gedaliah
   B. Jeremiah
   C. Maaseiah
   D. Pekahiah

8. Who was an Ethiopian?
   Jeremiah 39:16
   A. Ebed-melech
   B. Ir-nahash
   C. Pahath-moab
   D. Shethar-boznai

9. Who became governor of the cities of Judah?
   Jeremiah 40:5
   A. Cononiah
   B. Gedaliah
   C. Hananiah
   D. Igdaliah

10. Where did Jeremiah go to dwell?
    Jeremiah 40:6
    A. Keilah
    B. Mizpah
    C. Ophrah
    D. Rechah

11. Who was a son of a Maachathite?
    Jeremiah 40:8
    A. Ananiah
    B. Cononiah
    C. Hananiah
    D. Jezaniah

12. Who was the king of the Ammonites?
    Jeremiah 40:14
    A. King Baalis
    B. King Gaal
    C. King Jaakan
    D. King Maai

13. During which month was the governor of the cities of Judah murdered?

    Jeremiah 41:1–2

    A. 5th
    B. 7th
    C. 9th
    D. 11th

14. How many men from Shechem, Shiloh, and Samaria shaved their beards and rent their clothes?

    Jeremiah 41:5–7

    A. 8
    B. 80
    C. 800
    D. 8,000

15. How many of the men from Shechem, Shiloh, and Samaria did Ishmael spare?

    Jeremiah 41:8

    A. 4
    B. 6
    C. 8
    D. 10

16. Which king dug the pit Ishmael cast dead bodies into?

    Jeremiah 41:9

    A. King Asa
    B. King Koa
    C. King Pua
    D. King Zia

17. Who went to fight against Ishmael?

    Jeremiah 41:11–12

    A. Bilshan
    B. Elhanan
    C. Johanan
    D. Sheshan

18. How many men escaped with Ishmael?

    Jeremiah 41:15

    A. 4
    B. 6
    C. 8
    D. 10

19. Whom did Ishmael and his men flee to?

    Jeremiah 41:15

    A. The Ammonites
    B. The Edomites
    C. The Moabites
    D. The Perizzites

20. Which habitation is near Bethlehem?

    Jeremiah 41:17

    A. Chimham
    B. Jokneam
    C. Rhegium
    D. Sibraim

*Answers on page 770

AUGUST 21

Lesson 233
Today's Reading: *Jeremiah 42–44*
Period of Time: 587 BC
Author: Jeremiah

1. Who was Kareah's son?
   Jeremiah 42:1
   A. Hodevah
   B. Johanan
   C. Magdiel
   D. Quartus

2. Who was Hoshaiah's son?
   Jeremiah 42:1
   A. Cononiah
   B. Jezaniah
   C. Mattaniah
   D. Shebaniah

3. How many days after Jeremiah prayed for the people did the word of the LORD come to him?
   Jeremiah 42:4–7
   A. 5
   B. 10
   C. 15
   D. 20

4. Where did the people want to go?
   Jeremiah 42:14–19
   A. Egypt
   B. Japho
   C. Lakum
   D. Tabor

5. Who was Hoshaiah's son?
   Jeremiah 43:2
   A. Azariah
   B. Gemariah
   C. Sheariah
   D. Zechariah

6. Who was Neriah's son?
   Jeremiah 43:3
   A. Baruch
   B. Henoch
   C. Lamech
   D. Melech

7. Who was the captain of the guard?
   Jeremiah 43:6
   A. Nebajoth
   B. Nebuchadnezzar
   C. Nebushasban
   D. Nebuzaradan

8. Who was the son of Ahikam?
   Jeremiah 43:6
   A. Gedaliah
   B. Hezekiah
   C. Jahaziah
   D. Malchiah

9. Where did the people settle after being warned **not** to leave Judah?
   Jeremiah 43:4–8
   A. Bethlehem
   B. Jerusalem
   C. Palestine
   D. Tahpanhes

10. What did Jeremiah hide in the clay in the brickkiln?
    Jeremiah 43:9
    A. Brass idols
    B. Great stones
    C. Silver coins
    D. Wine jars

11. Who was the king of Babylon?
    Jeremiah 43:10
    A. King Nebai
    B. King Nebat
    C. King Nebuchadrezzar
    D. King Nebushasban

12. Where will the LORD kindle a fire?
    Jeremiah 43:12
    A. Along the city walls of Jerusalem
    B. By the groves in the wilderness
    C. In the houses of the gods of Egypt
    D. Upon the altars of Ashtoreh

13. Whose image does Jeremiah say the LORD shall break?

    Jeremiah 43:13

    A. Beth-she'mesh
    B. Chemosh
    C. Merodach
    D. Succothbenoth

14. Which town is located in Egypt?

    Jeremiah 44:1

    A. Bethel
    B. Chesil
    C. Migdol
    D. Peniel

15. Which other town is located in Egypt?

    Jeremiah 44:1

    A. Bethlehem
    B. Jerusalem
    C. Palestine
    D. Tahpanhes

16. What is yet another town located in Egypt?

    Jeremiah 44:1

    A. Eden
    B. Lehi
    C. Noph
    D. Shen

17. Where were the men from whose wives burned incense unto other gods?

    Jeremiah 44:15

    A. Memphis
    B. Nineveh
    C. Pathros
    D. Raamses

18. Which god did the people burn incense and pour drink offerings to?

    Jeremiah 44:17–25

    A. Ashima of Syria
    B. Diana of Ephesus
    C. Nibhaz of Samaria
    D. Queen of heaven

19. Who was the king of Egypt during the time of Jeremiah?

    Jeremiah 44:30

    A. Pharaoh-amenhotep
    B. Pharaoh-hophra
    C. Pharaoh-narmer
    D. Pharaoh-raamses

20. Who was a king of Judah?

    Jeremiah 44:30

    A. King Barachiah
    B. King Jeremiah
    C. King Pekahiah
    D. King Zedekiah

*Answers on page 770

AUGUST 22

Lesson 234
Today's Reading: *Jeremiah 45–48*
Period of Time: 587 BC
Author: Jeremiah

1. Who was Baruch's father?
   Jeremiah 45:1
   A. Hodaiah
   B. Kolaiah
   C. Neriah
   D. Pedaiah

2. During which year of Jehoiakim's reign did Jeremiah write a book?
   Jeremiah 45:1
   A. 2nd
   B. 3rd
   C. 4th
   D. 5th

3. Which king of Egypt is mentioned in Jeremiah 46:2?
   Jeremiah 46:2
   A. Pharaoh-aba
   B. Pharaoh-dedumose
   C. Pharaoh-khufu
   D. Pharaoh-necho

4. Where did Egypt battle Babylon?
   Jeremiah 46:2
   A. Bathrabbim
   B. Carchemish
   C. Hierapolis
   D. Michmethah

5. What does the LORD tell the army of Egypt to put on?
   Jeremiah 46:4
   A. Brigandines
   B. Habits
   C. Miters
   D. Yokes

6. Which two nations shall handle the shield in Egypt's army?
   Jeremiah 46:9
   A. Athenians and Syrians
   B. Ethiopians and Libyans
   C. Galatians and Thessalonians
   D. Parthians and Babylonians

7. Who shall handle and bend the bow in Egypt's army?
   Jeremiah 46:9
   A. The Arabians
   B. The Grecians
   C. The Lydians
   D. The Philippians

8. What was the daughter of Egypt to get in Gilead?
   Jeremiah 46:11
   A. Balm
   B. Coats
   C. Oil
   D. Wax

9. Who was the king of Babylon?
   Jeremiah 46:2, 46:13, 46:26
   A. King Berodachbaladan
   B. King Chushan-rishathaim
   C. King Nebuchadrezzar
   D. King Tiglath-pileser

10. Which city is located in Egypt?
    Jeremiah 46:14
    A. Damascus
    B. Nineveh
    C. Perezuzza
    D. Tahpanhes

11. Which one of the following is a real mountain?
    Jeremiah 46:18
    A. Mount Alexandria
    B. Mount Gaza
    C. Mount Sidon
    D. Mount Tabor

12. Which one of the following is a real mountain?

    Jeremiah 46:18

    A. Mount Carmel
    B. Mount Megiddo
    C. Mount Nazareth
    D. Mount Sychar

13. Which city shall become waste and desolate without an inhabitant?

    Jeremiah 46:19

    A. Cush
    B. Enam
    C. Lehi
    D. Noph

14. Which city did baldness come upon?

    Jeremiah 47:5

    A. Cana
    B. Gaza
    C. Hara
    D. Jaba

15. Who has been cut off with the remnant of its valley?

    Jeremiah 47:5

    A. Ashkelon
    B. Laodicea
    C. Pibeseth
    D. Togarmah

16. Who is confounded and dismayed?

    Jeremiah 48:1

    A. Bileam
    B. Dilean
    C. Kitron
    D. Misgab

17. Which is a city of Moab?

    Jeremiah 48:2

    A. Bithron
    B. Heshbon
    C. Lebanon
    D. Shimron

18. Where shall a voice of crying, spoiling, and great destruction come from?

    Jeremiah 48:3–5

    A. Engannim
    B. Horonaim
    C. Mahanaim
    D. Rephidim

19. Who shall go forth into captivity with his priests and his princes?

    Jeremiah 48:7–13

    A. Chemosh
    B. Mercurius
    C. Nisroch
    D. Tammuz

20. Which two of the following places shall a fire and flame come from?

    Jeremiah 48:45

    A. Cabbon and Bithron
    B. Dibon and Migron
    C. Heshbon and Sihon
    D. Kitron and Ekron

Answers on page 770

AUGUST 23

Lesson 235
Today's Reading: *Jeremiah 49–50*
Period of Time: 587–562 BC
Author: Jeremiah

1. Which land did the king of the Ammonites inherit?
   Jeremiah 49:1
   A. Land of Asshur
   B. Land of Gad
   C. Land of Levi
   D. Land of Judah

2. Where will an alarm of war be heard in Ammon?
   Jeremiah 49:2–3
   A. Accad
   B. Baalah
   C. Lydda
   D. Rabbah

3. Which city was to howl because Ai had been spoiled?
   Jeremiah 49:3
   A. Bithron
   B. Eltekon
   C. Heshbon
   D. Ziphron

4. Which place is located in Edom?
   Jeremiah 49:7, 49:20
   A. Addan
   B. Golan
   C. Paran
   D. Teman

5. Which place located in Edom does the LORD tell to flee, turn back, and dwell deep?
   Jeremiah 49:8
   A. Debir
   B. Decapolis
   C. Dedan
   D. Derbe

6. Whom are the Edomites descendants of?
   Jeremiah 49:8
   A. Asa
   B. Esau
   C. Jacob
   D. Lot

7. Which Edomite city will become desolate, a reproach, a waste, and a curse?
   Jeremiah 49:13, 49:22
   A. Bozrah
   B. Mearah
   C. Nimrah
   D. Ophrah

8. Upon which sea was the cry of a great noise heard?
   Jeremiah 49:21
   A. Black sea
   B. Green sea
   C. Red sea
   D. White sea

9. Which two cities were near Damascus?
   Jeremiah 49:23
   A. Carthage and Thyatira
   B. Hamath and Arpad
   C. Memphis and Thebes
   D. Pergamum and Athens

10. Who was a king of Damascus?
    Jeremiah 49:27
    A. King Ben-ha'dad
    B. King Hophra
    C. King Nero
    D. King Zedekiah

11. Which two kingdoms will the king of Babylon destroy?
    Jeremiah 49:28–33
    A. Alexandria and Tarsus
    B. Ephesus and Cyrene
    C. Kedar and Hazor
    D. Philadelphia and Corinth

12. Who was the king of Judah?

    Jeremiah 49:34

    A. King Ben-ha'dad
    B. King Hophra
    C. King Nebuchadnezzar
    D. King Zedekiah

13. Where will the LORD set up his throne?

    Jeremiah 49:38

    A. Elam
    B. Hara
    C. Neah
    D. Shen

14. Which false god will be confounded?

    Jeremiah 50:2

    A. Ashima
    B. Bel
    C. Dagon
    D. Merodach

15. Which false god will be broken into pieces?

    Jeremiah 50:2

    A. Ashima
    B. Bel
    C. Dagon
    D. Merodach

16. From which direction will an army come to destroy Babylon?

    Jeremiah 50:3–9, 50:41

    A. North
    B. South
    C. East
    D. West

17. Which king devoured Israel first?

    Jeremiah 50:17

    A. King of Assyria
    B. King of Grecia
    C. King of Nicomedia
    D. King of Persia

18. Who was the last king to devour Israel?

    Jeremiah 50:17

    A. King Asa
    B. King Darius
    C. King Jehoshaphat
    D. King Nebuchadnezzar

19. From which two places shall Israel feed once again?

    Jeremiah 50:19

    A. Akkad and Kish
    B. Byzantium and Miletus
    C. Carmel and Bashan
    D. Damascus and Lebanon

20. Upon which two mountains did the LORD say Israel's soul would be satisfied?

    Jeremiah 50:19

    A. Mount Ararat and Mount Nebo
    B. Mount Ephraim and Mount Gilead
    C. Mount Gerizim and Mount Pisgah
    D. Mount Horeb and Mount Sinai

*Answers on page 770

AUGUST 24

Lesson 236
Today's Reading: *Jeremiah 51–52*
Period of Time: 587–562 BC
Author: Jeremiah

1. What has Babylon been in the LORD's hand?
   Jeremiah 51:7
   A. A brass fan
   B. A golden cup
   C. A silver cord
   D. An iron fist

2. Who shall destroy Babylon?
   Jeremiah 51:11
   A. The Assyrians
   B. The Grecians
   C. The Medes
   D. The Romans

3. What is the daughter of Babylon like?
   Jeremiah 51:33
   A. A fat heifer
   B. A rusty plow
   C. A sharp sickle
   D. A threshing floor

4. Who has been taken?
   Jeremiah 51:41
   A. Shechem
   B. Sheloan
   C. Shephar
   D. Sheshach

5. Whom will the LORD punish in Babylon?
   Jeremiah 51:44
   A. Bel
   B. Chemosh
   C. Diana
   D. Mercurius

6. From which direction shall the spoilers come to destroy Babylon?
   Jeremiah 51:48
   A. North
   B. South
   C. East
   D. West

7. Who is the father of Seraiah?
   Jeremiah 51:59
   A. Beriah
   B. Jeziah
   C. Neriah
   D. Tobiah

8. Which river was Jeremiah to toss a book into?
   Jeremiah 51:63
   A. River Euphrates
   B. River Gihon
   C. River Jabbok
   D. River Ulai

9. How old was King Zedekiah when he began to reign in Judah?
   Jeremiah 52:1
   A. 16 years old
   B. 21 years old
   C. 37 years old
   D. 45 years old

10. Who was King Zedekiah's mother?
    Jeremiah 52:1
    A. Abigail
    B. Hamutal
    C. Ruth
    D. Vashti

11. Who was an evil king in the eyes of the LORD?
    Jeremiah 52:2
    A. King David
    B. King Jehoiakim
    C. King Solomon
    D. King Uzziah

12. Upon which plains was King Zedekiah captured by the army of the Chaldeans?
    Jeremiah 52:8
    A. Plains of Aven
    B. Plains of Dura
    C. Plains of Jericho
    D. Plains of Mamre

13. Which city is located in the land of Hamath?

    Jeremiah 52:9

    A. Cyprus
    B. Lystra
    C. Paphos
    D. Riblah

14. What did the king of Babylon do to King Zedekiah after he slew his sons?

    Jeremiah 52:10–11

    A. Burned him to death
    B. Cut off his feet
    C. Hung him to a wall
    D. Put out his eyes

15. Who was the captain of the guard?

    Jeremiah 52:12–26

    A. Naaman
    B. Nebuzaradan
    C. Nimrod
    D. Nogah

16. Which king made the 12 brasen bulls for the house of the LORD?

    Jeremiah 52:20

    A. King David
    B. King Jehoiakim
    C. King Solomon
    D. King Uzziah

17. Besides Seraiah, which priest was also put to death by the king of Babylon?

    Jeremiah 52:24–27

    A. Chenaniah
    B. Ismachiah
    C. Obadiah
    D. Zephaniah

18. What was the total number of Jews taken to Babylon?

    Jeremiah 52:30

    A. 832
    B. 3,023
    C. 4,600
    D. 9,200

19. Who became the king of Babylon after Nebuchadrezzar?

    Jeremiah 52:31

    A. King Evilmerodach
    B. King Jashubilehem
    C. King Mephibosheth
    D. King Parshandatha

20. Which former king of Judah was released from prison and kindly treated by the king of Babylon?

    Jeremiah 52:31–34

    A. King Jehoiachin
    B. King Menahem
    C. King Pekahiah
    D. King Zimri

*Answers on page 770

AUGUST 25

Lesson 237

Today's Reading: *Lamentations 1–2*
Period of Time: 610 BC
Author: Jeremiah

1. How does the city sit?
   Lamentations 1:1
   A. Arrogantly
   B. Peacefully
   C. Solitarily
   D. Tiredly

2. What personification is used to describe the city?
   Lamentations 1:1
   A. A garden
   B. A light
   C. A virgin
   D. A widow

3. What has the city become?
   Lamentations 1:1
   A. Commercial
   B. Lent
   C. Respective
   D. Tributary

4. How many of the city's lovers comfort her?
   Lamentations 1:2
   A. 1
   B. 10
   C. 100
   D. None

5. Who has gone into captivity because of affliction and great servitude?
   Lamentations 1:3
   A. Babylon
   B. Judah
   C. Media
   D. Persia

6. What does the city dwell among?
   Lamentations 1:3
   A. The heathen
   B. The kings
   C. The nobles
   D. The princes

7. What is the city doing?
   Lamentations 1:4
   A. Celebrating
   B. Mourning
   C. Sacrificing
   D. Worshipping

8. What are the city's princes like?
   Lamentations 1:6
   A. Harts that find no pasture
   B. Lions with no den
   C. Rams fallen from the mountain
   D. Scorpions that have no sting

9. What do the people seek?
   Lamentations 1:11
   A. Bread
   B. Gold
   C. Idols
   D. Wool

10. What has the LORD done to the virgin?
    Lamentations 1:15
    A. Fed her dainty meats
    B. Gave her away as a bride
    C. Placed his wing over her
    D. Trodden her as in a winepress

11. What is Jerusalem like?
    Lamentations 1:17
    A. A light upon a hill
    B. A menstruous woman
    C. A strong tower
    D. An adopted child

12. Which two of the following have gone into captivity?
    Lamentations 1:18
    A. Generals and kings
    B. Priests and elders
    C. Scribes and lawyers
    D. Virgins and young men

13. Which two of the following gave up the ghost in the city?

    Lamentations 1:19

    A. Generals and kings
    B. Priests and elders
    C. Scribes and lawyers
    D. Virgins and young men

14. What has the LORD done to the habitations of Jacob?

    Lamentations 2:1–4

    A. Bent his bow at them like an enemy
    B. Clapped his hands at them like thunder
    C. Ground them into meal like a miller
    D. Sowed them as seed like a husbandman

15. What did the LORD pour out?

    Lamentations 2:4

    A. His covering like a shadow
    B. His fury like fire
    C. His strength like a winepress
    D. His water like rain

16. What languished together?

    Lamentations 2:8

    A. The earth and the sun
    B. The hills and the mountains
    C. The rampart and the wall
    D. The sea and the river

17. What does the prophet say is poured upon the earth?

    Lamentations 2:11

    A. His blood
    B. His heart
    C. His liver
    D. His tears

18. What is the virgin daughter of Zion's breach like?

    Lamentations 2:13

    A. The brook
    B. The river
    C. The sea
    D. The waterway

19. What did men once call the city?

    Lamentations 2:15

    A. The great whore of Zion
    B. The mother of pearl
    C. The perfection of beauty
    D. The unblemished daughter

20. What is **not** to cease?

    Lamentations 2:18

    A. The apple of thine eye
    B. The honey under thine tongue
    C. The lemon upon thine skin
    D. The wheat in thine belly

*Answers on page 770

AUGUST 26

Lesson 238
Today's Reading: *Lamentations 3–5*
Period of Time: 610 BC
Author: Jeremiah

1. Where has the LORD set Jeremiah?
   Lamentations 3:6
   A. Along the coast
   B. In dark places
   C. Near the river
   D. Upon the mountain

2. What of Jeremiah's has the LORD made heavy?
   Lamentations 3:7
   A. His arm
   B. His chain
   C. His heart
   D. His shoes

3. What does Jeremiah say the LORD was like to him?
   Lamentations 3:10
   A. A bear lying in wait
   B. A hen collecting her chick
   C. A lion sifting its prey
   D. A worm eating his flesh

4. What does Jeremiah state he was like to God?
   Lamentations 3:12
   A. A cup for the drink
   B. A lamp for the darkness
   C. A mark for the arrow
   D. A pen for the paper

5. What did the LORD make Jeremiah drunk with?
   Lamentations 3:15
   A. Blood
   B. Fear
   C. Milk
   D. Wormwood

6. When does Jeremiah say it is good for a man to bear the yoke?
   Lamentations 3:27
   A. As a babe
   B. During the rain
   C. In his youth
   D. When he is old

7. What has the LORD made the people of Judah like in the midst of the people?
   Lamentations 3:45
   A. A close brother
   B. A favorite son
   C. A golden arm
   D. An offscouring

8. How does Jeremiah's enemy chase him?
   Lamentations 3:52
   A. Like a bird
   B. Like a hart
   C. Like a lion
   D. Like an ox

9. Where does Jeremiah say they have cut off his life and cast a stone upon him?
   Lamentations 3:53
   A. In the dungeon
   B. In the field
   C. In the temple
   D. In the vale

10. What has Jeremiah become to Israel?
    Lamentations 3:63
    A. Garlick
    B. Lunatick
    C. Musick
    D. Wick

11. What does Jeremiah say draws out the breast and gives suck to their young ones?

    Lamentations 4:3

    A. Arabian horses
    B. Evening wolves
    C. Mountain goats
    D. Sea monsters

12. What does Jeremiah say Israel has become cruel like?

    Lamentations 4:3

    A. Blue jays
    B. Eagles
    C. Ostriches
    D. Ravens

13. Whom does Jeremiah say Israel's punishment for sin is greater than?

    Lamentations 4:6

    A. Salem's sin
    B. Secacah's sin
    C. Sidon's sin
    D. Sodom's sin

14. Which one of the following was purer than snow?

    Lamentations 4:7

    A. The Benjamites
    B. The Levites
    C. The Nazarites
    D. The Shulamites

15. What does Israel wander like?

    Lamentations 4:14

    A. Blind men
    B. Goat herders
    C. Shepherds
    D. Vagabonds

16. What are the prosecutors swifter than?

    Lamentations 4:19

    A. Asps
    B. Eagles
    C. Greyhounds
    D. Leopards

17. Where did Edom dwell?

    Lamentations 4:21

    A. Land of Ai
    B. Land of No
    C. Land of Ur
    D. Land of Uz

18. Which two of the following have Jeremiah's people given the hand to?

    Lamentations 5:6

    A. Babylonians and Cretans
    B. Egyptians and Assyrians
    C. Grecians and Romans
    D. Libyans and Macedonians

19. What color is the skin of Jeremiah's people?

    Lamentations 5:10

    A. Black
    B. Red
    C. White
    D. Yellow

20. What walks upon the mountain of Zion because Zion is desolate?

    Lamentations 5:18

    A. Dragons
    B. Foxes
    C. Geese
    D. Peacocks

*Answers on page 770

AUGUST 27

Lesson 239
Today's Reading: *Ezekiel 1–4*
Period of Time: 595–594 BC
Author: Ezekiel

1. When did Ezekiel see the visions of God?
   Ezekiel 1:1
   A. 10th year, 3rd month, 6th day
   B. 20th year, 1st month, 4th day
   C. 30th year, 4th month, 5th day
   D. 40th year, 2nd month, 7th day

2. Which river was Ezekiel near?
   Ezekiel 1:1, 1:3
   A. River of Chebar
   B. River of living water
   C. River of the wilderness
   D. River of water of life

3. Which king was in captivity?
   Ezekiel 1:2
   A. King Asnappar
   B. King Jehoiachin
   C. King Nebuchadnezzar
   D. King Shalmaneser

4. What was Ezekiel's occupation?
   Ezekiel 1:3
   A. Butler
   B. Priest
   C. Shepherd
   D. Woodsman

5. Who was Ezekiel's father?
   Ezekiel 1:3
   A. Amzi
   B. Buzi
   C. Gehazi
   D. Uzzi

6. How many living creatures did Ezekiel see?
   Ezekiel 1:5
   A. 4
   B. 12
   C. 40
   D. 100

7. What did the right sides of the living creatures' faces look like?
   Ezekiel 1:10
   A. Apes and goats
   B. Cows and rams
   C. Men and lions
   D. Wolves and horses

8. What did the left sides of the living creatures' faces look like?
   Ezekiel 1:10
   A. Bears and owls
   B. Foxes and hawks
   C. Leopards and doves
   D. Oxen and eagles

9. What did the living creatures' appearances look like?
   Ezekiel 1:13
   A. Burning coals
   B. Glittering stars
   C. Running waters
   D. Shining metals

10. What type of stone was the color of the wheels?
    Ezekiel 1:16
    A. Amber
    B. Beryl
    C. Onyx
    D. Sapphire

11. What type of stone was the color of the throne?
    Ezekiel 1:26
    A. Amber
    B. Beryl
    C. Onyx
    D. Sapphire

12. What type of stone was the color of the likeness of the man?

    Ezekiel 1:27

    A. Amber
    B. Beryl
    C. Onyx
    D. Sapphire

13. What did the LORD tell Ezekiel he dwelled among?

    Ezekiel 2:6

    A. Bees
    B. Dragons
    C. Scorpions
    D. Unicorns

14. What did the roll taste like?

    Ezekiel 3:3

    A. Coriander
    B. Honey
    C. Salt
    D. Wormwood

15. Where did Ezekiel travel to?

    Ezekiel 3:15

    A. Bethhaccerem
    B. Hamathzobah
    C. Palestine
    D. Telabib

16. How many days did Ezekiel spend among the captives before the LORD spoke to him?

    Ezekiel 3:15

    A. 7
    B. 9
    C. 11
    D. 13

17. Which two of the following did Ezekiel use in his model of Jerusalem?

    Ezekiel 4:1–3

    A. A bar of soap and a bucket of water
    B. A hinge and a broken door
    C. A string of thread and a stick
    D. A tile and an iron pan

18. How many days did Ezekiel lie upon his left side?

    Ezekiel 4:4–5

    A. 140
    B. 230
    C. 390
    D. 470

19. How many days did Ezekiel lie on his right side?

    Ezekiel 4:6

    A. 10
    B. 20
    C. 30
    D. 40

20. What kind of dung was Ezekiel to use initially to bake the bread?

    Ezekiel 4:12–15

    A. Camel's dung
    B. Horse's dung
    C. Man's dung
    D. Pigeon's dung

*Answers on page 770

AUGUST 28

Lesson 240
Today's Reading: *Ezekiel 5–8*
Period of Time: 594 BC
Author: Ezekiel

1. What did Ezekiel use to cut his hair?
   Ezekiel 5:1
   A. A barber's razor
   B. A carpenter's saw
   C. A miller's stone
   D. A tailor's scissors

2. What was Ezekiel to do with the first 1/3rd of the cut hair?
   Ezekiel 5:2
   A. Burn it with fire
   B. Make twines with it
   C. Scatter it in the wind
   D. Smite it with a knife

3. What was Ezekiel to do with the second 1/3rd of the cut hair?
   Ezekiel 5:2
   A. Burn it with fire
   B. Make twines with it
   C. Scatter it in the wind
   D. Smite it with a knife

4. What was Ezekiel to do with the last 1/3rd of the cut hair?
   Ezekiel 5:2
   A. Burn it with fire
   B. Make twines with it
   C. Scatter it in the wind
   D. Smite it with a knife

5. What will the LORD scatter around the altars in the high places?
   Ezekiel 6:1–5
   A. Bones
   B. Fruit
   C. Meat
   D. Stones

6. Which place was near the desolate wilderness Ezekiel made reference to?
   Ezekiel 6:14
   A. Baalath
   B. Diblath
   C. Hamath
   D. Ramath

7. What has blossomed?
   Ezekiel 7:10
   A. The almond
   B. The lily
   C. The rod
   D. The valley

8. What has budded?
   Ezekiel 7:10
   A. Courage
   B. Innocence
   C. Pride
   D. Shame

9. Which musical instrument was used to make the troops ready for battle?
   Ezekiel 7:14
   A. Bell
   B. Drum
   C. Trumpet
   D. Viol

10. What shall those that escape to the mountains be like?
    Ezekiel 7:16
    A. Crows
    B. Doves
    C. Eagles
    D. Quails

11. What shall the survivor's knees be as weak as?
    Ezekiel 7:17
    A. Gruel
    B. Palsy
    C. Sheep
    D. Water

12. What did the LORD tell Ezekiel to make?

    Ezekiel 7:23

    A. A bridle
    B. A chain
    C. A girdle
    D. A yoke

13. When did the hand of the LORD fall upon Ezekiel?

    Ezekiel 8:1

    A. 3rd year, 3rd month, 7th day
    B. 6th year, 6th month, 5th day
    C. 9th year, 9th month, 1st day
    D. 12th year, 12th month, 3rd day

14. What was the color of the image?

    Ezekiel 8:2

    A. Amber
    B. Beryl
    C. Onyx
    D. Sapphire

15. Which gate was the seat of the image of jealousy near?

    Ezekiel 8:3–5

    A. North gate
    B. South gate
    C. East gate
    D. West gate

16. How many men carried censers?

    Ezekiel 8:11

    A. 40
    B. 70
    C. 150
    D. 200

17. Who was Jaazaniah's father?

    Ezekiel 8:11

    A. Elhanan
    B. Johanan
    C. Matthan
    D. Shaphan

18. Whom did the women weep for?

    Ezekiel 8:14

    A. Adrammelech
    B. Mammon
    C. Rimmon
    D. Tammuz

19. Approximately how many men were in the inner court of the LORD's house, between the porch and altar?

    Ezekiel 8:16

    A. 7
    B. 12
    C. 25
    D. 31

20. What did the men in the inner court worship?

    Ezekiel 8:16

    A. The Ashtoreth pole
    B. The black stone
    C. The moon
    D. The sun

*Answers on page 770

AUGUST 29

Lesson 241
Today's Reading: *Ezekiel 9–12*
Period of Time: 594 BC
Author: Ezekiel

1. How many men came from the way of the higher gate?
   Ezekiel 9:2
   A. 2
   B. 4
   C. 6
   D. 8

2. Which direction was the higher gate?
   Ezekiel 9:2
   A. North
   B. South
   C. East
   D. West

3. What did the man clothed in linen have by his side?
   Ezekiel 9:2, 9:11
   A. A double-edged sword
   B. A measuring reed
   C. A plum line
   D. A writer's inkhorn

4. What type of stone did the throne resemble?
   Ezekiel 10:1
   A. Amber
   B. Beryl
   C. Onyx
   D. Sapphire

5. What was the man clothed in linen to scatter over the city?
   Ezekiel 10:2
   A. Coals of fire
   B. Dead men's ashes
   C. Ropes made of hair
   D. Seeds to plant cedar trees

6. How many wheels were by the cherubims?
   Ezekiel 10:9
   A. 2
   B. 3
   C. 4
   D. 5

7. What type of stone was the color of the wheels?
   Ezekiel 10:9
   A. Amber
   B. Beryl
   C. Onyx
   D. Sapphire

8. What did the face of the first cherub look like?
   Ezekiel 10:14
   A. A cherub
   B. A lion
   C. A man
   D. An eagle

9. What did the face of the second cherub look like?
   Ezekiel 10:14
   A. A cherub
   B. A lion
   C. A man
   D. An eagle

10. What did the face of the third cherub look like?
    Ezekiel 10:14
    A. A cherub
    B. A lion
    C. A man
    D. An eagle

11. What did the face of the fourth cherub look like?
    Ezekiel 10:14
    A. A cherub
    B. A lion
    C. A man
    D. An eagle

12. Near which river did Ezekiel see the living creature?

    Ezekiel 10:15

    A. River of Ahava
    B. River of Arnon
    C. River of Chebar
    D. River of Jordan

13. Which gate did the spirit take Ezekiel to?

    Ezekiel 11:1

    A. North gate
    B. South gate
    C. East gate
    D. West gate

14. How many men did Ezekiel see at the gate?

    Ezekiel 11:1

    A. 3
    B. 7
    C. 12
    D. 25

15. Who was Jaazaniah's father?

    Ezekiel 11:1

    A. Azur
    B. Eber
    C. Omar
    D. Seir

16. Who was Pelatiah's father?

    Ezekiel 11:1

    A. Athaiah
    B. Benaiah
    C. Dalaiah
    D. Habaiah

17. What did the wicked men call Jerusalem?

    Ezekiel 11:2–3, 11:7

    A. A broken reed
    B. An injured eagle
    C. Kindling wood
    D. The caldron

18. Whose son died when Ezekiel prophesied?

    Ezekiel 11:13

    A. Athaiah's son
    B. Benaiah's son
    C. Dalaiah's son
    D. Habaiah's son

19. Where was Ezekiel taken by the Spirit of God to be with them of the captivity?

    Ezekiel 11:24

    A. Chaldea
    B. Idumaea
    C. Judaea
    D. Laodicea

20. Where will the LORD send the prince of Jerusalem?

    Ezekiel 12:8–13

    A. Aijalon
    B. Babylon
    C. Eltekon
    D. Heshbon

*Answers on page 771

AUGUST 30

Lesson 242
Today's Reading: *Ezekiel 13–15*
Period of Time: 594 BC
Author: Ezekiel

1. What does the LORD call Ezekiel?
   Ezekiel 13:2
   A. Son of God
   B. Son of man
   C. Son of Satan
   D. Son of woman

2. Which word is used to describe the prophets?
   Ezekiel 13:3
   A. Foolish
   B. Obedient
   C. Stupid
   D. Worthless

3. Which animals are the prophets like?
   Ezekiel 13:4
   A. Foxes
   B. Owls
   C. Scorpions
   D. Weasels

4. What did the prophets prophesy?
   Ezekiel 13:10
   A. The coming of the Messiah
   B. The end of the world
   C. The nation Israel would live in peace
   D. The rapture of the world

5. What does the LORD say the prophets used to build the wall?
   Ezekiel 13:10
   A. Gooey slime
   B. Mud plaster
   C. Tar pitch
   D. Untempered morter

6. What was **not** used by God to destroy the wall?
   Ezekiel 13:13
   A. A stormy wind
   B. A terrible earthquake
   C. An overflowing shower
   D. Great hailstones

7. What were the women prophets guilty of?
   Ezekiel 13:18
   A. Baking unleavened bread
   B. Not washing their hands before eating
   C. Sewing pillows to all armholes
   D. Touching diseased and dead bodies

8. What grain is mentioned that the women prophets were given to pollute God?
   Ezekiel 13:19
   A. Barley
   B. Flax
   C. Oats
   D. Wheat

9. What did the LORD say he would tear?
   Ezekiel 13:21
   A. Aprons
   B. Coats
   C. Girdles
   D. Kerchiefs

10. Where were the elders from that came to see Ezekiel?
    Ezekiel 14:1
    A. Assyria
    B. Babylon
    C. Egypt
    D. Israel

11. Where had the elders set up their idols?
    Ezekiel 14:3–7
    A. In their hearts
    B. In their homes
    C. In their streets
    D. In their temples

12. Which two of the following will the LORD make a man who does **not** turn away from all of his abominations?
    Ezekiel 14:8
    A. A beggar and a thief
    B. A cripple and an outcast
    C. A sign and a proverb
    D. A warlock and a charmer

13. What shall the punishment of the evil prophet be the same as?
    Ezekiel 14:10
    A. He that disobeys the prophet
    B. He that seeketh unto him
    C. The father who bore him
    D. The son of his loins

14. What is the *first* judgment mentioned upon the land when it grievously sinneth against God?
    Ezekiel 14:13–21
    A. Famine
    B. Noisome beasts
    C. Pestilence
    D. The sword

15. What is the *second* judgment mentioned upon the land when it grievously sinneth against God?
    Ezekiel 14:13–21
    A. Famine
    B. Noisome beasts
    C. Pestilence
    D. The sword

16. What is the *third* judgment mentioned upon the land when it grievously sinneth against God?
    Ezekiel 14:13–21
    A. Famine
    B. Noisome beasts
    C. Pestilence
    D. The sword

17. What is the *fourth* judgment mentioned upon the land when it grievously sinneth against God?
    Ezekiel 14:13–21
    A. Famine
    B. Noisome beasts
    C. Pestilence
    D. The sword

18. Which three men are mentioned as being in the land, but shall deliver neither son nor daughter?
    Ezekiel 14:13–21
    A. Isaac, Jacob, and Esau
    B. Noah, Daniel, and Job
    C. Peter, James, and John
    D. Saul, David, and Jonathan

19. Who shall comfort Israel concerning the evil God has brought upon Jerusalem?
    Ezekiel 14:22–23
    A. A king
    B. A prophet
    C. A remnant
    D. A savior

20. Which one of the following symbolizes the inhabitants of Jerusalem?
    Ezekiel 15:1–7
    A. The burning bush
    B. The green grass
    C. The mustard seed
    D. The vine tree

*Answers on page 771

AUGUST 31

Lesson 243
Today's Reading: *Ezekiel 16*
Period of Time: 594 BC
Author: Ezekiel

1. Where is Jerusalem's birth and nativity located?
   Ezekiel 16:3
   A. Land of Benjamin
   B. Land of Canaan
   C. Land of Pathros
   D. Land of Shinar

2. Who was Jerusalem's father?
   Ezekiel 16:3, 16:45
   A. An Amorite
   B. An Edomite
   C. An Ishmaelite
   D. An Oznite

3. Who was Jerusalem's mother?
   Ezekiel 16:3, 16:45
   A. A Canaanite
   B. A Garmite
   C. A Hittite
   D. A Timnite

4. How has the LORD multiplied Jerusalem?
   Ezekiel 16:7
   A. Like the apple of the tree
   B. Like the bud of the field
   C. Like the fish of the sea
   D. Like the rabbit of the pasture

5. What was the time as the LORD passed by Jerusalem?
   Ezekiel 16:8
   A. Time of grieving
   B. Time of harvest
   C. Time of love
   D. Time of sowing

6. What did the LORD clothe Jerusalem with?
   Ezekiel 16:10
   A. Badgers' skin
   B. Broidered work
   C. Fine linen
   D. Silk

7. What did the LORD shod Jerusalem with?
   Ezekiel 16:10
   A. Badgers' skin
   B. Broidered work
   C. Fine linen
   D. Silk

8. What did the LORD gird Jerusalem with?
   Ezekiel 16:10
   A. Badger's skin
   B. Broidered work
   C. Fine linen
   D. Silk

9. What did the LORD cover Jerusalem with?
   Ezekiel 16:10
   A. Badger's skin
   B. Broidered work
   C. Fine linen
   D. Silk

10. Which three items was Jerusalem fed that they now offer to their idols?
    Ezekiel 16:13, 16:19
    A. Bacon, eggs, and cheese
    B. Cake, nuts, and grasshoppers
    C. Flour, honey, and oil
    D. Meat, potatoes, and wine

11. What did Jerusalem put her trust in?
    Ezekiel 16:15
    A. Her beauty
    B. Her chariots
    C. Her footmen
    D. Her riches

12. What was found on Jerusalem's jeweled idols?
    Ezekiel 16:17
    A. Images of cherubims
    B. Images of eagles
    C. Images of lions
    D. Images of men

13. Whom did Jerusalem cause to pass through the fire?

    Ezekiel 16:20–21

    A. Children
    B. Elders
    C. Prisoners
    D. Slaves

14. Whom did Jerusalem commit fornication with?

    Ezekiel 16:26

    A. The Corinthians
    B. The Egyptians
    C. The Grecians
    D. The Persians

15. Who was ashamed of Jerusalem's lewd way?

    Ezekiel 16:27

    A. The Corinthians
    B. The Libertines
    C. The Philistines
    D. The Zebulunites

16. Whom did Jerusalem also play the whore with?

    Ezekiel 16:28

    A. The Assyrians
    B. The Barbarians
    C. The Parthians
    D. The Scythians

17. How will Jerusalem be judged?

    Ezekiel 16:38

    A. As beasts that devour the weak prey and shed blood
    B. As soldiers that spoil towns and shed blood
    C. As thieves that rob widow's homes and shed blood
    D. As women that break wedlock and shed blood

18. What proverb shall be used against Jerusalem?

    Ezekiel 16:44

    A. As is the father, so is his son.
    B. As is the mother, so is her daughter.
    C. As is the tree, so is its apple.
    D. As is the vine, so is its grape.

19. Who is Jerusalem's elder sister?

    Ezekiel 16:46–56

    A. Armenia
    B. Galatia
    C. Phrygia
    D. Samaria

20. Who is Jerusalem's younger sister?

    Ezekiel 16:46–56

    A. Samos
    B. Senir
    C. Sihon
    D. Sodom

*Answers on page 771

SEPTEMBER 1

Lesson 244
Today's Reading: *Ezekiel 17–19*
Period of Time: 594 BC
Author: Ezekiel

1. What did the LORD tell Ezekiel to do?
   Ezekiel 17:1–2
   A. Drink from a well
   B. Go naked upon the earth
   C. Sacrifice a lamb
   D. Tell a riddle

2. What type of bird appeared first?
   Ezekiel 17:3–6
   A. A blue bird
   B. A great eagle
   C. A red cardinal
   D. A scrawny dove

3. Where did the first bird fly to?
   Ezekiel 17:3
   A. Lebanon
   B. Magdala
   C. Rhegium
   D. Telebib

4. Where did the first bird plant a seed?
   Ezekiel 17:5
   A. Along a river
   B. By the highway
   C. In a fruitful field
   D. Upon a mountain

5. What type of tree did the first bird set the seed as?
   Ezekiel 17:5
   A. A cedar tree
   B. A maple tree
   C. A sycamore tree
   D. A willow tree

6. What kind of bird appeared after the first bird?
   Ezekiel 17:7–8
   A. A blue bird
   B. A great eagle
   C. A red cardinal
   D. A scrawny dove

7. What type of soil was the vine planted in?
   Ezekiel 17:8
   A. Good soil
   B. Rocky soil
   C. Sandy soil
   D. Swampy soil

8. Which direction will the wind come from causing the vine to wither?
   Ezekiel 17:10
   A. North
   B. South
   C. East
   D. West

9. What does the LORD call Israel?
   Ezekiel 17:12
   A. A virgin daughter
   B. An unfaithful wife
   C. The rebellious house
   D. The unprofitable son

10. Where were the princes of Israel taken to?
    Ezekiel 17:12
    A. Babylon
    B. Chilmad
    C. Lebanon
    D. Nineveh

11. Where did Israel send its ambassadors?
    Ezekiel 17:15
    A. Arpad
    B. Egypt
    C. Libya
    D. Mysia

12. From which tree shall the LORD crop off a tender twig?
    Ezekiel 17:22
    A. A cedar tree
    B. A maple tree
    C. A sycamore tree
    D. A willow tree

13. Where shall the LORD plant the tender twig?

    Ezekiel 17:22

    A. Upon a fertile field
    B. Upon a high mountain
    C. Upon a low valley
    D. Upon a narrow ditch

14. What have the fathers eaten?

    Ezekiel 18:2

    A. Bitter herbs
    B. Pigeon dung
    C. Rotten flesh
    D. Sour grapes

15. What will happen to the soul that sinneth?

    Ezekiel 18:20

    A. It shall die.
    B. It shall flourish.
    C. It shall lament.
    D. It shall rise.

16. Who besides the father shall also bear the iniquity of the father?

    Ezekiel 18:20

    A. The daughter
    B. The son
    C. The wife
    D. No one

17. What will happen if a wicked person turns from all the sins he has committed?

    Ezekiel 18:21

    A. He shall cry.
    B. He shall grieve.
    C. He shall live.
    D. He shall vomit.

18. What did the people say concerning God?

    Ezekiel 18:25, 18:29

    A. The Almighty does not exist.
    B. The LORD is my shepherd.
    C. The throne of God is unsearchable.
    D. The way of the LORD is not equal.

19. Which two things does the LORD tell Israel to make new?

    Ezekiel 18:31

    A. Their barn and hayfield
    B. Their field and pasture
    C. Their heart and spirit
    D. Their vesture and shoes

20. What did the LORD tell Ezekiel to do for the princes of Israel?

    Ezekiel 19:1

    A. Give them bread to eat.
    B. Take up a lamentation for them.
    C. Unbridle the bit in their mouth.
    D. Wash their feet.

*Answers on page 771

SEPTEMBER 2

Lesson 245
Today's Reading: *Ezekiel 20–21*
Period of Time: 593 BC
Author: Ezekiel

1. When did the elders visit Ezekiel?
   Ezekiel 20:1
   A. 4th year, 7th month, 9th day
   B. 5th year, 2nd month, 6th day
   C. 7th year, 5th month, 10th day
   D. 10th year, 3rd month, 8th day

2. Why did the elders visit Ezekiel?
   Ezekiel 20:1
   A. To arrest Ezekiel
   B. To bring Neriah a gift
   C. To cast stones at Baruch
   D. To enquire of the LORD

3. From which nation did the LORD bring Israel out of captivity?
   Ezekiel 20:6–10
   A. Egypt
   B. Joppa
   C. Ophir
   D. Salem

4. How did the LORD describe the Promised Land?
   Ezekiel 20:6
   A. A land flowing with milk and honey
   B. A land luxuriant in gold and silver
   C. A land rich in springs and minerals
   D. A land vibrant in fish and meat

5. Where did the LORD give Israel his statutes?
   Ezekiel 20:10–11
   A. Along the river of Jordan
   B. In the wilderness
   C. Near the temple wall
   D. Upon mount Ararat

6. What was the sign between God and Israel?
   Ezekiel 20:12, 20:20
   A. A pile of 12 rocks
   B. Angels dressed in white
   C. God's miracles
   D. The sabbaths

7. What was the name of the high place where Israel blasphemed the LORD?
   Ezekiel 20:27–29
   A. Bamah
   B. Obama
   C. Osama
   D. Samah

8. What did Israel do to her children?
   Ezekiel 20:31
   A. Crushed them with great stones
   B. Drowned them in the Nile
   C. Murdered them using swords
   D. Sacrificed them by fire to idols

9. Who shall pass under the rod?
   Ezekiel 20:27–37
   A. Israel
   B. Jakan
   C. Putiel
   D. Shilhi

10. Where will the house of Israel serve the LORD and bring their offerings?
    Ezekiel 20:40
    A. Above the fruited plain
    B. By the banks of the river of Jordan
    C. In King Solomon's banquet hall
    D. Upon the LORD's holy mountain

11. Which direction did the LORD tell Ezekiel to face?
    Ezekiel 20:46
    A. North
    B. South
    C. East
    D. West

12. Which city did the LORD tell Ezekiel to turn toward?

    Ezekiel 21:2

    A. Bethphage
    B. Capernaum
    C. Jerusalem
    D. Nicopolis

13. Who shall draw forth his sword?

    Ezekiel 21:3

    A. David
    B. God
    C. Michael
    D. Naaman

14. What shall be as weak as water?

    Ezekiel 21:7

    A. All arms
    B. All knees
    C. All necks
    D. All stomachs

15. Which one of the following is an Ammonite city?

    Ezekiel 21:20

    A. Bathrabbim
    B. Jotbathah
    C. Rabbath
    D. Tabbath

16. Which city is located within Judah?

    Ezekiel 21:20

    A. Damascus
    B. Lebanon
    C. Jerusalem
    D. Samaria

17. What did the king of Babylon use for divination in Ezekiel 21:21?

    Ezekiel 21:21

    A. A heart
    B. A liver
    C. A spleen
    D. An eye

18. Which wicked prince shall remove his crown?

    Ezekiel 21:25–26

    A. The prince of Assyria
    B. The prince of Babylon
    C. The prince of Egypt
    D. The prince of Israel

19. What word is repeated three times in Ezekiel 21:27?

    Ezekiel 21:27

    A. Blasphemy
    B. Cursed
    C. Overturn
    D. Verily

20. Who shall become fuel for the fire and be remembered no more?

    Ezekiel 21:28–32

    A. The Ammonites
    B. The Babylonians
    C. The Medes
    D. The Persians

*Answers on page 771

SEPTEMBER 3

Lesson 246
Today's Reading: *Ezekiel 22–23*
Period of Time: 593 BC
Author: Ezekiel

1. What does the LORD call Jerusalem?
   Ezekiel 22:2
   A. The bloody city
   B. The clean city
   C. The dirty city
   D. The holy city

2. What has the LORD made Jerusalem to the heathen?
   Ezekiel 22:4
   A. A breadbasket
   B. A haven
   C. A quiver
   D. A reproach

3. What has the LORD made Jerusalem to all countries?
   Ezekiel 22:4
   A. A burning
   B. A healing
   C. A mocking
   D. A shielding

4. What did the princes of Jerusalem see?
   Ezekiel 22:6–10
   A. Their city besieged
   B. Their father's nakedness
   C. Their ships ruined
   D. Their wells dried up

5. What has the house of Israel become to the LORD?
   Ezekiel 22:18
   A. Diamonds
   B. Dross
   C. Dung
   D. Dust

6. What will the LORD do to Jerusalem?
   Ezekiel 22:20–21
   A. Crush it
   B. Drown it
   C. Melt it
   D. Sell it

7. Who does the LORD say is like a roaring lion ravening the prey?
   Ezekiel 22:25
   A. Priests
   B. Princes
   C. Prophets
   D. Prostitutes

8. Who hid their eyes from the LORD's sabbaths?
   Ezekiel 22:26
   A. Priests
   B. Princes
   C. Prophets
   D. Prostitutes

9. Who are like wolves ravening the prey?
   Ezekiel 22:27
   A. Priests
   B. Princes
   C. Prophets
   D. Prostitutes

10. How many men formed a hedge and stood in the gap before the LORD?
    Ezekiel 22:30
    A. 10
    B. 20
    C. 30
    D. None

11. In the parable, how many daughters came from the same mother?
    Ezekiel 23:2
    A. 2
    B. 8
    C. 12
    D. None

12. Where did the daughters commit whoredom?

    Ezekiel 23:3

    A. Asia
    B. Egypt
    C. Greece
    D. Rome

13. Whom does Aholah represent?

    Ezekiel 23:4

    A. Babylon
    B. Corinth
    C. Jerusalem
    D. Samaria

14. Whom does Aholibah represent?

    Ezekiel 23:4

    A. Babylon
    B. Corinth
    C. Jerusalem
    D. Samaria

15. Who were Aholah's lovers?

    Ezekiel 23:5

    A. The Assyrians
    B. The Corinthians
    C. The Persians
    D. The Thessalonians

16. Who were Aholibah's lovers?

    Ezekiel 23:11–17

    A. The Athenians
    B. The Babylonians
    C. The Romans
    D. The Sidonians

17. What shall Aholibah do in her distress?

    Ezekiel 23:34

    A. Cut her wrists
    B. Drink a cup of hemlock
    C. Jump from a towering cliff
    D. Pluck off her breasts

18. What evil practice did the people of Jerusalem commit?

    Ezekiel 23:37

    A. They ate meat offered to idols.
    B. They drank water turned into wine.
    C. They offered their sons by fire.
    D. They shaved the corners of their beards.

19. Who placed bracelets upon the daughter's hands and crowns upon their heads?

    Ezekiel 23:42

    A. The Alexandrians
    B. The Bereans
    C. The Ethiopians
    D. The Sabeans

20. What is in the hand of the adulteresses?

    Ezekiel 23:45

    A. Blood
    B. Money
    C. Perfume
    D. Shame

*Answers on page 771

SEPTEMBER 4

Lesson 247
Today's Reading: *Ezekiel 24–26*
Period of Time: 590 BC
Author: Ezekiel

1. When did the word of the LORD come to Ezekiel?
   Ezekiel 24:1
   A. 2nd year, 6th month, 12th day
   B. 5th year, 3rd month, 7th day
   C. 9th year, 10th month, 10th day
   D. 14th year, 8th month, 21st day

2. What did the LORD call the house of Judah?
   Ezekiel 24:3
   A. The clamorous house
   B. The flirtatious house
   C. The rebellious house
   D. The treacherous house

3. What did the LORD tell Ezekiel to do?
   Ezekiel 24:3–5
   A. Baptize his followers
   B. Boil bones in a pot
   C. Bray like a donkey
   D. Bury a hatchet

4. Which one of Ezekiel's relatives died in the evening?
   Ezekiel 24:16–18
   A. His mother
   B. His son
   C. His uncle
   D. His wife

5. What was Ezekiel forbidden to do after his relative died?
   Ezekiel 24:16–18
   A. Bury the body
   B. Eat any food
   C. Mourn nor weep
   D. Wash his hands

6. From which direction would men come to conquer the Ammonites?
   Ezekiel 25:2–4
   A. North
   B. South
   C. East
   D. West

7. Where will the LORD make a stable for camels?
   Ezekiel 25:5
   A. Maralah
   B. Rabbah
   C. Selah
   D. Taralah

8. Who—along with Moab—said, "The house of Judah is like unto all the heathen"?
   Ezekiel 25:8
   A. Beer
   B. Hali
   C. Nain
   D. Seir

9. Which one of the following places is located in Moab?
   Ezekiel 25:9
   A. Hierapolis
   B. Kiriathaim
   C. Pihahiroth
   D. Trogyllium

10. Whom will the LORD punish for taking vengeance on the house of Judah?
    Ezekiel 25:12
    A. Edom
    B. Elim
    C. Etam
    D. Ezem

11. Which place will God make desolate?

    Ezekiel 25:13

    A. Addan
    B. Golan
    C. Haran
    D. Teman

12. Which place shall fall by the sword?

    Ezekiel 25:13

    A. Dedan
    B. Gozan
    C. Mahanehdan
    D. Padan

13. Which people along the sea coast shall the LORD furiously rebuke?

    Ezekiel 25:15–17

    A. The Corinthians
    B. The Nicolaitanes
    C. The Philistines
    D. The Thessalonians

14. Whom will the LORD cut off?

    Ezekiel 25:16

    A. The Cherethims
    B. The Horims
    C. The Nethinims
    D. The Zamzummims

15. When did the LORD speak to Ezekiel regarding Tyrus?

    Ezekiel 26:1–2

    A. 3rd year, 21st day
    B. 5th year, 14th day
    C. 9th year, 7th day
    D. 11th year, 1st day

16. What will Tyrus be like?

    Ezekiel 26:4

    A. The bottom of a sea
    B. The cracks of a cup
    C. The sides of a wall
    D. The top of a rock

17. Who will conquer Tyrus?

    Ezekiel 26:7

    A. Namaan
    B. Nebuchadrezzar
    C. Nicodemus
    D. Noadiah

18. Which musical instruments did Ezekiel say shall no longer be heard in Tyrus?

    Ezekiel 26:13

    A. Harps
    B. Lutes
    C. Pipes
    D. Viols

19. What does Ezekiel say regarding Tyre's future?

    Ezekiel 26:14

    A. It shall be built no more.
    B. Kings shall rise from there.
    C. People shall come to worship there.
    D. Sons shall slay dragons in its caves.

20. Who shall come down from their thrones, and lay away their robes, and put off their broidered garments?

    Ezekiel 26:16

    A. The kings of Egypt
    B. The princes of the sea
    C. The queen of Sheba
    D. The rulers of the Greeks

Answers on page 771

SEPTEMBER 5

Lesson 248
Today's Reading: *Ezekiel 27–28*
Period of Time: 590 BC
Author: Ezekiel

1. What did Tyrus say?
   Ezekiel 27:3
   A. "All beautiful women hail from Tyrus."
   B. "Beauty is in the eye of the beholder."
   C. "I am of perfect beauty."
   D. "We build beautiful ships."

2. What was the fir trees of Senir used for on ships?
   Ezekiel 27:5
   A. Anchors
   B. Masts
   C. Oars
   D. Ship boards

3. What were the cedars of Lebanon used for on ships?
   Ezekiel 27:5
   A. Anchors
   B. Masts
   C. Oars
   D. Ship boards

4. What were the oaks of Bashan used for on ships?
   Ezekiel 27:6
   A. Anchors
   B. Masts
   C. Oars
   D. Ship boards

5. Who made benches for the ships?
   Ezekiel 27:6
   A. The Ashurites
   B. The Hagarites
   C. The Mithnites
   D. The Sodomites

6. What were the benches made of?
   Ezekiel 27:6
   A. Beryl
   B. Gold
   C. Ivory
   D. Saphire

7. Where did the fine linen come from to make the ship's sails?
   Ezekiel 27:7
   A. Assyria
   B. Egypt
   C. Greece
   D. Libya

8. Besides Zidon, where were the mariners from?
   Ezekiel 27:8
   A. Arvad
   B. Gebal
   C. Judah
   D. Tyrus

9. Where were the ship's pilots from?
   Ezekiel 27:8
   A. Arvad
   B. Gebal
   C. Judah
   D. Tyrus

10. Where were the ship caulkers from?
    Ezekiel 27:9
    A. Arvad
    B. Gebal
    C. Judah
    D. Tyrus

11. Who was in the towers of Tyrus?
    Ezekiel 27:11
    A. The Ammonites
    B. The Gammadims
    C. The Shunammites
    D. The Zamzummims

12. Who traded using horses, horsemen, and mules?
    Ezekiel 27:14
    A. House of Abelbethmaachah
    B. House of Gomorrah
    C. House of Kibrothhattaavah
    D. House of Togarmah

13. Who traded using emeralds, coral, and agate?

    Ezekiel 27:16

    A. Arabia
    B. Mesopotamia
    C. Philadelphia
    D. Syria

14. Who traded using wheat, honey, oil, and balm?

    Ezekiel 27:17

    A. Arvad
    B. Gebal
    C. Judah
    D. Tyrus

15. Who traded using wine of Helbon and white wool?

    Ezekiel 27:18

    A. Damascus
    B. Emmaus
    C. Miletus
    D. Tarsus

16. Who traded using precious clothes for chariots?

    Ezekiel 27:20

    A. Dedan
    B. Hauran
    C. Nibshan
    D. Teman

17. Who traded using lambs, rams, and goats?

    Ezekiel 27:21

    A. Arabia
    B. Grecia
    C. Lycia
    D. Syria

18. What did the prince of Tyrus say?

    Ezekiel 28:2

    A. Bless the God of Israel.
    B. God only knows.
    C. I am a God.
    D. There is no god, but God.

19. Where had the king of Tyrus been to?

    Ezekiel 28:12–13

    A. Cush
    B. Eden
    C. Moab
    D. Zoan

20. What does the LORD call those that despise Israel?

    Ezekiel 28:20–24

    A. A burning ague
    B. A crumbling tower
    C. A hissing viper
    D. A pricking brier

Answers on page 771

SEPTEMBER 6

Lesson 249
Today's Reading: *Ezekiel 29–31*
Period of Time: 589–588 BC
Author: Ezekiel

1. When did Ezekiel prophesy against Egypt?
   Ezekiel 29:1
   A. 10th year, 10th month, 12th day
   B. 16th year, 6th month, 7th day
   C. 21st year, 2nd month, 19th day
   D. 27th year, 1st month, 1st day

2. What did the LORD call Pharaoh?
   Ezekiel 29:3
   A. The bloody lion
   B. The great dragon
   C. The leaky boat
   D. The weak rope

3. What did Pharaoh claim he made?
   Ezekiel 29:3, 29:9
   A. A city
   B. A desert
   C. A mountain
   D. A river

4. How many years would Egypt live in exile?
   Ezekiel 29:10–13
   A. 20
   B. 40
   C. 60
   D. 80

5. Where would the Egyptians return to?
   Ezekiel 29:14
   A. Land of Ephesus
   B. Land of Michmas
   C. Land of Pathros
   D. Land of Salamis

6. When did the word of the LORD come to Ezekiel regarding the wages for the army of Babylon?
   Ezekiel 29:17
   A. 10th year, 10th month, 12th day
   B. 16th year, 6th month, 7th day
   C. 21st year, 2nd month, 19th day
   D. 27th year, 1st month, 1st day

7. Who was the king of Babylon?
   Ezekiel 29:18, 30:10
   A. King Adonizedek
   B. King Ben-ha'dad
   C. King Nebuchadrezzar
   D. King Zechariah

8. In which city was every head made bald?
   Ezekiel 29:18
   A. Chios
   B. Hanes
   C. Jebus
   D. Tyrus

9. Where shall there be great pain?
   Ezekiel 30:4
   A. Ethiopia
   B. Galatia
   C. Philistia
   D. Samaria

10. Which nation was in alliance with Egypt?
    Ezekiel 30:5
    A. Chub
    B. Elon
    C. Gaza
    D. Hena

11. Which area will become utterly waste and desolate?
    Ezekiel 29:10, 30:6–9
    A. From the tower of Babel to Libya
    B. From the tower of Hananeel to Sidon
    C. From the tower of Penuel to Damascus
    D. From the tower of Syene to Ethiopia

12. Where will the LORD make the images to cease?
    Ezekiel 30:13
    A. Cush
    B. Edom
    C. Noph
    D. Zoan

13. In which city will the LORD set a fire?

    Ezekiel 30:14–16

    A. Cush
    B. Edom
    C. Noph
    D. Zoan

14. In which city will the LORD execute judgments?

    Ezekiel 30:14–16

    A. No
    B. Po
    C. So
    D. To

15. Upon which city will the LORD pour his fury?

    Ezekiel 30:15–16

    A. Pau
    B. Sin
    C. Tob
    D. Zer

16. Where will the LORD break the yokes of Egypt?

    Ezekiel 30:18

    A. Alexandria
    B. Memphis
    C. Tehaphnehes
    D. Zafarana

17. When did the LORD tell Ezekiel he had broken Pharaoh's arm?

    Ezekiel 30:20–26

    A. 10th year, 10th month, 10th day
    B. 11th year, 1st month, 7th day
    C. 12th year, 2nd month, 17th day
    D. 13th year, 7th month, 6th day

18. When did the LORD order Ezekiel to speak to Pharaoh?

    Ezekiel 31:1–2

    A. 9th year, 8th month, 7th day
    B. 10th year, 10th month, 11th day
    C. 11th year, 3rd month, 1st day
    D. 14th year, 7th month, 8th day

19. Who represented a cedar in Lebanon with fair branches and a high stature?

    Ezekiel 31:3

    A. The Assyrian
    B. The Babylonian
    C. The Chaldean
    D. The Grecian

20. Which trees envied the cedar in Lebanon?

    Ezekiel 31:3–18

    A. Trees of Beer
    B. Trees of Eden
    C. Trees of Hali
    D. Trees of Lehi

*Answers on page 771

SEPTEMBER 7

Lesson 250
Today's Reading: *Ezekiel 32–33*
Period of Time: 587 BC
Author: Ezekiel

1. When was Ezekiel ordered to take up a lamentation for Pharaoh, king of Egypt?
   Ezekiel 32:1–2
   A. 6th year, 6th month, 2nd day
   B. 12th year, 12th month, 1st day
   C. 18th year, 3rd month, 3rd day
   D. 24th year, 4th month, 4th day

2. What is Pharaoh compared to the first time?
   Ezekiel 32:2
   A. A blind camel of the desert
   B. A hyena scorning the great eagle
   C. A wild colt never ridden
   D. A young lion of the nations

3. What is Pharaoh compared to the second time?
   Ezekiel 32:2
   A. A great fish swallowing a man
   B. A hook in behemoth's mouth
   C. A net overflowing with fish
   D. A whale in the seas

4. What shall be upon the land of Egypt?
   Ezekiel 32:6
   A. Blood
   B. Frogs
   C. Gnats
   D. Lice

5. Who shall overthrow Egypt?
   Ezekiel 32:11
   A. Babylon
   B. Greece
   C. Rome
   D. Syria

6. When did the LORD order Ezekiel to wail for the multitude of Egypt?
   Ezekiel 32:17–18
   A. 4th year, 13th day
   B. 8th year, 14th day
   C. 12th year, 15th day
   D. 16th year, 16th day

7. What is the first nation that Ezekiel states has already been defeated?
   Ezekiel 32:22
   A. Asshur
   B. Cappadocia
   C. Pontus
   D. Rome

8. What is the second nation that Ezekiel states has already been defeated?
   Ezekiel 32:24
   A. Eden
   B. Elam
   C. Enam
   D. Ezem

9. What other two nations does Ezekiel state have already been defeated?
   Ezekiel 32:26
   A. Dimonah and Gebal
   B. Kibzaim and Lycia
   C. Meshech and Tubal
   D. Rakkath and Adria

10. What is the fifth nation that Ezekiel states has already been defeated?
    Ezekiel 32:29
    A. Ava
    B. Edom
    C. Horem
    D. Kedesh

11. What is the last nation that Ezekiel states has already been defeated?
    Ezekiel 32:30
    A. Ammon
    B. Heshmon
    C. Rimmon
    D. Zidon

12. Which musical instrument did Judah use to warn the people of danger?

    Ezekiel 33:3–5

    A. The bell
    B. The drum
    C. The trumpet
    D. The viola

13. Who shall die because of his iniquity?

    Ezekiel 33:18

    A. He who loves his family
    B. He who turns from righteousness
    C. He who works his field
    D. He who worships the LORD

14. Which man shall surely live?

    Ezekiel 33:19

    A. He who beats his slave
    B. He who cheats his workers
    C. He who robs the rich
    D. He who turns from his wickedness

15. When did one escape and tell Ezekiel, "The city is smitten"?

    Ezekiel 33:21

    A. 6th year, 9th month, 3rd day
    B. 12th year, 10th month, 5th day
    C. 18th year, 11th month, 7th day
    D. 24th year, 12th month, 9th day

16. What did the LORD do to Ezekiel before the messenger arrived?

    Ezekiel 33:21–22

    A. Made him dumb
    B. Made him eat grass
    C. Made him preach
    D. Made him walk naked

17. Who inherited the Promised Land?

    Ezekiel 33:24

    A. Abraham
    B. Cain
    C. Moses
    D. Noah

18. What shall those in forts and caves die of?

    Ezekiel 33:27

    A. Earthquakes
    B. Old age
    C. Pestilence
    D. Wounds

19. What is Ezekiel like unto the people?

    Ezekiel 33:32

    A. A carpenter
    B. A gardener
    C. A miller
    D. A singer

20. What will the people finally realize about Ezekiel?

    Ezekiel 33:33

    A. He was a fool.
    B. He was a king.
    C. He was a prophet.
    D. He was a scribe.

*Answers on page 771

SEPTEMBER 8

Lesson 251
Today's Reading: *Ezekiel 34–36*
Period of Time: 587 BC
Author: Ezekiel

1. Which one of the following did the LORD say he was displeased with in Israel?
   Ezekiel 34:2
   A. Bakers
   B. Carpenters
   C. Merchants
   D. Shepherds

2. What wandered through all the mountains and upon every hill?
   Ezekiel 34:6
   A. Dragons
   B. Sheep
   C. Unicorns
   D. Wild beasts

3. Which two of the following will the LORD destroy?
   Ezekiel 34:16
   A. The babes and children
   B. The fat and strong
   C. The poor and diseased
   D. The wealthy and elderly

4. What does the LORD say he judges between?
   Ezekiel 34:17, 34:22
   A. Cattle and cattle
   B. Doves and doves
   C. Fish and fish
   D. Snakes and snakes

5. What else does the LORD say he judges between?
   Ezekiel 34:17
   A. Cattle and she-goats
   B. Lambs and she bears
   C. Rams and he goats
   D. Sheep and he bears

6. What else will the LORD judge between?
   Ezekiel 34:20
   A. Fat bears and wild bears
   B. Fat cattle and lean cattle
   C. Fat lions and thin lions
   D. Fat mules and stubborn mules

7. How many shepherds shall the LORD set over his flock?
   Ezekiel 34:23
   A. 1
   B. 7
   C. 12
   D. 40

8. Whom does the LORD call his servant?
   Ezekiel 34:23
   A. David
   B. Joshua
   C. Moses
   D. Samuel

9. What shall the LORD bring upon the land?
   Ezekiel 34:26
   A. Divers earthquakes
   B. Great floods
   C. Plagues of locusts
   D. Showers of blessing

10. Which mountain will the LORD make desolate?
    Ezekiel 35:2–3
    A. Mount Ararat
    B. Mount Carmel
    C. Mount Seir
    D. Mount Tabor

11. What shall pursue those who have killed the children of Israel?
    Ezekiel 35:6
    A. Blood
    B. Lions
    C. Pestilence
    D. Snakes

12. Whom has the LORD spoken against in the fire of his jealousy?

    Ezekiel 36:5

    A. Carmel
    B. Gibeon
    C. Idumea
    D. Tophet

13. What has the land of Israel borne?

    Ezekiel 36:6

    A. The chastisement of the sons
    B. The iniquities of the prophets
    C. The reproach of the kings
    D. The shame of the heathen

14. What shall the mountains of Israel no longer devour?

    Ezekiel 36:8–14

    A. Groves
    B. Idols
    C. Men
    D. Rams

15. How did the house of Israel defile the land?

    Ezekiel 36:17

    A. Like a dung hill outside the city
    B. Like a pig living in a sty
    C. Like the ox that treadeth out the corn
    D. Like the uncleanness of a removed woman

16. What does Ezekiel say the LORD will sanctify?

    Ezekiel 36:23

    A. His land
    B. His name
    C. His people
    D. His spirit

17. What shall the LORD do to his people?

    Ezekiel 36:25

    A. Baptize them in the pool of Siloam
    B. Cleanse them upon the lavers of brass
    C. Sprinkle clean water upon them
    D. Wash them in the river of Jordan

18. What shall the LORD take from Israel?

    Ezekiel 36:26

    A. The broken foot
    B. The hissing tongue
    C. The iron fist
    D. The stony heart

19. What shall the land of Israel become like?

    Ezekiel 36:35

    A. The garden of Eden
    B. The kingdom of Solomon
    C. The lily of the valley
    D. The vineyard of Naboth

20. What shall the waste cities be filled with?

    Ezekiel 36:38

    A. Clusters of grapes
    B. Flocks of men
    C. Herds of cattle
    D. Pools of fish

*Answers on page 771

SEPTEMBER 9

Lesson 252
Today's Reading: *Ezekiel 37–38*
Period of Time: 587 BC
Author: Ezekiel

1. Where did the LORD take Ezekiel to?
   Ezekiel 37:1–7
   A. A cave
   B. A mountain
   C. A river
   D. A valley

2. What happened first?
   Ezekiel 37:1–7
   A. Breath entered the bones
   B. Dust became bones
   C. Sinews, flesh and skin covered the bones
   D. The bones came together

3. What happened second?
   Ezekiel 37:8
   A. Breath entered the bones
   B. Dust became bones
   C. Sinews, flesh and skin covered the bones
   D. The bones came together

4. What happened third?
   Ezekiel 37:9–10
   A. Breath entered the bones
   B. Dust became bones
   C. Sinews, flesh and skin covered the bones
   D. The bones came together

5. How did the bones become alive?
   Ezekiel 37:9–10
   A. An angel commanded the bones to live
   B. Ezekiel touched the bones
   C. Lightning shocked the bones
   D. The wind breathed upon the bones

6. What did the living bones represent?
   Ezekiel 37:11
   A. Egypt
   B. Israel
   C. Lebanon
   D. Syria

7. What will the LORD open?
   Ezekiel 37:12–13
   A. Bottles
   B. Doors
   C. Graves
   D. Prisons

8. Whom did the first stick represent?
   Ezekiel 37:16
   A. Babylon
   B. Ephraim
   C. Judah
   D. Tyrus

9. Whom did the second stick represent?
   Ezekiel 37:16
   A. Babylon
   B. Ephraim
   C. Judah
   D. Tyrus

10. In the end, how many sticks did Ezekiel hold in his hand?
    Ezekiel 37:17–22
    A. 1
    B. 2
    C. 3
    D. 4

11. How many nations will be in the Promised Land after the LORD gathers the children of Israel?
    Ezekiel 37:22
    A. 1
    B. 2
    C. 3
    D. 4

12. How many kings will be over the Promised Land after the LORD gathers the children of Israel?

    Ezekiel 37:22

    A. 1
    B. 2
    C. 3
    D. 4

13. How many nations did the people of Israel belong to before God gathered his people?

    Ezekiel 37:22

    A. 1
    B. 2
    C. 3
    D. 4

14. Who will be Israel's prince forever?

    Ezekiel 37:24–25

    A. Abel
    B. Benjamin
    C. Cain
    D. David

15. How many shepherds will be over Israel?

    Ezekiel 37:24–25

    A. 1
    B. 2
    C. 3
    D. 4

16. What will be in the midst of Israel forever?

    Ezekiel 37:26–28

    A. The flaming sword
    B. The LORD's sanctuary
    C. The mountain of love
    D. The river of life

17. Who is the chief prince of Meshech and Tubal?

    Ezekiel 38:2

    A. Asa
    B. Eli
    C. Gog
    D. Hur

18. How will the army of the north attack Israel?

    Ezekiel 38:1–9

    A. Like a bee
    B. Like a hornet
    C. Like a pestilence
    D. Like a storm

19. How will the army of the north cover Israel?

    Ezekiel 38:1–9, 38:16

    A. Like a blanket
    B. Like a cloud
    C. Like a flood
    D. Like a shadow

20. Who will be destroyed—along with his bands—with the sword, pestilence, great hailstones, fire, and brimstone?

    Ezekiel 38:18–22

    A. Asa
    B. Eli
    C. Gog
    D. Hur

Answers on page 771

SEPTEMBER 10

Lesson 253
Today's Reading: *Ezekiel 39–40*
Period of Time: 587–575 BC
Author: Ezekiel

1. Which two nations is Gog the chief prince of?
   Ezekiel 39:1
   A. Ammon and Uphaz
   B. Ethiopia and Berea
   C. Meshech and Tubal
   D. Ptolemais and Ono

2. What does Gog hold in his left hand?
   Ezekiel 39:3
   A. A bow
   B. A knife
   C. A mace
   D. A spear

3. What does Gog hold in his right hand?
   Ezekiel 39:3
   A. Arrows
   B. Brigandines
   C. Chains
   D. Treaties

4. Where will the LORD send a fire?
   Ezekiel 39:6
   A. Hukok
   B. Liddya
   C. Magog
   D. Pekod

5. What name does the LORD use for himself in Ezekiel 39:7?
   Ezekiel 39:7
   A. Deliverer
   B. Holy One in Israel
   C. The great God
   D. Word of life

6. How many years will it take Israel to burn Gog's weapons?
   Ezekiel 39:9
   A. 2
   B. 3
   C. 6
   D. 7

7. Where will Gog's army be slain?
   Ezekiel 39:11
   A. Valley of Berachah
   B. Valley of Gibeon
   C. Valley of the Passengers
   D. Valley of the son of Hinnom

8. What will they call the valley after Gog's army is slain there?
   Ezekiel 39:11, 39:15
   A. Valley of Baca
   B. Valley of Hamongog
   C. Valley of salt
   D. Valley of the giants

9. How many months will it take Israel to bury the dead bodies of Gog?
   Ezekiel 39:12
   A. 3
   B. 7
   C. 9
   D. 11

10. During which year of Israel's captivity did Ezekiel have the vision of the man?
    Ezekiel 40:1
    A. 7th
    B. 13th
    C. 19th
    D. 25th

11. What was the man's appearance like in the vision?
    Ezekiel 40:3
    A. Brass
    B. Gold
    C. Iron
    D. Silver

12. In addition to a measuring reed, what else was the man in the vision holding?

    Ezekiel 40:3

    A. A flaming sword
    B. A line of flax
    C. A purse with five coins
    D. A sack filled with flour

13. Which gate did the man in the vision measure first?

    Ezekiel 40:3–6

    A. North gate
    B. South gate
    C. East gate
    D. West gate

14. How many chambers were in the outward court?

    Ezekiel 40:17

    A. 10
    B. 20
    C. 30
    D. 40

15. Toward which gate of the Inner Court were the burnt offerings washed?

    Ezekiel 40:35–38

    A. North gate
    B. South gate
    C. East gate
    D. West gate

16. Which type of tree was upon each post and arch?

    Ezekiel 40:16–37

    A. Cedar tree
    B. Elm tree
    C. Oak tree
    D. Palm tree

17. How many tables were used to slay the *offerings*?

    Ezekiel 40:39

    A. 4
    B. 8
    C. 12
    D. 16

18. How many tables were used to slay the *sacrifices*?

    Ezekiel 40:41

    A. 4
    B. 8
    C. 12
    D. 16

19. Which chambers were located without the inner gate in the inner court at the side of the north?

    Ezekiel 40:44

    A. Craftsmen's chambers
    B. Hewers' chambers
    C. Priests' chambers
    D. Singers' chambers

20. Whose sons were priests—the keepers of the charge of the altar?

    Ezekiel 40:46

    A. Cain's sons
    B. Esau's sons
    C. Paul's sons
    D. Zadok's sons

*Answers on page 772

Lesson 254
Today's Reading: *Ezekiel 41–43*
Period of Time: 587–575 BC
Author: Ezekiel

SEPTEMBER 11

1. How broad was each post of the tabernacle measured in cubits?
   Ezekiel 41:1
   A. 2
   B. 3
   C. 5
   D. 6

2. How broad was the door of the tabernacle measured in cubits?
   Ezekiel 41:2
   A. 10
   B. 20
   C. 30
   D. 40

3. How broad was the most holy place measured in cubits?
   Ezekiel 41:4
   A. 10
   B. 20
   C. 30
   D. 40

4. How broad was each side chamber measured in cubits?
   Ezekiel 41:5
   A. 2
   B. 4
   C. 6
   D. 8

5. How many stories did the side chambers have?
   Ezekiel 41:6
   A. 2
   B. 3
   C. 4
   D. 5

6. What was the total number of side chambers on each floor?
   Ezekiel 41:6
   A. 10
   B. 20
   C. 30
   D. 40

7. How long was the house measured in cubits?
   Ezekiel 41:13
   A. 20
   B. 40
   C. 80
   D. 100

8. Which type of tree was between each cherub?
   Ezekiel 41:18
   A. A cedar tree
   B. A fig tree
   C. A maple tree
   D. A palm tree

9. Which two faces were on each cherub?
   Ezekiel 41:19
   A. A bear and a leopard
   B. A goat and a ram
   C. A lamb and a bullock
   D. A man and a lion

10. How many cubits high was the altar of wood?
    Ezekiel 41:22
    A. 2
    B. 3
    C. 4
    D. 5

11. How many cubits was the length of the altar of wood?
    Ezekiel 41:22
    A. 2
    B. 3
    C. 4
    D. 5

12. How many stories high were the galleries have?

    Ezekiel 42:3

    A. 3
    B. 6
    C. 9
    D. 12

13. What were the north and south chambers called?

    Ezekiel 42:13

    A. Anointed grottoes
    B. Holy chambers
    C. Prayer closets
    D. Sanctified tabernacles

14. What was the length measured in reeds on the east side?

    Ezekiel 42:16

    A. 100
    B. 300
    C. 500
    D. 700

15. From which direction did the glory of God appear?

    Ezekiel 43:2

    A. North
    B. South
    C. East
    D. West

16. What was the LORD's voice like?

    Ezekiel 43:2

    A. Blasting trumpets
    B. Clapping thunder
    C. Many waters
    D. Rushing chariots

17. Near which river did Ezekiel have a vision?

    Ezekiel 43:3

    A. River Ahava
    B. River Arnon
    C. River Chebar
    D. River Euphrates

18. How many horns did the altar have?

    Ezekiel 43:15, 43:20

    A. 4
    B. 8
    C. 12
    D. 16

19. What shall the priest cast upon the burnt offering?

    Ezekiel 43:24

    A. Frankincense
    B. Gold
    C. Myrrh
    D. Salt

20. How many days was the altar to be purged and purified?

    Ezekiel 43:26

    A. 7
    B. 14
    C. 21
    D. 28

*Answers on page 772

Lesson 255
Today's Reading: *Ezekiel 44–45*
Period of Time: 587–575 BC
Author: Ezekiel

SEPTEMBER 12

1. Which gate was shut?
   Ezekiel 44:1
   A. North gate
   B. South gate
   C. East gate
   D. West gate

2. Who shall eat bread before the LORD in the gate that is shut?
   Ezekiel 44:3
   A. The angel
   B. The king
   C. The prince
   D. The scribe

3. From which gate did Ezekiel see the glory of the LORD fill the house of the LORD?
   Ezekiel 44:4
   A. North gate
   B. South gate
   C. East gate
   D. West gate

4. What did the rebellious people bring into the sanctuary that was forbidden?
   Ezekiel 44:6–7
   A. Bulls
   B. Flour
   C. Oil
   D. Strangers

5. Whose sons kept the charge of the sanctuary when Israel went astray from God?
   Ezekiel 44:15
   A. Cyrus's sons
   B. Darius's sons
   C. Nebuchadnezzar's sons
   D. Zadok's sons

6. Which type of garments were the priests to wear in the inner court?
   Ezekiel 44:15–17
   A. Camel hair garments
   B. Flannel garments
   C. Herringbone garments
   D. Linen garments

7. Where were the priests to change out of their holy garments?
   Ezekiel 44:19
   A. Inside the holy chambers
   B. Inside the most holy place
   C. Inside the prayer grottoes
   D. Inside the sanctified tabernacles

8. What were priests allowed to do?
   Ezekiel 44:20
   A. Allow their locks to grow long
   B. Have a women's style of haircut
   C. Poll their heads
   D. Shave their heads

9. What were priests forbidden to do?
   Ezekiel 44:21
   A. Eat leavened bread
   B. Drink wine in the inner court
   C. Marry a priest's widow
   D. Ride a donkey

10. How many days was a priest considered unclean after touching a dead body?
    Ezekiel 44:25–26
    A. 1
    B. 3
    C. 7
    D. 10

11. How was the land to be divided?
    Ezekiel 45:1
    A. By age (oldest to youngest)
    B. By greatest to least in numbers
    C. By least to greatest in numbers
    D. By lot

12. How many chambers belonged to the Levites?
    Ezekiel 45:5
    A. 10
    B. 20
    C. 30
    D. 40

13. How many ephahs equal one homer?
    Ezekiel 45:11
    A. 6
    B. 10
    C. 33
    D. 50

14. How many gerahs equal a shekel?
    Ezekiel 45:12
    A. 10
    B. 20
    C. 30
    D. 40

15. How much of an ephah of wheat was to be given for every homer of wheat?
    Ezekiel 45:13
    A. 1/6
    B. 1/10
    C. 1/33
    D. 1/50

16. How many baths equal one homer?
    Ezekiel 45:14
    A. 6
    B. 10
    C. 33
    D. 50

17. How many lambs were to be offered out of 200?
    Ezekiel 45:15
    A. 1
    B. 7
    C. 20
    D. 50

18. On which day of the first month was the sanctuary to be cleansed?
    Ezekiel 45:18
    A. 1st
    B. 7th
    C. 14th
    D. 21st

19. On which day of the first month was the passover to be celebrated?
    Ezekiel 45:21
    A. 1st
    B. 7th
    C. 14th
    D. 21st

20. How many days was the passover to be celebrated?
    Ezekiel 45:21
    A. 2
    B. 3
    C. 6
    D. 7

Answers on page 772

SEPTEMBER 13

Lesson 256
Today's Reading: *Ezekiel 46–48*
Period of Time: 587–575 BC
Author: Ezekiel

1. Which gate was to remain closed during the six working days of the week?
   Ezekiel 46:1
   A. North gate
   B. South gate
   C. East gate
   D. West gate

2. Who shall prepare the prince's burnt offerings and peace offerings?
   Ezekiel 46:2
   A. Bondmen
   B. Generals
   C. Maidens
   D. Priests

3. How many *lambs*—without blemish—was the prince to offer as part of the burnt offering on the sabbath day?
   Ezekiel 46:4
   A. 2
   B. 4
   C. 6
   D. 8

4. How many *rams*—without blemish—was the prince to offer as part of the offering on the sabbath day?
   Ezekiel 46:4
   A. 1
   B. 3
   C. 5
   D. 7

5. How many *young bullocks*—without blemish—shall the prince offer in the day of the new moon?
   Ezekiel 46:6
   A. 1
   B. 3
   C. 5
   D. 7

6. How many *lambs*—without blemish—shall the prince offer in the day of the new moon?
   Ezekiel 46:6
   A. 3
   B. 6
   C. 9
   D. 12

7. How many *rams*—without blemish—shall the prince offer in the day of the new moon?
   Ezekiel 46:6
   A. 1
   B. 3
   C. 5
   D. 7

8. Which gate shall a person exit from if he enters through the north gate?
   Ezekiel 46:9
   A. North gate
   B. South gate
   C. East gate
   D. West gate

9. Which animal of the first year without blemish was to be offered daily for a burnt offering?
   Ezekiel 46:13
   A. A bullock
   B. A goat
   C. A lamb
   D. A ram

10. Besides the burnt offering, which other offering was made daily?
    Ezekiel 46:13–14
    A. A meat offering
    B. A peace offering
    C. A sin offering
    D. A trespass offering

11. When was a servant to return a gift of inheritance to the prince?

    Ezekiel 46:17

    A. Next day of atonement
    B. Next new moon
    C. Next sabbath month
    D. Next year of liberty

12. How was the trespass offering to be cooked?

    Ezekiel 46:20

    A. Baked
    B. Boiled
    C. Fried
    D. Roasted

13. Where did Ezekiel say men shall cast forth their nets and catch an abundance of fish?

    Ezekiel 47:10

    A. From Beersheba to Bethlehem
    B. From Engedi to Eneglaim
    C. From Jerusalem to Jericho
    D. From Zidon to Zoar

14. Who shall have two portions of land?

    Ezekiel 47:13

    A. Benjamin
    B. Gad
    C. Joseph
    D. Reuben

15. Which one of the following was a priest?

    Ezekiel 48:11

    A. Daniel
    B. Hoshea
    C. Jeremiah
    D. Zadok

16. What was the name of one of the gates on the *north* side?

    Ezekiel 48:31

    A. Asher
    B. Dan
    C. Levi
    D. Zebulun

17. What was the name of one of the gates on the *east* side?

    Ezekiel 48:32

    A. Asher
    B. Dan
    C. Levi
    D. Zebulun

18. What was the name of one of the gates on the *south* side?

    Ezekiel 48:33

    A. Asher
    B. Dan
    C. Levi
    D. Zebulun

19. What was the name of one of the gates on the *west* side?

    Ezekiel 48:34

    A. Asher
    B. Dan
    C. Levi
    D. Zebulun

20. What will be the name of the city surrounded by the twelve gates?

    Ezekiel 48:35

    A. The crown jewel
    B. The emerald city
    C. The great and terrible city
    D. The LORD is there

Answers on page 772

SEPTEMBER 14

Lesson 257
Today's Reading: *Daniel 1–2*
Period of Time: 607–604 BC
Author: Daniel

1. Who was the king of Judah when Jerusalem was besieged?
   Daniel 1:1
   A. King Jehoiakim
   B. King Nathan
   C. King Oded
   D. King Shemiah

2. Which Babylonian king besieged Jerusalem?
   Daniel 1:1
   A. King Jeroboam
   B. King Nebuchadnezzar
   C. King Sennacherib
   D. King Tiberius

3. Where were the temple treasures taken to?
   Daniel 1:2
   A. Land of Gennesaret
   B. Land of Merathaim
   C. Land of Rameses
   D. Land of Shinar

4. Who was master of the eunuchs?
   Daniel 1:3
   A. Aminadab
   B. Arphaxad
   C. Ashpenaz
   D. Augustus

5. How many years was Daniel and others to be provided a daily provision of the king's meat and wine?
   Daniel 1:5
   A. 3
   B. 6
   C. 9
   D. 12

6. What was Daniel's name changed to?
   Daniel 1:7
   A. Abednego
   B. Belteshazzar
   C. Meshach
   D. Shadrach

7. What was Hananiah's name changed to?
   Daniel 1:7
   A. Abednego
   B. Belteshazzar
   C. Meshach
   D. Shadrach

8. What was Mishael's name changed to?
   Daniel 1:7
   A. Abednego
   B. Belteshazzar
   C. Meshach
   D. Shadrach

9. What was Azariah's name changed to?
   Daniel 1:7
   A. Abednego
   B. Belteshazzar
   C. Meshach
   D. Shadrach

10. Who did the prince of the eunuchs set over Daniel?
    Daniel 1:11
    A. Belshazzar
    B. Eleazar
    C. Melzar
    D. Shenazar

11. How many days did Daniel eat pulse and drink water?
    Daniel 1:12–16
    A. 3
    B. 6
    C. 7
    D. 10

12. Which king was a Babylonian king?
    Daniel 1:21
    A. King Asnappar
    B. King Cyrus
    C. King Hiram
    D. King Jabin

13. What language did the Chaldeans use when speaking to the king?

    Daniel 2:4

    A. Aramaic
    B. Greek
    C. Hebrew
    D. Syriack

14. Who was the captain of the king's guard?

    Daniel 2:14

    A. Arioch
    B. Keilah
    C. Phallu
    D. Tartan

15. What was the image's head made of?

    Daniel 2:32

    A. Brass
    B. Gold
    C. Iron
    D. Silver

16. What was the image's breast and arm's made of?

    Daniel 2:32

    A. Brass
    B. Gold
    C. Iron
    D. Silver

17. What was the image's belly and thighs made of?

    Daniel 2:32

    A. Brass
    B. Gold
    C. Iron
    D. Silver

18. What were the image's legs made of?

    Daniel 2:33

    A. Brass
    B. Gold
    C. Iron
    D. Silver

19. What was the image's feet made of in addition to clay?

    Daniel 2:33

    A. Brass
    B. Gold
    C. Iron
    D. Silver

20. What destroyed the image?

    Daniel 2:34

    A. A great wind
    B. A stone
    C. An army
    D. An earthquake

*Answers on page 772

SEPTEMBER 15

Lesson 258
Today's Reading: *Daniel 3–4*
Period of Time: 570–563 BC
Author: Daniel

1. What was Nebuchadnezzar's image made of?
   Daniel 3:1
   A. Brass
   B. Gold
   C. Iron
   D. Silver

2. How many cubits in height was the image?
   Daniel 3:1
   A. 20
   B. 40
   C. 60
   D. 80

3. What was the breadth in cubits of the image?
   Daniel 3:1
   A. 6
   B. 12
   C. 18
   D. 24

4. Where was the image set up?
   Daniel 3:1
   A. Plain of Dura
   B. Plain of Moab
   C. Plain of Ono
   D. Plain of Zaanaim

5. When were the people to bow down and worship the image?
   Daniel 3:5–15
   A. During the feast of the passover
   B. Everyday at noon
   C. On the sabbath day
   D. Whenever music was played

6. Who told Nebuchadnezzar certain Jews refused to worship the image?
   Daniel 3:8
   A. Certain Chaldeans
   B. Certain Egyptians
   C. Certain Grecians
   D. Certain Romans

7. Who was one of the men found guilty of refusing to worship the image?
   Daniel 3:12
   A. Abiasaph
   B. Hananiah
   C. Magpiash
   D. Shadrach

8. How many times hotter was the furnace heated?
   Daniel 3:19
   A. 3
   B. 7
   C. 10
   D. 12

9. Who threw the men into the furnace?
   Daniel 3:20
   A. Governors
   B. Judges
   C. Princes
   D. Soldiers

10. What did the men wear inside the furnace?
    Daniel 3:21
    A. Oily rags
    B. Sheepskins
    C. Their own clothes
    D. Nothing

11. How many men were bound and cast into the fire?
    Daniel 3:21–24
    A. 3
    B. 6
    C. 9
    D. 12

12. How many men did Nebuchadnezzar see inside the fire?

    Daniel 3:24–25

    A. 2
    B. 3
    C. 4
    D. 5

13. Whom did Nebuchadnezzar say one of the men inside of the fire looked like?

    Daniel 3:25

    A. The beast with four heads
    B. The devil himself
    C. The prince of darkness
    D. The Son of God

14. What name was Daniel given?

    Daniel 4:8

    A. Abednego
    B. Belteshazzar
    C. Meshach
    D. Shadrach

15. What did Nebuchadnezzar see in the midst of the earth in his vision?

    Daniel 4:10

    A. A bush
    B. A lake
    C. A tree
    D. A well

16. How many *times* would pass over Nebuchadnezzar while his heart was like a beast's?

    Daniel 4:16

    A. 3
    B. 5
    C. 7
    D. 9

17. How long was Daniel astonied and his thoughts troubled him?

    Daniel 4:19

    A. 1 hour
    B. 2 days
    C. 3 months
    D. 4 years

18. What would Nebuchadnezzar eat while dwelling with beasts?

    Daniel 4:25

    A. Beatles
    B. Grass
    C. Locusts
    D. Meat

19. What did Daniel say would cause Nebuchadnezzar to become wet while living among the beasts?

    Daniel 4:25

    A. Brooks overflowing their banks
    B. Desert oases
    C. Rivers during the rainy season
    D. The dew of heaven

20. How many months after Daniel told Nebuchadnezzar he would dwell among beasts did it come to pass?

    Daniel 4:28–33

    A. 6
    B. 12
    C. 18
    D. 24

Answers on page 772

SEPTEMBER 16

Lesson 259
Today's Reading: *Daniel 5–6*
Period of Time: 538 BC
Author: Daniel

1. Who was the last king of Babylon?
   Daniel 5:1
   A. King Belringer
   B. King Belshazzar
   C. King Belteshazzar
   D. King Belwisher

2. How many lords did the king invite to the feast?
   Daniel 5:1
   A. 1,000
   B. 2,000
   C. 3,000
   D. 4,000

3. Where were the golden vessels from used for drinking wine?
   Daniel 5:3
   A. Chephirah
   B. Hannathon
   C. Jerusalem
   D. Ptolemais

4. What happened when the king saw the handwriting on the wall?
   Daniel 5:5–6
   A. His hand became leprous.
   B. His knees smote together.
   C. His neck stiffened.
   D. His tongue became loosed.

5. What was the *first* promise the king gave to anyone who could interpret the handwriting?
   Daniel 5:7, 5:16
   A. He would be a ruler in the kingdom.
   B. He would be clothed in scarlet.
   C. He would receive a gold necklace.
   D. He would wed the king's daughter.

6. What was the *second* promise the king gave to anyone who could interpret the handwriting?
   Daniel 5:7, 5:16
   A. He would be a ruler in the kingdom.
   B. He would be clothed in scarlet.
   C. He would receive a gold necklace.
   D. He would wed the king's daughter.

7. What was the *third* promise the king gave to anyone who could interpret the handwriting?
   Daniel 5:7, 5:16
   A. He would be a ruler in the kingdom.
   B. He would be clothed in scarlet.
   C. He would receive a gold necklace.
   D. He would wed the king's daughter.

8. Who told the king that Daniel could interpret the handwriting?
   Daniel 5:10–12
   A. The baker
   B. The butler
   C. The guard
   D. The queen

9. Who dwelled among the wild asses and ate grass like oxen?
   Daniel 5:11–21
   A. Berodachbaladan
   B. Chushan-rishatha'im
   C. Joshbekashah
   D. Nebuchadnezzar

10. Which one of the following means *God hath numbered thy kingdom, and finished it*?
    Daniel 5:26
    A. GLEDE
    B. MENE
    C. PERES
    D. TEKEL

11. Which one of the following means *Thou art weighed in the balances, and art found wanting?*
    Daniel 5:27
    A. GLEDE
    B. MENE
    C. PERES
    D. TEKEL

12. Which one of the following means *Thy kingdom is divided, and given to the Medes and Persians?*
    Daniel 5:28
    A. GLEDE
    B. MENE
    C. PERES
    D. TEKEL

13. What was King Darius' ethnicity?
    Daniel 5:31
    A. Babylonian
    B. Jewish
    C. Median
    D. Persian

14. How old was King Darius when he took the kingdom of Babylon?
    Daniel 5:31
    A. 61 years old
    B. 62 years old
    C. 63 years old
    D. 64 years old

15. How many princes did King Darius set over the whole kingdom?
    Daniel 6:1
    A. 30
    B. 60
    C. 90
    D. 120

16. How many presidents did King Darius set over the kingdom?
    Daniel 6:2
    A. 3
    B. 12
    C. 50
    D. 100

17. How many days could a person **not** ask a petition of any God or man?
    Daniel 6:7, 6:12
    A. 10
    B. 20
    C. 30
    D. 40

18. How many times a day did Daniel pray to God?
    Daniel 6:10
    A. 3
    B. 5
    C. 7
    D. 10

19. How was Daniel punished for praying to God?
    Daniel 6:16
    A. He was cast into a den of lions.
    B. He was hung from a tree.
    C. He was publicly scourged.
    D. He was sold as a slave.

20. What was King Cyrus' ethnicity?
    Daniel 6:28
    A. Babylonian
    B. Jewish
    C. Median
    D. Persian

*Answers on page 772

SEPTEMBER 17

Lesson 260
Today's Reading: *Daniel 7–8*
Period of Time: 538 BC
Author: Daniel

1. Who was the king of Babylon?
   Daniel 7:1
   A. King Belshazzar
   B. King Belteshazzar
   C. King Belushar
   D. King Belvedar

2. What did the *first* beast look like?
   Daniel 7:4
   A. A bear
   B. A dragon
   C. A leopard
   D. A lion

3. What did the *second* beast look like?
   Daniel 7:5
   A. A bear
   B. A dragon
   C. A leopard
   D. A lion

4. How many ribs were in the *second* beast's mouth?
   Daniel 7:5
   A. 3
   B. 6
   C. 9
   D. 12

5. What did the *third* beast look like?
   Daniel 7:6
   A. A bear
   B. A dragon
   C. A leopard
   D. A lion

6. How many heads did the *third* beast have?
   Daniel 7:6
   A. 2
   B. 4
   C. 7
   D. 10

7. How many horns did the *fourth* beast have?
   Daniel 7:7
   A. 10
   B. 20
   C. 30
   D. 40

8. What color was the cloth garment the Ancient of days wore?
   Daniel 7:9
   A. Blue
   B. Crimson
   C. Purple
   D. White

9. What was the hair of the Ancient of days like?
   Daniel 7:9
   A. Brass
   B. Fire
   C. Silk
   D. Wool

10. How long were the other beast's lives prolonged after the *fourth* beast was slain?
    Daniel 7:12
    A. A season
    B. A season and a time
    C. Two seasons
    D. Two seasons and a time

11. What do the four beasts represent?
    Daniel 7:17
    A. Kings
    B. Mountains
    C. Planets
    D. Seasons

12. Where was Daniel when he had the vision of the ram and the he goat?
    Daniel 8:2
    A. Bethshan
    B. Nibshan
    C. Shushan
    D. Zaashan

13. In which province was the palace located?

    Daniel 8:2

    A. Amam
    B. Bileam
    C. Elam
    D. Ibleam

14. Which river was Daniel by?

    Daniel 8:2

    A. River of Chebar
    B. River of Gad
    C. River of Pishon
    D. River of Ulai

15. Which direction did the he goat come from?

    Daniel 8:5

    A. North
    B. South
    C. East
    D. West

16. After how many days will the sanctuary be cleansed?

    Daniel 8:14

    A. 1,453
    B. 2,300
    C. 3,666
    D. 4,513

17. Who explained the vision of the ram and the he goat to Daniel?

    Daniel 8:16

    A. Emanuel
    B. Gabriel
    C. Michael
    D. Paltiel

18. Which kings do the ram's two horns represent?

    Daniel 8:20

    A. The kings of Assyria and Syria
    B. The kings of Grecia and Egypt
    C. The kings of Media and Persia
    D. The kings of Rome and Babylon

19. Whom does the rough goat represent?

    Daniel 8:21

    A. The king of Assyria
    B. The king of Grecia
    C. The king of Media
    D. The king of Rome

20. Who shall destroy the king of fierce countenance?

    Daniel 8:21–25

    A. The prince of devils
    B. The prince of evil
    C. The prince of princes
    D. The prince of the power of the air

*Answers on page 772

SEPTEMBER 18

Lesson 261
Today's Reading: *Daniel 9–10*
Period of Time: 538 BC
Author: Daniel

1. Who was King Darius' father?
   Daniel 9:1
   A. King Ahasuerus
   B. King Demetrius
   C. King Epaenetus
   D. King Hymenaeus

2. What was King Darius a seed of?
   Daniel 9:1
   A. The Assyrians
   B. The Babylonians
   C. The Egyptians
   D. The Medians

3. Which prophet does Daniel mention?
   Daniel 9:2
   A. Berechiah
   B. Isaiah
   C. Jeremiah
   D. Nehemiah

4. How many years would Jerusalem remain desolate?
   Daniel 9:2
   A. 7
   B. 70
   C. 700
   D. 7,000

5. Who touched Daniel about the time of the evening oblation?
   Daniel 9:21
   A. Ezekiel
   B. Gabriel
   C. Othniel
   D. Zabdiel

6. Who was the king of Persia?
   Daniel 10:1
   A. King Amos
   B. King Cyrus
   C. King Ehud
   D. King Haggi

7. What name was Daniel given?
   Daniel 10:1
   A. Belshazzar
   B. Belteshazzar
   C. Belushar
   D. Belwashar

8. How many weeks did Daniel mourn?
   Daniel 10:2–3
   A. 3
   B. 6
   C. 9
   D. 12

9. When did Daniel see a vision, and a great quaking fell upon him and others?
   Daniel 10:4–7
   A. 1st month, 24th day
   B. 2nd month, 6th day
   C. 3rd month, 18th day
   D. 4th month, 12th day

10. Which river was Daniel at when he saw the vision?
    Daniel 10:4
    A. River Euphrates
    B. River Gihon
    C. River Hiddekel
    D. River Pison

11. Where was the fine gold from that the man in the vision wore?
    Daniel 10:5
    A. Havilah
    B. Ophir
    C. Sheba
    D. Uphaz

12. What was the man in the vision's body like?
    Daniel 10:6
    A. Beryl
    B. Diamond
    C. Jasper
    D. Onyx

13. What was the man in the vision's face like?

    Daniel 10:6

    A. Coal
    B. Iron
    C. Lightning
    D. Mercury

14. What was the man in the vision's eyes like?

    Daniel 10:6

    A. Blades of grass
    B. Fields of gold
    C. Lamps of fire
    D. Streams of water

15. What was the man in the vision's arms and feet like?

    Daniel 10:6

    A. Brass
    B. Clay
    C. Gold
    D. Iron

16. What was the man in the vision's voice like?

    Daniel 10:6

    A. A brook
    B. A dragon
    C. A lion
    D. A multitude

17. How many days did the prince of the kingdom of Persia fight against the man in the vision?

    Daniel 10:13

    A. 3
    B. 10
    C. 17
    D. 21

18. Which chief prince came to help fight against the prince of the kingdom of Persia?

    Daniel 10:13

    A. Abimael
    B. Ishmael
    C. Michael
    D. Rephael

19. What did the heavenly creature look like that strengthened Daniel in *Daniel 10:18*?

    Daniel 10:18

    A. A bear
    B. A fox
    C. A lion
    D. A man

20. Who did the heavenly creature say would come?

    Daniel 10:20

    A. The prince of Assyria
    B. The prince of Grecia
    C. The prince of Rome
    D. The prince of Sidon

*Answers on page 772

SEPTEMBER 19

Lesson 262
Today's Reading: *Daniel 11–12*
Period of Time: 538 BC
Author: Daniel

1. What was King Darius' ethnicity?
   Daniel 11:1
   A. Babylonian
   B. Corinthian
   C. Libyan
   D. Median

2. What will be the total number of kings yet to be in Persia?
   Daniel 11:2
   A. 2
   B. 4
   C. 6
   D. 8

3. Which king of Persia will be the richest?
   Daniel 11:2
   A. 1st
   B. 2nd
   C. 3rd
   D. 4th

4. Which nation shall go to war against Persia?
   Daniel 11:2
   A. Assyria
   B. Ethiopia
   C. Grecia
   D. Syria

5. Whom shall the king's daughter of the south go to and ask for an agreement?
   Daniel 11:6
   A. The bishop of the south
   B. The duke of the east
   C. The general of the west
   D. The king of the north

6. Where will the captives be taken to?
   Daniel 11:8
   A. Egypt
   B. Ekron
   C. Ephesus
   D. Ethiopia

7. What will the king of the south be moved with?
   Daniel 11:11
   A. Choler
   B. Drollery
   C. Pangs
   D. Wit

8. What will he who replaces the king of the north be called?
   Daniel 11:20
   A. A builder of cities
   B. A destroyer of woods
   C. A raiser of taxes
   D. A warrior of peace

9. Where will ships come from against the king of the north?
   Daniel 11:30
   A. Chittim
   B. Ebongezer
   C. Memphis
   D. Thebes

10. What will he—the king of the north—be known for?
    Daniel 11:31
    A. The abomination that maketh desolate
    B. The builder of the hanging gardens
    C. The creator of a peace treaty in Canaan
    D. The fall of the Roman Empire

11. Whom will the king of the north speak marvelous things against?
    Daniel 11:36
    A. The ambassador of Babylon
    B. The chief of the princes
    C. The emperor of Rome
    D. The God of gods

12. Who did Gabriel say would escape from the king of the north?

    Daniel 11:41

    A. Cush and Alexandria
    B. Edom and Moab
    C. Sodom and Gomorrah
    D. Tyre and Sidon

13. Who did Daniel say would **not** escape from the king of the north?

    Daniel 11:42

    A. Assyria
    B. Egypt
    C. Greece
    D. Rome

14. Which two nations shall be at the king of the north's steps?

    Daniel 11:43

    A. The Asians and Syrians
    B. The Corinthians and Thessalonians
    C. The Libyans and Ethiopians
    D. The Persians and Babylonians

15. Which great prince will stand for the people of Israel?

    Daniel 12:1

    A. Abimael
    B. Ishmael
    C. Michael
    D. Rephael

16. What was Daniel told would increase?

    Daniel 12:4

    A. Births
    B. Knowledge
    C. Tombs
    D. Weddings

17. How many people did Daniel see on the banks of the river?

    Daniel 12:5

    A. 2
    B. 10
    C. 21
    D. 36

18. What color shall many people be made?

    Daniel 12:10

    A. Almond
    B. Black
    C. Scarlet
    D. White

19. How many days will pass between the end of the daily sacrifices and the abomination that maketh desolate?

    Daniel 12:11

    A. 912
    B. 1,290
    C. 2,019
    D. 9,120

20. How many days after the abomination that maketh desolate shall those who wait upon the LORD be blessed?

    Daniel 12:12

    A. 1,115
    B. 1,225
    C. 1,335
    D. 1,445

*Answers on page 772

SEPTEMBER 20

Lesson 263
Today's Reading: *Hosea 1–6*
Period of Time: 808–698 BC
Author: Hosea

1. Who was Hosea's father?
   Hosea 1:1
   A. Beeri
   B. Emmor
   C. Maath
   D. Pallu

2. Who was a king of Judah?
   Hosea 1:1
   A. King Ahaz
   B. King Elah
   C. King Jehu
   D. King Omri

3. Who was a king of Israel?
   Hosea 1:1
   A. King Amaziah
   B. King Hazael
   C. King Jeroboam
   D. King Manasseh

4. Who was Hosea's wife?
   Hosea 1:3
   A. Abigail
   B. Bernice
   C. Elizabeth
   D. Gomer

5. What was the name of Hosea's *first* child?
   Hosea 1:3–4
   A. Goliath
   B. Ichabod
   C. Jezreel
   D. Lebanah

6. What was the name of Hosea's *daughter*?
   Hosea 1:6
   A. Loammi
   B. Local
   C. Lois
   D. Loruhamah

7. What was the name of Hosea's *third* child?
   Hosea 1:9
   A. Loammi
   B. Local
   C. Lois
   D. Loruhamah

8. What was Hosea to say unto his brethren?
   Hosea 2:1
   A. Ammi
   B. Cal
   C. Is
   D. Ruhamah

9. What was Hosea to say unto his sisters?
   Hosea 2:1
   A. Ammi
   B. Cal
   C. Is
   D. Ruhamah

10. Which valley was to become a door of hope for Israel?
    Hosea 2:15
    A. Valley of Achor
    B. Valley of Eshcol
    C. Valley of Keziz
    D. Valley of Vision

11. What does Hosea say Israel will call the LORD?
    Hosea 2:16
    A. Abba
    B. Baali
    C. Ishi
    D. Yahweh

12. What does Hosea say Israel will no longer call the LORD?
    Hosea 2:16
    A. Abba
    B. Baali
    C. Ishi
    D. Yahweh

13. Besides a homer and a half of barley, how many pieces of silver did Hosea pay for the adulteress?

    Hosea 3:2

    A. 3
    B. 7
    C. 12
    D. 15

14. Why are God's people destroyed?

    Hosea 4:6

    A. They lack armies.
    B. They lack knowledge.
    C. They lack swords.
    D. They lack walls.

15. What does Hosea state Israel is like?

    Hosea 4:16

    A. A backsliding ass
    B. A backsliding colt
    C. A backsliding heifer
    D. A backsliding lamb

16. Where is the cornet to be blown?

    Hosea 5:8

    A. Beth-aven
    B. Gibeah
    C. Samaria
    D. Ramah

17. Where is the trumpet to be blown?

    Hosea 5:8

    A. Beth-aven
    B. Gibeah
    C. Samaria
    D. Ramah

18. Who was a king of Assyria?

    Hosea 5:13

    A. King Cyrus
    B. King Herod
    C. King Jareb
    D. King Zimri

19. What did Hosea say the LORD desired from his people?

    Hosea 6:6

    A. Burnt offerings
    B. Mercy
    C. Signs and wonders
    D. Tithes

20. Which city is polluted with blood and full of iniquity?

    Hosea 6:8

    A. Cyrene
    B. Gilead
    C. Ibleam
    D. Libnah

*Answers on page 772

SEPTEMBER 21

Lesson 264
Today's Reading: *Hosea 7–12*
Period of Time: 808–698 BC
Author: Hosea

1. What does Hosea say Ephraim is?
   Hosea 7:8

   A. A cake not turned
   B. A day without rain
   C. A horse with no name
   D. A well overflowing its rim

2. Which musical instrument does Hosea mention?
   Hosea 8:1

   A. The dulcimer
   B. The harp
   C. The organ
   D. The trumpet

3. What shall be broken in pieces?
   Hosea 8:6

   A. The bull of Bashan
   B. The calf of Samaria
   C. The cow of Ethiopia
   D. The heifer of Judah

4. Who shall bury the people of Israel?
   Hosea 9:1–6

   A. Damascus
   B. Ephraim
   C. Memphis
   D. Thyatira

5. What does Hosea say the days of Israel's corruptness are like?
   Hosea 9:7–9

   A. The days of Gethsemane
   B. The days of Gibeah
   C. The days of Goshen
   D. The days of Grecia

6. Where did God hate Israel for all of their wickedness?
   Hosea 9:15

   A. Emmaus
   B. Gilgal
   C. Hebron
   D. Irpeel

7. Who was the Assyrian king?
   Hosea 10:6

   A. King Balak
   B. King Hanun
   C. King Jareb
   D. King Mesha

8. Where were the high places Hosea called the sin of Israel located?
   Hosea 10:8

   A. Aven
   B. Beon
   C. Chun
   D. Elon

9. Who will ride?
   Hosea 10:11

   A. Egypt
   B. Ephraim
   C. Jacob
   D. Judah

10. Who shall plow?
    Hosea 10:11

    A. Egypt
    B. Ephraim
    C. Jacob
    D. Judah

11. Who shall break the clods?
    Hosea 10:11

    A. Egypt
    B. Ephraim
    C. Jacob
    D. Judah

12. Who spoiled Betharbel?
    Hosea 10:14

    A. Eleazar
    B. Ithamar
    C. Phinehas
    D. Shalman

13. Whom did Hosea say Israel sacrificed to?

    Hosea 11:2

    A. Baalim
    B. Castor
    C. Nergal
    D. Tophet

14. Which wind does Ephraim follow?

    Hosea 12:1

    A. North wind
    B. South wind
    C. East wind
    D. West wind

15. Whom did Ephraim make a covenant with?

    Hosea 12:1

    A. The Assyrians
    B. The Babylonians
    C. The Grecians
    D. The Phoenicians

16. What did Israel send Egypt?

    Hosea 12:1

    A. Almonds
    B. Horses
    C. Metals
    D. Oil

17. Where did Hosea say the LORD found Jacob?

    Hosea 12:2–4

    A. Bethel
    B. Bethlehem
    C. Bethphage
    D. Bethsaida

18. Who said, "I am become rich"?

    Hosea 12:8

    A. Accho
    B. Ephraim
    C. Gilgal
    D. Jericho

19. Where did Hosea say Israel sacrificed bullocks?

    Hosea 12:11

    A. Accho
    B. Ephraim
    C. Gilgal
    D. Jericho

20. Where did Jacob flee to?

    Hosea 12:12

    A. Adria
    B. India
    C. Lydia
    D. Syria

*Answers on page 772

SEPTEMBER 22

Lesson 265
Today's Reading: *Hosea 13–14, Joel 1–3*
Period of Time: Hosea, 808–698 BC; Joel, 808 BC
Authors: Hosea, Joel

1. What did Hosea say the men did when they sacrificed to idols?
   Hosea 13:2
   A. Cried upon the hawk
   B. Kissed the calves
   C. Laid wreaths over the horses
   D. Placed coins under the lion's paw

2. Where will pregnant women be ripped open?
   Hosea 13:16
   A. Assyria
   B. Ethiopia
   C. Persia
   D. Samaria

3. Who will Israel say will **not** save them?
   Hosea 14:3
   A. Asshur
   B. Edom
   C. Lebanon
   D. Moab

4. Who is Joel's father?
   Joel 1:1
   A. Hamuel
   B. Kemuel
   C. Pethuel
   D. Samuel

5. What has eaten what the palmerworm has left?
   Joel 1:4
   A. The caterpillar
   B. The locust
   C. The moth
   D. The wormwood

6. What has eaten what the cankerworm has left?
   Joel 1:4
   A. The caterpillar
   B. The locust
   C. The moth
   D. The wormwood

7. Whom does Joel mention *first*?
   Joel 1:5–13
   A. Drunkards
   B. Husbandmen
   C. Priests
   D. Scribes

8. Whom does Joel mention *second*?
   Joel 1:5–13
   A. Drunkards
   B. Husbandmen
   C. Priests
   D. Scribes

9. Whom does Joel mention *third*?
   Joel 1:5–13
   A. Drunkards
   B. Husbandmen
   C. Priests
   D. Scribes

10. Who will prophecy?
    Joel 2:28
    A. Handmaids
    B. Old men
    C. Sons and daughters
    D. Young men

11. Who shall dream dreams?
    Joel 2:28
    A. Handmaids
    B. Old men
    C. Sons and daughters
    D. Young men

12. Who shall see visions?
    Joel 2:28
    A. Handmaids
    B. Old men
    C. Sons and daughters
    D. Young men

13. Whom were the children of Judah sold to?

    Joel 3:6

    A. The Grecians
    B. The Libertines
    C. The Philistines
    D. The Sabeans

14. Whom will God sell the people of Tyre, Zidon, and along the coasts of Palestine to?

    Joel 3:4–8

    A. The Grecians
    B. The Libertines
    C. The Philistines
    D. The Sabeans

15. What is Israel to make into swords?

    Joel 3:10

    A. Machetes
    B. Plowshares
    C. Pruning hooks
    D. Rakes

16. What is Israel to make into spears?

    Joel 3:10

    A. Machetes
    B. Plowshares
    C. Pruning hooks
    D. Rakes

17. In which valley will the LORD judge the heathen?

    Joel 3:12

    A. Valley of Jehoshaphat
    B. Valley of Megiddo
    C. Valley of Rephaim
    D. Valley of Shittim

18. What shall the hills flow with?

    Joel 3:18

    A. Blood
    B. Honey
    C. Milk
    D. Wine

19. Which valley will be watered from the fountain coming forth out of the house of the LORD?

    Joel 3:18

    A. Valley of Jehoshaphat
    B. Valley of Megiddo
    C. Valley of Rephaim
    D. Valley of Shittim

20. Where dwelleth the LORD?

    Joel 3:21

    A. Cush
    B. Edom
    C. Moab
    D. Zion

*Answers on page 773

SEPTEMBER 23

Lesson 266
Today's Reading: *Amos 1–5*
Period of Time: 808 BC
Author: Amos

1. Where was Amos from?
   Amos 1:1
   A. Japho
   B. Minni
   C. Tekoa
   D. Uphaz

2. Who was the king of Judah?
   Amos 1:1
   A. King Artaxerxes
   B. King Ben-ha'dad
   C. King Jeroboam
   D. King Uzziah

3. Who was the king of Israel?
   Amos 1:1
   A. King Artaxerxes
   B. King Ben-ha'dad
   C. King Jeroboam
   D. King Uzziah

4. How many years would Amos prophecy before an earthquake would occur?
   Amos 1:1
   A. 2
   B. 4
   C. 6
   D. 8

5. Who was the king of Damascus?
   Amos 1:3–4
   A. King Artaxerxes
   B. King Ben-ha'dad
   C. King Jeroboam
   D. King Uzziah

6. Which remnant will perish?
   Amos 1:8
   A. Remnant of the Amorites
   B. Remnant of the Nazarites
   C. Remnant of the Philistines
   D. Remnant of the Sidonians

7. Who sold the captives of Israel to Edom?
   Amos 1:9
   A. Cnidus
   B. Jebus
   C. Pontus
   D. Tyrus

8. Which city is located in Edom?
   Amos 1:11–12
   A. Bozrah
   B. Chephirah
   C. Mearah
   D. Nimrah

9. Which city is located in Ammon?
   Amos 1:13–14
   A. Baalah
   B. Rabbah
   C. Senaah
   D. Ziddim

10. Which city is located in Moab?
    Amos 2:1–2
    A. Hammath
    B. Kirioth
    C. Minnith
    D. Nazareth

11. How much did Israel sell the poor for?
    Amos 2:6
    A. A bath of wine
    B. A loaf of bread
    C. A pair of shoes
    D. A silver shekel

12. Who was as tall as the cedars and as strong as the oaks?
    Amos 2:9
    A. The Amorites
    B. The Nazarites
    C. The Philistines
    D. The Sidonians

13. How many years did the LORD lead the Israelites through the wilderness?
    Amos 2:10

    A. 10
    B. 20
    C. 30
    D. 40

14. Who was **not** supposed to drink wine?
    Amos 2:11–12

    A. Amorites
    B. Nazarites
    C. Philistines
    D. Sidonians

15. Whose altar horns would be cut off and fall to the ground?
    Amos 3:14

    A. Altars of Bethel
    B. Altars of Bethmeon
    C. Altars of Bethpeor
    D. Altars of Bethshan

16. Whose inhabitants will the LORD lead away with hooks?
    Amos 4:1–2

    A. Bashan's inhabitants
    B. Hauran's inhabitants
    C. Kartan's inhabitants
    D. Midian's inhabitants

17. Which one of the following devoured the fig and olive trees?
    Amos 4:9

    A. The cankerworm
    B. The earthworm
    C. The palmerworm
    D. The silkworm

18. What did Amos say the LORD had made?
    Amos 5:8

    A. The three stars and Pluto
    B. The four stars and Jupiter
    C. The five stars and Mars
    D. The seven stars and Orion

19. Which musical instruments did Amos say the LORD will no longer hear the melody of?
    Amos 5:23

    A. Dulcimers
    B. Organs
    C. Pipes
    D. Viols

20. Which two false gods does Amos say Israel turned to?
    Amos 5:26

    A. Castor and Pollux
    B. Moloch and Chiun
    C. Rimmon and Nebo
    D. Succothbenoth and Mercurius

Answers on page 773

SEPTEMBER 24

Lesson 267
Today's Reading: *Amos 6–9, Obadiah 1*
Period of Time: Amos, 808 BC; Obadiah, 587 BC
Authors: Amos, Obadiah

1. Which two of the following were the chief of the nations?
   Amos 6:1
   A. Cush and Ethiopia
   B. Gaza and Persia
   C. Seir and Grecia
   D. Zion and Samaria

2. What has Israel turned the fruit of righteousness into?
   Amos 6:12
   A. Hemlock
   B. Jacinth
   C. Mint
   D. Spikenard

3. What was the LORD holding in his hand?
   Amos 7:7
   A. A balance
   B. A measuring reed
   C. A plumbline
   D. A saw

4. Who was the priest of Bethel?
   Amos 7:10
   A. Amaziah
   B. Hilkiah
   C. Pekahiah
   D. Shelemiah

5. Who was the king of Israel?
   Amos 7:10
   A. King Asnappar
   B. King Jeroboam
   C. King Nebuchadnezzar
   D. King Shishak

6. What was Amos' occupation?
   Amos 7:14
   A. He was a herdman.
   B. He was a plowman.
   C. He was a swordsman.
   D. He was a watchman.

7. What did Amos gather?
   Amos 7:14
   A. Fresh berries
   B. Olive oil
   C. Pine nuts
   D. Sycomore fruit

8. What was in the basket?
   Amos 8:1–2
   A. Autumn leaves
   B. Spring flowers
   C. Summer fruit
   D. Winter clothes

9. Who shall faint for thirst?
   Amos 8:13
   A. Fair virgins and young men
   B. Mighty princes and wise princesses
   C. Old kings and virtuous queens
   D. Pretty maidens and brave dukes

10. In which Samarian city did the people worship a false god?
    Amos 8:14
    A. Ava
    B. Dan
    C. Gad
    D. Hai

11. Where did God bring the Philistines from?
    Amos 9:7
    A. Caphtor
    B. Enhazor
    C. Pethor
    D. Tadmor

12. Where did God bring the Syrians from?
    Amos 9:7
    A. Ain
    B. Iim
    C. Kir
    D. Sin

13. Who will overtake the reaper?

    Amos 9:13

    A. The messenger
    B. The overseer of the vineyard
    C. The plowman
    D. The treader of grapes

14. Who will overtake him that soweth seed?

    Amos 9:13

    A. The messenger
    B. The overseer of the vineyard
    C. The plowman
    D. The treader of grapes

15. What shall the mountains drop?

    Amos 9:13

    A. Beer
    B. Honey
    C. Milk
    D. Wine

16. Whom are the Edomites descendants of?

    Obadiah 1:1–6

    A. Agag
    B. Esau
    C. Hiel
    D. Saul

17. Whose mighty men in Edom will be dismayed and cut off by slaughter?

    Obadiah 1:9

    A. Ahiman's mighty men
    B. Heman's mighty men
    C. Mehuman's mighty men
    D. Teman's mighty men

18. Which mountain will they of the south possess?

    Obadiah 1:19

    A. Mount of Agag
    B. Mount of Esau
    C. Mount of Hiel
    D. Mount of Saul

19. Who shall possess Gilead?

    Obadiah 1:19

    A. Asher
    B. Benjamin
    C. Judah
    D. Napthali

20. Where were the captives of Jerusalem being held?

    Obadiah 1:20

    A. Dibongad
    B. Eltolad
    C. Sepharad
    D. Zedad

Answers on page 773

SEPTEMBER 25

Lesson 268
Today's Reading: *Jonah 1–4, Micah 1–2*
Period of Time: Jonah, 808 BC; Micah, 759–698 BC
Authors: Jonah, Micah

1. Who was Jonah's father?
   Jonah 1:1
   A. Amittai
   B. Elienai
   C. Gilalai
   D. Jeremai

2. Where was Jonah fleeing to?
   Jonah 1:3
   A. Kithlish
   B. Lachish
   C. Magbish
   D. Tarshish

3. Where did Jonah board a ship?
   Jonah 1:3
   A. India
   B. Joppa
   C. Perga
   D. Sheba

4. What was Jonah doing when the storm came?
   Jonah 1:4–5
   A. Cooking in the galley
   B. Sleeping below deck
   C. Swabbing the deck
   D. Walking the plank

5. What did Jonah claim to be?
   Jonah 1:9
   A. Egyptian
   B. Greek
   C. Hebrew
   D. Persian

6. How many days and nights was Jonah in the belly of the great fish?
   Jonah 1:17
   A. 3
   B. 6
   C. 9
   D. 12

7. Which statement is true concerning Jonah in the belly of the great fish?
   Jonah 2:5
   A. A shark bit Jonah's foot.
   B. Jonah escaped by building a fire.
   C. There were men's bones inside the fish.
   D. Weeds were wrapped around Jonah's head.

8. In how many days did Jonah say the LORD was going to destroy Nineveh?
   Jonah 3:4
   A. 20
   B. 40
   C. 60
   D. 80

9. Approximately how many people inhabited Nineveh?
   Jonah 4:11
   A. 40,000
   B. 80,000
   C. 120,000
   D. 160,000

10. What was Micah's surname?
    Micah 1:1
    A. The Ephrathite
    B. The Gederathite
    C. The Morasthite
    D. The Suchathite

11. Who was **not** a king of Judah?
    Micah 1:1
    A. King Ahaz
    B. King Ben-ha'dad
    C. King Hezekiah
    D. King Jotham

12. Which two of the following places was Micah a prophet to?

    Micah 1:1

    A. Assyria and Ijeabarim
    B. Cilicia and Capernaum
    C. Galatia and Padan-aram
    D. Samaria and Jerusalem

13. Which house did Micah tell to roll in the dust?

    Micah 1:10

    A. House of Aphrah
    B. House of Ophrah
    C. House of Taberah
    D. House of Uzzensherah

14. Whose inhabitants shall pass away into captivity and have their shame naked?

    Micah 1:11

    A. Debir
    B. Jattir
    C. Machir
    D. Saphir

15. Whose inhabitants did **not** come forth in the mourning of Bethezel?

    Micah 1:11

    A. Baalgad
    B. Maachah
    C. Naamah
    D. Zaanan

16. Whose inhabitants waited carefully for good?

    Micah 1:12

    A. Machir's inhabitants
    B. Madian's inhabitants
    C. Maroth's inhabitants
    D. Mashal's inhabitants

17. Whose inhabitants did Micah tell to bind the chariot to the swift beast?

    Micah 1:13

    A. Laban's inhabitants
    B. Lachish's inhabitants
    C. Lakum's inhabitants
    D. Laodicea's inhabitants

18. Which city was called *the glory of Israel*?

    Micah 1:15

    A. Adullam
    B. Lebaoth
    C. Phrygia
    D. Ziphron

19. What did Micah tell the rebellious people to do?

    Micah 1:16

    A. Bake bread for their gods
    B. Give gifts to their soldiers
    C. Shave their heads bald
    D. Wear silk clothing

20. Which pastoral city does Micah make reference to?

    Micah 2:12

    A. Bozrah
    B. Gomorrah
    C. Timnathserah
    D. Uzzensherah

*Answers on page 773

SEPTEMBER 26

Lesson 269
Today's Reading: *Micah 3–7*
Period of Time: 759–698 BC
Author: Micah

1. Who does Micah say will be ashamed?
   Micah 3:7
   A. The charioteer
   B. The doorkeepers
   C. The innkeepers
   D. The seers

2. Who does Micah say will be confounded?
   Micah 3:7
   A. The archers
   B. The diviners
   C. The refiners
   D. The trumpeters

3. What does Micah say the people use to build up Zion?
   Micah 3:10
   A. Blood
   B. Mortar
   C. Sweat
   D. Tears

4. What will people use to make plowshares?
   Micah 4:3
   A. Machetes
   B. Rakes
   C. Spears
   D. Swords

5. What will people use to make pruninghooks?
   Micah 4:3
   A. Machetes
   B. Rakes
   C. Spears
   D. Swords

6. Where did Micah say the people would go and be redeemed from their enemies?
   Micah 4:10
   A. Armageddon
   B. Babylon
   C. Memphis
   D. Thebes

7. How shall the LORD gather his people?
   Micah 4:12
   A. As the eggs in the nest
   B. As the grapes on the vine
   C. As the lambs in the sheepfold
   D. As the sheaves on the floor

8. What will the LORD make Zion's horn?
   Micah 4:13
   A. Brass
   B. Gold
   C. Iron
   D. Silver

9. What will the LORD make Zion's hoofs?
   Micah 4:13
   A. Brass
   B. Gold
   C. Iron
   D. Silver

10. Who was little among the thousands of Judah?
    Micah 5:2
    A. Atarothaddar
    B. Bethlehem Ephratah
    C. Hamath-zobah
    D. Jegarsahadutha

11. How many shepherds shall be raised against Assyria?
    Micah 5:5
    A. 1
    B. 3
    C. 7
    D. 9

12. How many principal men shall be raised against Assyria?
    Micah 5:5
    A. 2
    B. 4
    C. 6
    D. 8

13. Who was the king of Moab?

    Micah 6:5

    A. King Balak
    B. King Beor
    C. King Birsha
    D. King Booz

14. Who was Balaam's father?

    Micah 6:5

    A. Balak
    B. Beor
    C. Birsha
    D. Booz

15. Which kings statutes were God's people guilty of keeping?

    Micah 6:16

    A. King Ben-ha'dad's statutes
    B. King Cyrus's statutes
    C. King Omri's statutes
    D. King Solomon's statutes

16. What did Micah's soul desire?

    Micah 7:1

    A. The best archer among men
    B. The first ripe fruit
    C. The last of the summer wine
    D. The swiftest horse

17. What does Micah say the best of men is like?

    Micah 7:4

    A. A brier
    B. A hornet
    C. A pin
    D. A scorpion

18. What does Micah say the most upright person is sharper than?

    Micah 7:4

    A. A barber's razor
    B. A needle's point
    C. A thorn hedge
    D. A two-edged sword

19. Whom will the *truth* be performed to?

    Micah 7:20

    A. Abraham
    B. David
    C. Isaac
    D. Jacob

20. Whom will the *mercy* be performed to?

    Micah 7:20

    A. Abraham
    B. David
    C. Isaac
    D. Jacob

*Answers on page 773

SEPTEMBER 27

Lesson 270
Today's Reading: *Nahum 1–3, Habakkuk 1–3*
Period of Time: Nahum, before 626 BC; Habakkuk, 609 BC
Authors: Nahum, Habakkuk

1. What was Nahum's surname?
   Nahum 1:1
   A. The Arbathite
   B. The Elkoshite
   C. The Izrahite
   D. The Uzzielite

2. What is the *dust* of God's feet?
   Nahum 1:3
   A. The clouds
   B. The earth
   C. The hills
   D. The mountains

3. What *quakes* at God's presence?
   Nahum 1:5
   A. The clouds
   B. The earth
   C. The hills
   D. The mountains

4. What *melts* at God's presence?
   Nahum 1:5
   A. The clouds
   B. The earth
   C. The hills
   D. The mountains

5. What *burns* at God's presence?
   Nahum 1:5
   A. The clouds
   B. The earth
   C. The hills
   D. The mountains

6. Who shall be led away captive; and her maids shall lead her as with the voice of doves?
   Nahum 2:7
   A. Eunice
   B. Huzzab
   C. Milcah
   D. Salome

7. Which two nations were the *strength* of No?
   Nahum 3:8–9
   A. Corinth and Cush
   B. Ethiopia and Egypt
   C. Libya and Lebanon
   D. Macedonia and Magog

8. Which two nations were the *helpers* of No?
   Nahum 3:8–9
   A. Ain and Janum
   B. Nod and Crete
   C. Put and Lubim
   D. Tob and Gebal

9. How shall the fire and sword eat up the inhabitants of Nineveh?
   Nahum 3:15
   A. Like the cankerworm
   B. Like the lioness
   C. Like the ox
   D. Like the swine

10. Which king's shepherds shall slumber and his nobles shall dwell in the dust?
    Nahum 3:18
    A. King of Assyria
    B. King of Lycia
    C. King of Media
    D. King of Persia

11. What are the Chaldeans' horses *swifter* than?
    Habakkuk 1:8
    A. Antelopes
    B. Greyhounds
    C. Leopards
    D. Unicorns

12. What are the Chaldeans' horses *fiercer* than?
    Habakkuk 1:8
    A. Bears
    B. Dogs
    C. Lions
    D. Wolves

13. What shall the Chaldean horsemen fly like?
    Habakkuk 1:8
    A. Bats
    B. Eagles
    C. Owls
    D. Vultures

14. Besides the creeping things, what else does the LORD make men like?
    Habakkuk 1:14
    A. Cattle of the hills
    B. Doves of the nest
    C. Fish of the sea
    D. Hornets of the wind

15. What will answer the stone that cries out in the wall?
    Habakkuk 2:11
    A. The beam out of the timber
    B. The door between the posts
    C. The roof beneath the stars
    D. The window facing the east

16. What is the prayer of Habakkuk upon?
    Habakkuk 3:1
    A. Shibboleth
    B. Shields
    C. Shiftlessness
    D. Shigionoth

17. Where did God come from?
    Habakkuk 3:3
    A. Addan
    B. Golan
    C. Haran
    D. Teman

18. Where did the Holy One come from?
    Habakkuk 3:3
    A. Mount Arafat
    B. Mount Carmel
    C. Mount Nebo
    D. Mount Paran

19. Whose tents did Habakkuk see in affliction?
    Habakkuk 3:7
    A. Cushan's tents
    B. Dothan's tents
    C. Naaran's tents
    D. Zanaan's tents

20. Where did Habakkuk see curtains tremble?
    Habakkuk 3:7
    A. Land of Goshen
    B. Land of Hepher
    C. Land of Midian
    D. Land of Shinar

*Answers on page 773

SEPTEMBER 28

Lesson 271
Today's Reading: *Zephaniah 1–3, Haggai 1–2*
Period of Time: Zephaniah, 629 BC; Haggai, 520 BC
Authors: Zephaniah, Haggai

1. Who was Zephaniah's father?
   Zephaniah 1:1
   A. Carmi
   B. Chuza
   C. Cushi
   D. Cyrus

2. Who was the king of Judah?
   Zephaniah 1:1
   A. King Bariah
   B. King Josiah
   C. King Neriah
   D. King Ramiah

3. Whose name will the LORD cut off along with the priests and the remnant of Baal?
   Zephaniah 1:4
   A. The Anakims
   B. The Avims
   C. The Caphtorims
   D. The Chemarims

4. Which idol—in addition to Baal—did the people worship?
   Zephaniah 1:5
   A. Ashima
   B. Chiun
   C. Dagon
   D. Malcham

5. At which gate will there be the noise of a cry?
   Zephaniah 1:10
   A. Benjamin's gate
   B. Fish gate
   C. Horse gate
   D. King's gate

6. Where were the merchant people cut down, and they that bear silver cut off?
   Zephaniah 1:11
   A. Maachah
   B. Magdala
   C. Maktesh
   D. Maralah

7. How shall the people of Jerusalem walk?
   Zephaniah 1:12–17
   A. Like blind men
   B. Like drunken men
   C. Like lame men
   D. Like strong men

8. Who shall be rooted up?
   Zephaniah 2:4
   A. Edrei
   B. Ekron
   C. Endor
   D. Ether

9. Who was an inhabitant along the sea coast?
   Zephaniah 2:5
   A. The Cherethites
   B. The Gershonites
   C. The Ishmaelites
   D. The Shimronites

10. Who shall dwell in the sea coast dwellings and cottages?
    Zephaniah 2:6
    A. Carpenters
    B. Innkeepers
    C. Lawyers
    D. Shepherds

11. Which nation shall be like Sodom?
    Zephaniah 2:9
    A. Gaza
    B. Edom
    C. Moab
    D. Zion

12. Who shall lodge with the cormorant in the upper lintels?
    Zephaniah 2:14
    A. The bittern
    B. The lapwing
    C. The turtledove
    D. The vulture

13. What are the judges of Nineveh like?

    Zephaniah 3:3

    A. Beastly dragons
    B. Cunning goats
    C. Dead lions
    D. Evening wolves

14. Who are the light and treacherous persons of Nineveh?

    Zephaniah 3:4

    A. The merchants
    B. The prophets
    C. The teachers
    D. The shepherds

15. Who was the king of Persia?

    Haggai 1:1

    A. King Achish
    B. King Baalis
    C. King Darius
    D. King Hazael

16. Who was the governor of Judah?

    Haggai 1:1

    A. Zerubbabel
    B. Zidkijah
    C. Zorobabel
    D. Zuriel

17. Who was the high priest of Judah?

    Haggai 1:1

    A. Joshua
    B. Malchishua
    C. Pua
    D. Shammua

18. How did the LORD punish Israel?

    Haggai 1:11

    A. He allowed an army to attack Israel.
    B. He flooded their land.
    C. He sent a drought upon the land.
    D. He unleashed locusts to devour crops.

19. How many measures did a man receive when he came for twenty?

    Haggai 2:16

    A. 5
    B. 10
    C. 15
    D. 20

20. How many vessels from the pressfat did a man receive when he came for fifty?

    Haggai 2:16

    A. 5
    B. 10
    C. 15
    D. 20

Answers on page 773

SEPTEMBER 29

Lesson 272
Today's Reading: *Zechariah 1–6*
Period of Time: 520–519 BC
Author: Zechariah

1. Who is Zechariah's father?
   Zechariah 1:1
   A. Bechorath
   B. Beeliada
   C. Ben-ha'dad
   D. Berechiah

2. What is the eleventh month called in the Hebrew calendar?
   Zechariah 1:7
   A. Abib
   B. Elul
   C. Nisan
   D. Sebat

3. What color was the horse the rider rode upon among the myrtle trees?
   Zechariah 1:8
   A. Black
   B. Brown
   C. Red
   D. White

4. How many years had the LORD showed indignation toward Jerusalem and the cities of Judah?
   Zechariah 1:12
   A. 70
   B. 140
   C. 400
   D. 800

5. What do the four horns represent?
   Zechariah 1:18–21
   A. Angels
   B. Droughts
   C. Enemies
   D. Plagues

6. What was the man holding in his hand?
   Zechariah 2:1
   A. A hammer
   B. A measuring line
   C. A sickle
   D. An anvil

7. What will the LORD be to Jerusalem?
   Zechariah 2:5
   A. A battering ram
   B. A destroyer
   C. A mother hen
   D. A wall of fire

8. Who was the high priest?
   Zechariah 3:1
   A. Joiada
   B. Joktan
   C. Joshua
   D. Jotham

9. What was the high priest wearing?
   Zechariah 3:3
   A. Filthy garments
   B. Shining white linen
   C. The high priest's garments
   D. Nothing, he was naked

10. What was the name of the LORD's servant?
    Zechariah 3:8
    A. The BRANCH
    B. The RIVER
    C. The SHEPHERD
    D. The WANDERER

11. How many eyes did the stone have?
    Zechariah 3:9
    A. 2
    B. 3
    C. 5
    D. 7

12. How many lamps did the candlestick have?

    Zechariah 4:2

    A. 3
    B. 7
    C. 10
    D. 12

13. How many olive trees stood next to the candlestick?

    Zechariah 4:3

    A. 2
    B. 7
    C. 10
    D. 12

14. Whose hands had laid the foundation upon the ruins to rebuild the LORD's house?

    Zechariah 4:9

    A. Isaiah's hands
    B. Jeremiah's hands
    C. Nehemiah's hands
    D. Zerubbabel's hands

15. What is the curse that goes forth over the face of the whole earth?

    Zechariah 5:1–3

    A. A floating dark cloud
    B. A flying roll
    C. A hovering vulture
    D. A soaring eagle

16. What carried the ephah?

    Zechariah 5:5–9

    A. 1 child
    B. 2 women
    C. 7 lambs
    D. 10 virgins

17. Where was the house concerning the ephah to be built?

    Zechariah 5:11

    A. Land of Egypt
    B. Land of Havilah
    C. Land of Shinar
    D. Land of Temani

18. How many chariots came out from between the two mountains?

    Zechariah 6:1

    A. 2
    B. 4
    C. 6
    D. 8

19. Which description describes the two mountains the chariots came between?

    Zechariah 6:1

    A. Mountains of brass
    B. Mountains of fire
    C. Mountains of prey
    D. Mountains of spices

20. Who was Zephaniah's son?

    Zechariah 6:14

    A. Cis
    B. Eli
    C. Hen
    D. Ira

Answers on page 773

SEPTEMBER 30

Lesson 273
Today's Reading: *Zechariah 7–10*
Period of Time: 518 BC
Author: Zechariah

1. Which king reigned during the time of Zechariah?
   Zechariah 7:1
   A. King Abimelech
   B. King Darius
   C. King Herod
   D. King Nahash

2. What is the ninth month in the Hebrew calendar?
   Zechariah 7:1
   A. Adar
   B. Bul
   C. Chisleu
   D. Elul

3. Which two men went to the house of God to pray?
   Zechariah 7:2
   A. Beeliada and Adrammelech
   B. Kushaiah and Jehoshaphat
   C. Potiphar and Onesiphorus
   D. Sherezer and Regemmelech

4. During which two months did the men want to know if Israel should continue to fast and mourn?
   Zechariah 7:1–5
   A. First and Tenth
   B. Second and Ninth
   C. Third and Eighth
   D. Fifth and Seventh

5. How many years had Israel been in captivity?
   Zechariah 7:5
   A. 70
   B. 80
   C. 90
   D. 100

6. What does the LORD say became like an adamant stone?
   Zechariah 7:12
   A. The bread in the streets
   B. The cedars of Lebanon
   C. The heart of each Jew
   D. The raiment of the Babylonians

7. What shall Jerusalem be called?
   Zechariah 8:3
   A. A city by the sea
   B. A city of truth
   C. A city put on a hill
   D. A city with no king

8. What shall the streets of Jerusalem be filled with?
   Zechariah 8:5
   A. Carts filled with goods
   B. Chariots of fire
   C. Children playing
   D. Corpses of Israel's enemies

9. What belonging to the Jews was to become strong?
   Zechariah 8:9, 8:13
   A. Their cattle
   B. Their hands
   C. Their plows
   D. Their walls

10. How many men from other nations shall go to pray with one Jew in Jerusalem?
    Zechariah 8:23
    A. 5
    B. 7
    C. 10
    D. 12

11. Which city was known for its abundance of gold and silver?
    Zechariah 9:3
    A. Assos
    B. Chios
    C. Jebus
    D. Tyrus

12. What shall dwell in Ashdod?
    Zechariah 9:6
    A. A bastard
    B. A murderer
    C. A thief
    D. A widow

13. Whose pride shall be cut off?
    Zechariah 9:6
    A. The Chaldeans' pride
    B. The Meholathites' pride
    C. The Philistines' pride
    D. The Shilonites' pride

14. What shall the future king of Jerusalem enter the city upon?
    Zechariah 9:9
    A. A chariot of gold
    B. A white donkey
    C. The back of a camel
    D. The foal of an ass

15. Whom shall the LORD cut off the chariot from?
    Zechariah 9:10
    A. Ephraim
    B. Midian
    C. Sidon
    D. Tyre

16. Which city shall the LORD cut off the horse from?
    Zechariah 9:10
    A. Corinth
    B. Jerusalem
    C. Philadelphia
    D. Thessalonica

17. What shall make the young men cheerful?
    Zechariah 9:17
    A. Bows
    B. Corn
    C. Horses
    D. Women

18. What shall make the maids cheerful?
    Zechariah 9:17
    A. New clothing
    B. New houses
    C. New jewelry
    D. New wine

19. The pride of which nation shall be brought down?
    Zechariah 10:11
    A. Assyria
    B. Edom
    C. Moab
    D. Syria

20. The scepter shall depart from which nation?
    Zechariah 10:11
    A. Egypt
    B. Midian
    C. Persia
    D. Rome

Answers on page 773

OCTOBER 1

Lesson 274
Today's Reading: *Zechariah 11–14*
Period of Time: 518 BC
Author: Zechariah

1. Which nation was famous for its cedar trees?
   Zechariah 11:1
   A. Assyria
   B. Egypt
   C. Greece
   D. Lebanon

2. Which nation was famous for its oak trees?
   Zechariah 11:2
   A. Bashan
   B. Cushan
   C. Dothan
   D. Eshean

3. Which river was Zechariah referring to when he said, "There is a voice of the howling of the shepherds"?
   Zechariah 11:3
   A. River of Arnon
   B. River of Hiddekel
   C. River of Jordan
   D. River of Kishon

4. What were the names of the two staves?
   Zechariah 11:7
   A. Astonishment and Altars
   B. Beauty and Bands
   C. Precious and Pots
   D. Resurrection and Roses

5. How many shepherds did the LORD cut off in one month?
   Zechariah 11:8
   A. 2
   B. 3
   C. 4
   D. 5

6. How many pieces of silver were paid to the shepherd for his wages?
   Zechariah 11:12
   A. 7
   B. 10
   C. 24
   D. 30

7. What did Zechariah do with the pieces of silver?
   Zechariah 11:13
   A. Cast them to the potter
   B. Gave them to the poor
   C. Tossed them into a well
   D. Traded them for gold

8. What did the LORD say he would turn Jerusalem into?
   Zechariah 12:2
   A. A cup of trembling
   B. A horn of oil
   C. A mountain of holiness
   D. A river of life

9. What did the LORD say he would make Jerusalem for all people?
   Zechariah 12:3
   A. A burdensome stone
   B. A city of refuge
   C. A dung port
   D. A ruinous heap

10. What did the LORD say he would smite with astonishment?
    Zechariah 12:4
    A. Every ass
    B. Every camel
    C. Every horse
    D. Every mule

11. What did the LORD say he would smite with madness?

    Zechariah 12:4

    A. Every horse rider
    B. Every keeper of flocks
    C. Every refiner of metals
    D. Every tax collector

12. What did the LORD say he would smite with blindness?

    Zechariah 12:4

    A. Every ass of the field
    B. Every camel of the desert
    C. Every cow of the herd
    D. Every horse of the people

13. Whom did the LORD say he would make like a hearth of fire among the wood?

    Zechariah 12:6

    A. The dukes of Edom
    B. The governors of Judah
    C. The kings of the earth
    D. The prophets of Baal

14. In which valley did the mourning of Hadadrimmon take place?

    Zechariah 12:11

    A. Valley of Charashim
    B. Valley of Hamongog
    C. Valley of Jezreel
    D. Valley of Megiddon

15. What will happen after the shepherd has been smote?

    Zechariah 13:7

    A. The master will be reviled.
    B. The sheep will be scattered.
    C. The shepherd will fall.
    D. The wolves will feast.

16. Where is the mount of Olives located?

    Zechariah 14:4

    A. North of Jerusalem
    B. South of Jerusalem
    C. East of Jerusalem
    D. West of Jerusalem

17. Who was king when a great earthquake struck Judah?

    Zechariah 14:5

    A. King Baasha
    B. King Jehoahaz
    C. King Nadab
    D. King Uzziah

18. What shall go out from Jerusalem on the day the LORD shall come and all the saints with him?

    Zechariah 14:8

    A. Bleeding streets
    B. Crying stones
    C. Living waters
    D. Raging fires

19. Which feast shall be celebrated by all nations annually in Jerusalem?

    Zechariah 14:16

    A. Feast of harvest
    B. Feast of ingathering
    C. Feast of tabernacles
    D. Feast of weeks

20. What shall be written upon the bells of the horses?

    Zechariah 14:20

    A. BABYLON THE GREAT
    B. HOLINESS UNTO THE LORD
    C. KING OF KINGS
    D. LORD OF LORDS

Answers on page 773

OCTOBER 2

Lesson 275
Today's Reading: *Malachi 1–4*
Period of Time: 416 BC
Author: Malachi

1. Who was Jacob's brother?
   Malachi 1:2
   A. Ebal
   B. Ehud
   C. Enan
   D. Esau

2. Which nation said, "We are impoverished, but we will return and build the desolate places?"
   Malachi 1:4
   A. Asia
   B. Edom
   C. Moab
   D. Syria

3. How were the priests despising the LORD's name?
   Malachi 1:6–7
   A. By blessing the meek
   B. By giving too much to the poor
   C. By living according to the law
   D. By offering polluted bread

4. Who would eventually offer—in every place—incense in God's name?
   Malachi 1:11
   A. Gentiles
   B. Jews
   C. Pharisees
   D. Sadducees

5. What did the LORD call himself?
   Malachi 1:14
   A. A great King
   B. A mighty Lord
   C. A noble Vine
   D. A wise Judge

6. What does the LORD say he shall spread upon Israel's faces?
   Malachi 2:3
   A. Ashes
   B. Dung
   C. Mud
   D. Oil

7. Whom did God call the messenger of the LORD of hosts?
   Malachi 2:7
   A. The judge
   B. The king
   C. The priest
   D. The prophet

8. Which covenant had the priests corrupted?
   Malachi 2:8
   A. The covenant of Adam
   B. The covenant of David
   C. The covenant of Levi
   D. The covenant of Noah

9. Who did Malachi say hath married the daughter of a strange god?
   Malachi 2:11
   A. Judah
   B. Naphtali
   C. Reuben
   D. Zebulun

10. What does the LORD compare his messenger of the covenant to first?
    Malachi 3:1–2
    A. A fisherman's net
    B. A potter's wheel
    C. A refiner's fire
    D. A woodcutter's axe

11. What does the LORD compare his messenger of the covenant to second?

    Malachi 3:1–2

    A. A butcher's meat
    B. A cupbearer's wine
    C. A fuller's soap
    D. A grinder's meal

12. Which two things were the people **not** giving, thus robbing God?

    Malachi 3:8

    A. Honey and bread to the poor
    B. Milk and meat to orphans
    C. Money and care to widows
    D. Tithes and offerings to God

13. What does the LORD say the land shall be if Israel turns back to God?

    Malachi 3:12

    A. A backslidden land
    B. A delightsome land
    C. A peculiar land
    D. A wonder land

14. Which book was written before the LORD?

    Malachi 3:16

    A. A book of covenant
    B. A book of law
    C. A book of prayer
    D. A book of remembrance

15. What does Malachi compare the coming day to?

    Malachi 4:1

    A. A bowl
    B. A cup
    C. An apron
    D. An oven

16. What does Malachi say shall have healing in his wings?

    Malachi 4:2

    A. The eagles upon the mount
    B. The ravens of the valley
    C. The Sun of righteousness
    D. The terrestrial bodies

17. How shall those that fear the LORD's name grow up?

    Malachi 4:2

    A. As calves of the stall
    B. As green stalks of grain
    C. As horses going into battle
    D. As trees planted by the waters

18. Where did Moses receive the LORD's commandments?

    Malachi 4:4

    A. Horeb
    B. Lebanon
    C. Moriah
    D. Olivet

19. Which prophet did God promise to send to Israel?

    Malachi 4:5

    A. Abraham
    B. Elijah
    C. Jonah
    D. Samuel

20. What is the last word in the Old Testament?

    Malachi 4:6

    A. Amen
    B. Curse
    C. Earth
    D. Heart

Answers on page 773

OCTOBER 3

Lesson 276
Today's Reading: *Matthew 1–4*
Period of Time: March 23, 5 BC–31 AD
Author: Matthew

1. What is the total number of generations from Abraham to Christ?
   Matthew 1:17
   A. 14
   B. 28
   C. 42
   D. 56

2. Who was Jesus' mother?
   Matthew 1:18
   A. Mahlah
   B. Mara
   C. Martha
   D. Mary

3. Which name means *God with us*?
   Matthew 1:23
   A. Emmanuel
   B. Jehovah
   C. Rock
   D. Shiloh

4. Where was Jesus born?
   Matthew 2:1
   A. Anem
   B. Bethlehem
   C. Jerusalem
   D. Shechem

5. Which gifts did the wise men bring to Jesus?
   Matthew 2:11
   A. Clothing, silver, and gold
   B. Expensive perfume, livestock, and silver
   C. Gold, frankincense, and myrrh
   D. Spices, jewels, and gold

6. Where did Joseph and his family flee to after Jesus was born?
   Matthew 2:13–14
   A. Bethany
   B. Egypt
   C. Galilee
   D. Nazareth

7. Who prophesied that Rachel would weep for her dead children?
   Matthew 2:17–18
   A. Daniel
   B. Ezekiel
   C. Isaiah
   D. Jeremy

8. Who was King Herod's son?
   Matthew 2:22
   A. Archelaus
   B. Cornelius
   C. Julius
   D. Lebbaeus

9. Which city did Jesus grow up in as a boy?
   Matthew 2:23
   A. Bethany
   B. Capernaum
   C. Gennesaret
   D. Nazareth

10. Who prophesied the coming of John the Baptist?
    Matthew 3:1–3
    A. Esaias
    B. Jeremy
    C. Micaiah
    D. Obadiah

11. What was John the Baptist's raiment made of?
    Matthew 3:4
    A. Beaver skin
    B. Camel's hair
    C. Fig leaves
    D. Wool

12. Which two foods were mentioned as being a part of John the Baptist's diet?
    Matthew 3:4
    A. Cucumbers and melons
    B. Fish and leeks
    C. Locusts and wild honey
    D. Nuts and berries

13. Which river did John the Baptist use to baptize people?

    Matthew 3:6

    A. River of Jordan
    B. River of Kanah
    C. River of Pison
    D. River of Ulai

14. What did John the Baptist call the Pharisees and Sadducees?

    Matthew 3:7

    A. Rats
    B. Vipers
    C. Weasels
    D. Worms

15. Who will baptize people with fire?

    Matthew 3:11

    A. God the father
    B. Holy Ghost
    C. Jesus
    D. John the Baptist

16. Which bird did the Holy Spirit look like as it descended upon Jesus during his baptism?

    Matthew 3:16

    A. A bat
    B. A bittern
    C. A cuckow
    D. A dove

17. How many days and nights did Jesus fast in the wilderness?

    Matthew 4:1–2

    A. 30
    B. 40
    C. 50
    D. 60

18. What did Jesus tell Satan after being tempted the *third* time?

    Matthew 4:8–10

    A. "Man shall not live by bread alone."
    B. "Thou shalt not tempt the LORD."
    C. "Thou shalt worship the Lord thy God."
    D. "Vengeance is mine."

19. Whom did Jesus tell he would make them fishers of men?

    Matthew 4:18–19

    A. Andrew and Simon
    B. James and John
    C. Philip and Matthew
    D. Thomas and Thaddaeus

20. Who was the father of James and John?

    Matthew 4:21

    A. Agee
    B. Jesse
    C. Nagge
    D. Zebedee

*Answers on page 773

OCTOBER 4

Lesson 277
Today's Reading: *Matthew 5–6*
Period of Time: 31 AD
Author: Matthew

1. Who did Jesus say would inherit the kingdom of heaven?
   Matthew 5:3, 5:10
   A. The meek
   B. The poor in spirit
   C. They that mourn
   D. Those that hunger and thirst for righteousness

2. Who did Jesus say would be comforted?
   Matthew 5:4
   A. The merciful
   B. The peacemakers
   C. They that mourn
   D. Those that hunger and thirst for righteousness

3. Who did Jesus say would inherit the earth?
   Matthew 5:5
   A. The meek
   B. The peacemakers
   C. The pure in heart
   D. They that mourn

4. Who did Jesus say would be filled?
   Matthew 5:6
   A. The poor in spirit
   B. The pure in heart
   C. They that mourn
   D. Those that hunger and thirst for righteousness

5. Who did Jesus say would obtain mercy?
   Matthew 5:7
   A. The merciful
   B. The poor in spirit
   C. The pure in heart
   D. They that mourn

6. Who did Jesus say would see God?
   Matthew 5:8
   A. The meek
   B. The merciful
   C. The poor in spirit
   D. The pure in heart

7. Who did Jesus say would be called the children of God?
   Matthew 5:9
   A. The meek
   B. The merciful
   C. The peacemakers
   D. They that mourn

8. What did Jesus say to do when others revile, lie about you, and persecute you for his sake?
   Matthew 5:11–12
   A. Get even with them
   B. Rejoice and be glad
   C. Slap them on the cheek
   D. Take them to court

9. What did Jesus call those who obey God's commands?
   Matthew 5:14–16
   A. Apostles from heaven
   B. Disciples of Christ
   C. Light of the world
   D. Saved from hell

10. Why did Jesus come to earth?
    Matthew 5:17
    A. To become famous
    B. To fulfil the law
    C. To rule the world
    D. To teach Satan a lesson

11. Who did Jesus say would be least in the kingdom of heaven?

    Matthew 5:19

    A. Whoever breaks God's commandments and teaches others to do so
    B. Whoever cares for the sick and ill, and casts out devils in his name
    C. Whoever gives their money to orphans, the needy, and widows
    D. Whoever visits those worthy of death in jails and prisons

12. Who did Jesus say would be great in the kingdom of heaven?

    Matthew 5:19

    A. Whoever does and teaches God's commandments
    B. Whoever does not care for the sick and ill, and casts out devils in his name
    C. Whoever does not give their money to orphans, the needy, and widows
    D. Whoever does not visit those worthy of death in jails and prisons

13. Whose righteousness does a person need to exceed in order to enter the kingdom of heaven?

    Matthew 5:20

    A. Angels and demons
    B. Priests and Levites
    C. Saints and sinners
    D. Scribes and Pharisees

14. Which one of the following is **not** one of the ten commandments?

    Matthew 5:21–44

    A. Thou shalt not commit adultery.
    B. Thou shalt not kill.
    C. Thou shalt not love thy enemies.
    D. Thou shalt not steal.

15. What is God's footstool?

    Matthew 5:35

    A. The clouds
    B. The earth
    C. The moon
    D. The sun

16. Where did Jesus say a person should pray?

    Matthew 6:6

    A. At church
    B. In a closet
    C. In a synagogue
    D. On a street

17. Which verse is **not** part of *The LORD's Prayer*?

    Matthew 6:9–13

    A. Give us this day
    B. Hallowed be thy name
    C. Let this cup pass from me
    D. Our Father

18. What did Jesus say moths and rust corrupt?

    Matthew 6:19

    A. Brass swords exposed to the air
    B. Clothes stored in the closet
    C. Iron pipes used for water
    D. Treasures upon earth

19. What is the light of the body?

    Matthew 6:22

    A. The eye
    B. The heart
    C. The mind
    D. The soul

20. What did Jesus say was more arrayed than Solomon and all his glory?

    Matthew 6:28–29

    A. Asters
    B. Carnations
    C. Daisies
    D. Lilies

*Answers on page 774

OCTOBER 5

Lesson 278
Today's Reading: *Matthew 7–9*
Period of Time: 31 AD
Author: Matthew

1. What did Jesus say a person must remove from his own eye before judging others?
   Matthew 7:1–5
   A. A beam
   B. A grain of sand
   C. A mote
   D. An Eye-patch

2. Which precious stones did Jesus say **not** to cast to swine?
   Matthew 7:6
   A. Diamonds
   B. Emeralds
   C. Pearls
   D. Rubies

3. Which gate did Jesus say leads to life?
   Matthew 7:13–14
   A. The broad gate
   B. The fish gate
   C. The king's gate
   D. The strait gate

4. Who did Jesus say appears in sheep's clothing but are actually ravening wolves?
   Matthew 7:15
   A. Earthly kings
   B. False prophets
   C. Religious teachers
   D. Tax collectors

5. How did Jesus heal the leper?
   Matthew 8:1–3
   A. He baptized him in water.
   B. He cast out a demon.
   C. He touched him.
   D. He used spit and dirt.

6. Where did Jesus meet the centurion?
   Matthew 8:5
   A. Capernaum
   B. Cappadocia
   C. Carchemish
   D. Caria

7. Which sickness did the centurion's servant have?
   Matthew 8:5–13
   A. Blindness
   B. Emerods
   C. Leprosy
   D. Palsy

8. How did Jesus heal the centurion's servant?
   Matthew 8:5–13
   A. He cast out a demon.
   B. He spoke the word.
   C. He touched him.
   D. He used spit and dirt.

9. Which one of Peter's relatives did Jesus heal?
   Matthew 8:14
   A. Peter's aunt
   B. Peter's daughter
   C. Peter's mother-in-law
   D. Peter's wife

10. Which prophet said that Jesus would take our infirmities and bare our sicknesses?
    Matthew 8:17
    A. Esaias
    B. Jeremy
    C. Obadiah
    D. Zechariah

11. Whom did Jesus tell, "Let the dead bury the dead"?
    Matthew 8:21–22
    A. A certain ruler
    B. A disciple
    C. A lawyer
    D. A scribe

12. What miracle did Jesus do while on a ship?
    Matthew 8:23–26
    A. He and Andrew walked on water.
    B. He brought the dead captain back to life.
    C. He calmed a raging storm.
    D. He caught a vast amount of fish.

13. How many men were demon-possessed in the country of the Gergesenes?

    Matthew 8:28

    A. 2
    B. 7
    C. 10
    D. Too many to count

14. What did the demons call Jesus?

    Matthew 8:29

    A. KING OF KINGS
    B. LORD OF LORDS
    C. Prince of Peace
    D. Son of God

15. Which animals did Jesus cast the demons into?

    Matthew 8:30–32

    A. Dogs
    B. Goats
    C. Rams
    D. Swine

16. How did the Gergesenes react to Jesus after he cast out the demons?

    Matthew 8:33–34

    A. They apologized to him.
    B. They attacked him with clubs.
    C. They besought him to leave.
    D. They threw him a great feast.

17. Who marveled when they saw Jesus heal a man sick of the palsy?

    Matthew 9:1–8

    A. The multitudes
    B. The Pharisees
    C. The Sadducees
    D. The scribes

18. Whom did Jesus tell at the receipt of custom to follow him?

    Matthew 9:9

    A. John
    B. Luke
    C. Mark
    D. Matthew

19. Who asked Jesus to bring his dead daughter back to life?

    Matthew 9:18

    A. A priest
    B. A ruler
    C. A servant
    D. A teacher

20. How many years did the woman suffer from a blood disorder before being healed by Jesus?

    Matthew 9:20–22

    A. 5
    B. 12
    C. 29
    D. 38

Answers on page 774

Lesson 279
Today's Reading: *Matthew 10–12*
Period of Time: 31 AD
Author: Matthew

OCTOBER 6

1. How many disciples did Jesus have?
   Matthew 10:1
   A. 3
   B. 7
   C. 12
   D. 40

2. Which one of the following was **not** an original disciple of Jesus?
   Matthew 10:2–4
   A. Andrew
   B. Barnabas
   C. James
   D. Simon

3. Which one of the following was **not** an original disciple of Jesus?
   Matthew 10:2–4
   A. Apollo
   B. Bartholomew
   C. Philip
   D. Thomas

4. Who was James' brother?
   Matthew 10:2
   A. John
   B. Paul
   C. Peter
   D. Thaddeus

5. Who was a publican?
   Matthew 10:3
   A. John
   B. Luke
   C. Mark
   D. Matthew

6. Who was Alphaeus' son?
   Matthew 10:3
   A. Jabez
   B. Jambres
   C. James
   D. Jannes

7. What was Lebbaeus' surname?
   Matthew 10:3
   A. Alphaeus
   B. Bartimaeus
   C. Thaddaeus
   D. Zeus

8. What was Simon's surname—**not** Simon Peter?
   Matthew 10:4
   A. The Canaanite
   B. The Hittite
   C. The Hivite
   D. The Perizite

9. Which disciple betrayed Jesus?
   Matthew 10:4
   A. Herod Antipas
   B. Judas Iscariot
   C. Pontius Pilate
   D. Porcius Festus

10. What did Jesus tell his disciples to be as wise as?
    Matthew 10:16
    A. Ants
    B. Foxes
    C. Owls
    D. Serpents

11. Which birds did Jesus tell his disciples to be as harmless as?
    Matthew 10:16
    A. Albatrosses
    B. Bitterns
    C. Cormorants
    D. Doves

12. What did Jesus say he came to send?
    Matthew 10:34
    A. A buckler
    B. A fire
    C. A flood
    D. A sword

13. How many disciples did John the Baptist send to Jesus?

    Matthew 11:2

    A. 2
    B. 4
    C. 6
    D. 12

14. Which city did Jesus say would go to hell?

    Matthew 11:23

    A. Capernaum
    B. Jericho
    C. Nineveh
    D. Shiloh

15. Which kind of bread did David and his men eat?

    Matthew 12:3–4

    A. Ezekiel
    B. Leavened
    C. Manna
    D. Shewbread

16. Whom did Jesus heal on the sabbath day in Matthew 12:10?

    Matthew 12:10

    A. A blind girl
    B. A deaf boy
    C. A man with a withered hand
    D. A woman with a fever

17. Who is the prince of the devils?

    Matthew 12:24–27

    A. Barabbas
    B. Beelzebub
    C. Boanerges
    D. Buzi

18. Which sin is unforgiveable?

    Matthew 12:31

    A. Adultery involving homosexuality
    B. Blasphemy against the Holy Ghost
    C. Killing innocent newborns and children
    D. Stealing from God's holy temples

19. How many days and nights was Jonas in the whale's belly?

    Matthew 12:39–40

    A. 2
    B. 3
    C. 6
    D. 7

20. Which king did the queen of the south visit?

    Matthew 12:42

    A. King David
    B. King Jehoshaphat
    C. King Solomon
    D. King Zedekiah

Answers on page 774

OCTOBER 7

Lesson 280
Today's Reading: *Matthew 13–14*
Period of Time: 31–32 AD
Author: Matthew

1. Where did Jesus tell the *Parable of the Sower*?
   Mathew 13:2
   A. At a well
   B. Inside a synagogue
   C. Near a farmer's house
   D. On a ship

2. What represents the devil in the *Parable of the Sower*?
   Mathew 13:3–19
   A. Birds
   B. Dogs
   C. Goats
   D. Lions

3. Which prophet said, "By hearing ye shall hear, and shall **not** understand"?
   Mathew 13:14
   A. Amos
   B. Balaam
   C. Daniel
   D. Esaias

4. What do the stony places represent in the *Parable of the Sower*?
   Mathew 13:3–21
   A. Faith or joy
   B. God or the Holy Ghost
   C. Salvation or sanctification
   D. Tribulation or persecution

5. What do the thorns represent in the *Parable of the Sower*?
   Mathew 13:3–22
   A. The cleansing from sin and all unrighteousness
   B. The deceitfulness of riches and the care of this world
   C. The pain in a sick person's side such as the thorn in Paul's side
   D. The road to hell which is paved with good intentions.

6. Which type of field were the tares sowed in?
   Mathew 13:24–25
   A. A barley field
   B. A flax field
   C. A rye field
   D. A wheat field

7. Which type of grain did Jesus say was similar to the kingdom of heaven?
   Mathew 13:31–32
   A. A fig seed
   B. A mustard seed
   C. A pomegranate seed
   D. An olive seed

8. In how many measures of meal did the woman in the *Parable of the Leaven* hide the leaven?
   Mathew 13:33
   A. 1 1/2
   B. 2
   C. 2 2/3
   D. 3

9. Who did Jesus say sows the good seed in the *Parable of the Tares Among the Wheat*?
   Mathew 13:37
   A. The children of the kingdom
   B. The good Samaritan
   C. The Son of man
   D. The twelve apostles

10. Whom did Jesus call the reapers?
    Mathew 13:39
    A. The angels
    B. The children of God
    C. The devil and his angels
    D. The seventy disciples

11. Who was Jesus' mother?
    Mathew 13:55
    A. Elizabeth
    B. Martha
    C. Mary
    D. Ruth

12. How many brothers did Jesus have?
    Mathew 13:55
    A. 3
    B. 4
    C. 5
    D. 7

13. Whom did Herod the tetrarch think Jesus was?
    Mathew 14:1–2
    A. Abraham
    B. Elijah
    C. John the Baptist
    D. Moses

14. Who was Herod's brother?
    Mathew 14:3
    A. Philip
    B. Pontius Pilate
    C. Quirinius
    D. Tiberius Caesar

15. Who asked for the head of John the Baptist in a charger?
    Mathew 14:6–11
    A. Herodias' daughter
    B. John the Baptist's ex-wife
    C. Pontius Pilate's father
    D. Tertullus' client

16. How many loaves of bread and fish did the disciples have?
    Mathew 14:17
    A. 2 loaves and 1 fish
    B. 4 loaves and 4 fish
    C. 5 loaves and 2 fish
    D. 10 loaves and 5 fish

17. How many baskets full of bread and fish were leftover after the meal?
    Mathew 14:20
    A. 6
    B. 12
    C. 18
    D. 24

18. Approximately how many men did Jesus feed with the fish and bread?
    Mathew 14:21
    A. 2,000
    B. 5,000
    C. 8,000
    D. 10,000

19. Which apostle became frightened when he walked on water?
    Mathew 14:25–31
    A. James
    B. John
    C. Peter
    D. Philip

20. Where did Jesus travel to after walking upon the sea?
    Mathew 14:32–34
    A. Land of Gennesaret
    B. Land of Havilah
    C. Land of Nod
    D. Land of Shinar

*Answers on page 774

OCTOBER 8

Lesson 281
Today's Reading: *Matthew 15–17*
Period of Time: 32 AD
Author: Matthew

1. What did the scribes and Pharisees ask Jesus?
   Mathew 15:1–2
   A. Are you the carpenter's son? And is your mother's name Mary?
   B. Art thou he that should come, or do we look for another?
   C. Is it possible for Satan to cast out Satan?
   D. Why do your disciples not wash their hands when they eat bread?

2. What did Jesus call the scribes and Pharisees?
   Mathew 15:7
   A. Adulterers
   B. Fornicators
   C. Hypocrites
   D. Vipers

3. Which prophet said that the people draw near to God with their mouth, but their heart was far away?
   Mathew 15:7–8
   A. Amos
   B. Esaias
   C. Nathan
   D. Samuel

4. Which disciple asked Jesus to explain the *Parable of the Blind Leading the Blind*?
   Mathew 15:14–15
   A. Peter
   B. Philip
   C. Simon the Zealot
   D. Thaddaeus

5. What did Jesus tell the Caananite woman?
   Mathew 15:21–24
   A. "Go, call thy husband, and come here."
   B. "I am not sent but unto the lost sheep of the house of Israel."
   C. "Neither do I condemn thee; go, and sin no more."
   D. "Thy brother shall rise again."

6. What did Jesus say was **not** right to take from children and give to the dogs?
   Mathew 15:26
   A. Bread
   B. Milk
   C. Playthings
   D. Shoes

7. How many days did Jesus heal the lame, blind, dumb, and maimed on the mountain?
   Mathew 15:29–32
   A. 3
   B. 4
   C. 5
   D. 7

8. In addition to a few fish, how many loaves of bread did the disciples have?
   Mathew 15:34
   A. 3
   B. 4
   C. 5
   D. 7

9. How many baskets of food were leftover after Jesus fed the multitude on the mountain?
   Mathew 15:37
   A. 3
   B. 4
   C. 5
   D. 7

10. How many men—besides women and children—did Jesus feed on the mountain?
    Mathew 15:37–38
    A. 2,000
    B. 3,000
    C. 4,000
    D. 5,000

11. Where did Jesus and the disciples travel to after feeding the second multitude?

    Mathew 15:39

    A. Machpelah
    B. Magdala
    C. Magog
    D. Masada

12. What sign did Jesus say a wicked and adulterous generation would receive?

    Mathew 16:4

    A. A red and lowring sky in the morning
    B. A red sky in the evening
    C. The sign of a red heifer
    D. The sign of the prophet Jonas

13. What was Jesus referring to when he told his disciples to beware of the leaven of the Pharisees and Sadducees?

    Mathew 16:6–12

    A. Their bread
    B. Their doctrine
    C. Their wine
    D. Their yeast

14. Which name was **not** mentioned by the disciples as to whom the people thought Jesus was?

    Mathew 16:13–14

    A. Azzur
    B. Elias
    C. Jeremias
    D. John the Baptist

15. Upon which apostle did Jesus say he would build his church?

    Mathew 16:17–18

    A. James, the son of Alphaeus
    B. James, the son of Zebedee
    C. Simon Barjona
    D. Simon the Zealot

16. Whom did Jesus tell, "Get thee behind me, Satan"?

    Mathew 16:23

    A. Ananias
    B. Caiaphas
    C. Peter
    D. Pontius Pilate

17. Which apostle was **not** present during the transfiguration?

    Mathew 17:1–2

    A. James
    B. John
    C. Peter
    D. Philip

18. Which two of the following men appeared during the transfiguration?

    Mathew 17:3

    A. Abraham and Isaac
    B. David and Solomon
    C. Moses and Elias
    D. Samuel and Saul

19. What was wrong with the man the apostles could **not** heal?

    Mathew 17:14–21

    A. He was a lunatic.
    B. He was a mute.
    C. He was blind.
    D. He was lame.

20. Where did Peter get the money to pay the taxes?

    Mathew 17:24–27

    A. From a bear's cave
    B. From a fish's mouth
    C. From a sparrow's nest
    D. From a unicorn's horn

*Answers on page 774

OCTOBER 9

Lesson 282
Today's Reading: *Matthew 18–20*
Period of Time: 32–33 AD
Author: Matthew

1. Who did Jesus say was greatest in the kingdom of heaven?
   Mathew 18:1–4
   A. He who forgives his debtors
   B. He who gives all of his riches to the poor
   C. He who humbles himself as a little child
   D. He who loves and cares for his family

2. What did Jesus say would be better for a person who offends a child who believes in him?
   Mathew 18:6
   A. Being burned with fire
   B. Being drowned at sea
   C. Being flogged in public
   D. Being put in jail

3. Who continuously watches over God's little children?
   Mathew 18:10
   A. Their angels
   B. Their family
   C. Their neighbors
   D. Their village

4. What is the moral of the *Parable of the Lost Sheep*?
   Mathew 18:11–14
   A. To beware of wolves in sheep clothing
   B. To watch over your money and investments
   C. That God's people should watch for his return
   D. That none of God's little children should perish

5. How should a person be treated if he neglects to hear the church concerning the wrong he has done?
   Mathew 18:15–17
   A. Like a criminal and a thief
   B. Like a heathen and a publican
   C. Like a lunatic and a fool
   D. Like a traitor and a backslider

6. Where shall people find Jesus?
   Mathew 18:20
   A. Anywhere two or more people gather in his name.
   B. In the desert
   C. In the secret chambers
   D. Wherever great signs and wonders are performed

7. How often did Jesus say a person should forgive a person who repents of his sin?
   Mathew 18:21–22
   A. 7 x 1
   B. 7 x 7
   C. 70 x 7
   D. 700 x 70

8. How many talents did the servant owe the king?
   Mathew 18:24
   A. 1,000
   B. 3,000
   C. 5,000
   D. 10,000

9. How much did the servant owe the man whom the king had released from his debt?
   Mathew 18:28
   A. 10 farthings
   B. 100 pence
   C. 200 shekels
   D. 2,000 talents

10. Which incident allows a man to divorce his wife?
    Mathew 19:9
    A. She becomes demon-possessed
    B. She cannot bare him an heir
    C. She commits fornication
    D. She steals from him

11. Who demanded that the little children be sent away?

    Mathew 19:13

    A. The disciples
    B. The elders
    C. The publicans
    D. The scribes

12. What did a certain rich man call Jesus?

    Mathew 19:16–22

    A. Everlasting Father
    B. Everlasting Light
    C. Good LORD
    D. Good Master

13. What did Jesus say it would be easier for a camel to go through than for a rich man to enter into the kingdom of God?

    Mathew 19:24

    A. A burning house
    B. A hole in a floor
    C. The cracks in a wall
    D. The eye of a needle

14. Who shall sit upon 12 thrones in heaven and judge the twelve tribes of Israel?

    Mathew 19:28

    A. The 12 apostles
    B. The 12 minor prophets
    C. The 12 major prophets
    D. The 12 sons of Jacob

15. What did Jesus say regarding many that are first?

    Mathew 19:30

    A. They shall be greatest in heaven.
    B. They shall be last.
    C. They shall receive treasure in heaven.
    D. They shall rule the world.

16. How much did the householder pay each laborer that worked in his vineyard?

    Mathew 20:1–16

    A. 1 farthing
    B. 1 penny
    C. 2 shekels
    D. 2 talents of gold

17. Which disciples' relative asked that her sons sit on each side of Jesus in the kingdom of God?

    Mathew 20:20–21

    A. The cousin of Thaddaeus and Judas
    B. The father of Andrew and Peter
    C. The mother of Zebedee's children
    D. The uncle of Nathanael and Bartholomew

18. What did a disciple need to be if he wanted to be the greatest among the disciples?

    Mathew 20:26

    A. Their king
    B. Their lord
    C. Their minister
    D. Their servant

19. What did a disciple need to be if he wanted to be chief among the disciples?

    Mathew 20:27

    A. Their king
    B. Their lord
    C. Their minister
    D. Their servant

20. How many blind men did Jesus heal as he left Jericho?

    Mathew 20:29–34

    A. 2
    B. 3
    C. 7
    D. 10

Answers on page 774

OCTOBER 10

Lesson 283
Today's Reading: *Matthew 21–22*
Period of Time: Sunday, March 29–Tuesday, March 31, 33 AD
Author: Matthew

1. Which village is located on the mount of Olives?
   Mathew 21:1
   A. Bethel
   B. Bethlehem
   C. Bethphage
   D. Bethsaida

2. What did Jesus tell the two disciples to bring him from a nearby village?
   Mathew 21:2
   A. A fine linen cloth
   B. A pitcher of water
   C. A Roman coin
   D. An ass and her colt

3. What did the multitude toss as Jesus traveled to Jerusalem?
   Mathew 21:8
   A. Branches from trees
   B. Garbage from their homes
   C. Rocks from the street
   D. Rose petals

4. What did the multitude say as Jesus traveled to Jerusalem?
   Mathew 21:9
   A. "Art thou he that should come or do we look for another?"
   B. "Blessed is he who comes in the name of the LORD."
   C. "From where hath this man this wisdom?"
   D. "Master, rebuke thy disciples."

5. What did the multitude call Jesus when the people of Jerusalem asked who he was?
   Mathew 21:10–11
   A. "The Alpha and the Omega"
   B. "The Everlasting God"
   C. "The King of Kings"
   D. "The prophet of Nazareth"

6. What did Jesus do at the temple?
   Mathew 21:12
   A. Bought turtledoves for the poor
   B. Gave a sin offering
   C. Overthrew the moneychangers' tables
   D. Prayed for the Jewish leaders

7. What did Jesus say the temple was supposed to be?
   Mathew 21:13
   A. The common hall
   B. The house of prayer
   C. The light on a hill
   D. The temple for all people

8. Where did Jesus go after departing the temple?
   Mathew 21:17
   A. Bethany
   B. Bethesda
   C. Bethuel
   D. Bethzur

9. What type of tree did Jesus curse?
   Mathew 21:19
   A. A fig tree
   B. A myrtle tree
   C. A sycamore tree
   D. An oak tree

10. What did Jesus say could be cast into the sea if a person had enough faith?
    Mathew 21:21
    A. A camel
    B. A mountain
    C. A town
    D. An army

11. Who did Jesus say would enter the kingdom of God before the chief priests?

    Mathew 21:23–31

    A. Generals and soldiers
    B. Judges and lawyers
    C. Kings and queens
    D. Publicans and harlots

12. Whom did the owner of the vineyard send first during the harvest?

    Mathew 21:33–34

    A. His brothers
    B. His servants
    C. His son
    D. His uncle

13. Whom did the owner of the vineyard send last during the harvest?

    Mathew 21:33–39

    A. His brother
    B. His servant
    C. His son
    D. His uncle

14. What did Jesus say the builders rejected?

    Mathew 21:42

    A. A carpenter
    B. A hammer
    C. A nail
    D. A stone

15. What did the king do to those who refused to attend his son's wedding?

    Mathew 22:2–7

    A. He refused to let their sons marry his daughters.
    B. He removed their clothes and sold them as slaves.
    C. He sent his army to slay them and burn their city.
    D. He took away their lands and sold their farms.

16. Which group did **not** believe in the resurrection?

    Mathew 22:23

    A. The Herodians
    B. The Pharisees
    C. The Saducees
    D. The scribes

17. How many brothers married the same woman in the story told to Jesus?

    Mathew 22:23–28

    A. 2
    B. 3
    C. 6
    D. 7

18. Who asked Jesus which commandment was the greatest?

    Mathew 22:35–36

    A. A lawyer
    B. A priest
    C. A rabbi
    D. A soldier

19. What did Jesus say was the greatest commandment?

    Mathew 22:35–37

    A. Love God with all your heart, soul, and mind.
    B. Love the sinner, hate the sin.
    C. Love your neighbor as yourself.
    D. Love yourself before all others.

20. Who did the Pharisees claim was Christ's father?

    Mathew 22:41–42

    A. Abraham
    B. David
    C. Isaac
    D. Jacob

*Answers on page 774

OCTOBER 11

Lesson 284
Today's Reading: *Matthew 23–24*
Period of Time: Tuesday, March 31, 33 AD
Author: Matthew

1. Whose seat did Jesus say the scribes and Pharisees like to sit in?
   Matthew 23:1–2
   A. Abraham's seat
   B. Isaac's seat
   C. Jacob's seat
   D. Moses' seat

2. What did Jesus say the scribes and Pharisees do to their garments?
   Matthew 23:1–5
   A. Dye them red
   B. Embroider the front of them
   C. Enlarge their borders
   D. Rent holes in them

3. What did Jesus say the scribes and Pharisees like to be called?
   Matthew 23:1–7
   A. Levi
   B. Preacher
   C. Rabbi
   D. Reverend

4. What title besides *master* did Jesus say we should **not** call another person?
   Matthew 23:9–10
   A. Brother
   B. Father
   C. Lord
   D. Rabbi

5. Who did Jesus say will be our servant?
   Matthew 23:11
   A. He that is greatest
   B. He that is least
   C. He that is strongest
   D. He that is weakest

6. What did Jesus say would happen to a person who exalts himself?
   Matthew 23:12
   A. He shall be abased.
   B. He shall gain confidence.
   C. He will become the master.
   D. He will lead the weak.

7. How many *woes* did Jesus announce upon the scribes and Pharisees?
   Matthew 23:13–29
   A. 4
   B. 5
   C. 6
   D. 8

8. Whose houses did Jesus say the scribes and Pharisees devour?
   Matthew 23:14
   A. The apostle's houses
   B. The Herodian's houses
   C. The Sadducee's houses
   D. The widow's houses

9. Which one of the following was **not** mentioned by Jesus as part of the Pharisees' tithe?
   Matthew 23:23
   A. Anise
   B. Cummin
   C. Garlic
   D. Mint

10. What did Jesus say the blind guides strain at?
    Matthew 23:24
    A. A camel
    B. A gnat
    C. A horse
    D. A locust

587

11. What did Jesus say the Pharisees' cup and platter contain?

    Mathew 23:25

    A. Extortion and excess
    B. Hope and love
    C. Mercy and truth
    D. Peace and joy

12. What did Jesus call the scribes and Pharisees?

    Mathew 23:33

    A. Devils
    B. Serpents
    C. Traitors
    D. Zealots

13. Whom did the scribes and Pharisees slay between the temple and the altar?

    Mathew 23:34–35

    A. Abel
    B. Judas
    C. Stephen
    D. Zacharias

14. Which city did Jesus lament over?

    Mathew 23:37

    A. Bethlehem
    B. Jerusalem
    C. Sidon
    D. Tyre

15. Where did Jesus go after departing from the temple?

    Mathew 24:1–3

    A. Mount of Beatitudes
    B. Mount of Megiddo
    C. Mount of Olives
    D. Mount of Transfiguration

16. Which prophet spoke of the abomination of desolation?

    Mathew 24:15

    A. Amos
    B. Daniel
    C. Malachi
    D. Zephaniah

17. From which direction will the Son of man appear?

    Mathew 24:27

    A. North
    B. South
    C. East
    D. West

18. Which of the following did Jesus **not** mention would occur after the tribulation?

    Mathew 24:29

    A. The days will wax longer.
    B. The moon shall not give her light.
    C. The powers of the heavens shall be shaken.
    D. The sun will be darkened.

19. What would be the sign of the coming of the Son of man?

    Mathew 24:30–31

    A. Angels and the sound of a trumpet
    B. Earthquakes will rattle the world
    C. Sands in the hourglass will be no more
    D. Satan will be thrown into the lake of fire

20. Whose days did Jesus say the end times would be similar to?

    Mathew 24:36–39

    A. Days of Elijah
    B. Days of Elisha
    C. Days of Isaiah
    D. Days of Noe

Answers on page 774

OCTOBER 12

Lesson 285
Today's Reading: *Matthew 25–26*
Period of Time: Tuesday, March 31–Thursday, April 2, 33 AD
Author: Matthew

1. How many virgins were wise?
   Matthew 25:1–2
   A. 2
   B. 3
   C. 4
   D. 5

2. What did the foolish virgins forget?
   Matthew 25:1–3
   A. Oil for their lamps
   B. The wedding cake
   C. Wedding presents
   D. Wood for the fire

3. When did the bridegroom arrive?
   Matthew 25:6
   A. Midnight
   B. Noon
   C. The sixth hour
   D. The third watch

4. How many talents did the man who was given five talents earn?
   Matthew 25:14–30
   A. 0
   B. 2
   C. 5
   D. 10

5. How many talents did the man who was given two talents earn?
   Matthew 25:14–30
   A. 0
   B. 2
   C. 5
   D. 10

6. How many talents did the man who was given one talent earn?
   Matthew 25:14–30
   A. 0
   B. 2
   C. 5
   D. 10

7. What did the man do to the unprofitable servant?
   Matthew 25:24–30
   A. Cast him into outer darkness
   B. Flogged him in public
   C. Gave him ten more talents
   D. Sold him, his wife, and his children

8. Who will accompany Jesus when he returns in glory?
   Matthew 25:31
   A. Abraham
   B. Holy angels
   C. Isaac
   D. Moses

9. How did Jesus say he would divide all nations?
   Matthew 25:31–32
   A. As a captain divides his swords and spears
   B. As a farmer divides his crops and weeds
   C. As a miner divides his gold and rocks
   D. As a shepherd divides his sheep and goats

10. What shall the unrighteous—and the devil and his angels—be cast into?
    Matthew 25:41–46
    A. Limbo
    B. Purgatory
    C. The everlasting fire
    D. The waters of Gehenna

11. Who was the high priest who would eventually preside over the Jewish trial of Jesus?
    Matthew 26:3
    A. Annanias
    B. Bukki
    C. Caiaphas
    D. Zacharias

12. Whose house in Bethany did Jesus lodge at?

    Matthew 26:6

    A. Simon of Cyrene's house
    B. Simon Peter's house
    C. Simon the leper's house
    D. Simon the sorcerer's house

13. Who did Jesus say would always be remembered whenever the gospel is preached?

    Matthew 26:7–13

    A. The apostle who betrayed him
    B. The high priest who arrested him
    C. The Roman ruler who crucified him
    D. The woman who anointed his body

14. Which disciple betrayed Jesus?

    Matthew 26:14–15

    A. James the less
    B. Judas Iscariot
    C. Simon Peter
    D. Simon the Zealot

15. How many pieces of silver were paid to the disciple that betrayed Jesus?

    Matthew 26:15

    A. 2
    B. 5
    C. 10
    D. 30

16. Upon which mountain did Jesus go after the passover meal?

    Matthew 26:30

    A. Mount of Beatitudes
    B. Mount of Olives
    C. Mount of the Holy Cross
    D. Mount of the Transfiguration

17. Which disciple did Jesus say would deny him thrice?

    Matthew 26:33–34

    A. Peter
    B. Philip
    C. Thaddaeus
    D. Thomas

18. Which of the following disciples went with Jesus when he went to pray at Gethsemane?

    Matthew 26:36–37

    A. Andrew and the sons of Hinnom
    B. James and the sons of Anak
    C. Nathanael and the sons of Thunder
    D. Peter and the sons of Zebedee

19. Whose ear was cut off?

    Matthew 26:51

    A. A disciple's ear
    B. A servant's ear
    C. A soldier's ear
    D. A thief's ear

20. What was Jesus falsely accused of during the Jewish trial?

    Matthew 26:57–65

    A. Assault
    B. Battery
    C. Blasphemy
    D. Treason

*Answers on page 774

Lesson 286
Today's Reading: *Matthew 27–28*
Period of Time: Friday, April 3–Thursday, May 14, 33 AD
Author: Matthew

OCTOBER 13

1. Who was governor during Jesus' crucifixion?
   Mathew 27:2
   A. Augustus
   B. Claudius
   C. Herod the Great
   D. Pontius Pilate

2. Which disciple betrayed Jesus for 30 pieces of silver?
   Mathew 27:3
   A. Andrew
   B. Bartholomew
   C. Judas
   D. Thomas

3. How did the disciple that betrayed Jesus die?
   Mathew 27:5
   A. He accidently drowned.
   B. He hanged himself.
   C. He was burned at the stake.
   D. He was stoned to death.

4. What was the name of the field the chief priests purchased?
   Mathew 27:7
   A. The archer's field
   B. The fuller's field
   C. The miller's field
   D. The potter's field

5. Which prophet prophesied the purchasing of the field?
   Mathew 27:9–10
   A. Jeremy
   B. Jesher
   C. Jethro
   D. Jeziah

6. Who told the governor to release Jesus after having a troublesome dream?
   Mathew 27:19
   A. His aunt
   B. His daughter
   C. His mother
   D. His wife

7. Whom did the governor release?
   Mathew 27:16–26
   A. Barabbas
   B. Barnabas
   C. Bartholomew
   D. Bartimaeus

8. In which hall did the Roman soldiers place upon Jesus a scarlet robe, a crown of thorns, and then mock him?
   Mathew 27:27–31
   A. The carpenter hall
   B. The common hall
   C. The custom hall
   D. The cyprus hall

9. Who carried Jesus' cross?
   Mathew 27:32
   A. Simon of Cyrene
   B. Simon Peter
   C. Simon the Leper
   D. Simon the Sorcerer

10. Where was Jesus crucified?
    Mathew 27:33
    A. Gehenna
    B. Gethsemane
    C. Golgotha
    D. Gomorrah

11. What did the soldiers do with Jesus' garments?
    Mathew 27:35
    A. Cast lots for them
    B. Donated them to the poor
    C. Made a flag from them
    D. Sold them in an auction

12. What did the soldiers write above Jesus' head?
    Mathew 27:37
    A. LET THIS BE A WARNING TO ALL
    B. THIS IS JESUS THE KING OF THE JEWS
    C. THIS MAN IS NO GOD
    D. WE WASH OUR HANDS OF THIS JUST MAN'S BLOOD

13. At what hour did Jesus die?
    Mathew 27:46
    A. Third
    B. Sixth
    C. Ninth
    D. Twelfth

14. What did the centurion say after seeing the dead saints come out of the graves?
    Mathew 27:51–54
    A. "It is finished."
    B. "The dead in Christ have risen."
    C. "Truly this was the Son of God."
    D. "What must I do to be saved?"

15. Who took Jesus' body and laid it in his own tomb?
    Mathew 27:57–60
    A. Amos of Tekoa
    B. Elimelech of Judah
    C. Goliath of Gath
    D. Joseph of Arimathaea

16. Which two of the following women were the first to arrive at Jesus' grave toward the end of the sabbath?
    Mathew 28:1
    A. Abigail and Martha
    B. Mary and Mary
    C. Tryphena and Tryphosa
    D. Vashti and Esther

17. What did the *countenance* of the angel who rolled away the stone look like?
    Mathew 28:2–3
    A. Fire
    B. Lightning
    C. Snow
    D. Sunshine

18. What did the chief priests tell the soldiers to tell others regarding Jesus' missing body?
    Mathew 28:11–15
    A. Jesus had a twin brother still living.
    B. Jesus wasn't dead and walked away on his own.
    C. Jesus' body was removed by the soldiers and buried in another grave.
    D. Jesus' disciples stole his body.

19. Where did Jesus meet the disciples after the resurrection?
    Mathew 28:16–17
    A. Galilee
    B. Geshur
    C. Gilead
    D. Gomorrah

20. Whom did Jesus tell his disciples to go and teach?
    Mathew 28:18–20
    A. All children
    B. All Jews
    C. All nations
    D. All rabbis

Answers on page 774

OCTOBER 14

Lesson 287
Today's Reading: *Mark 1–3*
Period of Time: 26–31 AD
Author: Mark

1. At which river did John the Baptist baptize people?
   Mark 1:5
   A. River of Arnon
   B. River of Jordan
   C. River of Kishon
   D. River of Pison

2. What was John the Baptist's clothing made of?
   Mark 1:6
   A. Camel's hair
   B. Fine cotton
   C. Sheep's wool
   D. Snake skin

3. What did John the Baptist's diet consist of?
   Mark 1:6
   A. Bread and water
   B. Fish and pulse
   C. Locusts and wild honey
   D. Meat and potatoes

4. What did John the Baptist say Jesus would use to baptize people?
   Mark 1:8
   A. Fire
   B. His blood
   C. Holy water
   D. The Holy Ghost

5. What town was Jesus from?
   Mark 1:9
   A. Bethlehem
   B. Jerusalem
   C. Nazareth
   D. Philadelphia

6. What descended upon Jesus after he was baptized?
   Mark 1:10
   A. A dove
   B. An angel
   C. Satan
   D. The Spirit

7. After being baptized, how many days did Jesus spend in the wilderness?
   Mark 1:12–13
   A. 20
   B. 40
   C. 90
   D. 120

8. Whom did Jesus meet in the wilderness?
   Mark 1:13
   A. Abraham
   B. Elijah
   C. Moses
   D. Satan

9. Who was Andrew's brother?
   Mark 1:16
   A. Judas, son of James
   B. Nathanael
   C. Simon
   D. Thaddaeus

10. What were Andrew and his brother's occupation?
    Mark 1:16
    A. Carpenters
    B. Fishermen
    C. Silversmiths
    D. Tent makers

11. Who was the father of James and John?
    Mark 1:19
    A. Alphaeus
    B. Philemon
    C. Timothy
    D. Zebedee

12. What did Peter's mother-in-law suffer from?
    Mark 1:30
    A. A fever
    B. Leprosy
    C. Palsy
    D. An unclean spirit

13. In which city was the paralytic lowered through the roof?

    Mark 2:1–4

    A. Adramyttium
    B. Capernaum
    C. Iconium
    D. Rhegium

14. Who was Levi's father?

    Mark 2:14

    A. Alpheus
    B. Cornelius
    C. Demetrius
    D. Epaenetus

15. Who was the high priest when David ate the shewbread?

    Mark 2:25–26

    A. Aaron
    B. Abiathar
    C. Ananias
    D. Annas

16. Whom did the Pharisees conspire with to destroy Jesus?

    Mark 3:6

    A. The Herodians
    B. The Romans
    C. The Sadducees
    D. The scribes

17. How many disciples did Jesus ordain?

    Mark 3:14

    A. 3
    B. 10
    C. 12
    D. 70

18. What does *Boanerges* mean?

    Mark 3:17

    A. Sons of God
    B. Sons of light
    C. Sons of man
    D. Sons of thunder

19. Which disciple betrayed Jesus?

    Mark 3:19

    A. Andrew
    B. Bartholomew
    C. Judas Iscariot
    D. Simon Peter

20. Whom did the scribes attribute Jesus' power to cast out devils to?

    Mark 3:22

    A. Beelzebub
    B. Elijah
    C. God
    D. John the Baptist

*Answers on page 774

Lesson 288
Today's Reading: *Mark 4–5*
Period of Time: 31 AD
Author: Mark

OCTOBER 15

1. What did Jesus teach from?
   Mark 4:1
   A. A balcony
   B. A coliseum
   C. A ship
   D. A tower

2. What do the fowls represent in the *Parable of the Sower*?
   Mark 4:2–4, 4:14–15
   A. Angels
   B. Kings
   C. Prophets
   D. Satan

3. What does the lack of roots represent in the *Parable of the Sower*?
   Mark 4:5–6, 4:16–17
   A. Affliction or persecution
   B. Disease or illness
   C. Family or friends
   D. Jobs or money

4. What do the thorns **not** represent in the *Parable of the Sower*?
   Mark 4:7, 4:18–19
   A. Cares of this world
   B. Deceitfulness of riches
   C. Gifts of the Holy Ghost
   D. Lusts of other things

5. What was the total number of Jesus' apostles?
   Mark 4:10
   A. 3
   B. 7
   C. 10
   D. 12

6. Where did Jesus say a candle should be placed?
   Mark 4:21
   A. In a closet
   B. On a candlestick
   C. Under a bed
   D. Under a bushel

7. Which seed did Jesus compare to the kingdom of God?
   Mark 4:30–31
   A. A fig seed
   B. A grape seed
   C. A mustard seed
   D. A wheat seed

8. What was Jesus doing on the ship when the storm came?
   Mark 4:36–41
   A. Dining
   B. Fishing
   C. Sleeping
   D. Teaching

9. How many sailors were lost at sea from the storm?
   Mark 4:36–41
   A. 0
   B. 213
   C. 1400
   D. 1912

10. Which Jews were raising swine?
    Mark 5:1–14
    A. The Damascenes
    B. The Gadarenes
    C. The Hagarenes
    D. The Nazarenes

11. Where was the demon-possessed man living?
    Mark 5:2
    A. A cave
    B. A dungeon
    C. The city dump
    D. The tombs

12. What did the demon-possessed man call Jesus?
    Mark 5:7
    A. Christ of God
    B. Holy Messiah
    C. Son of the most high God
    D. The carpenter's son

595

13. What was the name of the unclean spirit dwelling within the man?

    Mark 5:9

    A. Baal
    B. Beelzebub
    C. Centurion
    D. Legion

14. Which animals did Jesus cast the unclean spirit into?

    Mark 5:11

    A. Cats
    B. Dogs
    C. Goats
    D. Swine

15. What happened to the animals after the unclean spirit entered into them?

    Mark 5:13

    A. They drowned.
    B. They flew away.
    C. They tormented the villagers.
    D. They were destroyed by fire.

16. Approximately how many devils entered into the animals?

    Mark 5:13

    A. 1,000
    B. 2,000
    C. 3,000
    D. 4,000

17. Where did the demon-possessed man go after being healed?

    Mark 5:20

    A. Decapolis
    B. Hierapolis
    C. Neapolis
    D. Nicopolis

18. Who was the ruler of the synagogue?

    Mark 5:22

    A. Cornelius
    B. Jairus
    C. Lucius
    D. Titus

19. How many years did the woman have the issue of blood?

    Mark 5:25

    A. 7
    B. 12
    C. 20
    D. 38

20. What does *Talitha cumi* mean?

    Mark 5:41

    A. Damsel, I say unto thee, arise.
    B. Daughter, your faith has made thee whole.
    C. Maid, take up thy bed and walk.
    D. Woman, thou art loosed.

*Answers on page 774

Lesson 289
Today's Reading: *Mark 6–7*
Period of Time: 31–32 AD
Author: Mark

OCTOBER 16

1. What was Jesus' occupation?
   Mark 6:3
   A. Carpenter
   B. Fisherman
   C. Physician
   D. Stonecutter

2. Who was Jesus' mother?
   Mark 6:3
   A. Mary
   B. Merab
   C. Michal
   D. Miriam

3. How many brothers did Jesus have?
   Mark 6:3
   A. 1
   B. 2
   C. 3
   D. 4

4. Who was Jesus' brother?
   Mark 6:3
   A. Boaz
   B. Juda
   C. Luke
   D. Mark

5. What did the apostles take with them?
   Mark 6:8
   A. Bread
   B. Money
   C. Staffs
   D. Wine

6. Whom did King Herod think Jesus was?
   Mark 6:14–16
   A. Elijah
   B. John the Baptist
   C. Lemuel
   D. Moses

7. Whom did King Herod marry?
   Mark 6:17
   A. Hadassah
   B. Hannah
   C. Helah
   D. Herodias

8. Who was King Herod's brother?
   Mark 6:17
   A. Paul
   B. Peter
   C. Philemon
   D. Philip

9. Whose head was placed in a charger?
   Mark 6:16–28
   A. Alexander the Great's head
   B. Herod Aprippa I's head
   C. John the Baptist's head
   D. Simon the Sorcerer's head

10. How many loaves of bread did the apostles have?
    Mark 6:32–38
    A. 2
    B. 5
    C. 10
    D. 12

11. How many fishes did the apostles have?
    Mark 6:32–38
    A. 2
    B. 5
    C. 10
    D. 12

12. How many baskets of leftover food were collected?
    Mark 6:43
    A. 2
    B. 5
    C. 10
    D. 12

13. Approximately how many men were fed in the desert?

    Mark 6:44
    A. 50
    B. 500
    C. 5,000
    D. 50,000

14. During which watch at night did Jesus walk upon the sea?

    Mark 6:47–48
    A. 4th
    B. 5th
    C. 6th
    D. 7th

15. Where did Jesus travel to after walking upon the sea?

    Mark 6:47–53
    A. Armageddon
    B. Capernaum
    C. Gennesaret
    D. Samaria

16. What did Jesus call the scribes and Pharisees?

    Mark 7:1–6
    A. Generation of vipers
    B. Hypocrites
    C. Sons of Satan
    D. Wolves in sheep's clothing

17. What does *Corban* mean?

    Mark 7:11
    A. Gift
    B. Priest
    C. Rabbi
    D. Tabernacle

18. What did Jesus say defiles a man?

    Mark 7:14–23
    A. A person's relatives
    B. Eating unclean foods
    C. Not washing his hands
    D. Things from the heart

19. What was wrong with the Syrophenician woman's daughter?

    Mark 7:24–26
    A. She was dead.
    B. She was deaf.
    C. She was demon-possessed.
    D. She was mute.

20. What does *Ephphatha* mean?

    Mark 7:34
    A. Be closed
    B. Be opened
    C. Be tolerant
    D. Be wise

*Answers on page 775

OCTOBER 17

Lesson 290
Today's Reading: *Mark 8–9*
Period of Time: 32 AD
Author: Mark

1. How many days had the multitude been with Jesus?
   Mark 8:1–2
   A. 2
   B. 3
   C. 4
   D. 5

2. How many loaves of bread did the disciples have?
   Mark 8:5
   A. 2
   B. 3
   C. 5
   D. 7

3. How many baskets of the leftover bread and fish remained?
   Mark 8:8
   A. 3
   B. 5
   C. 7
   D. 12

4. Approximately how many people did Jesus feed?
   Mark 8:9
   A. 40
   B. 400
   C. 4,000
   D. 40,000

5. Where did Jesus go after feeding the multitude?
   Mark 8:10
   A. Dalmanutha
   B. Jerusalem
   C. Korazin
   D. Magdala

6. Who asked Jesus to show them a sign from heaven?
   Mark 8:11
   A. The Herodians
   B. The Pharisees
   C. The Romans
   D. The Sadducees

7. Where did Jesus heal a blind man?
   Mark 8:22–25
   A. Bethsaida
   B. Capernaum
   C. Decapolis
   D. Emmaus

8. What did the blind man say men looked like to him the first time?
   Mark 8:24
   A. Ghosts
   B. Locusts
   C. Scarecrows
   D. Trees

9. Who stated that Jesus was the Christ?
   Mark 8:27–29
   A. Andrew
   B. James
   C. Peter
   D. Thomas

10. On which day did Jesus say he would rise from the dead?
    Mark 8:31
    A. 2nd
    B. 3rd
    C. 4th
    D. 5th

11. Which apostle did Jesus rebuke?
    Mark 8:33
    A. Matthew
    B. Peter
    C. Philip
    D. Thomas

12. Which apostle was **not** present during the transfiguration?

    Mark 9:2

    A. James
    B. John
    C. Peter
    D. Thaddaeus

13. What color did Jesus' raiment become during the transfiguration?

    Mark 9:3

    A. Black as coal
    B. Green as grass
    C. Red as fire
    D. White as snow

14. Which two men appeared at the transfiguration?

    Mark 9:2–4

    A. Elias and Moses
    B. Jeremiah and Ezekiel
    C. Micah and Amos
    D. Zechariah and Zephaniah

15. What appeared during the transfiguration?

    Mark 9:7

    A. A cloud
    B. A dove
    C. A rainbow
    D. An angel

16. Who questioned the apostles?

    Mark 9:14–16

    A. The Herodians
    B. The Pharisees
    C. The Romans
    D. The scribes

17. Who drove out the dumb and deaf spirit?

    Mark 9:17–29

    A. Andrew
    B. Jesus
    C. Levi
    D. Peter

18. What did the apostles discuss in Capernaum?

    Mark 9:33–34

    A. How to save Jesus from crucifixion.
    B. Where to celebrate the Lord's passover.
    C. Which of them should be the greatest.
    D. Why Jesus had to wash their feet.

19. Which apostle told Jesus they forbid a man to cast out demons in Jesus' name?

    Mark 9:38

    A. John
    B. Judas Iscariot
    C. Simon Peter
    D. Thaddaeus

20. What did Jesus say a person should have within themselves?

    Mark 9:50

    A. Bread
    B. Leaven
    C. Salt
    D. Water

*Answers on page 775

Lesson 291
Today's Reading: *Mark 10–11*
Period of Time: 33 AD
Author: Mark

OCTOBER 18

1. Which coasts mentioned in Mark 10:1 did Jesus teach at?
   Mark 10:1
   A. Coasts of Decapolis
   B. Coasts of Galilee
   C. Coasts of Judaea
   D. Coasts of Magdala

2. Which group questioned Jesus about divorce?
   Mark 10:2–12
   A. The Herodians
   B. The Pharisees
   C. The Publicans
   D. The Sadducees

3. Whose idea was it to write a bill of divorcement?
   Mark 10:4
   A. Abraham
   B. David
   C. Gaius
   D. Moses

4. What did Jesus say was one flesh?
   Mark 10:6–9
   A. A family
   B. A married couple
   C. An unborn child and its mother
   D. The Israelite nation

5. Whom did the disciples rebuke?
   Mark 10:13–16
   A. A Roman centurion
   B. Parents of little children
   C. Satan
   D. Scribes and Pharisees

6. What did the rich man call Jesus?
   Mark 10:17
   A. Good Master
   B. Good Shepherd
   C. Rabbi
   D. Rabboni

7. What did Jesus say it was easier for a camel to go through than for a rich man to enter into the kingdom of God?
   Mark 10:25
   A. The eye of a needle
   B. The gates of hell
   C. The temple door
   D. The windows of heaven

8. Which statement did Jesus say?
   Mark 10:27
   A. "He who doesn't work doesn't eat."
   B. "The LORD giveth and the LORD taketh away."
   C. "The LORD helps those who help themselves."
   D. "With God all things are possible."

9. Which apostle told Jesus they had left everything to follow him?
   Mark 10:28
   A. Andrew
   B. John
   C. Peter
   D. Thomas

10. How many apostles did Jesus have?
    Mark 10:32
    A. 3
    B. 7
    C. 10
    D. 12

11. Which city did Jesus say he would be killed in?
    Mark 10:33–34
    A. Bethlehem
    B. Jericho
    C. Jerusalem
    D. Nazareth

12. On which day did Jesus say he would rise again?

    Mark 10:33–34

    A. 2nd
    B. 3rd
    C. 4th
    D. 5th

13. Which two men were the sons of Zebedee?

    Mark 10:35

    A. Andrew and Simon
    B. Bartholomew and Nathaniel
    C. Didymus and Thomas
    D. James and John

14. In which city did Jesus heal a blind man?

    Mark 10:46–52

    A. Bethany
    B. Cana
    C. Jericho
    D. Nazareth

15. What was the blind man's name that Jesus healed?

    Mark 10:46

    A. Barabbas
    B. Barnabas
    C. Bartholomew
    D. Bartimaeus

16. What was the blind man doing when Jesus went by?

    Mark 10:46

    A. Begging
    B. Collecting taxes
    C. Making brooms
    D. Prophesying

17. How many disciples did Jesus send to fetch the colt?

    Mark 11:1–7

    A. 2
    B. 7
    C. 10
    D. 12

18. What did the people shout as Jesus rode into Jerusalem?

    Mark 11:8–10

    A. "Blessed be the king of the Jews!"
    B. "He saved others; let him save himself!"
    C. "Hosanna in the highest!"
    D. "Physician, heal thyself!"

19. What type of tree did Jesus curse?

    Mark 11:13–21

    A. A dogwood tree
    B. A fig tree
    C. A palm tree
    D. A sycamore tree

20. What did Jesus say the religious leaders had turned the temple into?

    Mark 11:15–17

    A. A den of thieves
    B. A house of prayer
    C. The greatest temple
    D. The seventh wonder

Answers on page 775

OCTOBER 19

Lesson 292
Today's Reading: *Mark 12–13*
Period of Time: Tuesday, March 31, 33 AD
Author: Mark

1. How many sons did the owner of the vineyard have?
   Mark 12:1–6
   A. 1
   B. 3
   C. 7
   D. 12

2. What did the builders reject?
   Mark 12:10
   A. A brick
   B. A hammer
   C. A nail
   D. A stone

3. Whom did the Jewish leaders send to try to catch Jesus in his words?
   Mark 12:13
   A. Lawyers and priests
   B. Pharisees and Herodians
   C. Publicans and soldiers
   D. Scribes and Sadducees

4. What type of coin did the crowd give to Jesus?
   Mark 12:13–17
   A. A dime
   B. A farthing
   C. A gerah
   D. A penny

5. Whose image was on the coin?
   Mark 12:16
   A. Caesar's image
   B. Herod's image
   C. Jesus' image
   D. Pharaoh's image

6. Who questioned Jesus about the resurrection?
   Mark 12:18–27
   A. The Herodians
   B. The Pharisees
   C. The Publicans
   D. The Sadducees

7. Which one of the following was a Mosaic law concerning marriage?
   Mark 12:19–25
   A. A brother shall marry his late brother's childless widow.
   B. A man may remarry the woman he divorced.
   C. A man must marry a virgin.
   D. A man shall have no more than 10 wives.

8. How many times did the woman in the story of the resurrection marry?
   Mark 12:18–22
   A. 2
   B. 3
   C. 7
   D. 10

9. Whom did God speak to from a bush?
   Mark 12:26
   A. Andrew
   B. Isaac
   C. Moses
   D. Peter

10. Who asked Jesus, "Which is the first commandment of all?"
    Mark 12:28
    A. A scribe
    B. Peter
    C. Peter's mother-in-law
    D. The high priest

11. What did Jesus say is the first commandment?
    Mark 12:28–30
    A. Don't murder
    B. Keep holy the sabbath day
    C. Love the LORD thy God
    D. Love thy neighbor as thyself

12. What did Jesus say is the second commandment?

    Mark 12:31

    A. Don't murder
    B. Keep holy the sabbath day
    C. Love the LORD thy God
    D. Love thy neighbor as thyself

13. Who called Jesus his Lord and son?

    Mark 12:35–37

    A. Adam
    B. David
    C. Judas
    D. Peter

14. Whom did Jesus say loved to wear long clothing and devour widow's houses?

    Mark 12:38–40

    A. Herodians
    B. Publicans
    C. Scribes
    D. Tax collectors

15. How many mites did the widow put in the treasury?

    Mark 12:42–43

    A. 2
    B. 5
    C. 10
    D. 40

16. What did Jesus say would eventually happen to the temple?

    Mark 13:1–2

    A. A pagan king would make it his palace.
    B. It would be destroyed.
    C. Jews would convert it into a hospital.
    D. Romans would turn it into a prison.

17. Upon which mountain did Jesus teach the disciples about the end times?

    Mark 13:3–4

    A. Mount of Beatitudes
    B. Mount of Olives
    C. Mount of the Holy Cross
    D. Mount of Transfiguration

18. Which disciple was **not** mentioned as one of the disciples who questioned Jesus about the end times?

    Mark 13:3–4

    A. Andrew
    B. Bartholomew
    C. James
    D. John

19. Which prophet spoke of the abomination of desolation?

    Mark 13:14

    A. Amos
    B. Balaam
    C. Daniel
    D. Ezekiel

20. What was the last word Jesus spoke to his disciples regarding the end times?

    Mark 13:37

    A. Fight
    B. Hide
    C. Pray
    D. Watch

Answers on page 775

OCTOBER 20

Lesson 293
Today's Reading: *Mark 14–16*
Period of Time: Tuesday, March 31–Thursday, May 14, 33 AD
Author: Mark

1. Whose house did Jesus dine at in Bethany?
   Mark 14:3
   A. Simon of Cyrene's house
   B. Simon Peter's house
   C. Simon the leper's house
   D. Simon the sorcerer's house

2. Which disciple betrayed Jesus?
   Mark 14:10
   A. Bartholomew
   B. Judas Iscariot
   C. Judas, the son of James
   D. Thaddaeus

3. Whom did Jesus tell two of his disciples to meet in Jerusalem?
   Mark 14:13
   A. A man bearing a pitcher of water
   B. A man selling donkeys
   C. A woman holding an alabaster box
   D. A woman selling fine linen

4. What did Jesus and his disciples do when supper was over?
   Mark 14:18–26
   A. Cast lots
   B. Drank brandy
   C. Smoked cigars
   D. Sung a hymn

5. Where did Jesus go to pray?
   Mark 14:32
   A. Calvary
   B. East gate
   C. Gethsemane
   D. Valley of decision

6. What sign did the disciple use to betray Jesus?
   Mark 14:44
   A. A fig leaf
   B. A handshake
   C. A kiss
   D. A scarlet cord

7. What did a certain young man do after Jesus was arrested?
   Mark 14:51–52
   A. He claimed to be Jesus.
   B. He fled from the mob—naked.
   C. He spoke in tongues.
   D. He tried to bribe the guards.

8. What was Jesus falsely accused of during the Jewish trial?
   Mark 14:64
   A. Blasphemy
   B. Fornication
   C. Murder
   D. Treason

9. What was Peter accused of being?
   Mark 14:70
   A. A Babylonian
   B. A Chaldean
   C. A Galilean
   D. A Philippian

10. How many times did Peter deny knowing Jesus?
    Mark 14:66–72
    A. 2
    B. 3
    C. 4
    D. 5

11. Whom did Pilate release?
    Mark 15:15
    A. Barabbas
    B. Epaphras
    C. Matthias
    D. Zacharias

12. Where did the Roman soldiers take Jesus to?
    Mark 15:16
    A. The Amphitheater
    B. The Circus Maximus
    C. The Coliseum
    D. The Praetorium

13. What does *Golgotha* mean?

    Mark 15:22

    A. The common hall
    B. The emperor's dungeon
    C. The house of prayer
    D. The place of a skull

14. At which hour did they crucify Jesus?

    Mark 15:25

    A. 3rd
    B. 4th
    C. 5th
    D. 6th

15. At which hour did Jesus give up the ghost?

    Mark 15:34–37

    A. 6th
    B. 9th
    C. 10th
    D. 12th

16. Who said, "Truly this man was the Son of God"?

    Mark 15:39

    A. One of the high priest's maids
    B. Pontius Pilate's wife
    C. The centurion
    D. The high priest

17. Whom did Pilate release Jesus' body to?

    Mark 15:43

    A. Goliath of Gath
    B. Joseph of Arimathaea
    C. Queen of Sheba
    D. Saul of Tarsus

18. What did the young man inside the tomb tell Mary and Mary?

    Mark 16:5–6

    A. "He is dead."
    B. "He is in hell."
    C. "He is in Nazareth."
    D. "He is risen."

19. How many devils did Jesus cast out of Mary Magdalene?

    Mark 16:9

    A. 2
    B. 3
    C. 6
    D. 7

20. Which sign of a believer did Jesus **not** mention?

    Mark 16:17–18

    A. They are saved by their works.
    B. They shall cast out devils.
    C. They shall lay hands on the sick, and they shall recover.
    D. They shall speak with new tongues.

*Answers on page 775

Lesson 294
Today's Reading: *Luke 1*
Period of Time: 6–5 BC
Author: Luke

OCTOBER 21

1. Whom did Luke personally write this gospel to?
   Luke 1:1–3
   A. Tertullus
   B. Theophilus
   C. Trophimus
   D. Tychicus

2. Who was the king of Judaea?
   Luke 1:5
   A. King Agag
   B. King Darius
   C. King Herod
   D. King Rezin

3. Which priestly course did Zacharias belong to?
   Luke 1:5
   A. Course of Abia
   B. Course of Huppah
   C. Course of Jedaiah
   D. Course of Shecaniah

4. Whom was Elizabeth a descendant of?
   Luke 1:5
   A. Aaron
   B. Cyrus
   C. Potiphar
   D. Uriah

5. What was Zacharias doing when the angel appeared?
   Luke 1:8–11
   A. Burning incense
   B. Giving a sin offering
   C. Praying
   D. Reading scriptures

6. What name did the angel tell Zacharias to give to his unborn child?
   Luke 1:13
   A. James
   B. John
   C. Joseph
   D. Judas

7. What was the angel's name that visited Zacharias?
   Luke 1:19
   A. Abaddon
   B. Apollyon
   C. Gabriel
   D. Michael

8. What happened to Zacharias for doubting God?
   Luke 1:20
   A. He became blind.
   B. He became dumb.
   C. His body broke out in boils.
   D. His hand became leprous.

9. In which city did Mary live?
   Luke 1:26–27
   A. Bethany
   B. Bethlehem
   C. Jerusalem
   D. Nazareth

10. Whom was Mary espoused to?
    Luke 1:27
    A. Job
    B. Jonah
    C. Jonathan
    D. Joseph

11. What name did the angel tell Mary to give her unborn child?
    Luke 1:30–31
    A. Adam
    B. Immanuel
    C. Jesus
    D. Shiloh

12. What relationship was Elizabeth to Mary?
    Luke 1:36
    A. Her aunt
    B. Her cousin
    C. Her grandmother
    D. Her niece

13. What happened when Mary visited Elizabeth?

    Luke 1:41–44

    A. Elizabeth spoke in new tongues.
    B. Elizabeth suffered morning sickness.
    C. Elizabeth went into labor.
    D. Elizabeth's baby leaped in her womb.

14. Approximately how many months did Mary abide with Elizabeth?

    Luke 1:56

    A. 1
    B. 2
    C. 3
    D. 4

15. On which day was Elizabeth's baby circumcised?

    Luke 1:59

    A. 3rd
    B. 5th
    C. 7th
    D. 8th

16. What did Elizabeth's family and friends want to name the baby?

    Luke 1:59

    A. Abraham
    B. David
    C. John
    D. Zacharias

17. What did Elizabeth and Zacharias name the baby?

    Luke 1:60–63

    A. Abraham
    B. David
    C. John
    D. Zacharias

18. Which covenant did Zacharias refer to in his benediction?

    Luke 1:72–73

    A. The Abrahamic Covenant
    B. The Davidic Covenant
    C. The Mosaic Covenant
    D. The Noahic Covenant

19. What did Zacharias prophesy his son would be called?

    Luke 1:76

    A. The Alpha and the Omega
    B. The prophet of the Highest
    C. The Son of God
    D. The Son of man

20. Where did Zacharias' child dwell until the day of his showing unto Israel?

    Luke 1:80

    A. Deserts
    B. Forests
    C. Mountains
    D. Seas

*Answers on page 775

OCTOBER 22

Lesson 295
Today's Reading: *Luke 2–3*
Period of Time: 5–27 AD
Author: Luke

1. Who issued a decree that the world should be taxed?
   Luke 2:1
   A. Caesar Augustus
   B. Caesar Claudius
   C. Caesar Nero
   D. Caesar Tiberius

2. Who was the governor of Syria?
   Luke 2:2
   A. Cornelius
   B. Crispus
   C. Cyrenius
   D. Cyrus

3. Where did Joseph travel to pay his taxes?
   Luke 2:4
   A. Agrippias
   B. Bethlehem
   C. Jerusalem
   D. Nazareth

4. Whom did the angels tell that Christ had been born?
   Luke 2:8–14
   A. The carpenters
   B. The high priests
   C. The shepherds
   D. The wise men

5. What did Mary offer when her days of purification had ended?
   Luke 2:22–24
   A. 1 Bullock
   B. 1 Ewe
   C. 2 Rams
   D. 2 Turtledoves or 2 young pigeons

6. Who blessed Joseph and his family in Jerusalem after Jesus' birth?
   Luke 2:25–35
   A. Hanani
   B. Kareah
   C. Onesimus
   D. Simeon

7. What was the name of the 84-year-old prophetess in Jerusalem?
   Luke 2:36–38
   A. Anna
   B. Leah
   C. Mary
   D. Ruth

8. Which feast is mentioned that Jesus annually attended with his family?
   Luke 2:41
   A. Feast of harvest
   B. Feast of ingathering
   C. Feast of the passover
   D. Feast of trumpets

9. How many days did Jesus' family search for him in Jerusalem?
   Luke 2:46
   A. 2
   B. 3
   C. 4
   D. 5

10. Who had been reigning for fifteen years when the Word of God came unto John?
    Luke 3:1–2
    A. Augustus Caesar
    B. Claudius Caesar
    C. Nero Caesar
    D. Tiberius Caesar

11. Who was the governor of Judaea?

    Luke 3:1

    A. Claudius Lysias
    B. John Mark
    C. Pontius Pilate
    D. Sergius Paulus

12. Who was Herod's brother?

    Luke 3:1

    A. Philemon
    B. Philip
    C. Phlegon
    D. Phygellus

13. Which two men were the high priests?

    Luke 3:2

    A. Barnabas and Timothy
    B. Caiaphas and Annas
    C. Eutychus and Rufus
    D. Simon and Andrew

14. Who was Herod's sister-in-law?

    Luke 3:19

    A. Herodias
    B. Johanna
    C. Mary
    D. Susanna

15. Approximately how old was Jesus when he was baptized?

    Luke 3:21–23

    A. 1 years old
    B. 12 years old
    C. 21 years old
    D. 30 years old

16. Who was Joseph's father-in-law?

    Luke 3:23

    A. Heli
    B. Joel
    C. Nero
    D. Paul

17. Who was David's father?

    Luke 3:31–32

    A. Absalom
    B. Jesse
    C. Rehoboam
    D. Solomon

18. Who was Abraham's father?

    Luke 3:34

    A. Esau
    B. Jacob
    C. Isaac
    D. Thara

19. Who was Sem's father?

    Luke 3:36

    A. Abel
    B. Japheth
    C. Noe
    D. Reuben

20. Who was Seth's father?

    Luke 3:38

    A. Adam
    B. Cain
    C. Methuselah
    D. Nimrod

*Answers on page 775

Lesson 296
Today's Reading: *Luke 4–5*
Period of Time: 27–31 AD
Author: Luke

OCTOBER 23

1. How many days was Jesus tempted by the devil?
   Luke 4:2
   A. 10
   B. 20
   C. 30
   D. 40

2. Which is the *first* response Jesus gave the devil?
   Luke 4:3–4
   A. Man shall not live by bread alone.
   B. New wine should be put in old bottles.
   C. Thou shalt not tempt the LORD thy God.
   D. Thou shalt worship the LORD thy God.

3. Which is the *second* response Jesus gave the devil?
   Luke 4:5–8
   A. Man shall not live by bread alone.
   B. New wine should be put in new bottles.
   C. Thou shalt not tempt the LORD thy God.
   D. Thou shalt worship the LORD thy God.

4. Which is the *third* response Jesus gave the devil?
   Luke 4:9–12
   A. Man shall not live by bread alone.
   B. New wine should be put in new bottles.
   C. Thou shalt not tempt the LORD thy God.
   D. Thou shalt worship the LORD thy God.

5. In which town was Jesus raised as a boy?
   Luke 4:16
   A. Bethlehem
   B. Nazareth
   C. Sidon
   D. Tyre

6. Which book did Jesus read from in the synagogue?
   Luke 4:17–20
   A. Book of the prophet Esaias
   B. Book of the kings of Israel
   C. Chronicles of Samuel the seer
   D. Words of Shemaiah the prophet

7. How long did the drought in Israel last during the days of Elias?
   Luke 4:25
   A. 2 years and 4 months
   B. 3 years and 6 months
   C. 4 years and 8 months
   D. 5 years and 10 months

8. Which city is located in Sidon?
   Luke 4:26
   A. Capharsabba
   B. Joppa
   C. Sarepta
   D. Thecoa

9. Which one of the following men was a leper?
   Luke 4:27
   A. Benaiah of Kabzeel
   B. Naaman of Syria
   C. Saul of Tarsus
   D. Simon of Cyrene

10. What did the people in Jesus' hometown desire to do with him when he finished teaching?
    Luke 4:29
    A. Cast him into prison
    B. Feed him to lions
    C. Make him their king
    D. Throw him from a cliff

11. Which city in Galilee did Jesus travel to after leaving his hometown?

    Luke 4:31

    A. Capernaum
    B. Jerusalem
    C. Nazareth
    D. Sychar

12. Which one of Peter's relatives did Jesus heal?

    Luke 4:38–39

    A. His cousin
    B. His mother
    C. His mother-in-law
    D. His nephew

13. Whose ship did Jesus enter?

    Luke 5:3

    A. Ahab's ship
    B. Hiram's ship
    C. Jonah's ship
    D. Simon's ship

14. Who claimed to be a sinful man?

    Luke 5:8

    A. Judas
    B. Nathaniel
    C. Peter
    D. Thomas

15. Which apostles were business partners?

    Luke 5:10

    A. Andrew, Philip, and Simon the zealot
    B. Bartholomew, Mathew, and James the son of Alphaeus
    C. Simon, James, and John
    D. Thomas, Judas Iscariot, and Judas the son of James

16. What illness did the man who was lowered through the roof suffer from?

    Luke 5:18–19

    A. He had a palsy.
    B. He had leprosy.
    C. He was blind.
    D. He was demon-possessed.

17. What was Jesus accused of by the scribes and Pharisees?

    Luke 5:21

    A. Adultery
    B. Blasphemies
    C. Murder
    D. Stealing

18. What was Levi's occupation?

    Luke 5:27

    A. Blacksmith
    B. Carpenter
    C. Fisherman
    D. Publican

19. What did Jesus say to Levi?

    Luke 5:27

    A. "Follow me."
    B. "Get thee behind me, Satan."
    C. "I will make you a fisher of men."
    D. "Upon this rock I will build my church."

20. Who threw Jesus a great feast in his house?

    Luke 5:29

    A. James
    B. Levi
    C. Peter
    D. Thomas

Answers on page 775

OCTOBER 24

Lesson 297
Today's Reading: *Luke 6–7*
Period of Time: 31 AD
Author: Luke

1. What did David eat in the house of God?
   Luke 6:3–4
   A. Corn
   B. Fish
   C. Shewbread
   D. The sin offering

2. Why were the scribes and Pharisees in the synagogue mad at Jesus?
   Luke 6:6–11
   A. He had cast out the moneychangers.
   B. He healed a man on the sabbath.
   C. He turned the water into wine.
   D. He walked on water.

3. What was the total number of Jesus' apostles?
   Luke 6:13
   A. 3
   B. 4
   C. 7
   D. 12

4. Which apostle did Jesus name Peter?
   Luke 6:14
   A. Judas
   B. Matthew
   C. Philip
   D. Simon

5. Who was Peter's brother?
   Luke 6:14
   A. Andrew
   B. Bartholomew
   C. James
   D. Thomas

6. Which one of the following men was **not** an original apostle?
   Luke 6:14–16
   A. John
   B. Judas
   C. Paul
   D. Philip

7. Who was Alphaeus' son?
   Luke 6:15
   A. Bartholomew
   B. James
   C. Matthew
   D. Thomas

8. Which apostle betrayed Jesus?
   Luke 6:16
   A. Andrew
   B. Bartholomew
   C. John
   D. Judas Iscariot

9. Whom did Jesus say the kingdom of God belonged to?
   Luke 6:20
   A. The angels
   B. The poor
   C. The rich
   D. The wise

10. Who did Jesus say shall mourn and weep?
    Luke 6:25
    A. Those who believe now
    B. Those who hunger now
    C. Those who laugh now
    D. Those who thirst now

11. What did Jesus say to do to your enemies?
    Luke 6:27
    A. Flee from them
    B. Keep them close
    C. Kill them
    D. Love them

12. Which name did Jesus use when referring to God?
    Luke 6:35
    A. Almighty God
    B. God Almighty
    C. The Highest
    D. The Light

13. What did Jesus say happens when the blind lead the blind?

    Luke 6:39

    A. They become lost.
    B. They fall into a ditch.
    C. They go around in circles.
    D. They see with spiritual eyes.

14. What did Jesus say a tree was known by?

    Luke 6:44

    A. Its bark
    B. Its fruit
    C. Its leaves
    D. Its size

15. What did Jesus say a house should be built upon?

    Luke 6:48

    A. A rock
    B. Blood and sweat
    C. Love
    D. The earth

16. Who beseeched Jesus on behalf of his ill servant?

    Luke 7:1–10

    A. A centurion
    B. A Pharisee
    C. A priest
    D. A scribe

17. In which city did Jesus bring a dead man back to life?

    Luke 7:11–15

    A. Antioch
    B. Ephesus
    C. Laodicea
    D. Nain

18. Who did Jesus say was the greatest of the prophets?

    Luke 7:28

    A. Daniel
    B. Himself
    C. John the Baptist
    D. Moses

19. Who invited Jesus to his house for dinner?

    Luke 7:36

    A. A Pharisee
    B. A publican
    C. A Sadducee
    D. A scribe

20. What did the woman bring to the dinner?

    Luke 7:37

    A. An alabaster box of ointment
    B. Bitter herbs from her garden
    C. Her sick daughter
    D. The fatted calf

Answers on page 775

OCTOBER 25

Lesson 298
Today's Reading: *Luke 8*
Period of Time: 31 AD
Author: Luke

1. How many devils were cast out of Mary Magdalene?
   Luke 8:2
   A. 7
   B. 11
   C. 12
   D. 24

2. Who was Herod's steward?
   Luke 8:3
   A. Aziza
   B. Chuza
   C. Moza
   D. Shiza

3. Which two of the following women were healed of evil spirits and infirmities?
   Luke 8:2–3
   A. Delilah and Jechiliah
   B. Eunice and Bernice
   C. Joanna and Susanna
   D. Puah and Leah

4. What does the seed represent in the *Parable of the Sower*?
   Luke 8:5, 8:11
   A. The fig tree
   B. The Holy Ghost
   C. The weeds and tares
   D. The word of God

5. Who represents the fowls in the *Parable of the Sower*?
   Luke 8:5, 8:12
   A. The angels
   B. The apostles
   C. The devil
   D. The Jewish leaders

6. What represents the lack of roots in the *Parable of the Sower*?
   Luke 8:6, 8:13
   A. Fishing
   B. Marriage
   C. Scriptures
   D. Temptation

7. Which two of the following represents the thorns in the *Parable of the Sower*?
   Luke 8:7, 8:14
   A. Famines and earthquakes
   B. Riches and pleasures
   C. Sickness and disease
   D. Wars and rumors of wars

8. What was Jesus doing on the ship when the storm arrived?
   Luke 8:22–23
   A. Eating
   B. Fishing
   C. Sleeping
   D. Teaching

9. What type of clothing did the demon-possessed man wear?
   Luke 8:26–27
   A. Cotton
   B. Leather
   C. Wool
   D. None, he was naked

10. Where did the demon-possessed man live?
    Luke 8:27
    A. In the city
    B. In the desert
    C. In the tombs
    D. In the woods

11. What was the name of the devil inside the demon-possessed man?

    Luke 8:30

    A. Beelzebub
    B. Legion
    C. Lucifer
    D. Prince of Darkness

12. What happened to the swine?

    Luke 8:32–33

    A. They drowned in a lake.
    B. They flew across a field.
    C. They were set free.
    D. They were slaughtered.

13. What did the Gadarenes ask Jesus to do after he healed the demon-possessed man?

    Luke 8:34–37

    A. Baptize them
    B. Heal others
    C. Leave their city
    D. Teach them

14. What was the name of the ruler of the synagogue?

    Luke 8:41

    A. Jairus
    B. Jambres
    C. James
    D. Jannes

15. Approximately how old was the ruler of the synagogue's daughter?

    Luke 8:42

    A. 5 years old
    B. 12 years old
    C. 16 year sold
    D. 21 years old

16. How many years did the woman have a bleeding disorder?

    Luke 8:43

    A. 3
    B. 7
    C. 10
    D. 12

17. How was the woman with the bleeding disorder healed?

    Luke 8:44

    A. Jesus spoke the word and she was healed.
    B. Jesus touched her.
    C. She bathed in the river of Jordan as instructed by Jesus.
    D. She touched the border of Jesus' garment.

18. Which apostle did **not** accompany Jesus into the dead child's home?

    Luke 8:51

    A. Andrew
    B. James
    C. John
    D. Peter

19. What did the mourners do when Jesus told them the girl wasn't dead?

    Luke 8:53

    A. Called him a blasphemer
    B. Laughed at him
    C. Threw rocks at him
    D. Tried to throw him from a cliff

20. What did Jesus tell the parents to do after healing their daughter?

    Luke 8:55

    A. Feed her
    B. Flee the city
    C. Give a burnt offering
    D. Tell others what God has done

*Answers on page 775

OCTOBER 26

Lesson 299
Today's Reading: *Luke 9*
Period of Time: 31–32 AD
Author: Luke

1. What did Jesus tell the apostles to take with them for their journey?
   Luke 9:1–3
   A. Bread
   B. Scripts
   C. Two coats
   D. Nothing

2. Who beheaded John the Baptist?
   Luke 9:7–9
   A. Augustus Caesar
   B. Herod the tetrarch
   C. Pontius Pilate
   D. Porcius Festus

3. Which city owned the desert area where Jesus took the disciples?
   Luke 9:10
   A. Bethsaida
   B. Capernaum
   C. Jericho
   D. Jerusalem

4. How many loaves of bread and fishes did the apostles have?
   Luke 9:13
   A. 2 loaves and 5 fishes
   B. 3 loaves and 4 fishes
   C. 4 loaves and 3 fishes
   D. 5 loaves and 2 fishes

5. Approximately how many men came to the desert to see Jesus?
   Luke 9:11–14
   A. 500
   B. 5,000
   C. 10,000
   D. 15,000

6. How many baskets of leftover food did the apostles collect?
   Luke 9:17
   A. 2
   B. 6
   C. 12
   D. 24

7. Which apostle said that Jesus was *The Christ of God*?
   Luke 9:20
   A. James
   B. John
   C. Peter
   D. Thomas

8. On which day did Jesus say he would rise from the dead?
   Luke 9:22
   A. 2nd
   B. 3rd
   C. 4th
   D. 5th

9. Which apostle did **not** go up the mountain to pray with Jesus?
   Luke 9:28
   A. James
   B. John
   C. Peter
   D. Philip

10. Which two of the following men appeared during the transfiguration?
    Luke 9:28–30
    A. Abraham and Isaac
    B. Caleb and Joshua
    C. Ezekiel and Jeremiah
    D. Moses and Elias

11. Which apostle wanted to build three tabernacles?

    Luke 9:33

    A. Peter
    B. Philip
    C. Thaddaeus
    D. Thomas

12. What did the voice from the cloud say?

    Luke 9:35

    A. "I am the LORD thy God."
    B. "I AM WHO I AM."
    C. "This is my beloved Son: hear him."
    D. "Ye are cursed with a curse."

13. What did Jesus call those who lacked faith in healing a demon-possessed boy?

    Luke 9:37–41

    A. A brood of vipers and backbiters
    B. A faithless and perverse generation
    C. Hypocrites and naysayers
    D. Sons and daughters of the father of lies

14. What did Jesus say if a person received in his name they would also receive?

    Luke 9:48

    A. A child
    B. His mother and brothers
    C. The Law of Moses
    D. The leaven of the Pharisees

15. Which apostle told Jesus they saw a person casting out devils in Jesus' name?

    Luke 9:49

    A. Andrew
    B. Bartholomew
    C. James
    D. John

16. What did Jesus command the apostles to do if they saw someone casting out devils in his name?

    Luke 9:50

    A. Forbid him not
    B. Rebuke him
    C. Remove the log in his eye
    D. Stone him

17. Which two apostles asked Jesus if he was going to reign down fire upon a Samaritan village?

    Luke 9:52–54

    A. Andrew and Judas
    B. Bartholomew and Thaddaeus
    C. James and John
    D. Peter and Philip

18. What did the *first* villager say to Jesus?

    Luke 9:57–58

    A. Beware of the leaven of the Pharisees.
    B. Cast thy burden upon the Lord.
    C. I will follow you wherever you go.
    D. Let the dead bury the dead.

19. What did the *second* villager say to Jesus?

    Luke 9:59–60

    A. Let me go bury my father.
    B. Let me tell my family at home goodbye.
    C. Let my beloved come into the garden.
    D. Let my people go.

20. What did the *third* villager say to Jesus?

    Luke 9:61–62

    A. Let me go bury my father.
    B. Let me tell my family at home goodbye.
    C. Let my beloved come into the garden.
    D. Let my people go.

*Answers on page 775

OCTOBER 27

Lesson 300
Today's Reading: *Luke 10–11*
Period of Time: 32–33 AD
Author: Luke

1. How many disciples did Jesus send forth?
   Luke 10:1
   A. 40
   B. 50
   C. 70
   D. 100

2. How did Jesus send the disciples out?
   Luke 10:1
   A. Two and two
   B. Three and three
   C. Four and four
   D. Five and five

3. What did Jesus tell the disciples to take with them?
   Luke 10:4
   A. Purses
   B. Scrips
   C. Shoes
   D. Nothing

4. Which instruction did Jesus give the disciples he sent forth?
   Luke 10:4–8
   A. Do not eat or drink in people's houses.
   B. Do not go from house to house.
   C. Protect the lambs from the wolves.
   D. Stop and greet people along the way.

5. Which city did Jesus say it would be more tolerable for during the judgment than for a city that refuses to receive his disciples?
   Luke 10:10–12
   A. Cabul
   B. Joppa
   C. Sodom
   D. Taanach

6. Which two cities did Jesus cast woes upon?
   Luke 10:13
   A. Chorazin and Bethsaida
   B. Gibeah and Gibeon
   C. Hebron and Tekoa
   D. Maarath and Dothan

7. Which city did Jesus say would be brought down to hell?
   Luke 10:15
   A. Babylon
   B. Capernaum
   C. Gomorrah
   D. Pirathon

8. What did Jesus say the disciples should rejoice over?
   Luke 10:17–20
   A. Their ability to cast out demons.
   B. Their ability to heal the sick.
   C. Their gift of prophecy.
   D. Their names were written in heaven.

9. What did the lawyer call Jesus?
   Luke 10:25
   A. Master
   B. Messiah
   C. Rabbi
   D. Teacher

10. Where was the man in Jesus' story traveling to?
    Luke 10:30
    A. Jamnia
    B. Janoah
    C. Jericho
    D. Jerusalem

11. Who was the *first* person to pass the wounded man?
    Luke 10:30–31
    A. A Levite
    B. A priest
    C. A Samaritan
    D. A scribe

12. Who was the *second* person to pass the wounded man?

    Luke 10:30–32

    A. A Levite
    B. A priest
    C. A Samaritan
    D. A scribe

13. Who was Martha's sister?

    Luke 10:38–39

    A. Elizabeth
    B. Joanna
    C. Mary
    D. Susanna

14. Which statement is **not** part of *The Lord's Prayer*?

    Luke 11:2–4

    A. Forgive us our sins
    B. Lead us not into temptation
    C. Our Father
    D. Remove this cup from me

15. How many loaves of bread did the man ask for in the *Parable of the Persistent Friend In Need*?

    Luke 11:5

    A. 3
    B. 7
    C. 10
    D. 12

16. Whom did the crowd claim Jesus received his power from to cast out demons?

    Luke 11:14–19

    A. Abba Father
    B. Beelzebub
    C. Melchizedek
    D. Simon the sorcerer

17. How many unclean spirits did the unclean spirit bring with him to dwell inside the man?

    Luke 11:24–26

    A. 2
    B. 3
    C. 5
    D. 7

18. The sign of which prophet did Jesus say the evil generation would receive?

    Luke 11:29

    A. Annas
    B. Elias
    C. Jonas
    D. Ozias

19. Who did Jesus say would rise during the judgment and condemn the evil generation?

    Luke 11:31

    A. The bishop of the east
    B. The duke of the north
    C. The king of the west
    D. The queen of the south

20. What did Jesus call the scribes and Pharisees?

    Luke 11:44

    A. Fools
    B. Hypocrites
    C. Rabbis
    D. Snakes

Answers on page 775

Lesson 301
Today's Reading: *Luke 12–13*
Period of Time: 33 AD
Author: Luke

OCTOBER 28

1. What did Jesus warn his disciples to beware of?
   Luke 12:1

   A. The flour of the Herodians
   B. The honey of the Publicans
   C. The leaven of the Pharisees
   D. The oil of the Sadducees

2. How many farthings did Jesus say five sparrows cost?
   Luke 12:6

   A. 2
   B. 9
   C. 50
   D. 99

3. Which sin did Jesus say is unforgiveable?
   Luke 12:10

   A. Blasphemy against the Holy Ghost
   B. Committing adultery
   C. Murdering thy neighbor
   D. Not keeping the sabbath holy

4. Whom did Jesus warn of covetousness?
   Luke 12:13–15

   A. A disciple who stole a coat
   B. A man upset with his inheritance
   C. A ruler who overtaxed his subjects
   D. A woman accused of adultery

5. What did the rich man desire to do in the *Parable of the Rich Fool*?
   Luke 12:16–21

   A. Build bigger barns
   B. Feed the multitude
   C. Loan money to his servants
   D. Search for pearls in a field

6. Which birds did Jesus say neither sows nor reaps?
   Luke 12:24

   A. Doves
   B. Eagles
   C. Ravens
   D. Sparrows

7. Which king did Jesus say was never arrayed as much as a lily?
   Luke 12:27

   A. King David
   B. King Hezekiah
   C. King Pekah
   D. King Solomon

8. At what hour will the Son of man return?
   Luke 12:35–40

   A. 2nd
   B. 3rd
   C. 4th
   D. Nobody knows but God

9. Which apostle asked Jesus to explain the *Parable of the Faithful and Wise Steward*?
   Luke 12:41

   A. Andrew
   B. Peter
   C. Thaddeus
   D. Thomas

10. What did Jesus say he came to send upon the earth?
    Luke 12:49

    A. Fire
    B. Love
    C. Kindness
    D. Rain

11. What did Jesus say he came to give to the earth?

    Luke 12:51

    A. Division
    B. Gifts
    C. Peace
    D. Treasure

12. What did Jesus say happens when a cloud rises from the west?

    Luke 12:54

    A. Darkness covers the skies
    B. Heat comes to pass
    C. Rain is on the way
    D. Snow blankets the earth

13. What did Jesus say happens when the south wind blows?

    Luke 12:55

    A. Darkness covers the sky
    B. Heat comes to pass
    C. Rain is on the way
    D. Snow blankets the earth

14. Whose blood had Pilate mingled with their sacrifices?

    Luke 13:1

    A. Elamite blood
    B. Galilean blood
    C. Median blood
    D. Parthian blood

15. How many people were killed when the tower in Siloam fell?

    Luke 13:4

    A. 3
    B. 6
    C. 12
    D. 18

16. In Jesus' parable, what type of tree did the man plant in his vineyard?

    Luke 13:6

    A. Ash tree
    B. Box tree
    C. Elm tree
    D. Fig tree

17. How many years had the woman in the synagogue suffered from a spirit of infirmity?

    Luke 13:11, 13:16

    A. 2
    B. 7
    C. 14
    D. 18

18. Which plant seed did Jesus compare to the kingdom of God?

    Luke 13:18–19

    A. Apple seed
    B. Mustard seed
    C. Pomegranate seed
    D. Wheat seed

19. Whom did Jesus call a fox?

    Luke 13:31–32

    A. Anna
    B. Annas
    C. Herod
    D. Herodias

20. Which city did Jesus lament over?

    Luke 13:34–35

    A. Bethlehem
    B. Gadara
    C. Jerusalem
    D. Nazareth

*Answers on page 776

OCTOBER 29

Lesson 302
Today's Reading: *Luke 14–16*
Period of Time: 33 AD
Author: Luke

1. What did the man suffer from whom Jesus healed at one of the chief Pharisees' house?
   Luke 14:1–2
   A. A bleeding disorder
   B. Blindness
   C. Palsy
   D. The dropsy

2. Who did Jesus say would be exalted?
   Luke 14:7–11
   A. A humble person
   B. A man who is slow to speak
   C. A poor person
   D. A rich man

3. Whom did Jesus say to invite to a feast?
   Luke 14:12–14
   A. Family
   B. Friends
   C. Rich neighbors
   D. The poor

4. What was the *second* man's excuse for **not** attending the great supper?
   Luke 14:16–20
   A. He bought a piece of land.
   B. He bought five yoke of oxen.
   C. He recently married.
   D. He was blind.

5. What did Jesus say a person had to hate in order to be his disciple?
   Luke 14:26
   A. His family
   B. Money
   C. Jewish leaders
   D. Romans

6. Which one of the following was **not** one of Jesus' parables?
   Luke 14:28–35
   A. A King Making War
   B. A Man Building a Tower
   C. The Boy Who Cried Wolf
   D. The Savourless Salt

7. In the *Parable of the Lost Sheep*, how many sheep did the man own?
   Luke 15:3–4
   A. 9
   B. 10
   C. 99
   D. 100

8. In the *Parable of the Lost Piece of Silver*, how many pieces of silver did the woman own?
   Luke 15:8
   A. 9
   B. 10
   C. 99
   D. 100

9. In the *Parable of the Prodigal Son*, what occupation did the son have after spending his inheritance?
   Luke 15:11–16
   A. Farming barley
   B. Feeding swine
   C. Herding cattle
   D. Shearing sheep

10. Which one of the following did the father **not** give to his lost son?
    Luke 15:22
    A. A necklace
    B. A ring
    C. A robe
    D. Shoes

11. What did the father serve the lost son for supper?

    Luke 15:23–30

    A. Beef
    B. Deer
    C. Fish
    D. Turkey

12. Which relative was jealous of the lost son?

    Luke 15:25–32

    A. His mother
    B. His sister
    C. The elder brother
    D. The youngest brother

13. What did the lost son spend his inheritance money on?

    Luke 15:30

    A. Bad investments
    B. Gambling
    C. Harlots
    D. Liquor

14. Which employee was the rich man upset with?

    Luke 16:1–2

    A. His banker
    B. His cook
    C. His steward
    D. His treasurer

15. How many measures of oil did a man owe the rich man?

    Luke 16:5–6

    A. 10
    B. 100
    C. 1,000
    D. 10,000

16. How many measures of wheat did a man owe the rich man?

    Luke 16:7

    A. 40
    B. 60
    C. 80
    D. 100

17. Which one of the following statements did Jesus say regarding money?

    Luke 16:13

    A. "A penny saved is a penny earned."
    B. "Buy low, sell high."
    C. "Save for a rainy day."
    D. "Ye cannot serve God and mammon."

18. What was the beggar's name?

    Luke 16:20

    A. Cornelius
    B. Julius
    C. Lazarus
    D. Malchus

19. Whom did the rich man talk to in hell?

    Luke 16:22–31

    A. Abraham
    B. Gabriel
    C. Moses
    D. Satan

20. How many brothers did the rich man have?

    Luke 16:27–28

    A. 3
    B. 5
    C. 7
    D. 12

*Answers on page 776

Lesson 303
Today's Reading: *Luke 17–18*
Period of Time: 33 AD
Author: Luke

OCTOBER 30

1. Which punishment did Jesus say would be better for a person who harmed a child?
   Luke 17:1–2
   A. Being cast into the sea with a millstone around his neck
   B. Being hanged in public with other child abusers
   C. Being placed into a pit and then stoned to death
   D. Being stripped naked and made into a human torch

2. What are you suppose to do if someone trespasses against you?
   Luke 17:3–4
   A. Get even with him
   B. Ignore him
   C. Rebuke him
   D. Take him to court

3. Which tree did Jesus mention would obey a person of strong faith and plant itself in the sea?
   Luke 17:5–6
   A. Acacia tree
   B. Juniper tree
   C. Sycamine tree
   D. Terebinth tree

4. How many lepers did Jesus heal?
   Luke 17:11–14
   A. 7
   B. 10
   C. 40
   D. 70

5. Which leper thanked Jesus for healing him?
   Luke 17:15–16
   A. The Cretan
   B. The Galilean
   C. The Roman
   D. The Samaritan

6. Where did Jesus tell the Pharisees the kingdom of God was located?
   Luke 17:20–21
   A. Beyond the clouds
   B. In the seventh heaven
   C. Within them
   D. Nobody knows

7. What did Jesus compare his second coming to?
   Luke 17:22–24
   A. A catastrophic flood across the earth
   B. A flash of lightning across the sky
   C. A plague of locusts across a field
   D. A raging wildfire across a forest

8. Who entered the ark?
   Luke 17:27
   A. Coz
   B. Job
   C. Lot
   D. Noe

9. Who once lived in the city of Sodom?
   Luke 17:29
   A. Abraham
   B. Isaac
   C. Jacob
   D. Lot

10. How was Sodom destroyed?
    Luke 17:29
    A. Fire and brimstone came from heaven.
    B. God caused the earth to swallow it.
    C. Roman soldiers smote its inhabitants.
    D. The angels turned it into a pillar of salt.

11. Which birds did Jesus say would gather whenever there is a body?
    Luke 17:37
    A. Eagles
    B. Ravens
    C. Sparrows
    D. Vultures

12. Who appeared before the judge?

    Luke 18:1–5

    A. A beggar
    B. A merchant
    C. A thief
    D. A widow

13. Which two of the following went into the temple to pray?

    Luke 18:10

    A. A Pharisee and a publican
    B. A prophet and prophetess
    C. A Roman and an Arabian
    D. A scribe and a Sadducee

14. Which person felt he was better than the other person in the temple?

    Luke 18:11–12

    A. The Pharisee
    B. The prophet
    C. The Roman
    D. The scribe

15. Whom did Jesus' disciples rebuke?

    Luke 18:15

    A. Jesus' mother and brothers
    B. Scribes and lawyers
    C. The sick and lame
    D. Those that brought infants

16. What did a certain ruler call Jesus?

    Luke 18:18

    A. Almighty God
    B. Good Master
    C. Holy One
    D. Lord Jehovah

17. What did Jesus say was easier for a camel to go through than for a rich man to enter the kingdom of God?

    Luke 18:25

    A. A button's hole
    B. A house's door
    C. A needle's eye
    D. A viper's den

18. Which apostle told Jesus they had left everything to follow him?

    Luke 18:28

    A. James
    B. John
    C. Peter
    D. Thomas

19. On which day did Jesus say he would rise again?

    Luke 18:33

    A. Second day
    B. Third day
    C. Fourth day
    D. Fifth day

20. Near which city did Jesus heal a blind man?

    Luke 18:35–43

    A. Gomorrah
    B. Jericho
    C. Tyre
    D. Sidon

*Answers on page 776

OCTOBER 31

Lesson 304
Today's Reading: *Luke 19–20*
Period of Time: 33 AD
Author: Luke

1. In which town did Jesus meet Zacchaeus?
   Luke 19:1–2
   A. Jericho
   B. Jerusalem
   C. Nazareth
   D. Raphia

2. What was Zacchaeus' occupation?
   Luke 19:2
   A. Jailer
   B. Moneylender
   C. Publican
   D. Tentmaker

3. Which statement **best** describes Zacchaeus?
   Luke 19:3
   A. Comely
   B. Fat
   C. Little
   D. Ruddy

4. What type of tree did Zacchaeus climb?
   Luke 19:4
   A. Acacia tree
   B. Fig tree
   C. Sycomore tree
   D. Terebinth tree

5. How much did Zacchaeus say he gave to the poor?
   Luke 19:8
   A. 5%
   B. 10%
   C. 25%
   D. 50%

6. How many servants did the nobleman have?
   Luke 19:13
   A. 10
   B. 20
   C. 30
   D. 40

7. How many pounds did the *first* man earn?
   Luke 19:16
   A. 0
   B. 5
   C. 7
   D. 10

8. How many pounds did the *second* man earn?
   Luke 19:18
   A. 0
   B. 5
   C. 7
   D. 10

9. How many pounds did the *third* man earn?
   Luke 19:20–21
   A. 0
   B. 5
   C. 7
   D. 10

10. How many disciples did Jesus send to fetch the colt?
    Luke 19:29–30
    A. 2
    B. 5
    C. 10
    D. 12

11. From which mountain did Jesus descend riding upon the colt?
    Luke 19:37
    A. Mount of Olives
    B. Mount Pisgah
    C. Mount Tabor
    D. Mount Zion

12. Who told Jesus to rebuke his disciples?
    Luke 19:39
    A. The Herodians
    B. The Pharisees
    C. The Sadducees
    D. The scribes

13. What did Jesus say would immediately cry if his disciples held their peace?

    Luke 19:40

    A. Babies
    B. Clouds
    C. Disciples
    D. Stones

14. Whom did Jesus cast out of the temple?

    Luke 19:45

    A. The temple priests
    B. The temple prostitutes
    C. Those diseased with leprosy
    D. Those that bought and sold

15. What did the builders reject?

    Luke 20:17

    A. A beam
    B. A hammer
    C. A nail
    D. A stone

16. Whose image was on the coin?

    Luke 20:24

    A. Alexander's image
    B. Caesar's image
    C. Lazarus' image
    D. Pilate's image

17. Which group did **not** believe in any resurrection?

    Luke 20:27

    A. The Herodians
    B. The Pharisees
    C. The Sadducees
    D. The scribes

18. How many brothers married the same woman?

    Luke 20:28–33

    A. 3
    B. 7
    C. 10
    D. 12

19. Who called Christ his Lord and son?

    Luke 20:41–44

    A. Abraham
    B. David
    C. Isaiah
    D. Moses

20. Who did Jesus say devoured widows' houses?

    Luke 20:45–47

    A. Doctors
    B. Lawyers
    C. Scribes
    D. Soldiers

*Answers on page 776

NOVEMBER 1

Lesson 305
Today's Reading: *Luke 21–22*
Period of Time: Tuesday, March 31–Thursday, April 2, 33 AD
Author: Luke

1. How many mites did the widow give?
   Luke 21:1–2
   - **A.** 2
   - **B.** 3
   - **C.** 4
   - **D.** 5

2. What prophecy did Jesus give regarding the temple?
   Luke 21:5–6
   - **A.** It would be destroyed.
   - **B.** It would become a hospital.
   - **C.** It would become a palace.
   - **D.** It would become a prison.

3. What did Jesus say would come first?
   Luke 21:8–12
   - **A.** Famines and pestilences
   - **B.** Great earthquakes
   - **C.** Many claiming to be the Christ
   - **D.** Wars and commotions

4. What would be the sign Jerusalem was about to be destroyed?
   Luke 21:20
   - **A.** Armies would surround the city
   - **B.** Great signs would come from heaven
   - **C.** Mountains would quake
   - **D.** The Son of God would be crucified

5. What did Jesus call the last days of Jerusalem?
   Luke 21:22
   - **A.** Days of persecution
   - **B.** Days of prosperity
   - **C.** Days of thunder
   - **D.** Days of vengeance

6. What did Jesus call the end times?
   Luke 21:24
   - **A.** Times of the church
   - **B.** Times of the Gentiles
   - **C.** Times of the Jews
   - **D.** Times of the Romans

7. How shall Christ return?
   Luke 21:27
   - **A.** In a chariot
   - **B.** In a cloud
   - **C.** On a donkey
   - **D.** On a horse

8. Which tree does Jesus mention specifically in his parable?
   Luke 21:29
   - **A.** The almond tree
   - **B.** The fig tree
   - **C.** The palm tree
   - **D.** The sycamore tree

9. What did Jesus say would never be destroyed?
   Luke 21:33
   - **A.** Earth and sky
   - **B.** Heaven and hell
   - **C.** Jesus' words
   - **D.** The temple

10. What did Jesus compare his Second Coming to?
    Luke 21:35
    - **A.** A snare
    - **B.** A sparrow
    - **C.** A star
    - **D.** A sword

11. Upon which mountain did Jesus spend his nights?
    Luke 21:37
    - **A.** Mount Ararat
    - **B.** Mount Hermon
    - **C.** Mount Nebo
    - **D.** Mount of Olives

12. When did Jesus teach in the temple?
    Luke 21:38
    - **A.** Afternoon
    - **B.** Evening
    - **C.** Morning
    - **D.** Night

13. Which feast were the Jews celebrating?

    Luke 22:1

    A. Feast of harvest
    B. Feast of ingathering
    C. Feast of tabernacles
    D. Feast of unleavened bread

14. Whom did Satan enter into?

    Luke 22:3

    A. Andrew
    B. Bartholomew
    C. Judas Iscariot
    D. Simon Peter

15. Which two disciples did Jesus send to find the man with the pitcher of water?

    Luke 22:8–10

    A. Andrew and Philip
    B. Batholomew and Matthew
    C. James and Thomas
    D. Peter and John

16. Who did Jesus say would deny him three times?

    Luke 22:34

    A. Andrew
    B. James
    C. Nathaniel
    D. Peter

17. How many swords did the apostles have?

    Luke 22:38

    A. 2
    B. 3
    C. 11
    D. 12

18. Whose right ear was cut off?

    Luke 22:50

    A. The apostle's ear—who betrayed Jesus
    B. The high priest's ear
    C. The servant's ear—of the high priest
    D. The thief's ear

19. Who questioned Jesus first?

    Luke 22:54–71

    A. The Gentiles
    B. The Jews
    C. The Romans
    D. The Samaritans

20. Where was Peter from?

    Luke 22:59

    A. Decapolis
    B. Galilee
    C. Judea
    D. Samaria

*Answers on page 776

Lesson 306
Today's Reading: *Luke 23–24*
Period of Time: Friday, April 3–Thursday, May 14, 33 AD
Author: Luke

1. What did Pilate ask Jesus?
   Luke 23:3

   A. "Art thou the king of the Jews?"
   B. "Can thou interpret dreams?"
   C. "Can thou turn water into wine?"
   D. "Who is thy father?"

2. What did Pilate ask the multitude?
   Luke 23:6

   A. If Jesus fed them in the desert.
   B. If Jesus had a wife.
   C. If Jesus raised Lazarus from the dead.
   D. If Jesus was a Galilean.

3. Why was Herod glad to see Jesus?
   Luke 23:8

   A. He had longed to be baptized by Jesus.
   B. He hoped to see a miracle.
   C. They went to school together.
   D. They were half-brothers.

4. Why was Barabbas cast into prison?
   Luke 23:18–19, 23:25

   A. For claiming he was a king
   B. For not giving tribute to Caesar
   C. For sedition and murder
   D. For teaching false doctrines

5. Who asked, "What evil hath he done?"
   Luke 23:20–22

   A. Claudius
   B. Festus
   C. Nero
   D. Pilate

6. Who carried Jesus' cross?
   Luke 23:26

   A. Simon of Cyrene
   B. Simon Peter
   C. Simon the Sorcerer
   D. Simon the Zealot

7. What did Jesus compare himself to?
   Luke 23:31

   A. A castle upon a hill
   B. A child with no mother
   C. A green tree
   D. A king without a city

8. How many malefactors were crucified with Jesus?
   Luke 23:32–33

   A. 2
   B. 7
   C. 8
   D. 12

9. Where was Jesus crucified?
   Luke 23:33

   A. Bethlehem
   B. Calvary
   C. Gethsemane
   D. Mount of Olives

10. What did the soldiers do with Jesus' clothes?
    Luke 23:34

    A. Auctioned them
    B. Cast lots for them
    C. Donated them to the poor
    D. Made them into rags

11. What drink did the soldiers offer Jesus?
    Luke 23:36

    A. Beer
    B. Tea
    C. Vinegar
    D. Water

12. What sign did the Roman soldiers nail to the cross?
    Luke 23:36–38

    A. LET THIS BE A WARNING
    B. THERE IS NO GOD BUT CAESAR
    C. THIS IS JESUS OF NAZARETH
    D. THIS IS THE KING OF THE JEWS

13. Which statement did Jesus say to one of the malefactors?

    Luke 23:39–43

    A. "I am the way, the truth, and the life."
    B. "Rejoice for your name is written in heaven."
    C. "The gates of hell cannot prevail against me."
    D. "To day shalt thou be with me in paradise."

14. How many hours did darkness cover the earth during the crucifixion?

    Luke 23:44

    A. 2
    B. 3
    C. 4
    D. 5

15. What did the centurion say after Jesus died?

    Luke 23:47

    A. "Certainly this was a righteous man."
    B. "He saved others; himself he could not save."
    C. "The King is dead, long live the King."
    D. "This man was no friend to Caesar."

16. Whose sepulcher was Jesus' body placed into?

    Luke 23:50–53

    A. Joseph Barnabas' sepulcher
    B. Joseph Barsabbas' sepulcher
    C. Joseph of Arimathaea's sepulcher
    D. Joseph the Carpenter's sepulcher

17. What did the two men in shining garments at Jesus' tomb ask the women?

    Luke 24:4–5

    A. "When did these events in Jerusalem take place?"
    B. "Where did you move his body to?"
    C. "Who was Jesus?"
    D. "Why seek ye the living among the dead?"

18. Who spoke to Jesus on the way to Emmaus?

    Luke 24:13–18

    A. Chloe
    B. Cleopas
    C. Cleopatra
    D. Clopas

19. What did the apostles give Jesus to eat?

    Luke 24:42–43

    A. Baked lamb and bitter herbs
    B. Boiled eggs and a wedge of cheese
    C. Broiled Fish and a honeycomb
    D. Roasted meat and potatoes

20. From where did Jesus ascend to heaven?

    Luke 24:50–51

    A. Bethany
    B. Calvary
    C. Debir
    D. Elam

*Answers on page 776

NOVEMBER 3

Lesson 307
Today's Reading: *John 1–3*
Period of Time: 5 BC–30 AD
Author: John

1. What existed in the beginning?
   John 1:1
   A. The big bang
   B. The flesh
   C. The primordial soup
   D. The Word

2. Who did the people think John the Baptist was?
   John 1:21
   A. Eglon
   B. Ehud
   C. Elias
   D. Esaias

3. Which prophet said, "Make straight the way of the Lord"?
   John 1:23
   A. Eglon
   B. Ehud
   C. Elias
   D. Esaias

4. Who was sent to question John the Baptist?
   John 1:24–27
   A. The Herodians
   B. The Pharisees
   C. The Romans
   D. The Sadducees

5. Where was John baptizing at?
   John 1:28
   A. Areopagus
   B. Bethabara
   C. Macedonia
   D. Padan-aram

6. What did John the Baptist call Jesus when he saw him?
   John 1:29
   A. Holy One of Israel
   B. Jesus of Nazareth
   C. King of glory
   D. Lamb of God

7. How did the Spirit descend from heaven?
   John 1:32
   A. Like a dove
   B. Like an angel
   C. Like rainfall
   D. Like sunshine

8. What does the word *rabbi* mean?
   John 1:38
   A. Father
   B. Master
   C. Potter
   D. Treasurer

9. Who was Simon Peter's brother?
   John 1:40
   A. Andrew
   B. Nathanael
   C. Philip
   D. Thomas

10. What name did Jesus give to Simon Peter?
    John 1:42
    A. Abidan
    B. Benoni
    C. Cephas
    D. Daniel

11. Where were Philip, Andrew, and Peter from?
    John 1:44
    A. Apollonia
    B. Bethsaida
    C. Macedonia
    D. Palestina

12. Where did Jesus perform his first miracle?
    John 2:1–11
    A. Aven
    B. Beer
    C. Cana
    D. Elim

13. How many waterpots were filled?

    John 2:6

    A. 3
    B. 4
    C. 5
    D. 6

14. How many firkins did each waterpot contain?

    John 2:6

    A. 2 or 3
    B. 4 or 5
    C. 6 or 7
    D. 8 or 9

15. How many years did it take to build the temple?

    John 2:20

    A. 18
    B. 27
    C. 46
    D. 53

16. Which ruler of the Jews came to visit Jesus at night?

    John 3:1–2

    A. Annas
    B. Caiaphas
    C. Nicodemus
    D. Zacharias

17. What did Jesus tell the ruler of the Jews?

    John 3:3–8

    A. "Ye must be born again."
    B. "Ye must build your house upon rock."
    C. "Ye must give all that ye have to the poor."
    D. "Ye must resist the power of the Romans."

18. What did God give fallen man to prove he still loved us?

    John 3:16

    A. Bishops, evangelists, and ministers
    B. His only begotten Son
    C. Kings, governments, and rulers
    D. The laws of natural science

19. Where did Jesus baptize his disciples?

    John 3:22

    A. Arabia
    B. Galilee
    C. Idumaea
    D. Judaea

20. Which place is near Salim?

    John 3:23

    A. Aenon
    B. Lebanon
    C. Punon
    D. Sihon

Answers on page 776

NOVEMBER 4

Lesson 308
Today's Reading: *John 4–5*
Period of Time: 30–31 AD
Author: John

1. Which city in Samaria did Jesus travel to?
   John 4:5
   A. Sirion
   B. Smyrna
   C. Sochoh
   D. Sychar

2. At which well did Jesus speak to the Samaritan woman?
   John 4:6
   A. Benjamin's well
   B. Jacob's well
   C. Laban's well
   D. Simeon's well

3. During which hour did Jesus sit on the well?
   John 4:6
   A. 3rd
   B. 4th
   C. 5th
   D. 6th

4. Where were the disciples when Jesus spoke to the Samaritan woman?
   John 4:8
   A. At the river to baptize followers
   B. At the temple to teach people
   C. In the city to buy meat
   D. In the desert to cast out demons

5. What did Jesus say he would have given the Samaritan woman if she had asked?
   John 4:10
   A. A mansion in heaven
   B. A new husband
   C. Living water
   D. The bread of life

6. How many former husbands did the Samaritan woman have?
   John 4:18
   A. 2
   B. 3
   C. 4
   D. 5

7. What did the Samaritan woman call Jesus?
   John 4:19
   A. A king
   B. A prophet
   C. A rabbi
   D. A teacher

8. How shall true worshippers worship God?
   John 4:23–24
   A. In dance and in song
   B. In spirit and in truth
   C. In tithes and in offerings
   D. In works and in praise

9. What is the *Messias* called?
   John 4:25
   A. Christ
   B. King
   C. Master
   D. Servant

10. What color did Jesus say the fields were?
    John 4:35
    A. Black
    B. Green
    C. White
    D. Yellow

11. How many days did Jesus stay with the Samaritans?
    John 4:40
    A. 1
    B. 2
    C. 3
    D. 4

12. What name did the Samaritans call Jesus?

    John 4:39–42

    A. I AM
    B. Lamb of God
    C. Messiah the prince
    D. The Saviour of the world

13. Where did Jesus turn water into wine?

    John 4:46

    A. Aija
    B. Cana
    C. Nain
    D. Tyre

14. Where was the nobleman's son?

    John 4:46

    A. Capernaum
    B. Gibbethon
    C. Illyricum
    D. Perezzuza

15. At which hour was the nobleman's son healed?

    John 4:52

    A. 1st
    B. 3rd
    C. 5th
    D. 7th

16. What is the name of the pool located near the sheep market?

    John 5:2

    A. Bethesda
    B. Lower
    C. Siloah
    D. Upper

17. How many porches did the pool located near the sheep market have?

    John 5:2

    A. 5
    B. 10
    C. 15
    D. 20

18. How many years did the man waiting by the pool have the infirmity?

    John 5:5

    A. 16
    B. 29
    C. 38
    D. 42

19. Who did Jesus say bared witness to the truth?

    John 5:33–36

    A. John
    B. Luke
    C. Mark
    D. Matthew

20. Who did Jesus say was the Jew's accuser?

    John 5:45

    A. Abraham
    B. David
    C. Moses
    D. Noah

*Answers on page 776

NOVEMBER 5

Lesson 309
Today's Reading: *John 6–7*
Period of Time: 32 AD
Author: John

1. What is the other name for the sea of Galilee?
   John 6:1
   A. Sea of Cilicia
   B. Sea of Pamphylia
   C. Sea of the Philistines
   D. Sea of Tiberias

2. Which feast of the Jews was nigh when Jesus went up into a mountain with his disciples?
   John 6:3–4
   A. Feast of harvest
   B. Feast of ingathering
   C. Feast of the passover
   D. Feast of weeks

3. Which disciple did Jesus ask concerning buying bread for the multitude?
   John 6:5
   A. Bartholomew
   B. John
   C. Philip
   D. Thaddeus

4. Who was Simon Peter's brother?
   John 6:8
   A. Andrew
   B. Matthew
   C. Nathanael
   D. Thomas

5. How many barley loaves did the lad have?
   John 6:9
   A. 2
   B. 5
   C. 7
   D. 12

6. How many fish did the lad have?
   John 6:9
   A. 2
   B. 5
   C. 7
   D. 12

7. Approximately how many men did Jesus feed?
   John 6:10
   A. 3,000
   B. 5,000
   C. 7,000
   D. 9,000

8. How many baskets of barley bread were left over?
   John 6:13
   A. 2
   B. 5
   C. 7
   D. 12

9. Where did Jesus go alone after feeding the multitude?
   John 6:15
   A. To a desert
   B. To a mountain
   C. To a river
   D. To a well

10. Where were the disciples going by ship?
    John 6:17
    A. Capernaum
    B. Damascus
    C. Jerusalem
    D. Sidon

11. How many furlongs had the disciples rowed when they saw Jesus walking on the sea?
    John 6:19
    A. 5 or 10
    B. 15 or 20
    C. 25 or 30
    D. 35 or 40

12. What did the multitude call Jesus when they found him on the other side of the sea?

    John 6:25

    A. Alpha
    B. Deliverer
    C. King
    D. Rabbi

13. Who was Jesus' earthly father?

    John 6:42

    A. Gabriel
    B. Joseph
    C. Michael
    D. Zadok

14. Which disciple told Jesus, "Thou hast the words of eternal life"?

    John 6:66–69

    A. James
    B. Matthew
    C. Nathanael
    D. Peter

15. Which disciple would betray Jesus?

    John 6:70–71

    A. Andrew
    B. Bartholomew
    C. Judas Iscariot
    D. Thomas

16. Which feast was at hand when Jesus walked in Galilee, but would **not** walk in Jewry?

    John 7:1–2

    A. Feast of tabernacles
    B. Feast of trumpets
    C. Feast of unleavened bread
    D. Feast of weeks

17. Who encouraged Jesus to perform miracles at the feast in Judaea?

    John 7:3–10

    A. His brothers
    B. His father
    C. His mother
    D. His sisters

18. According to the scriptures, which town would Christ come from?

    John 7:42

    A. Ashdod
    B. Bethlehem
    C. Caesarea
    D. Damascus

19. Which Jewish ruler visited Jesus at night?

    John 7:50

    A. Annas
    B. Caiaphas
    C. Jahaziel
    D. Nicodemus

20. Where did the Jewish leaders say a prophet would **not** come from?

    John 7:52

    A. Decapolis
    B. Egypt
    C. Galilee
    D. Perea

Answers on page 776

NOVEMBER 6

Lesson 310
Today's Reading: *John 8–9*
Period of Time: 32 AD
Author: John

1. Upon which mountain did Jesus spend the night?

    John 8:1

    A. Mount Hor
    B. Mount Nebo
    C. Mount of Olives
    D. Mount Zemaraim

2. When did Jesus go to the temple?

    John 8:2

    A. Morning
    B. Noon
    C. Evening
    D. Midnight

3. What did Jesus do when the adulterous woman was brought to him?

    John 8:3–8

    A. He baptized her.
    B. He cast a demon out of her.
    C. He let her wash his feet.
    D. He wrote on the ground.

4. What did Jesus tell the adulterous woman?

    John 8:11

    A. "Daughter, thy faith hath made thee whole."
    B. "Find the priest and give a sin offering."
    C. "Go and sin no more."
    D. "Woman, thou art loosed."

5. What did Jesus call himself in *John 8:12*?

    John 8:12

    A. The Christ of God
    B. The light of the world
    C. The Son of the Father
    D. The Word of God

6. According to the law, how many witnesses must there be in order for a charge to be true?

    John 8:17

    A. 2
    B. 3
    C. 10
    D. 12

7. Which part of the temple did Jesus teach in?

    John 8:20

    A. The court of the Gentiles
    B. The court of the priests
    C. The holy place
    D. The treasury

8. Which question did the Jews ask among themselves regarding Jesus?

    John 8:22

    A. "Will he baptize all of us?"
    B. "Will he kill himself?"
    C. "Will he raise the dead?"
    D. "Will he turn water into wine?"

9. What will the truth do for you?

    John 8:32

    A. Blind you
    B. Convict you
    C. Make you free
    D. Send you to hell

10. Who did the Jews claim was their father?

    John 8:39

    A. Abraham
    B. David
    C. Jacob
    D. Moses

11. Who is the father of lies?

    John 8:44

    A. The devil
    B. The Father
    C. The Holy Ghost
    D. The Son

12. What did the Jews call Jesus?

    John 8:48

    A. A Herodian
    B. A Pharisee
    C. A Sadducee
    D. A Samaritan

13. How did Jesus heal the man who had been blind since birth?

    John 9:6

    A. He kissed his eyes.
    B. He put clay over his eyes.
    C. He spoke the word.
    D. He touched his eyes.

14. Where did Jesus tell the man healed of blindness to wash at?

    John 9:7

    A. Conduit of the upper pool
    B. Pool of Gibeon
    C. Pool of Siloam
    D. Waters of the lower pool

15. Who did the man healed of blindness say healed him when the Jews asked him?

    John 9:11

    A. Emmanuel
    B. Jesus
    C. Lucifer
    D. Satan

16. Whom did the Jews take the man healed of blindness to?

    John 9:13

    A. The Herodians
    B. The Pharisees
    C. The Sadducees
    D. The Samaritans

17. What did the Jewish leaders call Jesus?

    John 9:24

    A. A prophet
    B. A rabbi
    C. A sinner
    D. A teacher

18. What did the man healed of blindness tell the Jewish leaders?

    John 9:25

    A. "Bright is the shining sun."
    B. "Grace will lead me home."
    C. "He saved a wretch like me."
    D. "I was blind, now I see."

19. What did the leaders do when the healed man asked if they would become Jesus' disciples?

    John 9:28

    A. They answered yes.
    B. They asked if Jesus would heal them.
    C. They claimed to already be Jesus' disciples.
    D. They reviled him.

20. What did the leaders do when they made an end of their inquiry of the healed man?

    John 9:34

    A. They cast him out.
    B. They gave God the glory.
    C. They praised his parents.
    D. They stoned him.

*Answers on page 776

Lesson 311

Today's Reading: *John 10–11*
Period of Time: 32–33 AD
Author: John

NOVEMBER 7

1. Which name did Jesus use for himself?
   John 10:11
   A. The begotten shepherd
   B. The good shepherd
   C. The lonely shepherd
   D. The wise shepherd

2. What did Jesus say scatters the sheep?
   John 10:12
   A. The bear
   B. The fox
   C. The lion
   D. The wolf

3. How many folds will there be?
   John 10:16
   A. 1
   B. 3
   C. 7
   D. 12

4. Which feast during the winter did Jesus attend?
   John 10:22
   A. Feast of atonement
   B. Feast of firstfruits
   C. Feast of the dedication
   D. Feast of unleavened bread

5. Where did the Jews question Jesus in the temple?
   John 10:23–39
   A. Court of Gentiles
   B. Gate Beautiful
   C. Solomon's Porch
   D. Western Wall

6. How did the Jews try to kill Jesus?
   John 10:31
   A. By burning him
   B. By drowning him
   C. By hanging him
   D. By stoning him

7. Which town did Lazarus live in?
   John 11:1
   A. Bethany
   B. Jericho
   C. Nineveh
   D. Phrygia

8. Who was one of Lazarus' sisters?
   John 11:1
   A. Abi
   B. Jael
   C. Lydia
   D. Martha

9. Who anointed Jesus with ointment and wiped his feet with her hair?
   John 11:2
   A. Anna
   B. Lois
   C. Mary
   D. Ruth

10. How many days did Jesus abode in the same place after being informed Lazarus was sick?
    John 11:6
    A. 2
    B. 4
    C. 6
    D. 8

11. How many hours did Jesus say were in a day?
    John 11:9
    A. 8
    B. 12
    C. 16
    D. 24

12. Which disciple was also called Thomas?
    John 11:16
    A. Andrew
    B. Bartholomew
    C. Didymus
    D. Simon

13. Which town was about 15 furlongs from Jerusalem?

    John 11:18

    A. Bethany
    B. Jericho
    C. Nineveh
    D. Phrygia

14. Who went to meet Jesus when she heard Jesus was coming?

    John 11:20

    A. Dorcas
    B. Eunice
    C. Martha
    D. Vashti

15. What is the shortest verse in the Bible?

    John 11:35

    A. Jesus groaned.
    B. Jesus laughed.
    C. Jesus shouted.
    D. Jesus wept.

16. How many days had Lazarus been dead before Jesus brought him back to life?

    John 11:39

    A. 1
    B. 2
    C. 3
    D. 4

17. Whom did some of the Jews tell that Jesus had raised Lazarus from the dead?

    John 11:46

    A. The Herodians
    B. The Pharisees
    C. The Romans
    D. The Sadducees

18. Who was the high priest that year?

    John 11:49

    A. Caiaphas
    B. Elishama
    C. Jahaziel
    D. Phinehas

19. Which city did Jesus go to after he raised Lazarus from the dead?

    John 11:54

    A. Antioch
    B. Ephraim
    C. Iconium
    D. Samaria

20. Which feast were the Jews preparing for?

    John 11:55

    A. Feast of harvest
    B. Feast of the passover
    C. Feast of tabernacles
    D. Feast of weeks

*Answers on page 776

NOVEMBER 8

Lesson 312
Today's Reading: *John 12–13*
Period of Time: Saturday, March 28–Thursday, April 2, 33 AD
Author: John

1. In which town did Lazarus live?
   John 12:1
   A. Bethany
   B. Havilah
   C. Magdala
   D. Samaria

2. Who served supper at Lazarus' home?
   John 12:2
   A. Maacah
   B. Mahlah
   C. Martha
   D. Matred

3. Who anointed Jesus and wiped his feet with her hair?
   John 12:3
   A. Anna
   B. Jael
   C. Lois
   D. Mary

4. Who was Judas Iscariot's father?
   John 12:4
   A. Linus
   B. Nahum
   C. Peter
   D. Simon

5. How many pence was the pound of ointment of spikenard worth?
   John 12:3–5
   A. 100
   B. 200
   C. 300
   D. 400

6. What was Judas Iscariot's job as a disciple?
   John 12:6
   A. He cooked the food.
   B. He did the laundry.
   C. He kept the money.
   D. He was the lawyer.

7. Whom did Jesus raise from the dead?
   John 12:1, 12:9
   A. Crispus
   B. Erastus
   C. Lazarus
   D. Malchus

8. What type of tree branches did the crowd collect and use to greet Jesus?
   John 12:13
   A. Oak tree branches
   B. Palm tree branches
   C. Shittah tree branches
   D. Willow tree branches

9. What did the crowd call Jesus?
   John 12:13
   A. King of glory
   B. King of Israel
   C. King of kings
   D. King of saints

10. Which young animal did Jesus ride into Jerusalem?
    John 12:14–15
    A. Ass
    B. Camel
    C. Horse
    D. Mule

11. Who said the world had gone after Jesus?
    John 12:19
    A. The Herodians
    B. The Pharisees
    C. The Samaritans
    D. The Zealots

12. Which town was Philip from?
    John 12:20–21
    A. Bethsaida
    B. Jerusalem
    C. Philistia
    D. Sansannah

13. What did Jesus call Satan?

    John 12:31

    A. Son of the morning
    B. The prince of this world
    C. The tempter
    D. Wicked one

14. Which prophet did Jesus make reference to?

    John 12:38

    A. Esaias
    B. Hosea
    C. Malachi
    D. Zechariah

15. What did Jesus say he came to do?

    John 12:47

    A. Cleanse the temple
    B. Heal the sick
    C. Overthrow Herod
    D. Save the world

16. Which disciple would betray Jesus?

    John 13:2

    A. Andrew
    B. Judas Iscariot
    C. Philip
    D. Simon the Zealot

17. What did Jesus do when supper had ended?

    John 13:5–11

    A. Healed a woman of her infirmity
    B. Raised a man from the dead
    C. Threw out the money changers
    D. Washed the disciples feet

18. Which disciple did Jesus give the sop to?

    John 13:26

    A. James
    B. John
    C. Judas Iscariot
    D. Judas the son of James

19. Which new commandment did Jesus give?

    John 13:34

    A. Beat one another
    B. Cheat one another
    C. Hate one another
    D. Love one another

20. How many times would Peter deny knowing Jesus before the cock would crow?

    John 13:38

    A. 3
    B. 5
    C. 7
    D. 9

*Answers on page 776

NOVEMBER 9

Lesson 313
Today's Reading: *John 14–16*
Period of Time: Thursday, April 2, 33 AD
Author: John

1. What did Jesus say there are lots of in his Father's house?

   John 14:2

   A. Gardens
   B. Lights
   C. Mansions
   D. Servants

2. Who asked Jesus, "How can we know the way?"

   John 14:5

   A. Judas
   B. Philip
   C. Simon
   D. Thomas

3. Which statement did Jesus make?

   John 14:6

   A. "I am the way, the truth, and the life."
   B. "Just say no."
   C. "Let's roll."
   D. "Whatever you are, be a good one."

4. Who said to Jesus, "Show us the Father, and it sufficeth us"?

   John 14:8

   A. Judas
   B. Philip
   C. Simon
   D. Thomas

5. What name does Jesus use for the Holy Ghost?

   John 14:16, 14:26; 15:26

   A. Comforter
   B. Light
   C. Saviour
   D. Wonderful

6. Who asked Jesus, "Lord, how is it that thou wilt manifest thyself unto us, and **not** unto the world?"

   John 14:22

   A. Judas
   B. Philip
   C. Simon
   D. Thomas

7. What did Jesus say he would leave with the disciples—**not** as the world giveth?

   John 14:27

   A. Bread
   B. Miracles
   C. Peace
   D. Writings

8. Where did Jesus tell the disciples he was going?

   John 14:28

   A. To the city
   B. To the Father
   C. To the garden of Gethsemane
   D. To the home of Lazarus

9. What does Jesus call Satan?

   John 14:30

   A. A roaring lion
   B. The prince of this world
   C. The tempter
   D. Wicked one

10. What does Jesus call himself?

    John 15:1–5

    A. The branches
    B. The husbandman
    C. The vine
    D. The water

11. What does Jesus call the Father?

    John 15:1

    A. The branches
    B. The husbandman
    C. The vine
    D. The water

12. What does Jesus call his followers?

    John 15:5

    A. The branches
    B. The husbandman
    C. The vine
    D. The water

13. What does Jesus state those who reject him will be like?

    John 15:6

    A. Carcasses bleached in the desert
    B. Fruit rotted on a tree
    C. Grapes pressed into wine
    D. Wood burned in a fire

14. What was Jesus' commandment?

    John 15:12

    A. Be not a lender.
    B. Eat, drink, and be merry.
    C. Give all that you have to the poor.
    D. Love one another.

15. What did Jesus say is the greatest demonstration of love?

    John 15:13

    A. When a child prays to God
    B. When a disciple fasts for God
    C. When a man dies for his friends
    D. When a stranger cares for a babe

16. What did Jesus say would happen when he dies?

    John 16:20

    A. Jews will be loved by the world.
    B. Romans will be converted to Christianity.
    C. Sorrow will be turned into joy.
    D. Water will be changed into blood.

17. What must a person do if he desires something from God?

    John 16:23

    A. Ask the Father in Jesus' name
    B. Give a love offering
    C. Pay his tithes
    D. Show his good works

18. What did Jesus use to teach the disciples?

    John 16:25, 16:29

    A. Charts
    B. Graphs
    C. Illustrations
    D. Proverbs

19. What did Jesus say the disciples would do when others come for him?

    John 16:32

    A. Sail to Galilee
    B. Scatter
    C. Shout a great shout
    D. Stand by his side

20. What did Jesus say his disciples would always have in this world?

    John 16:33

    A. Happiness
    B. Joy
    C. Mammon
    D. Tribulation

*Answers on page 777

NOVEMBER 10

Lesson 314
Today's Reading: *John 17–18*
Period of Time: Thursday, April 2–Friday, April 3, 33 AD
Author: John

1. What did Jesus say he did **not** pray for?
   John 17:9

   A. The City of David
   B. The Jewish rulers
   C. The Roman Caesars
   D. The world

2. Whom did Jesus say he was unable to save?
   John 17:12

   A. The daughter of Jairus
   B. The mother-in-law of Peter
   C. The son of perdition
   D. The wife of Lot

3. What did Jesus ask the Father to do through his truth for his followers?
   John 17:17

   A. Baptize them
   B. Forgive them
   C. Redeem them
   D. Sanctify them

4. What name does Jesus use for God?
   John 17:25

   A. Majesty on high
   B. Righteous Father
   C. Shiloh
   D. The Rock of my refuge

5. Which brook did Jesus and his disciples cross to reach a garden?
   John 18:1

   A. Brook Besor
   B. Brook Cedron
   C. Brook Eshcol
   D. Brook Zered

6. How many times did Jesus ask, "Whom seek ye?"
   John 18:4–7

   A. 2
   B. 4
   C. 6
   D. 8

7. Whom did the mob say they were looking for?
   John 18:5

   A. Jesus of Nazareth
   B. King of Israel
   C. Prince of life
   D. Son of man

8. What did the mob do after Jesus said he was the one they were looking for?
   John 18:6

   A. Asked him to perform a miracle
   B. Cast stones at him
   C. Fell to the ground
   D. Rushed him with staves

9. Who cut off the high priest's servant's ear?
   John 18:10

   A. Simon of Cyrene
   B. Simon Peter
   C. Simon the sorcerer
   D. Simon the zealot

10. Who was the high priest's servant?
    John 18:10

    A. Aristarchus
    B. Eutychus
    C. Lazarus
    D. Malchus

11. Who was Annas' son-in-law?
    John 18:13

    A. Barabas
    B. Caiaphas
    C. Ezekias
    D. Nicolas

12. Who asked Peter the *first* time if he was one of Jesus' disciples?
    John 18:17

    A. A Roman soldier
    B. A servant of the high priest
    C. The damsel that kept the door
    D. The servants and officers

647

13. Which one of the following was the high priest?

    John 18:24

    A. Caiaphas
    B. Epaphras
    C. Lysanias
    D. Olympas

14. Who asked Peter the *second* time if he was one of Jesus' disciples?

    John 18:18, 18:25

    A. A Roman soldier
    B. A servant of the high priest
    C. The damsel that kept the door
    D. The servants and officers

15. Who asked Peter the *third* time if he was one of Jesus' disciples?

    John 18:26

    A. A Roman soldier
    B. A servant of the high priest
    C. The damsel that kept the door
    D. The servants and officers

16. What happened immediately after the third time Peter denied knowing Jesus?

    John 18:27

    A. The cock crew.
    B. The groundhog saw his shadow.
    C. The lamb lay by the lion.
    D. The raven pecked Peter's head.

17. Where was Jesus taken to?

    John 18:28

    A. The barracks
    B. The dungeon
    C. The hall of judgment
    D. The palace of the gods

18. What did *the Jewish rulers* call Jesus?

    John 18:30

    A. A benefactor
    B. A cofactor
    C. A malefactor
    D. A nonfactor

19. What did *Pilate* call Jesus?

    John 18:39

    A. The King of Israel
    B. The King of Jacob
    C. The King of kings
    D. The King of the Jews

20. Which one of the following was a robber?

    John 18:40

    A. Barabbas
    B. Barachel
    C. Barnabas
    D. Barsabas

Answers on page 777

NOVEMBER 11

Lesson 315
Today's Reading: *John 19–21*
Period of Time: Friday, April 3–Thursday, May 14, 33 AD
Author: John

1. What color was the robe the soldiers placed upon Jesus?
   John 19:2–5
   A. Blue
   B. Gold
   C. Purple
   D. Scarlet

2. Where did the soldiers take Jesus after they scourged him?
   John 19:9
   A. The dungeon underground
   B. The hotel Jerusalem
   C. The imperial palace
   D. The judgment hall

3. What is the Hebrew name for the place that is called *the Pavement*?
   John 19:13
   A. Agape
   B. Gabbatha
   C. Mammon
   D. Tittle

4. About which hour was it when Pilate said, "Behold your king!"?
   John 19:14
   A. 6th
   B. 8th
   C. 10th
   D. 12th

5. Who did the Jews say was their king?
   John 19:15
   A. Caesar
   B. God
   C. Jesus
   D. Pilate

6. What is the Hebrew name for *the place of a skull*?
   John 19:17
   A. Ephphatha
   B. Golgotha
   C. Hosanna
   D. Raca

7. How many people were crucified with Jesus?
   John 19:18
   A. 2
   B. 3
   C. 4
   D. 5

8. Who was Mary's (the sister of Jesus' mother) husband?
   John 19:25
   A. Amraphel
   B. Bigthana
   C. Cleophas
   D. Eliasaph

9. What did the Roman soldiers do to Jesus while he was on the cross?
   John 19:32–34
   A. Broke his legs
   B. Dressed his wounds
   C. Offered him water to drink
   D. Pierced his side with a spear

10. Who asked Pilate for the body of Jesus?
    John 19:38
    A. Joseph of Arimathaea
    B. Philip the evangelist
    C. Saul of Tarsus
    D. Uriah the Hittite

11. Who brought a mixture of myrrh and aloes for the body of Jesus?

    John 19:39

    A. Didymus
    B. Nicodemus
    C. Onesimus
    D. Trophimus

12. Who noticed the stone to Jesus' sepulcher had been removed?

    John 20:1

    A. Amos of Tekoa
    B. John the Baptist
    C. Mary Magdalene
    D. Rahab the harlot

13. How many angels were in the empty tomb?

    John 20:12

    A. 2
    B. 3
    C. 4
    D. 5

14. Who mistook Jesus for the gardener?

    John 20:1–15

    A. Martha
    B. Mary Magdalene
    C. Mary the sister of Lazarus
    D. Mary the wife of Cleopas

15. What does *rabboni* mean?

    John 20:16

    A. Farmer
    B. Gardener
    C. Master
    D. Prophet

16. Who was also called Didymus?

    John 20:24–25

    A. Andrew
    B. James
    C. Nathanael
    D. Thomas

17. Where did the disciples go fishing, according to John 21:1?

    John 21:1

    A. Sea of Chinneroth
    B. Sea of Cilicia
    C. Sea of the Philistines
    D. Sea of Tiberias

18. How many cubits was the disciples' boat from land?

    John 21:8

    A. 12
    B. 89
    C. 153
    D. 200

19. How many fish were in the disciples' net?

    John 21:11

    A. 12
    B. 89
    C. 153
    D. 200

20. How many times did Jesus ask Simon Peter if he loved him?

    John 21:15–17

    A. 2
    B. 3
    C. 4
    D. 5

*Answers on page 777

Lesson 316
Today's Reading: *Acts 1–3*
Period of Time: 33 AD
Author: Luke

NOVEMBER 12

1. Whom does Luke mention in the first verse?
   Acts 1:1
   A. Andronicus
   B. Fortunatus
   C. Philologus
   D. Theophilus

2. How many days did Jesus remain on earth before his ascension?
   Acts 1:3
   A. 20
   B. 40
   C. 60
   D. 80

3. What were the disciples to be baptized with in a few days?
   Acts 1:5
   A. Holy fire
   B. Holy Ghost
   C. Holy water
   D. Holy wine

4. How many men in white apparel stood by the disciples?
   Acts 1:10
   A. 2
   B. 7
   C. 12
   D. 21

5. Upon which mountain did the disciples witness the ascension?
   Acts 1:12
   A. Mount Moriah
   B. Mount Nebo
   C. Mount Olivet
   D. Mount Zion

6. Which one of the following women was present in the upper room?
   Acts 1:13–14
   A. Leah
   B. Mary
   C. Ruth
   D. Sara

7. Approximately how many people were gathered in the upper room?
   Acts 1:15
   A. 40
   B. 80
   C. 120
   D. 160

8. What does *Aceldama* mean?
   Acts 1:19
   A. Field of blood
   B. House of blood
   C. River of blood
   D. Valley of blood

9. Who was chosen to take Judas' bishoprick?
   Acts 1:16–26
   A. Barsabbas
   B. Joseph
   C. Justus
   D. Matthias

10. What appeared unto those in the upper room on the day of Pentecost?
    Acts 2:1–3
    A. Angelic beings as of armies
    B. Bright stars as of light
    C. Cloven tongues as of fire
    D. Prayers of saints as of rivers

11. What were those in the upper room called?
    Acts 2:7
    A. Egyptians
    B. Galileans
    C. Parthians
    D. Sidonians

12. Which city is located in Libya?

    Acts 2:10

    A. Cyrene
    B. Memphis
    C. Raamses
    D. Thebez

13. Who preached to the multitude on the day of Pentecost?

    Acts 2:14

    A. Andrew
    B. James
    C. John
    D. Peter

14. At what hour of the day did the people receive the baptism in the Holy Spirit?

    Acts 2:15

    A. 1st
    B. 2nd
    C. 3rd
    D. 4th

15. Which prophet said God would pour out his Spirit upon all flesh?

    Acts 2:16–21

    A. Hiel
    B. Joel
    C. Lael
    D. Ohel

16. How many people were baptized on the day of Pentecost?

    Acts 2:41

    A. 7
    B. 21
    C. 666
    D. 3,000

17. Which two disciples cured a lame man in the temple through the power of Christ?

    Acts 3:1–8

    A. Andrew and Philip
    B. Bartholomew and Thaddaeus
    C. James and Matthew
    D. Peter and John

18. At which gate was the lame man asking for alms?

    Acts 3:2

    A. Beautiful gate
    B. Dung gate
    C. Old gate
    D. Valley gate

19. Where did the two apostles and the lame man go after the lame man was healed?

    Acts 3:8–11

    A. Luke's home
    B. Pool of Bethesda
    C. Solomon's porch
    D. The upper room

20. Which one of the following was a prophet?

    Acts 3:24

    A. Samuel
    B. Sanballat
    C. Saph
    D. Sargon

Answers on page 777

NOVEMBER 13

Lesson 317
Today's Reading: *Acts 4–6*
Period of Time: 33 AD
Author: Luke

1. Approximately how many heard the word and believed?

   Acts 4:4

   A. 2,000
   B. 3,000
   C. 4,000
   D. 5,000

2. Who was the high priest?

   Acts 4:6

   A. Annas
   B. Jonas
   C. Ozias
   D. Tiras

3. Approximately how old was the impotent man who was healed?

   Acts 4:9–22

   A. 20 years old
   B. 40 years old
   C. 60 years old
   D. 80 years old

4. Which surname did the apostles give Joses?

   Acts 4:36

   A. Barnabas
   B. Caiaphas
   C. Epaphras
   D. Jeremias

5. Which country was Joses from?

   Acts 4:36

   A. Cyprus
   B. Emmaus
   C. Pontus
   D. Tarsus

6. Which couple lied to the Holy Ghost?

   Acts 5:1–10

   A. Ananias and Sapphira
   B. Aquila and Priscilla
   C. Boaz and Ruth
   D. John and Elisabeth

7. Who freed the apostles from prison?

   Acts 5:18–19

   A. The angel of the LORD
   B. The governor of Judaea
   C. The keeper of the prison
   D. The Roman centurion

8. Where did the apostles go after being set free from prison?

   Acts 5:25

   A. The mount of Olives
   B. The sea of Galilee
   C. The temple
   D. The upper room

9. Who was a doctor of the law?

   Acts 5:34

   A. Apollyon
   B. Gamaliel
   C. Hippocrates
   D. Luke

10. Approximately how many followers did Theudas have?

    Acts 5:36

    A. 100
    B. 200
    C. 300
    D. 400

11. Who had many followers during the days of the taxing?

    Acts 5:37

    A. Cyrus of Persia
    B. Joseph of Arimathaea
    C. Judas of Galilee
    D. Simon of Cyrene

12. Who complained that their widows were being neglected?

    Acts 6:1

    A. The Babylonians
    B. The Grecians
    C. The Parthians
    D. The Romans

13. How many men were chosen to serve tables during the daily ministration?

    Acts 6:1–5

    A. 3
    B. 7
    C. 12
    D. 24

14. Who was one of the chosen to serve tables during the daily ministration?

    Acts 6:2–5

    A. Gideon
    B. Jairus
    C. Nimrod
    D. Philip

15. Who was a proselyte of Antioch?

    Acts 6:5

    A. Artemas
    B. Cleopas
    C. Ezekias
    D. Nicolas

16. What was Stephen falsely accused of?

    Acts 6:11

    A. Adultery
    B. Blasphemy
    C. Murder
    D. Stealing

17. Which council did Stephen appear in front of?

    Acts 6:12

    A. The Greek Council
    B. The Herodian Council
    C. The Jewish Council
    D. The Roman Council

18. Where was Jesus from?

    Acts 6:14

    A. Bethel
    B. Heshbon
    C. Jerusalem
    D. Nazareth

19. Who delivered the customs to the Jews?

    Acts 6:14

    A. Abraham
    B. Eli
    C. Moses
    D. Zachariah

20. What did Stephen's face look like?

    Acts 6:15

    A. A baby's face
    B. A devil's face
    C. An angel's face
    D. An infidel's face

*Answers on page 777

Lesson 318
Today's Reading: *Acts 7–8*
Period of Time: 33–34 AD
Author: Luke

NOVEMBER 14

1. Where did Abraham go after leaving Mesopotamia?
   Acts 7:2
   A. Bethharran
   B. Charran
   C. Naaran
   D. Paran

2. Who lived in Mesopotamia during the time of Abraham?
   Acts 7:4
   A. The Chaldeans
   B. The Epicureans
   C. The Koreans
   D. The Sabeans

3. How many years did the LORD say Abraham's descendants would be in bondage and evil treated?
   Acts 7:6
   A. 100
   B. 200
   C. 300
   D. 400

4. How many days after Isaac was born did Abraham circumcise him?
   Acts 7:8
   A. 3
   B. 8
   C. 14
   D. 21

5. Who was sold as a slave by his brothers?
   Acts 7:9
   A. Elihoreph
   B. Hareph
   C. Joseph
   D. Sheleph

6. How many of Jacob's relatives moved to Egypt—including Jacob?
   Acts 7:14–15
   A. 15
   B. 35
   C. 55
   D. 75

7. Where was Jacob's body laid to rest?
   Acts 7:16
   A. Michri
   B. Rechab
   C. Sychem
   D. Zacher

8. How many months Moses was nourished in his father's house?
   Acts 7:20
   A. 2
   B. 3
   C. 4
   D. 5

9. Which one of Pharaoh's relatives raised Moses as her own son?
   Acts 7:21
   A. His daughter
   B. His mother
   C. His sister
   D. His wife

10. How old was Moses when he fled from Egypt?
    Acts 7:23–29
    A. 18 years old
    B. 21 years old
    C. 40 years old
    D. 80 years old

11. Where did Moses flee to?
    Acts 7:29
    A. Madian
    B. Madmannah
    C. Madmenah
    D. Madon

12. How many sons did Moses have?

    Acts 7:29

    A. 1
    B. 2
    C. 3
    D. 4

13. How many years did the children of Israel spend in the desert?

    Acts 7:36

    A. 20
    B. 40
    C. 60
    D. 80

14. Upon which mountain did Moses receive the lively oracles?

    Acts 7:38

    A. Mount Nebo
    B. Mount Olivet
    C. Mount Pisgah
    D. Mount Sina

15. Which two idols was Israel guilty of worshipping?

    Acts 7:43

    A. Diana and Queen of Heaven
    B. Jupiter and Mercurius
    C. Moloch and Remphan
    D. Nibhaz and Tartak

16. Upon whose feet did the witnesses place their clothes?

    Acts 7:58

    A. Andrew's feet
    B. John's feet
    C. Peter's feet
    D. Saul's feet

17. How was Stephen put to death?

    Acts 7:59

    A. He was crucified.
    B. He was hanged.
    C. He was poisoned.
    D. He was stoned.

18. Who was a sorcerer?

    Acts 8:9

    A. Salu
    B. Sem
    C. Simon
    D. Sosipater

19. Who was the queen of Ethiopia?

    Acts 8:27

    A. Candace
    B. Esther
    C. Nehushta
    D. Vashti

20. Where did Philip go after baptizing the Ethiopian eunuch?

    Acts 8:40

    A. Azotus
    B. Emmaus
    C. Pontus
    D. Tarsus

*Answers on page 777

Lesson 319
Today's Reading: *Acts 9–10*
Period of Time: 35–41 AD
Author: Luke

1. Where was Saul going when he saw the light from heaven?
   Acts 9:1–3
   A. Capernaum
   B. Damascus
   C. Jerusalem
   D. Tyre

2. Who spoke to Saul when he saw the light from heaven?
   Acts 9:4–5
   A. Jesus
   B. Michael the archangel
   C. The angel Gabriel
   D. The angel of the LORD

3. How many days was Saul without sight, and neither did eat nor drink?
   Acts 9:9
   A. 2
   B. 3
   C. 4
   D. 5

4. Who put his hands upon Saul to restore his sight?
   Acts 9:10–18
   A. Ananias
   B. Andronicus
   C. Annas
   D. Antipas

5. On which street was the house of Judas located?
   Acts 9:11
   A. Broadway
   B. First
   C. Main
   D. Straight

6. Where was Saul from?
   Acts 9:11
   A. Ephesus
   B. Miletus
   C. Pontus
   D. Tarsus

7. What did Saul do *first* after regaining his sight?
   Acts 9:18
   A. He ate meat.
   B. He preached in a synagogue.
   C. He spoke in tongues.
   D. He was baptized.

8. How did Saul escape from the Jews?
   Acts 9:23–25
   A. He dressed as a woman.
   B. He faked being a leper.
   C. He hid in a cart.
   D. He went over a wall.

9. Who took Saul to the apostles?
   Acts 9:27
   A. Barabbas
   B. Barnabas
   C. Barsabas
   D. Bartimaeus

10. Whom did Saul dispute with?
    Acts 9:29
    A. The Grecians
    B. The Ionians
    C. The Persians
    D. The Romans

11. In which city did Peter heal a man sick with the palsy?
    Acts 9:32–34
    A. Addan
    B. Enhaddah
    C. Lydda
    D. Middin

12. What was the name of the man sick with the palsy?
    Acts 9:33

    A. Aeneas
    B. Beninu
    C. Henoch
    D. Penuel

13. How many years had the man been sick with the palsy?
    Acts 9:33

    A. 8
    B. 18
    C. 28
    D. 38

14. Whom did Peter bring back from the dead?
    Acts 9:36–41

    A. Eutychus
    B. Lazarus
    C. Paul
    D. Tabitha

15. What was Simon of Joppa's occupation?
    Acts 9:43

    A. Rabbi
    B. Stonecutter
    C. Tanner
    D. Watchman

16. Who was a centurion in Caesarea?
    Acts 10:1

    A. Claudius
    B. Cornelius
    C. Crispus
    D. Cyrenius

17. What did Peter see in his vision?
    Acts 10:9–11

    A. A command to flee to Egypt
    B. A man from Macedonia
    C. A sheet being let down from heaven
    D. A vision of the glories of the third heaven

18. How many men from Caesarea sought Peter?
    Acts 10:19

    A. 2
    B. 3
    C. 4
    D. 5

19. What was the Apostle Simon's surname?
    Acts 10:5, 10:32

    A. Justus
    B. Mark
    C. Peter
    D. Thaddaeus

20. Which spiritual gift did the centurion, his kinsmen, and near friends receive?
    Acts 10:24–46

    A. The gift of exhortation
    B. The gift of prophecy
    C. The gift of tongues
    D. The gift of wisdom

Answers on page 777

Lesson 320

Today's Reading: *Acts 11–13*
Period of Time: 41–45 AD
Author: Luke

NOVEMBER 16

1. Which city was Peter in when he had the vision of the sheet and animals?
   Acts 11:4–5
   A. Corinth
   B. Ephesus
   C. Iconium
   D. Joppa

2. How many times did God tell Peter, "Slay and eat"?
   Acts 11:4–10
   A. 2
   B. 3
   C. 4
   D. 5

3. Which city were the three men from that came to fetch Peter?
   Acts 11:11–12
   A. Alexandria
   B. Caesarea
   C. Jerusalem
   D. Tarsus

4. What was Simon's surname?
   Acts 11:13
   A. James
   B. Mark
   C. Peter
   D. Stephen

5. Whose persecution sent men to preach to the Jews in Phenice, Cyprus, and Antioch?
   Acts 11:19
   A. James' persecution
   B. Mark's persecution
   C. Peter's persecution
   D. Stephen's persecution

6. Where was the church located that sent Barnabas to Antioch?
   Acts 11:22
   A. Alexandria
   B. Caesarea
   C. Jerusalem
   D. Tarsus

7. Where was Saul from?
   Acts 11:25
   A. Alexandria
   B. Caesarea
   C. Jerusalem
   D. Tarsus

8. Where were the disciples called Christians the first time?
   Acts 11:26
   A. Antioch
   B. Corinth
   C. Ephesus
   D. Smyrna

9. Which prophet told of a great dearth?
   Acts 11:27–28
   A. Agabus
   B. Enoch
   C. Nathan
   D. Uriah

10. Who was reigning when the dearth occurred?
    Acts 11:28
    A. Augustus Caesar
    B. Claudius Caesar
    C. Nero Caesar
    D. Tiberius Caesar

11. Which disciple did King Herod kill?
    Acts 12:1–2
    A. James
    B. Mark
    C. Peter
    D. Stephen

12. Which disciple did King Herod cast into prison?

    Acts 12:3–4

    A. Bartholomew
    B. Nathanael
    C. Peter
    D. Simeon

13. After which holiday was King Herod going to bring the imprisoned disciple forth to the people?

    Acts 12:4

    A. Christmas
    B. Easter
    C. Halloween
    D. Thanksgiving

14. Who was John's mother?

    Acts 12:12

    A. Dorcas
    B. Hadassah
    C. Mary
    D. Rhoda

15. Who answered the door and saw Peter?

    Acts 12:13

    A. Dorcas
    B. Hadassah
    C. Mary
    D. Rhoda

16. Who was the king's chamberlain?

    Acts 12:20

    A. Blastus
    B. Philetus
    C. Tertullus
    D. Zacchaeus

17. What was John's surname?

    Acts 12:12, 12:25

    A. James
    B. Mark
    C. Peter
    D. Stephen

18. Who was called Niger?

    Acts 13:1

    A. Bartholomew
    B. Nathanael
    C. Peter
    D. Simeon

19. Which false prophet went blind for a season?

    Acts 13:6–11

    A. Bar-jesus
    B. Ebed-melech
    C. Ir-nahash
    D. Shethar-boznai

20. Where did Paul and Barnabas go after leaving Antioch in Pisidia?

    Acts 13:14–51

    A. Corinth
    B. Ephesus
    C. Iconium
    D. Joppa

*Answers on page 777

NOVEMBER 17

Lesson 321
Today's Reading: *Acts 14–16*
Period of Time: 45–53 AD
Author: Luke

1. Whom did Peter heal in Lystra?
   Acts 14:8
   A. A man possessed by demons
   B. A man with crippled feet
   C. A woman blind since birth
   D. A woman with an issue of blood

2. What did the people of Lystra call *Barnabas*?
   Acts 14:12
   A. Apollo
   B. Jupiter
   C. Mercurius
   D. Poseidon

3. What did the people of Lystra call *Paul*?
   Acts 14:12
   A. Apollo
   B. Jupiter
   C. Mercurius
   D. Poseidon

4. How did the crowd try to kill Paul?
   Acts 14:19
   A. By drowning him in the river
   B. By hanging him from a tree
   C. By stoning him with stones
   D. By throwing him from a cliff

5. Where did Paul and Barnabas travel to after leaving Lystra?
   Acts 14:20
   A. Derbe
   B. India
   C. Joppa
   D. Spain

6. Where did the apostles and elders meet to discuss church issues?
   Acts 15:1–4
   A. Alexandria
   B. Caesarea
   C. Jerusalem
   D. Rome

7. Who spoke *first* at the meeting?
   Acts 15:7–11
   A. Barnabas and Paul
   B. James
   C. Mark
   D. Peter

8. Who spoke *second* at the meeting?
   Acts 15:12
   A. Barnabas and Paul
   B. James
   C. Mark
   D. Peter

9. Who spoke *last* at the meeting?
   Acts 15:13–21
   A. Barnabas and Paul
   B. James
   C. Mark
   D. Peter

10. What was Judas' surname?
    Acts 15:22
    A. Barsabas
    B. Jeremiah
    C. Matthias
    D. Tyrannus

11. Who accompanied Paul, Barnabas, and Judas to Antioch?
    Acts 15:22
    A. Silas
    B. Simon
    C. Sippai
    D. Sisera

12. What was John's surname?
    Acts 15:37
    A. Luke
    B. Mark
    C. Paul
    D. Saul

13. Which two men traveled through Syria and Cilicia?

    Acts 15:40–41

    A. Barnabas and Mark
    B. James and Timotheus
    C. Paul and Silas
    D. Thomas and Luke

14. What was Timotheus' mother's ethnicity?

    Acts 16:1

    A. Egyptian
    B. Greek
    C. Jewish
    D. Roman

15. What was Timotheus' father's ethnicity?

    Acts 16:1

    A. Egyptian
    B. Greek
    C. Jewish
    D. Roman

16. Which one of the following is a chief city of Macedonia?

    Acts 16:12

    A. Damascus
    B. Gomorrah
    C. Mattanah
    D. Philippi

17. Who was a seller of purple?

    Acts 16:14

    A. Lydia
    B. Naomi
    C. Rhoda
    D. Tamar

18. Approximately when did the earthquake shake the foundations of the prison?

    Acts 16:25–26

    A. At the sixth hour
    B. At noon
    C. At the twelfth hour
    D. At midnight

19. Whom did Paul baptize?

    Acts 16:27–33

    A. His cell mate
    B. His lawyer
    C. The judge who freed him
    D. The keeper of the prison

20. Which nation did Paul tell the magistrates he was a citizen of?

    Acts 16:37

    A. Crete
    B. Egypt
    C. Greece
    D. Rome

*Answers on page 777

NOVEMBER 18

Lesson 322
Today's Reading: *Acts 17–18*
Period of Time: 53–56 AD
Author: Luke

1. How many sabbath days did Paul preach in Thessalonica?
   Acts 17:1–3
   A. 2
   B. 3
   C. 4
   D. 5

2. Whose house in Thessalonica did the Jews assault?
   Acts 17:5
   A. Dekar's house
   B. Haman's house
   C. Jason's house
   D. Rufus's house

3. Who received the word with all readiness of mind and searched the scriptures daily?
   Acts 17:10–11
   A. The Bereans
   B. The Chaldeans
   C. The Epicureans
   D. The Sabeans

4. Whom did Paul order to meet him in Athens?
   Acts 17:14–15
   A. Barnabas and Cleo
   B. Luke and Peter
   C. Matthew and John
   D. Silas and Timotheus

5. Which philosophers questioned Paul?
   Acts 17:18
   A. The Confucians and the Buddhists
   B. The Epicureans and the Stoicks
   C. The Hindus and the Nazis
   D. The Platonists and Socratics

6. Which court of justice did the philosophers take Paul to?
   Acts 17:19
   A. Areopagus
   B. Domus Aurea
   C. Praetorium
   D. Senatus Populusque Romanus

7. Where did Paul preach to the Athenians?
   Acts 17:22
   A. Jupiter's cave
   B. Mars' hill
   C. Saturn's mountain
   D. Venus' valley

8. Which inscription was found on the altar Paul referred to in Athens?
   Acts 17:23
   A. TO THE GODDESS DIANA
   B. TO THE GREAT ZEUS
   C. TO THE SCALES OF JUSTICE
   D. TO THE UNKNOWN GOD

9. What was Dionysius' surname?
   Acts 17:34
   A. The Areopagite
   B. The Hittite
   C. The Levite
   D. The Perrizzite

10. Which Athenian woman became a believer in Jesus Christ?
    Acts 17:34
    A. Alanis
    B. Damaris
    C. Lois
    D. Persis

11. Where was Aquila born?
    Acts 18:2
    A. Cyprus
    B. Emmaus
    C. Miletus
    D. Pontus

12. Who commanded all Jews to depart from Rome?

    Acts 18:2

    A. Augustus
    B. Claudius
    C. Tiberius
    D. Titus

13. What was Paul's occupation?

    Acts 18:3

    A. Baker
    B. Carpenter
    C. Lawyer
    D. Tentmaker

14. Whose house was attached to a synagogue in Corinth?

    Acts 18:7

    A. Agabus' house
    B. Carpus' house
    C. Justus' house
    D. Titus' house

15. Who was the chief ruler of a synagogue in Corinth?

    Acts 18:8

    A. Carpus
    B. Cornelius
    C. Crispus
    D. Cyrus

16. How many months did Paul stay in Corinth?

    Acts 18:11

    A. 6
    B. 12
    C. 18
    D. 24

17. Who was the deputy of Achaia?

    Acts 18:12

    A. Dishan
    B. Festus
    C. Gallio
    D. Ithran

18. Who was the chief ruler of a synagogue that was beaten by the Greeks in Corinth?

    Acts 18:17

    A. Aphses
    B. Boanerges
    C. Hermogenes
    D. Sosthenes

19. Where did Paul shave his head?

    Acts 18:18

    A. Cenchrea
    B. Nazareth
    C. Philippi
    D. Syracuse

20. Where was Apollos born?

    Acts 18:24

    A. Alexandria
    B. Amphipolis
    C. Arimathaea
    D. Armageddon

*Answers on page 777

NOVEMBER 19

Lesson 323
Today's Reading: *Acts 19–20*
Period of Time: 56–60 AD
Author: Luke

1. Who preached the gospel in Corinth while Paul was in Ephesus?
   Acts 19:1
   A. Apollos
   B. Barkos
   C. Enos
   D. Keros

2. Approximately how many disciples received the baptism in the Holy Ghost in Ephesus?
   Acts 19:1–7
   A. 3
   B. 8
   C. 12
   D. 70

3. Who owned a school in Ephesus?
   Acts 19:9
   A. Archelaus
   B. Lebbaeus
   C. Onesimus
   D. Tyrannus

4. What did the people take from Paul to heal the sick?
   Acts 19:11–12
   A. Ashes or dirt
   B. Handkerchiefs or aprons
   C. Ointments or herbs
   D. Water or oil

5. How many sons did Sceva have?
   Acts 19:14
   A. 3
   B. 4
   C. 7
   D. 12

6. How many pieces of silver were the books worth that were burned?
   Acts 19:19
   A. 10,000
   B. 50,000
   C. 100,000
   D. 200,000

7. Whom did Paul send to Macedonia?
   Acts 19:22
   A. Augustus and Claudius
   B. Gaius and Epaenetus
   C. Secundus and Blastus
   D. Timotheus and Erastus

8. Who was a silversmith?
   Acts 19:24
   A. Cornelius
   B. Demetrius
   C. Silvanus
   D. Theophilus

9. Which two of Paul's traveling companions came with him from Macedonia?
   Acts 19:29
   A. Claudius and Secundus
   B. Eutychus and Augustus
   C. Gaius and Aristarchus
   D. Timotheus and Tychicus

10. Which Jewish man tried to quiet the crowd at Ephesus?
    Acts 19:33
    A. Adonibezek
    B. Ahasuerus
    C. Alexander
    D. Ammon

11. How many hours did the crowd cry out, "Great is Diana of the Ephesians"?

    Acts 19:34

    A. 1
    B. 2
    C. 3
    D. 4

12. Who eventually quieted the crowd?

    Acts 19:35–41

    A. The chief captain
    B. The deputy
    C. The sheriff
    D. The townclerk

13. Which planet did the Ephesians believe the image of Diana came from?

    Acts 19:35

    A. Jupiter
    B. Mars
    C. Neptune
    D. Saturn

14. Who was from Berea?

    Acts 20:4

    A. Alexander
    B. Bethgader
    C. Jesher
    D. Sopater

15. Who was from Thessalonica?

    Acts 20:4

    A. Aristarchus and Secundus
    B. Claudius and Augustus
    C. Gaius and Timotheus
    D. Tychicus and Trophimus

16. Who was from Derbe?

    Acts 20:4

    A. Augustus
    B. Claudius
    C. Gaius
    D. Titus

17. Who was from Asia?

    Acts 20:4

    A. Aristarchus and Secundus
    B. Claudius and Augustus
    C. Gaius and Timotheus
    D. Tychicus and Trophimus

18. On which day of the week did the disciples come together to break bread?

    Acts 20:7

    A. 1st
    B. 3rd
    C. 6th
    D. 7th

19. Whom did Paul bring back from the dead?

    Acts 20:9–12

    A. Dorcas
    B. Eutychus
    C. Lazarus
    D. Tabitha

20. Where did Luke meet Paul?

    Acts 20:13–14

    A. Assos
    B. Berea
    C. Corinth
    D. Damascus

Answers on page 777

NOVEMBER 20

Lesson 324
Today's Reading: *Acts 21–22*
Period of Time: 60 AD
Author: Luke

1. How many days did Paul stay in Ptolemais?
   Acts 21:7
   A. 1
   B. 7
   C. 10
   D. 28

2. Where did Paul travel to after leaving Ptolemais?
   Acts 21:8
   A. Berea
   B. Caesarea
   C. Idumaea
   D. Judaea

3. What was Philip's title?
   Acts 21:8
   A. Bishop
   B. Deacon
   C. Evangelist
   D. Missionary

4. How many daughters did Philip have?
   Acts 21:9
   A. 1
   B. 2
   C. 3
   D. 4

5. Who told Paul the Jews in Jerusalem would bind him?
   Acts 21:10–11
   A. Agabus
   B. Carpus
   C. Darius
   D. Festus

6. Who was the old disciple from Cyprus?
   Acts 21:16
   A. Jason
   B. Mnason
   C. Naasson
   D. Samson

7. Whom did Paul meet in Jerusalem?
   Acts 21:17–18
   A. Jabez
   B. Jacob
   C. James
   D. Jason

8. How many men were purified with Paul?
   Acts 21:23–26
   A. 4
   B. 8
   C. 12
   D. 16

9. How many days did it take to be purified?
   Acts 21:23–27
   A. 3
   B. 5
   C. 7
   D. 9

10. Who did the Jews suppose Paul had brought into the temple?
    Acts 21:29
    A. Lazarus
    B. Marcus
    C. Onesimus
    D. Trophimus

11. Which Roman official rescued Paul from the Jews?
    Acts 21:31–33
    A. The chief captain of the band
    B. The deputy of Jerusalem
    C. The governor of Palestine
    D. The senator from Rome

12. How many chains did the Romans use to bind Paul?
    Acts 21:33
    A. 1
    B. 2
    C. 3
    D. 4

13. How many murderers—supposedly—did a certain Egyptian lead into the wilderness?

    Acts 21:38

    A. 1,000
    B. 2,000
    C. 3,000
    D. 4,000

14. Where is Tarsus located?

    Acts 21:39

    A. Assyria
    B. Bithynia
    C. Cilicia
    D. Dalmatia

15. Who taught Paul the law of the fathers?

    Acts 22:3

    A. Ezekiel
    B. Gamaliel
    C. Jekuthiel
    D. Salathiel

16. Where was Paul traveling to when he saw the great light?

    Acts 22:5–6

    A. Cyprus
    B. Damascus
    C. Ephesus
    D. Miletus

17. Whom did God use to restore Paul's sight?

    Acts 22:12–13

    A. Ananias
    B. Ezekias
    C. Jeremias
    D. Lysanias

18. What did the man who restored Paul's sight call Jesus?

    Acts 22:14

    A. Doctor of Israel
    B. Glorious Healer
    C. Merciful Physician
    D. The Just One

19. Which one of the following was a martyr?

    Acts 22:20

    A. Jashen
    B. Manaen
    C. Stephen
    D. Reuben

20. Which nation did Paul tell the centurion he was a citizen of?

    Acts 22:25–29

    A. Babylon
    B. Greece
    C. Israel
    D. Rome

*Answers on page 777

NOVEMBER 21

Lesson 325
Today's Reading: *Acts 23–25*
Period of Time: 60–62 AD
Author: Luke

1. Who was the high priest?
   Acts 23:2, 24:1
   A. Ananias
   B. Jahaziel
   C. Nadab
   D. Zadok

2. What did Paul call the high priest?
   Acts 23:3
   A. A child of the devil
   B. A fiery serpent
   C. A murdering thief
   D. A whited wall

3. Which religious sect did Paul belong to?
   Acts 23:6
   A. Herodians
   B. Pharisees
   C. Sadducees
   D. Samaritans

4. Which religious sect did **not** believe in resurrections, angels, or spirits?
   Acts 23:8
   A. Herodians
   B. Pharisees
   C. Sadducees
   D. Samaritans

5. Approximately how many Jews vowed they would neither eat nor drink till they had killed Paul?
   Acts 23:12–13
   A. 4
   B. 40
   C. 400
   D. 4,000

6. Who warned Paul of the plot to murder him?
   Acts 23:12–16
   A. His brother
   B. His cousin
   C. His nephew
   D. His sister

7. How many centurions did the Roman chief captain call upon?
   Acts 23:22–23
   A. 2
   B. 4
   C. 6
   D. 8

8. How many Roman *soldiers* were ordered to escort Paul to Caesarea?
   Acts 23:23
   A. 50
   B. 100
   C. 150
   D. 200

9. How many Roman *horsemen* were ordered to escort Paul to Caesarea?
   Acts 23:23
   A. 10
   B. 30
   C. 50
   D. 70

10. How many Roman *spearmen* were ordered to escort Paul to Caesarea?
    Acts 23:23
    A. 100
    B. 200
    C. 300
    D. 400

11. During which hour of the night did the Roman army prepare to leave Jerusalem?
    Acts 23:23
    A. 1st
    B. 2nd
    C. 3rd
    D. 4th

12. Who was the Roman chief captain?

    Acts 23:26, 24:22

    A. Claudius Lysias
    B. Gaius Amafinius
    C. Marcus Aurelius
    D. Pontus Aquila

13. Where did the Roman *soldiers* part ways from Paul and the Roman *horsemen*?

    Acts 23:31–32

    A. Antipatris
    B. Hierapolis
    C. Memphis
    D. Ptolemais

14. What province was Paul from?

    Acts 23:34

    A. Bithynia
    B. Cilicia
    C. Lydia
    D. Phrygia

15. Who was an orator?

    Acts 24:1

    A. Lucius
    B. Publius
    C. Silvanus
    D. Tertullus

16. Which sect did the Jewish rulers claim Paul was the ringleader of?

    Acts 24:5

    A. The Babylonians
    B. The Epicureans
    C. The Nazarenes
    D. The Stoicks

17. Who was Felix's wife?

    Acts 24:24

    A. Claudia
    B. Drusilla
    C. Joanna
    D. Mara

18. What was Festus's first name?

    Acts 24:27

    A. Decius
    B. Lucius
    C. Marcus
    D. Porcius

19. Which king questioned Paul?

    Acts 25:13–27

    A. King Agabus
    B. King Agag
    C. King Agrippa
    D. King Agur

20. Who was the Roman emperor?

    Acts 25:21–25

    A. Augustus
    B. Florianus
    C. Probus
    D. Severus

*Answers on page 778

Lesson 326
Today's Reading: *Acts 26–28*
Period of Time: 62–65 AD
Author: Luke

NOVEMBER 22

1. Which religious sect did Paul belong to?
   Acts 26:5
   A. Herodians
   B. Pharisees
   C. Publicans
   D. Samaritans

2. What was the total number of Jewish tribes?
   Acts 26:7
   A. 12
   B. 28
   C. 35
   D. 44

3. Where was Paul traveling to when he saw a light from heaven?
   Acts 26:12–13
   A. Antioch
   B. Corinth
   C. Damascus
   D. Thessalonica

4. Who told Paul, "It is hard for thee to kick against the pricks"?
   Acts 26:14–15
   A. James
   B. Jesus
   C. John
   D. Judas

5. Who told Paul, "Much learning doth make thee mad"?
   Acts 26:24
   A. Agrippa
   B. Festus
   C. Julius
   D. Publius

6. Who told Paul, "Almost thou persuades me to be a Christian"?
   Acts 26:28
   A. Agrippa
   B. Festus
   C. Julius
   D. Publius

7. Who was a centurion of Augustus' band?
   Acts 27:1
   A. Agrippa
   B. Festus
   C. Julius
   D. Publius

8. Where was the ship from that Paul boarded in Caesarea?
   Acts 27:2
   A. Adramyttium
   B. Capernaum
   C. Praetorium
   D. Trogyllium

9. Who was a Macedonian of Thessalonica?
   Acts 27:2
   A. Achaicus
   B. Alphaeus
   C. Andronicus
   D. Aristarchus

10. Which town was located in Lycia?
    Acts 27:5
    A. Athens
    B. Lasea
    C. Myra
    D. Phenice

11. Which city was near The Fair Havens?
    Acts 27:8
    A. Athens
    B. Lasea
    C. Myra
    D. Phenice

12. Which city was a haven of Crete?

    Acts 27:12

    A. Athens
    B. Lasea
    C. Myra
    D. Phenice

13. What was the name of the tempestuous wind?

    Acts 27:14

    A. Africanushydon
    B. Blastomegaladon
    C. Cyclobelladon
    D. Euroclydon

14. How many souls were onboard the ship?

    Acts 27:37

    A. 134
    B. 190
    C. 258
    D. 276

15. On which island was Paul shipwrecked?

    Acts 28:1

    A. Cos
    B. Lesbos
    C. Melita
    D. Patmos

16. Why did the barbarians call Paul a god?

    Acts 28:3–6

    A. He appeared in a chariot of fire.
    B. He calmed a storm on the sea.
    C. He survived a poisonous snake bite.
    D. He walked upon the sea without sinking.

17. Whose father did Paul heal?

    Acts 28:7–8

    A. Augustus' father
    B. Festus' father
    C. Julius' father
    D. Publius' father

18. Which two symbols were on the ship from Alexandria?

    Acts 28:11

    A. Castor and Pollux
    B. Neptune and Poseidon
    C. Oceanus and Delphinus
    D. Remus and Romulus

19. How many days did Paul tarry in Syracuse?

    Acts 28:12

    A. 2
    B. 3
    C. 4
    D. 5

20. How many years did Paul dwell in his own hired house in Rome?

    Acts 28:16–30

    A. 2
    B. 3
    C. 4
    D. 5

*Answers on page 778

NOVEMBER 23

Lesson 327
Today's Reading: *Romans 1–3*
Period of Time: 60 AD
Author: Paul

1. What does Paul call himself?
   Romans 1:1
   A. A priest
   B. A prisoner
   C. A servant
   D. A slave

2. What does Paul say he has been called to be?
   Romans 1:1
   A. An apostle
   B. An evangelist
   C. An intercessor
   D. An orphan

3. Whose seed did Jesus come from according to the flesh?
   Romans 1:3
   A. David
   B. Ham
   C. Ishmael
   D. Japheth

4. Which two of the following have believers received from Jesus' resurrection?
   Romans 1:5
   A. Abandonment and deaconship
   B. Grace and apostleship
   C. Sorrow and ambassadorship
   D. Tribulations and discipleship

5. What does Paul say the believers in Rome have been called to be?
   Romans 1:7
   A. Angels
   B. Deacons
   C. Prophets
   D. Saints

6. Whom does Paul say he is indebted to?
   Romans 1:14
   A. Egyptians and Babylonians
   B. Greeks and Barbarians
   C. Jews and Hittites
   D. Romans and Assyrians

7. What does Paul say he is **not** ashamed of?
   Romans 1:16
   A. His criminal past
   B. His Jewish heritage
   C. The gospel of Christ
   D. The idols in his house

8. What kind of mind does God give those who commit homosexuality?
   Romans 1:24–28
   A. A reprobate mind
   B. A spotless mind
   C. An undefiled mind
   D. An untarnished mind

9. Whom shall the glory, honour, and peace come upon first who worketh good?
   Romans 2:10
   A. The Barbarian
   B. The Greek
   C. The Jew
   D. The Roman

10. What will God **not** do?
    Romans 2:11
    A. Forgive sins
    B. Heal diseases
    C. Love children
    D. Respect persons

11. How do Gentiles—who have never been taught—know Moses' law?
    Romans 2:14–15
    A. By being circumcised
    B. By learning Hebrew
    C. By nature
    D. By observing the stars

12. What does Paul say his enemies are guilty of?
    Romans 3:8
    A. Adultery
    B. Idolatry
    C. Murder
    D. Slander

13. What does Paul call the throats of sinners?

    Romans 3:13

    A. A bottomless pit
    B. A gluttonous hole
    C. A narrow passageway
    D. An open sepulchre

14. What does Paul say is under the lips of sinners?

    Romans 3:13

    A. The poison of asps
    B. The roots of evil
    C. The sweetness of deceit
    D. The taste of blood

15. What are the feet of sinners swift to do?

    Romans 3:15

    A. Dance for God
    B. Kick the goads
    C. Shed blood
    D. Walk the glory road

16. What does Paul say sinners have **not** known?

    Romans 3:17

    A. The path of liberty
    B. The road of freedom
    C. The trail of tears
    D. The way of peace

17. What do sinners come short of?

    Romans 3:23

    A. Evil
    B. God's glory
    C. Sinful pleasures
    D. Worldly wisdom

18. What does Paul call Jesus?

    Romans 3:25

    A. A professional
    B. A propitiation
    C. A prospect
    D. A protector

19. What is a man justified by without the deeds of the law?

    Romans 3:28

    A. Faith
    B. Liberty
    C. Tithes
    D. Works

20. What does Paul say believers do regarding the law?

    Romans 3:31

    A. Break the law
    B. Establish the law
    C. Forget the law
    D. Rewrite the law

Answers on page 778

NOVEMBER 24

Lesson 328
Today's Reading: *Romans 4–7*
Period of Time: 60 AD
Author: Paul

1. Who said, "Blessed is the man to whom the Lord will **not** impute sin"?
   Romans 4:6–8
   A. Abraham
   B. David
   C. Job
   D. Solomon

2. What was the sign Abraham received as a seal of the righteousness of his faith?
   Romans 4:9–11
   A. Circumcision
   B. Communion
   C. Conviction
   D. Crucifixion

3. What promise did God give to Abraham?
   Romans 4:16–18
   A. He would be the father of many nations.
   B. He would live to be 100 years old.
   C. His daughter would marry an Egyptian.
   D. His son would one day rule Egypt.

4. Approximately how many years old was Abraham when Sarah became pregnant?
   Romans 4:19
   A. 60
   B. 80
   C. 100
   D. 120

5. How is a believer justified?
   Romans 5:1
   A. By class
   B. By faith
   C. By traditions
   D. By works

6. What does tribulation worketh?
   Romans 5:3
   A. Doubt
   B. Fear
   C. Patience
   D. Trouble

7. What does experience worketh?
   Romans 5:4
   A. Blindness
   B. Folly
   C. Hope
   D. Simplicity

8. How did God commend his love toward us?
   Romans 5:8
   A. Christ died for us.
   B. God forsook us.
   C. He gave us Mother Nature.
   D. The Holy Spirit rebuked us.

9. What does a person need in order to stand in God's holy presence?
   Romans 5:11
   A. Atonement
   B. Prestige
   C. Riches
   D. Status

10. Through whose transgression did sin enter the world?
    Romans 5:12–14
    A. Abel's transgression
    B. Adam's transgression
    C. Cain's transgression
    D. Eve's transgression

11. How much does salvation cost a person?
    Romans 5:15–18
    A. A life of piety
    B. An arm and a leg
    C. His blood, sweat, and tears
    D. Nothing, it is free

12. What does baptism represent?
    Romans 6:3–5
    A. Cleanliness is next to Godliness
    B. Great deluge
    C. John the Baptist
    D. The believer buried and raised with Christ

13. What is crucified with Christ so that the body of sin might be destroyed?

    Romans 6:6

    A. Animals
    B. Our old man
    C. Thieves
    D. Zealots

14. What does a person become after being made free from sin?

    Romans 6:18

    A. Kings of holiness
    B. Lords of discipline
    C. Servants of righteousness
    D. Tyrants of sinners

15. What *is* the wages of sin?

    Romans 6:23

    A. Birth
    B. Death
    C. Hope
    D. Jealousy

16. What shall a woman be called who marries another man while her first husband is still alive?

    Romans 7:1–3

    A. A busybody
    B. A modern woman
    C. A prima donna
    D. An adulteress

17. Which commandment taught Paul **not** to lust?

    Romans 7:7

    A. Thou shalt have no other gods before me.
    B. Thou shalt keep holy the sabbath day.
    C. Thou shalt not covet.
    D. Thou shalt not steal.

18. What word does Paul use for lust?

    Romans 7:8

    A. Concupiscence
    B. Incontinence
    C. Nonsense
    D. Prurience

19. What does Paul say the law is?

    Romans 7:14

    A. Carnal
    B. Natural
    C. Ritual
    D. Spiritual

20. What does Paul call himself?

    Romans 7:24–25

    A. A business man
    B. A holy man
    C. A righteous man
    D. A wretched man

Answers on page 778

Lesson 329
Today's Reading: *Romans 8–10*
Period of Time: 60 AD
Author: Paul

NOVEMBER 25

1. What is **not** found in them who are in Christ?
   Romans 8:1
   A. Condemnation
   B. Purification
   C. Salvation
   D. Sanctification

2. What law does the law of the Spirit of life in Christ Jesus make the believer free from?
   Romans 8:2
   A. Signs and wonders
   B. Sin and death
   C. Tears and suffering
   D. Trials and tribulations

3. What is it to be carnally minded?
   Romans 8:6
   A. Birth
   B. Death
   C. Law
   D. Spirit

4. What is it to be spiritually minded?
   Romans 8:6
   A. Death and heaven
   B. Hope and darkness
   C. Life and peace
   D. Truth and hell

5. What is the carnal mind enmity against?
   Romans 8:7
   A. God
   B. Man
   C. Rulers
   D. Satan

6. What is dead because of sin if Christ be in you?
   Romans 8:10
   A. The body
   B. The mind
   C. The soul
   D. The spirit

7. What does Paul call believers?
   Romans 8:12
   A. Creditors
   B. Debtors
   C. Impostors
   D. Protestors

8. Which spirit does the believer receive?
   Romans 8:15
   A. Spirit of adoption
   B. Spirit of jealousy
   C. Spirit of pride
   D. Spirit of rebellion

9. Which name does Paul use for God?
   Romans 8:15
   A. Abba, Father
   B. Everlasting Father
   C. Father of lights
   D. Our Father

10. What was the creature made subject to?
    Romans 8:20
    A. Abasement
    B. Humbleness
    C. Modesty
    D. Vanity

11. What does Paul say he and other believers have received?
    Romans 8:23
    A. The bread and wine of Christ
    B. The firstfruits of the Spirit
    C. The gift of prophecy
    D. The tabernacle of God

12. What are believers saved by?
    Romans 8:24
    A. Deeds
    B. Fear
    C. Hope
    D. Law

13. Who was Isaac's wife?

    Romans 9:10

    A. Bathsheba
    B. Drusilla
    C. Priscilla
    D. Rebecca

14. Which one of Isaac's sons did God *love*?

    Romans 9:13

    A. David
    B. Hezekiah
    C. Jacob
    D. Solomon

15. Which one of Isaac's sons did God *hate*?

    Romans 9:13

    A. Cain
    B. Dathan
    C. Esau
    D. Korah

16. Whom did God raise up so that he could show his power and that God's name might be declared throughout all the earth?

    Romans 9:17

    A. Alexander the Great
    B. Caesar
    C. Nebuchadnezzar
    D. Pharaoh

17. Which prophet said God would call them his people who were **not** his people?

    Romans 9:25

    A. Amos
    B. Joel
    C. Osee
    D. Shem

18. What shall happen if a person confesses with his mouth and believes in his heart that God raised Lord Jesus from the dead?

    Romans 10:9

    A. He shall be an outcast.
    B. He shall be condemned.
    C. He shall be guilty.
    D. He shall be saved.

19. Which prophet asked, "Lord, who has believed our report?"

    Romans 10:16

    A. Ahijah
    B. Esaias
    C. Jonah
    D. Nahum

20. How does faith come to a person?

    Romans 10:17

    A. By becoming an ordained minister
    B. By denying worldly pleasures
    C. By doing more good than bad
    D. By hearing the word of God

*Answers on page 778

NOVEMBER 26

Lesson 330
Today's Reading: *Romans 11–14*
Period of Time: 60 AD
Author: Paul

1. Which tribe did Paul belong to?
   Romans 11:1
   A. The tribe of Benjamin
   B. The tribe of Reuben
   C. The tribe of Simeon
   D. The tribe of Zebulun

2. Who said, "Lord, they have killed thy prophets, and digged down thine altars, and I am left alone, and they seek my life"?
   Romans 11:2–3
   A. Amos
   B. Caleb
   C. Daniel
   D. Elias

3. How many men had **not** bowed the knee to the image of Baal?
   Romans 11:4
   A. 1,000
   B. 3,000
   C. 5,000
   D. 7,000

4. Who said, "Let their table be made a snare, and a trap, and a stumblingblock, and a recompence unto them"?
   Romans 11:9
   A. Abraham
   B. David
   C. Joseph
   D. Saul

5. Which kind of wild tree did Paul use in his illustration?
   Romans 11:17–24
   A. The ash tree
   B. The elm tree
   C. The dogwood tree
   D. The olive tree

6. Which name does Paul use for Jesus Christ?
   Romans 11:26
   A. The Life
   B. The Deliverer
   C. The Truth
   D. The Way

7. What is the believer to present his body as?
   Romans 12:1
   A. A holy god
   B. A living sacrifice
   C. A perfect specimen
   D. An anointed idol

8. How is the believer to be transformed?
   Romans 12:2
   A. By keeping the law
   B. By not borrowing money
   C. By renewing his mind
   D. By selling all he has for the poor

9. How is a person to use his gift of prophecy?
   Romans 12:6
   A. According to the proportion of faith
   B. According to the stars alignment
   C. According to the tea leaves
   D. According to the words of wizards

10. How is a person to use his gift of giving?
    Romans 12:8
    A. With diligence
    B. With simplicity
    C. Without dissimulation
    D. Without emulation

11. How is a person to rule?
    Romans 12:8
    A. With diligence
    B. With simplicity
    C. Without dissimulation
    D. Without emulation

12. How is a person to love?

    Romans 12:9

    A. With diligence
    B. With simplicity
    C. Without dissimulation
    D. Without emulation

13. What does Paul say a person is **not** to be slothful in?

    Romans 12:11

    A. Business
    B. Hygiene
    C. Meals
    D. Sleep

14. What does Paul say a person is **not** to be wise in?

    Romans 12:16

    A. Church
    B. Class
    C. Conceits
    D. Country

15. Whom does vengeance belong to?

    Romans 12:19

    A. The Lord
    B. The offender
    C. The prosecutor
    D. The victim

16. What is a person doing when he gives his enemy food or drink?

    Romans 12:20

    A. Fraternizing with the enemy
    B. Giving him poison
    C. Heaping coals of fire on his head
    D. Starving his own family

17. What does Paul say regarding rulers?

    Romans 13:3–4

    A. They are weak leaders.
    B. They do not bear the sword in vain.
    C. They live short lives.
    D. They overburden the people.

18. Which statement does Paul state regarding money?

    Romans 13:8

    A. "A penny saved is a penny earned."
    B. "Buy low, sell high."
    C. "Don't put all your eggs in one basket."
    D. "Owe no man any thing."

19. What shall every person appear before?

    Romans 14:10

    A. The doors of purgatory
    B. The gates of hell
    C. The judgment seat of Christ
    D. The pearly gates

20. What does Paul say the kingdom of God is **not**?

    Romans 14:17

    A. Darkness and light
    B. Hot and cold
    C. Love and hate
    D. Meat and drink

Answers on page 778

Lesson 331
Today's Reading: *Romans 15–16*
Period of Time: 60 AD
Author: Paul

NOVEMBER 27

1. Who said, "There shall be a root of Jesse, and he that shall rise to reign over the Gentiles; in him shall the Gentiles trust"?
   Romans 15:12
   A. Amos
   B. Esaias
   C. Hosea
   D. Moses

2. Where was Paul planning to travel to?
   Romans 15:24–28
   A. Asia
   B. Egypt
   C. Greece
   D. Spain

3. Where were the churches located that gave gifts to the poor saints in Jerusalem?
   Romans 15:26
   A. Corinth and Smyrna
   B. Ephesus and Laodicea
   C. Macedonia and Achaia
   D. Philadelphia and Thyatira

4. Whom does Paul call *a sister and a servant of the church in Cenchrea?*
   Romans 16:1
   A. Lydia
   B. Phebe
   C. Rahel
   D. Timna

5. Whom does Paul call *his helpers in Christ Jesus?*
   Romans 16:3
   A. Drusilla and Baara
   B. Jerusha and Rhoda
   C. Priscilla and Aquila
   D. Tabitha and Martha

6. Whom does Paul call *the firstfruits of Achaia unto Christ?*
   Romans 16:5
   A. Epaenetus
   B. Gaius
   C. Quartus
   D. Tertius

7. Who does Paul say *bestowed much labour on us?*
   Romans 16:6
   A. Jael
   B. Lois
   C. Mary
   D. Puah

8. Whom does Paul call *his kinsmen and fellow-prisoners?*
   Romans 16:7
   A. Andronicus and Junia
   B. Bartimaeus and Rezia
   C. Fortunatus and Uzzia
   D. Onesiphorus and Sia

9. Whom does Paul call *our helper in Christ?*
   Romans 16:9
   A. Arisai
   B. Irijah
   C. Prisca
   D. Urbane

10. Whom does Paul call *approved in Christ?*
    Romans 16:10
    A. Apelles
    B. Aphses
    C. Apollos
    D. Appaim

11. Whom does Paul call *my kinsman?*
    Romans 16:11
    A. Chilion
    B. Herodion
    C. Jadon
    D. Ziphion

12. Which two individuals does Paul say *labour in the Lord?*

    Romans 16:12

    A. Bathsheba and Bathshua
    B. Ephratah and Ephrath
    C. Julia and Junia
    D. Tryphena and Tryphosa

13. Who does Paul say *laboured much in the Lord?*

    Romans 16:12

    A. Persis
    B. Phuvah
    C. Pithon
    D. Putiel

14. Whose mother—besides his own—does Paul ask the church in Rome to salute?

    Romans 16:13

    A. Erastus' mother
    B. Nereus' mother
    C. Rufus' mother
    D. Timotheus' mother

15. Whose sister does Paul ask the church in Rome to salute?

    Romans 16:15

    A. Erastus' sister
    B. Nereus' sister
    C. Rufus' sister
    D. Timotheus' sister

16. Whom does Paul call *my workfellow?*

    Romans 16:21

    A. Erastus
    B. Nereus
    C. Rufus
    D. Timotheus

17. Who wrote the epistle to the Romans for Paul?

    Romans 16:22

    A. Epaenetus
    B. Gaius
    C. Quartus
    D. Tertius

18. Whom does Paul call *mine host?*

    Romans 16:23

    A. Epaenetus
    B. Gaius
    C. Quartus
    D. Tertius

19. Who was the chamberlain of the city?

    Romans 16:23

    A. Erastus
    B. Nereus
    C. Rufus
    D. Timotheus

20. Whom does Paul call *a brother?*

    Romans 16:23

    A. Epaenetus
    B. Gaius
    C. Quartus
    D. Tertius

Answers on page 778

NOVEMBER 28

Lesson 332

Today's Reading: *I Corinthians 1–4*
Period of Time: 59 AD
Author: Paul

1. Whom does Paul call *our brother*?
   I Corinthians 1:1
   - **A.** Sosthenes
   - **B.** Stephen
   - **C.** Suah
   - **D.** Sychem

2. Why did Paul write his first letter to the Corinthians?
   I Corinthians 1:10–11
   - **A.** There were divisions in the church
   - **B.** There were Gentiles in the church
   - **C.** There were Jews in the church
   - **D.** There were no deacons in the church

3. From whose house did the members of the church write to Paul about their situation?
   I Corinthians 1:11
   - **A.** Chloe's house
   - **B.** Esther's house
   - **C.** Priscilla's house
   - **D.** Sapphira's house

4. Whom did Paul baptize?
   I Corinthians 1:14
   - **A.** Crispus and Gaius
   - **B.** John and Andrew
   - **C.** Philip and Peter
   - **D.** Timothy and Silas

5. Whose household members did Paul baptize?
   I Corinthians 1:16
   - **A.** Barnabas' household members
   - **B.** Cleophas' household members
   - **C.** Stephanas' household members
   - **D.** Thomas' household members

6. What is the preaching of the cross to those who are saved?
   I Corinthians 1:18
   - **A.** The power of darkness
   - **B.** The power of eternity
   - **C.** The power of forgiveness
   - **D.** The power of God

7. Who required a sign before they would believe Jesus Christ was their savior?
   I Corinthians 1:22
   - **A.** The Asians
   - **B.** The Greeks
   - **C.** The Jews
   - **D.** The Romans

8. Who sought wisdom before they would believe that Jesus Christ was their savior?
   I Corinthians 1:22
   - **A.** The Asians
   - **B.** The Greeks
   - **C.** The Jews
   - **D.** The Romans

9. Whom was the preaching of Christ *a stumblingblock* to?
   I Corinthians 1:23
   - **A.** The Asians
   - **B.** The Greeks
   - **C.** The Jews
   - **D.** The Romans

10. Whom was the preaching of Christ *foolishness* to?
    I Corinthians 1:23
    - **A.** The Asians
    - **B.** The Greeks
    - **C.** The Jews
    - **D.** The Romans

11. Which has God chosen to confound the wise?
    I Corinthians 1:27
    - **A.** Babyish men
    - **B.** Devilish scribes
    - **C.** Foolish things
    - **D.** Nightmarish angels

12. Which one of the following does Paul say will **not** receive the things of the Spirit of God?

    I Corinthians 2:14

    A. The humble man
    B. The natural man
    C. The rich man
    D. The wise man

13. What does Paul call carnal Christians?

    I Corinthians 3:1

    A. Apprentices of the gospel
    B. Babes in Christ
    C. Ignoramus
    D. Meat eaters

14. Who does Paul say *planted*?

    I Corinthians 3:6

    A. Apollos
    B. Barnabas
    C. Mark
    D. Paul

15. Who does Paul say *watered*?

    I Corinthians 3:6

    A. Apollos
    B. Barnabas
    C. Mark
    D. Paul

16. Who does Paul say *gave the increase*?

    I Corinthians 3:6

    A. Boaz
    B. God
    C. Pharaoh
    D. Satan

17. What does Paul compare himself to?

    I Corinthians 3:10

    A. A cunning artificer
    B. A skillful workman
    C. A true craftsman
    D. A wise masterbuilder

18. What does Paul call those who are saved?

    I Corinthians 3:16–17

    A. The brethren of the new covenant
    B. The church elders
    C. The fruit of the Holy Ghost
    D. The temple of God

19. How does the world treat the apostles?

    I Corinthians 4:13

    A. As ambassadors of Christ
    B. As God's holy priests
    C. As sons of the Most High God
    D. As the filth of the world

20. Whom did Paul send to the Corinthian church?

    I Corinthians 4:17

    A. Bartimaeus
    B. Prochorus
    C. Timotheus
    D. Zacchaeus

Answers on page 778

NOVEMBER 29

Lesson 333

Today's Reading: *I Corinthians 5–8*
Period of Time: 59 AD
Author: Paul

1. Who was the church member fornicating with?
   I Corinthians 5:1
   A. His father's wife
   B. His mother's sister
   C. His sister
   D. His stepsister

2. Which one of the following symbolizes sin?
   I Corinthians 5:6–8
   A. Blood
   B. Dirt
   C. Leaven
   D. Wine

3. Which action should the church take to a church member that has become a fornicator, railer, or drunkard?
   I Corinthians 5:11
   A. Beat the devil out of him
   B. Do not keep company with him
   C. Look beyond his mistakes
   D. Take him with them on missionary trips

4. Who shall judge the world?
   I Corinthians 6:2
   A. The angels
   B. The kings
   C. The priests
   D. The saints

5. Paul says all things are lawful unto him, but all things are **not** what?
   I Corinthians 6:12
   A. Disagreeable
   B. Expedient
   C. Injurious
   D. Worthless

6. What is the Christian's physical body?
   I Corinthians 6:19
   A. A tomb for the soul
   B. An empty vessel
   C. Dust and ashes
   D. The temple of the Holy Ghost

7. What was Paul's marital status?
   I Corinthians 7:8
   A. Divorced
   B. Engaged
   C. Married
   D. Single

8. What did Paul say marriage is better than?
   I Corinthians 7:9
   A. To burn
   B. To die lonely
   C. To freeze at night
   D. To never have been kissed

9. Whom does Paul give credit to for the following quote: "Let not the wife depart from her husband"?
   I Corinthians 7:10–11
   A. Abraham
   B. Esaias
   C. God
   D. Noe

10. What does the believing wife do for the unbelieving husband?
    I Corinthians 7:14
    A. Condemns him
    B. Forsakes him
    C. Sanctifies him
    D. Worships him

11. What should the believing wife do if the unbelieving husband leaves her?
    I Corinthians 7:15
    A. Follow him
    B. Let him depart
    C. Rebuke him
    D. Slap his face

12. What does Paul call circumcision?
    I Corinthians 7:19
    A. A mark of the beast
    B. Cleanliness
    C. Godliness
    D. Nothing

13. What did Paul say about the time?
    I Corinthians 7:29
    A. "Time flies when you're having fun."
    B. "Time is money."
    C. "Time is short."
    D. "Time stands still for no man."

14. Who does Paul say cares for the things that belong to God?
    I Corinthians 7:32
    A. He that is married.
    B. He that is unmarried.
    C. He whose lips have never lied.
    D. He whose lips have never touched wine.

15. Who does Paul say cares for the things that are of the world?
    I Corinthians 7:33
    A. He that is married
    B. He that is unmarried
    C. He whose lips have never lied
    D. He whose lips have never touched wine

16. Which does Paul say is better?
    I Corinthians 7:37–38
    A. A daughter who weds
    B. A virgin daughter who never weds
    C. He that never had a daughter
    D. He that offers up his daughter to Molech

17. How long is a wife bound by the law?
    I Corinthians 7:39
    A. Until her husband dies
    B. Until her husband pays her bond
    C. Until she earns more than her husband
    D. Until she has more than one husband

18. What does knowledge do to a person?
    I Corinthians 8:1
    A. Commendeth him
    B. Edifieth him
    C. Maketh him rich
    D. Puffeth him up

19. How many true Gods are there?
    I Corinthians 8:4
    A. One
    B. Hundreds
    C. Thousands
    D. Millions

20. When does Paul say a believer should **not** eat meat bought at the market that has been offered to idols?
    I Corinthians 8:7–13
    A. If it has been ground up
    B. If it loses its red color
    C. If it offends a weak brother
    D. If it smells old

*Answers on page 778

NOVEMBER 30

Lesson 334

Today's Reading: *I Corinthians 9–11*
Period of Time: 59 AD
Author: Paul

1. What does Paul say concerning plowing?
   I Corinthians 9:10
   A. Plow in fertile soil
   B. Plow in hope
   C. Plow in the fall
   D. Plow in the spring

2. What does Paul say about those who preach the gospel?
   I Corinthians 9:14
   A. They are worst than an infidel.
   B. They love to hear themselves talk.
   C. They should live of the gospel.
   D. They work for filthy lucre.

3. What does Paul call himself?
   I Corinthians 9:19
   A. A bishop
   B. A fool
   C. A liar
   D. A servant

4. What does Paul say he was like to the Jew?
   I Corinthians 9:20
   A. A Jew
   B. A prisoner
   C. A Roman
   D. A teacher

5. What did Paul say he became to gain the weak?
   I Corinthians 9:22
   A. Poor
   B. Rich
   C. Strong
   D. Weak

6. What does Paul say he was made to all men so that he might by all means save a few?
   I Corinthians 9:22
   A. A doctor
   B. A god
   C. All things
   D. An angel

7. What does Paul compare himself to?
   I Corinthians 9:24–26
   A. A doctor in a hospital
   B. A fisherman in a boat
   C. A hunter in the wood
   D. A runner in a race

8. What does Paul say the righteous wish to obtain by living a holy life?
   I Corinthians 9:25
   A. An annunciation from heaven
   B. An incorruptible crown
   C. An oracle from God
   D. An ultra long life

9. What is Paul trying to avoid being?
   I Corinthians 9:27
   A. A castaway
   B. A disciple
   C. A minister
   D. A prisoner

10. How many died in one day for committing fornication?
    I Corinthians 10:8
    A. 23,000
    B. 58,000
    C. 74,000
    D. 96,000

11. What killed those who tempted Christ?
    I Corinthians 10:9
    A. Hail
    B. Plagues
    C. Serpents
    D. Tidal waves

12. Where were the Corinthians buying their meat?
    I Corinthians 10:25
    A. From the farmers
    B. From the hunters
    C. From the prophets
    D. From the shambles

13. What should a person do at a feast if a man weak in his Christian faith says the meat set before them has been offered to idols?

    I Corinthians 10:27–28

    A. Do not eat it
    B. Enjoy it with a cup of wine
    C. Make sure it is well done
    D. Season it with a little salt

14. Who is the head of every man?

    I Corinthians 11:3

    A. Christ
    B. Himself
    C. His father
    D. His wife

15. Who is the head of every woman?

    I Corinthians 11:3

    A. Her father
    B. Her husband
    C. Her mother
    D. Herself

16. Who is the head of Christ?

    I Corinthians 11:3

    A. Andrew
    B. Bartholomew
    C. God
    D. Satan

17. What is the glory of the husband?

    I Corinthians 11:7

    A. His children
    B. His father
    C. His son
    D. His wife

18. What is shameful to a man?

    I Corinthians 11:14

    A. Baldness
    B. Hats
    C. Long hair
    D. Silver hair

19. What were the Corinthians partaking of unworthily?

    I Corinthians 11:20–30

    A. Baptisms
    B. The Lord's supper
    C. Their honeymoons
    D. Their wedding ceremonies

20. Where were the Corinthians to eat their meals?

    I Corinthians 11:20–34

    A. At church suppers
    B. In their homes
    C. In their synagogues
    D. Near the temple

*Answers on page 778

DECEMBER 1

Lesson 335
Today's Reading: *I Corinthians 12–14*
Period of Time: 59 AD
Author: Paul

1. What did Paul call idols?
   I Corinthians 12:2
   - **A.** Crafty
   - **B.** Dumb
   - **C.** Powerful
   - **D.** Valuable

2. Paul said there are diversities of gifts but the same what?
   I Corinthians 12:4
   - **A.** God
   - **B.** Devil
   - **C.** Lord
   - **D.** Spirit

3. Paul said there are differences of administrations but the same what?
   I Corinthians 12:5
   - **A.** God
   - **B.** Devil
   - **C.** Lord
   - **D.** Spirit

4. Paul said there are diversities of operations but the same what which worketh all in all?
   I Corinthians 12:6
   - **A.** God
   - **B.** Devil
   - **C.** Lord
   - **D.** Spirit

5. What did Paul say there should **not** be in the body of Christ?
   I Corinthians 12:25
   - **A.** Any Gentile
   - **B.** Any Jew
   - **C.** Any schism
   - **D.** Any tongue

6. What is the *first* gift God gave the church?
   I Corinthians 12:28
   - **A.** Apostles
   - **B.** Diversities of tongues
   - **C.** Gifts of healings
   - **D.** Helps

7. What is the *second* gift God gave the church?
   I Corinthians 12:28
   - **A.** Apostles
   - **B.** Governments
   - **C.** Miracles
   - **D.** Prophets

8. What is the *third* gift God gave the church?
   I Corinthians 12:28
   - **A.** Gifts of healings
   - **B.** Helps
   - **C.** Miracles
   - **D.** Teachers

9. What is the *fourth* gift God gave the church?
   I Corinthians 12:28
   - **A.** Diversities of tongues
   - **B.** Governments
   - **C.** Miracles
   - **D.** Teachers

10. What is the *fifth* gift God gave the church?
    I Corinthians 12:28
    - **A.** Diversities of tongues
    - **B.** Gifts of healings
    - **C.** Governments
    - **D.** Helps

11. What is the *sixth* gift God gave the church?
    I Corinthians 12:28
    - **A.** Gifts of healings
    - **B.** Governments
    - **C.** Helps
    - **D.** Miracles

12. What is the *seventh* gift God gave the church?

    I Corinthians 12:28

    A. Diversities of tongues
    B. Governments
    C. Helps
    D. Prophets

13. What is the *eighth* gift God gave the church?

    I Corinthians 12:28

    A. Diversities of tongues
    B. Gifts of healings
    C. Miracles
    D. Teachers

14. Which is the greatest?

    I Corinthians 13:13

    A. Charity
    B. Faith
    C. Hope
    D. Joy

15. Whom does he that speaketh in an unknown tongue edify?

    I Corinthians 14:4

    A. Apostles
    B. Himself
    C. The church
    D. The unbelievers

16. Who are tongues a sign to?

    I Corinthians 14:22

    A. Apostles
    B. Himself
    C. The church
    D. The unbelievers

17. What is the maximum number who should speak in tongues during a worship service?

    I Corinthians 14:27

    A. 2
    B. 3
    C. 4
    D. 5

18. What is God the author of?

    I Corinthians 14:33

    A. Evil
    B. Lies
    C. Peace
    D. Sin

19. Who were to remain silent in the church, according to 1 Corinthians 14:34?

    I Corinthians 14:34

    A. Children
    B. Prisoners
    C. Strangers
    D. Women

20. How was a worship service to be done?

    I Corinthians 14:40

    A. Decently and in order
    B. Prayer, praise, then preaching
    C. Routinely and timely
    D. Spontaneously and with emotion

*Answers on page 778

DECEMBER 2

Lesson 336
Today's Reading: *I Corinthians 15–16*
Period of Time: 59 AD
Author: Paul

1. Over how many people saw Jesus at once after the resurrection?
   I Corinthians 15:6
   A. 100
   B. 300
   C. 400
   D. 500

2. What does Paul say he is **not** worthy to be called?
   I Corinthians 15:9
   A. A disciple
   B. A priest
   C. A teacher
   D. An apostle

3. What has Jesus become to those that slept?
   I Corinthians 15:20
   A. Candles
   B. Firstfruits
   C. Shadows
   D. Tabernacles

4. Through which man did death enter the world?
   I Corinthians 15:22
   A. Adam
   B. Cain
   C. Moses
   D. Noah

5. What is the last enemy that shall be destroyed?
   I Corinthians 15:26
   A. Blasphemy
   B. Death
   C. Hell
   D. Satan

6. Where were men forced to fight wild beasts?
   I Corinthians 15:32
   A. Damascus
   B. Ephesus
   C. Pontus
   D. Tarsus

7. Which musical instrument will signal the dead being raised incorruptible?
   I Corinthians 15:52
   A. The cornet
   B. The flute
   C. The organ
   D. The trumpet

8. What does Paul call sin?
   I Corinthians 15:56
   A. Birthing pains
   B. Light cast into darkness
   C. The sting of death
   D. Shadows falling upon the evil

9. What is the strength of sin?
   I Corinthians 15:56
   A. The darkness
   B. The idol
   C. The law
   D. The pit

10. Where were the churches located that Paul ordered to take up an offering?
    I Corinthians 16:1
    A. Cilicia
    B. Galatia
    C. Philadelphia
    D. Seleucia

11. On which day of the week were believers to collect money for the saints?
    I Corinthians 16:2
    A. 1st
    B. 3rd
    C. 6th
    D. 7th

12. The saints from which city were to receive the money the churches had collected?
I Corinthians 16:3
    A. Decapolis
    B. Hapharaim
    C. Jerusalem
    D. Nicopolis

13. What place was Paul planning to pass through?
I Corinthians 16:5
    A. Capernaum
    B. Illyricum
    C. Macedonia
    D. Pamphylia

14. Where was Paul planning on staying until Pentecost?
I Corinthians 16:8
    A. Ephesdammim
    B. Ephesus
    C. Ephratah
    D. Ephron

15. Whom did Paul tell the Corinthians **not** to despise?
I Corinthians 16:10–11
    A. Biztha
    B. Didymus
    C. Philemon
    D. Timotheus

16. Who agreed to travel to Corinth but at a more convenient time?
I Corinthians 16:12
    A. Apollos
    B. Barnabas
    C. Mark
    D. Shimeon

17. Whose house was known as the firstfruits of Achaia?
I Corinthians 16:15
    A. Annas' house
    B. Parmenas' house
    C. Stephanas' house
    D. Zenas' house

18. Who was one of the men who helped the church in Corinth?
I Corinthians 16:17
    A. Asyncritus
    B. Blastus
    C. Epaenetus
    D. Fortunatus

19. Which couple had a church that met in their home?
I Corinthians 16:19
    A. Aquila and Priscilla
    B. Chuza and Joanna
    C. Felix and Drusilla
    D. Jehoiada and Jehosheba

20. What does Paul say any man who does **not** love the Lord Jesus Christ shall be?
I Corinthians 16:22
    A. Anathema Marantha
    B. Gabbatha Ouches
    C. Nethinim Greaves
    D. Stacte Matrix

*Answers on page 778

DECEMBER 3

Lesson 337

Today's Reading: *II Corinthians 1–4*
Period of Time: 60 AD
Author: Paul

1. What title does Paul use for himself?
   II Corinthians 1:1
   - **A.** Apostle
   - **B.** Disciple
   - **C.** Prophet
   - **D.** Rabbi

2. Whom does Paul call *our brother*?
   II Corinthians 1:1
   - **A.** Abraham
   - **B.** Jupiter
   - **C.** Solomon
   - **D.** Timothy

3. Where was Corinth located?
   II Corinthians 1:1
   - **A.** In Achaia
   - **B.** In Dalmatia
   - **C.** In Macedonia
   - **D.** In Thrace

4. Where did Paul and his traveling companions nearly die?
   II Corinthians 1:8–9
   - **A.** Asia
   - **B.** Babylon
   - **C.** Egypt
   - **D.** Libya

5. Where was Paul planning on passing through on his way to and from Corinth?
   II Corinthians 1:16
   - **A.** Carthage
   - **B.** Macedonia
   - **C.** Rome
   - **D.** Spain

6. Besides Paul, which two of the following men preached Jesus Christ to the Corinthians?
   II Corinthians 1:19
   - **A.** Samson and Tidal
   - **B.** Sennacherib and Titus
   - **C.** Silvanus and Timotheus
   - **D.** Sosipater and Tiberius

7. Paul was **not** ignorant of whose devices?
   II Corinthians 2:11
   - **A.** Augustus' devices
   - **B.** Felix's devices
   - **C.** Satan's devices
   - **D.** Tiberius' devices

8. Who was Paul looking for in Troas?
   II Corinthians 2:12–13
   - **A.** Abram
   - **B.** Jonah
   - **C.** Mamre
   - **D.** Titus

9. What does Paul call the Corinthian believers?
   II Corinthians 3:3
   - **A.** The angels of Corinth
   - **B.** The epistle of Christ
   - **C.** The miracles of Peter
   - **D.** The rock of Gibraltar

10. What does Paul say kills in verse 3:6?
    II Corinthians 3:6
    - **A.** The envelope
    - **B.** The ink well
    - **C.** The letter
    - **D.** The pen

11. What does Paul say gives life in verse 3:6?
    II Corinthians 3:6
    - **A.** The elders
    - **B.** The gods
    - **C.** The soul
    - **D.** The spirit

12. Who put a vail over his face?
    II Corinthians 3:13
    - **A.** Moses
    - **B.** Rehob
    - **C.** Sihon
    - **D.** Tidal

13. What is found where the Spirit of the Lord is?

    II Corinthians 3:17

    A. Confusion
    B. Liberty
    C. Punishment
    D. Sacrifice

14. Who has blinded the minds of them which do **not** believe the gospel?

    II Corinthians 4:4

    A. Hezekiah, king of Judah
    B. Moses the lawgiver
    C. Pharaoh, king of Egypt
    D. The god of this world

15. Paul says we are *troubled on every side* but **not** what?

    II Corinthians 4:8

    A. Distressed
    B. Plundered
    C. Ravaged
    D. Vanquished

16. Paul says we are *perplexed* but **not** what?

    II Corinthians 4:8

    A. Ill-treated
    B. In despair
    C. Optimistic
    D. Virtuous

17. Paul says we are *persecuted* but **not** what?

    II Corinthians 4:9

    A. Assaulted
    B. Beaten
    C. Forsaken
    D. Shipwrecked

18. Paul says we are *cast down* but **not** what?

    II Corinthians 4:9

    A. Deflated
    B. Dejected
    C. Despised
    D. Destroyed

19. What is renewed in the believer day by day?

    II Corinthians 4:16

    A. The convicted man
    B. The inward man
    C. The strong man
    D. The wretched man

20. What does Paul call the things that are **not** seen?

    II Corinthians 4:18

    A. Abysmal
    B. Dangerous
    C. Eternal
    D. Mysterious

*Answers on page 779

Lesson 338

Today's Reading: *II Corinthians 5–8*
Period of Time: 60 AD
Author: Paul

DECEMBER 4

1. What do believers earnestly desire to be clothed with?
   II Corinthians 5:2
   A. Their house which is from heaven
   B. Their royal robes colored purple
   C. Their sackcloths
   D. Their white holy garments

2. What does the believer desire be swallowed up of life?
   II Corinthians 5:4
   A. Mammon
   B. Manna
   C. Moons
   D. Mortality

3. What has God given the believer?
   II Corinthians 5:5
   A. The best the world has to offer
   B. The earnest of the Spirit
   C. The prosperity gospel
   D. The wings of angels

4. What does the believer walk by?
   II Corinthians 5:7
   A. Faith
   B. Lamps
   C. Sight
   D. Tokens

5. What must all appear before?
   II Corinthians 5:10
   A. The book of the dead
   B. The howls of hell
   C. The judgment seat of Christ
   D. The pearly gates of heaven

6. What does the love of Christ do for believers?
   II Corinthians 5:14
   A. Belittleth us
   B. Constraineth us
   C. Destroyeth us
   D. Tormenteth us

7. What does a believer become if he has been saved by Christ?
   II Corinthians 5:17
   A. A burning flame
   B. A carnal Christian
   C. A new creature
   D. A shining star

8. Which ministry has God given us?
   II Corinthians 5:18
   A. Ministry of exhortation
   B. Ministry of incantation
   C. Ministry of materialization
   D. Ministry of reconciliation

9. Which title does Paul use for believers?
   II Corinthians 5:20
   A. Ambassadors for Christ
   B. Diplomats for peace
   C. Governors of love
   D. Representatives of heaven

10. Which sin was Jesus guilty of committing?
    II Corinthians 5:21
    A. Adultery
    B. Fornication
    C. Murder
    D. None

11. Which words are written in italics in 2 Corinthians 6:1?
    II Corinthians 6:1
    A. Beseech you
    B. In vain
    C. With him
    D. Ye receive

12. When is the day of salvation?
    II Corinthians 6:2
    A. Now
    B. Tomorrow
    C. Yesterday
    D. No man knows

13. Which hardship does Paul list first that a true minister will endure, yet remain a man of God?

    II Corinthians 6:3–5

    A. In afflictions
    B. In distresses
    C. In much patience
    D. In necessities

14. Which name does Paul use for Satan?

    II Corinthians 6:15

    A. Abaddon
    B. Belial
    C. Devil
    D. Lucifer

15. Where does Paul say the temple of God is located today?

    II Corinthians 6:16

    A. Beyond the second heaven
    B. In the center of the Garden of Eden
    C. Upon the mountain of Jerusalem
    D. Within the human body of all believers

16. Who came to Paul and gave him a good report concerning the church in Corinth?

    II Corinthians 7:6–7

    A. Cyrus
    B. Gaius
    C. Linus
    D. Titus

17. What did Paul do to make the Corinthians sorry?

    II Corinthians 7:8

    A. Sent them a letter
    B. Stole their money
    C. Stoned an adulterer
    D. Struck a brother

18. Where were the churches located that Paul commended on their giving?

    II Corinthians 8:1

    A. In Alexandria
    B. In Macedonia
    C. In Philistia
    D. In Samaria

19. How does Paul describe Jesus' financial status while he lived in the flesh upon the earth?

    II Corinthians 8:9

    A. He lived as a commoner.
    B. He lived in poverty.
    C. He lived luxuriously.
    D. He lived royally.

20. Which principle did Paul teach regarding giving?

    II Corinthians 8:10–15

    A. Give a tithe, which is a commandment.
    B. Give everything you have to evangelists.
    C. Give from what you have to those in need.
    D. Give until it hurts and then give more.

Answers on page 779

DECEMBER 5

Lesson 339
Today's Reading: *II Corinthians 9–13*
Period of Time: 60 AD
Author: Paul

1. What did Paul call the Corinthians' generous gift?
   II Corinthians 9:1–5
   A. A bounty
   B. A gratuity
   C. A present
   D. A ransom

2. What did Paul say regarding giving?
   II Corinthians 9:6
   A. Borrow if you must, in order to give.
   B. Give as if you are receiving.
   C. He that sows sparingly will reap sparingly.
   D. The LORD will bless you tenfold.

3. How is a person to give an offering?
   II Corinthians 9:7
   A. As a sign of one's wealth
   B. Knowing others are watching
   C. Not grudgingly, or of necessity
   D. To impress others

4. How did the church at Corinth describe Paul's letters?
   II Corinthians 10:10
   A. Arrogant and ridiculous
   B. Blasphemous and worldly
   C. Philosophical and scholarly
   D. Weighty and powerful

5. How did the church at Corinth describe Paul's bodily presence?
   II Corinthians 10:10
   A. Abused
   B. Lean
   C. Massive
   D. Weak

6. How did the church at Corinth describe Paul's speech?
   II Corinthians 10:10
   A. Contemptible
   B. Dynamic
   C. Energetic
   D. Wistful

7. How does Paul say he received his money so that he could serve the Corinthians?
   II Corinthians 11:8
   A. He auctioned church property.
   B. He held fundraisers at churches.
   C. He received wages from other churches.
   D. He stole offerings from churches.

8. What is Satan transformed into?
   II Corinthians 11:14
   A. A bearded goat
   B. A gray-headed monster
   C. A horned devil carrying a pitchfork
   D. An angel of light

9. How many times did Paul receive forty stripes save one from the Jews?
   II Corinthians 11:24
   A. 3
   B. 5
   C. 7
   D. 10

10. How many times was Paul beaten with rods?
    II Corinthians 11:25
    A. 2
    B. 3
    C. 4
    D. 5

11. How many times was Paul stoned?
    II Corinthians 11:25
    A. 1
    B. 3
    C. 6
    D. 10

12. How many times was Paul shipwrecked?
    II Corinthians 11:25
    A. 2
    B. 3
    C. 4
    D. 5

13. How long was Paul in the deep?
    II Corinthians 11:25
    A. A night and a day
    B. A week and a day
    C. A month and a week
    D. A year and a month

14. Who was the king of Damascus?
    II Corinthians 11:32
    A. King Aretas
    B. King Darius
    C. King Hophra
    D. King Nahash

15. How did Paul escape from Damascus?
    II Corinthians 11:33
    A. He dug a tunnel from his cell to the wood.
    B. He dressed as a Roman soldier and walked out the front gates.
    C. He hid beneath the straw in a delivery wagon.
    D. He was lowered in a basket through a window in a wall.

16. Which heaven does Paul state a man he once knew was taken to?
    II Corinthians 12:2
    A. 1st
    B. 2nd
    C. 3rd
    D. 4th

17. What bodily ailment did Paul complain of?
    II Corinthians 12:7
    A. A crippled hand
    B. A thorn in the flesh
    C. An infected foot
    D. An ulcer to the scalp

18. Whom did Paul send to the Corinthians?
    II Corinthians 12:18
    A. Herod
    B. Philip
    C. Titus
    D. Uriah

19. How many times had Paul already visited the Corinthians?
    II Corinthians 13:1
    A. 1
    B. 2
    C. 3
    D. 4

20. What did Paul tell the Corinthians they were **not** because Jesus Christ was in them?
    II Corinthians 13:5–7
    A. Apostles
    B. Bishops
    C. Deacons
    D. Reprobates

*Answers on page 779

DECEMBER 6

Lesson 340
Today's Reading: *Galatians 1–6*
Period of Time: 58 AD
Author: Paul

1. How many days did Paul abode with Peter?
   Galatians 1:18
   A. 5
   B. 15
   C. 25
   D. 35

2. Who is Jesus' brother?
   Galatians 1:19
   A. Jabez
   B. Jacob
   C. Jadon
   D. James

3. Who accompanied Paul and Titus to Jerusalem?
   Galatians 2:1
   A. Agrippa
   B. Barnabas
   C. Luke
   D. Mark

4. What was Titus' ethnicity?
   Galatians 2:3
   A. Greek
   B. Hebrew
   C. Roman
   D. Samaritan

5. Which three of the following men gave Paul the right hands of fellowship?
   Galatians 2:9
   A. Andrew, Judas, and Matthew
   B. Barnabas, Jude, and Reuben
   C. Issachar, Dan, and Marcus
   D. James, Cephas, and John

6. Where did Paul confront Peter for encouraging the Gentiles to live like Jews?
   Galatians 2:11–21
   A. Antioch
   B. Corinth
   C. Ephesus
   D. Thessalonica

7. What did Paul say he was dead to so that he might live unto God?
   Galatians 2:19
   A. The judge
   B. The jury
   C. The law
   D. The prosecutor

8. What was Abraham's belief in God accounted to him as?
   Galatians 3:6
   A. Corruptness
   B. Evil-mindedness
   C. Righteousness
   D. Vileness

9. What shall the just live by?
   Galatians 3:11
   A. Faith
   B. Hope
   C. Love
   D. Peace

10. How many years after the covenant with Abraham was the law given by Moses?
    Galatians 3:16–17
    A. 100
    B. 250
    C. 360
    D. 430

11. In whose hand was the law ordained by angels?
    Galatians 3:19
    A. A defendant's hand
    B. A judge's hand
    C. A mediator's hand
    D. A prosecutor' hand

12. What are believers no longer under after faith has come?

    Galatians 3:25

    A. A guard
    B. A schoolmaster
    C. A tyrant
    D. A warden

13. What does the Spirit of his Son into the hearts of the believer cry out?

    Galatians 4:6

    A. Abba, Father
    B. Everlasting Father
    C. Our Father
    D. Son of the Father

14. What does a servant become after becoming a believer?

    Galatians 4:7

    A. A brother
    B. A father
    C. A master
    D. A son

15. How did the Galatians receive Paul?

    Galatians 4:14

    A. As a cruel task master
    B. As a judge of the law
    C. As a vile prisoner
    D. As an angel of God

16. How many sons did Abraham have?

    Galatians 4:22

    A. 1
    B. 2
    C. 3
    D. 4

17. Which covenant gendereth to bondage?

    Galatians 4:24

    A. Agar
    B. Leah
    C. Ruth
    D. Sara

18. What is the one word the law is fulfilled in?

    Galatians 5:14

    A. Bite and devour one another.
    B. Love thy neighbor as thyself.
    C. Trust no one.
    D. You are most important.

19. What are love, joy, peace, longsuffering, gentleness, goodness, faith, meekness, and temperance called?

    Galatians 5:22–23

    A. A person who is a fruitcake
    B. A way to cultivate fruits
    C. The fruit of the Spirit
    D. The path to no fruition

20. What does Paul say he bears in his body?

    Galatians 6:17

    A. The courage of David
    B. The fountain of holiness
    C. The marks of the Lord Jesus
    D. The strength of Samson

Answers on page 779

Lesson 341
Today's Reading: *Ephesians 1–3*
Period of Time: 64 AD
Author: Paul

DECEMBER 7

1. What does Paul call himself in the introduction?
   Ephesians 1:1
   A. A disciple
   B. A prisoner
   C. A servant
   D. An apostle

2. What has God done for believers?
   Ephesians 1:5
   A. Forgotten them
   B. Judged them
   C. Predestinated them
   D. Ruined them

3. What else has God done for believers?
   Ephesians 1:5
   A. Adopted them
   B. Denied them
   C. Judged them
   D. Sacrificed them

4. What has Jesus Christ made known to the believer?
   Ephesians 1:9
   A. The exact day of his next coming
   B. The mystery of his will
   C. The name of His sisters
   D. The reason he married Martha

5. What has the believer been sealed with?
   Ephesians 1:13
   A. A holy kiss
   B. Caesar's mark
   C. The blood of animals
   D. The Holy Spirit

6. What spirit does God give the believer?
   Ephesians 1:17
   A. Spirit of fear and doubt
   B. Spirit of power and turmoil
   C. Spirit of tribulation and disease
   D. Spirit of wisdom and revelation

7. What is the spirit that now worketh in the children of disobedience?
   Ephesians 2:2
   A. The dark spirit of death
   B. The lying spirit of Babylon
   C. The prince of the power of the air
   D. The spirit of wisdom and understanding

8. What is grace?
   Ephesians 2:8
   A. A code name for Christ
   B. Any woman who attends church
   C. The gift of God
   D. The law

9. What is man **not** saved by?
   Ephesians 2:8–9
   A. Blood of Jesus
   B. Love of God
   C. Redemption
   D. Works

10. What has Jesus Christ abolished with his flesh?
    Ephesians 2:15
    A. The enmity
    B. The Gentiles
    C. The Jews
    D. The underworld

11. What are believers and saints?
    Ephesians 2:19
    A. Chaff in the wind
    B. Fellowcitizens
    C. Rulers of this world
    D. Smoke and ashes

12. What is Jesus Christ of the holy temple in the Lord?
    Ephesians 2:20–21
    A. The beam that supports the roof
    B. The chief corner stone
    C. The marble used for the floors
    D. The nails in the wood

13. What does Paul call himself in verse 3:1?

    Ephesians 3:1

    A. A heathen
    B. A prisoner
    C. A runner
    D. A warrior

14. Which ethnic group in general is Paul ministering to in Ephesus?

    Ephesians 3:1

    A. Africans
    B. Asians
    C. Gentiles
    D. Jews

15. What is Paul hoping the Ephesians will understand by reading his letter to them?

    Ephesians 3:4

    A. His disappointment in them
    B. How to celebrate the Lord's supper
    C. The mystery of Christ
    D. Why they must be baptized in water

16. Which mystery does Paul say has been hid in God since the beginning of the world?

    Ephesians 3:9

    A. The fellowship of the mystery
    B. The mystery of evolution
    C. The reason why God created man first
    D. The years it took to make the world

17. What does Paul **not** want the Ephesians to faint over?

    Ephesians 3:13

    A. His new Philistine wife
    B. His tribulations for them
    C. His vegetarian diet
    D. His white Greek toga

18. What does Paul say the love of Christ passeth?

    Ephesians 3:19

    A. Knowledge
    B. Philosophy
    C. Understanding
    D. Wisdom

19. What specifically does Paul pray the Ephesians may receive?

    Ephesians 3:19

    A. A pardon from Caesar
    B. Land from Augustus
    C. Ships from Tarshish
    D. The fullness of God

20. What is the last word in Ephesians 3:21?

    Ephesians 3:21

    A. Amen
    B. Glory
    C. Spirit
    D. You

*Answers on page 779

DECEMBER 8

Lesson 342
Today's Reading: *Ephesians 4–6*
Period of Time: 64 AD
Author: Paul

1. What does Paul call himself in verse 4:1?
   Ephesians 4:1
   A. A prisoner
   B. A slave
   C. A runner
   D. An apostle

2. How many baptisms are there?
   Ephesians 4:5
   A. 1
   B. 2
   C. 3
   D. 4

3. Where did Jesus go *first* after he died on the cross?
   Ephesians 4:9
   A. The cemeteries in Jerusalem
   B. The lower parts of the earth
   C. The summit of mount Mariah
   D. The third heaven

4. What is the believer to be renewed in?
   Ephesians 4:23
   A. The chamber of his soul
   B. The deepest part of his heart
   C. The innermost marrow of his bones
   D. The spirit of his mind

5. What should the believer **not** allow the sun to go down upon?
   Ephesians 4:26
   A. His body
   B. His fears
   C. His shadow
   D. His wrath

6. What specifically does Paul say **not** to grieve?
   Ephesians 4:30
   A. A cruel master
   B. A wedded wife
   C. An anointed king
   D. The Holy Spirit

7. How is the believer to follow God?
   Ephesians 5:1
   A. As an eagle
   B. As blind men
   C. As dear children
   D. As running water

8. What is Jesus' sacrifice similar to?
   Ephesians 5:2
   A. A deer panting for water
   B. A rain cloud in the desert
   C. A sweetsmelling savour
   D. A violent shaking of the earth

9. Who has **no** inheritance in the kingdom of Christ and of God, according to Ephesians 5:5?
   Ephesians 5:5
   A. A butler
   B. A high priest
   C. A soldier
   D. A whoremonger

10. How is the believer to walk?
    Ephesians 5:15
    A. Blindly
    B. Circumspectly
    C. Perilously
    D. Quietly

11. How are men to love their wives?
    Ephesians 5:28
    A. As beasts of burden
    B. As small children
    C. As their own bodies
    D. As unwashed pots

12. Who is the believer to honor?
    Ephesians 6:2
    A. His gods
    B. His money
    C. His parents
    D. His servants

13. What does the believer **not** wrestle against?

    Ephesians 6:12

    A. Flesh and blood
    B. Principalities and powers
    C. Rulers of the darkness of this world
    D. Spiritual wickedness in high places

14. What is the believer to girt his loins with?

    Ephesians 6:14

    A. Gospel of peace
    B. Righteousness
    C. Truth
    D. Ways of this world

15. What is the breastplate of the armour of God?

    Ephesians 6:14

    A. Gospel of peace
    B. Righteousness
    C. Truth
    D. Ways of this world

16. What is the believer to shod his feet with?

    Ephesians 6:15

    A. Gospel of peace
    B. Righteousness
    C. Truth
    D. Ways of this world

17. What is the shield of the armour of God?

    Ephesians 6:16

    A. Charity
    B. Faith
    C. Righteousness
    D. Truth

18. What is the helmet of the armour of God?

    Ephesians 6:17

    A. Love
    B. Salvation
    C. Self-control
    D. Temperance

19. Which title does Paul use for himself?

    Ephesians 6:20

    A. Ambassador in bonds
    B. Envoy of heaven
    C. Imperial diplomat
    D. Official of the highest court

20. Whom does Paul call a beloved brother and faithful minister in the Lord?

    Ephesians 6:21

    A. Onesimus
    B. Philetus
    C. Silvanus
    D. Tychicus

*Answers on page 779

DECEMBER 9

Lesson 343
Today's Reading: *Philippians 1–4*
Period of Time: 64 AD
Author: Paul

1. What title does Paul use for himself and Timothy in the introduction?
   Philippians 1:1
   A. Apostles
   B. Ministers
   C. Prisoners
   D. Servants

2. What does Paul say death is, if to live is Christ?
   Philippians 1:21
   A. Gain
   B. Hell
   C. Purgatory
   D. Satan

3. What does Paul state that Jesus took upon him the form of?
   Philippians 2:7
   A. A lord
   B. A priest
   C. A ruler
   D. A servant

4. What should happen when people hear the name of Jesus?
   Philippians 2:10
   A. Every knee should bow
   B. Great earthquakes should shake the world
   C. Pestilence should kill 1/3rd of man
   D. There should be wars and rumors of wars

5. What should every tongue confess?
   Philippians 2:11
   A. Jesus Christ is Lord.
   B. Not all sins are bad.
   C. The Bible is full of errors.
   D. There are many ways to heaven.

6. Whom was Paul sending to the Philippians?
   Philippians 2:19
   A. Barnabus
   B. Cornelius
   C. Onesimus
   D. Timotheus

7. Who had been sick?
   Philippians 2:25–27
   A. Augustus
   B. Claudius
   C. Epaphroditus
   D. Mercurius

8. What does Paul tell the Philippians to beware of?
   Philippians 3:2
   A. Cats
   B. Dogs
   C. Lions
   D. Snakes

9. On which day was Paul circumcised?
   Philippians 3:5
   A. 4th day
   B. 6th day
   C. 8th day
   D. 10th day

10. Which tribe did Paul belong to?
    Philippians 3:5
    A. Tribe of Benjamin
    B. Tribe of Judah
    C. Tribe of Naphtali
    D. Tribe of Zebulun

11. Which group did Paul belong to?
    Philippians 3:5
    A. The Herodians
    B. The Pharisees
    C. The Samaritans
    D. The Zealots

12. What does Paul count the things he gained or accomplished?
    Philippians 3:7
    A. Awards of success
    B. Loss for Christ
    C. Proof of his apostleship
    D. Treasures in heaven

13. What is the god of the enemies of the cross of Christ?

    Philippians 3:18–19

    A. Their ancestors
    B. Their belly
    C. Their intellect
    D. Their money

14. What is the glory of the enemies of the cross of Christ?

    Philippians 3:19

    A. Their honesty
    B. Their mercy
    C. Their shame
    D. Their works

15. Which two people does Paul ask that they be of the same mind in the Lord?

    Philippians 4:2

    A. Apphia and Atarah
    B. Dorcas and Lydia
    C. Euodias and Syntyche
    D. Mary and Martha

16. Whom does Paul call a fellowlabourer, and his name is also written in the book of life?

    Philippians 4:3

    A. Absalom
    B. Barjona
    C. Clement
    D. Didymus

17. What does Paul praise the Philippians for?

    Philippians 4:15

    A. Their caring for widows and orphans
    B. Their giving and receiving
    C. Their songs and worship
    D. Their teachings and praise

18. Where was Paul when the Philippians sent him gifts?

    Philippians 4:16

    A. Laodicea
    B. Philadelphia
    C. Smyrna
    D. Thessalonica

19. Who delivered the gifts from the Philippians to Paul?

    Philippians 4:18

    A. Aristobulus
    B. Belteshazzar
    C. Chedorlaomer
    D. Epaphroditus

20. At whose household did many of the saints salute the Philippians?

    Philippians 4:22

    A. Caesar's household
    B. Gideon's household
    C. Julius's household
    D. Thomas's household

*Answers on page 779

DECEMBER 10

Lesson 344
Today's Reading: *Colossians 1–4*
Period of Time: 64 AD
Author: Paul

1. Whom does Paul include in his greeting?
   Colossians 1:1
   A. Tiberius
   B. Timotheus
   C. Tirshatha
   D. Titus

2. Whom does Paul call *a dear fellowservant and a faithful minister of Christ?*
   Colossians 1:7, 4:12
   A. Cyrenius
   B. Epaphras
   C. Mordecai
   D. Silvanus

3. What does the blood of Christ give the believer?
   Colossians 1:14
   A. Divination
   B. Emaciation
   C. Irritation
   D. Redemption

4. Who is the image of the invisible God?
   Colossians 1:13–29
   A. Adam
   B. David
   C. Jesus
   D. Moses

5. Which church did Paul express great concern for besides the church in Colosse?
   Colossians 2:1
   A. Laodicea
   B. Philadelphia
   C. Sardis
   D. Thyatira

6. Which two of the following traditions of men does Paul warn the Colossians **not** to be deceived by?
   Colossians 2:8
   A. Geography and false balances
   B. History and family genealogies
   C. Philosophy and vain deceit
   D. Sociology and deceptive measures

7. What did the Mosaic diet, holydays, new moon festivals, and sabbath days represent?
   Colossians 2:16–17
   A. A shadow of things to come
   B. Eat, drink, and be merry
   C. Man must suffer to find himself
   D. Steps to take to be nearer to God

8. What did Paul tell the Colossians **not** to do?
   Colossians 2:18
   A. Confess their sins
   B. Drink red wine
   C. Eat leavened bread
   D. Worship angels

9. What does Paul call covetousness?
   Colossians 3:5
   A. Fun
   B. Idolatry
   C. Sacraments
   D. Weakness

10. What does Paul call charity?
    Colossians 3:14
    A. The bond of perfectness
    B. The deeds of the firstborn
    C. The greed of the poor
    D. The way to get into heaven

11. What are Christians to redeem?
    Colossians 4:5
    A. Their food
    B. Their homes
    C. Their masters
    D. Their time

12. What did Paul say to season their speech with?
Colossians 4:6
   A. Herbs
   B. Pepper
   C. Salt
   D. Vinegar

13. Whom did Paul call *a beloved brother, a faithful minister, and fellowservant in the Lord*?
Colossians 4:7
   A. Aristarchus
   B. Marcus
   C. Onesimus
   D. Tychicus

14. Whom did Paul call *a faithful and beloved brother, and a Colossian*?
Colossians 4:9
   A. Aristarchus
   B. Marcus
   C. Onesimus
   D. Tychicus

15. Whom does Paul call *my fellowprisoner*?
Colossians 4:10
   A. Aristarchus
   B. Marcus
   C. Onesimus
   D. Tychicus

16. Who was Barnabas' cousin?
Colossians 4:10
   A. Aristarchus
   B. Marcus
   C. Onesimus
   D. Tychicus

17. Who was among the circumcision?
Colossians 4:11
   A. Archippus
   B. Justus
   C. Luke
   D. Nymphas

18. Who was a beloved physician?
Colossians 4:14
   A. Archippus
   B. Justus
   C. Luke
   D. Nymphas

19. Whose house was also used as a church?
Colossians 4:15
   A. Archippus' house
   B. Justus' house
   C. Luke's house
   D. Nymphas' house

20. Whom did Paul ask the Colossians to tell on his behalf, "Take heed to the ministry which thou hast received in the Lord, that thou fulfil it"?
Colossians 4:17
   A. Archippus
   B. Justus
   C. Luke
   D. Nymphas

*Answers on page 779

DECEMBER 11

Lesson 345

Today's Reading: *I Thessalonians 1–5*
Period of Time: 54 AD
Author: Paul

1. Whom does Paul include in his salutation?
   I Thessalonians 1:1
   A. Agabus and Matthew
   B. Linus and Barnabas
   C. Silvanus and Timotheus
   D. Tyranus and Philemon

2. What does Paul call the work of the Thessalonians who believe in Christ?
   I Thessalonians 1:3
   A. A labour of love
   B. A work in progress
   C. Acts of the Apostles
   D. The work of iniquity

3. Where were the Thessalonians ensamples to other believers?
   I Thessalonians 1:7
   A. Jerusalem and Tabor
   B. Macedonia and Achai
   C. Pamphylia and Calno
   D. Tahpanhes and Lydda

4. In which city were Paul and his traveling companions shamefully entreated?
   I Thessalonians 2:2
   A. Caesarea
   B. Gomorrah
   C. Nazareth
   D. Philippi

5. What does Paul state his gentleness to the Thessalonians is like?
   I Thessalonians 2:7
   A. As a husbandman tilleth his land
   B. As a master careth for his dog.
   C. As a nurse cherisheth her children.
   D. As a rider nourisheth his horse

6. Where were the churches located when the Thessalonians became followers of Christ?
   I Thessalonians 2:14
   A. Caesarea
   B. Judaea
   C. Kadeshbarnea
   D. Laodicea

7. Who hindered Paul and his companions from going to Thessalonica?
   I Thessalonians 2:18
   A. Augustus
   B. Claudius
   C. Nero
   D. Satan

8. What does Paul and his companions call the believers in Thessalonica?
   I Thessalonians 2:20
   A. Our glory and joy
   B. Our kindred and spirit
   C. Our peace and love
   D. Our rock and fortress

9. Where did Paul and his companions stay instead of going to Thessalonica?
   I Thessalonians 3:1
   A. Athens
   B. Babylon
   C. Egypt
   D. Libya

10. Whom did Paul send to the Thessalonians?
    I Thessalonians 3:2
    A. Bartimaeus
    B. Nicodemus
    C. Timotheus
    D. Zacchaeus

11. Whose voice shall be heard when the LORD descends from heaven?
    I Thessalonians 4:16
    A. Abraham's voice
    B. David's voice
    C. Gabriel's voice
    D. The archangel's voice

12. Which musical instrument shall be played when the LORD descends from heaven?
    I Thessalonians 4:16
    A. Cymbals
    B. Psaltery
    C. Sackbut
    D. Trumpet

13. Who shall rise first when the LORD descends from heaven?
    I Thessalonians 4:16
    A. The dead in Christ
    B. The dead in hell
    C. The living adults
    D. The living children

14. What shall happen to believers when the LORD descends from heaven?
    I Thessalonians 4:17
    A. They will be caught up into the clouds.
    B. They will judge the living and the dead.
    C. They will rule the earth.
    D. They will suffer martyrdom.

15. What does Paul state the coming of the LORD will be like?
    I Thessalonians 5:2
    A. As a hen gathereth her chickens
    B. As a new moon is celebrated
    C. As a shepherd watereth his flock
    D. As a thief in the night

16. What does Paul state the pain of unbelievers will feel like when the LORD comes?
    I Thessalonians 5:3
    A. As a flood covereth the green earth
    B. As a sharp sword stuck in the bowels
    C. As travail upon a woman with child
    D. As wounded birds trapped in snares

17. What other name does Paul use for the believers in Thessalonica?
    I Thessalonians 5:5
    A. The brethren of peace
    B. The children of light
    C. The people of the cross
    D. The sons of thunder

18. What does Paul call the breastplate the believers in Thessalonica are to put on?
    I Thessalonians 5:8
    A. Covenant and truth
    B. Faith and love
    C. Peace and joy
    D. Urim and Thummim

19. What does Paul call the helmet the believers in Thessalonica are to put on?
    I Thessalonians 5:8
    A. The gospel of peace
    B. The hope of salvation
    C. The sign of faith
    D. The Word of God

20. What are the believers **not** to despise?
    I Thessalonians 5:20
    A. Beatings
    B. Bribes
    C. Prophesyings
    D. Slayings

Answers on page 779

Lesson 346
Today's Reading: *II Thessalonians 1–3*
Period of Time: 54 AD
Author: Paul

DECEMBER 12

1. Whom does Paul include in his salutation?
   II Thessalonians 1:1
   A. Barnabas and Mark
   B. Luke and John
   C. Silvanus and Timotheus
   D. Zechariah and Zacharias

2. What was growing exceedingly at the church in Thessalonica?
   II Thessalonians 1:3
   A. Their baptisms of the righteous
   B. Their faith in Jesus Christ
   C. Their membership in the church
   D. Their missionary outreach program

3. What was abounding at the church in Thessalonica?
   II Thessalonians 1:3
   A. Their building
   B. Their charity
   C. Their music
   D. Their school

4. What will God do to those who trouble the church in Thessalonica?
   II Thessalonians 1:6
   A. Crown them
   B. Forgive them
   C. Recompense them
   D. Thank them

5. What will Jesus use to destroy those who do **not** obey the gospel?
   II Thessalonians 1:7–9
   A. A drought
   B. A fire
   C. A pestilence
   D. An earthquake

6. What does Paul call the Thessalonians at the beginning of chapter 2?
   II Thessalonians 2:1
   A. Brethren
   B. Children
   C. Disciples
   D. Members

7. What does Paul mention in his prayer, hoping it will **not** happen to the Thessalonians?
   II Thessalonians 2:2
   A. The Jews discover their church.
   B. The Romans persecute them.
   C. They are shaken in mind.
   D. They turn to idols.

8. What must happen before the day of Christ is at hand?
   II Thessalonians 2:2–3
   A. A falling away shall occur.
   B. Israel will no longer be a nation.
   C. Men shall live in peace.
   D. Satan must repent of his evil sins.

9. What does Paul call the man of sin that shall appear before Christ's return?
   II Thessalonians 2:3
   A. King of fools
   B. Light of the world
   C. Prince of peace
   D. Son of perdition

10. What will the man of sin do?
    II Thessalonians 2:4
    A. Kneel in the temple of God
    B. Live a life of holiness and righteousness
    C. Proclaim he is God
    D. Resurrect the dead

11. What will the LORD use to destroy the one called Wicked?

    II Thessalonians 2:8

    A. The brightness of his coming
    B. The fires of hell
    C. The shout of the angels
    D. The tears of the martyrs

12. What shall God send the unrighteous?

    II Thessalonians 2:11

    A. Forgiving spirits
    B. Healing waters
    C. Peculiar people
    D. Strong delusion

13. What does Paul tell the church to continue to believe?

    II Thessalonians 2:15

    A. Evangelists claiming to be God
    B. Ministers showing signs and wonders
    C. Rabbis sent from Jerusalem
    D. Traditions the word has taught them

14. What does Paul hope will happen to the word?

    II Thessalonians 3:1

    A. It be taught only in Latin
    B. It may have free course
    C. It returns to God with few errors
    D. It will be revised soon

15. What does Paul claim to be to the church?

    II Thessalonians 3:9

    A. A god
    B. A judge
    C. A saint
    D. An ensample

16. What does Paul say concerning a person who is too lazy to work?

    II Thessalonians 3:10

    A. Bake him bread.
    B. Build a house for him.
    C. Do not feed him.
    D. Teach him to fish.

17. What does Paul call lazy people who walk disorderly among the righteous?

    II Thessalonians 3:11

    A. Busybodies
    B. Hypocrites
    C. Snobs
    D. Wolves

18. What does Paul state **not** to become weary from?

    II Thessalonians 3:13

    A. Avoiding church
    B. Being gluttonous
    C. Cursing heathens
    D. Doing well

19. How are the righteous to treat an unrighteous man?

    II Thessalonians 3:14–15

    A. Admonish him as a brother.
    B. Place him in a ward.
    C. Stone him to death.
    D. Treat him as an enemy.

20. Which name does Paul use for Jesus in the closing of his epistle?

    II Thessalonians 3:16

    A. Lord of glory
    B. Lord of peace
    C. Lord of righteousness
    D. Lord of sabaoth

Answers on page 779

DECEMBER 13

Lesson 347
Today's Reading: *I Timothy 1–4*
Period of Time: 65 AD
Author: Paul

1. Where was Timothy abiding?
   I Timothy 1:3

   A. Antioch
   B. Ephesus
   C. Nineveh
   D. Samaria

2. Where did Paul travel to after leaving Timothy?
   I Timothy 1:3

   A. Apollonia
   B. Lycaonia
   C. Macedonia
   D. Philadelphia

3. What did Paul tell Timothy **not** to pay heed to?
   I Timothy 1:4

   A. Barnabas' lies
   B. Fables and endless genealogies
   C. John's prophecies from Patmos
   D. Roman laws

4. What does Paul say some have turned to in place of the gospel?
   I Timothy 1:3–6

   A. Church doctrines
   B. Paul's epistles
   C. The Lost Testament
   D. Vain jangling

5. What were some false teachers mingling with the gospel?
   I Timothy 1:3–7

   A. Charity
   B. The law of Moses
   C. The Lord's supper
   D. Water baptism

6. What did Paul do to Christians before becoming one?
   I Timothy 1:13

   A. Fed them
   B. Clothed them
   C. Persecuted them
   D. Taught them

7. What does Paul claim he was before turning to Christ?
   I Timothy 1:15

   A. A demon-possessed man
   B. An Olympic champion
   C. The chief among sinners
   D. The prophet of Baal

8. What does Paul say a person does to his faith when he turns from Christ?
   I Timothy 1:19

   A. Buries it
   B. Glorifies it
   C. Magnifies it
   D. Shipwrecks it

9. Which two of the following men did Paul deliver unto Satan?
   I Timothy 1:20

   A. Hymenaeus and Alexander
   B. Lebbaeus and Eder
   C. Thaddaeus and Ader
   D. Zacchaeus and Bethgader

10. How many Gods are there?
    I Timothy 2:5

    A. One
    B. Hundreds
    C. Thousands
    D. Millions

11. How many mediators are there between God and men?

    I Timothy 2:5

    A. One
    B. Hundreds
    C. Thousands
    D. Millions

12. How are women to dress?

    I Timothy 2:9

    A. They are to braid their hair.
    B. They are to dress modestly.
    C. They are to wear gold rings.
    D. They are to wear pearl necklaces.

13. Who was deceived?

    I Timothy 2:13–14

    A. Adam
    B. Cain
    C. Eve
    D. Lucifer

14. Which church official is Paul referring to when he states, "Not given to wine?"

    I Timothy 3:1–7

    A. Bishop
    B. Elder
    C. Monk
    D. Usher

15. Which church official is Paul referring to when he states, "…not given to much wine?"

    I Timothy 3:8–13

    A. Clergyman
    B. Deacon
    C. Minister
    D. Reverend

16. What may a Christian consume?

    I Timothy 4:1–5

    A. Beef, but only if it is grilled
    B. Dairy products, but only if they are kosher
    C. Fish, but no shellfish
    D. Pork, if received with thanksgiving

17. Which of the following does Paul say to refuse?

    I Timothy 4:7

    A. Profane and old wives' fables
    B. Red meat and unleavened bread
    C. Shellfish and leavened bread
    D. Taxes and fines levied by Rome

18. What does Paul say about bodily exercise?

    I Timothy 4:8

    A. It availeth the body much good.
    B. It cleanseth the soul.
    C. It helpeth one to live longer.
    D. It profiteth little.

19. What did Paul tell Timothy?

    I Timothy 4:12

    A. "Do not be ashamed of thy leprosy."
    B. "God will correct thy stuttering lips."
    C. "Honor not thy pagan family."
    D. "Let no man despise thy youth."

20. Who laid their hands upon Timothy?

    I Timothy 4:14

    A. The high priest
    B. The king
    C. The presbytery
    D. The rabbis

*Answers on page 779

DECEMBER 14

Lesson 348
Today's Reading: *I Timothy 5–6*
Period of Time: 65 AD
Author: Paul

1. How is an *elderly man* to be treated?
   I Timothy 5:1
   A. As a brother
   B. As a father
   C. As a grandfather
   D. As an uncle

2. How is a *younger man* to be treated?
   I Timothy 5:1
   A. As a brother
   B. As a cousin
   C. As a neighbor
   D. As a nephew

3. How is an *elderly woman* to be treated?
   I Timothy 5:2
   A. As a grandmother
   B. As a mother
   C. As a sister
   D. As an aunt

4. How is a *younger woman* to be treated?
   I Timothy 5:2
   A. As a cousin
   B. As a niece
   C. As a sister
   D. As an aunt

5. Who are to care for the widows first?
   I Timothy 5:4
   A. The church or pastor
   B. The government or monasteries
   C. Their adult brothers or fathers
   D. Their adult children or nephews

6. What does Paul say a person is worse than who does **not** care for his own family?
   I Timothy 5:8
   A. A hypocrite
   B. A publican
   C. A snake
   D. An infidel

7. How old would a widow need to be in order to receive aid from the church?
   I Timothy 5:9
   A. 40 years old
   B. 50 years old
   C. 60 years old
   D. 70 years old

8. Who was to receive double honor?
   I Timothy 5:17
   A. Elders who ruled well
   B. Knights of the Holy Grail
   C. Missionaries over the age of 50
   D. Widows with more than two children

9. Which animal did Paul say was **not** to be muzzled?
   I Timothy 5:18
   A. The dog trained for the hunt
   B. The horse prepared for the battle
   C. The mule that ploweth the field
   D. The ox that treadeth out the corn

10. Where was a sinner to be rebuked?
    I Timothy 5:20
    A. Before all church members
    B. Behind closed doors
    C. In magistrate courts
    D. In the great hall of judgment

11. What did Paul tell Timothy to drink a little of for his stomach ailments and recurring infirmities?
    I Timothy 5:23
    A. Beer
    B. Milk
    C. Water
    D. Wine

12. How were servants under the yoke to treat their masters?

    I Timothy 6:1

    A. With contempt
    B. With honour
    C. With maleficence
    D. With wickedness

13. Which false doctrine were believers to forsake?

    I Timothy 6:5

    A. Gain is godliness.
    B. God loveth a cheerful giver.
    C. The rich ruleth over the poor.
    D. The wages of sin is death.

14. Which two of the following did Paul say should make a person content?

    I Timothy 6:8

    A. Air and a house
    B. Bread and water
    C. Food and raiment
    D. Wine and song

15. What is the root of all evil?

    I Timothy 6:10

    A. The desire to be famous
    B. The height of one's pride
    C. The love of money
    D. The wayward lust of the flesh

16. Who witnessed a good confession?

    I Timothy 6:13

    A. Herod
    B. Julius Caesar
    C. Pontius Pilate
    D. Tiberius Caesar

17. What name did Paul use regarding Jesus as ruler?

    I Timothy 6:15

    A. Potentate
    B. Prefect
    C. Proconsul
    D. Provost

18. Which title did Paul use regarding Jesus' kingship?

    I Timothy 6:15

    A. King of death
    B. King of kings
    C. King of the Jews
    D. King of the Romans

19. Which title did Paul use regarding Jesus' lordship?

    I Timothy 6:15

    A. Lord of bones
    B. Lord of lords
    C. Lord of the apes
    D. Lord of the flies

20. Which type of science did Paul tell Timothy to avoid?

    I Timothy 6:20

    A. Astronomy
    B. Chemistry
    C. Geology
    D. Pseudoscience

*Answers on page 779

Lesson 349
Today's Reading: *II Timothy 1–4*
Period of Time: 66 AD
Author: Paul

DECEMBER 15

1. Who was Timothy's grandmother?
   II Timothy 1:5
   A. Anna
   B. Jael
   C. Lois
   D. Noah

2. Who was Timothy's mother?
   II Timothy 1:5
   A. Esther
   B. Eunice
   C. Euodias
   D. Eve

3. Which spirit has God given to every Christian?
   II Timothy 1:7
   A. Spirit of a lying tongue
   B. Spirit of a sound mind
   C. Spirit of fear
   D. Spirit of the world

4. What did our Saviour Jesus Christ abolish?
   II Timothy 1:10
   A. Death
   B. Grace
   C. Hope
   D. Peace

5. Which two men turned away from Paul in Asia?
   II Timothy 1:15
   A. Apollyon and Sosthenes
   B. Chelluh and Epaenetus
   C. Meshullam and Aeneas
   D. Phygellus and Hermogenes

6. Who ministered to Paul in Rome and Ephesus?
   II Timothy 1:16–18
   A. Aristobulus
   B. Epaphroditus
   C. Nicodemus
   D. Onesiphorous

7. Who does Paul say must be the first to partake of the fruit?
   II Timothy 2:6
   A. The cupbearers
   B. The husbandmen
   C. The kings
   D. The stewards

8. Which king was Jesus a descendant of?
   II Timothy 2:8
   A. King Artaxerxes
   B. King Cyrus
   C. King David
   D. King Esarhaddon

9. What shall happen to us if we be dead with Jesus Christ?
   II Timothy 2:11
   A. We shall also live with him.
   B. We shall be better than everybody else.
   C. We shall die in our own transgressions.
   D. We shall live in prosperity on earth.

10. Which two men does Paul refer to as cankers to the word of truth?
    II Timothy 2:15–18
    A. Agabus and Epaphroditus
    B. Hymenaeus and Philetus
    C. Prochorus and Asyncritus
    D. Trophimus and Fortunatus

11. Which two Egyptian magicians withstood Moses?
    II Timothy 3:8
    A. Jairus and Putiel
    B. Jalaam and Shishak
    C. Jannes and Jambres
    D. Jarha and Necho

12. What are all scriptures in the holy Bible?

    II Timothy 3:16

    A. A collection of folktales
    B. Fables and myths
    C. Rules and idioms to live by
    D. The inspired words of God

13. Who forsook Paul and loved the world?

    II Timothy 4:10

    A. Demas
    B. Lucas
    C. Tiras
    D. Zenas

14. Who was present with Paul?

    II Timothy 4:11

    A. Ezra
    B. John
    C. Luke
    D. Omri

15. Whom did Paul want Timothy to bring to him?

    II Timothy 4:11

    A. Joel
    B. Levi
    C. Mark
    D. Ucal

16. In which city did Paul leave his cloke?

    II Timothy 4:13

    A. Debir
    B. Gimzo
    C. Sidon
    D. Troas

17. Besides his cloke, what else did Paul want Timothy to bring to him?

    II Timothy 4:13

    A. Books and parchments
    B. Horses and blankets
    C. Pots and victuals
    D. Swords and habergeons

18. Who was a coppersmith?

    II Timothy 4:14

    A. Alexander
    B. Bethgader
    C. Harnepher
    D. Sosipater

19. Who did Paul say abode in Corinth?

    II Timothy 4:20

    A. Blastus
    B. Erastus
    C. Festus
    D. Justus

20. Whom did Paul leave at Miletum because he was sick?

    II Timothy 4:20

    A. Didymus
    B. Nicodemus
    C. Onesimus
    D. Trophimus

Answers on page 780

DECEMBER 16

Lesson 350
Today's Reading: *Titus 1–3, Philemon 1*
Period of Time: Titus, 65 AD; Philemon, 64 AD
Author: Paul

1. What does Paul call Titus?
   Titus 1:4
   A. His brother
   B. His father
   C. His nephew
   D. His son

2. Which church office does Paul address?
   Titus 1:7
   A. Office of a bishop
   B. Office of a deacon
   C. Office of an evangelist
   D. Office of an usher

3. What does Paul call Jews who were teaching false doctrines?
   Titus 1:10
   A. They of the circumcision.
   B. They of the devil.
   C. They of the house of Israel.
   D. They of the Samaritan house.

4. What does Paul call the false teachers' wages?
   Titus 1:11
   A. Counterfeit balances
   B. Filthy lucre
   C. Fool's gold
   D. Unjust wages

5. What did a prophet of their own call the Cretians?
   Titus 1:12
   A. Easy goers
   B. Fiddle faddle
   C. Lazy bones
   D. Slow bellies

6. Whom is Paul addressing when he says they should be sober, grave, temperate, sound in faith, charity, and in patience?
   Titus 2:2
   A. Aged men
   B. Aged women
   C. Young men
   D. Young women

7. Whom is Paul addressing when he says they should **not** be false accusers, given to much wine, but should be teachers of good things?
   Titus 2:3
   A. Aged men
   B. Aged women
   C. Young men
   D. Young women

8. Whom is Paul addressing when he says they should be sober, love their children, be discreet, chaste, and keepers at home?
   Titus 2:4–5
   A. Aged men
   B. Aged women
   C. Young men
   D. Young women

9. Whom is Paul addressing when he says they should be sober minded, have a pattern of good works, showing uncorruptness, gravity, sincerity, and sound speech?
   Titus 2:6–8
   A. Aged men
   B. Aged women
   C. Young men
   D. Young women

10. What did Paul say servants should be to their masters?
    Titus 2:9
    A. Capricious
    B. Obedient
    C. Purloining
    D. Rebellious

11. What does Paul say God's people should be looking for?

    Titus 2:13

    A. The beast
    B. The blessed hope
    C. The city of gold
    D. The false prophet

12. Which term does Paul use to describe God's people?

    Titus 2:14

    A. Particular
    B. Peculiar
    C. Popular
    D. Pustular

13. Whom did Paul say he might send to Titus?

    Titus 3:12

    A. Either Artemas or Tychicus
    B. Either Demas or Linus
    C. Either Elymas or Narcissus
    D. Either Thomas or Tyrannus

14. Where did Paul plan to spend the winter?

    Titus 3:12

    A. Amphipolis
    B. Decapolis
    C. Nicopolis
    D. Pentapolis

15. Who was a lawyer?

    Titus 3:13

    A. Annas
    B. Jonas
    C. Stephanas
    D. Zenas

16. What does Paul call Timothy?

    Philemon 1:1

    A. His brother
    B. His father
    C. His nephew
    D. His son

17. Which two of the following individuals had a church that met in their home?

    Philemon 1:2

    A. Agrippa and Bernice
    B. Ananias and Sapphira
    C. Apphia and Archippus
    D. Augustus and Claudia

18. Whom does Paul call his son?

    Philemon 1:10

    A. Achaicus
    B. Bartimaeus
    C. Nicodemus
    D. Onesimus

19. Whom does Paul call a fellowprisoner?

    Philemon 1:23

    A. Aeneas
    B. Demas
    C. Epaphras
    D. Lucas

20. Whom did Paul include as a fellowlabourer?

    Philemon 1:24

    A. Festus
    B. Lucius
    C. Marcus
    D. Rufus

*Answers on page 780

DECEMBER 17

Lesson 351
Today's Reading: *Hebrews 1–5*
Period of Time: 64 AD
Author: Unknown

1. What did God mainly use to speak to the fathers at sundry times and in divers manners?
   Hebrews 1:1
   A. Animals
   B. Babies
   C. Kings
   D. Prophets

2. Who was appointed heir of all things?
   Hebrews 1:2
   A. Abraham
   B. Jesus
   C. Joseph
   D. Mary—mother of Jesus

3. Which name does the author use for God?
   Hebrews 1:3
   A. Almighty God
   B. Everlasting Father
   C. Majesty on high
   D. The great God

4. What are God's ministers?
   Hebrews 1:7
   A. A flame of fire
   B. A mighty wind
   C. A pouring rain
   D. A thunder bolt

5. What did God use to anoint Jesus?
   Hebrews 1:9
   A. Oil of gladness
   B. Olive oil
   C. Red wine
   D. River water

6. What never changes?
   Hebrews 1:10–12
   A. Earth
   B. God
   C. Heavens
   D. Vestures

7. Which adjective describes the way the angels spoke God's word?
   Hebrews 2:2
   A. Hesitant
   B. Indecisive
   C. Stedfast
   D. Uncertain

8. What does Jesus call those who are sanctified?
   Hebrews 2:11
   A. Babes
   B. Blasphemers
   C. Bread
   D. Brethren

9. Who had the power of death?
   Hebrews 2:14
   A. The angels bound in chains
   B. The angels in darkness
   C. The devil
   D. The fallen angels

10. What will Jesus do for those who are tempted?
    Hebrews 2:18
    A. Aggravate them
    B. Punish them
    C. Succour them
    D. Torment them

11. Which name does the author use for Jesus?
    Hebrews 3:1
    A. High God
    B. Most high God
    C. Son of the highest
    D. The Apostle and High Priest

12. Who was faithful to God?
    Hebrews 3:2
    A. Balaam
    B. Delilah
    C. Jezebel
    D. Moses

13. What should a person do if he hears Jesus' voice today in his heart?

    Hebrews 3:7–8

    A. Give an offering from the heart
    B. Harden not his heart
    C. Run and hide his heart
    D. Seek open-heart surgery

14. What does the author call those who follow Christ?

    Hebrews 3:14

    A. Foolish
    B. Partakers
    C. Vain
    D. Worldly

15. Which day of the week did God rest?

    Hebrews 4:4

    A. 1st
    B. 3rd
    C. 6th
    D. 7th

16. What is sharper than any twoedged sword?

    Hebrews 4:12

    A. The edge of a razor
    B. The lying tongue
    C. The word of God
    D. The work of Satan

17. Who was tempted in the Bible yet remained without sin?

    Hebrews 4:15

    A. Jesus
    B. Nabal
    C. Peter
    D. Sapphira

18. Who was called by God to be a high priest?

    Hebrews 5:1–4

    A. Aaron
    B. Abraham
    C. Achan
    D. Adam

19. Which priest does Jesus follow?

    Hebrews 5:6–10

    A. Caiaphas
    B. Melchisedec
    C. Nadab
    D. Zedekiah

20. What does the author call a person who is unskillful in the word of righteousness?

    Hebrews 5:13

    A. A babe
    B. A moron
    C. An April fool
    D. An ignoramus

*Answers on page 780

Lesson 352
Today's Reading: *Hebrews 6–9*
Period of Time: 64 AD
Author: Unknown

DECEMBER 18

1. What are believers to do besides learning the principles of the doctrine of Christ?
   Hebrews 6:1
   A. Abandon the missionary field
   B. Go on unto perfection
   C. Live ungodly knowing we are saved
   D. Stop reading the word of God

2. What should Hebrews **not** be inclined to be when laboring toward God's name?
   Hebrews 6:10–12
   A. Cheerful
   B. Faithful
   C. Peaceful
   D. Slothful

3. Whom did God bless and multiply his seed?
   Hebrews 6:13–15
   A. Abraham
   B. Chimham
   C. Jeroham
   D. Malcham

4. Which part of a ship does the author use as a simile for our eternal hope?
   Hebrews 6:19
   A. As an anchor of the soul
   B. As the mast of the spirit
   C. As the rudder of our conscious
   D. As the sail of our power

5. Which city was Melchisedec the king of?
   Hebrews 7:1
   A. Horem
   B. Rekem
   C. Salem
   D. Telem

6. How much did Abraham give to Melchisedec from the spoils of war?
   Hebrews 7:2–4
   A. 10%
   B. 30%
   C. 50%
   D. 100%

7. What is Melchisedec's other title?
   Hebrews 7:2
   A. King of faith
   B. King of joy
   C. King of meekness
   D. King of peace

8. Whose sons received the office of the priesthood?
   Hebrews 7:5
   A. Asher's sons
   B. Levi's sons
   C. Reuben's sons
   D. Zebulun's sons

9. Which tribe did Jesus belong to?
   Hebrews 7:14
   A. Tribe of Dan
   B. Tribe of Ephraim
   C. Tribe of Juda
   D. Tribe of Manasseh

10. What does Jesus' death and resurrection give the Hebrews?
    Hebrews 7:22
    A. A continuance of the law
    B. A set of new laws
    C. A surety of a better testament
    D. A testament based upon works

11. Which word describes our new high priest?
    Hebrews 7:26
    A. Atheistic
    B. Carnal
    C. Defiled
    D. Harmless

12. Why will men eventually stop teaching their neighbors about Jesus?

    Hebrews 8:11

    A. All show know him.
    B. It will be against the law.
    C. Man will eventually become uneducable.
    D. They're all going to hell anyway.

13. Where was the golden table located?

    Hebrews 9:2

    A. In the Gentile Court
    B. In the Holiest of All
    C. In the sanctuary
    D. In the women's Court

14. Where was the golden censer located?

    Hebrews 9:3–4

    A. In the Gentiles' court
    B. In the Holiest of all
    C. In the sanctuary
    D. In the women's court

15. What did the cherubims of glory shadow?

    Hebrews 9:5

    A. The brass altar
    B. The candlestick
    C. The mercyseat
    D. The shewbread

16. How many times during a year did the high priest enter the second tabernacle?

    Hebrews 9:7

    A. 1
    B. 6
    C. 7
    D. 12

17. What did the high priest take with him when he entered the second tabernacle?

    Hebrews 9:7

    A. Apples
    B. Blood
    C. Manna
    D. Wine

18. What is Jesus' role for the Hebrews regarding the new testament?

    Hebrews 9:15

    A. Executioner
    B. Judge
    C. Jury
    D. Mediator

19. When does a testament go into force?

    Hebrews 9:17

    A. After the testament is notarized
    B. After the testament is signed
    C. When a judge decides it is valid
    D. When the person is dead

20. Which one of the following statements is part of Hebrews 9:28, regarding Jesus' second coming?

    Hebrews 9:28

    A. He shall appear without bread to feed the hungry.
    B. He shall appear without sin unto salvation.
    C. He shall appear without victory and judgment upon the earth.
    D. He shall appear without water for the thirsty.

*Answers on page 780

Lesson 353

Today's Reading: *Hebrews 10–11*
Period of Time: 64 AD
Author: Unknown

DECEMBER 19

1. Which blood washes away sins?
   Hebrews 10:1–12
   A. Bull's blood
   B. Goat's blood
   C. Jesus' blood
   D. Sheep's blood

2. Whose will did Jesus come to do?
   Hebrews 10:9
   A. Abraham's will
   B. God the Father's will
   C. His own will
   D. The Holy Ghost's will

3. How many sacrifices did Jesus offer for sins for ever?
   Hebrews 10:12
   A. 1
   B. 2
   C. 3
   D. 4

4. Where does Jesus sit?
   Hebrews 10:12
   A. Behind God
   B. In front of God
   C. Left hand of God
   D. Right hand of God

5. What will Jesus' enemies become?
   Hebrews 10:13
   A. His chair
   B. His footstool
   C. His rug
   D. His table

6. Where does the LORD say he will *write* his laws?
   Hebrews 10:16
   A. In our hearts
   B. In our minds
   C. In our souls
   D. In our spirits

7. What does the LORD say he will remember no more?
   Hebrews 10:17
   A. Our names
   B. Our prayers
   C. Our sins
   D. Our works

8. Which part of the temple does Jesus' flesh represent?
   Hebrews 10:20
   A. The altar of incense
   B. The holy of holies
   C. The sanctuary
   D. The veil

9. What are we to do when we assemble together in the LORD's name?
   Hebrews 10:25
   A. Exhort one another
   B. Judge one another
   C. Pervert one another
   D. Tempt one another

10. What was the minimum number of witnesses needed under Moses' law to bring charges against a person?
    Hebrews 10:28
    A. 1-2
    B. 2-3
    C. 3-4
    D. 4-5

11. Whom does vengeance belong to?
    Hebrews 10:30
    A. God
    B. Nobody
    C. The victim
    D. The witness

12. What shall the just live by?

    Hebrews 10:38

    A. Faith
    B. Mammon
    C. Penance
    D. Works

13. Which one of the following does a person do when he refuses to stay on the path of righteousness?

    Hebrews 10:39

    A. He brings glory to God.
    B. He comes to his senses.
    C. He draws back unto perdition.
    D. He extinguishes the flames of hell.

14. Who offered unto God a more excellent sacrifice than his brother?

    Hebrews 11:4

    A. Abel
    B. Boaz
    C. Cain
    D. Doeg

15. Who walked with God and never died?

    Hebrews 11:5

    A. Emmor
    B. Enoch
    C. Eshek
    D. Ethan

16. Who built an ark?

    Hebrews 11:7

    A. Dumah
    B. Jonah
    C. Noah
    D. Toah

17. Who delivered a child in her old age?

    Hebrews 11:11

    A. Leah
    B. Mary
    C. Ruth
    D. Sara

18. Who was nearly offered up as a sacrifice?

    Hebrews 11:17–19

    A. Abraham
    B. David
    C. Isaac
    D. Paul

19. Who was hid for three months by his parents after he was born?

    Hebrews 11:23

    A. Abraham
    B. Ishmael
    C. Joseph
    D. Moses

20. Who was a harlot?

    Hebrews 11:31

    A. Abigail
    B. Delilah
    C. Priscilla
    D. Rahab

*Answers on page 780

DECEMBER 20

Lesson 354
Today's Reading: *Hebrews 12–13*
Period of Time: 64 AD
Author: Unknown

1. What does the book of Hebrews state we should do patiently?
   Hebrews 12:1
   A. Eat the meal set before us
   B. Live the life set before us
   C. Play the cards set before us
   D. Run the race set before us

2. Who is the author and finisher of our faith?
   Hebrews 12:2
   A. Adam
   B. David
   C. Jesus
   D. Moses

3. What are those who do **not** accept the LORD's chastisements called?
   Hebrews 12:8
   A. Bastards
   B. Heirs
   C. Owners
   D. Sons

4. Which name does the author use for God?
   Hebrews 12:9
   A. Abba Father
   B. Father of spirits
   C. Our Father
   D. Son of the Father

5. Who sold his birthright for a morsel of meat?
   Hebrews 12:16
   A. Esau
   B. Jude
   C. Paul
   D. Saul

6. What did Moses say when the LORD spoke to him upon the mountain?
   Hebrews 12:18–21
   A. Depart from me; for I am a sinful man.
   B. I exceedingly fear and quake.
   C. Thy will be done.
   D. We are consumed by thine anger.

7. What is another name for the city of the living God?
   Hebrews 12:22
   A. Babylon the Great
   B. City of pure gold
   C. Imperial Rome
   D. The heavenly Jerusalem

8. What is Jesus' role in the new covenant?
   Hebrews 12:24
   A. Accuser
   B. Jury
   C. Mediator
   D. Prosecutor

9. Whose offering did the LORD accept?
   Hebrews 12:24
   A. Abel's offering
   B. Abihu's offering
   C. Ahab's offering
   D. Ananias' offering

10. Which words are used in Hebrews to describe God?
    Hebrews 12:29
    A. A consuming fire
    B. A demanding taskmaster
    C. A tinkling cymbal
    D. A weeping father

11. Who are we **not** to forget to entertain?
    Hebrews 13:2
    A. Antichrists
    B. Gods
    C. Kings
    D. Strangers

12. What does the book of Hebrews say marriage is?
    Hebrews 13:4
    A. Adultery
    B. Fornication
    C. Honourable
    D. Madness

13. What are we to leave out of conversation?

    Hebrews 13:5

    A. Covetousness
    B. Politics
    C. Religion
    D. Science

14. Which statement did Jesus say?

    Hebrews 13:5

    A. "I will be glad to finally get out of here."
    B. "I will go and never look back."
    C. "I will never leave thee, nor forsake thee."
    D. "I will see you in heaven if you are good."

15. Who is the same yesterday, today, and for ever?

    Hebrews 13:8

    A. Adam
    B. Jesus Christ
    C. Satan
    D. Simon Peter

16. What are we to establish within our hearts?

    Hebrews 13:9

    A. Envy
    B. Grace
    C. Meat
    D. Sorrow

17. Where was Jesus crucified?

    Hebrews 13:12

    A. Along the Via Dolorosa
    B. Herod's judgment hall
    C. Outside the city gates
    D. The Upper Room

18. What are we to offer to God continually?

    Hebrews 13:15

    A. Animals
    B. Children
    C. Money
    D. Praise

19. Who does the author say is set at liberty?

    Hebrews 13:23

    A. Andrew
    B. John
    C. Philip
    D. Timothy

20. The people from which nation salute the Hebrews?

    Hebrews 13:24

    A. Greece
    B. Italy
    C. Persia
    D. Spain

*Answers on page 780

DECEMBER 21

Lesson 355
Today's Reading: *James 1–5*
Period of Time: 34–45 AD
Author: James

1. What should a person do if they fall into divers temptations?
   James 1:2
   A. Count it all joy
   B. Proceed with caution
   C. Try not to get caught
   D. Weep in silence

2. What does God give to all men liberally if they ask for it?
   James 1:5
   A. Children
   B. Land
   C. Riches
   D. Wisdom

3. Which name does James use when referring to *God*?
   James 1:17
   A. Creator of the ends of the earth
   B. Father of lights
   C. God of Abraham
   D. Mighty God of Jacob

4. Which name does James use when referring to *Jesus Christ*?
   James 2:1
   A. Chief shepherd
   B. Faithful and True
   C. Lord of glory
   D. The bridegroom

5. What rejoices against judgment?
   James 2:13
   A. Death
   B. Heaven
   C. Mercy
   D. Sin

6. What must faith have in order to be alive?
   James 2:17
   A. Belief
   B. Endorsement
   C. Riches
   D. Works

7. What trembles and believes in God?
   James 2:19
   A. The angels
   B. The devils
   C. The kings
   D. The saints

8. Who was called the *Friend of God*?
   James 2:23
   A. Abraham
   B. David
   C. Joseph
   D. Moses

9. Who was a harlot?
   James 2:25
   A. Rachel
   B. Rahab
   C. Rhoda
   D. Ruth

10. What is an unruly evil full of deadly poison?
    James 3:8
    A. The bridle
    B. The master
    C. The sun
    D. The tongue

11. What is friendship with the world?
    James 4:4
    A. Blessedness with God
    B. Enmity with God
    C. Peace with God
    D. Righteousness with God

12. What does James state life is like?

    James 4:14

    A. A river
    B. A sundial
    C. A vapour
    D. An hourglass

13. Which other name does James use for Jesus Christ?

    James 5:4

    A. Lord of atonement
    B. Lord of heaven
    C. Lord of lords
    D. Lord of sabaoth

14. What does James say is drawing nigh?

    James 5:8

    A. The anointing of the saints
    B. The bereaving of the mothers
    C. The coming of the Lord
    D. The darkening of the day

15. Who stands before the door?

    James 5:9

    A. The judge
    B. The jury
    C. The prosecutor
    D. The witness

16. Who was a patient man?

    James 5:11

    A. Ham
    B. Job
    C. Lot
    D. Nun

17. What is a person to do when afflicted?

    James 5:13

    A. Fast
    B. Fight
    C. Pray
    D. Run

18. What is a person to do when merry?

    James 5:13

    A. Be silent
    B. Confess their sins
    C. Give alms
    D. Sing psalms

19. What does the effectual fervent prayer of a righteous man do?

    James 5:16

    A. Availeth much
    B. Bringeth shame
    C. Causeth death
    D. Doeth naught

20. Who prayed that it might **not** rain, and it rained **not** for three years and six months?

    James 5:17

    A. Elias
    B. Hermas
    C. Jeremias
    D. Silas

*Answers on page 780

DECEMBER 22

Lesson 356
Today's Reading: *I Peter 1–5*
Period of Time: 66 AD
Author: Peter

1. Which one of the following is a province that Peter mentions in his opening?
   I Peter 1:1
   A. Azotus
   B. Miletus
   C. Pontus
   D. Tarsus

2. What is more precious than gold?
   I Peter 1:7
   A. The great sea
   B. The life of the blood
   C. The land of Israel
   D. The trial of your faith

3. What lives and abides forever?
   I Peter 1:23
   A. The earth
   B. The heavens
   C. The pain of a woman in travail
   D. The word of God

4. What does Peter state all flesh is like?
   I Peter 1:24
   A. Dust
   B. Grass
   C. Leather
   D. Teeth

5. What did the builders disallow?
   I Peter 2:7
   A. The beam
   B. The hammer
   C. The pillar
   D. The stone

6. What does Peter call those who have been born again?
   I Peter 2:9
   A. A royal army
   B. A royal family
   C. A royal nation
   D. A royal priesthood

7. Which name does Peter use for Jesus Christ?
   I Peter 2:25
   A. The gardener and guardian angel
   B. The light of the world and prince of peace
   C. The Shepherd and Bishop of our souls
   D. The tempter and son of the morning

8. Who was Abraham's wife?
   I Peter 3:6
   A. Deborah
   B. Keturah
   C. Sarah
   D. Zipporah

9. How is a person to give an answer for the reason for their hope in Jesus Christ?
   I Peter 3:15
   A. With agony and doubt
   B. With joy and pride
   C. With meekness and fear
   D. With reverence and doom

10. How many souls were saved during the world-wide flood?
    I Peter 3:20
    A. 8
    B. 88
    C. 888
    D. 8,888

11. What shall cover a multitude of sins?
    I Peter 4:8
    A. Fervent charity
    B. Mighty works
    C. Spiritual tongues
    D. Zealous wonders

12. How should a man speak?
    I Peter 4:11
    A. As the kings of old
    B. As the oracles of God
    C. As the priests of Baal
    D. As the sages of time

13. What are Christians to be to the flock of God?

    I Peter 5:2–3

    A. Anti-Semitics
    B. Ensamples
    C. Hooks
    D. Shearers

14. What will Jesus Christ give to Christians that never fades?

    I Peter 5:4

    A. A crown of glory
    B. A mantle of honor
    C. A robe of righteousness
    D. A shield of faith

15. What are Christians to be clothed in?

    I Peter 5:5

    A. Black
    B. Humility
    C. Purple
    D. Rags

16. What does God give to the humble?

    I Peter 5:5

    A. Condemnation
    B. Famine
    C. Grace
    D. War

17. What is the devil similar to?

    I Peter 5:8

    A. A bleating lamb
    B. A cunning fox
    C. A howling wolf
    D. A roaring lion

18. Whom does Peter call a faithful brother?

    I Peter 5:12

    A. Rufus
    B. Silvanus
    C. Theophilus
    D. Zacchaeus

19. Which church does Peter mention in 1 Peter 5:13?

    I Peter 5:13

    A. Church in Babylon
    B. Church in Laodicea
    C. Church in Philadelphia
    D. Church in Smyrna

20. Whom does Peter call his son?

    I Peter 5:13

    A. Marcus
    B. Quartus
    C. Secundus
    D. Tiberius

*Answers on page 780

DECEMBER 23

Lesson 357
Today's Reading: *II Peter 1–3*
Period of Time: 66 AD
Author: Peter

1. What does corruption enter the world through?
   II Peter 1:4
   A. Fame
   B. Glory
   C. Honor
   D. Lust

2. What are we to add to our *faith*?
   II Peter 1:5
   A. Charity
   B. Godliness
   C. Temperance
   D. Virtue

3. What are we to add to our *knowledge*?
   II Peter 1:6
   A. Charity
   B. Godliness
   C. Temperance
   D. Virtue

4. What are we to add to our *patience*?
   II Peter 1:6
   A. Charity
   B. Godliness
   C. Temperance
   D. Virtue

5. What are we to add to our *brotherly kindness*?
   II Peter 1:7
   A. Charity
   B. Godliness
   C. Temperance
   D. Virtue

6. What is a person called who lacks such things as faith, knowledge, patience, and kindness?
   II Peter 1:9
   A. Blind
   B. Frugal
   C. Rich
   D. Wise

7. What does Peter call his physical body?
   II Peter 1:13–14
   A. A rock
   B. A sacrifice
   C. A tabernacle
   D. A vapour

8. How did the Apostles learn about Jesus Christ?
   II Peter 1:14–16
   A. They were caught up on a cloud with him.
   B. They were eyewitnesses of his majesty.
   C. They were instructed by Paul.
   D. They were taught by the religious leaders.

9. What did the LORD call Jesus Christ?
   II Peter 1:17
   A. His beloved Son
   B. His eternal glory
   C. His everlasting Spirit
   D. His soul brother

10. How did the prophets receive their prophecies?
    II Peter 1:21
    A. They discovered scrolls in a cave.
    B. They found tablets buried in the ground.
    C. They learned from the scribes.
    D. They were moved by the Holy Ghost.

11. What does Peter call the teachings of false prophets?
    II Peter 2:2
    A. Hilarious rubbish
    B. Intrusive paths
    C. Pernicious ways
    D. Tabloid trash

12. Where are the fallen angels?
    II Peter 2:4
    A. Going to and fro in the earth
    B. In chains of darkness
    C. Roaming the earth
    D. Trapped in the lake of fire

13. Who was called a preacher of righteousness?

    II Peter 2:5

    A. Abraham
    B. Joseph
    C. Moses
    D. Noah

14. Which two cities were turned into ashes?

    II Peter 2:6

    A. Babylon and Nineveh
    B. Ramses and Thebes
    C. Sodom and Gomorrah
    D. Tyre and Sidon

15. Who is the son of Bosor?

    II Peter 2:15

    A. Balaam
    B. Elnaam
    C. Jalaam
    D. Naam

16. Which one of the following will return to its own vomit?

    II Peter 2:22

    A. The asp
    B. The dog
    C. The rat
    D. The sow

17. What will destroy the heavens and the earth?

    II Peter 3:7

    A. Darkness
    B. Fire
    C. Ice
    D. Water

18. How many years are but one day to the LORD?

    II Peter 3:8

    A. 1
    B. 10
    C. 100
    D. 1,000

19. What does Peter say the coming day of the LORD will come as?

    II Peter 3:10

    A. A thief in the night
    B. A vapour of gas
    C. A walk in the moonlight
    D. A yuletide carol

20. What does Peter call Paul?

    II Peter 3:15

    A. His son
    B. My friend in Christ
    C. Our beloved brother
    D. Your teacher

*Answers on page 780

DECEMBER 24

Lesson 358
Today's Reading: *I John 1–5*
Period of Time: 90–95 AD
Author: John

1. What does John call Jesus Christ?
   I John 1:1
   A. Ancient of days
   B. Deliverer
   C. Omega
   D. The Word of life

2. What is God?
   I John 1:5
   A. Anger
   B. Evil
   C. Light
   D. Unclean

3. What cleanses us from all sin?
   I John 1:7
   A. The blood of Jesus Christ
   B. The gifts of the church
   C. The good deeds we do
   D. The Lord's supper

4. Who is our advocate with the Father?
   I John 2:1
   A. Father Abraham
   B. Jesus Christ
   C. Mary the mother of Jesus
   D. Moses

5. What is Jesus Christ for our sins?
   I John 2:2
   A. The apportion
   B. The corroboration
   C. The propitiation
   D. The triangulation

6. Who has known him that is from the beginning?
   I John 2:13
   A. Fathers
   B. Little children
   C. Mothers
   D. Young men

7. Who has overcome the wicked one?
   I John 2:13
   A. Fathers
   B. Little children
   C. Mothers
   D. Young men

8. Who has known the Father?
   I John 2:13
   A. Fathers
   B. Little children
   C. Mothers
   D. Young men

9. Who does John say their unction is from?
   I John 2:20
   A. The Holy one
   B. The son of the morning
   C. The tempter
   D. The wicked one

10. Which sin was Jesus guilty of?
    I John 3:5
    A. Adultery
    B. Lying
    C. Murder
    D. None

11. Who slew his brother?
    I John 3:12
    A. Abel
    B. Cain
    C. Paul
    D. Saul

12. What is God?
    I John 4:8
    A. Fear
    B. Hate
    C. Love
    D. Mean

13. Why did the Father send the Son?

    I John 4:14

    A. To be the Saviour of the world
    B. To defeat the Roman Empire
    C. To find the lost tribe of Israel
    D. To overthrow the Jewish council

14. What was the Son of God when he came to dwell among us?

    I John 5:6

    A. He was a spirit.
    B. He was an angel.
    C. He was water and blood.
    D. He was Yahweh in the spirit.

15. Who beareth witness to the Son?

    I John 5:6

    A. The Apostles
    B. The Deacons
    C. The Prophets
    D. The Spirit

16. Who are the three that bear record in heaven?

    I John 5:7

    A. The Father, the Word, and Holy Ghost
    B. The Heavenly host, Gabrielle, and Michael
    C. The Mother, the Archangel, and Joseph
    D. The Shepherd, the Lamb, and the Sheep

17. Which three are one?

    I John 5:7

    A. The Brother, the Son, and the Spirit
    B. The Father, the Word, and the Holy Ghost
    C. The Mother, the Father, and the Son
    D. The Sister, the Archangel, and the Victory

18. Which three bear witness in the earth?

    I John 5:8

    A. The dirt, the sun, and the heaven
    B. The Father, the Son, and the heavens
    C. The Spirit, the water, and the blood
    D. The trees, the grass, and the mountains

19. Which three agree in one?

    I John 5:8

    A. The Father, the Mother, and the Son
    B. The Brother, the Uncle, and the Cousin
    C. The Holy Ghost, Mary, and Joseph
    D. The Spirit, the water, and the blood

20. What are we to keep ourselves from?

    I John 5:21

    A. Fruit
    B. Idols
    C. Pork
    D. Work

Answers on page 780

Lesson 359

Today's Reading: II *John 1, III John 1, Jude 1*
Period of Time: II John and III John, 90–95 AD; Jude, 66 AD
Authors: John, Jude

DECEMBER 25

1. Whom does John greet in his opening?
   II John 1:1
   A. The elect lady
   B. The perfect lady
   C. The woman of the day
   D. The woman of the night

2. Which commandment, since the beginning, does John mention?
   II John 1:5
   A. Beat one another
   B. Cheat one another
   C. Hate one another
   D. Love one another

3. What does John call those who do **not** believe Jesus Christ came in the flesh?
   II John 1:7
   A. Achievers
   B. Believers
   C. Conceivers
   D. Deceivers

4. What do those who abideth in the doctrine of Christ receive?
   II John 1:9
   A. Infamy and chastisement
   B. Misery and boredom
   C. The Father and the Son
   D. The world and all its riches

5. What are we to do if a person denies the doctrine of Christ?
   II John 1:10
   A. Bid him God speed
   B. Receive him not into your house
   C. Treat him like a brother
   D. Whip him with cords

6. Whom is John's third epistle addressed to?
   III John 1:1
   A. Gaius
   B. Julius
   C. Lucius
   D. Publius

7. What does John say we should do?
   III John 1:3
   A. Deny the truth
   B. Make up the truth
   C. Run from the truth
   D. Walk in the truth

8. What does John say we are to be to the truth?
   III John 1:8
   A. Antichrists
   B. Commanders
   C. Fellowhelpers
   D. Rebels

9. Who refused to receive John?
   III John 1:9
   A. Aphses
   B. Diotrephes
   C. Hermes
   D. Sosthenes

10. Who gave a good report of all men?
    III John 1:12
    A. Claudius
    B. Demetrius
    C. Mercurius
    D. Tiberius

11. Who is Jude's brother?
    Jude 1:1
    A. James
    B. Matthew
    C. Peter
    D. Thomas

12. What were ungodly men turning the grace of God into?

    Jude 1:4

    A. Immaculateness
    B. Lasciviousness
    C. Straightforwardness
    D. Virtuousness

13. Which nation did the LORD deliver Israel from?

    Jude 1:5

    A. Egypt
    B. Greece
    C. Libya
    D. Spain

14. Where are the angels who kept **not** their first estate?

    Jude 1:6

    A. Agonizing in the lake of fire
    B. Going to and fro in the earth
    C. In everlasting chains under darkness
    D. Worshiping the father of lies in hell

15. Which two cities were destroyed because of their fornications?

    Jude 1:7

    A. Babylon and Nineveh
    B. Gog and Magog
    C. Sodom and Gomorrah
    D. Tyre and Sidon

16. Who is the archangel?

    Jude 1:9

    A. Abaddon
    B. Gabriel
    C. Lucifer
    D. Michael

17. Whose body did the archangel and the devil dispute over?

    Jude 1:9

    A. Adam's body
    B. Jacob's body
    C. Moses' body
    D. Noah's body

18. Which prophet turned against God's people for money?

    Jude 1:11

    A. Balaam
    B. Haggai
    C. Nathan
    D. Samuel

19. Who was the seventh from Adam?

    Jude 1:14

    A. Cainan
    B. Enoch
    C. Lamech
    D. Mathusala

20. What does Jude call those who shall walk after their own ungodly lusts in the last time?

    Jude 1:18

    A. Concocters
    B. Gawkers
    C. Hawkers
    D. Mockers

*Answers on page 780

DECEMBER 26

Lesson 360
Today's Reading: *Revelation 1–3*
Period of Time: 95 AD
Author: John

1. Where were the seven churches located?
   Revelation 1:4, 1:11
   A. Africa
   B. Antarctica
   C. Asia
   D. Australia

2. How many Spirits are before God's throne?
   Revelation 1:4
   A. 7
   B. 14
   C. 21
   D. 28

3. On which island did John write the Book of Revelation?
   Revelation 1:9
   A. Crete
   B. Patmos
   C. Rhodes
   D. Samos

4. How did John describe Jesus' hair?
   Revelation 1:14
   A. Black as coal
   B. Gray as clouds
   C. Red as cherries
   D. White as snow

5. What was Jesus holding in his right hand?
   Revelation 1:16, 1:20
   A. 3 bowls
   B. 7 stars
   C. 10 commandments
   D. 12 arrows

6. What did the candlesticks represent?
   Revelation 1:20
   A. Apostles
   B. Beasts
   C. Churches
   D. Dragons

7. What was the Church of Ephesus guilty of?
   Revelation 2:1–4
   A. Being too wealthy
   B. Leaving its first love
   C. Selling idols
   D. Worshiping Satan

8. Whose deeds did Jesus and the Church of Ephesus hate?
   Revelation 2:6
   A. The Alexandrians' deeds
   B. The Manahethites' deeds
   C. The Nicolaitanes' deeds
   D. The Shuthalhites' deeds

9. What did Jesus call the blasphemers who claimed they were Jews, but were not?
   Revelation 2:8–9
   A. The chapel upon the hill
   B. The church of God
   C. The synagogue of Satan
   D. The temple of the LORD

10. How many days would some of the members of the church in Smyrna have tribulation?
    Revelation 2:8–10
    A. 3
    B. 5
    C. 7
    D. 10

11. Whom did Jesus call a faithful martyr?
    Revelation 2:12–13
    A. Antipas
    B. Elishah
    C. Matthew
    D. Timothy

12. Which church was guilty of the doctrine of Balaam?

    Revelation 2:12–14

    A. Church in Ephesus
    B. Church in Jerusalem
    C. Church in Laodicea
    D. Church in Pergamos

13. What did Jesus say he would give to those who overcame to eat?

    Revelation 2:17

    A. Fish
    B. Manna
    C. Pomegranates
    D. Quail

14. What was to be written upon the white stone?

    Revelation 2:17

    A. A new commandment
    B. A new covenant
    C. A new doctrine
    D. A new name

15. What were Jesus' feet like?

    Revelation 2:18

    A. Fine brass
    B. Molded clay
    C. Polished silver
    D. Strong like iron

16. Who called herself a prophetess?

    Revelation 2:20

    A. Esther
    B. Jezebel
    C. Keturah
    D. Ruth

17. What did Jesus promise to give to those who overcome and do his work unto the end?

    Revelation 2:24–28

    A. The evening shade
    B. The midnight moon
    C. The morning star
    D. The noonday sun

18. Which church did Jesus say was dead?

    Revelation 3:1

    A. Church in Sardis
    B. Church in Smyrna
    C. Church in Pergamos
    D. Church in Philadelphia

19. Which church did Jesus set an open door in front of that no man can shut?

    Revelation 3:7–8

    A. Church in Ephesus
    B. Church in Laodicea
    C. Church in Pergamos
    D. Church in Philadelphia

20. Which church did Jesus say was lukewarm?

    Revelation 3:14–16

    A. Church in Laodicea
    B. Church in Sardis
    C. Church in Smyrna
    D. Church in Thyatira

Answers on page 780

Lesson 361
Today's Reading: *Revelation 4–8*
Period of Time: 95 AD
Author: John

DECEMBER 27

1. What did the first voice sound like?
   Revelation 4:1
   A. A lion
   B. A river
   C. A trumpet
   D. A waterfall

2. What surrounded the throne?
   Revelation 4:3
   A. A band of cherubims
   B. A flaming sword
   C. A rainbow
   D. A white fence

3. How many seats surrounded the throne?
   Revelation 4:4
   A. 6
   B. 12
   C. 18
   D. 24

4. What were the seven Spirits of God?
   Revelation 4:5
   A. Seven angels
   B. Seven bowls
   C. Seven elders
   D. Seven lamps

5. How many beasts were in the midst of the throne?
   Revelation 4:6
   A. 4
   B. 6
   C. 8
   D. 10

6. How many wings did each beast have?
   Revelation 4:8
   A. 4
   B. 6
   C. 8
   D. 10

7. How many horns did the lamb have?
   Revelation 5:6
   A. 7
   B. 14
   C. 21
   D. 28

8. What were the golden vials full of odours?
   Revelation 5:8
   A. The blood of martyrs
   B. The cries of God's children
   C. The diseases of man
   D. The prayers of saints

9. What color was the horse that appeared when the *first seal* was opened?
   Revelation 6:1–2
   A. Black
   B. Pale
   C. Red
   D. White

10. What color was the horse that appeared when the *second seal* was opened?
    Revelation 6:3–4
    A. Black
    B. Pale
    C. Red
    D. White

11. What color was the horse that appeared when the *third seal* was opened?
    Revelation 6:5
    A. Black
    B. Pale
    C. Red
    D. White

12. What color was the horse that appeared when the *fourth seal* was opened?

    Revelation 6:7–8
    A. Black
    B. Pale
    C. Red
    D. White

13. What happened when the *sixth seal* was opened?

    Revelation 6:12
    A. There was a great earthquake.
    B. There was a great plague.
    C. There was a great thunderstorm.
    D. There was a great war.

14. What was the total number of those that were sealed of all the tribes of the children of Israel?

    Revelation 7:4
    A. 72,000
    B. 144,000
    C. 216,000
    D. 288,000

15. What did those wearing white robes hold in their hands?

    Revelation 7:9
    A. Arrows
    B. Palms
    C. Rocks
    D. Stars

16. Approximately how many minutes of silence were there in heaven after the *seventh seal* was opened?

    Revelation 8:1
    A. 10
    B. 20
    C. 30
    D. 40

17. What happened when the *first angel* blew his trumpet?

    Revelation 8:7
    A. 1/3rd part of the sea became blood
    B. 1/3rd part of the sun, moon, and stars were smitten
    C. 1/3rd part of the trees were burnt up, and all green grass was burnt up
    D. 1/3rd part of the waters became wormwood

18. What happened when the *second angel* blew his trumpet?

    Revelation 8:8
    A. 1/3rd part of the sea became blood
    B. 1/3rd part of the sun, moon, and stars were smitten
    C. 1/3rd part of the trees were burnt up, and all green grass was burnt up
    D. 1/3rd part of the waters became wormwood

19. What happened when the *third angel* blew his trumpet?

    Revelation 8:10–11
    A. 1/3rd part of the sea became blood
    B. 1/3rd part of the sun, moon, and stars were smitten
    C. 1/3rd part of the trees were burnt up, and all green grass was burnt up
    D. 1/3rd part of the waters became wormwood

20. What happened when the *fourth angel* blew his trumpet?

    Revelation 8:12
    A. 1/3rd part of the sea became blood
    B. 1/3rd part of the sun, moon, and stars were smitten
    C. 1/3rd part of the trees were burnt up, and all green grass was burnt up
    D. 1/3rd part of the waters became wormwood

*Answers on page 781

DECEMBER 28

Lesson 362
Today's Reading: *Revelation 9–12*
Period of Time: 95 AD
Author: John

1. What was given the key to the bottomless pit?
   Revelation 9:1
   A. A beast
   B. A demon
   C. A star
   D. An eagle

2. What came out of the smoke?
   Revelation 9:2–3
   A. Horses
   B. Locusts
   C. Scorpions
   D. Snakes

3. How many months were those without the seal of God in their foreheads tormented?
   Revelation 9:4–5
   A. 5
   B. 20
   C. 25
   D. 30

4. What is the *Hebrew* name of the angel of the bottomless pit?
   Revelation 9:11
   A. Abaddon
   B. Ginnethon
   C. Pithon
   D. Sihon

5. What is the *Greek* name of the angel of the bottomless pit?
   Revelation 9:11
   A. Apelles
   B. Aphses
   C. Apollos
   D. Apollyon

6. What was the mighty angel with the little book clothed in?
   Revelation 10:1–2
   A. A breastplate
   B. A cloud
   C. A robe
   D. A tunic

7. What did the mighty angel's feet look like?
   Revelation 10:1
   A. Blankets of snow
   B. Furnaces of smoke
   C. Pillars of fire
   D. Sheets of ice

8. What did the mighty angel put his *right foot* upon?
   Revelation 10:2
   A. The bottomless pit
   B. The earth
   C. The mountain
   D. The sea

9. What did the little book taste like?
   Revelation 10:10
   A. Bread
   B. Honey
   C. Milk
   D. Wine

10. What happened after John ate the book?
    Revelation 10:10
    A. His belly became bitter
    B. His eyes became opened
    C. His hand became withered
    D. His tongue became loosed

11. What was given to the Gentiles?
    Revelation 11:2
    A. The altar
    B. The most holy place
    C. The outer court
    D. The temple of God

12. How many days shall the two witnesses give prophecies in the city?

    Revelation 11:3

    A. 7
    B. 40
    C. 666
    D. 1,260

13. What is the spiritual name of the great city?

    Revelation 11:8

    A. Babylon and Sidon
    B. Nineveh and Tyre
    C. Rome and Gomorrah
    D. Sodom and Egypt

14. How many men were slain in the earthquake?

    Revelation 11:13

    A. 7,000
    B. 93,000
    C. 150,000
    D. 1,000,000

15. How many elders sat before God on their seats?

    Revelation 11:16

    A. 24
    B. 400
    C. 36,000
    D. 150,000

16. What was the *first great wonder* to appear in heaven?

    Revelation 12:1–2

    A. A flaming star
    B. A man with a reed
    C. A pregnant woman
    D. A ram with 10 horns

17. What color was the great dragon?

    Revelation 12:3

    A. Black
    B. Pale
    C. Red
    D. White

18. Who fought against the dragon?

    Revelation 12:7

    A. David
    B. Gabriel
    C. Jesus
    D. Michael

19. What are the two names of the great dragon?

    Revelation 12:9

    A. Alpha and Omega
    B. Devil and Satan
    C. King and Lord
    D. Mercy and Truth

20. Whose mouth did the water come from?

    Revelation 12:15

    A. The horse
    B. The serpent
    C. The tortoise
    D. The unicorn

*Answers on page 781

DECEMBER 29

Lesson 363
Today's Reading: *Revelation 13–16*
Period of Time: 95 AD
Author: John

1. How many heads did the beast out of the sea have?
   Revelation 13:1
   A. 5
   B. 7
   C. 12
   D. 24

2. What name was written upon the heads of the beast out of the sea?
   Revelation 13:1
   A. Almighty
   B. Blasphemy
   C. Holy
   D. Mystery

3. Which book contains the names of those upon the earth that will **not** worship the beast?
   Revelation 13:8
   A. The book of A-Z
   B. The book of life
   C. The book of the dead
   D. The book of the martyrs

4. How many horns did the beast out of the earth have?
   Revelation 13:11
   A. 2
   B. 7
   C. 10
   D. 12

5. What is the number of the beast?
   Revelation 13:18
   A. 274
   B. 490
   C. 666
   D. 823

6. Which mountain did the Lamb stand upon?
   Revelation 14:1
   A. Mount Gilboa
   B. Mount Jearim
   C. Mount Lebanon
   D. Mount Sion

7. How many men stood with the Lamb upon the mountain?
   Revelation 14:1
   A. 144,000
   B. 350,265
   C. 562,053
   D. 912,318

8. What is written upon the foreheads of those who stood upon the mountain with the Lamb?
   Revelation 14:1
   A. Everlasting King
   B. Holy Unto the LORD
   C. The Lamb's father's name
   D. Washed in the blood of the Son

9. What did the men who stood with the Lamb have in common?
   Revelation 14:4
   A. They were all Gentiles.
   B. They were all Jews.
   C. They were all soldiers.
   D. They were all virgins.

10. What did the one like the Son of man sitting upon a white cloud hold in his hand?
    Revelation 14:14
    A. A harp
    B. A little book
    C. A sharp sickle
    D. A two-edged sword

11. How many angels appeared carrying vials?
    Revelation 15:1
    A. 3
    B. 7
    C. 10
    D. 13

12. What song, besides the song of the Lamb, did the saints with harps sing?
    Revelation 15:3
    A. The Song of David
    B. The Song of Joshua
    C. The Song of Moses
    D. The Song of Solomon

13. What were the angels with the vials clothed in?
    Revelation 15:6
    A. Blue linen and golden breastplates
    B. Purple linen and golden crowns
    C. Red linen and golden halos
    D. White linen and golden girdles

14. What was the *first* vial poured upon?
    Revelation 16:2
    A. The air
    B. The cattle
    C. The Devil
    D. The earth

15. What was the *second* vial poured upon?
    Revelation 16:3
    A. The air
    B. The rivers
    C. The sea
    D. The sun

16. What was the *fourth* vial poured upon?
    Revelation 16:8
    A. The air
    B. The rivers
    C. The sea
    D. The sun

17. Which river was the *sixth* vial poured upon?
    Revelation 16:12
    A. River Euphrates
    B. River Gihon
    C. River Hiddekel
    D. River Pison

18. How many unclean spirits came out of the mouth of the dragon?
    Revelation 16:13
    A. 2
    B. 3
    C. 12
    D. 24

19. Where did the Dragon gather his army to battle the Lamb?
    Revelation 16:16
    A. Armageddon
    B. Jericho
    C. Michmash
    D. Ziklag

20. What was the *seventh* vial poured upon?
    Revelation 16:17
    A. The air
    B. The rivers
    C. The sea
    D. The sun

*Answers on page 781

DECEMBER 30

Lesson 364
Today's Reading: *Revelation 17–19*
Period of Time: 95 AD
Author: John

1. What color was the beast that the great whore sat upon?
   Revelation 17:3
   A. Black
   B. Pale
   C. Scarlet
   D. White

2. How many heads did the beast have?
   Revelation 17:3
   A. 3
   B. 5
   C. 7
   D. 10

3. How many horns did the beast have?
   Revelation 17:3
   A. 3
   B. 5
   C. 7
   D. 10

4. Which golden object did the great whore hold in her hand?
   Revelation 17:4
   A. A book
   B. A cup
   C. A mirror
   D. A scepter

5. What was the great whore drinking?
   Revelation 17:6
   A. Blood
   B. Champagne
   C. Water
   D. Wine

6. Where did the beast come from?
   Revelation 17:8
   A. The bottomless pit
   B. The dragon's mouth
   C. The great sea
   D. The river Euphrates

7. What does each of the heads on the beast represent?
   Revelation 17:9
   A. Fountains
   B. Mountains
   C. Rivers
   D. Seas

8. How many kings does the angel say have already fallen?
   Revelation 17:10
   A. 2
   B. 3
   C. 5
   D. 7

9. How many kings does the angel say remain?
   Revelation 17:10
   A. 1
   B. 2
   C. 3
   D. 4

10. How many kings does the angel say are yet to come?
    Revelation 17:10
    A. 1
    B. 2
    C. 3
    D. 4

11. What is the name of the fallen city?
    Revelation 18:2
    A. Baalathbeer
    B. Babel
    C. Babylon
    D. Bashan

12. What was the stone like that the angel cast into the sea?

    Revelation 18:21

    A. A limestone
    B. A millstone
    C. A sandstone
    D. A tombstone

13. How many beasts fell down and worshipped God with the 24 elders?

    Revelation 19:4

    A. 1
    B. 2
    C. 3
    D. 4

14. What great event will occur in heaven?

    Revelation 19:6–9

    A. The battle for heaven
    B. The marriage supper of the Lamb
    C. The throne of God is destroyed
    D. The virgin queen is cast to the earth

15. What are the two names of the rider upon the first horse?

    Revelation 19:11

    A. Awesome and Terrible
    B. Everlasting and Good
    C. Faithful and True
    D. Peace and Joy

16. What was the other name of the rider upon the first horse?

    Revelation 19:13

    A. The Final Authority
    B. The King of Time
    C. The Prince of the Night
    D. The Word of God

17. What color were the horses of the armies which were in heaven?

    Revelation 19:14

    A. Black
    B. Pale
    C. Red
    D. White

18. Where was KING OF KINGS AND LORD OF LORDS written upon the rider of the horse?

    Revelation 19:16

    A. On his bow and arrows
    B. On his helmet and breastplate
    C. On his sword and shield
    D. On his vesture and thigh

19. What did the angel standing in the sun call out to?

    Revelation 19:17

    A. The fowls in the midst of heaven
    B. The beasts upon the earth
    C. The cherubims in heaven
    D. The dragons of the sea

20. Which two of the following were cast alive into a lake of fire burning with brimstone?

    Revelation 19:20

    A. The archangel and his host
    B. The beast and false prophet
    C. The pale rider and his horse
    D. The sun and the moon

*Answers on page 781

Lesson 365

Today's Reading: *Revelation 20–22*
Period of Time: 95 AD
Author: John

---

1. What did the angel's key open?
   Revelation 20:1
   A. The bottomless pit
   B. The door of the Rock
   C. The gates to the New Jerusalem
   D. The pearly gates

2. Which one of the following is one of Satan's names?
   Revelation 20:2
   A. Abba
   B. Light of the world
   C. Old serpent
   D. Prince of the kings of the earth

3. How many years will Satan be bound?
   Revelation 20:2
   A. 250
   B. 500
   C. 750
   D. 1,000

4. How long will Satan be loosed after he is released?
   Revelation 20:3
   A. A little season
   B. A long season
   C. A year and three months
   D. A year and a half

5. Which two of the following nations are enemies of God?
   Revelation 20:8
   A. Bethlehem and Jerusalem
   B. Gog and Magog
   C. Sodom and Gomorrah
   D. Tyre and Sidon

6. Where will Satan spend eternity?
   Revelation 20:10
   A. In limbo
   B. In purgatory
   C. In the lake of fire and brimstone
   D. In the nine circles of hell

7. Which two of the following will spend eternity with Satan?
   Revelation 20:10
   A. The archangel and Gabriel
   B. The beast and false prophet
   C. The two witnesses
   D. The virgin and her unborn child

8. Where will God judge the dead?
   Revelation 20:11–12
   A. At the pearly gates
   B. In the common hall
   C. Near the outer court of the temple
   D. Upon the great white throne

9. Which book will God use to judge the dead?
   Revelation 20:12
   A. The book of good and evil
   B. The book of life
   C. The book of light and darkness
   D. The book of the dead

10. What is the second death?
    Revelation 20:14
    A. Christ is crucified a second time
    B. Death and hell are cast into the lake of fire
    C. Man pays for his sins in limbo
    D. The earth is flooded once more

11. What did John call the holy city coming down from heaven?
    Revelation 21:2
    A. Babylon
    B. City of the King
    C. New Jerusalem
    D. Utopia

12. What did God call himself?
    Revelation 21:6
    A. Alpha and Omega
    B. Beelzebub and Apollyon
    C. Legion and the Adversary
    D. Son of the morning and Belial

13. How many plagues did the vials contain?
    Revelation 21:9
    A. 3
    B. 4
    C. 6
    D. 7

14. How many gates surrounded the holy city?
    Revelation 21:12
    A. 4
    B. 8
    C. 12
    D. 24

15. What was written upon the foundations of the holy city?
    Revelation 21:14
    A. The names of the 12 apostles
    B. The names of the 12 months
    C. The names of the 12 nations
    D. The names of the 12 tribes

16. What did the angel use to measure the city?
    Revelation 21:15
    A. A carpenter's square
    B. A golden reed
    C. A plum line
    D. A silver tripod

17. What was the length of the city in furlongs?
    Revelation 21:16
    A. 6,000
    B. 8,000
    C. 10,000
    D. 12,000

18. How many manners of fruit did the tree of life bare?
    Revelation 22:2
    A. 3
    B. 6
    C. 9
    D. 12

19. Who is the bright and morning star?
    Revelation 22:16
    A. Abraham
    B. Gabriel
    C. Jesus
    D. Satan

20. What is the last word in the Bible?
    Revelation 22:21
    A. Amen
    B. Faith
    C. Save
    D. World

Answers on page 781

January 1	January 2	January 3	January 4	January 5	January 6
Lesson 1	Lesson 2	Lesson 3	Lesson 4	Lesson 5	Lesson 6
1. C	1. B	1. A	1. A	1. B	1. A
2. D	2. A	2. D	2. D	2. B	2. C
3. C	3. B	3. B	3. B	3. C	3. C
4. B	4. B	4. A	4. A	4. C	4. B
5. B	5. D	5. C	5. C	5. D	5. A
6. B	6. A	6. A	6. C	6. A	6. D
7. B	7. D	7. C	7. A	7. C	7. B
8. A	8. C	8. B	8. D	8. B	8. D
9. C	9. A	9. B	9. A	9. A	9. B
10. A	10. C	10. D	10. C	10. D	10. D
11. D	11. D	11. C	11. B	11. D	11. A
12. A	12. D	12. C	12. D	12. A	12. C
13. A	13. B	13. A	13. C	13. D	13. D
14. D	14. B	14. D	14. B	14. C	14. B
15. D	15. C	15. A	15. D	15. C	15. A
16. B	16. A	16. D	16. B	16. A	16. C
17. C	17. C	17. B	17. D	17. A	17. B
18. D	18. A	18. C	18. C	18. B	18. D
19. A	19. D	19. D	19. B	19. B	19. C
20. C	20. C	20. B	20. A	20. D	20. A

January 7	January 8	January 9	January 10	January 11	January 12
Lesson 7	Lesson 8	Lesson 9	Lesson 10	Lesson 11	Lesson 12
1. C	1. B	1. C	1. B	1. A	1. A
2. D	2. A	2. D	2. C	2. D	2. B
3. D	3. D	3. C	3. C	3. C	3. C
4. D	4. C	4. D	4. C	4. B	4. D
5. A	5. A	5. A	5. A	5. B	5. A
6. D	6. C	6. B	6. D	6. C	6. C
7. B	7. A	7. A	7. B	7. D	7. D
8. B	8. D	8. B	8. B	8. A	8. A
9. A	9. B	9. B	9. D	9. B	9. B
10. C	10. D	10. C	10. D	10. D	10. D
11. A	11. A	11. D	11. A	11. C	11. C
12. D	12. B	12. D	12. A	12. A	12. A
13. A	13. C	13. A	13. B	13. B	13. B
14. B	14. B	14. A	14. D	14. C	14. C
15. C	15. D	15. B	15. C	15. D	15. A
16. B	16. C	16. B	16. A	16. A	16. D
17. C	17. B	17. C	17. C	17. C	17. B
18. B	18. A	18. A	18. B	18. A	18. B
19. C	19. C	19. C	19. A	19. D	19. C
20. A	20. D	20. D	20. D	20. B	20. D

January 13	January 14	January 15	January 16	January 17	January 18
Lesson 13	Lesson 14	Lesson 15	Lesson 16	Lesson 17	Lesson 18
1. A	1. B	1. C	1. B	1. C	1. A
2. B	2. C	2. A	2. D	2. A	2. A
3. C	3. C	3. B	3. A	3. B	3. C
4. A	4. D	4. D	4. C	4. C	4. D
5. C	5. A	5. A	5. B	5. C	5. D
6. A	6. B	6. D	6. B	6. D	6. B
7. D	7. D	7. D	7. C	7. B	7. C
8. D	8. A	8. C	8. D	8. D	8. B
9. B	9. D	9. B	9. B	9. B	9. C
10. B	10. D	10. A	10. A	10. A	10. B
11. D	11. A	11. B	11. D	11. B	11. D
12. C	12. C	12. B	12. A	12. A	12. A
13. A	13. B	13. B	13. C	13. C	13. C
14. B	14. A	14. A	14. C	14. D	14. D
15. A	15. D	15. A	15. B	15. D	15. A
16. C	16. C	16. D	16. D	16. A	16. B
17. B	17. B	17. C	17. A	17. A	17. B
18. D	18. B	18. C	18. A	18. C	18. C
19. D	19. A	19. C	19. D	19. D	19. A
20. C	20. C	20. D	20. C	20. B	20. D

January 19	January 20	January 21	January 22	January 23	January 24
Lesson 19	Lesson 20	Lesson 21	Lesson 22	Lesson 23	Lesson 24
1. B	1. A	1. C	1. A	1. C	1. C
2. A	2. C	2. B	2. B	2. D	2. A
3. D	3. D	3. C	3. C	3. D	3. B
4. C	4. B	4. D	4. B	4. B	4. D
5. B	5. A	5. A	5. B	5. A	5. D
6. A	6. D	6. C	6. A	6. C	6. B
7. D	7. D	7. D	7. D	7. D	7. C
8. C	8. C	8. A	8. C	8. D	8. A
9. D	9. B	9. B	9. A	9. C	9. C
10. A	10. A	10. D	10. B	10. B	10. D
11. B	11. C	11. B	11. A	11. C	11. B
12. C	12. B	12. B	12. D	12. A	12. A
13. D	13. B	13. D	13. D	13. A	13. B
14. B	14. C	14. A	14. D	14. B	14. C
15. C	15. A	15. A	15. C	15. A	15. A
16. A	16. D	16. C	16. C	16. D	16. B
17. A	17. D	17. D	17. C	17. B	17. A
18. B	18. C	18. B	18. D	18. C	18. D
19. D	19. B	19. C	19. A	19. A	19. D
20. C	20. A	20. A	20. B	20. B	20. C

January 25	January 26	January 27	January 28	January 29	January 30
Lesson 25	Lesson 26	Lesson 27	Lesson 28	Lesson 29	Lesson 30
1. C	1. D	1. C	1. B	1. D	1. B
2. B	2. C	2. B	2. A	2. B	2. B
3. D	3. C	3. C	3. A	3. A	3. B
4. A	4. B	4. A	4. C	4. D	4. A
5. A	5. B	5. C	5. D	5. C	5. A
6. C	6. A	6. A	6. B	6. B	6. B
7. D	7. A	7. A	7. D	7. A	7. D
8. C	8. D	8. B	8. B	8. D	8. A
9. D	9. D	9. B	9. C	9. B	9. C
10. A	10. A	10. D	10. D	10. D	10. D
11. B	11. C	11. C	11. D	11. B	11. D
12. B	12. C	12. B	12. C	12. A	12. A
13. C	13. D	13. D	13. A	13. C	13. C
14. A	14. A	14. D	14. C	14. A	14. D
15. A	15. B	15. A	15. D	15. C	15. C
16. D	16. B	16. B	16. A	16. D	16. C
17. C	17. A	17. D	17. B	17. B	17. B
18. B	18. B	18. D	18. A	18. C	18. D
19. B	19. C	19. A	19. C	19. C	19. A
20. D	20. D	20. C	20. B	20. A	20. C

January 31	February 1	February 2	February 3	February 4	February 5
Lesson 31	Lesson 32	Lesson 33	Lesson 34	Lesson 35	Lesson 36
1. B	1. B	1. B	1. B	1. C	1. A
2. C	2. A	2. B	2. A	2. A	2. B
3. D	3. D	3. B	3. A	3. B	3. C
4. B	4. C	4. D	4. D	4. C	4. D
5. C	5. A	5. D	5. D	5. D	5. A
6. A	6. B	6. D	6. C	6. A	6. B
7. A	7. A	7. A	7. C	7. B	7. A
8. D	8. C	8. A	8. A	8. A	8. C
9. D	9. C	9. A	9. B	9. D	9. D
10. C	10. D	10. C	10. B	10. A	10. C
11. D	11. B	11. C	11. D	11. C	11. A
12. C	12. D	12. C	12. B	12. D	12. D
13. A	13. C	13. B	13. C	13. B	13. B
14. B	14. A	14. A	14. D	14. B	14. C
15. A	15. B	15. D	15. A	15. B	15. D
16. D	16. D	16. C	16. C	16. A	16. A
17. C	17. D	17. D	17. B	17. D	17. B
18. A	18. C	18. A	18. D	18. C	18. D
19. B	19. B	19. C	19. C	19. D	19. B
20. B	20. A	20. B	20. A	20. C	20. C

February 6 Lesson 37	February 7 Lesson 38	February 8 Lesson 39	February 9 Lesson 40	February 10 Lesson 41	February 11 Lesson 42
1. B	1. D	1. A	1. A	1. D	1. C
2. B	2. C	2. A	2. D	2. B	2. D
3. A	3. B	3. A	3. C	3. C	3. A
4. D	4. D	4. A	4. B	4. C	4. B
5. C	5. A	5. C	5. B	5. D	5. D
6. C	6. C	6. A	6. A	6. D	6. C
7. A	7. A	7. B	7. B	7. A	7. A
8. D	8. B	8. C	8. D	8. C	8. D
9. C	9. D	9. D	9. B	9. B	9. B
10. D	10. B	10. B	10. C	10. C	10. C
11. B	11. D	11. D	11. C	11. B	11. A
12. B	12. A	12. D	12. D	12. A	12. B
13. B	13. A	13. B	13. D	13. A	13. B
14. C	14. C	14. B	14. C	14. D	14. A
15. A	15. B	15. C	15. A	15. D	15. D
16. A	16. C	16. D	16. B	16. C	16. C
17. A	17. D	17. D	17. A	17. A	17. B
18. D	18. C	18. B	18. A	18. B	18. A
19. C	19. A	19. C	19. D	19. A	19. C
20. D	20. B	20. C	20. C	20. B	20. D

February 12 Lesson 43	February 13 Lesson 44	February 14 Lesson 45	February 15 Lesson 46	February 16 Lesson 47	February 17 Lesson 48
1. B	1. D	1. D	1. C	1. A	1. C
2. B	2. A	2. B	2. C	2. D	2. D
3. A	3. B	3. D	3. A	3. D	3. A
4. D	4. C	4. D	4. B	4. D	4. B
5. C	5. A	5. A	5. D	5. C	5. D
6. D	6. B	6. A	6. B	6. C	6. C
7. B	7. C	7. D	7. D	7. B	7. A
8. A	8. D	8. C	8. B	8. B	8. B
9. C	9. D	9. D	9. A	9. A	9. D
10. D	10. A	10. B	10. A	10. C	10. B
11. A	11. B	11. A	11. C	11. D	11. C
12. B	12. C	12. C	12. D	12. B	12. A
13. D	13. A	13. B	13. C	13. B	13. B
14. C	14. C	14. C	14. D	14. C	14. C
15. C	15. B	15. C	15. B	15. A	15. D
16. D	16. B	16. C	16. C	16. A	16. A
17. C	17. D	17. A	17. A	17. D	17. B
18. B	18. A	18. A	18. B	18. B	18. D
19. A	19. C	19. B	19. D	19. C	19. A
20. A	20. D	20. B	20. A	20. A	20. C

February 18	**February 19**	**February 20**	**February 21**	**February 22**	**February 23**
Lesson 49	Lesson 50	Lesson 51	Lesson 52	Lesson 53	Lesson 54
1. A	1. C	1. C	1. C	1. D	1. A
2. A	2. D	2. A	2. B	2. B	2. C
3. C	3. D	3. B	3. A	3. B	3. C
4. C	4. D	4. D	4. D	4. A	4. A
5. D	5. A	5. A	5. C	5. A	5. A
6. C	6. B	6. C	6. D	6. C	6. D
7. B	7. C	7. C	7. B	7. D	7. D
8. A	8. B	8. B	8. A	8. C	8. C
9. B	9. A	9. A	9. C	9. A	9. D
10. D	10. B	10. C	10. A	10. B	10. B
11. B	11. A	11. A	11. D	11. A	11. C
12. A	12. B	12. B	12. D	12. C	12. B
13. B	13. C	13. D	13. B	13. D	13. B
14. C	14. A	14. D	14. C	14. B	14. C
15. B	15. A	15. D	15. B	15. C	15. B
16. D	16. C	16. C	16. A	16. C	16. B
17. C	17. B	17. B	17. A	17. A	17. A
18. D	18. D	18. B	18. D	18. D	18. D
19. D	19. D	19. A	19. B	19. D	19. D
20. A	20. C	20. D	20. C	20. B	20. A

February 24	**February 25**	**February 26**	**February 27**	**February 28**	**March 1**
Lesson 55	Lesson 56	Lesson 57	Lesson 58	Lesson 59	Lesson 60
1. A	1. B	1. D	1. C	1. B	1. C
2. C	2. A	2. A	2. C	2. C	2. A
3. B	3. C	3. C	3. B	3. A	3. C
4. D	4. D	4. B	4. A	4. A	4. B
5. B	5. A	5. B	5. D	5. B	5. B
6. B	6. D	6. D	6. A	6. D	6. D
7. C	7. C	7. C	7. B	7. A	7. C
8. C	8. D	8. A	8. C	8. B	8. B
9. A	9. B	9. B	9. D	9. D	9. D
10. A	10. C	10. A	10. B	10. C	10. A
11. C	11. B	11. D	11. D	11. C	11. D
12. D	12. A	12. A	12. C	12. C	12. A
13. C	13. C	13. A	13. D	13. D	13. B
14. B	14. B	14. C	14. A	14. A	14. A
15. A	15. D	15. D	15. B	15. B	15. C
16. B	16. A	16. C	16. A	16. D	16. D
17. D	17. D	17. D	17. D	17. C	17. A
18. D	18. B	18. B	18. C	18. A	18. D
19. A	19. C	19. C	19. A	19. D	19. C
20. D	20. A	20. B	20. B	20. B	20. B

March 2	March 3	March 4	March 5	March 6	March 7
Lesson 61	Lesson 62	Lesson 63	Lesson 64	Lesson 65	Lesson 66
1. A	1. B	1. D	1. A	1. B	1. A
2. C	2. B	2. C	2. A	2. A	2. D
3. D	3. A	3. D	3. D	3. A	3. C
4. C	4. D	4. A	4. D	4. A	4. D
5. B	5. B	5. C	5. D	5. D	5. C
6. D	6. C	6. C	6. C	6. A	6. B
7. B	7. D	7. A	7. C	7. C	7. A
8. D	8. B	8. B	8. B	8. B	8. A
9. A	9. A	9. B	9. D	9. D	9. A
10. B	10. C	10. B	10. B	10. C	10. D
11. A	11. C	11. D	11. B	11. C	11. C
12. D	12. C	12. C	12. C	12. C	12. C
13. C	13. A	13. A	13. A	13. D	13. B
14. C	14. B	14. B	14. B	14. B	14. B
15. D	15. A	15. A	15. B	15. C	15. A
16. C	16. D	16. A	16. A	16. D	16. B
17. A	17. D	17. B	17. A	17. B	17. D
18. B	18. C	18. D	18. C	18. D	18. C
19. B	19. A	19. D	19. D	19. A	19. B
20. A	20. D	20. C	20. C	20. B	20. D

March 8	March 9	March 10	March 11	March 12	March 13
Lesson 67	Lesson 68	Lesson 69	Lesson 70	Lesson 71	Lesson 72
1. A	1. C	1. B	1. C	1. A	1. C
2. D	2. B	2. C	2. B	2. B	2. D
3. A	3. A	3. D	3. C	3. D	3. A
4. D	4. D	4. A	4. A	4. D	4. A
5. C	5. C	5. D	5. C	5. D	5. D
6. D	6. D	6. B	6. C	6. D	6. A
7. B	7. B	7. C	7. D	7. A	7. C
8. D	8. A	8. B	8. D	8. C	8. A
9. C	9. D	9. A	9. B	9. C	9. D
10. B	10. B	10. A	10. B	10. A	10. B
11. A	11. D	11. D	11. A	11. C	11. A
12. D	12. C	12. C	12. A	12. B	12. B
13. C	13. B	13. B	13. B	13. A	13. C
14. C	14. D	14. A	14. A	14. B	14. D
15. B	15. C	15. C	15. B	15. B	15. C
16. C	16. A	16. D	16. A	16. B	16. B
17. A	17. B	17. C	17. D	17. C	17. B
18. B	18. A	18. A	18. D	18. D	18. B
19. A	19. C	19. B	19. C	19. A	19. C
20. B	20. A	20. D	20. D	20. C	20. D

March 14	**March 15**	**March 16**	**March 17**	**March 18**	**March 19**
Lesson 73	Lesson 74	Lesson 75	Lesson 76	Lesson 77	Lesson 78
1. A	1. C	1. D	1. D	1. C	1. C
2. C	2. D	2. B	2. C	2. C	2. D
3. D	3. A	3. A	3. A	3. A	3. C
4. B	4. B	4. C	4. C	4. B	4. D
5. D	5. D	5. A	5. B	5. D	5. B
6. C	6. B	6. D	6. B	6. B	6. A
7. B	7. C	7. C	7. A	7. C	7. B
8. A	8. A	8. B	8. D	8. D	8. A
9. D	9. D	9. C	9. A	9. B	9. C
10. B	10. B	10. D	10. D	10. D	10. A
11. C	11. A	11. B	11. C	11. B	11. D
12. B	12. C	12. A	12. D	12. D	12. A
13. A	13. B	13. D	13. B	13. A	13. A
14. C	14. D	14. A	14. A	14. C	14. B
15. A	15. C	15. C	15. C	15. A	15. B
16. C	16. A	16. B	16. B	16. C	16. C
17. D	17. B	17. A	17. D	17. B	17. D
18. B	18. A	18. B	18. B	18. A	18. D
19. A	19. D	19. D	19. A	19. A	19. B
20. D	20. C	20. C	20. C	20. D	20. C

March 20	**March 21**	**March 22**	**March 23**	**March 24**	**March 25**
Lesson 79	Lesson 80	Lesson 81	Lesson 82	Lesson 83	Lesson 84
1. D	1. A	1. B	1. C	1. A	1. C
2. C	2. D	2. C	2. D	2. C	2. D
3. A	3. C	3. B	3. B	3. A	3. A
4. B	4. B	4. A	4. A	4. D	4. B
5. C	5. D	5. B	5. C	5. B	5. D
6. C	6. C	6. D	6. D	6. B	6. B
7. B	7. B	7. C	7. B	7. B	7. A
8. A	8. B	8. D	8. A	8. D	8. A
9. D	9. A	9. D	9. B	9. C	9. C
10. A	10. C	10. C	10. D	10. D	10. D
11. B	11. C	11. A	11. A	11. A	11. C
12. A	12. C	12. D	12. C	12. B	12. A
13. C	13. B	13. A	13. D	13. C	13. B
14. A	14. D	14. B	14. A	14. A	14. B
15. B	15. D	15. A	15. C	15. A	15. C
16. D	16. A	16. C	16. B	16. D	16. A
17. B	17. A	17. C	17. B	17. C	17. B
18. D	18. A	18. A	18. A	18. D	18. C
19. D	19. D	19. D	19. C	19. B	19. D
20. C	20. B	20. B	20. D	20. C	20. D

March 26	**March 27**	**March 28**	**March 29**	**March 30**	**March 31**
Lesson 85	Lesson 86	Lesson 87	Lesson 88	Lesson 89	Lesson 90
1. B	1. C	1. B	1. C	1. B	1. C
2. D	2. B	2. C	2. B	2. D	2. A
3. C	3. A	3. D	3. A	3. A	3. C
4. D	4. D	4. A	4. D	4. C	4. D
5. D	5. B	5. C	5. D	5. C	5. B
6. B	6. C	6. A	6. C	6. A	6. D
7. A	7. A	7. C	7. D	7. B	7. C
8. C	8. C	8. A	8. A	8. C	8. A
9. C	9. B	9. B	9. B	9. C	9. A
10. A	10. A	10. B	10. B	10. A	10. B
11. B	11. D	11. B	11. C	11. B	11. D
12. A	12. B	12. D	12. A	12. D	12. D
13. A	13. A	13. D	13. C	13. A	13. C
14. C	14. A	14. A	14. A	14. D	14. A
15. B	15. D	15. A	15. A	15. B	15. A
16. C	16. B	16. C	16. D	16. A	16. C
17. B	17. C	17. D	17. C	17. C	17. B
18. D	18. C	18. D	18. B	18. D	18. D
19. A	19. D	19. C	19. B	19. B	19. B
20. D	20. D	20. B	20. D	20. D	20. B

April 1	**April 2**	**April 3**	**April 4**	**April 5**	**April 6**
Lesson 91	Lesson 92	Lesson 93	Lesson 94	Lesson 95	Lesson 96
1. C	1. C	1. D	1. D	1. C	1. C
2. C	2. A	2. B	2. D	2. B	2. B
3. D	3. B	3. D	3. C	3. C	3. C
4. C	4. B	4. C	4. A	4. B	4. A
5. B	5. D	5. B	5. B	5. A	5. A
6. D	6. A	6. A	6. C	6. B	6. D
7. A	7. C	7. B	7. A	7. A	7. D
8. B	8. A	8. B	8. A	8. C	8. B
9. A	9. B	9. C	9. B	9. D	9. D
10. D	10. C	10. D	10. D	10. B	10. B
11. B	11. B	11. C	11. B	11. A	11. C
12. D	12. B	12. A	12. C	12. D	12. A
13. A	13. C	13. D	13. C	13. A	13. C
14. A	14. A	14. D	14. D	14. C	14. B
15. B	15. D	15. A	15. C	15. D	15. A
16. B	16. D	16. B	16. B	16. B	16. D
17. C	17. C	17. C	17. B	17. C	17. A
18. C	18. A	18. A	18. A	18. D	18. D
19. D	19. D	19. C	19. A	19. A	19. B
20. A	20. D	20. A	20. D	20. D	20. C

April 7 Lesson 97	**April 8** Lesson 98	**April 9** Lesson 99	**April 10** Lesson 100	**April 11** Lesson	**April 12** Lesson 102
1. D	1. C	1. B	1. D	1. C	1. D
2. B	2. B	2. C	2. A	2. C	2. D
3. C	3. C	3. A	3. C	3. B	3. B
4. A	4. B	4. B	4. B	4. C	4. B
5. D	5. A	5. A	5. D	5. D	5. C
6. A	6. D	6. B	6. D	6. D	6. A
7. B	7. A	7. C	7. C	7. B	7. A
8. C	8. D	8. D	8. B	8. D	8. D
9. A	9. D	9. A	9. A	9. A	9. B
10. A	10. B	10. C	10. D	10. D	10. C
11. A	11. A	11. D	11. C	11. A	11. A
12. D	12. C	12. C	12. C	12. B	12. B
13. B	13. A	13. A	13. B	13. B	13. A
14. C	14. B	14. D	14. C	14. C	14. D
15. D	15. D	15. C	15. A	15. A	15. C
16. B	16. C	16. B	16. D	16. C	16. C
17. B	17. B	17. D	17. A	17. A	17. A
18. C	18. D	18. A	18. A	18. A	18. B
19. D	19. A	19. B	19. B	19. D	19. D
20. C	20. C	20. D	20. B	20. B	20. C

April 13 Lesson 103	**April 14** Lesson 104	**April 15** Lesson 105	**April 16** Lesson 106	**April 17** Lesson 107	**April 18** Lesson 108
1. D	1. A	1. D	1. B	1. D	1. C
2. A	2. A	2. C	2. A	2. B	2. D
3. A	3. C	3. A	3. B	3. C	3. C
4. B	4. B	4. B	4. D	4. A	4. A
5. D	5. D	5. A	5. B	5. D	5. D
6. A	6. B	6. B	6. A	6. A	6. D
7. B	7. D	7. D	7. B	7. A	7. B
8. C	8. C	8. D	8. A	8. A	8. B
9. B	9. A	9. C	9. D	9. C	9. C
10. C	10. A	10. B	10. C	10. B	10. A
11. C	11. D	11. A	11. C	11. D	11. B
12. A	12. B	12. C	12. D	12. D	12. C
13. C	13. D	13. D	13. D	13. A	13. D
14. B	14. B	14. B	14. C	14. C	14. B
15. B	15. B	15. A	15. A	15. B	15. A
16. D	16. C	16. C	16. B	16. D	16. B
17. D	17. A	17. A	17. D	17. B	17. A
18. A	18. D	18. B	18. C	18. B	18. C
19. C	19. C	19. C	19. A	19. C	19. D
20. D	20. C	20. D	20. C	20. C	20. A

April 19	April 20	April 21	April 22	April 23	April 24
Lesson 109	Lesson 110	Lesson 111	Lesson 112	Lesson 113	Lesson 114
1. A	1. C	1. D	1. A	1. B	1. B
2. B	2. D	2. C	2. B	2. C	2. C
3. A	3. C	3. C	3. C	3. A	3. D
4. C	4. B	4. D	4. D	4. D	4. D
5. C	5. B	5. B	5. B	5. B	5. A
6. D	6. D	6. D	6. C	6. A	6. A
7. B	7. A	7. A	7. A	7. C	7. C
8. C	8. C	8. B	8. D	8. D	8. B
9. B	9. B	9. C	9. C	9. C	9. B
10. D	10. A	10. D	10. B	10. D	10. A
11. D	11. A	11. D	11. A	11. B	11. C
12. A	12. C	12. A	12. D	12. A	12. D
13. C	13. D	13. B	13. D	13. C	13. D
14. A	14. A	14. A	14. A	14. A	14. C
15. D	15. D	15. A	15. C	15. D	15. A
16. D	16. A	16. B	16. B	16. B	16. B
17. A	17. B	17. A	17. B	17. B	17. D
18. B	18. D	18. C	18. A	18. D	18. C
19. B	19. C	19. B	19. D	19. A	19. A
20. C	20. B	20. C	20. C	20. C	20. B

April 25	April 26	April 27	April 28	April 29	April 30
Lesson 115	Lesson 116	Lesson 117	Lesson 118	Lesson 119	Lesson 120
1. B	1. A	1. B	1. C	1. A	1. D
2. D	2. B	2. A	2. D	2. B	2. D
3. C	3. D	3. C	3. A	3. C	3. C
4. C	4. C	4. C	4. D	4. D	4. B
5. A	5. A	5. C	5. C	5. A	5. C
6. D	6. B	6. A	6. B	6. B	6. B
7. A	7. D	7. C	7. C	7. C	7. C
8. A	8. C	8. A	8. D	8. D	8. A
9. B	9. B	9. C	9. D	9. D	9. A
10. B	10. C	10. D	10. C	10. C	10. B
11. C	11. A	11. A	11. A	11. A	11. A
12. A	12. D	12. D	12. B	12. B	12. D
13. C	13. A	13. B	13. A	13. B	13. D
14. B	14. B	14. D	14. B	14. D	14. B
15. D	15. C	15. B	15. C	15. C	15. C
16. C	16. D	16. D	16. B	16. B	16. A
17. D	17. C	17. B	17. A	17. A	17. C
18. A	18. B	18. D	18. B	18. A	18. B
19. D	19. D	19. B	19. A	19. D	19. A
20. B	20. A	20. A	20. D	20. C	20. D

May 1
Lesson 121
1. D
2. D
3. A
4. A
5. C
6. C
7. C
8. B
9. C
10. B
11. B
12. A
13. A
14. D
15. D
16. B
17. A
18. B
19. C
20. D

May 2
Lesson 122
1. B
2. D
3. C
4. A
5. A
6. B
7. D
8. C
9. C
10. C
11. B
12. B
13. A
14. B
15. D
16. D
17. D
18. A
19. C
20. A

May 3
Lesson 123
1. A
2. A
3. B
4. C
5. C
6. A
7. B
8. A
9. B
10. B
11. D
12. C
13. D
14. C
15. C
16. D
17. D
18. A
19. B
20. D

May 4
Lesson 124
1. A
2. B
3. C
4. D
5. D
6. B
7. C
8. A
9. D
10. C
11. B
12. A
13. B
14. D
15. C
16. D
17. A
18. C
19. B
20. A

May 5
Lesson 125
1. B
2. B
3. C
4. C
5. B
6. A
7. D
8. D
9. C
10. C
11. D
12. A
13. A
14. A
15. D
16. A
17. C
18. B
19. D
20. B

May 6
Lesson 126
1. D
2. C
3. D
4. C
5. C
6. D
7. D
8. B
9. C
10. B
11. A
12. B
13. A
14. A
15. A
16. B
17. D
18. A
19. B
20. C

May 7
Lesson 127
1. A
2. C
3. B
4. D
5. D
6. C
7. A
8. B
9. B
10. C
11. A
12. C
13. D
14. A
15. B
16. D
17. D
18. A
19. C
20. B

May 8
Lesson 128
1. A
2. C
3. A
4. C
5. D
6. B
7. C
8. D
9. A
10. B
11. C
12. D
13. D
14. A
15. B
16. D
17. B
18. C
19. B
20. A

May 9
Lesson 129
1. D
2. A
3. D
4. B
5. A
6. C
7. D
8. C
9. C
10. B
11. D
12. C
13. B
14. C
15. D
16. B
17. A
18. A
19. A
20. B

May 10
Lesson 130
1. C
2. D
3. B
4. D
5. B
6. A
7. B
8. C
9. C
10. D
11. B
12. D
13. A
14. D
15. A
16. C
17. A
18. A
19. C
20. B

May 11
Lesson 131
1. C
2. D
3. B
4. C
5. B
6. C
7. D
8. A
9. D
10. B
11. C
12. B
13. A
14. A
15. A
16. C
17. D
18. A
19. D
20. B

May 12
Lesson 132
1. A
2. B
3. C
4. B
5. B
6. C
7. B
8. D
9. D
10. C
11. A
12. A
13. B
14. D
15. C
16. A
17. C
18. A
19. D
20. D

May 13	**May 14**	**May 15**	**May 16**	**May 17**	**May 18**
Lesson 133	Lesson 134	Lesson 135	Lesson 136	Lesson 137	Lesson 138
1. B	1. A	1. C	1. A	1. B	1. B
2. A	2. D	2. A	2. D	2. D	2. C
3. D	3. B	3. B	3. B	3. A	3. A
4. D	4. D	4. C	4. B	4. C	4. D
5. C	5. C	5. D	5. B	5. A	5. D
6. B	6. A	6. C	6. B	6. B	6. D
7. C	7. C	7. B	7. B	7. D	7. B
8. A	8. C	8. A	8. C	8. C	8. A
9. A	9. B	9. D	9. A	9. C	9. C
10. C	10. A	10. D	10. A	10. B	10. B
11. B	11. C	11. D	11. C	11. A	11. C
12. A	12. A	12. B	12. A	12. D	12. A
13. B	13. D	13. A	13. D	13. D	13. D
14. D	14. D	14. C	14. D	14. C	14. B
15. B	15. B	15. B	15. C	15. B	15. A
16. C	16. B	16. A	16. D	16. A	16. C
17. D	17. A	17. D	17. C	17. B	17. C
18. A	18. B	18. A	18. D	18. C	18. A
19. C	19. D	19. C	19. A	19. D	19. D
20. D	20. C	20. B	20. C	20. A	20. B

May 19	**May 20**	**May 21**	**May 22**	**May 23**	**May 24**
Lesson 139	Lesson 140	Lesson 141	Lesson 142	Lesson 143	Lesson 144
1. D	1. A	1. A	1. A	1. D	1. D
2. D	2. C	2. B	2. A	2. C	2. B
3. C	3. A	3. A	3. C	3. B	3. A
4. A	4. A	4. B	4. D	4. A	4. C
5. B	5. C	5. C	5. B	5. B	5. A
6. C	6. C	6. D	6. B	6. A	6. A
7. C	7. A	7. D	7. B	7. A	7. D
8. A	8. C	8. C	8. C	8. A	8. D
9. B	9. B	9. B	9. C	9. B	9. D
10. B	10. C	10. C	10. C	10. C	10. B
11. A	11. D	11. B	11. D	11. C	11. C
12. D	12. D	12. D	12. A	12. B	12. C
13. A	13. B	13. A	13. D	13. B	13. A
14. A	14. B	14. D	14. C	14. D	14. C
15. C	15. A	15. A	15. B	15. D	15. C
16. B	16. D	16. D	16. A	16. A	16. A
17. D	17. D	17. A	17. A	17. D	17. B
18. D	18. D	18. C	18. B	18. C	18. D
19. C	19. B	19. C	19. D	19. C	19. B
20. B	20. B	20. B	20. D	20. D	20. B

May 25	**May 26**	**May 27**	**May 28**	**May 29**	**May 30**
Lesson 145	Lesson 146	Lesson 147	Lesson 148	Lesson 149	Lesson 150
1. B	1. B	1. B	1. B	1. A	1. C
2. A	2. A	2. A	2. B	2. A	2. B
3. A	3. A	3. C	3. D	3. C	3. D
4. B	4. D	4. C	4. B	4. C	4. C
5. B	5. C	5. C	5. C	5. B	5. D
6. D	6. C	6. B	6. B	6. D	6. C
7. D	7. D	7. D	7. A	7. B	7. D
8. B	8. A	8. A	8. D	8. A	8. A
9. A	9. A	9. D	9. D	9. C	9. B
10. D	10. B	10. B	10. C	10. A	10. A
11. C	11. D	11. D	11. A	11. D	11. C
12. A	12. C	12. B	12. C	12. A	12. B
13. A	13. C	13. D	13. A	13. D	13. A
14. C	14. D	14. B	14. C	14. B	14. B
15. C	15. A	15. D	15. B	15. B	15. B
16. D	16. C	16. C	16. A	16. D	16. D
17. C	17. B	17. A	17. D	17. C	17. A
18. C	18. B	18. A	18. D	18. C	18. C
19. D	19. B	19. A	19. C	19. B	19. A
20. B	20. D	20. C	20. A	20. D	20. D

May 31	**June 1**	**June 2**	**June 3**	**June 4**	**June 5**
Lesson 151	Lesson 152	Lesson 153	Lesson 154	Lesson 155	Lesson 156
1. D	1. C	1. B	1. D	1. D	1. D
2. A	2. A	2. A	2. C	2. B	2. A
3. C	3. D	3. D	3. A	3. C	3. A
4. B	4. B	4. B	4. D	4. C	4. C
5. B	5. D	5. A	5. D	5. B	5. C
6. C	6. D	6. C	6. A	6. A	6. D
7. A	7. C	7. A	7. C	7. C	7. B
8. C	8. B	8. B	8. D	8. A	8. A
9. D	9. A	9. B	9. C	9. B	9. B
10. A	10. B	10. D	10. A	10. D	10. C
11. B	11. C	11. A	11. B	11. D	11. D
12. D	12. D	12. C	12. B	12. D	12. B
13. B	13. A	13. C	13. A	13. B	13. A
14. C	14. D	14. D	14. C	14. D	14. D
15. A	15. C	15. B	15. D	15. B	15. C
16. A	16. A	16. A	16. B	16. A	16. B
17. C	17. B	17. D	17. A	17. A	17. A
18. D	18. C	18. C	18. B	18. C	18. B
19. D	19. B	19. D	19. C	19. A	19. C
20. B	20. A	20. C	20. B	20. C	20. D

June 6 Lesson 157	**June 7** Lesson 158	**June 8** Lesson 159	**June 9** Lesson 160	**June 10** Lesson 161	**June 11** Lesson 162
1. A	1. A	1. C	1. A	1. D	1. B
2. C	2. C	2. C	2. D	2. C	2. A
3. D	3. D	3. A	3. A	3. B	3. A
4. B	4. A	4. D	4. D	4. D	4. D
5. C	5. B	5. B	5. D	5. B	5. B
6. C	6. C	6. C	6. B	6. C	6. A
7. B	7. B	7. D	7. C	7. C	7. D
8. B	8. B	8. B	8. C	8. B	8. A
9. A	9. D	9. B	9. B	9. A	9. D
10. C	10. D	10. D	10. A	10. D	10. C
11. A	11. C	11. D	11. A	11. A	11. D
12. B	12. A	12. A	12. C	12. D	12. C
13. B	13. D	13. D	13. D	13. C	13. C
14. A	14. D	14. A	14. B	14. B	14. C
15. D	15. B	15. A	15. C	15. A	15. B
16. D	16. C	16. A	16. C	16. A	16. D
17. D	17. A	17. B	17. D	17. D	17. B
18. A	18. C	18. C	18. B	18. C	18. C
19. D	19. A	19. B	19. A	19. A	19. A
20. C	20. B	20. C	20. B	20. B	20. B

June 12 Lesson 163	**June 13** Lesson 164	**June 14** Lesson 165	**June 15** Lesson 166	**June 16** Lesson 167	**June 17** Lesson 168
1. B	1. A	1. D	1. D	1. D	1. D
2. D	2. D	2. B	2. A	2. D	2. A
3. C	3. C	3. C	3. C	3. A	3. D
4. D	4. B	4. C	4. C	4. D	4. C
5. D	5. A	5. D	5. D	5. B	5. A
6. A	6. D	6. D	6. B	6. C	6. C
7. B	7. B	7. C	7. B	7. D	7. D
8. B	8. D	8. C	8. B	8. C	8. C
9. A	9. C	9. A	9. C	9. D	9. B
10. C	10. C	10. B	10. C	10. A	10. D
11. B	11. C	11. A	11. B	11. A	11. C
12. D	12. D	12. B	12. B	12. B	12. B
13. D	13. D	13. A	13. C	13. C	13. A
14. C	14. A	14. B	14. A	14. B	14. A
15. C	15. B	15. B	15. D	15. A	15. B
16. A	16. B	16. A	16. A	16. B	16. B
17. C	17. B	17. A	17. A	17. C	17. D
18. A	18. C	18. D	18. D	18. B	18. C
19. A	19. A	19. D	19. A	19. C	19. A
20. B	20. A	20. C	20. D	20. A	20. B

June 18	**June 19**	**June 20**	**June 21**	**June 22**	**June 23**
Lesson 169	Lesson 170	Lesson 171	Lesson 172	Lesson 173	Lesson 174
1. A	1. D	1. D	1. C	1. B	1. A
2. B	2. A	2. B	2. B	2. C	2. D
3. B	3. C	3. A	3. D	3. B	3. C
4. A	4. C	4. A	4. C	4. D	4. B
5. A	5. D	5. C	5. B	5. D	5. B
6. D	6. A	6. B	6. A	6. D	6. A
7. D	7. B	7. C	7. B	7. C	7. C
8. B	8. A	8. A	8. C	8. C	8. D
9. D	9. B	9. B	9. D	9. D	9. C
10. D	10. A	10. C	10. D	10. B	10. B
11. B	11. C	11. A	11. A	11. B	11. D
12. A	12. C	12. B	12. C	12. D	12. C
13. B	13. D	13. D	13. C	13. A	13. C
14. C	14. C	14. D	14. B	14. C	14. A
15. C	15. D	15. C	15. A	15. B	15. A
16. C	16. B	16. D	16. D	16. A	16. D
17. C	17. B	17. B	17. A	17. A	17. A
18. A	18. A	18. C	18. A	18. A	18. B
19. D	19. D	19. A	19. D	19. A	19. B
20. C	20. B	20. D	20. B	20. C	20. D

June 24	**June 25**	**June 26**	**June 27**	**June 28**	**June 29**
Lesson 175	Lesson 176	Lesson 177	Lesson 178	Lesson 179	Lesson 180
1. A	1. B	1. D	1. A	1. B	1. D
2. B	2. B	2. A	2. C	2. B	2. D
3. A	3. C	3. C	3. B	3. D	3. B
4. C	4. A	4. D	4. D	4. D	4. B
5. D	5. C	5. C	5. A	5. C	5. A
6. B	6. D	6. B	6. C	6. C	6. B
7. C	7. B	7. A	7. B	7. A	7. C
8. B	8. A	8. C	8. D	8. A	8. B
9. D	9. A	9. D	9. C	9. B	9. A
10. D	10. B	10. B	10. D	10. A	10. C
11. A	11. D	11. A	11. B	11. B	11. A
12. A	12. D	12. B	12. A	12. B	12. D
13. C	13. D	13. A	13. A	13. C	13. B
14. C	14. C	14. C	14. B	14. D	14. D
15. B	15. C	15. D	15. C	15. A	15. D
16. B	16. C	16. B	16. B	16. C	16. C
17. C	17. A	17. C	17. C	17. D	17. C
18. D	18. D	18. B	18. A	18. A	18. A
19. A	19. B	19. A	19. D	19. D	19. C
20. D	20. A	20. D	20. D	20. C	20. A

June 30	**July 1**	**July 2**	**July 3**	**July 4**	**July 5**
Lesson 181	Lesson 182	Lesson 183	Lesson 184	Lesson 185	Lesson 186
1. B	1. A	1. A	1. D	1. A	1. D
2. C	2. D	2. A	2. B	2. D	2. C
3. B	3. D	3. B	3. A	3. D	3. A
4. D	4. A	4. B	4. A	4. A	4. C
5. A	5. B	5. C	5. C	5. B	5. B
6. C	6. B	6. A	6. C	6. C	6. D
7. A	7. C	7. C	7. A	7. A	7. C
8. C	8. C	8. C	8. C	8. C	8. B
9. A	9. B	9. B	9. C	9. B	9. B
10. B	10. D	10. D	10. A	10. C	10. C
11. B	11. C	11. A	11. B	11. A	11. D
12. C	12. D	12. B	12. A	12. C	12. A
13. A	13. C	13. A	13. B	13. D	13. A
14. D	14. D	14. B	14. D	14. C	14. C
15. C	15. A	15. C	15. B	15. D	15. D
16. D	16. B	16. D	16. C	16. B	16. B
17. D	17. B	17. D	17. D	17. B	17. A
18. D	18. A	18. D	18. D	18. A	18. A
19. B	19. A	19. C	19. D	19. D	19. D
20. A	20. C	20. D	20. B	20. B	20. B

July 6	**July 7**	**July 8**	**July 9**	**July 10**	**July 11**
Lesson 187	Lesson 188	Lesson 189	Lesson 190	Lesson 191	Lesson 192
1. A	1. A	1. B	1. B	1. B	1. A
2. D	2. B	2. D	2. D	2. B	2. B
3. C	3. A	3. D	3. B	3. C	3. D
4. B	4. D	4. C	4. C	4. C	4. A
5. D	5. B	5. A	5. A	5. D	5. A
6. A	6. C	6. B	6. C	6. D	6. C
7. B	7. B	7. C	7. A	7. D	7. D
8. A	8. A	8. B	8. A	8. A	8. B
9. B	9. D	9. A	9. A	9. A	9. C
10. B	10. C	10. C	10. A	10. A	10. C
11. A	11. C	11. C	11. C	11. B	11. B
12. D	12. D	12. B	12. B	12. C	12. D
13. B	13. B	13. D	13. D	13. B	13. A
14. C	14. A	14. A	14. C	14. C	14. B
15. C	15. D	15. A	15. B	15. D	15. A
16. D	16. D	16. D	16. B	16. D	16. D
17. A	17. A	17. B	17. D	17. A	17. D
18. C	18. C	18. C	18. D	18. A	18. C
19. D	19. B	19. D	19. D	19. C	19. C
20. C	20. C	20. A	20. C	20. B	20. B

July 12 Lesson 193	**July 13** Lesson 194	**July 14** Lesson 195	**July 15** Lesson 196	**July 16** Lesson 197	**July 17** Lesson 198
1. D	1. B	1. D	1. D	1. C	1. B
2. B	2. C	2. C	2. C	2. A	2. C
3. D	3. C	3. B	3. B	3. D	3. D
4. C	4. C	4. A	4. B	4. A	4. D
5. A	5. D	5. D	5. A	5. B	5. D
6. D	6. A	6. A	6. A	6. D	6. C
7. A	7. A	7. B	7. D	7. A	7. C
8. C	8. B	8. C	8. B	8. B	8. A
9. C	9. D	9. B	9. D	9. A	9. C
10. B	10. D	10. D	10. D	10. C	10. A
11. B	11. D	11. A	11. C	11. D	11. D
12. A	12. D	12. A	12. D	12. B	12. A
13. D	13. C	13. C	13. B	13. C	13. A
14. C	14. B	14. C	14. C	14. B	14. A
15. A	15. A	15. B	15. B	15. C	15. B
16. B	16. A	16. D	16. A	16. C	16. B
17. A	17. B	17. B	17. C	17. D	17. B
18. C	18. B	18. A	18. C	18. B	18. B
19. B	19. A	19. D	19. A	19. D	19. C
20. D	20. C	20. C	20. A	20. A	20. D

July 18 Lesson 199	**July 19** Lesson 200	**July 20** Lesson 201	**July 21** Lesson 202	**July 22** Lesson 203	**July 23** Lesson 204
1. C	1. A	1. D	1. A	1. C	1. B
2. A	2. D	2. A	2. D	2. C	2. B
3. B	3. A	3. A	3. A	3. A	3. A
4. A	4. C	4. B	4. C	4. A	4. D
5. D	5. B	5. A	5. D	5. A	5. A
6. B	6. A	6. C	6. B	6. C	6. C
7. C	7. C	7. C	7. A	7. C	7. A
8. C	8. C	8. D	8. D	8. B	8. C
9. B	9. D	9. A	9. D	9. D	9. A
10. D	10. D	10. D	10. B	10. C	10. C
11. C	11. B	11. D	11. C	11. B	11. A
12. A	12. B	12. C	12. C	12. D	12. D
13. D	13. D	13. B	13. C	13. D	13. D
14. B	14. C	14. B	14. B	14. B	14. B
15. C	15. A	15. C	15. B	15. B	15. C
16. A	16. D	16. D	16. B	16. B	16. B
17. B	17. B	17. B	17. C	17. A	17. D
18. D	18. B	18. A	18. D	18. D	18. C
19. A	19. C	19. C	19. A	19. D	19. B
20. D	20. A	20. B	20. A	20. A	20. D

July 24 Lesson 205	**July 25** Lesson 206	**July 26** Lesson 207	**July 27** Lesson 208	**July 28** Lesson 209	**July 29** Lesson 210
1. A	1. A	1. C	1. D	1. A	1. C
2. B	2. B	2. A	2. B	2. D	2. A
3. C	3. D	3. B	3. C	3. B	3. B
4. D	4. D	4. A	4. A	4. B	4. A
5. C	5. C	5. B	5. C	5. C	5. B
6. C	6. C	6. C	6. D	6. D	6. D
7. B	7. A	7. B	7. B	7. C	7. D
8. B	8. C	8. B	8. D	8. D	8. B
9. B	9. A	9. D	9. B	9. D	9. B
10. A	10. C	10. C	10. B	10. A	10. C
11. C	11. A	11. A	11. A	11. A	11. C
12. A	12. D	12. A	12. D	12. C	12. C
13. B	13. D	13. B	13. C	13. C	13. A
14. D	14. C	14. A	14. D	14. B	14. D
15. D	15. A	15. D	15. A	15. A	15. B
16. A	16. B	16. C	16. A	16. A	16. A
17. C	17. B	17. D	17. A	17. D	17. D
18. D	18. B	18. D	18. C	18. B	18. D
19. D	19. D	19. C	19. C	19. C	19. A
20. A	20. B	20. D	20. B	20. B	20. C

July 30 Lesson 211	**July 31** Lesson 212	**August 1** Lesson 213	**August 2** Lesson 214	**August 3** Lesson 215	**August 4** Lesson 216
1. D	1. D	1. C	1. B	1. B	1. A
2. C	2. C	2. B	2. B	2. A	2. C
3. B	3. D	3. D	3. A	3. C	3. B
4. D	4. A	4. B	4. A	4. B	4. C
5. B	5. A	5. B	5. C	5. D	5. B
6. A	6. D	6. D	6. B	6. B	6. D
7. B	7. B	7. C	7. C	7. D	7. B
8. D	8. B	8. A	8. D	8. D	8. D
9. A	9. C	9. C	9. B	9. C	9. B
10. C	10. C	10. D	10. C	10. C	10. C
11. D	11. A	11. D	11. A	11. A	11. A
12. D	12. B	12. A	12. D	12. D	12. C
13. C	13. B	13. B	13. D	13. D	13. A
14. C	14. C	14. A	14. A	14. A	14. D
15. C	15. B	15. D	15. C	15. B	15. A
16. A	16. D	16. C	16. A	16. C	16. A
17. A	17. A	17. A	17. D	17. B	17. B
18. B	18. D	18. A	18. D	18. A	18. D
19. B	19. C	19. B	19. C	19. A	19. D
20. A	20. A	20. C	20. B	20. C	20. C

August 5 Lesson 217	**August 6** Lesson 218	**August 7** Lesson 219	**August 8** Lesson 220	**August 9** Lesson 221	**August 10** Lesson 222
1. B	1. A	1. B	1. C	1. C	1. C
2. A	2. D	2. D	2. A	2. A	2. D
3. B	3. C	3. B	3. B	3. B	3. D
4. D	4. B	4. A	4. D	4. B	4. D
5. B	5. A	5. C	5. B	5. B	5. A
6. A	6. C	6. B	6. C	6. B	6. C
7. C	7. D	7. C	7. A	7. C	7. D
8. A	8. D	8. D	8. B	8. D	8. B
9. B	9. B	9. D	9. D	9. A	9. C
10. D	10. A	10. A	10. B	10. D	10. A
11. C	11. A	11. A	11. A	11. D	11. A
12. C	12. B	12. A	12. A	12. B	12. C
13. D	13. C	13. D	13. D	13. A	13. B
14. D	14. A	14. C	14. D	14. A	14. B
15. D	15. C	15. B	15. C	15. D	15. A
16. C	16. B	16. C	16. A	16. A	16. A
17. B	17. B	17. A	17. B	17. C	17. B
18. A	18. D	18. D	18. C	18. C	18. C
19. A	19. C	19. B	19. C	19. D	19. B
20. C	20. D	20. C	20. D	20. C	20. D

August 11 Lesson 223	**August 12** Lesson 224	**August 13** Lesson 225	**August 14** Lesson 226	**August 15** Lesson 227	**August 16** Lesson 228
1. C	1. C	1. C	1. C	1. C	1. D
2. A	2. D	2. C	2. D	2. B	2. A
3. A	3. A	3. A	3. B	3. C	3. C
4. D	4. A	4. D	4. C	4. B	4. B
5. A	5. A	5. D	5. A	5. D	5. C
6. B	6. C	6. A	6. D	6. D	6. B
7. A	7. C	7. D	7. C	7. A	7. D
8. B	8. A	8. C	8. A	8. A	8. C
9. B	9. B	9. A	9. A	9. A	9. D
10. A	10. D	10. C	10. D	10. A	10. A
11. D	11. B	11. D	11. D	11. D	11. B
12. C	12. D	12. B	12. C	12. C	12. A
13. C	13. B	13. A	13. C	13. C	13. B
14. C	14. B	14. B	14. B	14. B	14. C
15. C	15. B	15. A	15. B	15. D	15. D
16. D	16. C	16. C	16. A	16. B	16. C
17. D	17. D	17. D	17. B	17. B	17. D
18. B	18. A	18. B	18. A	18. A	18. A
19. D	19. D	19. B	19. B	19. D	19. B
20. B	20. C	20. B	20. D	20. C	20. A

August 17 Lesson 229	August 18 Lesson 230	August 19 Lesson 231	August 20 Lesson 232	August 21 Lesson 233	August 22 Lesson 234
1. C	1. C	1. B	1. C	1. B	1. C
2. A	2. A	2. C	2. D	2. B	2. C
3. D	3. B	3. D	3. C	3. B	3. D
4. D	4. D	4. A	4. D	4. A	4. B
5. C	5. D	5. C	5. D	5. A	5. A
6. B	6. A	6. B	6. C	6. A	6. B
7. C	7. B	7. A	7. B	7. D	7. C
8. A	8. B	8. B	8. A	8. A	8. A
9. D	9. A	9. C	9. B	9. D	9. C
10. C	10. D	10. D	10. B	10. B	10. D
11. D	11. C	11. D	11. D	11. C	11. D
12. D	12. D	12. A	12. A	12. C	12. A
13. A	13. C	13. A	13. B	13. A	13. D
14. A	14. C	14. B	14. B	14. C	14. B
15. B	15. C	15. C	15. D	15. D	15. A
16. A	16. B	16. D	16. A	16. C	16. D
17. B	17. D	17. D	17. C	17. C	17. B
18. B	18. A	18. A	18. C	18. D	18. B
19. C	19. B	19. C	19. A	19. B	19. A
20. B	20. A	20. B	20. A	20. D	20. C

August 23 Lesson 235	August 24 Lesson 236	August 25 Lesson 237	August 26 Lesson 238	August 27 Lesson 239	August 28 Lesson 240
1. B	1. B	1. C	1. B	1. C	1. A
2. D	2. C	2. D	2. B	2. A	2. A
3. C	3. D	3. D	3. A	3. B	3. D
4. D	4. D	4. D	4. C	4. B	4. C
5. C	5. A	5. B	5. D	5. B	5. A
6. B	6. A	6. A	6. C	6. A	6. B
7. A	7. C	7. B	7. D	7. C	7. C
8. C	8. A	8. A	8. A	8. D	8. C
9. B	9. B	9. A	9. A	9. A	9. C
10. A	10. B	10. D	10. C	10. B	10. B
11. C	11. B	11. B	11. D	11. D	11. D
12. D	12. C	12. D	12. C	12. A	12. B
13. A	13. D	13. B	13. D	13. C	13. B
14. B	14. D	14. A	14. C	14. B	14. A
15. D	15. B	15. B	15. A	15. D	15. A
16. A	16. C	16. C	16. B	16. A	16. B
17. A	17. D	17. C	17. D	17. D	17. D
18. D	18. C	18. C	18. B	18. C	18. D
19. C	19. A	19. C	19. A	19. D	19. C
20. B	20. A	20. A	20. B	20. C	20. D

August 29 Lesson 241	**August 30** Lesson 242	**August 31** Lesson 243	**September 1** Lesson 244	**September 2** Lesson 245	**September 3** Lesson 246
1. C	1. B	1. B	1. D	1. C	1. A
2. A	2. A	2. A	2. B	2. D	2. D
3. D	3. A	3. C	3. A	3. A	3. C
4. D	4. C	4. B	4. C	4. A	4. B
5. A	5. D	5. C	5. D	5. B	5. B
6. C	6. B	6. B	6. B	6. D	6. C
7. B	7. C	7. A	7. A	7. A	7. C
8. A	8. A	8. C	8. C	8. D	8. A
9. C	9. D	9. D	9. C	9. A	9. B
10. B	10. D	10. C	10. A	10. D	10. D
11. D	11. A	11. A	11. B	11. B	11. A
12. C	12. C	12. D	12. A	12. C	12. B
13. C	13. B	13. A	13. B	13. B	13. D
14. D	14. A	14. B	14. D	14. B	14. C
15. A	15. B	15. C	15. A	15. C	15. A
16. B	16. D	16. A	16. D	16. C	16. B
17. D	17. C	17. D	17. C	17. B	17. D
18. B	18. B	18. B	18. D	18. D	18. C
19. A	19. C	19. D	19. C	19. C	19. D
20. B	20. D	20. D	20. B	20. A	20. A

September 4 Lesson 247	**September 5** Lesson 248	**September 6** Lesson 249	**September 7** Lesson 250	**September 8** Lesson 251	**September 9** Lesson 252
1. C	1. C	1. A	1. B	1. D	1. D
2. C	2. D	2. B	2. D	2. B	2. D
3. B	3. B	3. D	3. D	3. B	3. C
4. D	4. C	4. B	4. A	4. A	4. A
5. C	5. A	5. C	5. A	5. C	5. D
6. C	6. C	6. D	6. C	6. B	6. B
7. B	7. B	7. C	7. A	7. A	7. C
8. D	8. A	8. D	8. B	8. A	8. C
9. B	9. D	9. A	9. C	9. D	9. B
10. A	10. B	10. A	10. B	10. C	10. A
11. D	11. B	11. D	11. D	11. A	11. A
12. A	12. D	12. C	12. C	12. C	12. A
13. C	13. D	13. D	13. B	13. D	13. B
14. A	14. C	14. A	14. D	14. C	14. D
15. D	15. A	15. B	15. B	15. D	15. A
16. D	16. A	16. C	16. A	16. B	16. B
17. B	17. A	17. B	17. A	17. C	17. C
18. A	18. C	18. C	18. C	18. D	18. D
19. A	19. B	19. A	19. D	19. A	19. B
20. B	20. D	20. B	20. C	20. B	20. C

September 10	September 11	September 12	September 13	September 14	September 15
Lesson 253	Lesson 254	Lesson 255	Lesson 256	Lesson 257	Lesson 258
1. C	1. D	1. C	1. C	1. A	1. B
2. A	2. A	2. C	2. D	2. B	2. C
3. A	3. B	3. A	3. C	3. D	3. A
4. C	4. B	4. D	4. A	4. C	4. A
5. B	5. B	5. D	5. A	5. A	5. D
6. D	6. C	6. D	6. B	6. B	6. A
7. C	7. D	7. A	7. A	7. D	7. D
8. B	8. D	8. C	8. B	8. C	8. B
9. B	9. D	9. B	9. C	9. A	9. D
10. D	10. B	10. C	10. A	10. C	10. C
11. A	11. A	11. D	11. D	11. D	11. A
12. B	12. A	12. B	12. B	12. B	12. C
13. C	13. B	13. B	13. B	13. D	13. D
14. C	14. C	14. B	14. C	14. A	14. B
15. A	15. C	15. A	15. D	15. B	15. C
16. D	16. C	16. B	16. C	16. D	16. C
17. A	17. C	17. A	17. B	17. A	17. A
18. B	18. A	18. A	18. D	18. C	18. B
19. D	19. D	19. C	19. A	19. C	19. D
20. D	20. A	20. D	20. D	20. B	20. B

September 16	September 17	September 18	September 19	September 20	September 21
Lesson 259	Lesson 260	Lesson 261	Lesson 262	Lesson 263	Lesson 264
1. B	1. A	1. A	1. D	1. A	1. A
2. A	2. D	2. D	2. B	2. A	2. D
3. C	3. A	3. C	3. D	3. C	3. B
4. B	4. A	4. B	4. C	4. D	4. C
5. B	5. C	5. B	5. D	5. C	5. B
6. C	6. B	6. B	6. A	6. D	6. B
7. A	7. A	7. B	7. A	7. A	7. C
8. D	8. D	8. A	8. C	8. A	8. A
9. D	9. D	9. A	9. A	9. D	9. B
10. B	10. B	10. C	10. A	10. A	10. D
11. D	11. A	11. D	11. D	11. C	11. C
12. C	12. C	12. A	12. B	12. B	12. D
13. C	13. C	13. C	13. B	13. D	13. A
14. B	14. D	14. C	14. C	14. B	14. C
15. D	15. D	15. A	15. C	15. C	15. A
16. A	16. B	16. D	16. B	16. B	16. D
17. C	17. B	17. D	17. A	17. D	17. A
18. A	18. C	18. C	18. D	18. C	18. B
19. A	19. B	19. D	19. B	19. B	19. C
20. D	20. C	20. B	20. C	20. B	20. D

September 22 Lesson 265	**September 23** Lesson 266	**September 24** Lesson 267	**September 25** Lesson 268	**September 26** Lesson 269	**September 27** Lesson 270
1. B	1. C	1. D	1. A	1. D	1. B
2. D	2. D	2. A	2. D	2. B	2. A
3. A	3. C	3. C	3. B	3. A	3. D
4. C	4. A	4. A	4. B	4. D	4. C
5. B	5. B	5. B	5. C	5. C	5. B
6. A	6. C	6. A	6. A	6. B	6. B
7. A	7. D	7. D	7. D	7. D	7. B
8. C	8. A	8. C	8. B	8. C	8. C
9. B	9. B	9. A	9. C	9. A	9. A
10. C	10. B	10. B	10. C	10. B	10. A
11. B	11. C	11. A	11. B	11. C	11. C
12. D	12. A	12. C	12. D	12. D	12. D
13. A	13. D	13. C	13. A	13. A	13. B
14. D	14. B	14. D	14. D	14. B	14. C
15. B	15. A	15. D	15. D	15. C	15. A
16. C	16. A	16. B	16. C	16. B	16. D
17. A	17. C	17. D	17. B	17. A	17. D
18. C	18. D	18. B	18. A	18. C	18. D
19. D	19. D	19. B	19. C	19. D	19. A
20. D	20. B	20. C	20. A	20. A	20. C

September 28 Lesson 271	**September 29** Lesson 272	**September 30** Lesson 273	**October 1** Lesson 274	**October 2** Lesson 275	**October 3** Lesson 276
1. C	1. D	1. B	1. D	1. D	1. C
2. B	2. D	2. C	2. A	2. B	2. D
3. D	3. C	3. D	3. C	3. D	3. A
4. D	4. A	4. D	4. B	4. A	4. B
5. B	5. C	5. A	5. B	5. A	5. C
6. C	6. B	6. C	6. D	6. B	6. B
7. A	7. D	7. B	7. A	7. C	7. D
8. B	8. C	8. C	8. A	8. C	8. A
9. A	9. A	9. B	9. A	9. A	9. D
10. D	10. A	10. C	10. C	10. C	10. A
11. C	11. D	11. D	11. A	11. C	11. B
12. A	12. B	12. A	12. D	12. D	12. C
13. D	13. A	13. C	13. B	13. B	13. A
14. B	14. D	14. D	14. D	14. D	14. B
15. C	15. B	15. A	15. B	15. D	15. C
16. A	16. B	16. B	16. C	16. C	16. D
17. A	17. C	17. B	17. D	17. A	17. B
18. C	18. B	18. D	18. C	18. A	18. C
19. B	19. A	19. A	19. C	19. B	19. A
20. D	20. C	20. A	20. B	20. B	20. D

October 4 Lesson 277	**October 5** Lesson 278	**October 6** Lesson 279	**October 7** Lesson 280	**October 8** Lesson 281	**October 9** Lesson 282
1. B	1. A	1. C	1. D	1. D	1. C
2. C	2. C	2. B	2. A	2. C	2. B
3. A	3. D	3. A	3. D	3. B	3. A
4. D	4. B	4. A	4. D	4. A	4. D
5. A	5. C	5. D	5. B	5. B	5. B
6. D	6. A	6. C	6. D	6. A	6. A
7. C	7. D	7. C	7. B	7. A	7. C
8. B	8. B	8. A	8. D	8. D	8. D
9. C	9. C	9. B	9. C	9. D	9. B
10. B	10. A	10. D	10. A	10. C	10. C
11. A	11. B	11. D	11. C	11. B	11. A
12. A	12. C	12. D	12. B	12. D	12. D
13. D	13. A	13. A	13. C	13. B	13. D
14. C	14. D	14. A	14. A	14. A	14. A
15. B	15. D	15. D	15. A	15. C	15. B
16. B	16. C	16. C	16. C	16. C	16. B
17. C	17. A	17. B	17. B	17. D	17. C
18. D	18. D	18. B	18. B	18. C	18. C
19. A	19. B	19. B	19. C	19. A	19. D
20. D	20. B	20. C	20. A	20. B	20. A

October 10 Lesson 283	**October 11** Lesson 284	**October 12** Lesson 285	**October 13** Lesson 286	**October 14** Lesson 287	**October 15** Lesson 288
1. C	1. D	1. D	1. D	1. B	1. C
2. D	2. C	2. A	2. C	2. A	2. D
3. A	3. C	3. A	3. B	3. C	3. A
4. B	4. B	4. C	4. D	4. D	4. C
5. D	5. A	5. B	5. A	5. C	5. D
6. C	6. A	6. A	6. D	6. D	6. B
7. B	7. D	7. A	7. A	7. B	7. C
8. A	8. D	8. B	8. B	8. D	8. C
9. A	9. C	9. D	9. A	9. C	9. A
10. B	10. B	10. C	10. C	10. B	10. B
11. D	11. A	11. C	11. A	11. D	11. D
12. B	12. B	12. C	12. B	12. A	12. C
13. C	13. D	13. D	13. C	13. B	13. D
14. D	14. B	14. B	14. C	14. A	14. D
15. C	15. C	15. D	15. D	15. B	15. A
16. C	16. B	16. B	16. B	16. A	16. B
17. D	17. C	17. A	17. B	17. C	17. A
18. A	18. A	18. D	18. D	18. D	18. B
19. A	19. A	19. B	19. A	19. C	19. B
20. B	20. D	20. C	20. C	20. A	20. A

October 16	**October 17**	**October 18**	**October 19**	**October 20**	**October 21**
Lesson 289	Lesson 290	Lesson 291	Lesson 292	Lesson 293	Lesson 294
1. A	1. B	1. C	1. A	1. C	1. B
2. A	2. D	2. B	2. D	2. B	2. C
3. D	3. C	3. D	3. B	3. A	3. A
4. B	4. C	4. B	4. D	4. D	4. A
5. C	5. A	5. B	5. A	5. C	5. A
6. B	6. B	6. A	6. D	6. C	6. B
7. D	7. A	7. A	7. A	7. B	7. C
8. D	8. D	8. D	8. C	8. A	8. B
9. C	9. C	9. C	9. C	9. C	9. D
10. B	10. B	10. D	10. A	10. B	10. D
11. A	11. B	11. C	11. C	11. A	11. C
12. D	12. D	12. B	12. D	12. D	12. B
13. C	13. D	13. D	13. B	13. D	13. D
14. A	14. A	14. C	14. C	14. A	14. C
15. C	15. A	15. D	15. A	15. B	15. D
16. B	16. D	16. A	16. B	16. C	16. D
17. A	17. B	17. A	17. B	17. B	17. C
18. D	18. C	18. C	18. B	18. D	18. A
19. C	19. A	19. B	19. C	19. D	19. B
20. B	20. C	20. A	20. D	20. A	20. A

October 22	**October 23**	**October 24**	**October 25**	**October 26**	**October 27**
Lesson 295	Lesson 296	Lesson 297	Lesson 298	Lesson 299	Lesson 300
1. A	1. D	1. C	1. A	1. D	1. C
2. C	2. A	2. B	2. B	2. B	2. A
3. B	3. D	3. D	3. C	3. A	3. D
4. C	4. C	4. D	4. D	4. D	4. B
5. D	5. B	5. A	5. C	5. B	5. C
6. D	6. A	6. C	6. D	6. C	6. A
7. A	7. B	7. B	7. B	7. C	7. B
8. C	8. C	8. D	8. C	8. B	8. D
9. B	9. B	9. B	9. D	9. D	9. A
10. D	10. D	10. C	10. C	10. D	10. C
11. C	11. A	11. D	11. B	11. A	11. B
12. B	12. C	12. C	12. A	12. C	12. A
13. B	13. D	13. B	13. C	13. B	13. C
14. A	14. C	14. B	14. A	14. A	14. D
15. D	15. C	15. A	15. B	15. D	15. A
16. A	16. A	16. A	16. D	16. A	16. B
17. B	17. B	17. D	17. D	17. C	17. D
18. D	18. D	18. C	18. A	18. C	18. C
19. C	19. A	19. A	19. B	19. A	19. D
20. A	20. B	20. A	20. A	20. B	20. B

October 28	**October 29**	**October 30**	**October 31**	**November 1**	**November 2**
Lesson 301	Lesson 302	Lesson 303	Lesson 304	Lesson 305	Lesson 306
1. C	1. D	1. A	1. A	1. A	1. A
2. A	2. A	2. C	2. C	2. A	2. D
3. A	3. D	3. C	3. C	3. C	3. B
4. B	4. B	4. B	4. C	4. A	4. C
5. A	5. A	5. D	5. D	5. D	5. D
6. C	6. C	6. C	6. A	6. B	6. A
7. D	7. D	7. B	7. D	7. B	7. C
8. D	8. B	8. D	8. B	8. B	8. A
9. B	9. B	9. D	9. A	9. C	9. B
10. A	10. A	10. A	10. A	10. A	10. B
11. A	11. A	11. A	11. A	11. D	11. C
12. C	12. C	12. D	12. B	12. C	12. D
13. B	13. C	13. A	13. D	13. D	13. D
14. B	14. C	14. A	14. D	14. C	14. B
15. D	15. B	15. D	15. D	15. D	15. A
16. D	16. D	16. B	16. B	16. D	16. C
17. D	17. D	17. C	17. C	17. A	17. D
18. B	18. C	18. C	18. B	18. C	18. B
19. C	19. A	19. B	19. B	19. B	19. C
20. C	20. B	20. B	20. C	20. B	20. A

November 3	**November 4**	**November 5**	**November 6**	**November 7**	**November 8**
Lesson 307	Lesson 308	Lesson 309	Lesson 310	Lesson 311	Lesson 312
1. D	1. D	1. D	1. C	1. B	1. A
2. C	2. B	2. C	2. A	2. D	2. C
3. D	3. D	3. C	3. D	3. A	3. D
4. B	4. C	4. A	4. C	4. C	4. D
5. B	5. C	5. B	5. B	5. C	5. C
6. D	6. D	6. A	6. A	6. D	6. C
7. A	7. B	7. B	7. D	7. A	7. C
8. B	8. B	8. D	8. B	8. D	8. B
9. A	9. A	9. B	9. C	9. C	9. B
10. C	10. C	10. A	10. A	10. A	10. A
11. B	11. B	11. C	11. A	11. B	11. B
12. C	12. D	12. D	12. D	12. C	12. A
13. D	13. B	13. B	13. B	13. A	13. B
14. A	14. A	14. D	14. C	14. C	14. A
15. C	15. D	15. C	15. B	15. D	15. D
16. C	16. A	16. A	16. B	16. D	16. B
17. A	17. A	17. A	17. C	17. B	17. D
18. B	18. C	18. B	18. D	18. A	18. C
19. D	19. A	19. D	19. D	19. B	19. D
20. A	20. C	20. C	20. A	20. B	20. A

November 9	**November 10**	**November 11**	**November 12**	**November 13**	**November 14**
Lesson 313	Lesson 314	Lesson 315	Lesson 316	Lesson 317	Lesson 318
1. C	1. D	1. C	1. D	1. D	1. B
2. D	2. C	2. D	2. B	2. A	2. A
3. A	3. D	3. B	3. B	3. B	3. D
4. B	4. B	4. A	4. A	4. A	4. B
5. A	5. B	5. A	5. C	5. A	5. C
6. A	6. A	6. B	6. B	6. A	6. D
7. C	7. A	7. A	7. C	7. A	7. C
8. B	8. C	8. C	8. A	8. C	8. B
9. B	9. B	9. D	9. D	9. B	9. A
10. C	10. D	10. A	10. C	10. D	10. C
11. B	11. B	11. B	11. B	11. C	11. A
12. A	12. C	12. C	12. A	12. B	12. B
13. D	13. A	13. A	13. D	13. B	13. B
14. D	14. D	14. B	14. C	14. D	14. D
15. C	15. B	15. C	15. B	15. D	15. C
16. C	16. A	16. D	16. D	16. B	16. D
17. A	17. C	17. D	17. D	17. C	17. D
18. D	18. C	18. D	18. A	18. D	18. C
19. B	19. D	19. C	19. C	19. C	19. A
20. D	20. A	20. B	20. A	20. C	20. A

November 15	**November 16**	**November 17**	**November 18**	**November 19**	**November 20**
Lesson 319	Lesson 320	Lesson 321	Lesson 322	Lesson 323	Lesson 324
1. B	1. D	1. B	1. B	1. A	1. A
2. A	2. B	2. B	2. C	2. C	2. B
3. B	3. B	3. C	3. A	3. D	3. C
4. A	4. C	4. C	4. D	4. B	4. D
5. D	5. D	5. A	5. B	5. C	5. A
6. D	6. C	6. C	6. A	6. B	6. B
7. D	7. D	7. D	7. B	7. D	7. C
8. D	8. A	8. A	8. D	8. B	8. A
9. B	9. A	9. B	9. A	9. C	9. C
10. A	10. B	10. A	10. B	10. C	10. D
11. C	11. A	11. A	11. D	11. B	11. A
12. A	12. C	12. B	12. B	12. D	12. B
13. A	13. B	13. C	13. D	13. A	13. D
14. D	14. C	14. C	14. C	14. D	14. C
15. C	15. D	15. B	15. C	15. A	15. B
16. B	16. A	16. D	16. C	16. C	16. B
17. C	17. B	17. A	17. C	17. D	17. A
18. B	18. D	18. D	18. D	18. A	18. D
19. C	19. A	19. D	19. A	19. B	19. C
20. C	20. C	20. D	20. A	20. A	20. D

November 21 Lesson 325	**November 22** Lesson 326	**November 23** Lesson 327	**November 24** Lesson 328	**November 25** Lesson 329	**November 26** Lesson 330
1. A	1. B	1. C	1. B	1. A	1. A
2. D	2. A	2. A	2. A	2. B	2. D
3. B	3. C	3. A	3. A	3. B	3. D
4. C	4. B	4. B	4. C	4. C	4. B
5. B	5. B	5. D	5. B	5. A	5. D
6. C	6. A	6. B	6. C	6. A	6. B
7. A	7. C	7. C	7. C	7. B	7. B
8. D	8. A	8. A	8. A	8. A	8. C
9. D	9. D	9. C	9. A	9. A	9. A
10. B	10. C	10. D	10. B	10. D	10. B
11. C	11. B	11. C	11. D	11. B	11. A
12. A	12. D	12. D	12. D	12. C	12. C
13. A	13. D	13. D	13. B	13. D	13. A
14. B	14. D	14. A	14. C	14. C	14. C
15. D	15. C	15. C	15. B	15. C	15. A
16. C	16. C	16. D	16. D	16. D	16. C
17. B	17. D	17. B	17. C	17. C	17. B
18. D	18. A	18. B	18. A	18. D	18. D
19. C	19. B	19. A	19. D	19. B	19. C
20. A	20. A	20. B	20. D	20. D	20. D

November 27 Lesson 331	**November 28** Lesson 332	**November 29** Lesson 333	**November 30** Lesson 334	**December 1** Lesson 335	**December 2** Lesson 336
1. B	1. A	1. A	1. B	1. B	1. D
2. D	2. A	2. C	2. C	2. D	2. D
3. C	3. A	3. B	3. D	3. C	3. B
4. B	4. A	4. D	4. A	4. A	4. A
5. C	5. C	5. B	5. D	5. C	5. B
6. A	6. D	6. D	6. C	6. A	6. B
7. C	7. C	7. D	7. D	7. D	7. D
8. A	8. B	8. A	8. B	8. D	8. C
9. D	9. C	9. C	9. A	9. C	9. C
10. A	10. B	10. C	10. A	10. B	10. B
11. B	11. C	11. B	11. C	11. C	11. A
12. D	12. B	12. D	12. D	12. B	12. C
13. A	13. B	13. C	13. A	13. A	13. C
14. C	14. D	14. B	14. A	14. A	14. B
15. B	15. A	15. A	15. B	15. B	15. D
16. D	16. B	16. B	16. C	16. D	16. A
17. D	17. D	17. A	17. D	17. B	17. C
18. B	18. D	18. D	18. C	18. C	18. D
19. A	19. D	19. A	19. B	19. D	19. A
20. C	20. C	20. C	20. B	20. A	20. A

December 3	**December 4**	**December 5**	**December 6**	**December 7**	**December 8**
Lesson 337	Lesson 338	Lesson 339	Lesson 340	Lesson 341	Lesson 342
1. A	1. A	1. A	1. B	1. D	1. A
2. D	2. D	2. C	2. D	2. C	2. A
3. A	3. B	3. C	3. B	3. A	3. B
4. A	4. A	4. D	4. A	4. B	4. D
5. B	5. C	5. D	5. D	5. D	5. D
6. C	6. B	6. A	6. A	6. D	6. D
7. C	7. C	7. C	7. C	7. C	7. C
8. D	8. D	8. D	8. C	8. C	8. C
9. B	9. A	9. B	9. A	9. D	9. D
10. C	10. D	10. B	10. D	10. A	10. B
11. D	11. C	11. A	11. C	11. B	11. C
12. A	12. A	12. B	12. B	12. B	12. C
13. B	13. C	13. A	13. A	13. B	13. A
14. D	14. B	14. A	14. D	14. C	14. C
15. A	15. D	15. D	15. D	15. C	15. B
16. B	16. D	16. C	16. B	16. A	16. A
17. C	17. A	17. B	17. A	17. B	17. B
18. D	18. B	18. C	18. B	18. A	18. B
19. B	19. B	19. B	19. C	19. D	19. A
20. C	20. C	20. D	20. C	20. A	20. D

December 9	**December 10**	**December 11**	**December 12**	**December 13**	**December 14**
Lesson 343	Lesson 344	Lesson 345	Lesson 346	Lesson 347	Lesson 348
1. D	1. B	1. C	1. C	1. B	1. B
2. A	2. B	2. A	2. B	2. C	2. A
3. D	3. D	3. B	3. B	3. B	3. B
4. A	4. C	4. D	4. C	4. D	4. C
5. A	5. A	5. C	5. B	5. B	5. D
6. D	6. C	6. B	6. A	6. C	6. D
7. C	7. A	7. D	7. C	7. C	7. C
8. B	8. D	8. A	8. A	8. D	8. A
9. C	9. B	9. A	9. D	9. A	9. D
10. A	10. A	10. C	10. C	10. A	10. A
11. B	11. D	11. D	11. A	11. A	11. D
12. B	12. C	12. D	12. D	12. B	12. B
13. B	13. D	13. A	13. D	13. C	13. A
14. C	14. C	14. A	14. B	14. A	14. C
15. C	15. A	15. D	15. D	15. B	15. C
16. C	16. B	16. C	16. C	16. D	16. C
17. B	17. B	17. B	17. A	17. A	17. A
18. D	18. C	18. B	18. D	18. D	18. B
19. D	19. D	19. B	19. A	19. D	19. B
20. A	20. A	20. C	20. B	20. C	20. D

December 15 Lesson 349	**December 16** Lesson 350	**December 17** Lesson 351	**December 18** Lesson 352	**December 19** Lesson 353	**December 20** Lesson 354
1. C	1. D	1. D	1. B	1. C	1. D
2. B	2. A	2. B	2. D	2. B	2. C
3. B	3. A	3. C	3. A	3. A	3. A
4. A	4. B	4. A	4. A	4. D	4. B
5. D	5. D	5. A	5. C	5. B	5. A
6. D	6. A	6. B	6. A	6. B	6. B
7. B	7. B	7. C	7. D	7. C	7. D
8. C	8. D	8. D	8. B	8. D	8. C
9. A	9. C	9. C	9. C	9. A	9. A
10. B	10. B	10. C	10. C	10. B	10. A
11. C	11. B	11. D	11. D	11. A	11. D
12. D	12. B	12. D	12. A	12. A	12. C
13. A	13. A	13. B	13. C	13. C	13. A
14. C	14. C	14. B	14. B	14. A	14. C
15. C	15. D	15. D	15. C	15. B	15. B
16. D	16. A	16. C	16. A	16. C	16. B
17. A	17. C	17. A	17. B	17. D	17. C
18. A	18. D	18. A	18. D	18. C	18. D
19. B	19. C	19. B	19. D	19. D	19. D
20. D	20. C	20. A	20. B	20. D	20. B

December 21 Lesson 355	**December 22** Lesson 356	**December 23** Lesson 357	**December 24** Lesson 358	**December 25** Lesson 359	**December 26** Lesson 360
1. A	1. C	1. D	1. D	1. A	1. C
2. D	2. D	2. D	2. C	2. D	2. A
3. B	3. D	3. C	3. A	3. D	3. B
4. C	4. B	4. B	4. B	4. C	4. D
5. C	5. D	5. A	5. C	5. B	5. B
6. D	6. D	6. A	6. A	6. A	6. C
7. B	7. C	7. C	7. D	7. D	7. B
8. A	8. C	8. B	8. B	8. C	8. C
9. B	9. C	9. A	9. A	9. B	9. C
10. D	10. A	10. D	10. D	10. B	10. D
11. B	11. A	11. C	11. B	11. A	11. A
12. C	12. B	12. B	12. C	12. B	12. D
13. D	13. B	13. D	13. A	13. A	13. B
14. C	14. A	14. C	14. C	14. C	14. D
15. A	15. B	15. A	15. D	15. C	15. A
16. B	16. C	16. B	16. A	16. D	16. B
17. C	17. D	17. B	17. B	17. C	17. C
18. D	18. B	18. D	18. C	18. A	18. A
19. A	19. A	19. A	19. D	19. B	19. D
20. A	20. A	20. C	20. B	20. D	20. A

December 27	**December 28**	**December 29**	**December 30**	**December 31**
Lesson 361	Lesson 362	Lesson 363	Lesson 364	Lesson 365
1. C	1. C	1. B	1. C	1. A
2. C	2. B	2. B	2. C	2. C
3. D	3. A	3. B	3. D	3. D
4. D	4. A	4. A	4. B	4. A
5. A	5. D	5. C	5. A	5. B
6. B	6. B	6. D	6. A	6. C
7. A	7. C	7. A	7. B	7. B
8. D	8. D	8. C	8. C	8. D
9. D	9. B	9. D	9. A	9. B
10. C	10. A	10. C	10. A	10. B
11. A	11. C	11. B	11. C	11. C
12. B	12. D	12. C	12. B	12. A
13. A	13. D	13. D	13. D	13. D
14. B	14. A	14. D	14. B	14. C
15. B	15. A	15. C	15. C	15. A
16. C	16. C	16. D	16. D	16. B
17. C	17. C	17. A	17. D	17. D
18. A	18. D	18. B	18. D	18. D
19. D	19. B	19. A	19. A	19. C
20. B	20. B	20. A	20. B	20. A

Name: _____

Date: _____

Lesson Number: _____   Test Page Numbers: _____   Answer Key Page Number: _____

Directions: First fold the sheet in half at the center of the paper. Second, take the pre-test by bubbling in your answers. Third, grade your test using the answer key found in *Daily Bible Study 101: Questions & Answers* and mark any incorrect answers on your answer sheet. Fourth, read today's assignment in your Bible, and also take review notes. When you are ready, take the Post-test. Finally, grade your paper by marking the number of incorrect answers as you did in step three. Use the grading scale to determine your final score.

Pretest

#				
1.	Ⓐ	Ⓑ	Ⓒ	Ⓓ
2.	Ⓐ	Ⓑ	Ⓒ	Ⓓ
3.	Ⓐ	Ⓑ	Ⓒ	Ⓓ
4.	Ⓐ	Ⓑ	Ⓒ	Ⓓ
5.	Ⓐ	Ⓑ	Ⓒ	Ⓓ
6.	Ⓐ	Ⓑ	Ⓒ	Ⓓ
7.	Ⓐ	Ⓑ	Ⓒ	Ⓓ
8.	Ⓐ	Ⓑ	Ⓒ	Ⓓ
9.	Ⓐ	Ⓑ	Ⓒ	Ⓓ
10.	Ⓐ	Ⓑ	Ⓒ	Ⓓ
11.	Ⓐ	Ⓑ	Ⓒ	Ⓓ
12.	Ⓐ	Ⓑ	Ⓒ	Ⓓ
13.	Ⓐ	Ⓑ	Ⓒ	Ⓓ
14.	Ⓐ	Ⓑ	Ⓒ	Ⓓ
15.	Ⓐ	Ⓑ	Ⓒ	Ⓓ
16.	Ⓐ	Ⓑ	Ⓒ	Ⓓ
17.	Ⓐ	Ⓑ	Ⓒ	Ⓓ
18.	Ⓐ	Ⓑ	Ⓒ	Ⓓ
19.	Ⓐ	Ⓑ	Ⓒ	Ⓓ
20.	Ⓐ	Ⓑ	Ⓒ	Ⓓ

Pretest Score

Number of questions missed = _____

Personal goal for the post-test = _____

Posttest

#				
1.	Ⓐ	Ⓑ	Ⓒ	Ⓓ
2.	Ⓐ	Ⓑ	Ⓒ	Ⓓ
3.	Ⓐ	Ⓑ	Ⓒ	Ⓓ
4.	Ⓐ	Ⓑ	Ⓒ	Ⓓ
5.	Ⓐ	Ⓑ	Ⓒ	Ⓓ
6.	Ⓐ	Ⓑ	Ⓒ	Ⓓ
7.	Ⓐ	Ⓑ	Ⓒ	Ⓓ
8.	Ⓐ	Ⓑ	Ⓒ	Ⓓ
9.	Ⓐ	Ⓑ	Ⓒ	Ⓓ
10.	Ⓐ	Ⓑ	Ⓒ	Ⓓ
11.	Ⓐ	Ⓑ	Ⓒ	Ⓓ
12.	Ⓐ	Ⓑ	Ⓒ	Ⓓ
13.	Ⓐ	Ⓑ	Ⓒ	Ⓓ
14.	Ⓐ	Ⓑ	Ⓒ	Ⓓ
15.	Ⓐ	Ⓑ	Ⓒ	Ⓓ
16.	Ⓐ	Ⓑ	Ⓒ	Ⓓ
17.	Ⓐ	Ⓑ	Ⓒ	Ⓓ
18.	Ⓐ	Ⓑ	Ⓒ	Ⓓ
19.	Ⓐ	Ⓑ	Ⓒ	Ⓓ
20.	Ⓐ	Ⓑ	Ⓒ	Ⓓ

Posttest Score

Number of questions missed = _____

Scoring Scale

*Number of questions missed

0-2 = Excellent   3-4 = Good   5-6 = Fair

7-8 = Poor   > 8 = Review and try again

MASTER FOR DUPLICATION Copyright © 2016 Bridan Publishing

Notes

Preface

1. Bloom. *Questions for the Revised Bloom's Taxonomy*. Handout. Print.
2. Bauer, page xxiv.
3. Ibid.
4. Scofield, C. I., and E. Schuyler, page vi.
5. Ussher, James, Larry Pierce, and Marion Pierce. *The Annals of the World*. Green Forest, AR: Master Books, 2003. Print.
6. Ham, Wieland, and Snelling, pages 89-102.
7. Johnson, page 114.
8. Some Scientists Alive Today Who Accept the Biblical Account of Creation. N.p., n.d. Web. 13 Aug. 2016.
9. *The Book of Acts*, 17:10-12.
10. *The Book of Joshua*, 1:8.
11. *The Gospel According to Mark*, 14:49.
12. *The Book of Acts*, 2:41-47.

Works Cited

Bauer, Susan Wise. Preface. *The History of the Ancient World: From The Earliest Accounts To The Fall of Rome*. New York: W. W. Norton, 2007.

Bloom, Benjamin. *Questions for the Revised Bloom's Taxonomy (from Quick Flip Questions for the Revised Bloom's Taxonomy EDUPRESS EP 729 - www.edupress.com)*. Handout. SUN. Colorado. Success Unlimited. 2008.

Ham, Ken, Carl Wieland, and Andrew Snelling. *The Answers Book: Answers to the 12 Most-asked Questions on Genesis and Creation/Evolution*. Qld., Australia: Creation Science Foundation, 1998.

http://timkienthuc.blogspot.com/2012/02/questions-for-revised-blooms-taxonomy.html

Johnson, Phillip E. *Darwin on Trial*. 2nd Edition ed. Downers Grove, IL: InterVarsity Press. 1993.

Scofield, C. I., and E. Schuyler. English. Introduction. *The New Scofield Reference Bible...Authorized King James Version. With Introductions, Annotations, Subject Chain References, and Such Word Changes in the Text as Will Help the Reader*. London: n.p., 1967.

http://creation.com/scientists-alive-today-who-accept-the-biblical-account-of-creation

The Holy Bible Containing the Old and New Testament Translated Out of the Original Tongues and With the Former Translations Diligently Compared and Revised by His Majesty's Special Command. Appointed to be Read in Churches. Authorized King James Version. Cambridge. 1769.

Permissions

- Most of the dates used for the timeline are based upon *The Annals of the World* by James Ussher, Larry and Marion Pierce; ISBN Numbers 13: 978-0-89051-360-6; 10: 089051-360-0; LCN 2003106357. 2003; pages 17-19, 26-64, 67-104, 107-155, 160-161; 773-874. Used with permission from the publisher - Master Books. The other dates are based upon the author's opinions.
- The author also wishes to thank Unsplash.com | www.unsplash.com, especially Simon Caspersen (page 785) and Daniel Roe (page 786) for permission to use their photographs.

Acknowledgements

I WOULD LIKE TO FIRST THANK GOD for without him I am nothing. Next, I want to thank my parents who made tremendous sacrifices in order to give me and my siblings better childhoods than they had growing up. Furthermore, I would like to give a heartfelt thanks to my lovely bride Shelby who has supported me throughout this project. And thanks to Danielle and Brianna, my beautiful daughters, who sacrificed their time with me so I could complete this book.

To my mentor and friend, John Wiseman, who has taught me more than words can say about Bible interpretation and doctrines. Also, Nolan Moore, my brother-in-law and former pastor, who has since retired from the pulpit, for his faithfulness in preaching and teaching the Word of God. To Myra Fishback for her unending encouragement and support.

Thank you to the current and former Bearden High School English teachers, especially Connie Francis, and all the rest of my colleagues, including Cassandra Dowd, who shared their knowledge on the art of writing. It is truly an honor to be part of a school devoted to excellence in teaching and learning.

To Paul Cowell, the owner and innkeeper at Whitestone Country Inn in Roane County, Tennessee. Paul's advice on cover design, printing, publishing, and promotion have been invaluable. I am truly grateful for your advice and friendship.

Book Rev. Casaus as a Speaker

Learn to Teach Like the Master.

- Learn the 5 secrets to great teaching
- Discover how to increase attendance in your classes
- Make Jesus' master plan your master plan
- Gain knowledge on how to prepare effective lesson plans
- Acquire the skills you need to teach like a professional

Filled with knowledge and Godly wisdom, Rev. Casaus is a polished and experienced speaker that connects with audiences of every age. He also teaches at both high school and college levels. Rev. Casaus provides attendees who want to teach like professionals to high schoolers, college age or adults, to leave with a personal vision for goals, tactics, and the motivation to be and build better disciples for tomorrow.

Pastors, associate pastors, small group leaders, and those who teach Bible studies to high school students up to adults will benefit from Rev. Casaus' teaching.

CONTACT
To schedule Rev. Casaus, visit **bridanpublishing.com**

And they shall not teach every man his neighbour, and every man his brother, saying, Know the Lord: for all shall know me, from the least to the greatest.
- Hebrews 8:11

Book Rev. Casaus to Preach at Your Church

Read, Heed, and Succeed

Brother Casaus delivers a powerful sermon on what it means to be successful in the eyes of the LORD and how individuals can achieve this success. His is not a pie in the sky myth, but a compelling message about how to put your trust in God and obey Him in order to reap His blessings. Brother Casaus teaches how God calls, commissions and comforts those who are willing to serve Him. Contact us today to let Rev. Casaus serve you and your congregation.

CONTACT
To schedule Rev. Casaus, visit **bridanpublishing.com**

And they shall not teach every man his neighbour, and every man his brother, saying, Know the Lord: for all shall know me, from the least to the greatest.
- Hebrews 8:11

DAILY BIBLE STUDY 101:

Holy Bible

King James Version

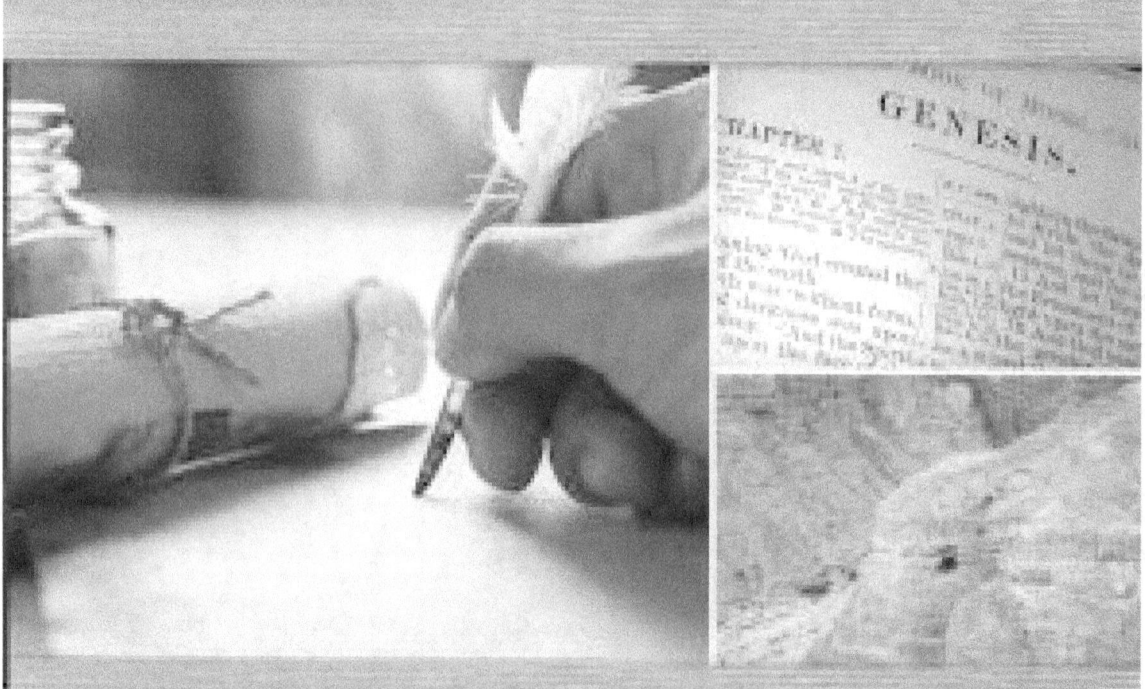

DAILY BIBLE STUDY 101:
Bible Outlines

Reggie Casaus

A great companion to
Daily Bible Study 101: Daily Devotional

- Over 7,000 multiple choice questions and answers

- Daily reading plans

- And more! Designed to help you dig deep and allow the Word to take root in your heart and mind

Available at most local and online bookstores.

About the Author

Reverend Reggie Casaus is a graduate of Berean School of the Bible. Filled with knowledge and Godly wisdom, Rev. Casaus is a polished and experienced speaker, teacher, ordained pastor and author that connects with audiences of every age. He has taught at both high school and college levels, at Bearden High School in Knoxville, Tennessee and Roane State Community College in Harriman, Tennessee. Daily Bible Study 101: Daily Devotional is his second book, and companion to his first, Daily Bible Study 101: Questions & Answers. Both volumes are available in local and online bookstores. Reach Rev. Casaus at **bridanpublishing.com**

www.ingramcontent.com/pod-product-compliance
Lightning Source LLC
Chambersburg PA
CBHW080401300426
44113CB00015B/2372